British Athletics

with Amateur Athletic Club Champio
and UK Year Lists

Peter Lovesey and Keith Morbey

Historical Series Booklet No. 17   (2016)

National Union of Track Statisticians

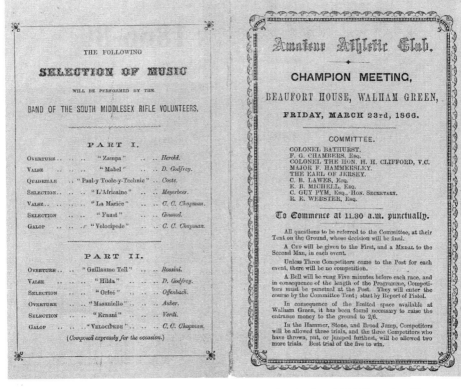

Rear (left) and front (right) covers of the programme for the first AAC Championships.

British Athletics 1866-80

Copyright © 2016 Peter Lovesey and Keith Morbey

All Rights Reserved

ISBN 978-0-904612-22-6

Published in 2016 by the National Union of Track Statisticians, web site www.nuts.org.uk

Cover illustration: The 1867 Oxford v Cambridge match at Beaufort House, Walham Green, the first year the sports were held in London. The winner of the shot was Richard Waltham (Cambridge). All the throwers wore cricket flannels. 'The weight-putters took up a lot of time,' one report complained, 'for they were allowed six throws apiece.'

CONTENTS

Pole Leaping at the Agricultural Hall, Islington, 1871. The event is the annual Cumberland & Westmoreland Wrestling Society meeting and the competitors are dressed in wrestling costume rather than athletics kit. Philip Winder (Kendal) was the winner with 10ft 1in. The favourite, David Anderson, broke his pole and sprained his ankle, a not uncommon hazard of hard landings.

4

For more details see the NUTS web-site at www.nuts.org.uk.
Most of the booklets that cover men include mini biographies of athletes who were active during the 1866-80 period, for example 7 in the Mile and many more in the field events.

Alfred Loder (Cambridge UAC, left) and High Upcher (Oxford U) leading in the Oxford v Cambridge hurdles at Lillie Bridge in 1875. Loder, once called 'the most graceful performer who ever topped timber' won by a foot in 16 4/5 sec. The modern style of hurdling was evolved by an Oxford man, A.C.M.Croome, the winner in 1886.

ACKNOWLEDGEMENTS

As long ago as 1969, Dave Terry and Peter Lovesey of the NUTS published UK best performer lists for the years from 1866 onwards based on work in the British Museum Newspaper Library at Colindale. These pioneering lists were confined to amateurs and intended to cover each year to 1918, but they stalled at 1875. Even so, they became the foundation for the present publication, now much extended to include professional marks and the leading performances for each event. The present work takes the process on to 1880. Its stately progress has for years been a subject of amusement at the annual meeting of the NUTS historical group.

Peter Matthews, Chairman of the NUTS, and Ian Tempest have been the prime movers in producing the Historical Series booklets which now form a marvellous event-by-event record of our sport. Without the encouragement and gentle chivvying from Peter and Ian it is doubtful if the present book would ever have been completed.

In 2003, the late Ian Buchanan published *The AAA Championships 1880-1939* as No. 7 in the series, and he was most helpful in sharing his findings of earlier material. The period 1866-79 was when the first national Championships were founded and run by the old Amateur Athletic Club, which the AAA replaced. We have relied mainly on newspaper reports and other printed and online sources. The difficulty is that the newspapers don't necessarily agree on results. Trevor Clowes spent many hours at Colindale finding a way through the myriad variations in reporting of the Championship meetings. His notes clarified many anomalies and we are immensely grateful for his contribution.

In 1999, Keith Morbey rashly offered to begin compiling an index and the first version was finished in a matter of months. Inevitably questions came up about full names and birthdates and soon he was as involved as Lovesey was. More so, when he started researching the Scottish and Border Games for professional results that became so comprehensive that we decided to list them separately for the field events. Keith's contributions over recent years have been so substantial (notwithstanding his work on the *1930-1939 UK Men's Ranking Lists, Historical Series Booklet No. 11*) that there is no question that he should be credited as joint author of this booklet.

We have also been fortunate in recent years to have had the invaluable contribution of Ari Törmä, the Finnish statistician and historian, author of a series of deeply researched statistical studies of the various track and field events, but on an international scale. Working mainly on the internet, accessing digitised newspapers through the British Library's website, Ari double-checked our findings and came up with a number of extra marks for each year.

A German historian, Hubert Hamacher, was meanwhile working on his own international study of the years 1880 to 1900, published first as two volumes in German, and then in an English language version, *Athletics at the End of the Nineteenth Century*, in 2011. Hubert travelled Europe researching in libraries and inevitably came to Colindale where the British Newspaper Library was housed. As well as making notes on the period of his published work, he researched the earlier years and later corresponded extensively with Peter Lovesey comparing his notes with the draft lists. His suggestions, painstakingly handwritten when he was over ninety years old, were exceptionally helpful.

It was encouraging, too, to discover that other historians working independently were making studies that overlapped the period we were researching. The late Eric Cowe, a respected authority on the history of women's athletics, became interested in the earliest known annual sports meetings, the Scottish Border games, and compiled lists that were published in Track Stats, first in 1985, covering the period 1827-1842. In 1992 and 1993 he extended his researches to cover the high jump and triple jump up to 1875.

For the history of the amateurs in Scotland we are indebted to the Rev John W. Keddie, whose *Scottish Athletics 1883-1933* actually has much helpful information about the era before the SAAA was founded.

Ireland is justly proud of its role in the history of the sport. Dublin University held its first athletic sports in College Park as early as 1857. The world's first international athletics meetings were between England and Ireland in 1876 and 1877. The Irish led the world in field events for several decades and there is a wealth of material published by Irish athletics historians. Patriotic Irishmen may be irked to find their countrymen included in United Kingdom lists, but in the years of our study all of Ireland was governed from Britain so it was realistic to extend this study to performances made in the Emerald Isle. It may be added that without the Irish, certain field events, notably the triple jump, would scarcely feature. The Irish historians have been generous with their assistance. Tony O'Donoghue, author of *1873-1914 Irish Championship Athletics*, is a meticulous researcher and has been a steady support for many years. Colm Murphy, who began with several booklets about athletics at his own Queen's College, Cork, has in recent years produced a series of books bringing the story of the Irish Championships up to 1999. Colm shared with us his own privately compiled list of Irish performances year by year. And Cyril Smyth, of Trinity College, Dublin, has provided much information about the pioneering athletes of the university.

In any project such as ours, the groundwork was done and the task made easier by the researchers of earlier generations and here we wish to pay tribute to distinguished and inspiring historians of the past, particularly H.F.Wilkinson, William McCombie Smith, Montague Shearman, F.A.M.Webster, Harold Abrahams, Roberto Quercetani and Norris and Ross McWhirter. In the twenty-first century, the most notable and reliable general history is *Running through the Ages*, by Edward S. Sears, now in its second edition (2015).

A number of specialised books relevant to our research were written in more recent years on nineteenth century athletics and we have been grateful to consult them. Harry Berry's *A Very Peculiar Practice: a history of the hammer throw in the British Isles 1850 to 1914* and *A History of the Pole Vault in the British Isles* (Parts One and Two) list annual performances collected from newspaper archives before it was possible to access them electronically. Warren Roe's *Front Runners* (2002) is a beautifully documented history of the Hackney Wick running ground, and Kevin Kelly did a comparable job for Garratt Lane with *Robert Sadler and the Lost Copenhagen Running Grounds* (2013). Richard O. Watson published *'Choppy' Warburton: long distance runner and trainer of cycling champions* (2006). Warren Roe's several booklets include two that come into our time-frame: *Jack White 'The Gateshead Clipper' 1837-1910* and *Edward 'Teddy' Mills 'Young England' 1841-1894.* Rob Hadgraft wrote *Deerfoot: Athletics' Noble Savage* (2007); and *Beer and Brine: the Making of Walter George, Athletics' First Superstar* (2006). More recently Dave Day and his colleagues at Manchester Metropolitan University have produced some ground-breaking books on the period, of which *Sporting Lives* (2011) and *Pedestrianism* (2014) are outstanding examples. The Irish historians (in addition to those mentioned above) include Séamus Ó Riain, the author of *Maurice Davin (1842-1927): First President of the GAA* (2004) and Kieran Sheedy *Peerless Tom Malone* (2000). The Scottish Highland Games are well covered in Charlie Allan's *Donald Dinnie: the First Sporting Superstar* (1999); and Tom Carruthers' *Golf Club Maker: Thomas Carruthers 1840-1924* (2004) and *Tom Carruthers: Running for Money* (2012).

Peter Radford, the NUTS President, marked the 150th anniversary of the 1866 inaugural championship meeting by publishing an illustrated booklet recording the day's events as they unfolded. *1866 and all that . . .* is a fine companion volume to our own work and we have been happy to share our material with Peter: peter.radford@mail.com.

Ever since the founding of the NUTS in 1958 the publication of material on the history of the sport has been one of its outstanding achievements. As well as the *NUTS Annual* and the event booklets, we publish a magazine originally entitled *NUTS Notes*, later *Track Stats*, and we are much indebted to the editors Andrew Huxtable (1963-79), Tim Lynch-Staunton (1980-94) and Bob Phillips (since 1995). Andrew and Bob have published significant works of their own on historical athletics. In addition to those already named, numerous other individuals answered our queries and contributed to the present work, notably Richard Bond, Lars Falkmo, Stan Greenberg, Richard Hymans, Tom McNab, Bill Mallon, Paul S. Marshall, Wilf Morgan, Glenn Piper, the late Don Potts, Hamish Thomson, Chris Thorne, David M. Thurlow, Mel Watman, Clive Williams, Alex Wilson and Colin Young. Kevin Kelly has been particularly helpful in providing illustrations for the final publication. Finally, we are profoundly grateful to Stuart Mazdon, who undertook the unenviable task of converting our rough-hewn lists to book form. The design delights the authors and is entirely of his making.

INTRODUCTION

The world's first national championships for amateurs were organised by the Amateur Athletic Club from 1866 to 1879. In the latter year London Athletic Club staged a rival championship meeting. In 1880, the Amateur Athletic Association was founded and took over. The annual championships have been continuous ever since except for the war years. A booklet by the late Ian Buchanan, *The AAA Championships 1880-1939*, published by the NUTS in 2003, listed the top six in each event. So the present booklet concentrates on the pre-history, the period of the AAC Championships, a significant stage when meetings were increasing in number, clubs were being formed, new tracks built and many of the rules and procedures of modern athletics established.

The AAC was set up as a club with the aim of running an annual championship meeting. It never aspired to govern the sport, as did the AAA. The founder and main organiser for the fourteen years of its existence was John Graham Chambers (1843-83), a remarkable young Welshman who as an undergraduate was largely responsible for founding and running the Oxford and Cambridge meeting in 1864. Thanks in large part to Chambers, the basic programme of track and field was established in these years, taking the best from a variety of traditions including school and college sports, the highland games and pedestrianism (professional athletics). When the AAC announced its programme in December, 1865, it created a template that would later be followed by national bodies around the world and by the Olympic movement. This was Chambers' concept of a balanced championship meeting: 100yds, 440yds, 880yds, 1 mile, 4 miles, 7 miles walk, 120yds hurdles over ten flights, 3ft 6in high, high running jump, long running leap and high pole jump, putting the weight (16lb) and throwing the hammer (16lb). The weights and the height of the hurdles remain the same even in our modern version of the sport. Other events ancient in origin, the discus and javelin, were added at later dates.

In 1866, most athletics was professional in the sense that there was a long-established system of competition for money prizes, mainly for running and walking, known as pedestrianism. But it would be a mistake to compare the "professionals" of Victorian times with the elite of modern athletes who can earn a good living from the sport. The majority were part-timers working in other occupations. Even the best of them generally listed jobs other than pedestrianism on the census forms.

Distinct from this working class sport, the public schools, military colleges, civil service and universities had been developing competitive athletics as a recreational pastime. They practised a range of events, emulating the running, jumping and throwing typical of Scottish Highland and Border Games. When the AAC announced its championship meeting it was thought necessary to call the participants *gentlemen amateurs*. This was intended to define both their class and their aspiration as lovers of sport as distinct from the pedestrians, chasers after cash prizes. There were exceptions: a few working class men gained entry in the 1870s, but the majority of the entrants were out of the top drawer.

The events in a Victorian athletics meeting might sound familiar, but a modern spectator travelling back in time would find much that was surprising. First and most obvious was what was worn. The rules required that athletes were properly attired. In the earliest meetings at the universities, cricket flannels were the norm. By the time of the championships of 1866, short-sleeved tops covered the shoulders and loose drawers extended below the knees. Spiked shoes had been in use by professionals since the mid 1840s and were worn by many amateurs in the 1860s. Tracksuits were unknown. Competitors turned up in topcoats and hats. Often such covering was needed, because the university athletics season started in the frosts of February and was over in April. The AAC Championships were held a day or so after the Oxford v Cambridge meeting in March or early April. The weather was not often conducive to fast times. By breaking the close link with the universities insisted on by Chambers, the AAA from 1880 onwards made the annual championships a July meeting and altogether warmer.

The track surfaces were originally turf and remained so for many provincial meetings, but cinders were used at the main metropolitan venues. Purpose-built running tracks as we know them had been introduced about 1835 at Sheffield's Hyde Park and London's Lord's cricket ground. On these tracks – which could vary in size from 440 yards to approximately 1/3 mile – the events were generally started by pistol shot, but sometimes word of mouth. There was no rule about the number of false starts, except that someone who 'broke' could be put back a yard, but at the discretion of the starter. As many as a dozen or more false starts might occur before the field got away. Timekeepers held stopwatches accurate to the nearest fifth of a second.

Lanes for the 100 yards were marked with strings staked at about knee length. In all other races there were no lanes. Thus a 220 or 440 yards started with a charge for the pole position, then a waiting game and an extra surge at the end. All runners used a standing start until the 1890s.

Handicap running became increasingly popular in the period of our study. The handicappers were experts who kept records of performers and gave starts calculated to ensure that everyone had a chance of winning and the races were as close as possible. The "scratch" man was reckoned to be the fastest and thus the only one who ran the full distance. In our ranking lists we have included performances from scratch but not by athletes given starts. In theory it is possible to estimate the time a handicapped runner might have achieved, but we have followed the principle that each runner listed should have run the full distance.

The ethos about distance running was different from the modern idea that everyone (except pacemakers) should strive to complete the race. If a Victorian felt at some stage that he stood no chance of winning it was acceptable to stop running and retire. It was rare for everyone to last the course.

Hurdling was over sheep hurdles staked into the turf and they didn't topple when hit. In 1895 when the London Athletic Club athletes first saw the collapsible structures used in America they called them 'clothes-horse hurdles'. The standard height of 3ft 6in became the norm. The 120 yards races were always over turf, generally down the centre of the ground. 440 yards was only possible at meetings over grass courses and was sometimes over 3ft 6in hurdles, but generally 3ft 0in.

Steeplechasing had so many variations as to barriers and distance that we have not attempted to make year lists for this event.

Field events, too, had their own nineteenth century character. A modern high jumper using the flop style would be disqualified for diving head first. A jumper like Marshall Brooks ran straight at the bar and tucked his legs under him as he sailed over six feet. Organisers sometimes provided landing areas of tan (crushed bark) or sand. Mattresses were introduced later, notably in the pole jump, and were for softies. The poles used by the vaulters were made of ash or hickory and gave no spring, so the extra power supplied by a modern fibre glass pole makes the modern event almost another discipline. The poles had a spike in the end that gave some purchase for the jump. A controversial "climbing" technique was developed that enabled skilful athletes to haul themselves higher by moving their hands as the pole reached the vertical.

The long jump was the event closest to the modern form, but was generally known as the broad jump or running jump. The Victorians all used the "sail" style still favoured by many modern athletes. The measurement was taken to the jumper's heelmarks, so it was important to avoid making a mark with any other part of the anatomy and so recording a no-jump.

Opposite: The map shows the proximity of major athletics venues in West Brompton. The Beaufort House track is the irregular oval around and through the rifle range of the South Middlesex Rifle Volunteers with the house itself to the west. Amateur athletics were held there from 1864 to 1869, with the track shown here probably being 3 laps to the mile. The irregular rectangle of the Lillie Bridge track is immediately to the east, around the cricket ground. The inaugural meeting there was the AAC Championships of 1869. The majority of the map is from the 1865-1871 period, but the south-eastern quadrant is from 1894, by which time many fields and orchards had been built upon. There we see the familiar shape of a track on the Stamford Bridge Athletic Grounds, built by London AC in 1877. The two fields labelled 90 and 91 in the far north-west corner of the map, north of The Hermitage, were the original location of the Star Running Grounds where professional races were held. In 1879 that area was developed for housing and the Star Grounds moved south of the river to Battersea. For more details of these grounds and others, see *Played in London*, published by English Heritage, and www.runtrackdir.com.

199

200

Monbury Chapel
(Church of England)

B.M.243

WEST LONDON EXTENSION RY

Stamford Bridge
Athletic Grounds

Pavilion

B.M.19.3

P.H.

Chelsea
Station L.X

B.M.19.5

B.M. Posty. Boro. Bdy.

FULHAM EXTENSION

METROPOLITAN DISTRICT RY

97

London Road
Car Company's
Depot

B.M.55

Pond

W.S.T.

Lillie Bridge
Cricket Ground

96

WEST LONDON EXTENSION RAIL

Brom. & Fulham Junction

92

95

94 Range

Rifle Ground

101

100

Waltham Green
Station

89

91

90

The Hermitage

Brandon
House

Horse Tank

Cinder Tank

Pond

Walham Green

132

The Hermitage

86

183

M

A

The triple jump, known mainly in this period as the hop, step and leap or hop, step and jump, was rarely contested in England, except in certain schools and among some Lancashire professionals. It was more popular in Scottish highland games and in Ireland. A variant technique, using two hops and a jump, was found by some to be more efficient, and was allowed except when judges were particularly vigilant. Press reports generally fail to state which technique was used, so we have included both forms in our lists.

The shot put is an ancient event developed from throwing heavy stones or cannonballs for distance. The weight became standardised at 16lb, but heavier weights of 22lb and more were used in the Highlands. The throwing area in England was originally between two lines seven feet apart, but in Scotland this was six inches more. In 1878 John Chambers introduced the seven-foot circle for the championship meeting, but from 1882 the AAA used a seven-foot square. Only in the Olympic year of 1908 did they concede that Chambers had it right and reverted to the circle.

The discus and javelin were introduced in Britain for the 1908 Olympics, and weren't practised in the period of our study.

Hammer-throwers used wooden-handled implements and the rules permitted shafts of any length and an unlimited run or turning area until about 1876 when the length of the handle was restricted to 3ft 6in and the seven-foot run was introduced. The seven-foot circle dates from 1878. In the Scottish Games turns were not permitted. A nine-foot circle was permitted in England from 1887 to 1907. There was no "cage" but accidents were rare.

Another feature of the early championship meetings was the low turnout of competitors and this continued into the early AAA meetings. They didn't enter unless they expected to win. When a top performer was known to be competing, the field would sometimes be reduced to one or two. The 100yds and 120yds hurdles generally had enough entrants to justify qualifying heats, but most other events would be down to a maximum of six. In the year Marshall Brooks high-jumped 6ft 2½ at the Oxford and Cambridge meeting, no one challenged him for the AAC title. 'Walk-overs' for one athlete of exceptional ability are known to have occurred in the mile, 4 miles, 7 miles walk, pole jump, long jump, shot and hammer.

The lists that follow are sufficiently comprehensive to indicate the standard of Victorian athletics, but it should be stated that in many provincial meetings times were not taken or jumps and throws measured. It is frustrating to historians to read reports of well-known athletes competing and credited only with their finishing order. In Scottish Games, the jumps and throws were usually measured, but it was not the tradition to time any of the races. Fine runners like Hindle, McLeavy and Cummings were regulars there, and must have performed well, but we will never know how well.

In recent years many newspapers have been digitised, making it possible to search more efficiently, and it is certain that fresh performances will come to light as time goes on. We decided to publish in the 150th year since the AAC first held a championship meeting. We hope future historians will add to our pioneering effort.

Peter Lovesey became an athletics enthusiast watching the 1948 Olympics. In the 1960s he wrote about the history of the sport for Athletics Arena and Athletics Weekly and joined the NUTS. His first book, *The Kings of Distance* (1968), was about five great runners from Deerfoot to Zatopek. He wrote the *Official Centenary History of the AAA* (1979) and has published two bibliographies, *The Guide to British Track & Field Literature* (1969, with Tom McNab) and *An Athletics Compendium* (2001, with Andrew Huxtable and Tom McNab). He is a crime novelist: website www.peterlovesey.com.

Keith Morbey first became interested in athletics listening to the radio commentary of the Wooderson–Andersson encounter from White City in 1945. A lifetime interest followed and he joined the NUTS as its Hampshire correspondent in 1959 after National Service as an RAF Russian linguist. A short spell in repertory followed and he has been acting in Amateur Dramatics ever since. He wrote under the name 'Old Timer' in Athletics Arena and in 1964, following a conversation with Stan Greenberg decided to specialise in relay statistics. For several years he was Archivist for The Ghost Club and is now a Ghost Club consultant.

THE AMATEUR ATHLETIC CLUB CHAMPIONSHIPS

DATES & VENUES

1866	Friday 23 March	Beaufort House, West Brompton, London
1867	Monday 15 April	Beaufort House
1868	Fri/Sat 19/20 June	Beaufort House
1869	Saturday 3 April	Lillie Bridge, West Brompton, London
1870	Fri/Sat 8/9 April	Lillie Bridge
1871	Monday 3 April	Lillie Bridge
1872	Wednesday 27 March	Lillie Bridge
1873	Saturday 5 April	Lillie Bridge
1874	Monday 30 March	Lillie Bridge
1875	Monday 22 March	Lillie Bridge
1876	Monday 10 April	Lillie Bridge
1877	Monday 26 March	Lillie Bridge
1878	Monday 15 April	Lillie Bridge
1879	Monday 7 April	Lillie Bridge

In 1879 London Athletic Club organised a rival Championship Meeting at Stamford Bridge, London, on Saturday 14 and Monday 16 June.

100 YARDS

1866 23 March. 3 heats. 13 competitors.
Heat 1
1. C.H.Prest — London AC — 10¾
2. A.J.A.Wilkinson — Anomalies CC — 1 ft
3. W.F.Maitland — Oxford UAC — close
4. R.F.C.Villiers — Barnes FC

Heat 2
1. C.G.Emery — Civil Service — 10¾
2. W.Collett — London AC — ½ yd
ac J.Lowther — Public Schools C
ac R.W.Smith — Royal Horse Artillery

Heat 3
1. T.M.Colmore — Oxford UAC — 10½
2. R.W.Vidal — Oxford UAC — 1 yd
3. M.E.Jobling — Northumberland CC — close
4. B.B.Connolly — Cambridge UAC
5. H.J.V.Philpott — Twickenham RC

FINAL
1. T.M.Colmore — Oxford UAC — 10½
2. R.W.Vidal — Oxford UAC — 6 in
3. W.Collett — London AC — ½ yd
4. C.G.Emery — Civil Service
5. A.J.A.Wilkinson — Anomalies CC
C.H.Prest (London AC) did not start

1867 15 April. 3 heats. 7 competitors.
Heat 1
1. J.H.Ridley — Eton College — 11.0
2. C.G.Emery — London AC — ½ yd

Heat 2
1. W.Collett — London AC — 11¼
2. J.Somervell — Oxford UAC — 2 yd

Heat 3
1= W.H.MacLaren — Manchester AC — 10¾
1= R.W.Vidal — Oxford UAC — 10¾
3. W.C.Clifford — 48th Regiment — close

FINAL
1. J.H.Ridley — Eton College — 10¾
2. W.Collett — London AC — 1 yd
3. R.W.Vidal — Oxford UAC — 1 ft
4. W.H.MacLaren — Manchester AC — 1 ft

1868 Heats 19 June, final 20 June. 6 competitors
Heat 1
1. W.M.Tennent — Manchester AC — 10.0 w
2. E.J.Colbeck — London AC — 4 yd
3. W.H.Betts — London AC — 2 ft

Heat 2
1. W.H.MacLaren — Manchester AC — 10 3/5
2. W.Collett — London AC — 4 ft
3. F.G.Templer — Harrow School — 2 yd

FINAL
1. W.M.Tennent — Manchester AC — 10 1/5
2. E.J.Colbeck — London AC — 1 ft
3. W.H.MacLaren — Manchester AC — 1½ yd
4. W.Collett — London AC

1869 3 April. 6 competitors
Heat 1
1. W.F.Eaton — Civil Service — 10 3/5
2. J.H.Hague — Enfield Lock — 2 ft
3. J.C.Butler — Amateur AC — 2 yd
4. W.J.F.Morgan — Unattached

Heat 2
1. J.G.Wilson — Oxford UAC — NTT
2. E.G.Loder — Eton College — 6 in
Both certain to qualify, so they jogged over

FINAL
1. J.G.Wilson — Oxford UAC — 10 2/5
2= E.G.Loder — Eton College — 1 yd
2= J.H.Hague — Enfield Lock — 1 yd
4. W.F.Eaton — Civil Service
Run-off for second place: 1. Loder 10 2/5 2. Hague 1 ft

1870 Heats 8 April, final 9 April. 11 competitors.
Heat 1
1. R.Matthews   London AC   w.o.

Heat 2
1. W.Collett	London AC	10 2/5
2. A.J.Baker	London AC	6 in/1 ft
3. G.P.Butcher	London AC	1 ft
4. C.E.Watson	Amateur AC	close

Heat 3
1. F.O.Philpott	Oxford UAC	10 2/5
2= R.Clement	Red Rovers FC	2 yd
2= E.J.Colbeck	London AC	2 yd

Heat 4
1. A.J.Eames	London AC	1 yd
2= J.V.Fitzgerald	Oxford UAC	½ yd
2= C.J.Curteis	London AC	½ yd

Second Round
Heat 1
1. A.J.Baker	London AC	10 1/5
2. F.O.Philpott	Oxford UAC	1 ft
3. W.Collett	London AC	6 in
4. J.V.Fitzgerald	Oxford UAC	
5. C.J.Curteis	London AC	

Heat 2
1. E.J.Colbeck	London AC	10 2/5
2. A.J.Eames	London AC	1 yd
3. R.Clement	Red Rovers FC	1 ft
4. R.Matthews	London AC	1 ft

FINAL
1. A.J.Baker	London AC	10 1/5
2. F.O.Philpott	Oxford UAC	1 ft
3. E.J.Colbeck	London AC	½ yd
4. A.J.Eames	London AC	½ yd

1871 3 April. No heats. 5 competitors.
1. J.G.Wilson	Oxford UAC	10 2/5
2. E.J.Davies	Cambridge UAC	2 yd
3. T.C.Hooman	Wanderers FC	2 yd
4. H.S.Dalbiac	RMA	
W.Collett	London AC	dnf (fell)

1872 27 March. 7 competitors.
Heat 1
1. W.A.Dawson	Cambridge UAC	10¼
2. G.R.Johnstone	London AC	2½ yd
3. H.M.Tennent	Amateur AC	2 yd
4. E.H.Cameron	Royal Engineers	

Heat 2
1. R.Philpot	Cambridge UAC	10 2/5
2. A.W.L.Brodie	Cambridge UAC	1 ft
3. W.H.Palmer	Lewisham CC	3 yd

FINAL
1. W.A.Dawson	Cambridge UAC	10½
2. R.Philpot	Cambridge UAC	2½ yd
3. G.R.Johnstone	London AC	1½ yd
4. A.W.L.Brodie	Cambridge UAC	½ yd

1873 5 April. 6 competitors
Heat 1
1. J.Potter	South London H	10 3/5
2. W.E.Tomkin	Eton College	1 yd
3. A.Hatfield	Eton College	8 yd

Heat 2
1= G.R.Johnstone	Amateur AC	10 3/5
1= A.W.Oldfield	Birmingham AC	10 3/5
3. A.A.Yorke	Sherwood AC	1½ yd

FINAL
1. J.Potter	South London H	10 2/5
2. A.W.Oldfield	Birmingham AC	½ yd
3. G.R.Johnstone	Amateur AC	4 ft

W.E.Tomkin (Eton College) did not start

1874 30 March. 9 competitors
Heat 1
1. A.H.Pearson	Notts City FC	10 1/5
2. E.J.Davies	Cambridge UAC	2 ft
3. C.Atkins	Cheltenham	3 yd
4. H.R.S.De Moist	London AC	

Heat 2
1. J.Potter	London AC	10¼
2. J.D.Ogilby	Irish Champion AC	1 yd
3. G.A.Templer	Cambridge UAC	2 yd
4. R.E.Newport	Oxford UAC	
5. W.E.Tomkin	Eton College	

FINAL
1. E.J.Davies	Cambridge UAC	10½
2. J.Potter	London AC	1 ft
3. A.H.Pearson	Notts City FC	inches
4. J.D.Ogilby	Irish Champion AC	close

1875 22 March. No heats. 3 competitors.
FINAL
1. J.Potter	South London H	10 3/5
2. H.Lucas	South London H	6 in/½ yd
3. W.C.R.Bedford	Cambridge UAC	6 in

1876 10 April. 6 competitors.
Heat 1
1. M.Shearman	Oxford UAC	10 1/5
2. H.Lucas	South London H	2½ yd
3. A.Powles	South London H	½ yd

Heat 2
1. E.M.Salmon	Cambridge UAC	10 3/5
2. E.J.Davies	Cambridge UAC	½ yd
3. C.A.W.Gilbert	London AC	

FINAL
1. M.Shearman	Oxford UAC	10 3/5
2. E.M.Salmon	Cambridge UAC	¾ yd
3. E.J.Davies	Cambridge UAC	
4. H.Lucas	South London H	

1877 26 March. 7 competitors.
Heats started by word of mouth.
Heat 1

1. E.C.Trepplin	Oxford UAC	10 2/5
2. H.H.Sturt	London AC	3 yd
3. H.Crossley	Leyton FC	2 yd
4. H.T.Hicks	102nd Fusiliers	9-10 yd

Heat 2

1. E.M.Salmon	Cambridge UAC	10 4/5
2. H.Macdougall	London AC	1 yd
3. J.G.Alkin	Nuneaton FC	1½ yd

FINAL

1. H.Macdougall	London AC	10 2/5
2. E.M.Salmon	Cambridge UAC	1 ft
3. E.C.Trepplin	Oxford UAC	1 yd
4. H.H.Sturt	London AC	1 yd

Several sources state that Macdougall false-started, but there was no recall.

1878 15 April. 4 competitors
Heat 1

E.Baddeley	Cambridge UAC	w.o.
L.Junker	London AC/Russia	w.o.

Heat 2

H.Macdougall	London AC	w.o.
G.L.Spencer	Cambridge UAC	w.o.

FINAL

1. L.Junker	London AC/Russia	10 1/5
2. G.L.Spencer	Cambridge UAC	2½ yd
3. H.Macdougall	London AC	1 yd
4. E.Baddeley	Cambridge UAC	

1879 7 April. No heats. 3 competitors
FINAL

1. M.R.Portal	Oxford UAC	10 3/5
2. E.Storey	Cambridge UAC	1 ft
3. E.L.Lucas	Cambridge UAC	2 yd

1879
LAC Championship 14 June. 4 competitors

1. C.L.Lockton	London AC	10 1/5
2. H.Allan	London AC	2½ yd
3. H.Crossley	London AC	close
4. H.M.Massey	St Thomas's Hosp	close

440 YARDS

1866 23 March. 3 competitors

1. J.H.Ridley	Eton College	55.0
2. A.J.A.Wilkinson	Anomalies CC	6 yd
3. C.W.Beardsell	Huddersfield	

1867 15 April. 4 competitors

1. J.H.Ridley	Eton College	52¾
2. R.W.Vidal	Oxford UAC	¾ yd
3. E.J.Colbeck	London AC	1 ft
4. W.H.MacLaren	Manchester AC	1 ft

1868 20 June. 3 competitors

1. E.J.Colbeck	London AC	50 2/5
2. W.H.MacLaren	Manchester AC	12 yd
H.J.Chinnery	London AC	dnf

Colbeck set a world best time despite colliding with a sheep on the track.

1869 3 April. 5 competitors

1. E.J.Colbeck	London AC	53 3/5
2. W.G.Grace	London AC	10 yd
3. F.T.Down	Oxford UAC	5 yd
4. J.C.Butler	Amateur AC	10 yd
5. H.C.Needham	Grenadier Guards	

1870 9 April. 3 competitors

1. A.R.Upcher	Cambridge UAC	52 3/5
2. E.J.Colbeck	London AC	53 1/5
3. A.G.Clarke	South Essex AC	

Times in Bell's Life *are 52 2/5 and 53.0*

1871 3 April. 3 competitors

1. A.R.Upcher	Cambridge UAC	51 4/5
2. W.Page	London AC	4 yd
3. H.S.Dalbiac	RMA	5 yd

1872 27 March. 4 competitors

1. R.Philpot	Cambridge UAC	52 4/5
2. A.W.L.Brodie	Cambridge UAC	1½ yd
3. E.G.Loder	Cambridge UAC	4 yd
4. W.Page	London AC	3 yd

1873 3 April. 3 competitors

1. A.R.Upcher	Cambridge UAC	53 2/5
2. C.D.Risbee	Northampton AC	8 to 10 yd
3. J.C.MacLean	Carlton FC	5 yd

1874 30 March. 4 competitors

1. G.A.Templer	Cambridge UAC	53¾
2. J.Potter	London AC	4 yd
3. G.W.Gower	GW Railway CC	6 yd
4. A.L.Pelham	Amateur AC	close

1875 22 March. 3 competitors

1. F.T.Elborough	London AC	51.0
2. A.R.Lewis	Cambridge UAC	5 yd
3. J.Potter	South London H	1 ft

1876 10 April. 2 competitors

1. F.T.Elborough	London AC	52 2/5
2. A.R.Lewis	Cambridge UAC	4 yd

1877 26 March. 3 competitors

1. F.T.Elborough	London AC	51 2/5
2. W.H.Churchill	Cambridge UAC	5 yd
3. H.W.Hill	London AC	4 yd

1878 15 April. 4 competitors

1. J.Shearman	London AC	52 4/5
2. M.Shearman	Oxford UAC	1 yd
3. W.H.Churchill	Cambridge UAC	6 yd
4. H.H.Sturt	London AC	

1879 7 April. 3 competitors

1. E.Storey	Cambridge UAC	51 2/5
2. M.R.Portal	Oxford UAC	1 ft
3. F.W.Fellowes	Burton FC	20 yd

1879

LAC Championship 14 June. 4 competitors

1. H.R.Ball	London AC	51 4/5
2. S.H.Baker	London AC	1½ yd
3. H.H.Sturt	London AC	½ yd
4. S.D.A.Stoneham	Beckenham CC	

880 YARDS

1866 23 March. 4 competitors

1. P.M.Thornton	London AC	2:05.0
2. W.C.Gibbs	Cambridge UAC	10 yd
E.B.Michell	Oxford UAC	dnf
W.Collett	London AC	dnf

Note: Bell's Life gave 2:07.0

1867 15 April. 4 competitors

1. W.J.Frere	Oxford UAC	2:10.0
2. W.D.Hogarth	Liverpool AC	3 yd
3. A.King	London AC	walked in
F.G.Pelham	Cambridge UAC	dnf

1868 19 June. 4 competitors

1. E.J.Colbeck	London AC	2:02.0
2. A.King	London AC	4½ yd
3. W.R.M.Bethune	Civil Service	3½ yd
H.S.Dixon	Civil Service	dnf

1869 3 April. 4 competitors

1. R.V.Somers-Smith	Oxford UAC	2:02.6
2. E.J.Colbeck	London AC	2 yd
3. W.B.Newson	German Gym S	12 yd
4. W.G.Grace	London AC	5 yd

1870 9 April. 6 competitors

1. R.V.Somers-Smith	Oxford UAC	2:02.0
2. A.J.C.Dowding	Oxford UAC	1½ yd
3. A.L.Pelham	Cambridge UAC	12 yd
4. G.A.Templer	Cambridge UAC	several yd
5. E.J.Colbeck	London AC	15 yd
W.F.Eaton	Amateur AC	dnf

1871 3 April. 2 competitors

1. A.L.Pelham	Cambridge UAC	2:06.0
2. A.J.C.Dowding	Oxford UAC	1 ft

1872 27 March. 6 competitors

1= T.Christie	Oxford UAC	2:00.4
1= G.A.Templer	Cambridge UAC	2:00.4
3. A.L.Pelham	Cambridge UAC	8 yd
4. H.S.Dixon	London AC	
A.E.W.D.Forbes	ex-Eton College	dnf
C.C.Armitage	S.Norwood AC	dnf

World best performance.

1873 5 April. 6 competitors

1. A.L.Pelham	Cambridge UAC	2:05.5
2. G.A.Templer	Cambridge UAC	3 yd
3. J.W.Moore	Birmingham AC	1½ yd
J.Bolton	Liverpool AC	dnf
H.W.Murray	Amateur AC	dnf
H.S.Dixon	London AC	dnf

The time is given as 2:04.8 in Bell's Life

1874 30 March. 3 competitors

1. E.A.Sandford	Oxford UAC	2:04.0
2. F.W.Todd	Irish Champion AC	3 yd
3. J.W.Moore	Birmingham AC	1 yd

1875 22 March. 5 competitors

1. E.A.Sandford	Oxford UAC	2:04.2
2. H.A.Bryden	Clapham Rovers FC	1 yd
3. F.W.Todd	Irish Champion AC	3 yd
4. H.W.Hill	London AC	
C.C.Cumberbatch	Cambridge UAC	dnf

1876 10 April. 6 competitors

1. F.T.Elborough	London AC	2:03.0
2. A.L.Pelham	Royal Agric College	1 yd
3. H.A.Bryden	London AC	2 yd
ac C.H.T.Metcalfe	Oxford UAC	
ac W.Cunliffe	Cambridge UAC	
F.W.Todd	Irish Champion AC	dnf

1877 26 March. 2 competitors

1. F.T.Elborough	London AC	2:00.0
2. A.L.Pelham	Amateur AC	3 yd

Time given as 1:59.8 in Bell's Life

1878 15 April. 4 competitors

1= H.A.Whately	Oxford UAC	2:03.4
1= L.Knowles	Cambridge UAC	2:03.4
3. J.D.Sadler	London AC	4 yd
ac W.W.Bolton	Cambridge UAC	

1879 7 April. 4 competitors

1. W.W.Bolton	Cambridge UAC	2:03.6
2. L.Knowles	Cambridge UAC	3 yd
3. C.J.Johnstone	Cambridge UAC	17 yd
4. W.E.Pedley	Royal Ind Eng Coll	1 yd

1879

LAC Championship 14 June. 3 competitors

1. C.Hazen Wood	London AC	2:01.2
2. N.Turner	London AC	5 yd
3. W.E.Pedley	Royal Ind Eng Coll	15 yd

ONE MILE

1866 23 March. 4 competitors
1. C.B.Lawes   Cambridge UAC   4:39.0
2. W.P.Bowman   Oxford UAC   12 yd
   W.M.Chinnery   London AC   dnf
ac R.F.C.Villiers   Barnes FC

1867 15 April. 3 competitors
1. S.G.Scott   Oxford UAC   4:42.0
2. C.H.K.Long   Cambridge UAC   6 in
3. W.M.Chinnery   London AC   walked in

1868 19 June. 2 competitors
1. W.M.Chinnery   London AC   4:33.2
2. E.M.Hawtrey   Eton College   27 yd

1869 3 April. 2 competitors
1. W.M.Chinnery   London AC   4:50.0
2. G.A.Templer   Cambridge UAC   5:01.5

1870 9 April. 3 competitors
1. R.H.Benson   Oxford UAC   4:54.6
2. E.A.Bartlett   Oxford UAC   4:57.6
3. T.R.Hewitt   Cambridge UAC   5:02.0

1871 3 April. 4 competitors
1. W.M.Chinnery   London AC   4:31.8
2. T.Christie   Oxford UAC   20 yd
3. E.M.Hawtrey   Cambridge UAC   30 yd
4. H.A.MacNaghten   Cambridge UAC

1872 27 March. 4 competitors
1. C.H.Mason   London AC   4:42.25
2. T.R.Hewitt   Oxford UAC   8 yd
3. E.M.Hawtrey   Cambridge UAC   8 yd
   A.E.W.D.Forbes   ex-Eton College dnf

1873 5 April. 4 competitors
1. W.Slade   London AC   4:32.6

2. E.A.Sandford   Oxford UAC   3 yd
3. J.W.Moore   Birmingham AC   30 yd
4. A.E.W.D.Forbes   Amateur AC

1874 30 March. 2 competitors
1. W.Slade   London AC   4:43.0
   E.B.Grimmer   Norwich AC   dnf

1875 22 March. 3 competitors
1. W.Slade   Amateur AC   4:35.4
   T.R.Hewitt   Cambridge UAC   dnf
   W.Y.Winthrop   Cambridge UAC   dnf

1876 10 April. 2 competitors
1. W.Slade   London AC   4:35.2
2. H.J.Lee-Evans   ex-Cambridge UAC 27 yd

1877 26 March. 1 competitor
1. W.Slade   London AC   4:29.2 (w.o.)
*Slade, unchallenged, ran a partly-paced mile. Time
4:29.5 in another source.*

1878 15 April. 4 competitors
1. A.F.Hills   Oxford UAC   4:28.8
2. J.Gibb   London AC   2½ yd
3. H.J.Lee-Evans   ex-Cambridge UAC 60 yd
ac E.B.Grimmer   St John's, Norwich

1879 7 April. 3 competitors
1. B.R.Wise   Oxford UAC   4:29.0
2. H.C.Jenkins   Oxford UAC   15 yd
3. C.J.Johnstone   Cambridge UAC   100 yd

1879
LAC Championship 14 June. 3 competitors
1. W.G.George   Moseley H   4:26.6
ac S.K.Holman   London AC
ac C.Hazen Wood   London AC   dnf

FOUR MILES

1866 23 March. 10 competitors
1. R.C.Garnett   Cambridge UAC   21:41.0
2. E.Royds   Eton College   15 yd
3. B.C.Molloy   London Rowing C
   K.T.Digby   London AC   dnf
   G.A.Montgomerie Oxford   dnf
   C.F.Farran   London Rowing C   dnf
   F.Witty   London AC   dnf
   F.St J.N.Barne   Scots Fusilier Guards dnf
   C.W.Beardsell   Huddersfield   dnf
ac? D.Moffatt   Oxford UAC
ac? W.S.Cadman   Cambridge UAC
World best performance. Several sources give 21:42.0

1867 15 April. 6 competitors
1. G.G.Kennedy   Cambridge UAC   22:12.5
2. J.W.Fletcher   Oxford UAC   15 yd
3. J.G.Webster   London AC   150 yd
   J.A.Allanson   London AC   dnf
   M.H.Holworthy   Amateur AC   dnf
   E.P.Hood   Oxford UAC   dnf

1868 20 June. 4 competitors
1. W.M.Chinnery   London AC   21:12.0
2. J.Snow   Manchester AC   270 yd
   W.Gilmour   London AC   dnf
   H.S.Dixon   Civil Service   dnf
World best performance. Several sources give 21:11.0

1869 3 April. 4 competitors
1. W.M.Chinnery   London AC   21:30.0
2. E.M.Hawtrey   Cambridge UAC   21:35.0
   W.Gilmour   London AC   dnf
   J.G.Webster   Twickenham RC   dnf

1870 9 April. 6 competitors
1. H.C.Riches   London AC   21:24.0
2. E.M.Hawtrey   Cambridge UAC   21:25.6
3. A.Hardy   London AC   500 yd
   F.V.Rainsford   London AC   dnf
   J.G.Webster   Twickenham RC   dnf
   D.E.Young   ??   dnf

1871 3 April. 3 competitors

1. J.Scott	London AC	20:38.0
2. A.Wheeler	London Gym Soc	22:02.0
3. F.V.Rainsford	London AC	23:37.0

World best performance

1872 27 March. 7 competitors

1. J.B.Edgar	Isle of Man	21:31.25
2. A.Wheeler	German Gym Soc	21:44.0
3. J.Powell	Barnes FC	22:22.0
J.E.Matthews	London AC	dnf
P.J.Burt	Amateur AC	dnf
C.J.Michod	London AC	dnf
A.F.Somerville	Cambridge UAC	dnf

1873 5 April. 6 competitors

1. A.F.Somerville	Cambridge UAC	21:38.0
2. A.Wheeler	Stoke on Trent	21:48.0e
E.Kensington	Royal Artillery	dnf
C.H.Mason	London AC	dnf
C.H.Larrette	South London H	dnf
F.Richardson	Stratford	dnf

1874 30 March. 9 competitors

1. W.Slade	Amateur AC	20:52.0
2. J.E.Warburton	Haslingden AC	30 yd
3. A.E.R.Micklefield	Cambridge UAC	450 yd
A.Wheeler	North London H	dnf
G.F.Congreve	Amateur AC	dnf
A.C.Courtney	Irish Champion AC	dnf
J.E.Matthews	London AC	dnf
A.Gilmour	Cambridge UAC	dnf
C.H.Larrette	South London H	dnf

1875 22 March. 6 competitors

1. J.Gibb	South London H	21:09.4
W.Slade	Amateur AC	dnf
C.W.L.Bulpett	Oxford UAC	dnf
P.H.Stenning	Clevedon FC	dnf
P.M.Ward	Farnham Club	dnf
J.Swift	West Kent CB	dnf

1876 10 April. 4 competitors

1. A.Goodwin	Oxford UAC	21:17.2
2. C.H.Mason	London AC	3 yd
3. J.C.Bendixen	South London H	120 yd
A.P.Smith	London AC	dnf

1877 26 March. 1 competitor

1. J.Gibb	South London H	walk over

Gibb ran for 2 2/3 miles (2 miles in 10:15) and was declared the winner.

1878 15 April. 2 competitors

1. J.Gibb	London AC	20:29.8
A.P.Smith	London AC	dnf

1879 7 April. 2 competitors

1. J.E.Warburton	Stoke Victoria AC	20:41.6
2. J.Harris	Middlesborough BC	22:15.6

1879
LAC Championship 14 June. 3 competitors

1. W.G.George	Moseley H	20:52.2
C.H.Mason	London AC	dnf
W.Stevenson	London AC	dnf

10 MILES

1879
LAC Championship 16 June. 4 competitors

1. C.H.Mason	London AC	56:31.6
2. G.E.Stanley	Spartan H	57:51.8
C.F.Turner	Spartan H	dnf
W.Stevenson	London AC	dnf

2 MILES STEEPLECHASE

1879
LAC Championship 16 June. 3 competitors

1. H.M.Oliver	Moseley H	11:49.2
2. C.L.O'Malley	Ilex SC	70 yd
3. R.S.Benson	Royal Sch of Mines	100 yd

120 YARDS HURDLES

1866 23 March. 11 competitors

Heat 1

1. D.P.Morgan	Oxford UAC	18½
2. C.G.Emery	Civil Service	12 yd
3. R.W.Smith	Royal Horse Artillery	1 yd

Heat 2

1. T.Milvain	Oxford UAC	18.0
2. J.B.Martin	Oxford UAC	2½ yd
3. M.E.Jobling	Northumberland CC	well beaten

Heat 3

1. C.N.Jackson	Oxford UAC	18½
2. L.M.Tiffany	Cambridge UAC	1 yd
3. W.H.D.Haggard	Oxford UAC	
4. A.King	Oxford UAC	
R.W.Vidal	Oxford UAC	dnf (fell)

FINAL

1. T.Milvain	Oxford UAC	17¾
2. L.M.Tiffany	Cambridge UAC	½ yd
3. J.B.Martin	Oxford UAC	
4. C.N.Jackson	Oxford UAC	
5. C.G.Emery	Civil Service	
D.P.Morgan	Oxford UAC	dnf (fell)

1867 15 April. 15 competitors

Heat 1

1. A.J.Law	Cambridge UAC	21¾
2. A.Hillyard	Oxford UAC	1 yd
3. E.Butler	Lobndon AC	some distance

Heat 2

1. H.M.Thompson	Cambridge UAC	19.0
2. R.W.Vidal	Oxford UAC	1 yd
3. A.King	Oxford UAC	
4. A.E.Molineux	Oxford UAC	

Heat 3
1. C.N.Jackson	Oxford UAC	18½
2. T.Milvain	Amateur AC	2 yd
3. C.G.Emery	London AC	close
4. R.Babington	Civil Service	

Heat 4
1= R.Fitzherbert	Cambridge UAC	18½
1= J.B.Martin	London AC	18½
3. E.Havers	Ingatestone CC	well beaten
4. M.E.Jobling	Northumberland CC	

FINAL
1. A.J.Law	Cambridge UAC	18.0
2. H.M.Thompson	Cambridge UAC	6 in
3. C.N.Jackson	OUAC	2 ft
4. R.Fitzherbert	Cambridge UAC	1 ft
5. J.B.Martin	London AC	1 ft

1868 19 June. 6 competitors
Heat 1
1. W.F.P.Moore	Amateur AC	18 3/5
2. W.H.Betts	London AC	12 yd
3. W.F.Eaton	Civil Service	6 in

Heat 2
1. W.H.MacLaren	Manchester AC	17 3/5
2. W.M.Tennent	Manchester AC	2 yd
3. C.Pitt-Taylor	Cambridge UAC	½ yd

*A run-off for second place was ordered after an
objection, and Tennent 17 2/5 beat Pitt-Taylor.*

FINAL
1. W.M.Tennent	Manchester AC	17 2/5
2. W.H.MacLaren	Manchester AC	½ yd
3. W.F.P.Moore	Amateur AC	5 yd
4. W.H.Betts	London AC	close up

1869 3 April. 6 competitors
Heat 1
1. G.R.Nunn	Guy's Hospital	18½
2. E.E.Toller	Cambridge UAC	2 yd
3. A.Hillyard	Oxford UAC	1 yd
4. H.C.Needham	Grenadier Guards	

Heat 2
| 1. W.F.Eaton | Civil Service | 20 3/5 |
| 2. J.G.Elliott | German Gym Soc | |

FINAL
1. G.R.Nunn	Guy's Hospital	18 3/5
2. E.E.Toller	Cambridge UAC	4 yd
3. W.F.Eaton	Civil Service	6 in
4. J.G.Elliott	German Gym Soc	

1870 9 April. 9 competitors
Heat 1
1. J.L.Stirling	Cambridge UAC	17.0
2. F.O.Philpott	Oxford UAC	2 yd
3. E.S.Garnier	Oxford UAC	4 yd
4. G.R.Nunn	United Hospitals AC	

Heat 2
1. E.E.Toller	London AC	18 1/5
2. I.A.Lewis	Guy's Hospital	2½ yd
3. C.W.Nicholas	South Essex AC	2 yd
4. A.G.Clarke	South Essex AC	
5. A.R.Jackson	South Norwood AC	

FINAL
1. J.L.Stirling	Cambridge UAC	17.0
2. F.O.Philpott	Oxford UAC	5 yd
3. E.E.Toller	London AC	4 yd
4. I.A.Lewis	Guy's Hospital	

1871 3 April. 5 competitors
1. E.S.Garnier	Oxford UAC	16 3/5
2. W.C.Davies	Cambridge UAC	3 yd
3. A.R.Upcher	Cambridge UAC	3 yd
4. H.W.Beauchamp	Cambridge UAC	
5. F.P.Chappell	Oxford UAC	

1872 27 March. 8 competitors
Heat 1
1. J.L.Stirling	London AC	17 1/5
2. E.S.Garnier	Oxford UAC	inches
3. J.Brockbank	Cambridge UAC	
4. T.Kitson	Upton Park FC	

Heat 2
1. H.W.Beauchamp	Cambridge UAC	17 1/5
2. E.S.Prior	Cambridge UAC	well beaten
3. W.F.P.Moore	Amateur AC	
H.M.Tennent	Amateur AC	dnf

FINAL
1. J.L.Stirling	London AC	16 4/5
2. E.S.Garnier	Oxford UAC	½ yd
3. H.W.Beauchamp	Cambridge UAC	2 yd
4. E.S.Prior	Cambridge UAC	

1873 5 April. 5 competitors
1. H.K.Upcher	Oxford UAC	16 2/5
2= E.S.Garnier	Oxford UAC	½ yd
2= J.H.A.Reay	Amateur AC	½ yd
4. E.S.Prior	Cambridge UAC	
5. E.J.Rice	Northampton AC	

1874 30 March. 6 competitors
Heat 1
1. H.K.Upcher	Oxford UAC	16 3/5
2. C.J.Spencer	Notts FC	2 yd
3. W.C.R.Bedford	Cambridge UAC	1 yd

Heat 2
1= J.H.A.Reay	London AC	16 4/5
1= H.W.Beauchamp	Kings Lynn FC	16 4/5
3. H.Macdougall	Kings Lynn FC	a few yd

FINAL
1. H.K.Upcher	Oxford UAC	16½
2. J.H.A.Reay	London AC	3 yd
3. H.W.Beauchamp	Kings Lynn FC	1 yd
C.J.Spencer	Notts FC	dnf

1875 22 March. 6 competitors
Heat 1
1. A.B.Loder	Cambridge UAC	17 2/5	
2. C.A.Bayly	Oxford UAC	1 yd	
3. C.L.Lockton	Merchant Taylors' Sch	1 yd	

Heat 2
1. H.K.Upcher	Oxford UAC	18 3/5	
2. W.C.R.Bedford	Cambridge UAC	1 yd	
3. G.Willmore	Crystal Palace AC	1 ft	

FINAL
1. H.K.Upcher	Oxford UAC	16 4/5
2. A.B.Loder	Cambridge UAC	1 ft
3. C.A.Bayly	Oxford UAC	1 yd
4. W.C.R.Bedford	Cambridge UAC	close

1876 10 April. 3 competitors
1. A.B.Loder	Cambridge UAC	16 2/5
2. J.H.A.Reay	London AC	3 yd
3. F.J.W.Wood	ex-Harrow Sch	3-4 yd

1877 26 March. 5 competitors
Heat 1
1. J.H.A.Reay	London AC	17 1/5
2. E.M.Salmon	Cambridge UAC	1 yd
3. C.A.W.Gilbert	London AC	½ yd

Heat 2
1. S.F.Jackson	Oxford UAC	walk over (23.0)
2. H.Macdougall	London AC	walk over

FINAL
1. J.H.A.Reay	London AC	17 1/5
2. S.F.Jackson	Oxford UAC	3 yd

3. H.Macdougall	London AC
4. E.M.Salmon	Cambridge UAC

1878 15 April. 7 competitors
Heat 1
1. C.L.Lockton	London AC	16 4/5
2. A.A.Barker	London AC	2 yd
3. H.Macdougall	London AC	2 yd
4. C.A.W.Gilbert	Oxford UAC	

Heat 2
1. S.F.Jackson	Oxford UAC	16 2/5
2. S.Palmer	Cambridge UAC	½ yd
3. H.Allan	London AC	5 yd

FINAL
1. S.Palmer	Cambridge UAC	16 1/5
2= S.F.Jackson	Oxford UAC	3 yd
2= C.L.Lockton	London AC	3 yd
4. A.A.Barker	London AC	

Bell's Life stated, "The official time was 16 1/5, but our representative and several others made it a fraction inside 16 seconds." Subsequently ratified as a British (and in effect world) record of 16.0.

1879 7 April. 2 competitors
1. S.Palmer	Cambridge UAC	17 2/5
2. C.A.W.Gilbert	Oxford UAC	12 yd

1879
LAC Championship 14 June. 4 competitors
1. C.L.Lockton	London AC	16 3/5
2. H.Allan	London AC	2 yd
3. F.J.W.Wood	London AC	6 in
4. H.W.Strachan	London AC	

7 MILES WALK

1866 23 March. 4 competitors
1. J.G.Chambers	Public Schools C	59:32.0
2. R.M.McKerrell	Cambridge UAC	60 yd
3. W.Doig	Cambridge UAC	15 yd
H.F.Montgomery	Oxford UAC	dnf

1867 15 April. 6 competitors
1. T.H.Farnworth	Liverpool AC	58:18.0
2. J.G.Chambers	Amateur AC	6 in
3. T.W.Thompson	London AC	a good lap
R.M.H.Williams	Civil Service	dnf
ac F.Stuart	Greenwich	
ac J.Westell	London AC	

1868 20 June. 3 competitors
1. W.Rye	London AC	57:40.0
2. T.S.Griffith	City AAC	58:00.0
3. H.F.Wilkinson	London AC	a mile

1869 3 April. 2 competitors
1. T.S.Griffith	South Essex AC	58:35.0
2. C.E.Broad	Brixton AC	1:04:02.0

1870 9 April. 4 competitors
1. T.S.Griffith	South Essex AC	55:30.0
2. R.H.Nunn	London AC	55:55.0
3. J.E.Bentley	London AC	57:01.0
H.W.Petherick	Addiscombe	dnf

World best performance

1871 3 April. 2 competitors
1. J.Francis	South Essex AC	58:09.0
J.E.Bentley	London AC	disq

1872 27 March. 5 competitors
1. T.R.Hogg	London AC	57:22.0
2. H.W.Steib	Preston Gym S	5 yd
3. J.A.Jobling	Northumberland CC	600 yd
A.Gilmour	Cambridge UAC	dnf
B.Ferguson	RA College	disq

1873 5 April. 5 competitors
1. W.J.Morgan	Atalanta RC	54:56.0
H.W.Steib	Preston Gym S	dnf
A.Gilmour	Amateur AC	dnf
G.Duxfield	Southport	dnf
E.A.Dawes	Romford	dnf

World best performance. Bell's Life gives 54:57, but four other sources agree on 54:56

1874 30 March. 1 competitor
1. W.J.Morgan   Atalanta RC   55:26.8

1875 22 March. 3 competitors
1. W.J.Morgan   Atalanta RC   53:47.0
   H.Webster   Stoke Victoria AC   dnf
   J.H.Becke   Oxford UAC   dnf
World best performance

1876 10 April. 2 competitors
1. H.Venn   London AC   55:11.8
   W.J.Morgan   Atalanta RC   dnf

1877 26 March. 5 competitors
1. H.Webster   Knotty Ash   53:59.6
2. W.J.Morgan   Atalanta RC   1 ft

3. S.W.Mitcalfe   London RC   55:06.0
4. H.Venn   London AC   55:35.0
ac J.Miles   Garston FC   dnf

1878 15 April. 3 competitors
1. H.Venn   London AC   52:25.0
   G.A.Jones   West London H   dnf
   H.Webster   Liverpool   dnf

1879 7 April. 1 competitor
1. H.Webster   Stoke Victoria AC   52:34.5
World best performance

1879
LAC Championship 14 June. 1 competitor
1. H.Venn   London AC   56:10.6

HIGH JUMP

1866 23 March. 4 competitors
1= T.G.Little   Cambridge UAC   5'9   1.753
1= J.H.T.Roupell   Cambridge UAC   5'9   1.753
3. C.E.Green   Cambridge UAC   5'6   1.676
4. R.W.Smith   Royal Horse Artillery   5'4   1.626
World best performance

1867 15 April. 4 competitors
1= C.E.Green   Cambridge UAC   5'8   1.727
1= T.G.Little   Cambridge UAC   5'8   1.727
3= Sir V.A.Brooke   Amateur AC   5'6   1.676
3= F.W.Parsons   Oxford UAC   5'6   1.676

1868 19 June. 4 competitors
1. R.J.C.Mitchell   Manchester AC   5'8   1.727
2. C.G.Pym   Civil Service   5'6   1.676
3. F.W.Parsons   Oxford UAC   5'2   1.575
4. J.G.Hoare   Cambridge UAC

1869 3 April. 2 competitors
1. J.G.Hoare   Cambridge UAC   5'2   1.575
2. J.A.Harwood   London AC   5'0   1.524

1870 9 April. 6 competitors
1. R.J.C.Mitchell   Manchester AC   5'9   1.753
2= E.Bergman   Oxford UAC   5'5   1.651
2= J.A.Harwood   London AC   5'5   1.651
4. R.L.N.Michell   Oxford UAC   5'3   1.600
5= R.G.Graham   London RC   5'1   1.549
5= C.W.Nicholas   South Essex AC   5'1   1.549
World best performance

1871 3 April. 4 competitors
1. R.J.C.Mitchell   Manchester AC   5'9½   1.765
2. J.A.Harwood   London AC   5'6   1.676
3. C.Mason   South Lincoln AC   5'1½   1.562
4. W.F.Curteis   Cambridge UAC
World best performance
Harwood 5'3½ in Bell's Life

1872 27 March. 4 competitors
1. E.S.Prior   Cambridge UAC   5'4   1.626
2. F.H.Woods   Oxford UAC   5'3   1.600
3. J.F.M.Bland   Trinity Coll Dublin
4. J.A.Harwood   London AC

1873 5 April. 8 competitors
1. J.B.Hurst   Louth AC   5'6   1.676
2= J.A.Harwood   London AC   5'4   1.626
2= E.S.Prior   Cambridge UAC   5'4   1.626
2= J.Y.Watson   German Gym Soc   5'4   1.626
2= F.H.Woods   Oxford UAC   5'4   1.626
6. G.A.Hingeston   Rly Clearing Hse AC   5'2   1.575
ac J.G.Alkin   Watford
ac W.E.Tomkin   Eton College

1874 30 March. 3 competitors
1. M.J.Brooks   Oxford UAC   5'11   1.803
2. T.Davin   Irish Champion AC   5'10   1.778
3. J.Y.Watson   London AC   5'7   1.702
World best performance

1875 22 March. 1 competitor
1. M.G.Glazebrook   Oxford UAC   5'11   1.803
Equal world best performance

1876 10 April. 1 competitor
1. M.J.Brooks   Oxford UAC   6'0   1.829

1877 26 March. 4 competitors
1. G.W.Blathwayt   Cambridge UAC   5'6   1.676
2= J.G.Alkin   Nuneaton CC   5'3¼   1.607
2= H.E.Kayll   Nuneaton CC   5'3¼   1.607
2= H.W.Strachan   London AC   5'3¼   1.607

1878 15 April. 4 competitors
1. T.H.Tomlinson   Northumberland CC   5'10¼   1.784
2. G.W.Blathwayt   Cambridge UAC   5'9   1.753

1879 7 April. 2 competitors
1. R.H.Macaulay   Cambridge UAC   5'9½   1.765
2. T.H.Tomlinson   Derby   5'6½   1.689

1879
LAC Championship 14 June. 4 competitors
1= W.Hall   Ariel RC, Bristol   5'9   1.753
1= R.E.Thomas   Liverpool Gym   5'9   1.753
3= H.W.Strachan   London AC   5'5½   1.664
3= F.J.W.Wood   London AC   5'5½   1.664

STATIONS COUNT FROM THE TURF.

11.30. 100 YARDS.   1st Heat.

1. Lieut.-Colonel WYNNE ..   Grenadier Guards..   ..   ..
2. A. J. WILKINSON   ..   Anomalies C. C. ..   ..   *violet*
3. C. H. PREST   ..   London   ..   ..   ..
4. W. F. MAITLAND ..   ..   Christ Church, Oxford ..   ..   *blue and white*
5. Hon. R. VILLIERS   ..   Oxford   ..   ..   ..

                     2nd Heat.

6. JAS. LOWTHER   ..
7. R. W. SMITH   ..   Horse Artillery   ..   ..   ..
8. W. COLLETT   ..   London Rowing Club   ..   *white, black sash*
9. C. EMERY ..   ..   Civil Service   ..   ..   *scarlet*

                     3rd Heat.

10. T. M. COLEMORE..   ..   Brazenose College, Oxford   ..   *white and black*
11. C. GUY PYM   ..   Civil Service   ..   ..   *blue and orange*
12. R. W. VIDAL   ..   St. John's College, Oxford   ..   *blue and white*
13. H. J. PHILPOTT ..   ..   *dark blue*
14. J. E. JOBLING   ..   Northumberland Cricket Club..   *blue and white*

The first and second in the trial heats to run in the final heat.

11.45. HURDLE RACE. 120 yards, over 10 flights of Hurdles.

                     1st Heat.

1. D. MORGAN   ..   ..   Magdalen Hall, Oxford ..   ..   *green*
2. C. H. PREST   ..   ..
3. R. W. SMITH   ..   ..   Horse Artillery   ..   ..   ..
4. C. EMERY ..   ..   Civil Service   ..   ..   *scarlet*

                     2nd Heat.

5. J. E. JOBLING   ..   Northumberland Cricket Club..   *blue and white*
6. Lieut.-Colonel WYNNE ..   Grenadier Guards   ..   ..
7. J. B. MARTIN   ..   *magenta*
8. T. MILVAINE   ..   Trinity Hall, Cambridge..   ..   *black and white*

                     3rd Heat.

9. H. W. THOMPSON   ..   Trinity College, Cambridge   ..   *blue and white*
10. L. TIFFANY   ..   Emmanuel College, Cambridge..   *light*
11. R. W. VIDAL   ..   St. John's College, Oxford   ..   *blue and white*
12. W. H. HAGGARD..   ..   Magdalen College, Oxford   ..   *black and white*
13. C. W. JACKSON ..   ..   Magdalen Hall, Oxford   ..   ..   *cherry*

The first and second in the trial heats to run in the final.

12.0. SEVEN MILES WALKING RACE.

1. R. M. McKERREL   ..   Trinity College, Cambridge   ..   *black, skull & cross bones*
2. J. G. CHAMBERS ..   ..   Public Schools Club   ..   ..
3. H. F. MONTGOMERY   ..   Christ Church, Oxford   ..   ..   *dark blue*
4. W. DOIG ..   ..   St. John's College, Cambridge ..   *light blue*
5. F. YOUNG ..   ..   2nd Life Guards ..   ..   *cherry and white*

Two cautions will be given, at the third the competitor will be disqualified.

1.10. 100 YARDS.   Final Heat.

1   3   5
2   4   6

1.30. PUTTING THE WEIGHT.   16 lbs.

1. Captain FRASER ..   ..   *grey and blue*
2. G. ELLIOT ..   ..   Trinity College, Cambridge   ..   *light blue*
3. C. C. CHESTON ..   ..   Merton College, Oxford ..   ..   *white with red cross*

The weight must be delivered from the shoulder, with either hand, seven feet run allowed ; no throw to count if delivered or followed with either foot over the mark; all throws will be measured by lines drawn parallel to the scratch.

The original AAC Championships programme from 1866. The pole jump was a late addition to the day's schedule.

2.0. HIGH JUMP.

1	R. W. SMITH	Horse Artillery	
2	J. C. LITTLE	Peterhouse, Cambridge	dark blue and white
3	C. E. GREEN	Trinity College, Cambridge	red, black and blue
4	J. H. S. ROUPELL	Trinity College, Cambridge	black and white

Three trials at each height, the majority of competitors to decide at what height the bar shall first be placed, and how much it shall be raised for each jump.

2.20. THROWING THE HAMMER.   16 lbs.

1	Captain FRASER		grey and blue
2	D. MOFFAT	Christ Church College. Oxford	white, blue stripes
3	D. MORGAN	Magdalen College, Oxford	green
4	R. JAMES	Jesus College, Oxford	red and black

Any method of throwing will be allowed, but the competitor will not be allowed to cross a certain line before the delivery of the hammer.

3.0. BROAD JUMP.

1	R. FITZHERBERT	St. John's College, Cambridge	red, black and blue
2	R. W. SMITH	Horse Artillery	
3	J. G. LITTLE	Peterhouse, Cambridge	dark blue and white
4	J. R. BOYLE		white, red sash
5	J. LOWE	Jesus College, Cambridge	black and red
6	W. F. MAITLAND	Christ Church College, Oxford	blue and white

3.30. ONE MILE.

1	C. B. LAWES	Trinity College, Cambridge	light blue
2	R. M. CHINNERY	London Athletic Club	green and gold
3	W. H. B. BOWMAN	University College, Oxford	
4	Earl of JERSEY	Baliol College, Oxford	
5	Hon. R. VILLIERS	Oxford	

3.45. QUARTER OF A MILE.

1	C. GUY PYM	Civil Service	orange and blue
2	C. W. BEARDSELL		black & white, blue hoop
3	A. J. WILKINSON	Anomalies C. C.	violet
4	JOHN H. RIDLEY	Eton	scarlet

4.0. HURDLE RACE.   Final Heat.

1		3	5
2		4	6

4.15. HALF-A-MILE.

1	P. M. THORNTON	London	light blue
2	W. C. GIBBS	Jesus College. Cambridge	red and black
3	W. COLLETT	London Rowing Club	white, black sash
4	E. B. MICHELL	Magdalen College, Oxford	

4.30. FOUR MILES.

1	C. W. BEARDSELL		black & white, blue hoop
2	P. C. GARNETT	Trinity College, Cambridge	light blue
3	K. T. DIGBY	London Athletic Club	green and silver
4	B. C. MOLLOY	London Rowing Club	mauve and black
5	C. F. FARRAN	London Rowing Club	rose
6	F. WITTY	London Athletic Club	blue, black stripes
7	Captain BARNES	Scots Fusilier Guards	pink and white
8	D. MOFFAT	Christchurch College, Oxford	
9	A. H. JOHNSON	Exeter College, Oxford	
10	E. ROYDS	Eton	white and scarlet
11	Hon. G. MONTGOMERIE	Oxford	

Note that, unlike today and more like a horse-racing event, each runner had a different kit, even those from the same club.

POLE JUMP

1866 23 March. 3 competitors
1. F. or J. Wheeler Wandsworth   10'0   3.05
2. C.C.Ewbank   Cambridge UAC   9'6   2.90
3. R.E.Lambert   Civil Service   8'3   2.51

1867 15 April. 2 competitors
1. W.F.P.Moore   London AC   9'3   2.82
2. E.Gurney   Cambridge UAC   9'0   2.74

1868 19 June. 3 competitors
1. R.J.C.Mitchell   Manchester AC   10'6½   3.21
2. W.F.P.Moore   London AC   10'0½   3.06
3. A.Lubbock   Amateur AC   8'6   2.59
World best performance

1869 3 April. 1 competitor
1. R.G.Graham   London Rowing C   9'3   2.82

1870 9 April. 3 competitors
1. R.J.C.Mitchell   Manchester AC   10'3   3.12
2. E.Bergman   Oxford UAC   10'2   3.10
3. R.G.Graham   London Rowing C   9'0   2.74

1871 3 April. 3 competitors
1. R.J.C.Mitchell   Manchester AC   10'1   3.07
2. W.F.P.Moore   London AC   9'7   2.92
3. W.F.Curteis   Cambridge UAC   9'6   2.90

1872 27 March. 2 competitors
1. H.C.Fellowes   Lichfield College   9'6   2.90
2. W.F.P.Moore   Amateur AC   9'4   2.84

1873 5 April. 6 competitors
1. W.Kelsey   Hull AC   10'6   3.20

2. C.E.Leeds   Amateur AC   10'2   3.10
ac J.Trotter   Cambridge UAC   9'0+ 2.74+
ac A.E.Deck   St Bart's Hosp   9'0+ 2.74+
ac P.St.J.Hough   Ham   9'0+ 2.74+
ac J.B.Woolley   Gipsies FC   9'0+ 2.74+
All competitors cleared 9'0/2.74 or better

1874 30 March. 5 competitors
1. E.Woodburn   Ulverston CC   10'7   3.23
2= H.M.Fyffe   South London H   10'4   3.15
2= R.W.Sabin   Culworth AC   10'4   3.15
2= W.Kelsey   Hull CC   10'4   3.15
5. J.B.Woolley   Crystal Palace AC   9'10 3.00
World best performance

1875 Not held

1876 10 April. 2 competitors
1. H.W.Strachan   London AC   10'1   3.07
2. C.W.Gaskin   Wisbech CC   9'1   2.77

1877 26 March. 2 competitors
1. H.E.Kayll   Nuneaton CC   10'9   3.28
2. H.W.Strachan   London AC   10'6   3.20

1878 15 April. 1 competitor
1. H.W.Strachan   London AC   10'0   3.05

1879 7 April. 1 competitor
1. F.W.D.Robinson Beccles AC   10'0   3.05

1879
London AC Championship Not held

LONG JUMP

1866 23 March. 4 competitors
1. R.Fitzherbert   Cambridge UAC   19'8   5.99
2. T.G.Little   Cambridge UAC   19'4   5.89
3. R.W.Smith   Royal Horse Artillery
4. J.B.S.Boyle   Lincoln's Inn

1867 15 April. 2 competitors
1. R.Fitzherbert   Cambridge UAC   19'4½ 5.91
2. T.G.Little   Cambridge UAC   19'2   5.84

1868 20 June. 4 competitors
1. R.J.C.Mitchell   Manchester AC   19'8½ 6.01
2. E.Havers   Ingatestone AC   10'6   5.92
ac W.M.Tennent   Manchester AC
ac W.H.Betts   London AC

1869 3 April. 2 competitors
1. A.C.Tosswill   Oxford UAC   19'7   5.97
2. J.H.Hague   Enfield Lock   17'4   5.28

1870 9 April. 7 competitors
1. R.J.C.Mitchell   Manchester AC   19'11¾ 6.09
2. E.G.Loder   Cambridge UAC   19'2   5.84
3. E.Havers   Ingatestone CC   19'1   5.82
4. F.O.Philpott   Oxford UAC   18'10   5.74

5. E.Bergman   Oxford UAC   18'9   5.71
6. C.W.Nicholas   South Essex AC   18'6   5.64
7. I.A.Lewis   Guy's Hospital   18'2½   5.55

1871 3 April. 10 competitors
1= E.J.Davies   Cambridge UAC   20'4   6.20
1= R.J.C.Mitchell   Manchester AC   20'4   6.20
3. J.A.Ornsby   Oxford UAC   20'3   6.17
4. H.S.Ferguson   RMA   18'9   5.71
ac G.P.Rogers   London AC
ac W.F.P.Moore   London AC
ac W.F.Curteis   Cambridge UAC
ac E.G.Loder   Cambridge UAC
ac S.H.Gatty   Oxford UAC
ac W.W.Mann   South Norwood AC

1872 27 March. 4 competitors
1. E.J.Davies   Cambridge UAC   22'7   6.88
2. R.L.Dixon   Cambridge UAC   20'3   6.17
3. W.A.Dawson   Cambridge UAC   19'0+   5.79+
4. H.C.Fellowes   Lichfield College
World best performance

1873 5 April. 1 competitor
1. C.L.Lockton   Thames H & H   19'4   5.89

1874 30 March. 5 competitors
1. E.J.Davies   Cambridge UAC   22'5   6.83
2. H.K.Upcher   Oxford UAC   20'0+   6.10+
3. W.Kelsey   Hull CC
4. W.B.Pattison   Gipsies FC
5. E.Woodburn   Ulverston CC

1875 22 March. 2 competitors
1. C.L.Lockton   Merchant Taylors' S 20'10¼ 6.36
2. H.K.Upcher   Oxford UAC   20'4½   6.21

1876 10 April. 4 competitors
1. J.G.Alkin   Nuneaton CC   21'3   6.48
2. W.E.Tomkin   ex-Eton College   21'0   6.40
3. F.J.W.Wood   ex-Harrow Sch   20'2½   6.16
ac H.W.Strachan   London AC

1877 26 March. 2 competitors
1. J.G.Alkin   Nuneaton CC   20'6¾   6.27
2. H.W.Strachan   London AC   19'8   5.99

1878 15 April. 5 competitors
1. E.Baddeley   Cambridge UAC   22'8   6.91
2. G.E.Fowler   Birmingham AC   22'2   6.76
ac H.W.Strachan   London AC
ac C.W.M.Kemp   Oxford UAC
ac J.G.Alkin   London AC

1879 7 April. 2 competitors
1. W.G.Elliott   Cambridge UAC   20'10½   6.36
2. S.F.Prest   Durham ARC   19'2   5.84
The winner cleared 21'4½/6.51 afterwards in an exhibition jump

1879
London AC Championship 14 June. 4 competitors
1. C.L.Lockton   London AC   22'1½   6.74
2. H.Crossley   London AC   20'5   6.22
3. G.E.Fowler   Birmingham AC   19'9   6.02
4. B.St.J.Hough   ex-Merchant Taylors' 19'7½ 5.98

SHOT

1866 23 March. 2 competitors
1. C.G.L.Fraser   Metropolitan Police 34'10 10.62
2. G.W.Elliot   Cambridge UAC   30'4   9.25
Shot weighed 18lb 10oz owing to an error

1867 15 April. 6 competitors
1. J.Stone   Liverpool Gym   36'6   11.13
2. R.Waltham   Cambridge UAC   33'1½   10.10
3. W.F.P.Moore   London AC   33'1   10.08
ac R.N.Gream   62nd Regiment
ac P.Halkett   London AC
ac C.B.Lawes   Amateur AC
World best performance

1868 20 June. 4 competitors
1. J.Stone   Liverpool AC   37'11   11.56
2. R.J.C.Mitchell Manchester AC   36'0   10.97
ac W.F.P.Moore   London AC
ac G.R.Nunn   Guy's Hospital
World best performance

1869 3 April. 2 competitors
1. H.A.Leeke   Cambridge UAC   31'4½   9.56
2. A.Macfie   Birmingham AC   30'2   9.19

1870 9 April. 5 competitors
1. R.J.C.Mitchell Manchester AC   38'0   11.58
2. E.L.Phelps   Cambridge UAC   32'5   9.88
ac H.A.Leeke   Cambridge UAC
ac R.Sherwood   London AC
ac F.B.Soden   London AC

1871 3 April. 9 competitors
1. R.J.C.Mitchell Manchester AC   38'8½   11.80
2. E.J.Bor   RMA   37'5½   11.42
3. H.W.R.Domvile   Oxford UAC   35'5   10.79
ac T.Bolton   Rochdale AC
ac A.W.Churchward Cambridge UAC
ac M.H.C.Shelton   Cambridge UAC
ac W.F.P.Moore   London AC
ac H.A.Leeke   Cambridge UAC
ac F.B.Soden   Amateur AC

1872 27 March. 4 competitors
1. E.J.Bor   London AC   42'5   12.93
2. W.F.P.Moore   Amateur AC   35'3   10.74
3. H.W.R.Domvile   Oxford UAC   35'0   10.67
4. N.J.Littleton   Cambridge UAC
World best performance

1873 5 April. 3 competitors
1. E.J.Bor   Royal Engineers   40'0   12.19
2. T.J.Stone   Newton-le-Willows 38'7   11.76
3. W.F.P.Moore   Amateur AC   36'9   11.20

1874 30 March. 4 competitors
1. W.F.P.Moore   Amateur AC   39'11   12.17
2. T.J.Stone   Liverpool AC   39'3   11.96
3. N.J.Littleton   Cambridge UAC   38'1½   11.62
4. S.S.Brown   Oxford UAC   36'0+   10.97+

1875 22 March. 2 competitors
1. T.J.Stone   Liverpool AC   39'10   12.14
ac W.Y.Winthrop   London AC   no valid mark

1876 10 April. 2 competitors
1. T.J.Stone   Newton-le-Willows 38'7½   11.77
2. W.Y.Winthrop   London AC   34'11   10.64

1877 26 March. 2 competitors
1. T.J.Stone   Newton-le-Willows 38'2   11.63
2. W.Y.Winthrop   Amateur AC   36'2   11.02

1878 15 April. 1 competitor
1. W.Y.Winthrop   London AC   38'10   11.84

1879 7 April. 2 competitors
1. A.H.East   Cambridge UAC   37'7½   11.47
2. H.W.Macaulay   Oxford UAC   35'9   10.90

1879
London AC Championship 14 June. 2 competitors
1. W.Y.Winthrop   London AC   39'5   12.01
2. R.E.Thomas   Liverpool Gym   35'4   10.77

HAMMER

1866 23 March. 4 competitors
1. R.J.James   Cambridge UAC   78'4   23.88
2. D.P.Morgan   Oxford UAC   75'0   22.86
ac D.Moffatt   Oxford UAC
ac C.G.L.Fraser   Metropolitan Police

1867 15 April. 5 competitors
1. P.Halkett   London AC   94'7   28.83
2. J.R.Eyre   Cambridge UAC   94'1   28.68
3. G.R.Thornton   Cambridge UAC   93'2   28.40
ac R.N.Gream   62nd Regiment
ac D.Moffatt   Oxford UAC

1868 19 June. 4 competitors
1. H.A.Leeke   Cambridge UAC   99'6   30.33
2. D.Moffatt   Amateur AC   96'9   29.49
3. P.Halkett   London AC   93'3   28.42
4. H.W.Richardson   West Kent AC
World best performance, unlimited run

1869 3 April. 5 competitors
1. W.A.Burgess   Oxford UAC   102'3   31.17
2. H.A.Leeke   Cambridge UAC   99'4   30.28
3. F.U.Waite   Oxford UAC   96'6   29.41
4. T.Batson   Oxford UAC   95'5   29.08
5. D.Moffatt   Oxford UAC   81'4   24.79

1870 9 April. 4 competitors
1. H.A.Leeke   Cambridge UAC   102'0   31.09
2. F.U.Waite   Oxford UAC   101'11 31.06
3. W.A.Burgess   Oxford UAC   100'4   30.58
4. M.H.C.Shelton   Cambridge UAC   88'6   26.97

1871 3 April. 7 competitors
1. W.A.Burgess   Oxford UAC   105'5   32.13
2. A.W.Churchward   Cambridge UAC   102'2   31.14
3. H.A.Leeke   Cambridge UAC   100'4   30.58
ac S.H.Gatty   Oxford UAC
ac D.Moffatt   Oxford UAC
ac H.F.Nicholl   Oxford UAC
ac M.H.C.Shelton   Cambridge UAC

1872 27 March. 6 competitors
1. H.A.Leeke   ex-Cambridge UAC   111'7   34.01
2. J.Paterson   Cambridge UAC   111'1   33.86
3. W.A.Burgess   Oxford UAC   105'3   32.08
4. E.S.Garnier   Oxford UAC   104'8   31.90
5. C.M.Thompson   Cambridge UAC   103'6   31.55
ac D.Moffatt   Amateur AC
World best performance, unlimited run. Leeke also
threw 108'0 and Paterson 110'5, but it is not known if
these throws were prior to those listed above.

1873 5 April. 1 competitor
1. J.Paterson   Cambridge UAC   108'0   32.92

1874 30 March. 5 competitors
1. S.S.Brown   Oxford UAC   120'0   36.58
2. W.A.Burgess   Oxford UAC   119'8   36.47
3. J.Paterson   Cambridge UAC   116'10 35.61
4. H.A.Leeke   ex-Cambridge UAC   100'+   30.48+
5. G.H.Hales   Cambridge UAC   100'+   30.48+

1875 22 March. 4 competitors
1. W.A.Burgess   ex-Oxford UAC   103'9   31.62
2. J.D.Todd   Oxford UAC   101'6   30.94
3. S.S.Brown   Oxford UAC   98'0   29.87
4. W.Y.Winthrop   Cambridge UAC

1876 10 April. 2 competitors
1. G.H.Hales   Cambridge UAC   96'3   29.34
2. T.J.Stone   Newton-le-Willows   85'8   26.11
World best performance, seven-foot area

1877 26 March. 1 competitor
1. G.H.Hales   Cambridge UAC   110'0   33.53
World best performance, seven-foot area

1878 15 April. 2 competitors
1. E.Baddeley   Cambridge UAC   98'10   30.12
2. W.A.Burgess   ex-Oxford UAC   88'7   27.00

1879 Not held

1879
London AC Championship 14 June. 2 competitors
1. W.A.Burgess   ex-Oxford UAC   96'9   29.49
2. W.Y.Winthrop   London AC   93'7   28.52

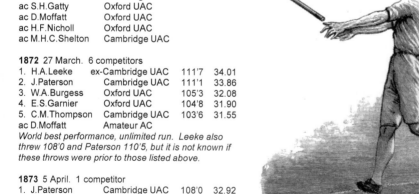

INTRODUCTION TO THE LISTS

A sharp distinction was made between amateurs and professionals (marked p) in this era, but both classes of athlete used the same tracks and often the same timekeepers, so we decided as the lists evolved that in the running events it was of more interest to include everyone. The field events are treated differently because the vast majority of so-called professionals were competing in the highland and border games in different conditions and with slightly different rules in the case of the throws.

Timing was usually to the nearest one-fifth of a second, sometimes to the nearest quarter-second and occasionally (but frequently in school sports) to the nearest second. In the 100yds, 220yds and 120yds hurdles lists we give the winning times in fractions when known, but for ease of comparison from 440yds and upwards subdivisions of seconds are expressed in decimals.

A difficulty we encountered was that place times were seldom taken for events of less than 10 miles. Most press reports give the second athlete's distance behind the winner and a further distance for the gap to the third placed athlete. Estimates in newspapers can vary. Any attempt to estimate times for the non-winning athletes depends on the accuracy of the reporting. **Maintained average speed** is a formula devised by Keith Morbey and based on the following principles:
1. If only one estimate is located then that has to be taken as accurate.
2. Where two different estimates are found the more conservative one is accepted.
3. If more than two are found a consensus is taken. For example with estimates of 1, 1½, 2 and 4 yards, the choice is 2 yards.
4. Reliable local sources are sometimes preferred to national reports.
5. Having decided the best estimate, a calculation of the time is made.
6. In sprints an athlete should be moving at optimum speed from start to finish, but in longer races most runners will try to spurt as they approach the finish.
7. This presumed finishing spurt is factored into the calculation. If in a half-mile race won in 1:50.0 sec the second finisher is ten yards behind he will have covered 870yds in 110sec. By using the formula: *Distance in Yards divided by Time in Seconds times 45/22* his time can be expressed in miles per hour. We can extrapolate this speed to a time for the full distance by using the formula: *Distance in Yards divided by mph times 45/22*. However, this presupposes that the runner completes the race at the same average speed he used for the first 870yds. The reality is that he would probably be speeding up over the last few yards. As a result the formula makes the estimate a conservative one.
8. Because it deals in average speeds the formula can be used for all distances.
9. The formula has given good results where it has been possible to compare an estimated time with a subsequently discovered 'actual' time. The estimate is often a fraction slower, showing that the formula gives a conservative result.

Hurdle races varied as to distance and the height and number of hurdles. We have confined our study to the events a modern follower of the sport would recognise.

Making imperial to **metric conversions** for horizontal distances in a fair manner relies on knowing the method of measurement, i.e. whether the mark was rounded to the nearest imperial unit (be it ¼-, ½- or 1-inch) or strictly rounded down to the next lower unit. However there were no rules at the time to define the rounding method and it may well have varied from meeting to meeting. Therefore we have converted metric distances to the nearest centimetre, which agrees with the method used by Ari Törmä in his lists up to 1865. In the high jump, where the bar is set at a precise height, we have followed the practice in recent ATFS publications of converting to the nearest millimetre. In the pole vault, heights tend to be whole inches, and the accuracy of measurement would have been less than in the high jump so rounding to the nearest centimetre has again been used.

A variety of implements were used in the **shot put**, also known as throwing the weight, cannonball, or (notably in Scotland) the stone. The weights varied considerably, but we have listed only performances with 16lb except, listed separately, when throws with heavier weights in Scotland were sometimes superior to the standard 16lb. In the games there were often separate competitions for "light" and "heavy" weights, but there was no consistency. "Light" might be anything from 10 to 16lb. "Heavy" might be from 16 to 24¾lb. From 1866 in the UK the throwing area was a pair of lines 7ft apart until in 1878 John Chambers introduced the 7ft circle for the championships. The throwing area in the highland games was 6 inches more (at 7ft 6in). Because the games were held in fields uneven surfaces might affect performances. We have tried to indicate notorious slopes, such as Bridge of Allan 'held on ground so steep that the chief difficulty was . . . to keep from going over the stance' (McCombie Smith). In Border games, according to the same authority, a standing throw was used, but the thrower was allowed to step forward from 6 to 8 feet over the mark.

The **hammer** was originally a sledge hammer. Spherical heads were introduced later. The run-up was unlimited until 1876 when it was confined to two lines 7ft apart and in 1878 to a 7ft circle. In highland games a standing style was used in the years under study. The thrower swung the hammer in a circle above his head prior to releasing it. The "light" and "heavy" categories for competition applied as they did for the shot. There was a variation in Ireland, where Maurice Davin threw one-handed. A longer shaft results in a longer throw and for a time in Scotland and the rest of Britain this was tested to excess, trenches being dug to allow the over-long hammers to swing freely.

We have included a section called **Other Events,** mostly for non-standard distances and disciplines, showing the single best known performances of the year. The lists include performances made in other countries by British athletes, among them recent immigrants to the US and Canada.

Abbreviations and Glossary

AAC – Amateur Athletic Club Championships
challenge – special challenge event
college – confined to college members
CU – Cambridge University
e – estimated time
ENGvIRL – England versus Ireland
ex – exhibition
heavy – programmed as heavy implement event
hc – handicap event
HHL – hop, hop and leap
HSL – hop, step and leap
ht – heat
i – indoor competition
ICAC – Irish Champion Athletic Club
int – intermediate time
IRLvENG – Ireland versus England
LAC – London Athletic Club
light – programmed as light implement event
local – confined to local residents
NCAA – Northern Counties AA Championships
nd – unknown day and month
open – open competition
OU – Oxford University
OvC – Oxford versus Cambridge Universities
p – professional
QC – Queen's College
r1 – race one of two
r2 – race two of two
rA – race A
rB – race B
RMA – Royal Military Academy, Woolwich
RMC – Royal Military College, Sandhurst
ro – run off after tied result
sf – semi final
u – unofficial
wo – walkover
= – tied result

Venues with abbreviations

Aberdeen (CC) – Aberdeenshire Cricket Club Ground, Holburn
Aberdeen (RG) – Recreation Grounds, Inches
Birmingham (AC) – Aston Cross Grounds
Birmingham (ALG) – Aston Lower Grounds, Trinity Road
Birmingham (PR) – Portland Road Ground, Edgbaston
Dublin (CP) – College Park, Trinity College
Dublin (EG) – Exhibition Grounds, Iveagh Gardens
Dublin (LCG) – Leinster Cricket Ground, Rathmines
Dublin (LR) – Lansdowne Road, Ballsbridge
Edinburgh (ACG) – Academicals Cricket Ground, Raeburn Place
Edinburgh (GP) – Greenhill Park, Morningside
Edinburgh (Pow) – Powderhall Grounds, Broughton
Glasgow (Ac) – Academicals Club Ground, Kelvinside
Glasgow (Alex) – Alexandra Athletic Club Ground, Kennyhill Park
Glasgow (HP) – Hampden Park, Mount Florida
Glasgow (QP) – Queen's Park Recreation Ground, Crosshill
Glasgow (Shaw) – Shawfield Recreation Grounds
Glasgow (Spr) – Springfield Recreation Grounds, London Road
Glasgow (Sto) – Stonefield Recreation Grounds, South Wellington (now Lawmoor) Street, Govan
Glasgow (VC) – Vale of Clyde Recreation Grounds, Govan Road
Glasgow (WSCG) – West of Scotland Cricket Ground, Hamilton Crescent, Partick
London (Ag Hall) – Agricultural Hall, Islington
London (BH) – Beaufort House, Walham Green
London (Bow) – Prince of Wales Ground, Old Ford, Bow
London (CP) – Crystal Palace
London (HW) – Hackney Wick, Victoria Park
London (LB) – Lillie Bridge, West Brompton
London (Oval) – Kennington Oval
London (SB) – Stamford Bridge, Chelsea
London (Star) – Star Grounds, Fulham
London (WL) – West London Cricket Ground, Brompton
Manchester (Cir) – The Circus, Peter Street
Manchester (City) – City Grounds, Ashton New Road, Bradford
Manchester (Cope) – Copenhagen Grounds, Newton Heath
Manchester (Long) – Longsight
Manchester (Pom) – Pomona Gardens, Hulme
Manchester (RG) – Race Ground, Broughton
Manchester (RO) – Royal Oak Grounds, Newton Heath
Manchester (WR) – Manley Park, Whalley Range
New York (MSG) – Madison Square Garden
Sheffield (BL) – Bramall Lane
Sheffield (HP) – Hyde Park
Sheffield (QG) – Queen's Ground, Hillsborough

100 Yards

10.0	Hector Gurdon-Rebow (Colchester)	7.11.46	1	Colchester			10 Jan
10.0	John Prothero (OU)	c43	1	Oxford			13 Feb
10.0	Cecil Hornby (ex-Harrow Sch)	25.07.43	1	Tonbridge			15 Mar
10.0	James Fairlie (CU)	28.12.48	1	Glenalmond			28 Apr
10.0	Frank Barker (Brentwood)	27.11.45	1	Brentwood			7 Jul
10.0	J.W.George (Reading)		1	Streatley			1 Aug
10.0	J. Thompson (Horsley)		1	Horsley			24 Aug
10.0	Pte Closs (15th Hussars)		1	Aldershot			23 Oct
10.0	Benjamin Connolly (CU)	10.09.45	1	Cambridge			7 Nov
10.0	Edward Potter (Newton Abbot)		1	Newton Abbot			24 Nov
10 1/5	Edward Nolan (OU)	01.07.45	1ht2	Oxford			2 Mar
10 1/5	Robert Vidal (OU)	19.02.43	1=	Oxford	OvC		10 Mar
10 1/5	Thomas Colmore (OU)	13.01.45	1=	Oxford	OvC		10 Mar
10 ¼	William Maitland (OU)	6.05.44	1	Oxford			20 Feb
10 ¼	John Smith (OU)	45	1	Oxford			27 Nov
10 ¼	William Allen (CU)	c47	1	Cambridge			1 Dec

Note
Connolly "under ten seconds with the wind" (*Bell's Life*); "a yard inside evens" (*Illustrated Sporting News*);
"in a trifle under 10 seconds, running with the wind" (*Cambridge Independent Press*)

School sports

10.0	Francis Dickson (Cheltenham Coll)	15.11.47	1	Cheltenham	4 May
10.0	Arthur Atkins (ex-Cheltenham Coll)	30.09.45	1	Cheltenham	5 May
10.0	Richard Deane (Royal Naval Academy)	30.04.48	1	Gosport	8 May
10.0	Banks (Cliffe House Sch)		1	Lewes	24 May
10.0	A. Payne (Cheltenham Gr Sch)		1	Cheltenham	26 May
10.0	Wyles (Independent Coll)		1	Taunton	20 Jun
10 ¼	Leonard Howell (Winchester Coll)	6.08.48	1	Winchester	22 Mar

220 Yards

23.0	William Collett (LAC)	18.06.43	1	London (WL)	24 Nov
23 ¼	Charles Emery (LAC)	c43	1	London (BH)	19 May
23.5 e	Emery		2	London (WL)	24 Nov
23.8 e	W.A.Simpson (LAC)		2	London (BH)	19 May
24.0	Percy Thornton (LAC)	29.12.41	1	London (WL)	24 Feb
24.0	Duncan Stewart (Edinburgh U)		1	Edinburgh (GP)	27 Jun
24.1 e	Simpson		2	London (WL)	24 Feb
24 ½	Collett		1	London (WL)	25 Aug
25.0	Charles Bauchope (Edinburgh U)	46	1	Edinburgh (GP)	27 Jun
25.2 e	Simpson		2ht2hc	London	14 Apr
25 ½	Harry Staughton (Uppingham Sch/AUS)	11.10.48	1	Uppingham	4 May
25 ½	Joshua Brooke (Huddersfield)	6.06.46	1	Huddersfield	23 Jun

(12/8)

Notes
Estimates: Emery 4y down on 23.0; Simpson "nearly 5y" down on 23¼ (19/05); 1y down on 25.0 (14/04);
and ½y down on 24.0 (24/02)

440 Yards

52.0 e	Guy Pym (LAC)	11.02.41	3hc	London (WL)	24 Feb
52.0	John Laing (OU)	1.04.46	1	Blackheath	27 Jun
52.5 p	Hugh Holland (Norley)	43	1	Chester	20 Sep
52.75	Pym		1	London (BH)	4 May
52.9 e p	John Hitchen (Barrow)	40	2	Chester	20 Sep
53.2	Charles Fell (OU/NZL)	5.08.44	1	London (BH)	17 Feb
53.25 p	Daniel Sconce (Chester)	47	1	Chester	20 Sep
53.5	Francis Pelham (CU)	18.10.44	1	Cambridge	3 Mar
53.5	Robert Vidal (OU)	19.02.43	1	London (BH)	3 May
53.5	Pym		1ht1	London (BH)	4 May
54.0	Francis Cheetham (CU)	45	1	Cambridge	26 Feb
54.0	Thomas Viccars (Leicester)	45	1	Leicester	24 May
54.0	Edward Colbeck (LAC)	21.12.47	1ht4hc	London (WL)	3 Nov

(13/11)

54.2 e	Henry Chinnery (LAC)	26.06.47	2	London (BH)	17 Feb
54.5	Mark Jobling (Northumberland)	43	1	Sheffield (BL)	7 May

54.5	Sam Haywood (19th W. Yorks Volunteers)	c43	1	Sheffield		26 Sep
54.7 e	Edward Nolan (OU)	01.07.45	2	Oxford	OvC	10 Mar
55.0	John Ridley (Eton College)	23.06.48	1	London (BH)	AAC	23 Mar
55.0	John Martin (LAC)	10.06.41	1	Woolwich		9 May

Notes
Estimates: Pym 1½y down on 51.75; Hitchen 3y down on 52.5; Chinnery 8y down on 53.2;
Nolan 3y down on 54.25.

880 Yards

2:00.25 p	William Richards (Bridgend)	11.10.38	1	Manchester (RO)		4 Aug
2:00.6 e p	John Neary (IRL)	41	2	Manchester (RO)		4 Aug
2:02.0 p	Robert McKinstray (Ayr)	18.04.37	int	Manchester (RO)		30 Jun
2:03.0	Pte McCulloch (Maybole)		1	Ayr		4 Aug
2:04.0 p	Neary		1	Manchester (Cope)		22 Dec
2:04.8 e p	Richards		2	Manchester (Cope)		22 Dec
2:05.0	Percy Thornton (LAC)	29.12.41	1	London (BH)	AAC	23 Mar
2:06.0 p	George Walsh (Royton)	3.02.44	1	Oldham		18 Aug
2:06.0	John Laing (OU)	1.04.46	1	Oxford		3 Nov
2:06.5	Charles Lawes (OU)	3.10.43	1	Oxford		21 Feb
2:06.7 e	William Gibbs (CU)	28.07.45	2	Oxford		21 Feb
2:06.9 e	Thornton		3	Oxford		21 Feb
2:07.0 p	William Riley (Blackburn)	48	1	Burnley		13 Oct
2:07.0	Walter Chinnery (LAC)	19.08.43	1	Cambridge		16 Nov
		(14/11)				
2:07.5 p	Joseph Snow (Manchester)	c46	1	Everton, Lancs		1 Sep
2:07.5 e p	W. Barnes (Shaw)	28.05.44	2	Oldham		18 Aug
2:07.6 e p	James Hooton (Liverpool Gym)	c42	2	Everton, Lancs		1 Sep
2:07.8 e p	James Coupe (Rawtenstall)	c43	2	Burnley		13 Oct
2:09.0	Thomas Little (CU)	15.02.45	1	Cambridge		29 Nov
2:09.5	Mark Jobling (Civil Service)	43	1	London (BH)		4 May
2:09.8 e	Edward Colbeck (LAC)	21.12.47	2	Cambridge		29 Nov
2:10.0	Henry Shorting (Tonbridge)	15.01.47	1	Tonbridge		15 Mar
2:10.0 p	Joe Tuck (Lambeth)	c42	1	London (WL)		17 Mar
2:10.0 p	Tommy Cox (Chatham)	09.44	1	London (HW)		18 Dec

Notes
2:05.0 by Thornton also reported as 2:07.0
2:06.0 by Laing also reported as 2:04.0 and 2:10.0
Neary was credited with 1:51.5 from an 8½y start at Crystal Palace on 13 Oct, but "the distance, however, was doubtful" *(Bell's Life)*
Estimates: Neary 2½y down on 2:00.25; Richards 5y down on 2:04.0; Gibbs 1y down on 2:06.5; Thornton 2y down on 2:06.5; Barnes 10y down on 2:06.0; Hooton ½y down on 2:07.5; Coupe 5y down on 2:07.0; Colbeck 5y down on 2:09.0.
Intermediate times: 2:02.0 by McKinstray in a ¾ mile race, won by Richards, in 3:07.0. Richards and James Nuttall (Stockport) must also have been close to 2:02.0, as they overtook McKinstray soon after.

Mile

4:36.25 p	Ike Hughes (Manchester)	9.04.46	1	Manchester (RO)		24 Nov
4:37.0	Percy Thornton (CU)	29.12.41	1	London (BH)		17 Feb
4:37.2 e p	William Bell (Newcastle)		2	Manchester (RO)		24 Nov
4:38.0	Richard Thornton (ex-Harrow Sch)	9.10.47	1	St Servan, FRA		Sep
4:39.0	Walter Chinnery (LAC)	19.08.43	1hc	London (BH)		24 Feb
4:39.0	Charles Lawes (LAC)	3.10.43	1	London (BH)	AAC	23 Mar
4:40.2 e	Chinnery		2	London (BH)		17 Feb
4:41.0 e	William Bowman (OU)	25.09.45	2	London (BH)	AAC	23 Mar
4:41.0 p	Bob Rogers (Chelsea)	12.01.46	1	Manchester (RO)		29 Dec
4:42.0	Henry Dayrell (Clifton)	12.43	1hc	Clifton		22 Sep
4:43.5	John Laing (OU)	1.04.46	1	Oxford		15 Nov
4:45.0	James Kerr (Bristol)		1	Clifton		20 Oct
		(12/11)				
4:46.0	Mark Jobling (Northumberland)	43	1	Sheffield (BL)		7 May
4:47.9 e	Charles Long (CU)	19.04.45	2	Cambridge		5 Mar
4:48.0 p	John Fleet (Manchester)	6.04.45	int	Manchester (RO)		3 Nov
4:48.0 e	William Gibbs (CU)	28.07.45	3	Oxford	OvC	10 Mar
4:49.0	Edward Ingham (Wellington Coll)	18.03.47	1	Wellington		13 Mar

4:50.0		Stewart Douglas (Winchester Coll)	23.06.48	1	Winchester	24 Mar
4:50.0	p	Robert McKinstray (Ayr)	18.04.37	int	Manchester (RO)	31 Mar
4:50.0		William Easton (Bristol)	47	1	Clifton	9 Jun
4:50.0	p	Charles Nurse (Brighton)	c40	int*	London (CP)	1 Aug
4:50.0		George Barnes (Brighton C)	9.03.47	1	Brighton	17 Sep
4:50.0	p	Alec Austin (Woolwich)	44	1	Gravesend	22 Sep

Doubtful

4:32.0	Arthur Irvin (Rossall School)	10.03.48	1	Fleetwood	12 Mar

Notes

Estimates: Bell 6y down on 4:36.25; Chinnery 20y down on 4:37; Bowman 12y down on 4:39 (23/03); Long 5y down on 4:47; Gibbs 15y 1ft down on 4:45.4.

Intermediate times: Fleet in the first mile of an 11 mile race; McKinstray in a 2 mile race; Nurse in a 2 mile race.

* Nurse entered as an amateur and was afterwards disqualified as a professional.

2 Miles

9:57.0	p	Robert McKinstray (Ayr)	18.04.37	1	Manchester (RO)		31 Mar
10:03.0	p	John Fleet (Manchester)	6.04.45	int	Manchester (RO)		3 Nov
10:06.0	p	James Sanderson (Whitworth)	28.12.37	inthc	Oldham		13 Jan
10:10.0	p	Harry Andrews (Monmouth)	28.05.31	int	London (BH)		30 Apr
10:15.0		James Molloy (Kingston RC/IRL)	19.08.37	1	St Servan, FRA		Sep
10:17.0	p	Billy Mills (Bethnal Green)	09.43	int	London (HW)		19 Mar
10:17.4	e p	John Cooper (Bethnal Green)	c35	int	London (HW)		19 Mar
10:20.0		John Laing (OU)	1.04.46	1=	Oxford		10 Mar
10:20.0		Charles Long (CU)	19.04.45	1=	Oxford		10 Mar
10:21.5	e	Thomas Little (CU)	15.02.45	3	Oxford		10 Mar
10:25.0	p	Mills		int	London (HW)		26 Mar
10:25.0	p	Henry Guy (Bow)	19.08.46	int	London (Bow)		1 Sep
		(12/11)					
10:25.4	e p	Edward Golder (Canterbury)	1.07.43	int	London (HW)		26 Mar
10:29.0	p	Tom Roberts (Birmingham)		1	Birmingham (AC)		2 Apr
10:29.8	e p	W. Hill (Lye Waste)	c25	2	Birmingham (AC)		2 Apr
10:30.0	p	William Virtue (Bedfordbury)	21.07.47	int	London (BH)		30 Apr
10:34.0	p	John Brighton (Norwich)	14.07.32	int	Manchester (RO)		17 Nov
10:37.3	e	Arthur Johnson (OU)	8.02.45	2	Oxford		3 Mar
10:37.9	e	William Bowman (OU)	25.09.45	3	Oxford		3 Mar
10:52.0	p	Charles Nurse (Brighton)	c40	1	Margate		1 Oct
10:52.4	e	Frederick Witty (LAC)	6.08.43	2	Margate		1 Oct
10:59.0		William Gibbs (CU)	28.07.45	1	Clifton		4 Aug
11:00.0		Richard Garnett (CU)	18.02.43	int	London (BH)	AAC	23 Mar

Notes

Nurse was a professional in an amateur race.

Estimates: Cooper 2y down on 10:17 (19/03); Little 8y down on 10:20.0; Golder 2y down on 10:25.0; Hill 4y down on 10:29; Johnson 50y and Bowman 53y down on 10:28.2; Witty 2y down on 10:52.

Intermediate times: Fleet and Brighton in 11 mile races against time; Sanderson in a 6 mile race; Mills and Cooper in 5 mile races (19/03); Andrews, Mills (26/03); Guy, Golder, Garnett and Virtue in 4 mile races.

3 Miles

15:19.0	p	James Sanderson (Whitworth)	28.12.37	inthc	Oldham		13 Jan
15:19.0	p	John Fleet (Manchester)	6.04.45	int	Manchester (RO)		3 Nov
15:39.0	p	Harry Andrews (Monmouth)	28.05.31	int	London (BH)		30 Apr
15:50.0	p	John Cooper (Bethnal Green)	c35	int	London (HW)		19 Mar
15:50.4	e p	Billy Mills (Bethnal Green)	09.43	int	London (HW)		19 Mar
15:56.0	p	Mills		int	London (HW)		14 May
15:56.4	e p	Cooper		int	London (HW)		14 May
15:57.0	p	Mills		int	London (HW)		26 Mar
15:57.4	e p	Edward Golder (Canterbury)	1.07.43	int	London (HW)		26 Mar
16:00.0	p	John Brighton (Norwich)	14.07.32	int	Manchester (RO)		17 Nov
		(10/7)					
16:05.2	e p	Henry Guy (Bow)	19.08.46	int	London (Bow)		1 Sep
16:14.0		John Goodman (Liverpool)	c47	1	Liverpool		18 Oct
16:20.0	p	Charles Guilder (Gravesend)	c40	1	Gravesend		9 Jul
16:27.0		Richard Garnett (CU)	18.02.43	int	London (BH)	AAC	23 Mar
16:30.0	p	Pat Canavan (Dublin/IRL)		1=hc	Birmingham		1 Jan

Notes
Estimates: Mills 2y down on 15:50.0 (19/03); Cooper 2y down on 15:56.0; Golder 2y down on 15:57.0; Guy 1y down on 16:05.0
Intermediate times: Sanderson in a 6 mile race; Fleet and Brighton in 11 mile runs against time; Cooper and Mills (19/03 & 14/05) in 5 mile races; Andrews, Mills (26/03), Guy, Golder and Garnett in 4 mile races.

4 Miles

20:34.75 p	James Sanderson (Whitworth)	28.12.37	inthc	Oldham			13 Jan
20:40.0 p	John Fleet (Manchester)	6.04.45	int	Manchester (RO)			3 Nov
21:12.0 p	John Brighton (Norwich)	14.07.32	int	Manchester (RO)			17 Nov
21:13.0 p	Harry Andrews (Monmouth)	28.05.31	1	London (BH)			30 Apr
21:17.0 p	Edward Golder (Canterbury)	1.07.43	1	London (HW)			26 Mar
21:35.0 p	John Cooper (Bethnal Green)	c35	int	London (HW)			14 May
21:40.0 p	Henry Guy (Bow)	19.08.46	1=	London (Bow)			1 Sep
21:40.0 p	Billy Mills (Bethnal Green)	09.43	1=	London (Bow)			1 Sep
21:41.0	Richard Garnett (CU)	18.02.43	1	London (BH)	AAC		23 Mar
21:43.8 e	Edward Royds (Eton College)	9.10.47	2	London (BH)	AAC		23 Mar

Estimate: Royds 15y down on 21:41
Intermediate times: Sanderson in a 6 mile race; Fleet and Brighton in 11 mile races against time; Cooper in a 5 mile race.

6 Miles

31:22.0 p	James Sanderson (Whitworth)	28.12.37	inthc	Oldham	13 Jan
32:13.0 p	John Fleet (Manchester)	6.04.45	int	Manchester (RO)	3 Nov
32:23.0 p	John Brighton (Norwich)	14.07.32	int	Manchester (RO)	17 Nov
33:24.0 p	Charles Guilder (Gravesend)	c40	int	Gravesend	30 Jul
34:43.25 p	James Radcliffe (Rochdale)	06.33	1hc	Oldham	13 Jan

Notes
The terms of the Oldham race were for Sanderson to run 6½ miles while Radcliffe ran 6.
Intermediate times in races at 10 miles (30/07) and 11 miles (3/11; 17/11).

10 Miles

54:37.0 p	John Brighton (Norwich)	14.07.32	int	Manchester (RO)	17 Nov
55:04.0 p	Charles Guilder (Gravesend)	c40	wo	Gravesend	30 Jul

Note: Intermediate time in a match to run 11 miles in 1 hour.

120 Yards Hurdles

16.0	Edward Havers (Ingatestone)	c44	1	Brentwood		7 Jul
16 2/5 w	Louis Tiffany (CU/USA)	10.10.44	1	Cambridge		6 Mar
17 ¼	Charles Fell (OU/NZL)	5.08.44	1	Oxford		2 Nov
17 ¾	Thomas Milvain (CU)	4.05.44	1	London (BH)	AAC	23 Mar
17.9 e	Tiffany		2	London (BH)	AAC	23 Mar
18.0	Arthur Wilmot (OU)	14.02.45	1	Oxford		6 Feb
18.0	David Morgan (OU)	43	1	Oxford		2 Mar
18.0	Tiffany		1ht1	Cambridge		3 Mar
18.0	Milvain		1ht2	London (BH)	AAC	23 Mar
18.0	T. Nicol (Horsley)		1	Horsley		24 Aug
18.0	Frederick O'Grady (OU)	20.04.47	1ht2	Oxford		2 Nov
18.0	John Smith (OU)	45	1	Oxford		27 Nov
	(12/9)					
18.1 e	Edmund Page (OU)	44	2	Oxford		27 Nov
18.4 e	John Martin (OU)	10.06.41	2ht2	London (BH)	AAC	23 Mar
18 ½	Robert Vidal (OU)	19.02.43	1ht3	Oxford		2 Mar
18 ½	Clement Jackson (OU)	2.04.46	1ht3	London (BH)	AAC	23 Mar
18 ½	Arthur Bartley (OU)	16.03.48	1	Oxford		16 Nov
18 ½	Maurice Kingsley (CU)	9.02.47	1	Cambridge		24 Nov

Notes
The 16.0 by Havers at a minor meeting was not regarded as a record.
Tiffany's 16.6 was "with the wind which was blowing more than half a gale" *(The Field)*. Vidal was given 18.8ht on 2/03 by *The Field*.
Estimates: Page ½y down on 18.0; Martin 2½y down on 18.0; Tiffany ½y down on 17.75.

440 Yards Hurdles

15 flights
Doubtful (seems exceptionally fast):

1:03.25		Frederick Smith (Dublin U/IRL)		1	Dublin (CP), IRL		30 May

20 flights

1:14.0		William Morris (RMA Woolwich)		1	Woolwich		9 May
1:14.3 e		J. Walter Joyce (RMA Woolwich)		2	Woolwich		9 May
1:14.9 e		H.P.Russell (RMA Woolwich)		3	Woolwich		9 May

Note: Joyce 1½y and Russell 5y down on 1:14.0.

High Jump

5'9	1.753		Thomas Little (CU)	15.02.45	1=	London (BH)	AAC	23 Mar
5'9	1.753		John Roupell (CU)	13.07.45	1=	London (BH)	AAC	23 Mar
5'9	1.753		Little		1	Sheffield (BL)		7 May
5'9	1.753		Henry Brooke (German Gym Soc)	07.48	1=	Islington		26 Nov
5'9	1.753		John Harwood (German Gym Soc)	22.06.45	1=	Islington		26 Nov
5'8	1.727		Roupell		1	Cambridge		5 Mar
5'7	1.702		John Moir (Edinburgh U)	43	1	Edinburgh (GP)		27 Jun
5'7	1.702		Arthur Fowle (Hertford)	c37	1	Hertford		25 Jul
5'6½	1.689		Charles Green (CU)	26.08.46	2=	Cambridge		5 Mar
5'6½	1.689		Little		2=	Cambridge		5 Mar
5'6	1.676		Roupell		1	Oxford	OvC	10 Mar
5'6	1.676		Edward Cave (Blandford)	c49	1=	Blandford		2 Aug
5'6	1.676		James Quirk (Blandford)	5.03.50	1=	Blandford		2 Aug
5'5½	1.664		Little		1	Cambridge		24 Feb
5'5½	1.664		Robert Mitchell (Stacksteads)	14.07.47	1	Llandudno		25 Jun

(15/10)

5'5	1.651		George Thornton (CU)	23.03.45	4	Cambridge	5 Mar
5'5	1.651		Hon George Villiers (Barnes FC)	27.09.47	1=	Barnes	24 Mar
5'5	1.651		Robert Graham (Barnes FC)	c44	1=	Barnes	24 Mar
5'5	1.651		John Hoare (CU)	16.03.47	1	Cambridge	27 Nov

Gymnastic trial indoors

5'7	1.702 i		G. Stephens (Liverpool)		1	Liverpool Gym	28 Mar
5'6	1.676 i		J. Robertson (Liverpool)		1	Liverpool Gym	8 Feb
5'5	1.651 i		Joseph Taylor (Liverpool)		2	Liverpool Gym	28 Mar

Doubtful

5'11	1.803		J. Lewis (Totnes)		1	Chudleigh	26 Sep
5'10	1.778		William Warner (CU)	29.08.44	2	Chudleigh	26 Sep

High Jump: Highland & Border

5'10	1.778	p	John Bell (Hawick)	c39	1=	Galashiels	28 Jul
5'10	1.778	p	Gavin Tait (Douglas)	34	1=	Galashiels	28 Jul
5'9	1.753	p	Donald Dinnie (Aboyne)	8.06.37	1	Kilbride	13 Jul
5'9	1.753	p	Samuel Muir (Stewarton)	c41	1	Johnstone	14 Jul
5'9	1.753	p	Andrew Milne (Forfar)	24.11.39	1	Dundee	28 Jul
5'9	1.753	p	Milne		1	Alloa	8 Aug
5'8	1.727	p	Muir		1	Maryhill	16 Jun
5'8	1.727	p	G. Tait		2=	Kilbride	13 Jul
5'8	1.727	p	William Tait (Douglas)	36	2=	Kilbride	13 Jul
5'8	1.727	p	Campbell Currie (Stewarton)	c39	2=	Johnstone	14 Jul
5'8	1.727	p	G. Tait		2=	Johnstone	14 Jul
5'8	1.727	p	W. Tait		1	Peebles	21 Jul
5'8	1.727	p	Dinnie		2	Dundee	28 Jul
5'8	1.727	p	Muir		1	Barrhead	4 Aug
5'8	1.727	p	Muir		2	Alloa	8 Aug
5'8	1.727	p	Bell		3	Alloa	8 Aug
5'8	1.727	p	Dinnie		1	Leith	28 Aug
5'8	1.727	p	Dinnie		1	Birnam	30 Aug
5'8	1.727	p	Dinnie		1=	Airdrie	10 Sep
5'8	1.727	p	G. Tait		1=	Airdrie	10 Sep
5'8	1.727	p	Muir		1=	Airdrie	10 Sep
5'8	1.727	p	G. Tait		1	Calderbank	11 Sep

(22/7)

5'7	1.702	p	James Wright (Perth)	15.01.45	2	Birnam	30 Aug
5'6½	1.689	p	John Scott (Galashiels)		2	Gorebridge	15 Sep
5'6	1.676	p	John Kean (Castle Eden)	c44	1	Newcastle	4 Apr
5'6	1.676	p	David Milne (Forfar)	28.12.42	3	Birnam	30 Aug
5'5	1.651	p	Alexander Campbell (Strathbraan)		4	Birnam	30 Aug

Pole Vault

10'0	3.05		F. or J. Wheeler (Wandsworth)		1	London (BH) AAC	23 Mar
9'9	2.97		George Bayley (Stalybridge)	45	1=	Manchester (RG)	4 Aug
9'9	2.97		Sydney Hyde (Dukinfield)	c41	1=	Manchester (RG)	4 Aug
9'7	2.92		F. Worthington (Tonbridge)		1	Tunbridge Wells	6 Apr
9'6	2.89		Christopher Ewbank (CU)	10.03.45	2	London (BH) AAC	23 Mar
9'6	2.89		Bayley		1	Llandudno	26 Jun
9'6	2.89		Cruikshank (Blandford)		1	Blandford	2 Aug
9'5	2.87		Henry St Quintin	c46	1	Cirencester	17 Oct
9'4	2.84		James Quirk (Blandford)	5.03.50	2	Blandford	2 Aug
9'3½	2.83		Worthington		1	Tonbridge	15 Mar
9'3	2.82		Robert Mitchell (Stacksteads)	14.07.47	2	Llandudno	26 Jun
9'2	2.79		Mitchell		1	Sheffield (BL)	7 May
9'2	2.79		William Pearson (Blandford)		3	Blandford	2 Aug
9'1	2.77		William Curteis (Tonbridge Sch)	28.01.49	2	Tunbridge Wells	6 Apr
9'1	2.77		Lynham (QC Galway/IRL)		1=	Galway, IRL	23 Apr
9'1	2.77		Woods (QC Galway/IRL)		1=	Galway, IRL	23 Apr
9'1	2.77		Avison Scott (Brighton College)	18.07.48	1	Brighton	20 Sep
9'0	2.74		Henry Gataker (RMA Woolwich)	12.09.47	1	Woolwich	9 May
9'0	2.74		Worthington		1	Canterbury	22 May

(19/15)

Notes
Height cleared by Bayley and Hyde (4/08) also given as 9'11½ (*A History of the Pole Vault*, H. Berry)
Bell's Life has Ewbank's AAC jump as 9'3, not 9'6
Worthington of Tonbridge is listed in 3 meetings with initials A, F and C. F occurs again in 1867.

Pole Vault: Lakeland, Highland & Border

10'2½	3.11	p	John Allison (Kendal)	8.02.43	1	Blackburn	4 Aug
10'0	3.05	p	David Anderson (Alnwick)	c46	1	Wooler	25 Jul
10'0	3.05	p	Thomas Shevels (Durham)	c47	1=	Coxhoe	17 Sep
10'0	3.05	p	W. Lawson (Middlesbrough)		1=	Coxhoe	17 Sep
9'10	3.00	p	Allison		1	Liverpool	22 May
9'10	3.00	p	David Johnstone (Lochead)		1=	Hawick	9 Jun
9'10	3.00	p	Robert Taylor (Hawick)		1=	Hawick	9 Jun
9'10	3.00	p	Anderson		1	Eglingham	3 Nov
9'9	2.97	p	Robert Musgrave (Cockermouth)	11.10.41	1	Stockton	21 May
9'9	2.97	p	Johnstone		1	Newcastleton	20 Jul
9'8	2.94	p	Robert Porter (Innerleithen)		1	Innerleithen	12 Aug
9'8	2.94	p	Johnstone		1	Talkin Tarn	17 Aug
9'7	2.92	p	William Jamieson (Penrith)	c35	2	Innerleithen	12 Aug

(13/9)

9'6	2.89	p	William Hall (Brampton)		1	Jarrow	22 May
9'6	2.89	p	Samuel Rigg (Kendal)	c46	1	Ulverston	28 Aug
9'4	2.84	p	W. Allen (Hawick)		3	Hawick	9 Jun
9'4	2.84	p	David Thomson (Galashiels)		3	Galashiels	28 Jul
9'4	2.84	p	David Milne (Forfar)	28.12.42	1	Birnam	30 Aug
9'4	2.84	p	Robert Scott (Innerleithen)		1	Dalkeith	29 Sep
9'3	2.82	p	Robert Poustie (Duntrune)	41	1	Rollo's Pier	14 Jul
9'3	2.82	p	Anderson Turner (Salsburgh)	17.03.38	2	Dalkeith	29 Sep
9'3	2.82	p	George Tickell (Thornthwaite)	42	1	Keswick	24 Oct
9'2	2.79	p	Henry Knox (Blyth)	41	2	Eglingham	3 Nov
9'0	2.74	p	William Telford (Brampton)	45	1	Stockton	22 May
9'0	2.74	p	John Clark (Langholm)		2	Newcastleton	20 Jul
9'0	2.74	p	Matthew Middlemist (Jedburgh)	c39	3=	Peebles	21 Jul
9'0	2.74	p	Alexander McGhee (Biggar)		3=	Peebles	21 Jul
9'0	2.74	p	Robert Thomson (Lochgelly)		1	Kelly	14 Sep

Indoors

10'6	3.20 i p		Musgrave		1	London (Ag Hall)	30 Mar
10'3	3.12 i p		Philip Winder (Kendal)	13.12.47	2=	London (Ag Hall)	30 Mar

10'3   3.12 i p   James Baines (Penrith)   2=   London (Ag Hall)   30 Mar
Note: Musgrave is said in *Sporting Chronicle Annuals* to have cleared 10'10½ this year at Cockermouth (nd).

Long Jump

20'8	6.30	Thomas Little (CU)	15.02.45	1	Sheffield (BL)		7 May
20'6	6.25	Robert Mitchell (Stacksteads)	14.07.47	2	Sheffield (BL)		7 May
20'6	6.25	Mitchell		1	Llandudno		26 Jun
20'4	6.20	Little		1	Oxford	OvC	10 Mar
20'0	6.10	Percy Wright (Colchester)		1	Colchester		9 May
20'0	6.10	George Bayley (Stalybridge)	45	2	Llandudno		26 Jun
19'11	6.07	William Maitland (OU)	6.05.44	2	Oxford	OvC	10 Mar
19'10	6.05	Charles Corfe (CU)	8.06.47	1	Cambridge		27 Nov
19'9	6.02	Lewin Norris (Grantham)	5.11.47	1	Grantham		5 Apr
19'9	6.02	Edmund Phelps (CU)	14.12.47	1	Cambridge		23 Nov
19'8	5.99	Little		1	Cambridge		5 Mar
19'8	5.99	Alick Tosswill (OU)	21.01.45	3	Oxford	OvC	10 Mar
19'8	5.99	Richard Fitzherbert (CU)	12.04.46	1	London (BH)	AAC	23 Mar
19'6	5.94	James Turner (OU)	16.10.46	1	St Servan, FRA		Sep
			(14/11)				
19'5½	5.93	Charles Absolom (CU)	7.06.46	1	Cambridge		24 Nov
19'4	5.89	Arthur Law (CU)	21.03.44	1	Tunbridge Wells		6 Apr
19'4	5.89	Avison Scott (Brighton College)	18.07.48	1	Brighton		20 Sep
19'3	5.87	John Wilson (Durham Sch)	19.07.48	1	Durham		14 May
19'2	5.84	George Owen (Rotherham)	22.02.42	1	Rotherham		26 Aug
19'1¾	5.84	George Savile (Rossall School)	26.04.47	1	Fleetwood		12 Mar

Long Jump: Highland & Border

19'4	5.89	p	Samuel Muir (Stewarton)	c41	1	Alloa	8 Aug
19'2½	5.85	p	Gavin Tait (Douglas)	34	1	Berwick-on-Tweed	24 Sep
19'1½	5.83	p	John Bell (Hawick)	c39	1	Newcastleton	20 Jul
19'0	5.79	p	Andrew Milne (Forfar)	24.11.39	1	Dundee	28 Jul

Triple Jump

May include performances achieved with two hops and a jump

41'6½	12.66	Edward Havers (Ingatestone)	c44	1	Brentwood	7 Jul
40'7	12.37	Pte McCart (78th Regt)		1	Gibraltar, GIB	11 Oct
40'6½	12.36	Bombardier Watson (Royal Artillery)		2	Gibraltar, GIB	11 Oct
40'1	12.22	Edward Grace (Marshfield)	28.11.41	1	Clifton	25 Aug

Triple Jump: Highland & Border

May include performances achieved with two hops and a jump

46'11	14.30	p	John Bell (Hawick)	c39	1	Hawick	8 Jun
46'9	14.25	p	Gavin Tait (Douglas)	34	1	Calderbank	11 Sep
46'9	14.25	p	James Young (Alva)	c47	1	Dalkeith	29 Sep
46'8¾	14.24	p	Tait		2	Hawick	8 Jun
46'7	14.20	p	Tait		1	Newcastleton	20 Jul
46'6	14.17	p	Young		2	Newcastleton	20 Jul
46'5	14.15	p	Young		1	Alloa	8 Aug
46'1	14.05	p	Young		1	Gorebridge	15 Sep
45'10	13.97	p	Tait		1	Berwick-on-Tweed	24 Sep
45'8	13.92	p	Young		1	Jedburgh	10 Aug
45'6	13.87	p	Samuel Muir (Stewarton)	c41	1	Barrhead	4 Aug
45'6	13.87	p	Muir		2	Calderbank	11 Sep
				(12/4)			
43'0	13.11	p	Campbell Currie (Stewarton)	c39	2	Barrhead	4 Aug
42'8	13.00	p	Robert Knox (Newstead)	17.09.47	1	St Boswells	14 Jul
41'9	12.73	p	John Allan (Alnwick)		3	Airdrie	11 Sep
41'2	12.55	p	Donald Dinnie (Aboyne)	8.06.37	1	Bridge of Allan	4 Aug
40'7	12.37	p	William Weir		3	Motherwell	11 Aug
40'5	12.32	p	Robert Porter (Innerleithen)		1	Edinburgh	15 Sep
40'4	12.29	p	R.J.Calder		2=	West Calder	25 Jul
40'4	12.29	p	John Wilson		2=	West Calder	25 Jul
40'4	12.29	p	Robert Johnston (Whitburn)		2	Roslin	18 Aug
40'3	12.27	p	Peter Barratt (Hawick)		3	Peebles	21 Jul
40'3	12.27	p	William Tait (Glendoch)	36	2	Perth	25 Aug

Shot

37'5	11.40	William Walker (Tunbridge Wells)	14.12.48	1	Tunbridge Wells		6 Apr
36'0	10.97	Archibald McKerracher (Edinburgh U)	27.09.42	1	Edinburgh		27 Jun
34'10*	10.62	Charles Fraser (Glenlivet)	c39	1	London (BH)	AAC	23 Mar
34'9	10.59	Henry Lugard (Tunbridge Wells)	27.04.49	2	Tunbridge Wells		6 Apr
34'6	10.52	William Boyd (OU)	c45	1	Oxford		27 Nov
33'6	10.21	Henry Richardson (Eltham)		1	Eltham		28 May
33'5	10.19	Brooke Cunliffe (Eltham)	12.06.48	2	Eltham		28 May
32'10½	10.02	George Elliot (CU)	13.05.44	1	Oxford	OvC	10 Mar
32'9½	9.99	Richard Waltham (CU)	25.02.46	2	Oxford	OvC	10 Mar
32'1	9.78	Fraser		1	London (BH)		19 May
32'0	9.75	Charles Absolom (CU)	7.06.46	1	Cambridge		1 Dec
31'9½	9.69	Waltham		1	Cambridge		5 Mar
31'6¾	9.62	Elliot		2	Cambridge		5 Mar
		(13/10)					
30'11	9.42	David Morgan (OU)	43	1	Oxford		3 Mar
30'11	9.42	Reginald Willis (Great Shelford)	48	1	Cirencester		17 Oct

Weight unstated

38'5	11.71	Arthur Davies (OU)	9.04.43	1	Oxford	13 Feb
33'6	10.21	John Thomas (OU)	c44	2	Oxford	13 Feb
33'0	10.06	Henry Hallett (Tonbridge)	41	1	Tonbridge	15 Mar
33'0	10.06	Captain Burnaby (Royal Horse Guards)		1	Windsor	10 May

Throwing the cannonball

33'2	10.11	Henry Cloete (Victoria Coll)	c46	1	St Helier	19 Apr
32'7½	9.94	Francis Thomson (Victoria Coll)	47	2	St Helier	19 Apr

22lb stone

35'0	10.67	David Lundie (St Andrews U)	23.11.46	1	St Andrews	7 Apr
31'0	9.45	W. Duff (St Andrews U)		2	St Andrews	7 Apr

Note
* Fraser's throw in the AAC sports was with a shot weighing 18lb 10oz.
Reports of the result in the CU Sports on 5/03 in *Bell's Life* and *The Athlete for 1866* give Elliot 1st and Waltham 2nd, but we have followed *The Field* and the *CUAC Record Book*.

Shot: Highland & Border
Includes 16lb stone & ball

44'10	13.67	p	Donald Dinnie (Aboyne)	8.06.37	1	Calderbank	11 Sep
44'5	13.54	p	Dinnie		1	Johnstone	14 Jul
42'11	13.08	p	Allan Mather (Busby)		1	Busby	15 Sep
42'8	13.00	p	John George (Tarland)	46	2	Johnstone	14 Jul
42'7	12.98	p	Dinnie		1	New Stevenston	13 Aug
42'3	12.88	p	Dinnie		1	Maryhill	16 Jun
42'2½	12.87	p	Dinnie		1	Alexandria	15 Sep
42'0	12.80	p	William Tait (Glendoch)	36	2	Maryhill	16 Jun
41'10	12.75	p	James Paton (Murthly)	33	3	Maryhill	16 Jun
41'9	12.73	p	Tait		2	Calderbank	11 Sep
41'3	12.57	p	George		4	Maryhill	16 Jun
41'0	12.50	p	Francis Strachan (Drum)	c37	1	Lumphanan	21 Jul
41'0	12.50	p	Tait		2	Alexandria	15 Sep
			(13/6)				
38'0	11.58	p	John Moir (Strathdon)	27.07.42	1	Colquhonnie	21 Aug
37'8½*	11.49	p	James Fleming (Blair Castle)	18.09.40	2	Perth	25 Aug
37'3½	11.37	p	William McGregor (Asloun House)		2	Colquhonnie	21 Aug
37'1	11.30	p	James Kennedy (Edinburgh)		1	Edinburgh	15 Sep
37'2	11.33	p	Charles Emslie (Wester Craigievar)		2	Lumphanan	21 Jul
36'8	11.18	p	Thomas Ogilvie (Drum)		3	Lumphanan	21 Jul
36'6	11.13	p	Charles Hogarth (Busby)		2	Busby	15 Sep
35'9	10.90	p	John Dunlop (Busby)		3	Busby	15 Sep
34'11½	10.66	p	Peter Bremner (Glenkindie)	20.01.42	3	Colquhonnie	21 Aug
34'4	10.46	p	W. Mitchell (Clachinturn)		1	Abergeldie	26 Jul
34'2	10.41	p	James Brown (Leith)		2	Edinburgh	15 Sep
34'0	10.36	p	J. Christie (Edinburgh)		3	Edinburgh	15 Sep
33'4	10.16	p	John Cameron (Sloch)		1	Grantown-on-Spey	10 Aug
33'4	10.16	p	William McKenzie		3	Alexandria	15 Sep

Note: * correct weight assumed from evidence of other years

Weight unstated

43'7	13.28	p	Dinnie		1	Forfar	10 Aug
40'8	12.40	p	William Cattanach (Glengairn)	c35	1	Ballater	25 Jul
35'2	10.72	p	James Leighton (Kilmindie)		1	Forfar (local)	10 Aug
34'7	10.54	p	Peter Keith (Marcus)	c40	2	Forfar (local)	10 Aug

17lb by performer

43'10	13.36	p	Dinnie		1	Inverary	8 Aug
33'4	10.16	p	A. Black (Glendarvell)		1	Inverary (local)	7 Aug

18lb by performer

38'8	11.79	p	Dinnie		1	Berwick-on-Tweed	24 Sep
35'6½	10.83	p	Tait		2	Berwick-on-Tweed	24 Sep

20lb by performer

37'1	11.30	p	James Michie (Corrie)	20.10.46	1	Tomintoul	30 Aug

21lb by performer

37'0	11.28	p	Richard Young (Kersknowe)		1	Galashiels	28 Jul

22lb by performer

42'6	12.95	p	Dinnie		1	Dundee	28 Jul
38'10	11.84	p	George		2	Coatbridge	17 Sep
38'6	11.73	p	Tait		3	Coatbridge	17 Sep
37'10	11.53	p	Fleming		2	Birnam	30 Aug
35'1	10.69	p	Paton		3	Dunkeld	25 Jul
34'8	10.57	p	Michie		m	Knockandhu	23 Aug

Hammer

91'2½	27.80	David Morgan (OU)	43	1	Oxford		2 Mar
90'9	27.66	Robert Martin (Dublin U/IRL)	17.06.46	u	Dublin (CP), IRL		30 May
90'8	27.64	Richard James (CU)	27.05.44	1	Cambridge		3 Mar
89'8	27.33	George Thornton (CU)	23.03.45	2	Cambridge		3 Mar
87'7	26.70	Thornton		1	Oxford	OvC	10 Mar
86'9	26.44	James		2	Oxford	OvC	10 Mar
86'8	26.42	Walter Croker (OU)	2.01.45	1	Oxford		14 Mar
86'6	26.37	Morgan		3	Oxford	OvC	10 Mar
86'5	26.34	Reginald Rudyerd (Tonbridge Sch)	28.12.48	1	Tonbridge		22 Mar
86'0	26.21	Reginald Marsden (OU)	15.07.45	1	Oxford		19 Nov
85'2	25.96	Thornton		1	Cambridge		26 Nov
85'0	25.91	John Reynard-Cookson (Harrow Sch)	c48	1	Harrow		24 Mar
			(12/8)				
84'10	25.86	William Walker (Tonbridge Sch)	14.12.48	2	Tonbridge		22 Mar
84'0	25.60	David Lundie (St Andrews U)	23.11.46	1	St Andrews		7 Apr
80'0	24.38	Henry Leeke (CU)	6.02.46	1	Cambridge		1 Dec
78'11	24.05	Charles Corfe (CU)	8.06.47	2	Cambridge		26 Nov
78'4½	23.89	Douglas Moffatt (OU)	31.07.43	3	Oxford		2 Mar
78'4½	23.89	George Osborne (CU)	1.04.42	3	Cambridge		3 Mar

Weight unstated

95'6	29.11	J. Simpson (Leicester)		1	Leicester	24 May

Notes
Martin's 90'9 was in a competition undecided, as the hammer broke. The *Fife Herald* has Lundie's throw as 87'6. Simpson's weight unstated performance gains some credence in the light of the 1867 competition in Leicester, when he beat William Burgess into third place.

Hammer: Highland & Border

102'10	31.34	p	Donald Dinnie (Aboyne)	8.06.37	1	Clova	21 Aug
98'3½*	29.96	p	Dinnie		1	Dunkeld	25 Jul
94'0	28.65	p	John George (Tarland)	46	1	Inverness	20 Sep
93'8	28.55	p	Dinnie		1	Alexandria	15 Sep
93'2	28.40	p	James Fleming (Blair Castle)	18.09.40	2	Inverness	20 Sep
92'9	28.27	p	Dinnie		1	Dundee	28 Jul
92'0	28.04	p	Dinnie		1	Braemar (open)	6 Sep
91'10½	28.00	p	James Paton (Murthly)	33	1	Glenisla	17 Aug

91'8	27.94	p	Dinnie		1	Coatbridge	17 Sep
91'3½	27.83	p	Dinnie		1	Johnstone	14 Jul
90'0*	27.43	p	Dinnie		1	Leith	28 Aug
				(11/4)			
88'8	27.03	p	William Tait (Douglas)	36	2	Coatbridge	17 Sep
86'6	26.37	p	Charles Hogarth (Busby)		1	Busby	15 Sep
82'7	25.17	p	William Cattanach (Glengairn)	c35	2	Braemar (open)	6 Sep
82'0	24.99	p	James Duncan (Clova)		2	Clova	21 Aug
79'9	24.31	p	Alexander Robertson (Doonie)		3	Clova	21 Aug
79'8	24.28	p	Charles Emslie (Wester Craigievar)		1	Lumphanan	21 Jul
78'4	23.88	p	Charles McHardy (Dumbarton)	34	2	Barrhead	4 Aug

Ten throws allowed:

104'1½	31.74	p	James Kennedy (Invergowrie)	c36	1	Invergowrie	10 Jan
102'6	31.24	p	William Stewart (Pitlochry)	29	2	Invergowrie	10 Jan

18lb by performer

80'7	24.56	p	Donald McIntyre (Glenorchy)		1	Glenorchy	30 Aug
79'7	24.26	p	Archibald McIntyre (Glenorchy)		2	Glenorchy	30 Aug

Note: *correct weight assumed from evidence of other years.

The Civil Service Sports at Beaufort House, 1866, the most fashionable meeting of the year. In the first AAC Championships at the same venue a gust of wind blew the canvas cover off the grandstand.

Other Events

150 Yards

15.75	Henry Dunlop (Dublin U/IRL)		1ht3	Dublin (CP), IRL	30 May

200 Yards

21.0	p	George Mole (Sheffield)	6.08.42	1	Manchester (RO)	3 Jul
21.5		Henry Sewell (CU)	21.08.47	1	Cambridge	28 Nov
21.5		Edward Colbeck (LAC)	21.12.47	1	Cambridge	30 Nov

300 Yards
33.5   William Collett (LAC)   18.06.43   1hc   London (Bow)   17 Nov

600 Yards
1:19.0   Walter Chinnery (LAC)   19.08.43   1   London (BH)   5 May

¾ Mile
3:07.0 p   William Richards (Bridgend)   11.10.38   1   Manchester (RO)   30 Jun

1 Hour
11m 00y p   John Brighton (Norwich)   14.07.32   1   Manchester (RO)   17 Nov
in a match against time completed in 59:52.0

1 Mile Walk
6:50.0 p   George Topley (Chatham)   29.10.45   int   London (WL)   12 Mar

2 Miles Walk
14:08.0 p   George Topley (Chatham)   29.10.45   int   London (WL)   12 Mar

7 Miles Walk
50:52.0 p   George Topley (Chatham)   29.10.45   int   London (WL)   12 Mar
[in scheduled match of 21 miles, won after 13, when his opponent, Jem Miles, retired]

Cricket Ball
113y 2ft 0in 103.94   Brooke Cunliffe (RMA)   12.06.48   1   Camberley   27 Sep

Oxford and Cambridge on Christ Church Meadows, 1866. The 2 miles ended in a dead heat
between Laing (Oxford) and Long (Cambridge). The crowd mobbed them and three runners were
unable to finish. Heavy betting on the result led to 'awful strife, the sounds of which, dinning into
the midnight, I can still hear' (C.N.Jackson, writing in 1901). It was ruled that neither university
should host the match in future and it was moved to London the next year.

1867 UK Year List

100 Yards

10.0	William Tennent (Manchester AC)	6.10.45	1	Buersil	15 Jun
10 1/5	Charles Corfe (CU)	8.06.47	1sf1	Cambridge	29 Mar
10 1/5	Edward Pitman (CU)	11.02.45	1	Cambridge	30 Mar
10.2 e	William MacLaren (Manchester AC)	50	2	Buersil	15 Jun
10 ¼	Richard Fitzherbert (CU)	12.04.46	1	Cambridge	16 Mar
10 ¼	Thomas Colmore (OU)	13.01.45	1ht1	Oxford	22 Mar
10 ¼	Colmore		1	Oxford	23 Mar
10 ¼ e	Mitchell Templeton (CU)	23.07.46	2	Cambridge	30 Mar
10 ¼	William Collett (LAC)	18.06.43	1	Richmond	5 Apr
10 ¼	John Duckworth (Haslingden)	44	1	Birmingham (PR)	26 Jun
10 ¼	MacLaren		1	Huddersfield	13 Jul
10 ¼	John Ridley (CU)	23.06.48	1ht2	Cambridge	20 Nov
10 ¼	Ridley		1	Cambridge	20 Nov
10 ¼	Stewart Douglas (OU)	23.06.48	1	Oxford	29 Nov
10 ¼	Tennent		1	Oxford	3 Dec

Notes

Fifty Years of Sport gives 10¼ for the Oxford v Cambridge result (Pitman, 12 April), but most other sources give 10 2/5. *The Field* credits Tennent with 10.0 on 3 Dec, but *Bell's Life* has 10¼.
Estimates: MacLaren 1y down on 10.0; Templeton inches down on 10.2.

Doubtful

9.0	Ensign Neale (80th Staffs Volunteers)		1	Aldershot	24 Sep

"A cutting wind from the north west." (*Sheldrake's Aldershot & Sandhurst Military Gazette*). Two others deadheated only 3 yards back.

10.0	Pte D. Dundas (93rd Highlanders)		1	Jhansi, IND	c18 Mar
10.0	Godfrey Brameld (Loughborough)	10.09.48	1	Loughborough	4 Jun
10.0	Colour Sgt Jones (56th Regt)		1rB	Aldershot	10 Sep
10.0	Pte W. Langall (56th Regt)		1fA	Aldershot	10 Sep
10.0	Sergeant Archer (80th Staffs Volunteers)		1	Aldershot	24 Sep

Aldershot marks were suspiciously fast (see 9.0 above). All of the above appear to have been timed to the nearest second

School Sports

10.0	John Yockney (Clifton Coll)	27.01.50	1	Clifton	5 Apr
10.0	George Collister (King William's Coll)	5.05.48	1	Douglas, IOM	10 Apr
10.0	John Baines (Cheltenham Coll)	10.12.47	1	Cheltenham	3 May
10.0	Baines		1	Cheltenham	4 May
10.0	R. Judd (City of London Sch)		1	London (BH)	13 May
10.0	Griffith (St Peter's Sch)		1	York	22 Jun
10.0	William Ironmonger (Derby GS)	48	1	Derby	22 Jul
10.0	Walker (Brentwood Sch)		1	Brentwood	8 Oct
10 ¼	Arthur Jennings (Radley College)	19.12.49	1	Radley	3 Apr
10 ¼	Edward Hoare (Tonbridge Sch)	23.08.49	1	Tonbridge	15 Apr

220 Yards

22 ¾	Edward Colbeck (LAC)	21.12.47	1	London (WL)	31 May
23.2 e	William Collett (LAC)	18.06.43	2	London (WL)	31 May
23 ¼	Charles Emery (LAC)	c43	1	Liverpool	29 Jun
23 ¼	John Duckworth (Haslingden)	44	1hc	Liverpool	10 Aug
23.4 e	Duckworth		2	Liverpool	29 Jun
23 ½	Collett		1	London (WL)	2 Mar
23 ¾	Thomas Allingham (Victoria United)	31.03.43	1	Tufnell Park	21 Sep
23.8 e	Emery		2	London (WL)	2 Mar
24.0	Thomas Pigott (Civil Service)	5.03.40	1ht1	London (BH)	17 May
24.0	Thomas Omond (Edinburgh U)	27.04.46	1	Edinburgh (GP)	26 Jun
24.0	William MacLaren (Manchester AC)	50	1	Haslingden	27 Jul
24.0 e	William Palmer (Nicholson's United CC)	c47	2	Tufnell Park	21 Sep
24.2 e	Alexander Dunlop (Edinburgh U)	3.10.48	2	Edinburgh (GP)	26 Jun

Notes

Estimates: Collett 4y down on 22.75; Duckworth 1½y down on 23.25; Emery 2y down on 23.5; Palmer 2y down on 23.75; Dunlop 1y down on 24.0.

440 Yards

51.0	p	Frank Hewitt (Millwall)		8.05.45	1	Manchester (RO)		13 May
51.4		Francis Pelham (CU)		18.10.44	1	Cambridge		28 Mar
51.5		Montagu Knight (OU)		26.10.44	1	Oxford		23 Mar
51.5		Thomas Little (CU)		15.02.45	1	Cambridge		25 Mar
51.6	e p	George Mole (Walsall)		6.06.42	2	Manchester (RO)		13 May
51.7	e	Edward Pitman (CU)		11.02.45	2	Cambridge		28 Mar
51.8		Pitman			1	London (BH)	OvC	12 Apr
51.8	e	William Maitland (OU)		6.05.44	2	Oxford		23 Mar
52.0		Pitman			1	Cambridge		21 Mar
52.0	e	William Frere (OU)		30.10.45	3	Oxford		23 Mar
52.0		John Muggeridge (CU)		7.07.46	1	Tonbridge		15 Apr
			(11/9)					
52.5		John Ridley (CU)		23.06.48	1	Cambridge		27 Nov
52.8	e p	Siah Albison (Bowlee)		26.04.40	2	Manchester (RO)		11 May
52.9	e	Robert Vidal (OU)		19.02.43	2	London (BH)	AAC	15 Apr
53.0	p	John Rothwell (Bury)		23.06.42	1	Manchester (RO)		26 Jan
53.0		George Sams (CU)		29.01.42	1	Cambridge		23 Mar
53.0		Edward Hoare (Tonbridge Sch)		23.08.49	1	Tonbridge		15 Apr
53.0	e	Edward Colbeck (LAC)		21.12.47	3	London (BH)	AAC	15 Apr

Notes
Estimates: Mole 4½y down on 51.0; Pitman 2½y down on 51.4; Maitland 2y down on 51.5; Frere 4y down on 51.5; Albison 2½y down on 52.5; Vidal ¾y & Colbeck a further 1ft down on 52.75.

880 Yards

1:55.75	p	James Nuttall (Stockport)	28.12.41	1hc	Manchester (Cope)		31 Aug
1:58.0	p	Harry Whitehead (Hyde)	26.04.47	1	Manchester (City)		28 Dec
1:59.0	e p	Bob Rogers (Chelsea)	12.01.46	2	Manchester (City)		28 Dec
2:01.0		William Gair (Edinburgh U)	9.12.46	1	Edinburgh (GP)		26 Jun
2:01.8	e	Arthur King (LAC)	c46	3hc	London (WL)		23 Feb
2:01.9	e	James Paulin (Thames RC)	c44	4hc	London (WL)		23 Feb
2:02.5		Francis Pelham (CU)	18.10.44	1	Cambridge		23 Mar
2:02.5	e	William Bowman (OU)	25.09.45	2hc	Oxford		4 Dec
2:02.8		Pelham		1	Cambridge		29 Mar
2:03.0	p	John Bell (14th F Highland Volunteers)		1	Dundee		20 Jul
2:03.0	e	William Frere (OU)	30.10.45	3hc	Oxford		4 Dec
			(11/10)				
2:03.25	p	Edward Mills (Bethnal Green)	25.08.41	1	London (WL)		22 Jun
2:03.3	e	Thomas Little (CU)	15.02.45	2	Cambridge		29 Mar
2:03.5	p	John Fleet (Manchester)	6.04.45	1	Manchester (City)		25 May
2:03.75	p	Joe Tuck (Lambeth)	c42	2	London (WL)		22 Jun
2:04.4	e p	John Heywood (Rochdale)	11.06.45	2	Manchester (City)		25 May
2:05.25		Edward Colbeck (LAC)	21.12.47	1	London (WL)		12 Oct
2:05.25	p	Robert McKinstray (Ayr)	18.04.37	int	Manchester (RO)		2 Nov
2:05.8	e	Walter Chinnery (LAC)	19.08.43	2hc	London (WL)		30 Nov
2:06.6	e	Montagu Knight (OU)	26.10.44	2	Oxford		22 Mar
2:07.0	p	J. Sherwood (Worcester)		1	Nottingham		25 Mar
2:07.0		John Brockbank (Shrewsbury Sch)	22.08.48	1	Shrewsbury		10 Jul

Notes
In Nuttall's record-breaking race, John Fleet (10y start) finished 2y down.
Estimates: Rogers 7y down on 1:58; King 16y & Paulin 17y down on 1:59.5; Bowman 3y down on 2:02; Frere 7y down on 2:02; Little 3y down on 2:02.8; Heywood 6y down on 2:03.5; Chinnery 6in down on 2:05.75; Knight ½y down on 2:06.5.
Intermediate time: McKinstray in 1½ mile race

Mile

4:28.75	p	John Fleet (Manchester)	6.04.45	1	Manchester (RO)		14 Sep
4:29.6	e p	John Neary (IRL)	41	2	Manchester (RO)		14 Sep
4:30.0	p	Robert McKinstray (Ayr)	18.04.37	int	Manchester (RO)		3 Aug
4:31.0	p	McKinstray		1	Manchester (RO)		1 Jun
4:34.0		William Gibbs (CU)	28.07.45	1	Cambridge		9 Mar
4:34.7	e	Thomas Little (CU)	15.02.45	2	Cambridge		9 Mar
4:35.25	p	Robert Hindle (Paisley)	46	1	Bridge of Allan		3 Aug
4:36.0		Walter Chinnery (LAC)	19.08.43	5hc	London (WL)		12 Oct

4:36.6	Edward Royds (CU)	9.10.47	1	Cambridge		28 Mar
4:36.66	Charles Long (CU)	19.04.45	1	Cambridge		20 Mar
4:36.8 e	Long		2	Cambridge		28 Mar
4:37.0	Little		1	Cambridge		23 Mar
4:37.3 e	Royds		2	Cambridge		20 Mar
4:38.0	Edmond Farran (Dublin U/IRL)	27.08.47	1	Dublin (CP), IRL		23 May
4:38.0	Chinnery		1	Oxford		27 Nov
		(15/10)				
4:38.2 e	Gilbert Kennedy (CU)	9.05.44	3	Cambridge		20 Mar
4:40.4	Samuel Scott (OU)	20.05.47	1	London (BH)	OvC	12 Apr
4:40.7 e p	William Park (Glasgow)		2hc	Edinburgh		18 May
4:42.0	Edward Bevir (RMA Woolwich)	2.06.47	1	Woolwich		8 May
4:43.0 e	John Fletcher (OU)	11.05.47	3	London (BH)	OvC	12 Apr
4:43.0	John Martin (LAC)	10.06.41	1	London (BH)		27 Apr
4:45.0 p	Charles Cooper (Leeds)		int	Manchester (RO)		4 May
4:45.0	Pte T. McKenna (1st 13th Regt)		1	Gibraltar, GIB		17 Oct
4:46.0	William Batchelor (CU)	14.11.46	1	Cambridge		29 Nov
4:46.5	John Laing (OU)	1.04.46	1	Oxford		22 Mar
4:47.0	William Bowman (OU)	25.09.45	2	Oxford		27 Nov
4:47.5	Mark Jobling (Northumberland)	43	1	Birmingham (PR)		26 Jun
4:48.0 e	Edward Mapplebeck (Birmingham AC)	6.04.45	2	Birmingham (PR)		26 Jun

Notes
The Field gave Gibbs 4:31.0 at Cambridge on 9/03.
Estimates: Neary 5y down on 4:28.75; Little 4y down on 4:34; Royds 4y down on 4:36.66; Long 1y down on 4:36.6 (28/03); Kennedy 10y down on 4:36.66; Park 4y down on 4:40; Fletcher 16y down on 4:40.4; Mapplebeck 3y down on 4:47.5.
Intermediate times: McInstray in a 1½ mile race, won in 7:02.5; Cooper in a 4 mile race.

2 Miles

9:52.0 p	John Fleet (Manchester)	6.04.45	1	London (HW)		4 Mar
9:59.0	Roland Michell (OU)	14.02.47	1	London (BH)	OvC	12 Apr
9:59.1 e	Charles Long (CU)	19.04.45	2	London (BH)	OvC	12 Apr
10:01.7 e	John Morgan (OU)	19.08.47	3	London (BH)	OvC	12 Apr
10:04.0 p	William Lang (Middlesbrough)	22.12.38	int	London (HW)		6 May
10:04.5 e p	Fleet		int	London (HW)		6 May
10:10.0	Gilbert Kennedy (CU)	9.05.44	1	Cambridge		30 Mar
10:10.0 e p	Charles Cooper (Leeds)		int	Manchester (RO)		4 May
10:10.2 e	Long		2	Cambridge		30 Mar
10:17.0	Walter Chinnery (LAC)	19.08.43	1	Canterbury		11 Jun
10:18.0 p	Billy Mills (Bethnal Green)	09.43	1	London (WL)		10 Aug
10:20.0	John Quirk (Dublin U/IRL)	18.08.47	1	Dublin (CP), IRL		22 May
		(12/10)				
10:25.5 p	William Park (Glasgow)		int	Glasgow		2 Nov
10:25.9 e p	William Bell (Newcastle)		int	Glasgow		2 Nov
10:27.0	James Allanson (Civil Service)	43	1	London (BH)		17 May
10:31.1 e	John Laing (OU)	1.04.46	2	Oxford		23 Mar
10:35.0	W. Carter (Oxford)		1	Oxford		22 Apr
10:35.0 p	Henry Guy (Bow)	19.08.46	1	London (Bow)		18 May
10:35.0 p	John Brighton (Norwich)	14.07.32	int	London (HW)		21 Oct

Doubtful:

10:22.0	Henry Dickinson (Shrewsbury Sch)	3.02.50	1	Shrewsbury		9 Jul
10:23.5 e	Percy Hibbert (Shrewsbury Sch)	27.01.50	2	Shrewsbury		9 Jul

Notes
Estimates: Long 1ft down on 9:59.0 [some accounts say 10:00]; Morgan 15y down on 9:59; Fleet 2y down on 10:04; Long 1y down on 10:10; Bell 1y down on 10:25.5; Laing 6y down on 10:30.
Intermediate times: Lang & Fleet in a 10 mile race; Cooper in a 5 mile race; Park & Bell in a 6 mile race; Brighton in a 10 mile race.

3 Miles

15:24.0 p	William Lang (Middlesbrough)	22.12.38	int	London (HW)		6 May
15:24.4 e p	John Fleet (Manchester)	6.04.45	int	London (HW)		6 May
15:37.0	John Morgan (OU)	19.08.47	1	Oxford		29 Nov
15:39.0	Roland Michell (OU)	14.02.47	2	Oxford		29 Nov

15:45.0	p	John Brighton (Norwich)	14.07.32	int	Manchester (RO)		16 Mar
15:46.0	p	William Park (Glasgow)		int	Glasgow		2 Nov
15:46.4 e p		William Bell (Newcastle)		int	Glasgow		2 Nov
16:00.0	p	Brighton		int	London (HW)		21 Oct
16:00.1	p	Lang		int	London (HW)		21 Oct
16:14.0	p	Park		int	Glasgow (Sto)		25 May
16:20.0		John Fletcher (OU)	11.05.47	int	London (BH)		27 Apr
16:35.5		Charles Dodworth (Bramhall FC)	c47	1	Sheffield (BL)		6 May
16:48.0		Fletcher		int	London (BH)	AAC	15 Apr

Notes
Estimates: Fleet 2y down on 15:24.0; Bell 1y down on 15:46.0.
Intermediate times: Fletcher in 4 mile race; Lang and Fleet in 10 mile races; Brighton in a 1 hour match (16/03) and 10 mile race (21/10); Park and Bell in 6 mile races; Fletcher in a 4 mile race.

4 Miles

21:11.0	p	John Fleet (Manchester)	6.04.45	int	London (HW)		6 May
21:11.4 e p		William Lang (Middlesbrough)	22.12.38	int	London (HW)		6 May
21:13.25	p	William Park (Glasgow)		int	Glasgow		2 Nov
21:13.6 e p		William Bell (Newcastle)		int	Glasgow		2 Nov
21:40.0	p	John Brighton (Norwich)	14.07.32	int	London (HW)		21 Oct
21:53.25	p	Park		int	Glasgow (Sto)		25 May
21:57.0		John Fletcher (OU)	11.05.47	1	London (BH)		27 Apr
22:12.5		Gilbert Kennedy (CU)	9.05.44	1	London (BH)	AAC	15 Apr
22:15.4 e		Fletcher		2	London (BH)	AAC	15 Apr

Notes
Estimates: Lang 2y down on 21:11.0; Bell 1y down on 2:13.25; Fletcher 15y down on 22:12.5
Intermediate times in races at 6 miles (25/05; 2/11) and 10 miles (6/05; 21/10)

6 Miles

32:23.0	p	John Fleet (Manchester)	6.04.45	int	London (HW)	6 May
32:23.4 e p		William Lang (Middlesbrough)	22.12.38	int	London (HW)	6 May
32:52.25	p	William Park (Glasgow)		1	Glasgow	2 Nov
33:00.0	p	John Brighton (Norwich)	14.07.32	int	London (HW)	21 Oct
34:01.25	p	Park		1	Glasgow (Sto)	25 May

Notes
Estimates: Lang 2y down on 32:23.0. The 21/10 race was won by Lang, who stayed in contact with Brighton throughout, probably not more than 5y behind at this stage.
Intermediate times in 10 mile races.

10 Miles

| 56:40.0 | p | William Lang (Middlesbrough) | 22.12.38 | 1 | London (HW) | 21 Oct |
| 56:45.9 e p | | John Brighton (Norwich) | 14.07.32 | 2 | London (HW) | 21 Oct |

Note: Estimate: Brighton 30y down.

120 Yards Hurdles

16 ½		Arthur Hillyard (OU)	16.01.45	1	Oxford	22 Feb
16 ½		Hillyard		1	Oxford	23 Mar
16 ½		Arnold Kirke-Smith (Cheltenham Coll)	23.04.50	1	Cheltenham	4 May
16.6 e		Clement Jackson (OU)	2.04.46	2	Oxford	22 Feb
16.7 e		Jackson		2	Oxford	23 Mar
16 ¾		William MacLaren (Manchester AC)	50	1	Rotherham	22 Aug
16.9 e		Arthur Walkden (Mansfield)	45	2	Rotherham	22 Aug
17.0 e		Thomas Milvain (CU)	4.05.44	3	Oxford	22 Feb
17.0		Jackson		1=ht2	Oxford	22 Feb
17.0		Hillyard		1=ht2	Oxford	22 Feb
17.0		Hillyard		1=ht1	Oxford	22 Mar
17.0		William Phipps (OU)	15.02.47	1=ht1	Oxford	22 Mar
		(12/7)				
17 ½		Hugh Price (OU)	8.03.44	1ht4	Oxford	22 Feb
17 ½		Arthur Molineux (OU)	5.02.46	1ht2	Oxford	1 Mar
17 ½		Henry Thompson (CU)	30.08.45	1	Cambridge	23 Mar
17 ½		Edward Colbeck (LAC)	21.12.47	1	London (WL)	12 Oct

School Sports

16 ½		Kirke-Smith	23.04.50	1	Cheltenham	4 May

Doubtful:

16.0		Swainson Akroyd (Reigate)	13.11.48	1	Reigate	27 Apr

Equalled the best on record, but was disregarded. Slight incline.

Notes
Estimates: Jackson 2ft down on 16.5 (22/02) and 1y down on 16.5 (23/03); Milvain 3y down on 16.5; Walkden 1y down on 16.75.

440 Yards Hurdles

1:07.0	Noel Paterson (Eltham CC)	11.06.44	1	Eltham	27 Apr
1:07.0	William Murray (Dublin U/IRL)		1=	Dublin (CP), IRL	22 May
1:07.0	Frederick Smith (Dublin U/IRL)		1=	Dublin (CP), IRL	22 May

12 flights (3ft high - and twice over water)

1:07.0	William MacLaren (Manchester AC)	50	1	Huddersfield	13 Jul

20 flights

1:08.0	William Morris (RMA Woolwich)		1	Woolwich	8 May
1:09.5e	J. Walter Joyce (RMA Woolwich)		2	Woolwich	8 May

Note
John Lawrence's Annual gave 1:08.0 for the dead heat between Murray and Smith.
Estimate: Joyce 9y down on 1:08.0

High Jump

5'9	1.753	Thomas Little (CU)	15.02.45	1	London (BH)	OvC	12 Apr
5'8	1.727	Charles Green (CU)	26.08.46	2=	London (BH)	OvC	12 Apr
5'8	1.727	Frederick O'Grady (OU)	20.04.47	2=	London (BH)	OvC	12 Apr
5'8	1.727	Green		1=	London (BH)	AAC	15 Apr
5'8	1.727	Little		1=	London (BH)	AAC	15 Apr
			(5/3)				
5'7	1.702	Frederick Parsons (OU)	8.10.46	4	London (BH)	OvC	12 Apr
5'7	1.702	Robert Mitchell (Stacksteads)	14.07.47	1	Buersil		15 Jun
5'7	1.702	Pte Fellows (King's Dragoon Guards)		1	Aldershot		10 Oct
5'6½	1.689	Robert Smith (RHA, Woolwich)		2	London (BH)		27 Apr
5'6	1.676	Sir Victor Brooke (AAC)	5.01.43	3=	London (BH)	AAC	15 Apr
5'6	1.676	John Harwood (LAC)	22.06.45	3	London (BH)		27 Apr
5'6	1.676	Edward Bergman (Bristol)	8.02.49	1	Bruton		5 Jun
5'6	1.676	Thomas Wilson (Liverpool)		1	Liverpool		11 Jun
5'6	1.676	John Duckworth (Haslingden)	44	1	Liverpool		29 Jun
5'6	1.676	William Halliley (Bedford Commercial Sch)	16.09.51	1	Bedford		30 Aug
5'6	1.676	Cpl McCormack (King's Dragoon Guards)		2	Aldershot		10 Oct

Note
The jump by Fellows at Aldershot is given as 5'9 in *Bell's Life*, but we have taken the result from *Sheldrake's Aldershot & Sandhurst Military Gazette*.

Doubtful

5'10	1.778 i	Richard Mayor (Liverpool Gym Soc)	c40	1	Liverpool	29 Mar
5'10	1.778 i	Mayor		1	Liverpool	4 Feb
5'9	1.753 i	George Stone (Liverpool Gym Soc)	8.04.47	2	Liverpool	4 Feb
5'9	1.753 i	Mayor		1=	Liverpool	15 Nov
5'9	1.753 i	Stone		1=	Liverpool	15 Nov
5'8	1.727 i	Stone		2	Liverpool	29 Mar

Jumping was over a cord. Mayor was beaten by Duckworth (5'6/1.676) and Harwood on 29 Jun.

High Jump: Highland & Border

5'9	1.753	p	Gavin Tait (Douglas)	34	1=	Barrhead	27 Jul
5'9	1.753	p	Samuel Muir (Stewarton)	c41	1=	Barrhead	27 Jul
5'9	1.753	p	G. Tait		1	Edinburgh	14 Sep
5'8	1.727	p	G. Tait		1	Maryhill	15 Jun
5'8	1.727	p	John Bell (Hawick)	c39	1=	Galashiels	20 Jul
5'8	1.727	p	G. Tait		1=	Galashiels	20 Jul
5'8	1.727	p	Bell		1	Langholm	27 Jul

5'8	1.727	p	William Tait (Glendoch)	36	3	Barrhead	27 Jul
5'8	1.727	p	Andrew Milne (Forfar)	24.11.39	1	Lochgelly	2 Aug
5'8	1.727	p	Muir		1=	Bridge of Allan	3 Aug
5'8	1.727	p	G. Tait		1=	Bridge of Allan	3 Aug
5'8	1.727	p	W. Tait		1=	Bridge of Allan	3 Aug
5'8	1.727	p	G. Tait		1	Alloa	14 Aug
5'8	1.727	p	Milne		1=	Alva	15 Aug
5'8	1.727	p	Muir		1=	Alva	15 Aug
5'8	1.727	p	W. Tait		1	Lanark	28 Sep
				(16/5)			
5'7	1.702	p	James Wright (Perth)	15.01.45	2	Lochgelly	2 Aug
5'7	1.702	p	Donald Dinnie (Aboyne)	8.06.37	4	Bridge of Allan	3 Aug
5'6	1.676	p	Owen Toy (Forfar/IRL)	c46	2	Dundee	20 Jul

Pole Vault

10'0	3.05	Robert Horne (Kendal)	c47	1=	Manchester (RG)	6 Jul
10'0	3.05	Sydney Hyde (Dukinfield)	c41	1=	Manchester (RG)	6 Jul
9'9	2.97	Edward Bergman (Bristol)	8.02.49	1	Bristol	28 Sep
9'8	2.95	Robert Mitchell (Stacksteads)	14.07.47	1	Rochdale	15 Jun
9'8	2.95	Mitchell		1	Barnsley	24 Aug
9'6	2.90	Edmund Gurney (CU)	23.03.47	1	Cambridge	28 Mar
9'6	2.90	Arthur Angell (Winchester)	44	1=	Winchester	10 Sep
9'6	2.90	Montague Palmer (Newbury)	50	1=	Winchester	10 Sep
9'6	2.90	Alfred Lubbock (MCC)	31.10.45	1	Blackheath	5 Oct
9'5	2.87	J. Plowman (German Gym Soc)		1	Birmingham (PR)	26 Jun
9'5	2.87	Hyde		2	Barnsley	24 Aug
9'4½	2.86	John Gurney (Repton Sch)	19.06.49	1	Repton	6 Apr
9'4	2.84	Warren Warren (Cheltenham Coll)	12.03.49	1	Cheltenham	4 May
9'4	2.84	William Pennington (Kendal)	24.05.48	1	Haslingden	27 Jul
9'4	2.84	Edward Townshend (RMC Sandhurst)	48	1	Sandhurst	11 Sep
9'4	2.84	William Powell Moore (LAC)	23.04.46	2	Blackheath	5 Oct

Pole Vault: Lakeland, Highland & Border

10'7½	3.24	p	David Anderson (Alnwick)	c46	1	Newton-on-the-Moor	Aug
10'4	3.15	p	John Allison (Kendal)	8.02.43	1	Blackburn	15 Jun
10'3	3.12	p	Anderson		1	Glanton	3 Aug
10'3	3.12	p	Anderson		1=	Berwick-on-Tweed	5 Aug
10'3	3.12	p	Robert Musgrave (Cockermouth)	11.10.41	1=	Berwick-on-Tweed	5 Aug
10'2	3.10	p	Robert Taylor (Appletreehall, Hawick)		1	Jedburgh	9 Aug
10'1	3.07	p	Musgrave		ex	Stockton	11 Jun
10'1	3.07	p	David Johnstone (Lochead)		2	Jedburgh	9 Aug
10'1	3.07	p	John Forbes (Banff)		1	Huntly	6 Sep
10'0	3.05	p	Anderson		1	Felton	30 Sep
				(10/6)			
9'8	2.95	p	Jacob Field (Galashiels)		2=	Galashiels	20 Jul
9'8	2.95	p	Anderson Turner (Salsburgh)	17.03.38	2=	Galashiels	20 Jul
9'7	2.92	p	James Stewart (Lochee)		1	Dundee	20 Jul
9'7	2.92	p	Robert Russell (Crofthead)		1	Wishaw	23 Jul
9'6	2.90	p	W. Lawson (Middlesbrough)		1	Stockton	11 Jun
9'6	2.90	p	William Ewing (Alexandria)	c47	1	Johnstone	13 Jul
9'6	2.90	p	William Fleming (Gartsherrie)	c48	2=	Wishaw	23 Jul
9'6	2.90	p	Walter Pollock (Chapelhall)	c43	2=	Wishaw	23 Jul
9'6	2.90	p	John Ashcroft (Ashbank)		2=	Langholm	27 Jul
9'6	2.90	p	John Graham (Kirklinton)		2=	Langholm	27 Jul
9'6	2.90	p	David Milne (Forfar)	28.12.42	1	Forfar	9 Aug
9'6	2.90	p	Samuel Rigg (Kendal)	c46	ex	Manchester (RO)	27 Aug

Indoors

10'5	3.17	i p	Allison	8.02.43	1=	London (Ag Hall)	19 Apr
10'5	3.17	i p	Musgrave	11.10.41	1=	London (Ag Hall)	19 Apr
9'6	2.90	i p	James Baines (Penrith)		3=	London (Ag Hall)	19 Apr
9'6	2.90	i p	Mark Shearman (Keswick)	c49	3=	London (Ag Hall)	19 Apr

Notes
Musgrave and Allison were credited with 11'6/3.51 at the Agricultural Hall on 19 April by the *Illustrated Sporting News and Westmoreland Gazette*; *Bell's Life* made it 11'0/3.35; another source 10'5/3.17. The latter is closer to

their other performances during 1867, and is preferred by Harry Berry in *A History of the Pole Vault in the British Isles.*

Long Jump

20'9	6.32	John Wilson (Durham)		19.07.48	1	Durham		6 Apr
20'5	6.22	Robert Mitchell (Stacksteads)		14.07.47	1	Liverpool		20 May
20'5	6.22	John Duckworth (Haslingden)		44	1	Haslingden		27 Jul
20'3	6.17	Frank Foers (Rotherham)		43	1	Rotherham		22 Aug
20'2	6.15	Charles Absolom (CU)		7.06.46	1	London (BH)	OvC	12 Apr
20'1	6.12	William Maitland (OU)		6.05.44	2	London (BH)	OvC	12 Apr
20'0½	6.11	Lancelot Watson (Rotherham)		c44	2	Rotherham		22 Aug
20'0	6.10	Foers			1	Rotherham		1 Aug
			(8/7)					
19'10¼	6.05	Lewin Norris (CU)		5.11.47	2	Cambridge		29 Mar
19'9	6.02	P.A.Brindley (Leeds)			2	Haslingden		27 Jul
19'8	5.99	Edward Havers (Ingatestone)		c44	1	Ingatestone		18 May
19'5	5.92	Thomas Little (CU)		15.02.45	3	London (BH)	OvC	12 Apr
19'5	5.92	Francis Philpott (OU)		17.05.48	1	Oxford		9 Nov
19'4½	5.91	Richard Fitzherbert (CU)		12.04.46	1	London (BH)	AAC	15 Apr
19'4	5.89	Gordon Millington (Rugby School)		c48	1	Rugby		9 May

Indoors

20'0	6.10 i	William Ramsay (Liverpool Gym Soc)	c47	1	Liverpool		29 Mar

Long Jump: Highland & Border

21'5½	6.54	p	Samuel Muir (Stewarton)		c41	1	Alloa	14 Aug
21'2	6.45	p	Muir			1	Whitburn	16 Jul
20'9	6.32	p	Muir			1	West Calder	31 Jul
20'9	6.32	p	Robert Knox (Newstead)		17.09.47	1	Jedburgh	9 Aug
20'8	6.30	p	Gavin Tait (Douglas)		34	1	Biggar	18 Jun
20'8	6.30	p	James Young (Alva)		c47	2	Alloa	14 Aug
20'7	6.27	p	Andrew Milne (Forfar)		24.11.39	2	West Calder	31 Jul
20'7	6.27	p	Thomas Carruthers (Yetholm)		27.04.40	3	Alloa	14 Aug
20'4	6.20	p	John Bell (Hawick)		c39	1	Berwick	5 Aug
20'0	6.10	p	Tait			2	Whitburn	16 Jul
20'0	6.10	p	Carruthers			3	West Calder	31 Jul
20'0	6.10	p	Bell			2	Jedburgh	9 Aug
				(12/7)				

Triple Jump

Both lists may include performances achieved with two hops and a jump

41'0	12.50	George Keller (Cork/IRL)		c49	1	Queenstown/IRL	25 Sep
39'10	12.14	John Haines (Cheltenham Coll)		23.03.50	1	Cheltenham	3 May
39'3	11.96	R. Walker (56th Regt)			1	Aldershot	10 Sep

Triple Jump: Highland, Border & Lancashire Professional

48'5	14.76	p	James Young (Alva)	c47	1	Jedburgh	9 Aug
48'3	14.71	p	Young		1	Aboyne	31 Aug
47'9	14.55	p	Robert Knox (Newstead)	17.09.47	2	Jedburgh	9 Aug
47'0	14.33	p	Young		1	Dalkeith	28 Sep
46'10	14.27	p	Knox		2	Dalkeith	28 Sep
46'9	14.25	p	Samuel Muir (Stewarton)	c41	1	Riggend	3 Sep
46'7	14.20	p	John Bell (Hawick)	o39	1	Galashiels	20 Jul
46'5	14.15	p	Knox		2	Galashiels	20 Jul
46'5	14.15	p	Muir		1	Bridge of Allan	3 Aug
45'8	13.92	p	Muir		1	Barrhead	27 Jul
45'8	13.92	p	Knox		1	Berwick-on-Tweed	5 Aug
45'7	13.89	p	Bell		2	Berwick-on-Tweed	5 Aug
45'5	13.84	p	Knox		1	Hawick	7 Jun
45'1	13.74	p	Bell		2	Hawick	7 Jun
45'1	13.74	p	Young		1	Alva	15 Aug
45'0	13.72	p	Gavin Tait (Douglas)	34	1	Burntisland	10 Jul
				(16/5)			
44'6	13.56	p	Andrew Milne (Montrose)	24.11.39	1	Dundee	20 Jul
43'7	13.28	p	Robert Neilston (Greenock)		1	Greenock	12 Jun
43'5	13.23	p	William Tait (Douglas)	36	3	Bridge of Allan	3 Aug

43'4	13.21	p	Owen Toy (Forfar/IRL)	c46	2	Burntisland		10 Jul
42'10½	13.07	p	Neil McKay (Innerleithen)	6.01.46	1	Peebles		13 Jul
42'10	13.06	p	Adam Bennett (Alva)		2	Peebles		13 Jul
42'7	12.98	p	James Henderson (Lochgelly)		2	Lochgelly		2 Aug
42'7	12.98	p	David Milne (Forfar)	28.12.42	1	Forfar		9 Aug
42'6	12.95	p	Henry Hayhurst (Blackburn)	44	1	Blackburn		14 Jun
42'5	12.93	p	Peter Barratt (Hawick)		1	Arniston		17 Aug
42'2	12.85	p	R. Edmundson (Blackburn)		2	Blackburn		14 Jun
42'0	12.80	p	Henry Swailes (Church)	c40	3	Blackburn		14 Jun
41'7	12.67	p	Alexander Fleming (Glasgow)		3	Barrhead		27 Jul
41'6	12.65	p	Campbell Currie (Stewarton)	c39	2	Kilmarnock		28 Sep
41'0	12.50	p	R.J.Calder		3	West Calder		31 Jul
41'0	12.50	p	Robert Johnston (Whitburn)		3	Motherwell		24 Aug
41'0	12.50	p	Malcolm McGregor (Alexandria)	c45	2	Vale of Leven		7 Sep

Shot

37'7	11.46		John Stone (Liverpool AC)	25.08.42	1	Liverpool		29 Jun
36'6	11.13		Stone		1	London (BH)	AAC	15 Apr
35'7	10.85		George Young (King William's Coll)	29.08.49	1	Douglas, IOM		10 Apr
34'9	10.59		Richard Waltham (CU)	25.02.46	1	London (BH)	OvC	12 Apr
34'8	10.57		George Nunn (Guy's Hosp)	c45	1	London (BH)		1 Jun
34'8	10.57		Philip Mules (Edinburgh U)	43	1	Edinburgh (GP)		26 Jun
34'4	10.46		William Powell Moore (LAC)	23.04.46	1	London (WL)		12 Oct
33'10	10.31		J.R.Hartley (German Gym Soc)		1	Birmingham (PR)		25 Jun
33'8	10.26		Patrick Halkett (London Scottish)	2.04.37	1	Islington		27 Apr
33'8	10.26		Charles Bauchope (Edinburgh U)	46	1	Edinburgh		5 Jul
33'7	10.24		David Lundie (St Andrews U)	23.11.46	1	St Andrews		23 Mar
33'1½	10.10		Waltham		2	London (BH)	AAC	15 Apr
33'1	10.08		Powell Moore		3	London (BH)	AAC	15 Apr
33'0	10.06		Waltham		1	Cambridge		23 Mar
32'11	10.03		Thomas Batson (OU)	18.05.46	2	London (BH)	OvC	12 Apr

18lb

39'7	12.06		William Glen (93rd Highland Regt)		1	Jhansi, IND		18 Mar

Later competed in Highland Games

Doubtful

42'7	12.98		H. Coventry (Woolston)		1	Tewkesbury		13 Aug

Shot: Highland & Border
Includes 16lb stone & ball

45'7	13.89	p	Donald Dinnie (Aboyne)	8.06.37	1	Aboyne	31 Aug
43'2	13.16	p	James Fleming (Tullymet)	18.09.40	1	Maryhill	15 Jun
43'2	13.16	p	William Tait (Douglas)	36	1	Edinburgh	14 Sep
43'1	13.13	p	John George (Cromar)	46	2	Edinburgh	14 Sep
42'4	12.90	p	George		1	Vale of Leven	7 Sep
42'3	12.88	p	Tait		2	Maryhill	15 Jun
41'3¾	12.59	p	George		1	Glasgow	31 Jul
41'1¾	12.54	p	Tait		2	Glasgow	31 Jul
41'0	12.50	p	Tait		1	Holytown	1 Jul
40'8*	12.40	p	Tait		1	Motherwell	24 Aug
40'6	12.34	p	George		1	Johnstone	13 Jul
40'5	12.32	p	Tait		1	Edinburgh	20 Jul
40'4	12.29	p	Charles Danford (Falkirk)		3	Glasgow	31 Jul
40'0+	12.19	p	Angus McKenzie (Tannadice)		1	Forfar	9 Aug
				(14/6)			
38'10	11.84	p	James Kennedy (Edinburgh)	c36	2	Edinburgh	20 Jul
38'7	11.76	p	James Wilson sen. (Tillyfourie)		1	Monymusk	2 Aug
38'5	11.71	p	William Bremner (Inverkindie)	3.01.47	2	Aboyne	31 Aug
38'0*	11.58	p	Easton Watson (Whitburn)	c46	2	Motherwell	24 Aug
37'6	11.43	p	John Moir (Strathdon)	27.07.42	3	Aboyne	31 Aug
36'10+	11.23	p	Peter Keith (Marcus)	c40	2	Forfar	9 Aug
36'8	11.18	p	Samuel Benzies (Tillyfourie)		2	Monymusk	2 Aug
36'0	10.97	p	W. Marshall		3	Holytown	1 Jul
36'0*	10.97	p	John Linn (Carnbrae)		3	Motherwell	24 Aug
35'11	10.95	p	George Wilson (Leochel-Cushnie)		1	Lumphanan	3 Aug

35'10	10.92	p	Alexander Grant (Birkhall)		2	Lumphanan	3 Aug
35'8	10.87	p	D. Johnston (Edinburgh)		3	Edinburgh	20 Jul
35'6	10.82	p	Gavin Tait (Douglas)	34	2	Vale of Leven	7 Sep
35'3	10.74	p	Thomas Rattray (Culsalmond)	c43	1	Upper Garioch	27 Aug

Notes
+16½lb ball at Forfar on 9 Aug.
*correct weight assumed from evidence of other years

Weight unstated

41'3	12.57	p	W. Tait		1	Carlops	17 Aug

18lb by performer

42'11	13.08	p	Dinnie		1	Forfar	9 Aug
42'6	12.95	p	W. Tait		2	Forfar	9 Aug
42'0	12.80	p	George		3	Forfar	9 Aug
36'10	11.23	p	George McPherson (Cabrach)		1	Milltown	25 Dec
36'3	11.05	p	John Forbes (Cabrach)		2	Milltown	25 Dec
35'10	10.92	p	William Fraser (Clunas)		3	Nairn	10 Aug
35'10	10.92	p	William McGregor (Candacraig)		1	Colquhonnie	20 Aug

22lb by performer

41'10	12.75	p	Fleming		1	Dundee	20 Jul
41'2	12.55	p	Dinnie		2	Dundee	20 Jul
39'7	12.06	p	George		2	Bridge of Allan	3 Aug
39'6	12.04	p	W. Tait		2	Dunkeld	24 Jul
36'9	11.20	p	Kennedy		1	Arniston	17 Aug

Doubtful (slope)

49'4	15.04	p	Dinnie		1	Bridge of Allan	3 Aug
48'8	14.83	p	George		2	Bridge of Allan	3 Aug
48'2	14.68	p	W. Tait		3	Bridge of Allan	3 Aug

Hammer

98'10	30.12	John Eyre (CU)	29.01.45	1	London (BH)	OvC	12 Apr
97'3	29.64	George Thornton (CU)	23.03.45	2	London (BH)	OvC	12 Apr
94'7	28.83	Patrick Halkett (LAC)	2.04.37	1	London (BH)	AAC	15 Apr
94'5	28.78	Eyre		1	Cambridge		29 Nov
94'1	28.68	Eyre		2	London (BH)	AAC	15 Apr
93'2	28.40	Thornton		3	London (BH)	AAC	15 Apr
93'0	28.35	Halkett		1	Aldershot		20 Sep
92'10	28.30	Thornton		1	Cambridge		29 Mar
90'10	27.69	Walter Croker (OU)	2.01.45	3	London (BH)	OvC	12 Apr
90'0	27.43	Sgt Harrington (4th Dragoon Guards)		2	Aldershot		20 Sep

(10/5)

88'2	26.87	David Lundie (St Andrews U)	23.11.46	1	St Andrews		23 Mar
88'0	26.82	John Stritch (Dublin U/IRL)	44	1	Dublin (CP), IRL		23 May
88'0	26.82	Sgt Fleming (4th Dragoon Guards)		3	Aldershot		20 Sep
86'8½	26.43	Henry Leeke (CU)	6.02.46	3	Cambridge		29 Mar
85'7	26.09	William Collins (Radley College)	16.10.48	1	Radley		3 Apr
84'0	25.60	George Mills (OU)	19.01.47	1	Oxford		15 Nov
83'0	25.30	David Bethune, The Master of Lindsay	18.04.32	1	Worlabye		11 Apr
81'1	24.71	Archibald Menzies (St Andrews U)		2	St Andrews		23 Mar
80'0	24.38	Douglas Moffatt (OU)	31.07.43	1	Oxford		2 Mar
80'0	24.38	Fairfax Wade (Radley College)	16.07.51	2	Radley		3 Apr

Weight unstated

102'5	31.22	J. Simpson (Leicester)		1	Leicester		30 May
99'7	30.35	Edward Gittins (Leicester)	47	2	Leicester		30 May

Hammer: Highland & Border

107'10	32.87	p	Donald Dinnie (Aboyne)	8.06.37	1	Aboyne	31 Aug
106'0*	32.31	p	William Tait (Douglas)	36	1	Barrhead	27 Jul
105'10	32.26	p	Dinnie		1	Rollo's Pier	28 Sep
105'0*	32.00	p	John George (Cromar)	46	2	Barrhead	27 Jul
103'7**	31.57	p	Dinnie		1	Forfar	9 Aug
100'10	30.73	p	Dinnie		1	Dundee	20 Jul
100'0	30.48	p	James Fleming (Tullymet)	18.09.40	2	Dundee	20 Jul

98'11**	30.15	p	Tait		2	Forfar	9 Aug
98'3	29.95	p	James Michie (Glenlivet)	20.10.46	1	Lumphanan	17 Aug
97'7*	29.74	p	Dinnie		1	Dunkeld	24 Jul
97'5½*	29.71	p	Dinnie		1	Birnam	29 Aug
96'10**	29.51	p	George		3	Forfar	9 Aug
				(12/5)			
92'4*	28.14	p	Charles Danford (Blair Atholl)		3	Dunkeld	24 Jul
91'8	27.94	p	William Bremner (Inverkindie)	3.01.47	2	Aboyne	31 Aug
90'0**	27.43	p	Angus McKenzie (Tannadice)		1	Forfar (local)	9 Aug
89'0	27.13	p	Samuel Benzies (Tillyfourie)		1	Monymusk	2 Aug
88'9	27.05	p	John McKay (Bathgate)		1	Riggend	3 Sep
87'1	26.54	p	James Wilson jun. (Tillyfourie)		2	Monymusk	2 Aug
86'10	26.47	p	James Wilson sen. (Tillyfourie)		3	Monymusk	2 Aug
85'0*	25.91	p	Alexander Grant (Birkhall)		3	Aboyne	31 Aug
84'3	25.68	p	George Wilson (Leochel-Cushnie)		2	Lumphanan	17 Aug
83'11	25.58	p	James Esson (Aboyne)		3	Lumphanan	17 Aug
82'3	25.07	p	James Paton (Murthly)	33	1	Glenisla (champion)	23 Aug
81'7	24.87	p	William Scott (Brechin)		3	Dundee	20 Jul
81'0*	24.69	p	Donald McDonald (Murthly)		3	Birnam	29 Aug
80'3	24.46	p	Thomas Ogilvie (Drum)		1	Lumphanan	3 Aug

Notes
*correct weight assumed from evidence of other years
**16½lb hammer at Forfar.

Weight unstated

109'6	33.38	p	Tait		1	Holytown	1 Jul
107'1	32.64	p	George		2	Holytown	1 Jul
107'0	32.61	p	Tait		1	Motherwell	24 Aug
97'0	29.57	p	John Linn (Carnbrae)		2	Motherwell	24 Aug
95'0	28.96	p	J. McLeod (Bathgate)		3	Holytown	1 Jul
93'0	28.35	p	Robert Johnston (Whitburn)		3	Motherwell	24 Aug

Other Events

110 Yards

11.0		William MacLaren (Manchester AC)	50	1	Haslingden	27 Jul

150 Yards

15.0 p		Frank Hewitt (Millwall)	8.05.45	1	Manchester (RO)	8 Jun

200 Yards

20.5		John Duckworth (Haslingden AC)	44	1	Birmingham (PR)	26 Jun

300 Yards

35.2e		Edward Colbeck (LAC)	21.12.47	2hc	London (WL)	16 Mar

"A short yard" down on 35.0.

600 Yards

1:15.6		Edward Colbeck (LAC)	21.12.47	1	London (BH)	18 May

1½ Miles

6:59.0 p		John Fleet (Manchester)	6.04.45	1	Manchester (RO)	23 Feb

1 Mile Walk

7:04.0 p		George Davison (Hoxton)	2.09.44	int	London (WL)	5 Oct

[in a 10 mile match with Stockwell, won in 1:21:23]

2 Miles Walk

13:57.0 p		George Topley (Chatham)	29.10.45	int	London (WL)	1 Jul

[in scheduled 21 mile match won at 8 miles, when Spooner retd]

7 Miles Walk

50:42.0 p		George Topley (Chatham)	29.10.45	int	London (WL)	1 Jul

[in scheduled 21 mile match won at 8 miles, when Spooner retd]

Cricket Ball

117y 0ft 0in	106.98	William Grave (Athenaeum & Hightown)	48	1	Manchester (RG)	6 Jul

[*The Sporting Chronicle* gives 122y 0ft 0in/111.56]

1868 UK Year List

100 Yards

10.0	John Tennent (OU/AUS)	31.07.46	1	London (BH)	OvC	3 Apr
10.0 w?	William Tennent (Manchester AC)	6.10.45	1ht1	London (BH)	AAC	19 Jun
10.0	Arthur Gwatkin (CU)	17.07.50	1	Cambridge		14 Nov
10 1/10	Charles Absolom (CU)	7.06.46	1=	Cambridge		19 Mar
10 1/10	Charles Corfe (CU)	8.06.47	1=	Cambridge		19 Mar
10.1/10	Absolom		1ro	Cambridge		19 Mar
10 1/5	J. Tennent		1	Oxford		14 Mar
10.2 e	Corfe		2ro	Cambridge		19 Mar
10.2 e	John Ridley (CU)	23.06.48	3	Cambridge		19 Mar
10 1/5	Edward Colbeck (LAC)	21.12.47	1	London (BH)		25 Apr
10 1/5	Benjamin Connolly (Guy's Hosp)	10.09.45	1	London (BH)		11 Jun
10 1/5	W. Tennent		1	London (BH)	AAC	20 Jun
		(12/8)				
10 ¼	Francis Philpott (OU)	17.05.48	1ht2	Oxford		13 Mar
10 ¼	Sharpley Bainbridge (Lincoln)	c47	1	Lincoln		9 May
10 ¼	Francis Cross (King's College Hosp)	26.11.48	1	London (BH)		11 Jun
10 ¼	James Statham (Manchester)	50	1	Liverpool		20 Jun
10 ¼	C.B.Johnson (Norwich)		1	Lowestoft		10 Sep
10 ¼	Thomas Matthews	45	1hc	Clifton		12 Sep
10 ¼	Edwin White (Basingstoke)	9.06.45	1	Basingstoke		22 Sep
10 ¼	William Goodfellow (CU/NZL)	16.09.50	1sf2	Cambridge		14 Nov

Doubtful:

10.0	T. Sturgeon		1	Tamalpore, IND	3 Jan
10.0	Henry Foley (Frome)	c48	1	Frome	30 Apr
10.0	Henry Callaghan (RMC Sandhurst)		1=	Camberley	25 Sep
10.0	Reginald Lousada (RMC Sandhurst)	50	1=	Camberley	25 Sep
10.0	Higgins (Royal Agric Coll)		1	Cirencester	21 Oct
10.0	Lousada		1	Camberley	26 Sep
10 ¼	George Peake (OU)	6.03.46	1	Oxford	10 Dec

Sandhurst course said to be downhill. In Peake's race "the wind favoured the runners very much" (*Bell's Life*)

School Sports

10.0	John Harrison (Wellington Coll)	22.03.51	1	Crowthorne	15 Mar
10.0	Lewis Evans (C.O. Sch, Canterbury)	9.07.51	1	Canterbury	28 Apr
10.0	Thomas Clerk (Wimbledon School)	c50	1	Wimbledon	30 May

Australian Aboriginal cricketer on tour

10 ¼	Jungunjinanuke ('Dick-a-Dick') (AUS)		1	Sheffield (BL)	12 Aug

Notes

Absolom and Corfe were given 10.0 in *The Times,* 10.1 in *Bell's Life* and 10.2 in *The Field;* the dead-heat was run off in 10.1 (10.0 in *The Times;* 10.2 in *The Field*), Absolom winning by ½y; Ridley ½y down;
Gwatkin's 10.0 in the Cambridge Freshmen's sports was said by *Bell's* to have been agreed by all timekeepers.
The Field credited J.O.R.Fairlie with 10.0 in a heat of the OU Sports on 13 March, but *Bell's Life* made it 10.5.

220 Yards

23.0	Charles Bauchope (Edinburgh U)	46	1	London (WL)	10 Oct
23 ¼	John Potter (Western CC)	48	1	Manchester (SAL)	27 Jun
23 ½ p	John Rothwell (Bury)	23.06.42	1	Manchester (Cope)	14 Nov
23.7 e	William Collett (LAC)	18.06.43	2	London (WL)	10 Oct
23.8 e p	G. Rushton (Whitworth)		2	Manchester (Cope)	14 Nov
24.0	Thomas Pigott (Civil Service)	5.03.40	1ro	London (BH)	30 May
24 2/5	Walter Eaton (Civil Service)	7.04.48	1=	London (BH)	30 May
24 2/5	Pigott		1-	London (BH)	30 May
24.5 e	Eaton		2ro	London (BH)	30 May
25.0	Thomas Stretch (Ormskirk)	28.01.51	1	Ormskirk	16 May
25 1/5	Harry Tomlinson (Civil Service)	11.06.46	1ht2	London (BH)	30 May

Doubtful:

22.0	William Gair (Edinburgh U)	9.12.46	1	Edinburgh (GP)	18 Jun
22.3 e	H.D.Parry (Edinburgh U)	c47	2	Edinburgh (GP)	18 Jun

Notes

Estimates: Collett 6y down on 23.0; Rushton 2y down on 23.5; Eaton 4y down on 24.0. Parry 2y down.

440 Yards

50.25		Edward Colbeck (LAC)	21.12.47	1hc	London (BH)		17 Jun
50.4		Colbeck		1	London (BH)	AAC	20 Jun
50.9 e p		Frank Hewitt (Sheffield)	8.05.45	1hc	Sheffield (HP)		2 May
51.0		John Ridley (CU)	23.06.48	1	London (BH)	OvC	3 Apr
51.0		Henry Chinnery (LAC)	26.06.47	1	Wimbledon		30 May
51.25		Colbeck		1hc	London (LB)		25 Apr
51.25		Ridley		1	Cambridge		18 Mar
51.4 e		William Frere (OU)	30.10.45	2	London (BH)	OvC	3 Apr
51.5 e		Arthur Lambert (CU)	17.01.47	2	Cambridge		18 Mar
51.8 e		Charles Corfe (CU)	8.06.47	3	Cambridge		18 Mar
51.8 e		Lambert		3	London (BH)	OvC	3 Apr
51.9 e		Alexander Finlay (CU)	24.09.44	4	Cambridge		18 Mar
51.9 e		William MacLaren (Manchester AC)	50	2	London (BH)	AAC	20 Jun
52.0		Ridley		1	Oxford		14 Mar
		(14/9)					
52.5	p	William Pounder (Rawtenstall)	9.06.46	1	Manchester (Cope)		1 Jan
52.5	p	Harry Whitehead (Hyde)	26.04.47	1	Manchester (Cope)		25 Jan
52.5		Thomas Bainbridge (CU)	47	1	Cambridge		21 Feb
52.5 e		Gilbert Grace (LAC)	18.07.48	2	Oxford		14 Mar
52.5		Thomas Omond (OU)	27.04.46	1	Oxford		20 Nov

Noteworthy foreign mark:

51.5	*John Harris (Australia)*		1hc	*Ballarat, AUS*		*26 Dec*

Notes

Colbeck's 50.25 was in a handicap match with A. King (LAC); his 50.4 in the AAC included a collision with a sheep.
Hewitt started 10y back in a 440y and ran 450y in 52.0.
Estimates: Frere 3y down on 51.0; Lambert 5ft down on 51.25 (18 Mar) and 6y down on 51.0 (3 Apr); MacLaren 12y down on 50.4; Corfe 4y down on 51.25; Finlay 5y down on 51.25; Grace 4y down on 52.0.

880 Yards

1:58.75	p	Bob Rogers (Chelsea)	12.01.46	1	London (WL)		15 Jun
1:58.8 e p		David Binns (Bingley)	20.08.41	2	London (WL)		15 Jun
2:00.0		Walter Chinnery (LAC)	19.08.43	1	Nottingham		7 May
2:02.0		Edward Colbeck (LAC)	21.12.47	1	London (BH)	AAC	19 Jun
2:02.0		Chinnery		2hc	London (BH)		28 Nov
2:02.5	p	Frank Hewitt (Sheffield)	8.05.45	1hc	Sheffield (BL)		13 Apr
2:02.7 e		Arthur King (LAC)	c46	2	London (BH)	AAC	19 Jun
		(7/6)					
2:03.2 e		Walter Bethune (Civil Service)	19.02.45	3	London (BH)	AAC	19 Jun
2:03.3 e p		Albert Bird (Sheffield)	15.08.46	3hc	Sheffield (BL)		13 Apr
2:03.5		Henry Gurney (CU)	7.09.47	1	Cambridge		11 Nov
2:04.0		William Frere (OU)	30.10.45	1	Oxford		13 Mar
2:04.1 e		Robert Somers-Smith (OU)	23.05.48	2	Oxford		13 Mar
2:04.3 e		Thomas Bainbridge (CU)	47	2	Cambridge		11 Nov
2:04.3 e p		Tom Small (Hornsey)	11.03.43	2hc	London (HW)		24 Dec
2:04.8		Arthur Lambert (CU)	17.01.47	1	Cambridge		19 Mar
2:06.0		William Bowman (OU)	25.09.45	1	Oxford		6 Mar

Notes

Chinnery's 2:00.0 was not credited as a record in the press; Wilkinson, in *Modern Athletics*, credits Frere with 2:02.6 in the Oxford Sports on 13 Mar, with Somers-Smith 6in down, but other reports give 2:04.0.
Estimates: Binns 6in down on 1:58.75; King 4.5y down on 2:02; Bethune 8y down on 2:02; Somers-Smith 6in down on 2:04; Bainbridge 5y down on 2:03.5; Small 2y down on 2:04.

Mile

4:23.5	p	John Fleet (Manchester)	6.04.45	1	Manchester (City)		10 Apr
4:26.6 e p		Robert McKinstray (Ayr)	18.04.37	2	Manchester (City)		10 Apr
4:28.8		William Gibbs (CU)	28.07.45	1	London (BH)	OvC	3 Apr
4:29.0	p	Bob Rogers (Chelsea)	12.01.46	1	London (WL)		18 May
4:29.0		Walter Chinnery (LAC)	19.08.43	1	London (BH)		30 May
4:29.4 e p		James Nuttall (Stockport)	28.12.41	2	London (WL)		18 May
4:29.6		Chinnery		1	Cambridge		10 Mar
4:30.4 e		Chinnery		1hc	Oxford		9 Dec

4:31.2 e	John Laing (OU)	1.04.46	2	London (BH)	OvC	3 Apr
4:32.0	Edward Mapplebeck (Birmingham AC)	6.04.45	1	Birmingham (PR)		10 Oct
4:32.7 e	Francis Pelham (CU)	18.10.44	2	Cambridge		10 Mar
4:32.9 e	Edward Hawtrey (ex-Eton College)	10.10.47	2	London (BH)		30 May
4:33.2	Chinnery		4hc	London (BH)		25 Apr
4:33.2	Chinnery		1	London (BH)	AAC	19 Jun
4:33.8	Gibbs		1	Cambridge		17 Mar
4:34.3 e	William Bowman (OU)	25.09.45	3	London (BH)	OvC	3 Apr
4:35.0	Sidney Styles (Salisbury)	23.11.48	1	Salisbury		28 Mar
	(17/12)					
4:36.6 e p	Ike Hughes (Manchester)	9.04.46	2	Manchester (RO)		8 Feb
4:37.0 e	Edward Royds (CU)	9.10.47	2	Cambridge		17 Mar
4:38.0	Christie (Newbury)		1	Newbury		4 Aug
4:40.0	Frost (King's Lynn)		1hc	King's Lynn		10 Apr
4:40.0	Thomas Hewitt (CU)	18.11.49	1	Cambridge		14 Nov

Notes
Gibbs's time on 3 Apr given as 4:31.75 in *Bell's Life;* but Wilkinson in *Modern Athletics* states "the author, who was standing against the railings in a line with the winning post, made it as above (4:28.8), which he believes to be correct, as two "clockers", one a professional, in other parts of the ground, and with whom he had no communication till afterwards, made it the same".
Estimates: McKinstray 20y down on 4:23.5; Nuttall 2y down on 4:29; Chinnery, penalised 20y, ran 4:33.4; Laing 15y down on 4:28.8; Pelham 20y down on 4:29.6; Hawtrey 25y down on 4:29.0; Bowman 35y down on 4:28.8; Hughes 1ft down on 4:36.5; Royds 20y down on 4:33.8.

2 Miles

10:02.0 p	George Hazael (Deptford)	22.11.44	int	London (Bow)		6 Jul
10:03.0 p	Hazael		int	London (Bow)		26 Dec
10:03.2 e p	Edward Mills (Bethnal Green)	25.08.41	int	London (Bow)		26 Dec
10:07.0 p	Edward Golder (Bethnal Green)	1.07.43	int	London (Bow)		6 Jul
10:16.0	Edward Mapplebeck (Birmingham AC)	6.04.45	1	Birmingham (PR)		24 Jun
10:18.0 p	Jack White (Gateshead)	1.03.37	int	London (HW)		17 Feb
10:18.0	John Morgan (OU)	19.08.47	int	London (BH)	OvC	3 Apr
10:18.4 e p	William Lang (Middlesbrough)	22.12.38	int	London (HW)		17 Feb
10:19.8 e	Roland Michell (OU)	14.02.47	int	London (BH)	OvC	3 Apr
10:26.7 e	Henry Edmunds (Birmingham AC)		2	Birmingham (PR)		24 Jun
	(10/9)					
10:28.0	Walter Chinnery (LAC)	19.08.43	int	London (BH)	AAC	20 Jun
10:28.0	Joseph Snow (Manchester AC)	c46	int	London (BH)	AAC	20 Jun
10:32.0	George Stephenson (Norton)		1	Sheffield (BL)		13 Apr
10:34.5	Montague Collins (Oxford)	31.01.48	1	Oxford		13 Apr
10:41.25	John Collins (Atlas CC)	c48	1hc	Liverpool		20 Jun
10:43.0	George Norman (St George's Hosp)	42	1	London (BH)		12 Jun
10:44.0 p	William Gentleman (Bethnal Green)	c41	int	London (HW)		18 May
10:45.0	Augustus Micklefield (CU)	12.07.46	int	Cambridge		19 Mar
10:45.1 e	Edward Royds (CU)	9.10.47	int	Cambridge		19 Mar
10:45.2 e	Gilbert Kennedy (CU)	9.05.44	int	Cambridge		19 Mar
10:47.0 p	Samuel Sutton (Clerkenwell)	42	1	London (HW)		16 May
10:48.0	John Quirk (Trinity Coll Dublin/IRL)	18.08.47	1	Dublin (CP), IRL		6 May
10:52.0	R.E.Harris (Canterbury)		1	Canterbury		2 Jun
10:54.0	Henry Wetherall (OU)	49	1	Oxford		3 Dec

Notes
Estimates: Mills 1y down on 10:03; Lang 2y down on 10:18; Michell 10y down on 10:18, Edmunds 60y down on 10:16; Royds and Kennedy close behind 10:45.
Intermediate times: Morgan, Michell, Micklefield, Royds and Kennedy in 3m; Hazael, Mills, Golder, Chinnery, Snow in 4m; White, Lang, Gentleman in 10m.

3 Miles

15:05.0 p	George Hazael (Deptford)	22.11.44	int	London (Bow)		26 Dec
15:20.2	John Morgan (OU)	19.08.47	1	London (BH)	OvC	3 Apr
15:30.0 p	Hazael	22.11.44	int	London (Bow)		6 Jul
15:32.0 p	Jack White (Gateshead)	1.03.37	int	London (HW)		17 Feb
15:32.0 p	Edward Golder (Bethnal Green)	1.07.43	int	London (Bow)		6 Jul
15:33.0 p	William Lang (Middlesbrough)	22.12.38	int	London (HW)		17 Feb
15:37.75	Walter Chinnery (LAC)	19.08.43	1	Sheffield (BL)		4 May

15:38.0	Morgan		1	Oxford		14 Mar
15:45.0	Chinnery		1	Nottingham		7 May
15:55.4	Edward Royds (CU)	9.10.47	1	Cambridge		19 Mar
15:56.2 e	Augustus Micklefield (CU)	12.07.46	2	Cambridge		19 Mar
15:56.9 e	Gilbert Kennedy (CU)	9.05.44	3	Cambridge		19 Mar

Notes
Morgan's 15:38 at Oxford is as given in the *OUAC Handbook* (1900); it was variously reported as 15:28 (*Bell's*), 15:38.5 (*The Times*) and 15:39.6 (*Wilkinson*).
Estimate: Micklefield 4y and Kennedy 8y down on 15:55.4.
Intermediate times: Hazael and Golder in 4m, won by Hazael 'at his leisure', no time taken; White and Lang in 10m.

4 Miles

20:32.0 p	Jack White (Gateshead)	1.03.37	int	London (HW)		17 Feb
20:33.0 p	William Lang (Middlesbrough)	22.12.38	int	London (HW)		17 Feb
21:11.0	Walter Chinnery (LAC)	19:08.43	1	London (BH)	AAC	20 Jun
21:15.0 p	George Hazael (Deptford)	22.11.44	1hc	Canterbury		2 Jun
21:30.0 p	William Gentleman (Bethnal Green)	c41	int	London (HW)		18 May

Note: Intermediate times all in 10 mile races.

6 Miles

31:29.0 p	Jack White (Gateshead)	1.03.37	int	London (HW)	17 Feb
31:29.3 e p	William Lang (Middlesbrough)	22.12.38	int	London (HW)	17 Feb

Notes
Intermediate times in 10 mile race.
Estimate: Lang 1½y down.

10 Miles

53:50.0 p	William Lang (Middlesbrough)	22.12.38	1	London (HW)	17 Feb
53:57.4 e p	Jack White (Gateshead)	1.03.37	2	London (HW)	17 Feb
56:19.75 p	William Park (Glasgow)		1	Glasgow (Sto)	3 Oct

Note: Estimate: White 40y down on 53:50.0.

120 Yards Hurdles

16 2/5	Charles Pitt-Taylor (CU)	2.03.47	1	London (BH)	OvC	3 Apr
16 ⅔	Pitt-Taylor		1ht1	Cambridge		28 Nov
16.9 e	Lewis Newnham (OU)	46	2	London (BH)	OvC	3 Apr
17.0	Pitt-Taylor		1	Cambridge		28 Nov
17.1 e	William Keeling (OU)	48	2ht1	Cambridge		28 Nov
17 1/5	George Nunn (Guy's Hosp)	c45	1	London (CP)		18 Jul
17 ¼	Pitt-Taylor		1ht1	Cambridge		18 Mar
17.3 e	Arthur Hillyard (OU)	16.01.45	3	London (BH)	OvC	3 Apr
17 2/5	Hillyard		1	Oxford		13 Mar
17.4 e	Henry Thompson (CU)	30.08.45	2ht1	Cambridge		18 Mar
17 2/5	Arthur Lambert (CU)	17.01.47	1ht2	Cambridge		18 Mar
17 2/5	William Tennent (Manchester AC)	6.10.45	1ht2ro	London (BH)	AAC	19 Jun
17 2/5	Tennent		1	London (BH)	AAC	20 Jun
17.5 e	William MacLaren (Manchester AC)	50	2	London (BH)	AAC	20 Jun
	(14/9)					
17.6 e	William Cooper (CU)	26.12.47	2ht2	Cambridge		18 Mar
17.6 e	Gilbert Grace (LAC)	18.07.48	2ht1hc	Blackheath		6 Jun
17 4/5	Richard Fitzherbert (CU)	12.04.46	1=	Cambridge		19 Mar
18.0	John Laing (OU)	1.04.46	1	Oxford		5 Mar
18.0	William Leak (Eton College)	51	1	Eton		3 Nov

Doubtful

17.0	Henry Foley (Trowbridge)	48	1	Frome	30 Apr
18.0	Charles Tylecote (Clifton Coll)	13.11.47	1ht1ro	Clifton	19 Mar
18.0	Herbert Bodington (Clifton Coll)	23.07.49	1ht4	Clifton	19 Mar
18.0	George Arthur (Clifton Coll)	19.01.51	1	Clifton	19 Mar

Apparently timed to nearest second at Frome and nearest half-second at Clifton.

Notes
There was a run-off for second place in heat 2 of the AAC Championship.
Estimates: Newnham 3y down on 16.4; Keeling 3y down on 16.66 (28/11); Hillyard 6y down on 16.4; Thompson 2ft down on 17.25; Grace 1y down on 17.4; MacLaren ½y down on 17.4; Cooper 1y down on 17.4;

220 Yards Hurdles

28.4		Edward Havers (Ingatestone CC)	c44	1	Ingatestone	23 May
28.6 e		P. Benton (Ingatestone)		2	Ingatestone	23 May
30.5		Arthur Walkden (Mansfield)	45	1	Manchester (SAL)	27 Jun
30.8 e		Charles Pickering (Hulme)	22.02.48	2	Manchester (SAL)	27 Jun
30.9 e		James Hooton (Liverpool)	c42	3	Manchester (SAL)	27 Jun
31.5		Joseph Barnes (LAC)	c42	1	Barnes	28 Mar
31.8 e		Robert Graham (London RC)	c44	2	Barnes	28 Mar
32.0		Barnes		1ht2	Barnes	28 Mar
32.0		J. Tyler (Loughborough)		1	Loughborough	9 Jun
32.1 e		William Barsby (Loughborough)	c43	2	Loughborough	9 Jun
32.75		Mark Jobling (LAC)	43	1ht1	Barnes	28 Mar

Notes
Estimates: Benton 1½y down on 28.4; Pickering 2y down on 30.5; Hooton 2y and inches down on 30.5; Graham 2y down on 31.5; Barsby ½y down on 32.0.

440 Yards Hurdles

1:04.0		Horatio Holt Hart (RMA Woolwich/IRL)	9.08.50	1	Eltham	25 Apr
1:04.1 e		J.K.Berkeley (LAC)		2	Eltham	25 Apr
1:04.8 e		Dudley St Leger Hill (RMA Woolwich)	20.11.48	3	Eltham	25 Apr
1:05.5		Frederick Slade (Eltham)	49	1	Etham	25 Apr
1:05.8 e		Joseph Green (Eltham)	28.04.46	2	Eltham	25 Apr
1:06.0		Henry Riches (LAC)	26.11.46	1hc	Hammersmith	30 May

Notes
Estimates: Berkeley inches down on 1:04; Hill 5y and some inches down on 1:04; Green 2y down on 1:05.5.

20 hurdles

1:08.2		Mackenzie Churchill (50th Regt)	1	Woolwich	6 May
1:08.6 e		William Morris (ex-RMA Woolwich)	2	Woolwich	6 May

Note: Estimate: Morris 2y down on 1:08.2

High Jump

5'8¼	1.734	Charles Green (CU)	26.08.46	1=	Cambridge		19 Mar
5'8¼	1.734	John Hoare (CU)	16.03.47	1=	Cambridge		19 Mar
5'8	1.727	Guy Pym (LAC)	11.02.41	1	London (BH)		30 May
5'8	1.727	Robert Mitchell (Rossendale)	14.07.47	1	London (BH)	AAC	20 Jun
5'8	1.727	Mitchell		1	Manchester (SAL)		27 Jun
5'8	1.727	Richard Mayor (Liverpool Gym Soc)	c40	1	Bootle		1 Aug
5'8	1.727	Gerald Stephens (Basingstoke)	44	1	Newbury		4 Aug
5'7½	1.715	Hoare		1	Cambridge		9 Mar
5'7½	1.715	Mitchell		1	Sheffield (BL)		4 May
5'7½	1.715	Maurice Davin (Carrick-on-Suir/IRL)	29.06.42	1	Kilsheelan, IRL		24 Apr
5'7¼	1.708	Hoare		1	Tunbridge Wells		4 Apr
5'7	1.702	Frederick Parsons (OU)	8.10.46	1	Oxford		18 Feb
5'7	1.702	Frederick O'Grady (OU)	20.04.47	1	London (BH)	OvC	3 Apr

(13/9)

5'6½	1.689	John Hickson (Brookfield CC)	47	1	Highgate	25 Apr
5'6	1.676	John Harwood (German Gym Soc)	22.06.45	1	Islington	21 Mar
5'6	1.676	William Curteis (Tonbridge Sch)	28.01.49	1	Tunbridge Wells	4 Apr
5'6	1.676	Sydney Abbott (Civil Service)	c43	2	London (BH)	30 May
5'6	1.676	Edward Bergman (Bristol)	8.02.49	1	Clifton	13 Jun
5'6	1.676	John Duckworth (Haslingden)	44	2	Manchester (SAL)	27 Jun
5'6	1.676	Hon George Villiers (Grenadier Guards)	27.09.47	1	The Curragh, IRL	22 Sep

Indoors

5'10	1.778 i	Hugh Miller (Liverpool Gym Soc/IRL)	43	1	Liverpool	28 Mar
5'8	1.727 i	Mayor		1	Liverpool	8 Dec

Australian Aboriginal cricketers on tour:

5'8	1.727	Pripumuarraman ('Charley Dumas') (AUS)		1=	Gravesend	1 Jun

| 5'8 | 1.727 | | Grougarrong ('Jimmy Mosquito') (AUS) | | c47 | 1= | Gravesend | | 1 Jun |
| 5'6 | 1.676 | | Jungunjinanuke ('Dick-a-Dick') (AUS) | | | 3 | Gravesend | | 1 Jun |

Note: Wyndham Lawrence was credited with 5'7 at the Cheltenham College Sports on 1 May, but this was over a rope and said to have been worth "some five or six inches less" (Wilkinson: *Modern Athletics*, 1868)

High Jump: Highland and Border

5'10	1.778	p	John Allison (Kendal)	8.02.43	1	Liverpool	2 Jun
5'10	1.778	p	Donald Dinnie (Aboyne)	8.06.37	1=	Alloa	12 Aug
5'10	1.778	p	Robert McIlvein (42nd Highlanders)		1=	Alloa	12 Aug
5'10	1.778	p	Andrew Milne (Forfar)	24.11.39	1=	Alloa	12 Aug
5'10	1.778	p	Gavin Tait (Douglas)	34	1=	Alloa	12 Aug
5'8	1.727	p	Dinnie		1=	Dundee	25 Jul
5'8	1.727	p	Milne		1=	Dundee	25 Jul
5'7	1.702	p	Dinnie		1=	Greenock	3 Jul
5'7	1.702	p	Tait		1=	Greenock	3 Jul
5'7	1.702	p	McIlvein		1	Kirkintilloch	17 Jul
5'7	1.702	p	Dinnie		1	Johnstone	18 Jul
5'7	1.702	p	Dinnie		1	Denny	5 Sep
			(12/5)				
5'6	1.676	p	Samuel Muir (Stewarton)	c41	2=	Johnstone	18 Jul
5'6	1.676	p	David Milne (Forfar)	28.12.42	3	Dundee	25 Jul
5'6	1.676	p	James Wright (Perth)	15.01.45	1=	Perth	22 Aug

Notes
Donald Dinnie in his memoirs claimed a jump of 6'1 at Turriff, Aberdeenshire. The *Aberdeen Journal* gave the Alloa jumps as 5'9.

Pole Vault

10'6½	3.21		Robert Mitchell (Manchester AC)	14.07.47	1	London (BH)	AAC	19 Jun
10'6	3.20		Mitchell		1	Huddersfield		18 Jul
10'0½	3.06		William Powell Moore (LAC)	23.04.46	2	London (BH)	AAC	19 Jun
10'0	3.05		Alfred Lubbock (AAC)	31.10.45	1	Blackheath		6 Jun
			(4/3)					
9'6	2.90		Charles Leeds (OU)	45	1	Oxford		12 Mar
9'6	2.90		William Curteis (Tonbridge Sch)	28.01.49	1	Tunbridge Wells		14 Apr
9'6	2.90		Edward Bergman (Bristol)	8.02.49	1	Clifton		13 Jun
9'6	2.90		Francis Whelan (Sheffield FC)	47	2	Huddersfield		18 Jul
9'6	2.90		Piper M. Martin (71st Highlanders)		1	The Curragh, IRL		22 Sep

Over a rope

| 9'6 | 2.90 | | Montague Palmer (Newbury Gymnasium) | 50 | 1 | Newbury | 3 Aug |

Note: Powell Moore [10'0½] given 10'1½ in *Bell's*, 10'1 in *The Sportsman*.

Pole Vault: Lakeland, Highland & Border

10'3	3.12	p	David Anderson (Alnwick)	c46	1	Glenton	3 Aug
10'3	3.12	p	Anderson		1	Alloa	12 Aug
10'1	3.07	p	Anderson		1	Jedburgh	7 Aug
10'0	3.05	p	John Allison (Kendal)	8.02.43	1	Manchester (WR)	13 Apr
10'0	3.05	p	Robert Musgrave (Cockermouth)	11.10.41	1	Stockton	1 Jun
10'0	3.05	p	Musgrave		1	Newcastle	2 Jun
10'0	3.05	p	Anderson		1	Edinburgh	8 Aug
10'0	3.05	p	David Milne (Forfar)	28.12.42	2	Alloa	12 Aug
10'0	3.05	p	Anderson		1	Armiston	15 Aug
			(9/4)				
9'10	3.00	p	Mark Shearman (Keswick)	c49	1=	Carlisle	8 Jul
9'10	3.00	p	James Waugh (Carlisle)	c49	1=	Carlisle	8 Jul
9'9	2.97	p	William Hall (Brampton)		2=	Newcastle	2 Jun
9'9	2.97	p	Thomas Shevels (Durham)	c47	2=	Newcastle	2 Jun
9'9	2.97	p	William Renwick (Galashiels)		1	Galashiels	18 Jul
9'9	2.97	p	Robert Thomson (Lochgelly)		1	Lochgelly	1 Aug
9'8	2.95	p	Samuel Rigg (Kendal)	c46	2	Liverpool	2 Jun
9'8	2.95	p	Isaac Tyson (Carlisle)	46	4	Carlisle	8 Jul
9'8	2.95	p	John Ashcroft (Canonbie)		2=	Galashiels	18 Jul
9'8	2.95	p	Jacob Field (Galashiels)		2=	Galashiels	18 Jul
9'8	2.95	p	John Crosbie (Hundalee Mill)		2	Jedburgh	7 Aug

9'7	2.92	p	William Ewing (Bonhill)	c47	1=	Alexandria		25 Jul
9'7	2.92	p	Malcolm McGregor (Alexandria)	c45	1=	Alexandria		25 Jul
9'7	2.92	p	D. Donald (Dundee)		2=	Dundee		25 Jul
9'7	2.92	p	James Stewart (Lochee)		2=	Dundee		25 Jul
9'6	2.90	p	John Cooling (Stott Park/IRL)	44	3	Liverpool		2 Jun
9'6	2.90	p	James Henderson (Lochgelly)		2	Lochgelly		1 Aug
9'6	2.90	p	James Fleming (Blair Atholl)	18.09.40	1=	Wishaw		27 Aug
9'6	2.90	p	Anthony Hall (Edinburgh)	c46	1=	Wishaw		27 Aug
9'6	2.90	p	Anderson Turner (Salsburgh)	17.03.38	1=	Wishaw		27 Aug

Indoors

| 10'3 | 3.12 i | p | Allison | 8.02.43 | 1 | London (Ag Hall) | | 10 Apr |
| 10'2 | 3.10 i | p | James Baines (Penrith) | | 2 | London (Ag Hall) | | 10 Apr |

Long Jump

21'4	6.50		Alick Tosswill (OU)	21.01.45	1	Oxford		14 Mar
21'2¼	6.46		Tosswill		1	London (BH)	OvC	3 Apr
21'2	6.45		Charles Absolom (CU)	7.06.46	1	Richmond		18 Apr
21'1	6.43		Richard Waltham (CU)	25.02.46	2	London (BH)	OvC	3 Apr
21'0	6.40		Robert Mitchell (Manchester AC)	14.07.47	1	Chesterfield		1 Jun
20'7½	6.29		Waltham		1	Cambridge		18 Mar
20'7	6.27		Francis Philpott (OU)	17.05.48	2	Oxford		14 Mar
20'2	6.15		Absolom		2	Cambridge		18 Mar
20'2	6.15		Edward Havers (Ingatestone CC)	c44	1	Barnes		28 Mar
20'1½	6.13		Absolom		3	London (BH)	OvC	3 Apr
20'1	6.12		Havers		2	Richmond		18 Apr
20'1	6.12		Tosswill		1	Reigate		18 Apr
20'0	6.10		Henry Wilcox (Rossall School)	14.10.49	1	Fleetwood		25 Feb
20'0	6.10		William MacLaren (Manchester AC)	50	1	Birmingham (PR)		24 Jun
19'11	6.07		Henry Fellowes (Beighton)	22.11.51	1	Beccles		1 Jul
19'10	6.05		Charles Devis (Birmingham AC)	30.04.50	1	Birmingham (PR)		4 Oct
19'9	6.02		William Curteis (Tonbridge Sch)	28.01.49	1	Tunbridge Wells		14 Apr
19'9	6.02		Macbeth (South London)		1	Peckham		4 Sep
19'8½	6.01		Mitchell		1	London (BH)	AAC	20 Jun
19'8	5.99		Richard James (OU)	c48	1hc	Oxford		3 Dec

Ancillary (record) jump:

| 20'11½ | 6.39 | | Tosswill | | - | Oxford | | 14 Mar |

His series was 20'8½ - 20'3 - 20'11½ - 21'4.

Extra Jump

| 21'0 | 6.40 | | Tosswill | | ex | Reigate | | 18 Apr |

Note
Accounts of Waltham's jumping in the Oxford v Cambridge match differ, but Wilkinson in *Modern Athletics* states that he cleared 21'1 with his third jump, and Tosswill surpassed it by 1¼ in with his fifth.

Long Jump: Highland & Border

20'5	6.22	p	Samuel Muir (Stewarton)	c41	1	Dalkeith	29 Aug
20'4½	6.21	p	James Young (Hawick)	c47	1	Hawick	5 Jun
20'4	6.20	p	Muir		1	Alloa	12 Aug
20'2	6.15	p	Robert Knox (Newstead)	17.09.47	2	Alloa	12 Aug
19'9	6.02	p	David Milne (Forfar)	28.12.42	3	Alloa	12 Aug
19'9	6.02	p	Knox		2	Dalkeith	29 Aug
19'8	5.99	p	Knox		2	Hawick	5 Jun
19'8	5.99	p	Muir		1	Barrhead	27 Jun
19'8	5.99	p	Milne		1	Forfar	7 Aug

Triple Jump

42'0	12.80		William O'Sullivan (Roskeen/IRL)		1	Mallow, IRL	9 Jun
41'5½	12.64		Wilfred Creswick (Sheffield)	c45	1	Liverpool	20 Jun
40'5	12.32		John Duckworth (Haslingden)	44	2	Liverpool	20 Jun

Triple Jump: Highland, Border & Lancashire Professional

47'1	14.35	p	Robert Knox (Newstead)	17.09.47	1	Jedburgh	7 Aug
46'2	14.07	p	Knox		1	Armiston	15 Aug
46'0	14.02	p	Knox		1	Alloa	12 Aug
45'11	14.00	p	James Young (Alva)	c47	1	Hawick	5 Jun
45'8	13.92	p	Knox		1	Galashiels	18 Jul
45'2½	13.78	p	Samuel Muir (Stewarton)	c41	1	Dalkeith	29 Aug
45'2	13.77	p	Young		1	Newcastleton	5 Aug
45'1	13.74	p	Knox		2	Hawick	5 Jun
			(8/3)				
43'7	13.28	p	Andrew Milne (Montrose)	24.11.39	1	Kirkintilloch	17 Jul
43'6	13.26	p	Neil McKay (Innerleithen)	6.01.46	1	Peebles	18 Jul
43'0	13.11	p	Malcolm McGregor (Alexandria)	c45	2	Barrhead	27 Jun
42'11	13.08	p	Thomas Carruthers (Yetholm)	27.04.40	2	Peebles	18 Jul
42'10½	13.07	p	Peter Barratt (Hawick)		2	St Boswells	11 Jul
42'9	13.03	p	Robert McIlvein (42nd Highlanders)		1	Bridge of Allan (local)	1 Aug
42'7	12.98	p	Peter Campbell (Alexandria)	c43	2	Bridge of Allan (local)	1 Aug
42'7	12.98	p	Gavin Tait (Douglas)	34	2	Tillicoultry	14 Aug
42'6	12.95	p	John Bell (Hawick)	c39	2	Earlstoun	1 Aug
42'3	12.88	p	David Milne (Forfar)	28.12.42	1	Rollo's Pier	18 Jul
41'10	12.75	p	Donald Dinnie (Aboyne)	8.06.37	2=	Denny	5 Sep
41'7	12.67	p	J. Storey (Pendleton)		1	Manchester (RO)	24 Aug
41'4	12.60	p	J. Noble		1	Broughton	1 Aug
41'4	12.60	p	J. Knot (Edinburgh)		2	Edinburgh	8 Aug
40'9	12.42	p	D. Donald (Dundee)		2	Dundee	25 Jul
40'8	12.40	p	Thomas Wood (Innerleithen)		2=	Innerleithen	1 Aug
40'6	12.34	p	F. Eliott		1	Portobello	5 Sep
40'5	12.32	p	John Toy (Dundee)	c46	2	Rollo's Pier	18 Jul
40'3	12.27	p	Alexander Fleming (Glasgow)		3	Whitburn	21 Jul
40'3	12.27	p	William Wareham (Hurst)	46	2	Manchester (RO)	24 Aug
40'2	12.24	p	Pringle		1	Penicuik	1 Aug

Note: *The Scotsman* gives 45'3/13.79 for Muir at Dalkeith on 29/08.

Shot

37'11	11.56		John Stone (Liverpool AC)	25.08.42	1	London (BH)	AAC	20 Jun
36'6	11.13		Pte Riddle (71st Highlanders)		1	Dublin, IRL		9 Jun
36'4	11.07		Richard Waltham (CU)	25.02.46	1	Cambridge		24 Feb
36'0	10.97		Waltham		1	Cambridge		17 Mar
36'0	10.97		Robert Mitchell (Manchester AC)	14.07.47	2	London (BH)	AAC	20 Jun
35'9	10.90		David Lundie (St Andrews U)	23.11.46	1	St Andrews		28 Mar
35'0	10.67		Pte J. Mooney (65th Regt/IRL)		1	Dublin, IRL		3 Jun
35'0	10.67		George Nunn (Guy's Hosp)	c45	1	London (BH)		12 Jun
			(8/7)					
34'11½	10.66		Pte Weir (Royal Engineers)		1	Cork, IRL		20 Jun
34'9½	10.60		William Powell Moore (LAC)	23.04.46	1	London (BH)		27 Jun
34'9	10.59		D. McRae (Edinburgh U)		1	Edinburgh (GP)		18 Jun
34'7	10.54		Thomas Batson (OU)	18.05.46	1	Oxford		14 Mar
34'1	10.39		William R. Burgess (OU)	c45	2	Oxford		14 Mar
33'10	10.31		Herbert Hodges (CU)	14.01.47	1	Cambridge		21 Feb
33'7½	10.25		Patrick Halkett (LAC)	2.04.37	2	London (BH)		27 Jun
33'6	10.21		Charles Absolom (CU)	7.06.46	2	Cambridge		17 Mar
33'0	10.06		William Trahair (Penzance)		1	Penzance		16 Sep
33'0	10.06		William Prince (CU)	c46	1	Cambridge		28 Nov

Extra throw:

37'0	11.28		George Nunn (Guy's Hosp)	c45		London (BH)	12 Jun

Shot: Highland & Border
Includes 16lb stone and ball

45'6	13.87	p	Donald Dinnie (Aboyne)	8.06.37	1	Johnstone	18 Jul
45'2	13.77	p	John George (Dumbarton)	46	2	Johnstone	18 Jul
44'9	13.64	p	James Fleming (Blair Atholl)	18.09.40	1	Balfron	18 Jul
44'2½*	13.47	p	Dinnie		1	West Calder	29 Jul
43'7	13.28	p	George		1	Edinburgh	8 Aug
43'1	13.13	p	George		1	Aboyne	24 Sep

42'5*	12.93	p	George		2	West Calder	29 Jul
42'4*	12.90	p	Dinnie		1	Forfar	7 Aug
41'9	12.73	p	Charles Emslie (Wester Craigievar)		1	Culsalmond	22 Sep
41'7¾	12.69	p	Fleming		2	Aboyne	24 Sep
40'2	12.24	p	William Stewart (Perth)	29	2	Balfron	18 Jul
				(11/5)			
39'0*	11.89	p	Alexander Grant (Birkhall)		1	Lumphanan	1 Aug
38'9*	11.81	p	William Bremner (Strathdon)	3.01.47	2	Lumphanan	1 Aug
38'2	11.63	p	Peter McHardy (Glasgow)	c48	3	Balfron	18 Jul
37'8½	11.49	p	John Moir (Strathdon)	27.07.42	3	Aboyne	24 Sep
37'8*	11.48	p	Peter Keith (Marcus)	c40	1	Forfar (local)	7 Aug
37'8	11.48	p	Peter Bremner (Glenbucket)	20.01.42	1	Glenkindie	22 Sep
37'4*	11.38	p	James Esson (Aboyne)		3	Lumphanan	1 Aug
36'8*	11.18	p	James Moon		2hc	Perth	22 Aug
36'7	11.15	p	Alexander Bowie (Keith Hall)	44	2	Culsalmond	22 Sep
36'5*	11.10	p	James Leighton (Kingston)		2	Forfar (local)	7 Aug
36'3*	11.05	p	Andrew Hunter (Forfar)		3	Forfar (local)	7 Aug
35'9*	10.90	p	William Scott (Cargill)		2	Forfar	7 Aug
35'9	10.90	p	R. Ross (Glenkindie)		2	Glenkindie	22 Sep
34'10½	10.63	p*	James Sime (West Calder)		3	West Calder	29 Jul
34'9	10.59	p	William Grieve (Badenscoth)		3	Culsalmond	22 Sep

Note
*correct weight assumed from evidence of other years

Weight unstated

43'9	13.33	p	Dinnie		1	Pathhead	6 Aug
36'0	10.97	p	D. Irvine (St Martin's)		1	Balbeggie	19 Sep
35'4	10.77	p	William Mackie (Kennethmont)		1	Lumsden	14 Aug
35'2	10.72	p	Alexander Paterson (Rhynie)		2	Lumsden	14 Aug
34'9	10.59	p	Andrew Milne (Montrose)	24.11.39	2	Pathhead	6 Aug

17lb by performer

38'2	11.63	p	W. Bremner		1	Colquhonnie	24 Aug
35'4	10.77	p	James Findlay (Craigedhu)	c52	2	Colquhonnie	24 Aug

18lb by performer

42'0	12.80	p	Dinnie		1	Nairn	8 Aug
37'4½	11.39	p	William Fraser (Clunas)		2	Nairn	8 Aug

21lb by performer

40'3	12.27	p	Dinnie		1	Huntly	11 Sep

22lb stone/ball by performer

41'4	12.60	p	Dinnie		1	Kirkintilloch	17 Jul
41'0	12.50	p	Fleming		2	Dundee	25 Jul
40'7	12.37	p	George		2	Kirkintilloch	17 Jul
37'0	11.28	p	Donald McDonald (Murthly)		3	Dunkeld	24 Jul
35'10	10.92	p	John Scott (Dunkeld)		2	Tillicoultry	14 Aug
35'8	10.87	p	W. Scott		3	Dundee	25 Jul

23lb ball by performer

36'0	10.97	p	Dinnie		1	Whitburn	21 Jul

24lb stone by performer

37'7	11.46	p	Dinnie		1	Coupar Angus	16 Jul
35'9	10.90	p	Fleming		2	Coupar Angus	16 Jul

Doubtful

49'10½	15.20	p	Dinnie		1	Greenock	3 Jul
46'6	14.17	p	Fleming		2	Greenock	3 Jul
46'4½	14.14	p	George		3	Greenock	3 Jul
45'11	14.00	p	Fleming		1	Bridge of Allan	1 Aug
45'0	13.72	p	Dinnie		2	Bridge of Allan	1 Aug
44'7	13.59	p	George		3	Bridge of Allan	1 Aug
39'5	12.01	p	Pte Clark (42nd Regt)		1	Bridge of Allan (local)	1 Aug
38'9	11.81	p	Robert McIlvein (42nd Highlanders)		2	Bridge of Allan (local)	1 Aug

The weight at Greenock was said to be 16lb, but all three were some way in excess of known form, so presumably the ground sloped. Bridge of Allan had a notorious slope.

Notes: Dinnie wrote: "It was in 1868 that I made my great 'rut' on Lord Charles Kerr's Bowling Green, Kinnoull, Perth. I put a stone weighing 16lb 2oz 49ft 6in – equal to over 50ft with the real weight." McCombie Smith states in *The Athletes and Athletic Sports of Scotland* (1891) that this was in private practice.

Hammer

99'6	30.33	Thomas Batson (OU)	18.05.46	1	London (BH)	OvC	3 Apr
99'6	30.33	Henry Leeke (CU)	6.02.46	1	London (BH)	AAC	19 Jun
98'8	30.07	Leeke		2	London (BH)	OvC	3 Apr
97'11	29.84	William A. Burgess (OU)	27.12.46	1	Oxford		8 Dec
97'2	29.62	John Eyre (CU)	29.01.45	3	London (BH)	OvC	3 Apr
96'9	29.49	Douglas Moffatt (AAC)	31.07.43	2	London (BH)	AAC	19 Jun
95'10	29.21	Robert Mitchell (Manchester AC)	14.07.47	1	Huddersfield		18 Jul
94'7	28.83	Leeke		1	Cambridge		18 Mar
93'3	28.42	Patrick Halkett (LAC)	2.04.37	3	London (BH)	AAC	19 Jun
91'0	27.74	David Lundie (St Andrews U)	23.11.46	1	St Andrews		28 Mar
		(10/8)					
89'11	27.41	George Mills (OU)	19.01.47	2	Oxford		8 Dec
89'9¾	27.37	Richard Waltham (CU)	25.02.46	2	Cambridge		18 Mar
89'8	27.33	John Jones (Huddersfield AC)		2	Huddersfield		18 Jul
89'0	27.13	Mortimer Shelton (CU)	14.09.48	1	Cambridge		28 Nov
88'8	27.03	Fairfax Wade (Radley College)	16.07.51	1	Radley		6 Mar
88'0	26.82	John Stritch (Trinity Coll Dublin/IRL)	44	1	Dublin (CP), IRL		5 May
87'6	26.67	George Nunn (Guy's Hosp)	c45	1	London (BH)		11 Jun
87'3	26.59	Charles Corfe (CU)	8.06.47	1	Cambridge		23 Nov

Hammer: Highland & Border

111'2	33.88	p	Donald Dinnie (Aboyne)	8.06.37	1	Johnstone	18 Jul
101'9*	31.01	p	Dinnie		1	Dunkeld	24 Jul
101'0	30.78	p	Dinnie		1	Coupar Angus	16 Jul
100'7	30.66	p	Dinnie		1	Kirkintilloch	17 Jul
99'11*	30.45	p	James Fleming (Blair Atholl)	18.09.40	2	Dunkeld	24 Jul
97'6*	29.72	p	Dinnie		1	Leith	4 Aug
97'5	29.69	p	Dinnie		1	Birnam	27 Aug
96'9	29.49	p	Dinnie		1	Dumbarton	15 Aug
96'6*	29.41	p	Dinnie		1	Forfar	7 Aug
95'10	29.21	p	Fleming		2	Coupar Angus	16 Jul
94'1	28.68	p	John George (Renfrew)	46	2	Johnstone	18 Jul
			(11/3)				
93'0	28.35	p	Peter Bremner (Glenbucket)	20.01.42	1	Colquhonnie	24 Aug
90'0	27.43	p	Charles Emslie (Wester Craigievar)		1	Culsalmond	22 Sep
89'8	27.33	p	Alexander Grant (Birkhall)		1	Lumphanan	1 Aug

Note: *correct weight assumed from evidence of other years. Forfar may have been 16½lb

Weight unstated

110'0	33.53	p	Charles Danford (Maddiston)		1	Muiravonside (heavy)	6 Aug
98'9	30.10	p	Dinnie		1	Tillicoultry	14 Aug
97'6	29.72	p	George		1	Edinburgh	8 Aug
96'0	29.26	p	Donald McDonald (Murthly)		1	Blair Castle	2 Sep
94'3	28.73	p	D. Irvine (St Martin's)		1	Balbeggie	19 Sep
93'9	28.57	p	Dinnie		1	Lochgelly	1 Aug
90'5	27.56	p	J. Campbell (Collace)		2	Balbeggie	19 Sep
90'4	27.53	p	James Donald (Stoneywood)		1	Stoneywood (light)	18 Jul

17lb by performer

111'0	33.83	p	Dinnie		1	Dundee	25 Jul
95'9	29.18	p	Fleming		2	Dundee	25 Jul
93'7	28.52	p	Danford		3	Dundee	25 Jul
92'9	28.27	p	George		2	Greenock	3 Jul

18lb by performer

101'6	30.94	p	Dinnie		3hc	Perth	22 Aug
99'10	30.43	p	Fleming		1hc	Perth	22 Aug
88'0	26.82	p	George		3	Kirkintilloch	17 Jul

20lb by performer

90'2	27.48	p	Dinnie		1	Ballater	22 Jul

Other Events

150 Yards
15.5   Joseph Barnes (LAC)   c42   1   London (BH)   25 Apr

200 Yards
20.5   George Peake (OU)   6.03.46   1   Oxford   10 Dec

300 Yards
32.5   p   J. Ashon (Hollinwood)   25.03.40   1   Manchester (Cope)   27 Jun

600 Yards
1:19.0   Joseph Barnes (LAC)   c42   1   London (BH)   23 May

1½ Miles
7:03.0   p   John Fleet (Manchester)   6.04.45   1   Manchester (RO)   18 Jul

25 Miles
3:17:05   p   Henry Smalley (Birmingham)   18.02.32   int   Birmingham (AC)   19 Oct
In 50 miles match, in which his opponent retired

1 Mile Walk
6:55.0   Walter Rye (LAC)   31.10.43   int   London (BH)   30 Apr
From scratch in 3 miles handicap

2 Miles Walk
14:42.0   p   James Miles (Brixton)   24.07.40   int   London (HW)   29 Jun
In 8 miles match won by G. Davison

7 Miles Walk
56:24.0   p   George Davison (Hoxton)   2.09.44   int   London (WL)   18 Jul
In a match to walk 21 miles in 3 hours

Cricket Ball
125y 0ft 0in   114.30   W. Rose (Athenaeum CC)   1   Manchester (SAL)   27 Jun

The Oxford and Cambridge match at Lillie Bridge in 1869. Races were often run clockwise. It was not until the twentieth century that anti-clockwise running became the norm. Note the wall on the western side protecting athletes and spectators from the Beaufort House rifle range next door.

100 Yards

10.0		Charles Greenwood (Durham U)	1.03.48	1	Durham	27 Feb
10.0		William Cross (W of Scotland CC)	c51	1	Glasgow (WSCG)	17 Apr
10.0		John Duckworth (Haslingden)	44	1	Ormskirk	15 May
10.1	e	Cecil Eccles (Liverpool)	47	2	Ormskirk	15 May
10.1	e	Alexander Allfrey (West Kent FC)	12.02.48	2=hc	Blackheath	4 Jun
10 1/5		John Wilson (OU)	19.07.48	1	London (LB) OvC	18 Mar
10 1/5		Charles Corfe (CU)	8.06.47	1ht3	Cambridge	5 Mar
10 1/5		Francis Cator (RMC Sandhurst)	7.06.51	1ht3	Sandhurst	23 Sep
10 1/5		Walter Eaton (Civil Service)	7.04.48	1	London (BH)	15 May
10.2	e	James Statham (Salford)	50	3	Ormskirk	15 May
10 1/5		Brown Fletcher (South Essex AC)	c45	1ht2hc	Blackheath	4 Jun
10 1/5		John Whelan (Sheffield FC)	c48	1ht2	Huddersfield	12 Jun
10 1/5		Robert Philpot (CU)	12.06.50	1	Cambridge	20 Nov

School Sports

10.0	J. Healy (Stonyhurst Coll/IRL)		1	Dublin, IRL	30 Mar
10.0	J. Howard (Grantham Gr Sch)		1	Grantham	21 Apr
10.0	Arthur Malden (QE School, Ipswich)	50	1	Ipswich	10 May
10.0	G. Hine (Northwich)	53	1	Northwich	5 Jun
10.0	A.R.Goodwyn (Donington Gr Sch)		1	Donington, Lincs	25 Jun

Wind assisted?

10 1/5	Francis Philpott (OU)	17.05.48	1ht1	Oxford	25 Feb

"The wind was in favour of the runners" (*Bell's Life*)

Downhill

10.0	W. Hackingley (1st Battn 25th Regt)		1ht2	Aldershot	8 Jul
10.0	Hackingley		1	Aldershot	8 Jul
10.0	Ferdinand Tidmarsh (23rd Foot)	21.05.45	1	Aldershot	8 Jul
10 1/5	William Armstrong (Dublin U/IRL)		1=	Dublin (CP), IRL	10 Jun
10 1/5	George Butcher (LAC)	17.02.47	1=	Dublin (CP), IRL	10 Jun

Notes
Wilson given 10.0 (with James Strachan 2y down) in *The Field,* but 10 1/5 in *Bell's*, Shearman, Wilkinson and *Fifty Years of Sport*. Eccles ½y and Statham 2ft 6in down on 10.0; Allfrey ½y down on 10.0. *Bell's Life* made the Dublin dead-heat 10 2/5. We have followed *John Lawrence's Annual*.

220 Yards

23 2/5		Walter Eaton (Civil Service)	7.04.48	1	London (BH)	15 May
23.5	e	Frederick Hartung (LAC)	29.05.46	3ht1hc	South Norwood	12 Jun
23.9	e	Thomas Pigott (Civil Service)	5.03.40	2	London (BH)	15 May
24.0	p	Robert Hindle (Paisley)	46	1	Barrhead	24 Jul
24.1	e	Arthur Badcock (Civil Service)	12.07.47	3	London (BH)	15 May
24.4	e p	Gavin Tait (Douglas)	34	2	Barrhead	24 Jul
24 ½		John Duckworth (Haslingden)	44	1	Manchester (SAL)	3 Jul
24 ½	p	Harry Whitehead (Hyde)	26.04.47	1ht1	Barrhead	24 Jul
24.6	e p	Hindle		2ht1	Barrhead	24 Jul
24 3/5		George Butcher (LAC)	17.02.47	1hc	London (BH)	4 Dec

School Sports

24 3/5	H. Bradbury (Kensington Sch)	c50	1	London (LB)	5 Jun

Doubtful:

22 ½	J. Godfrey (Chatham)		1	Milton Chapel	26 Jul

Notes
Hartung 6y down on 22.8; Pigott 4y down on 23.4; Badcock 5½y down on 23.4; Tait 3y down on 24.0; Hindle ½y down on 24.5.

440 Yards

51.0		Charles Corfe (CU)	8.06.47	1	Cambridge	8 Mar
51.3	e	Abbot Upcher (CU)	19.10.49	2	Cambridge	8 Mar
51.5	p	James Nuttall (Manchester)	28.12.41	1	Manchester (RO)	17 Jul
51.75	p	Harry Whitehead (Hyde)	26.04.47	1	Manchester (RO)	18 Dec
51.9	e p	George Walsh (Royton)	3.02.44	2	Manchester (RO)	18 Dec
52.0	e	Archibald Mitchell (CU)	14.08.50	3	Cambridge	8 Mar
52.0	p	David Binns (Bingley)	20.08.41	1	Manchester (RO)	5 Apr

52.2	Gilbert Grace (LAC)	18.07.48	1hc	London (BH)		10 Apr
53.0	John Wilson (OU)	19.07.48	1	Oxford		27 Feb
53.0	Upcher		1	London (LB)	OvC	18 Mar
		(10/9)				
53.25	Arthur Pollock (South Norwood & Brixton AC)	c49	1	London (LB)		1 Jun
53.3 e p	William Ainscow (Manchester)	c45	2	Manchester (RO)		17 Jul
53.5 e	Robert Somers-Smith (OU)	23.05.48	2	Oxford		27 Feb
53.5	Charles Pickering (Hulme)	22.02.48	1	Knutsford		31 Jul
53.6 e	Arthur Jeffreys (OU)	7.04.48	3	London (LB)	OvC	18 Mar
53.6	Edward Colbeck (LAC)	21.12.47	1	London (LB)	AAC	3 Apr
53.6 e	John Cockerell (LAC)	c46	2	London (LB)		1 Jun

School Sports

| 53.0 | William Dawson (Marlborough Coll) | 3.12.50 | 1 | Marlborough | 3 Apr |
| 53.7 e | William Dixon (Marlborough Coll) | 10.01.51 | 2 | Marlborough | 3 Apr |

Notes
Bell's Life made the Oxford v Cambridge time slower, at 53.4.
Estimates: Upcher 2y down on 51.0; Walsh 1y down on 51.75; Mitchell 8y down on 51.0; Somers-Smith 4y down on 53.0; Cockerell 2½y down on 53.25; Jeffreys 4y down on 53.0; Dixon 5y down on 53.0.

880 Yards

1:59.0 p	Frank Hewitt (Millwall)	8.05.45	1hc	Sheffield (HP)		28 Jun
1:59.0 p	John Fleet (Manchester)	6.04.45	1	Sheffield (HP)		14 Aug
1:59.2 e p	Albert Bird (Sheffield)	15.08.46	2	Sheffield (HP)		14 Aug
2:00.0 p	Bird		1	Sheffield (HP)		1 Feb
2:01.8	Robert Somers-Smith (OU)	23.05.48	1	Oxford		26 Feb
2:02.0	Walter Chinnery (LAC)	19.08.43	1	London (BH)		15 May
2:02.5 p	Bird		1	Sheffield (HP)		9 Aug
2:02.6	Somers-Smith		1	London (LB)	AAC	3 Apr
2:02.8 e p	Fleet		2	Sheffield (HP)		9 Aug
2:03.0 e	Edward Colbeck (LAC)	21.12.47	2	London (LB)	AAC	3 Apr
		(10/6)				
2:03.1 e	Arthur Dowding (OU)	23.11.48	2	Oxford		26 Feb
2:04.0	Ellis Ashmead Bartlett (OU)	24.08.49	1	Cambridge		22 Feb
2:04.0	Henry Gurney (CU)	7.09.47	1	Cambridge		23 Feb
2:04.2 e	Thomas Bainbridge (CU)	47	2	Cambridge		22 Feb
2:04.2	Sydenham Dixon (Civil Service)	4.05.48	1	London (LB)		21 May
2:04.6 e	William Blandford Newson (Germ. Gym S)	7.11.47	3	London (LB)	AAC	3 Apr
2:04.8 e	Fairfax Hassard (Royal Engineers)	13.10.48	2	London (LB)		21 May
2:05.0	F. Ward (Cambridge)		1	Cambridge		29 Mar
2:05.3 e	Archibald Mitchell (CU)	14.08.50	2	Cambridge		6 Mar
2:05.3 e	Gilbert Grace (LAC)	18.07.48	4	London (LB)	AAC	3 Apr
2:05.5 p	Robert Hindle (Paisley)	46	1	Barrhead		24 Jul
2:05.8	James Becke (Northampton)	48	1	Northampton		8 Jun
2:06.0	Charles Kenyon (West Derby)	18.11.48	1	Farnworth		28 Aug

Doubtful (under 17 race):
| 2:04.0 | Hollis (Cuckfield) | c53 | 1 | Cuckfield | 25 Aug |

Notes
Estimates: Bird 1y down on 1:59; Fleet 1½y down on 2:02.5; Colbeck 2½y down on 2:06; Dowding 9y down on 2:01.8; Newson 14y down on 2:06; Bainbridge 1y down on 2:04; Grace 19y down on 2:02.6; Hassard 4y down on 2:04.2; Mitchell 3y down on 2:04.8.

Mile

4:29.5 p	Albert Bird (Sheffield)	15.08.46	1	Sheffield (HP)		22 Mar
4:30.0 p	Bob Rogers (Chelsea)	12.01.46	1	London (Bow)		3 Apr
4:30.2 e p	Frank Hewitt (Millwall)	8.05.45	2	Sheffield (HP)		22 Mar
4:30.4	Walter Chinnery (LAC)	19.08.43	3hc	London (BH)		10 Apr
4:33.6	Robert Somers-Smith (OU)	23.05.48	1	Oxford		25 Feb
4:34.5 p	James Childerhouse (Deptford)	15.05.49	1	London (Bow)		25 Jan
4:34.9 e	Samuel Scott (OU)	20.05.47	2	Oxford		25 Feb
4:35.0 p	John Neary (Manchester/IRL)	41	int	Manchester (RO)		26 Jun
4:35.0	Haine (Eastbourne)		1	Eastbourne		17 Aug
4:35.0	T. Crow (Tottenham House CC)		1=	Willesden		18 Sep
4:35.0	John May (Tottenham House CC)	c42	1=	Willesden		18 Sep

(11/11)

4:35.1	e p	Edward Mills (Bethnal Green)	25.08.41	2	London (Bow)		25 Jan
4:35.1	e	Arthur Clarke (OU)	22.12.48	3	Oxford		25 Feb
4:35.2		Edward Royds (CU)	9.10.47	1	London (LB)	OvC	18 Mar
4:35.4	e p	John Fleet (Manchester)	6.04.45	int	Manchester (RO)		26 Jun
4:35.8	e	Thomas Wootten (Tottenham House CC)	6.08.47	3	Willesden		18 Sep
4:38.7	e	John Laing (OU)	1.04.46	3=	London (LB)	OvC	18 Mar

Notes

Through an error in measurement, Chinnery ran 7y over the mile, which equates to 4:29.4e.
Estimates: Hewitt 4y down on 4:29.5; Scott 8y down on 4:33.6; Mills 3½y down on 4:34.5; Clarke 9y down on 4:33.6; Fleet 2½y down on 4:35; Wootten 5y down on 4:35; Laing 22y down on 4:35.2.
Intermediate times: in match race at 1½ m [26/06].

2 Miles

9:54.8	p	Billy Mills (Bethnal Green)	09.43	int	London (LB)		16 Aug
9:59.0	p	George Hazael (Deptford)	22.11.44	int	London (Bow)		25 Oct
10:07.0	p	Alfred Markham (Marylebone)	c48	int	London (Bow)		10 Apr
10:07.2	p	Hazael		int	London (HW)		8 Nov
10:07.4	e p	Mills		int	London (HW)		8 Nov
10:07.8	e p	Robert McKinstray (Ayr)	18.04.37	int	London (HW)		8 Nov
10:11.0		Edward Mapplebeck (Birmingham AC)	6.04.45	1	Birmingham (PR)		10 Jul
10:12.0		James Edgar (Douglas, IOM)	23.02.51	1	Douglas, IOM		24 Aug
10:14.0	p	Jack White (Gateshead)	1.03.37	int	London (Star)		27 Dec
10:15.0		John Morgan (OU)	19.08.47	int	Oxford		18 Feb

(10/8)

10:16.0		Edgar Kensington (Royal Artillery)	4.09.42	1	London (LB)		21 May
10:16.4	e	Charles Kenyon (West Derby)	18.11.48	2	Douglas, IOM		24 Aug
10:20.0		James Warburton (Haslingden)	13.11.45	1	Haslingden		31 Jul
10:21.1	e p	Bob Rogers (Chelsea)	12.01.46	int	London (Star)		27 Dec
10:25.0	e p	Joe Rowe (Hackney)	c46	int	London (HW)		8 Nov
10:25.4	e p	Edward Golder (Canterbury)	1.07.43	int	London (HW)		24 May
10:28.2	e p	James Childerhouse (Deptford)	15.05.49	int	London (Star)		27 Dec
10:28.5	e p	William Gentleman (Bethnal Green)	c41	int	London (HW)		8 Nov
10:29.2	e	Alfred Goodier (Manchester)	47	2	Manchester (SAL)		3 Jul
10:29.4	e p	Edward Mills (Bethnal Green)	25.08.41	int	London (Bow)		29 Mar
10:31.0		Joseph Snow (Sale)	c46	1	Knutsford		31 Jul
10:32.6	e	Hubert Reynolds (Liverpool)	20.02.49	3	Knutsford		31 Jul
10:35.0		Edward Hawtrey (LAC)	10.10.47	int	London (BH)		27 Feb
10:35.0		Tyrrell Paine (CU)	15.10.49	int	London (LB)	OvC	18 Mar
10:42.0	p	John Brighton (Norwich)	14.07.32	int	London (Bow)		25 Oct
10:42.6		Charles Michod (Civil Service)	9.10.49	1	London (BH)		15 May
10:43.4	e	H. Strafford (Civil Service)		2	London (BH)		15 May
10:44.0		George Stephenson (Norton FC)		int	Sheffield (BL)		3 May

Notes

Estimates: Billy Mills 1y, McKinstray 2y, Rowe 100y & Gentleman 120y down on 10:07.2 (8/11); Kenyon 25y down on 10:12.0 (24/08); Rogers 40y & Childerhouse 60y down on 10:14.0; Golder 2y down on 10:25.0; Goodier 5y down on 10:28.25 (3/07); E. Mills 2y down on 10:29.0; Reynolds 6y down on 10:31.0; Strafford 4y down on 10:42.6.
Intermediate times in races at 3 miles [18/02, 27/02, 18/03 and 3/05]; 4 miles [10/04, 24/05, 16/08, and 27/12 (Star)]; 5 miles [27/12 (HW)]; and 10 miles [29/03, 25/10 and 8/11]

3 Miles

15:13.2	p	George Hazael (Deptford)	22.11.44	int	London (HW)		8 Nov
15:13.4	e p	Billy Mills (Bethnal Green)	09.43	int	London (HW)		8 Nov
15:15.0	p	Hazael		int	London (Bow)		25 Oct
15:21.4	p	Mills		int	London (LB)		16 Aug
15:32.0		John Morgan (OU)	19.08.47	1hc	Oxford		18 Feb
15:32.0	p	Alfred Markham (Marylebone)	c48	int	London (Bow)		10 Apr
15:34.0	p	Jack White (Gateshead)	1.03.37	int	London (Star)		27 Dec
15:34.6		Morgan		1	London (LB)	OvC	18 Mar
15:36.2	p	Robert McKinstray (Ayr)	18.04.37	int	London (HW)		27 Dec
15:36.8	e p	Hazael		int	London (HW)		27 Dec
15:40.0	p	Mills		int	London (HW)		24 May

(11/6)

15:40.2 e p	Edward Golder (Canterbury)	1.07.43	int	London (HW)		24 May
15:44.4 e p	Edward Mills (Bethnal Green)	25.08.41	int	London (Bow)		29 Mar
15:50.0	Edward Hawtrey (LAC)	10.10.47	1	London (BH)		27 Feb
15:58.0	Tyrrell Paine (CU)	15.10.49	1	Cambridge		8 Mar

Notes
Estimates: Billy Mills 1y down on 15:13.2; Hazael 3y on 15:36.2; Golder 1y on 15:40.0; Edward Mills 2y on 15:44.0.
Intermediate times in races at 4 miles [10/04, 24/05, 16/08 and 27/12 (Star)]; 5 miles [25/10; 27/12 (HW)]; 10 miles [29/03 and 8/11]

4 Miles

20:28.4 p	Robert McKinstray (Ayr)	18.04.37	int	London (HW)		27 Dec
20:28.8 e p	George Hazael (Deptford)	22.11.44	int	London (HW)		27 Dec
20:34.0 p	Hazael		int	London (Bow)		29 Mar
20:35.0 p	Hazael		int	London (Bow)		25 Oct
20:43.4 p	Hazael		int	London (HW)		8 Nov
20:43.4 p	Billy Mills (Bethnal Green)	09.43	int	London (HW)		8 Nov
20:55.0 p	Edward Mills (Bethnal Green)	25.08.41	int	London (Bow)		29 Mar
20:57.0 p	B. Mills		1	London (HW)		24 May
20:58.8 e p	Edward Golder (Canterbury)	1.07.43	2	London (HW)		24 May
21:05.0 p	E. Mills		1hc	London (HW)		2 Aug
21:08.25 p	Hazael		int	London (Bow)		22 Nov
21:11.9 e p	B. Mills		int	London (Bow)		22 Nov
21:16.0 p	Jack White (Gateshead)	1.03.37	1	London (Star)		27 Dec
21:30.0	Walter Chinnery (LAC)	19.08.43	1	London (LB)	AAC	3 Apr
21:35.0	Edward Hawtrey (LAC)	10.10.47	2	London (LB)	AAC	3 Apr

Notes
Estimates: Hazael 2y down on 20:28.4; Golder 10y on 20:57.0; Billy Mills 20y on 21:08.25.
Intermediate times in races at 5 miles [25/10, 27/12]; and 10 miles [29/03, 8/11 and 22/11]

6 Miles

31:35.4 p	George Hazael (Deptford)	22.11.44	int	London (HW)	8 Nov
31:35.6 pe	Billy Mills (Bethnal Green)	09.43	int	London (HW)	8 Nov
33:35.0 p	John Brighton (Norwich)	14.07.32	int	London (Bow)	6 Dec

Notes
Estimate: Mills 1y down on 31:35.4
Intermediate times in races at 10 miles. Brighton against a velocipedist, unfinished.

10 Miles

53:55.6 p	George Hazael (Deptford)	22.11.44	1	London (HW)	8 Nov
53:56.0 pe	Billy Mills (Bethnal Green)	09.43	2	London (HW)	8 Nov
55:32.5 p	Hazael		1	Manchester (Cope)	15 May

Note: Estimate: Mills 2y down.

120 Yards Hurdles

17.0	William Cooper (CU)	26.12.47	1	Cambridge		8 Mar
17.0	John Stirling (CU)	5.11.49	1	Cambridge		20 Nov
17 1/5	Arthur Hillyard (OU)	16.01.45	1	Oxford		26 Feb
17 1/5	Francis Philpott (OU)	17.05.48	1	London (LB)	OvC	18 Mar
17.2 e	Philpott		2	Cambridge		20 Nov
17 ½	Francis Whelan (Sheffield)	47	1	Sheffield (BL)		3 May
17 ½	Philpott		1ht1hc	Oxford		17 Nov
17 ½	William Walker (OU)	14.12.48	1	Oxford		19 Nov
		(8/6)				
17 3/5	Frederick Williamson (OU)	46	1ht2	Oxford		25 Feb
17 3/5	Ernest Toller (CU)	11.11.47	1ht1	Cambridge		5 Mar
17 3/5	Walter Eaton (Civil Service)	7.04.48	1	Hammersmith		1 May
17 3/5	William Lindsay (Civil Service)	3.08.47	1	London (BH)		15 May
17 3/5	William Huddleston (Lincoln)	6.03.49	1ht1	Leeds		11 Sep
17 3/5	R.F.S.Walker (RMC)		1	Camberley		23 Sep
17.7 e	Arnold Graves (Civil Service/IRL)	17.11.47	2	London (BH)		15 May
17.8 e	John Ornsby (Doncaster Gr Sch)	1.09.50	2	Sheffield (BL)		3 May

17 4/5	Edward Rice (Northampton)	c51	1	Northampton	8 Jun
17 4/5	James Quirk (OU)	5.03.50	1	Oxford	13 Nov
17.8 e	Louis Jackson (OU)	30.04.49	2	Oxford	19 Nov

School Sports (conditions unknown)

16.0	A.R.Goodwyn (Donington Gr Sch)		1	Donington, Lincs	25 Jun
17 1/5	Charles Wood (Cheltenham Coll)	1.07.51	1	Cheltenham	7 May
17 ¾	Arthur Stewart (QE School, Ipswich)	16.06.50	1	Ipswich	10 May
17.8 e	Arthur Malden (QE School, Ipswich)	50	2	Ipswich	10 May

Notes
Stirling was given 17.2 in *Bell's Life*, so Philpott (¾y down) would have been 17.4; Graves a few inches down on 17.6; Ornsby 2y down on 17.5; Jackson 2y down on 17.5; Malden 6in down on 17.75.

220 Yards Hurdles

27.25	John Sykes (Rochdale)	c48	1	Farnworth	28 Aug
27.4 e	William Desborough (Gateacre)	46	2	Farnworth	28 Aug
27.7 e	Charles Grundy (Claughton)	c50	3	Farnworth	28 Aug
31.0	Arthur Walkden (Manchester AFC)	45	1	Manchester (SAL)	3 Jul
32.0	Edmund Stretch (Ormskirk)	13.08.49	1	Ormskirk	15 May
32.0	W. Taylor (Bridlington)		1ht2	Farnworth	28 Aug
32.0	Grundy		1ht3	Farnworth	28 Aug
32.1 e	Bennet Greig (Rusholme)	15.10.49	2ht3	Farnworth	28 Aug
33.0	Stretch		1ht1	Ormskirk	15 May
33.0	Desborough		1ht1	Farnworth	28 Aug

Notes
Desborough ½y down on 27.25; Grundy 3½y down on 27.25; Greig 1ft down on 32.0.

12 flights

28.6	H. Wilton (Upton Park FC)		1	West Ham	10 Apr
28.8 e	Newton Nixon (Upton Park FC)	c48	2	West Ham	10 Apr
29.6	Millner Jutsum (Upton Park FC)	8.11.44	1ht2	West Ham	10 Apr
29.8 e	Henry Compton (Upton Park FC)		2ht2	West Ham	10 Apr
31.0	Nixon		1ht1	West Ham	10 Apr
31.3 e	Wilton		2ht1	West Ham	10 Apr

Notes
Nixon 1y down on 28.6; Compton 1y down on 29.6; Wilton 2y down on 31.0.

440 Yards Hurdles

1:04.0	Thomas Lee (Liverpool)		1	Burnley	7 Aug
1:04.5 e	John Sykes (Rochdale)	c48	2	Burnley	7 Aug
1:05.0	John Aston (Manchester)		1	Didsbury	19 Jun
1:05.0	William Craig (Uddingston)		1r1	East Kilbride	31 Jul
1:05.5	John Duckworth (Haslingden)	44	1	Ormskirk	15 May
1:06.5	Andrew Calderwood (East Kilbride)	11.04.49	1r2	East Kilbride	31 Jul
1:06.6 e	John Orr (East Kilbride)	c51	2r2	East Kilbride	31 Jul
1:08.0	Frederick Slade (Eltham CC)	49	1	Eltham	22 May
1:09.3 e	Noel Paterson (Eltham CC)	11.06.44	2	Eltham	22 May
1:09.5 e	Thomas Miller (Eltham CC)	c45	3	Eltham	22 May

12 flights

1:08.75	A. Atkinson (DCC Manchester)		1	Bradford	24 Jul
1:09.0	Lee		1	Douglas, IOM	24 Jul
1:09.7 e	James Moorhouse (Huddersfield AC)	c45	2	Douglas, IOM	24 Jul

15 flights:

1:07.2	Charles Watson (King's College Hosp)	21.03.49	1	London (LB)	17 Jun

School Sports (conditions unknown)

1:07.0	Henry Wace (Shrewsbury Sch)	21.09.53	1	Shrewsbury	14 Apr
1:08.0	Percy Hibbert (Shrewsbury Sch)	27.01.50	1	Shrewsbury	17 Jun

Notes
Sykes 3y down on 1:04; Orr ½y down on 1:06.5; Paterson 8y down on 1:08; Miller 9y down on 1:08.
Craig also competed as a professional.

High Jump

5'8	1.727	Robert Mitchell (Rossendale)	14.07.47	1	Sheffield (BL)	3 May
5'8	1.727	Hugh Miller (Liverpool Atlas AC/IRL)	c43	1	Liverpool	26 Jun
5'7½	1.715	James Bland (Dublin U/IRL)	6.04.50	1	Dublin (CP), IRL	10 Jun
5'7	1.702	Francis Corbett (Manchester AC)	c46	2=	Liverpool	26 Jun
5'7	1.702	John Duckworth (Haslingden)	44	2=	Liverpool	26 Jun
5'7	1.702	Charles Grundy (Liverpool)	c50	2=	Liverpool	26 Jun
5'7	1.702	Duckworth		1	Manchester (SAL)	3 Jul
5'6½	1.689	Roland Michell (OU)	14.02.47	1	Oxford	25 Feb
5'6½	1.689	John Ornsby (Doncaster Gr Sch)	1.09.50	1	Doncaster	mid Mar
5'6	1.676	Joseph Greaves (Manchester)	50	2	Manchester (SAL)	3 Jul
5'6	1.676	G. Widdett (Herne Bay)		1	Herne Bay	19 Jul

Indoors

5'10	1.778 i	Duckworth		1	Preston	15 Dec

Doubtful

5'6	1.676 i	W. Barber		1hc	Lambeth	1 Dec

[Indoors, at Lambeth St Baths. "Although the peg stood at 5'6, the bail itself dropped 2 or 3 inches in the centre]

High Jump: Highland & Border

5'10½	1.791	p	Andrew Milne (Forfar)	24.11.39	1	Dundee	21 Aug
5'10	1.778	p	John Black (Carmichael)		1=	Blantyre	15 Jul
5'10	1.778	p	Gavin Tait (Douglas)	34	1=	Blantyre	15 Jul
5'10	1.778	p	William Tait (Glendoch)	36	1=	Blantyre	15 Jul
5'10	1.778	p	Donald Dinnie (Aboyne)	8.06.37	1=	Forfar	6 Aug
5'10	1.778	p	Milne		1=	Forfar	6 Aug
5'9½	1.765	p	Dinnie		2	Dundee	21 Aug
5'9	1.753	p	Samuel Muir (Stewarton)	c41	1	West Calder	28 Jul
5'9	1.753	p	Muir		1	Alloa	11 Aug
5'9	1.753	p	Robert McIlvein (42nd Highlanders)		1	Edinburgh	14 Aug
			(10/7)				
5'8	1.727	p	Jackson (Glasgow)		1	Gateshead	30 Mar
5'7	1.702	p	James Fleming (Ballinluig)	18.09.40	2=	Coupar Angus	15 Jul
5'7	1.702	p	Donald McDonald (Murthly)		2=	Coupar Angus	15 Jul
5'7	1.702	p	David Anderson (Alnwick)	c46	1	Galashiels	24 Jul
5'7	1.702	p	John Toy (Dundee)	c46	4=	Forfar	6 Aug
5'6	1.676	p	James Black (Glasgow)		3	Kirkintilloch	16 Jul
5'6	1.676	p	David Milne (Forfar)	28.12.42	3	Dundee	21 Aug
5'6	1.676	p	Anthony Hall (Edinburgh)	c46	1=	Carlops	14 Aug
5'6	1.676	p	Matthew Middlemist (Jedburgh)	c39	1=	Carlops	14 Aug
5'6	1.676	p	Alexander Robson (Denholm)	c47	2	Galashiels	24 Jul

Note

A medal of Dinnie's states that he was champion of Perth with a high leap of 5'11 this year.

Pole Vault

9'10	3.00		Robert Mitchell (Rossendale)	14.07.47	1	Haslingden	31 Jul
9'8	2.95		Edmund Gurney (CU)	23.03.47	1	Norwich	24 May
9'8	2.95	p	Samuel Rigg (Kendal)	c46	2=	Haslingden	31 Jul
9'8	2.95		John Thwaites (Bolton)	c45	2=	Haslingden	31 Jul
9'6	2.90		Charles Down (RMC Sandhurst)	03.50	1	Woolwich	8 May
9'6	2.90		Arnold Graves (Civil Service/IRL)	17.11.47	1	London (BH)	15 May
9'6	2.90		Frederick Barber (Norfolk FBC, Sheffield)	c47	1=	Nottingham	17 May
9'6	2.90		Francis Whelan (Sheffield FC)	47	1=	Nottingham	17 May

School Sports

9'6	2.90	William Calvert (Donington Gr Sch)		1	Donington, Lincs	25 Jun
9'3	2.82	Gould (St James's Collegiate Sch)		1	Jersey	31 May
9'2½	2.81	John Ornsby (Doncaster Gr Sch)	1.09.50	1	Doncaster	20 Mar

Note

Rigg competed professionally, but was not debarred from this amateur meeting.

Pole Vault: Lakeland, Highland & Border

10'8	3.25	p	David Anderson (Alnwick)	c46	1	Alva	12 Aug
10'6	3.20	p	Anderson		1	Leith	10 Aug
10'5	3.17	p	Anderson		1	Gateshead	30 Mar
10'4	3.15	p	Thomas Bell (Thornthwaite)		1	Cleator Moor	8 Jun
10'4	3.15	p	William Ewing (Bonhill)	c47	1	Dumbarton	14 Aug
10'4	3.15	p	Anderson		1	Edinburgh	14 Aug
10'2	3.10	p	Anderson		1	Tillicoultry	13 Aug
10'2	3.10	p	William Borland (Kilbarchan)	c48	2=	Dumbarton	14 Aug
10'2	3.10	p	Malcolm McGregor (Bonhill)	c45	2=	Dumbarton	14 Aug
			(9/5)				
9'10	3.00	p	John Cooling (Stott Park/IRL)	44	1	Liverpool	17 May
9'10	3.00	p	William Young		1	Kirkintilloch	16 Jul
9'10	3.00	p	R. Thomson (West Calder)		2	West Calder	28 Jul
9'9	2.97	p	J. Best (Edinburgh)		2	Galashiels	24 Jul
9'9	2.97	p	William Crichton (Coupar Angus)	05.49	1	Forfar	6 Aug
9'9	2.97	p	J. Bruce		1	Dundee	7 Aug
9'8	2.95	p	William Renwick (Galashiels)		3	Galashiels	24 Jul
9'8	2.95	p	Anderson Turner (Salsburgh)	17.03.38	3=	West Calder	28 Jul
9'8	2.95	p	James Campbell (West Calder)		3=	West Calder	28 Jul
9'8	2.95	p	Samuel Muir (Stewarton)	c41	2	Alloa	11 Aug
9'7	2.92	p	James Ewing (Bonhill)		2=	Kirkintilloch	16 Jul
9'7	2.92	p	David Milne (Forfar)	28.12.42	2	Forfar	6 Aug
9'7	2.92	p	James Stewart (Lochee)		1	Blairgowrie	26 Jul
9'6	2.90	p	John Wilson (Hutton Roof)	c46	2	Liverpool	17 May
9'6	2.90	p	Anthony Hall (Edinburgh)	c46	1	Carlops	14 Aug
9'6	2.90	p	J. Stenhouse (Galashiels)		3	Edinburgh	14 Aug
9'6	2.90	p	Robert Poustie (Duntrune)	41	2=	Dundee	21 Aug
9'6	2.90	p	Robert Scott (Innerleithen)		3	Dalkeith	11 Sep

Indoors

10'5	3.17 i	p	Robert Musgrave (Cockermouth)	11.10.41	1	London (Ag Hall)	26 Mar
10'4	3.15 i	p	John Allison (Kendal)	8.02.43	1	Manchester	3 May
10'2	3.10 i	p	Anderson		2	London (Ag Hall)	26 Mar
9'6	2.90 i	p	James Baines (Penrith)		3=	London (Ag Hall)	26 Mar
9'6	2.90 i	p	Mark Shearman (Keswick)	c49	3=	London (Ag Hall)	26 Mar

Note: Musgrave was given 11'6, Anderson 11'4, James Baines & Mark Shearman 10'6, at the Agricultural Hall on 26/03 by *Lloyd's Weekly Newspaper*

Long Jump

22'2	6.76	Alick Tosswill (OU)	21.01.45	1	Oxford		27 Feb
21'1¾	6.45	John Duckworth (Haslingden)	44	1	Burnley		7 Aug
21'1½	6.44	Edward Bergman (OU)	8.02.49	1	Oxford		13 Nov
21'0	6.40	Duckworth		1	Liverpool		26 Jun
20'9	6.32	Henry Tidy (Middleton)	47	1	Atherstone		5 Jul
20'8	6.30	Richard Waltham (CU)	25.02.46	1	London (LB)	OvC	18 Mar
20'7¾	6.29	Francis Philpott (OU)	17.05.48	2	Oxford		27 Feb
20'7½	6.29	John Maxwell-Lyte (OU)	20.06.50	2	Oxford		13 Nov
20'6½	6.26	John Ornsby (OU)	1.09.50	3	Oxford		13 Nov
20'1½	6.13	James Brookes (OU)	47	3	Oxford		27 Feb
20'1	6.12	William Mann (Eltham)	17.11.49	1	Eastbourne		17 Aug
20'0	6.10	Ornsby		1	Sheffield		3 May
20'0	6.10	Ivor Lewis (Guy's Hosp)	21.05.48	ex	London (LB)		17 Jun
		(13/11)					
19'11	6.07	William Walker (OU)	14.12.48	4	Oxford		27 Feb
19'11	6.07	Henry Fellowes (Beighton)	22.11.51	1	Lowestoft		5 Aug
19'10½	6.06	Noel Lucas (OU)	25.12.49	1	Oxford		18 Nov

Long Jump: Highland & Border

20'6	6.25	p	Robert Knox (Newstead)	17.09.47	1	Jedburgh	6 Aug
20'5	6.22	p	Samuel Muir (Stewarton)	c41	1	Dalkeith	29 Aug
20'5	6.22	p	Muir		1=	Dalkeith	11 Sep
20'5	6.22	p	James Young (Alva)	c47	1=	Dalkeith	11 Sep
20'0	6.10	p	Muir		1	Whitburn	13 Jul

Triple Jump

42'3	12.88	Dr Murphy (Egmont/IRL)		1	Liscarroll, IRL	29 Jun
41'6	12.65	E.P.Collis (IRL)		1	Cork, IRL	15 Oct
41'2	12.55	D. Donovan (Cork/IRL)		1	Cork (open), IRL	14 May
41'1	12.52	Gilbert Grace (Bristol)	18.07.48	1	Clifton	25 Sep
41'0	12.50	Dudley Fitzgerald (QC Cork/IRL)	c48	2	Cork (college), IRL	14 May
41'0	12.50	Joseph Walsh (IRL)		2	Cork, IRL	15 Oct
40'11	12.47	William O'Sullivan (Roskeen/IRL)		1	Mallow, IRL	24 May
40'11	12.47	John Joyce (QC Cork/IRL)	4.07.49	3	Cork (college), IRL	14 May
40'0	12.19	C.W.Prebble (Dagnall Park AC)		1	Dagnall Park	3 Jul
40'0	12.19	Edward Grace (Bristol)	28.11.41	1	Clifton	25 Sep

Note
Bell's Life lists two competitions at the QC Cork sports on 14/5, but it seems they competed together. *Bell's* gives Donovan 41'2. The *Cork Examiner* has Donovan on 41'6, Fitzgerald 41'0 and John Joyce (father of the writer, James Joyce) 40'11. However, *Bell's* does not list Joyce.

Triple Jump: Highland & Border

46'9	14.25	p	Robert Knox (Newstead)	17.09.47	1	Jedburgh	6 Aug
46'6	14.17	p	James Black (Glasgow)		1	Kirkintilloch	16 Jul
46'6	14.17	p	Samuel Muir (Stewarton)	c41	1	West Calder	28 Jul
46'4	14.12	p	Muir		1	Paisley	25 Sep
46'3	14.10	p	James Todd (Glasgow)		2	Kirkintilloch	16 Jul
46'3	14.10	p	James Young (Alva)	c47	1	Wishaw	9 Sep
46'2	14.07	p	Knox		1	Hawick	11 Jun
46'0	14.02	p	John Bell (Hawick)	c39	2	Hawick	11 Jun
46'0	14.02	p	Knox		1	Tillicoultry	13 Aug
45'10	13.97	p	Alexander Robson (Denholm)	c47	2	Jedburgh	6 Aug
			(10/7)				
45'0	13.72	p	James Rough (Kilbarchan)	c46	1	Dalry	4 Aug
44'8	13.61	p	William Borland (Edinburgh)	c48	2	Paisley	25 Sep
44'1	13.44	p	Thomas Carruthers (Yetholm)	27.04.40	2	Lasswade	18 Sep
44'0½	13.42	p	Gavin Tait (Douglas)	34	1	Hawick	9 Jun
43'9	13.33	p	James Goddard (Hawick)	c49	1	St Boswells	17 Jul
43'8	13.31	p	Peter Campbell (Alexandria)	c43	1	Denny	28 Aug
43'7	13.28	p	Robert Neilston (Greenock)		1	Greenock	12 Jun
43'7	13.28	p	David Milne (Forfar)	28.12.42	3	Forfar	6 Aug
43'5	13.23	p	Robert McIlvein (42nd Highlanders)		3	West Calder	28 Jul
43'3	13.18	p	Peter McCallum		3	Barrhead	24 Jul
43'0	13.11	p	W.A.Ramsay (Singleton)		1	Singleton, Lancs	29 Sep
42'11	13.08	p	John Toy (Dundee)	c46	4	Forfar	6 Aug
42'6	12.95	p	Andrew Milne (Montrose)	24.11.39	1	Dundee	21 Aug
42'2	12.85	p	Robert Drysdale (Tillicoultry)		1	Clackmannan	29 Jun
42'0	12.80	p	A. Lamberdon		3	Crofthead	27 Aug
41'8	12.70	p	James Johnstone (Alloa)		1	Dunfermline	17 Jul
41'8	12.70	p	J. McGregor (Maryhill)		3	Kelvinside	17 Jul
41'8	12.70	p	Alexander Fleming (Glasgow)		2	Whittingham	23 Aug
41'7	12.67	p	William Craig (Uddingston)		2	Springburn	18 Sep
41'4	12.60	p	John Allan (Alnwick)		1	Glanton	2 Aug
41'3	12.57	p	J. McIntyre (Cardross)		4	Barrhead	24 Jul
41'2	12.55	p	William Tait (Glendoch)	36	3	Muiravonside	26 Jun
41'0	12.50	p	G.W.Wood (Singleton)		2	Singleton, Lancs	29 Sep

Shot

39'0	11.89	J. Elliott (Sunderland RVC)		1	Sunderland	22 May
38'6	11.73	William Trahair (Penzance)		1	Penzance	23 Sep
38'0	11.58	Richard Waltham (CU)	25.02.46	1	Cambridge	5 Mar
37'6	11.43	William Mackenzie (Edinburgh U)	c51	1	Leeds	11 Sep
37'0	11.28	Joseph Rowley (Queensferry)		1	Didsbury	19 Jun
36'9	11.20	John Rowland (Didsbury CC)	44	2	Didsbury	19 Jun
36'0	10.97	Rowland		2	Leeds	11 Sep
35'11	10.95	Waltham		1	Cambridge	24 Feb
35'7	10.85	Edmund Phelps (CU)	14.12.47	1	Cambridge	16 Nov
34'6	10.52	Alexander Pringle (Edinburgh U)	c42	1	Edinburgh	23 Jun
34'4½	10.48	John Burgess (Brookfield CC)	22.09.48	1	Highgate	8 May

34'4½	10.48		William Forsyth (Edinburgh U)		c49	2	Edinburgh	23 Jun

18lb with follow

34'4	10.46		Edward Bor (RMA Woolwich/IRL)		25.08.50	1	Woolwich	5 May

Note
The puts by Elliott and Trahair were not reported as beating Waltham's amateur record, and must be treated with reserve.

Shot: Highland & Border
Includes 16lb stone and ball

43'7	13.28	p	Donald Dinnie (Aboyne)		8.06.37	1	Aboyne (champion)	31 Aug
43'6	13.26	p	James Fleming (Ballinluig)		18.09.40	2	Aboyne (champion)	31 Aug
43'0	13.11	p	Fleming			1	Nairn	14 Aug
42'4	12.90	p	Fleming			1	Kelvinside	17 Jul
42'3	12.88	p	Dinnie			1	West Calder	28 Jul
41'8	12.70	p	Alexander Bowie (Keith Hall)		44	1	Culsalmond	26 Aug
40'7	12.37	p	R.D.Garden (Culsalmond)			2	Culsalmond	26 Aug
40'7	12.37	p	Fleming			1	Aboyne	31 Aug
				(8/4)				
39'9½	12.13	p	William Tait (Glendoch)		36	2	West Calder	28 Jul
38'10	11.84	p	Robert Scott (Strathallan)			1	Bridge of Allan (local)	7 Aug
38'9	11.81	p	William Fraser (Clunas)			2	Nairn	14 Aug
38'7	11.76	p	Thomas Rattray (Culsalmond)		c43	3	Culsalmond	26 Aug
38'5	11.71	p	James Blair (Wishaw)			3	West Calder	28 Jul
38'4	11.68	p	Alexander Grant (Aboyne)			1	Ballater	28 Jul
38'4*	11.68	p	Charles Emslie (Wester Craigievar)			1	Monymusk	9 Aug
37'9	11.51	p	James Michie (Glenlivet)		20.10.46	3	Nairn	14 Aug
37'4	11.38	p	Peter Bremner (Glenbucket)		20.01.42	1	Lumphanan	7 Aug
36'10	11.23	p	Peter McHardy (Glasgow)		c48	3	Kelvinside	17 Jul
36'8½	11.19	p	John Moir (Auchernach)		27.07.42	3	Aboyne	31 Aug
36'0½	10.99	p	J. Wilson (Glasgow)			3	Kelvinside	17 Jul
35'11	10.95	p	John McLeod (Baillieston)			2=	New Stevenston	19 Jul
35'11*	10.95	p	William Law (Tough)			2	Monymusk	9 Aug
35'9	10.90	p	James Esson (Aboyne)			2	Ballater	28 Jul
35'9	10.90	p	James Strang (East Kilbride)		c50	1	Busby	14 Aug
35'8	10.87	p	George Mearns (Kincardine)			2	Lumphanan	7 Aug
35'6	10.82	p	Cpl Clark (42nd Regiment)			4	West Calder	28 Jul
35'2	10.72	p	Charles Stewart (Glenmuick)			3	Ballater	28 Jul
34'11*	10.64	p	Lewis Stewart (Kemnay)			3	Monymusk	9 Aug
34'10	10.62	p	William Robertson (Aberdeen)			4	Ballater	28 Jul
34'6	10.52	p	James Lindsay (Crofthead)			5	West Calder	28 Jul
34'5	10.49	p	James Melrose (Peebles)		17.04.47	2	Musselburgh	11 Aug

Note: *correct weight assumed from evidence of other years

Weight unstated

42'3	12.88	p	Dinnie		1	Dunkeld (champion)	24 Jul
37'2	11.33	p	James Smith		1	Leochel-Cushnie	17 Aug
36'7	11.15	p	George Wilson (Leochel-Cushnie)		3	Leochel-Cushnie	17 Aug

17lb

41'4	12.60	p	Dinnie		1	Newcastle	18 May

18lb

41'2	12.55	p	John Anderson (Edinburgh)		1	Lasswade	18 Sep
40'1	12.22	p	Dinnie		1	Edinburgh	14 Aug
39'4	11.99	p	Clark		2	Lasswade	18 Sep
37'5	11.40	p	Tait		3	Edinburgh	14 Aug

22lb

41'8	12.70	p	Dinnie		1	Arniston	14 Aug
41'6	12.65	p	Tait		1	East Kilbride	31 Jul
39'5	12.01	p	Donald McDonald (Murthly)		2	Dunkeld	24 Jul
38'6	11.73	p	Fleming		2	Birnam	26 Aug
36'5	11.10	p	John MacLagan (Dunfermline)		3	Alloa	11 Aug
36'3	11.05	p	John George (Tarland)	46	1	Dumbarton	14 Aug
36'1½	11.01	p	William Strang (East Kilbride)	c48	2	East Kilbride	31 Jul

36'0	10.97	p	Edward Hunter (Uddingston)			3	East Kilbride	31 Jul
35'10	10.92	p	Samuel Muir (Stewarton)		c41	3	Arniston	14 Aug

Doubtful (see 1868 note)

49'2	14.99	p	Dinnie			1	Greenock	12 Jun
47'5	14.45	p	Fleming			2	Greenock	12 Jun
47'2	14.38	p	George			3	Greenock	12 Jun
40'3	12.27	p	John McLean (Greenock)			1	Greenock (local)	12 Jun
38'6	11.73	p	James Murray (Greenock)			2	Greenock (local)	12 Jun
37'11	11.56	p	Alexander Ritchie (Greenock)			3	Greenock (local)	12 Jun

Hammer

103'11	31.67	Henry Leeke (CU)	6.02.46	1	London (LB)	OvC	18 Mar
102'3	31.17	William A. Burgess (OU)	27.12.46	1	London (LB)	AAC	3 Apr
101'5	30.91	Francis Waite (OU)	24.09.46	2	London (LB)	OvC	18 Mar
99'4	30.28	Leeke		2	London (LB)	AAC	3 Apr
98'9¾	30.12	Waite		2hc	Cambridge		2 Dec
98'6	30.02	Leeke		1	Cambridge		6 Mar
97'10	29.82	Waite		1	Oxford		25 Feb
97'10	29.82	Leeke		1	Derby		25 Sep
96'6	29.41	Mortimer Shelton (CU)	14.09.48	3	London (LB)	OvC	18 Mar
96'6	29.41	Waite		3	London (LB)	AAC	3 Apr
95'5	29.08	Thomas Batson (OU)	18.05.46	4	London (LB)	AAC	3 Apr
95'1	28.98	Stephen Gatty (OU)	9.10.49	2	Oxford		25 Feb
		(12/6)					
93'2	28.40	Edward Baily (Harrow School)	18.01.52	1	Harrow		20 Mar
90'9	27.66	John Rowland (Didsbury CC)	44	1	Leeds		11 Sep
90'0	27.43	Henry Richardson (West Kent FC)		1	Chislehurst		8 May
89'10	27.38	Alaric Churchward (CU)	11.46	2	Cambridge		24 Nov
89'1	27.15	Samuel Lucas (OU)	30.12.47	3hc	Oxford		20 Nov
88'9	27.05	George Mills (OU)	19.01.47	2hc	Cambridge		11 Nov
88'4	26.92	Richard Waltham (CU)	25.02.46	3	Cambridge		6 Mar

Additional Junior Mark:

87'1½	26.56	Fairfax Wade (Radley College)	16.07.51	1	Radley		4 Mar

Notes
In the Oxford v Cambridge match, Waite also threw 100'9/30.71.
In the AAC, Burgess threw 85'8 – 94'7 – 97'4 – 97'5 – 102'3; Leeke 86'8 – 91'3 – 95'9 – 97'5 – 99'4; Waite 88'5 – 87'6 – 96'6 – 89'6; Batson 94'3 – 95'5.
In the Oxford University Sports on 25 Feb, Burgess (3rd) and Mills (4th) are said to have thrown "over 90'0" (no other details).

Hammer: Highland & Border

111'0	33.83	p	Donald Dinnie (Aboyne)	8.06.37	1	Dunkeld champion	26 Jul
110'10*	33.78	p	Dinnie		1	Forfar	6 Aug
107'8	32.82	p	Dinnie		1	Coupar Angus	15 Jul
106'0	32.31	p	James Fleming (Ballinluig)	18.09.40	1	Nairn	14 Aug
103'9	31.62	p	Dinnie		1	Aboyne	31 Aug
103'0	31.39	p	Dinnie		1	Balfron	17 Jul
102'7*	31.27	p	Fleming		2	Forfar	6 Aug
102'4	31.19	p	Fleming		1	Kelvinside	17 Jul
102'0	31.09	p	Fleming		1	Dunkeld	24 Jul
102'0	31.09	p	Fleming		2	Dunkeld	26 Jul
101'8	30.99	p	Dinnie		1	Birnam	26 Aug
100'10	30.73	p	Donald McDonald (Murthly)		2	Dunkeld	24 Jul
			(12/3)				
99'0*	30.18	p	James Anderson		1	Barrhead	24 Jul
98'8	30.07	p	Alexander McLay (Bonhill)		2	Kelvinside	17 Jul
96'5*	29.39	p	William Bremner (Glenbucket)	3.01.47	1	Lumphanan	21 Aug
94'3	28.73	p	William Tait (Glendoch)	36	1	Springburn	18 Sep
93'9*	28.57	p	Alexander Grant (Aboyne)		3	Forfar	6 Aug
93'5	28.47	p	John George (Renfrew)	46	1	Dumbarton	14 Aug
89'9	27.36	p	Peter McHardy (Glasgow)	c48	3	Kelvinside	17 Jul
89'9	27.36	p	James Michie (Glenlivet)	20.10.46	2	Inverness	23 Sep

Note: *correct weight assumed from evidence of other years

Weight unstated

114'0	34.75	p	Dinnie		1	Muiravonside (heavy)	26 Jun
112'2	34.19	p	Dinnie		1	Perth	11 Sep
107'8	32.82	p	Dinnie		1	Blairgowrie	26 Jul
106'0	32.31	p	Fleming		1	Bridge of Allan	7 Aug
100'9	30.71	p	Dinnie		1	Edinburgh	14 Aug
97'8	29.77	p	John MacLagan (Dunkeld)		2	Bridge of Allan	7 Aug
91'5	27.86	p	William McCombie Smith (Lumphanan)	7.09.47	1	Leochel-Cushnie	17 Aug
91'3	27.81	p	Peter Bremner (Glenbucket)	20.01.42	2	Leochel-Cushnie	17 Aug
89'4	27.23	p	James Smith		3	Leochel-Cushnie	17 Aug

17lb by performer

105'0	32.00	p	Dinnie		1	Dundee	21 Aug
96'2	29.31	p	Fleming		2	Dundee	21 Aug

18lb by performer

106'6	32.46	p	Dinnie		1	Leith	10 Aug
92'9	28.27	p	Fleming		2	Greenock	12 Jun

22lb by performer

101'8	30.99	p	Dinnie		1	Birnam	26 Aug
93'3	28.42	p	Fleming		2	Birnam	26 Aug

Other Events

150 Yards

15.4		Gilbert Grace (LAC)	18.07.48	1hthc	London (BH)	10 Apr

200 Yards

20.4		Abbot Upcher (CU)	19.10.49	1	Cambridge	13 Nov

300 Yards

32.5	p	Harry Whitehead (Hyde)	26.04.47	1	Kelvinside	19 Jul
33.8		Sgt Russell (Royal Horse Artillery)		1	Aldershot	8 Jul

600 Yards

1:20.0	C. Benwell (Dagnall Park)		1	Dagnall Park	3 Jul

1000 Yards

2:31.0	John Quirk (Dublin U/IRL)	18.08.47	1	Dublin (CP), IRL	10 Jun

1½ Miles

6:57.0	p	John Fleet (Manchester)	6.04.45	1	Manchester (RO)	26 Jun

5 Miles

25:56.0	p	George Hazael (Deptford)	22.11.44	int	Bow	25 Oct

1 Mile Walk

7:05.0	p	George Davison (Hoxton)	2.09.44	int	London (HW)	1 Nov

In a 2 hour match

2 Miles Walk

14:46.0	Thomas Griffith (South Essex AC)	c39	1	Bideford	30 Aug

7 Miles Walk

54:10.0	p	George Davison (Hoxton)	2.09.44	int	London (HW)	6 Dec

In a 21 mile match

Cricket Ball

117y 0ft 6in	107.14	Gilbert Grace (LAC)	18.07.48	1	London (Oval)	30 Aug

W.G.Grace's prize was a cricket outfit and bat.

1870 UK Year List

100 Yards

10.0	p	Frank Hewitt (Millwall)	8.05.45	1	Melbourne, AUS		7 Mar
10.0		William Dawson (CU)	3.12.50	1	Cambridge		11 Mar
10.0		Alfred Baker (LAC)	10.12.46	1ro	London (LB)		2 Apr
10.0		John Tobin (Lismore AC/IRL)	29.11.47	1	Cork, IRL		7 Apr
10.0		John Wilson (OU)	19.07.48	1	London (LB)	OvC	7 Apr
10.0		Thomas Jones (Birmingham AC)	c49	1	Birmingham (PR)		23 Jul
10.0		Charles Pickering (Manchester AC)	22.02.48	1	Knutsford		30 Jul
10.1	e	Egerton Clarke (CU)	11.07.47	2	London (LB)	OvC	7 Apr
10.1	e	F. Marryatt (65th Regt/IRL)		2	Cork, IRL		7 Apr
10 1/8		John Duckworth (Haslingden AC)	44	1	Ormskirk		21 May
			(10/10)				
10.2	e	Robert Lock (CU)	15.07.48	2=	Cambridge		11 Mar
10.2	e	John Stirling (CU)	5.11.49	2=	Cambridge		11 Mar
10 1/5		Edward Colbeck (LAC)	21.12.47	1=	London (LB)		2 Apr
10 1/5		C. Kitchen (Marshall & Snelgrove)		1	St John's Wood		24 Sep
10 1/5		William Collett (LAC)	18.06.43	1	London (LB)		22 Oct
10 1/5		Charles Heath (OU)	26.08.51	1ht1	Oxford		18 Nov

Downhill & wind-assisted:

9 ¾	p	George Mole (Walsall)	6.06.42	1	Liverpool		25 Jun

Doubtful

10.0	John Harrison (QC Galway/IRL)		1	Galway, IRL		29 Mar
10.0	Abbot Upcher (CU)	19.10.49	1	Beccles		6 Jul
10.0	D. Peirce (St David's College)		1	Lampeter		28 Oct

Notes
Hewitt was timed at 9¾, 10.0 and 10¼. Baker's 10.0 was in a run-off after tying with Colbeck in 10 1/5.
Estimates: Lock & Stirling 1y down on 10.0; Clarke ½y down on 10.0; Marryatt "the merest fluke" down on 10.0.

220 Yards

23 1/5		Thomas Hooman (Wanderers FBC)	28.12.50	1	Walthamstow		1 Oct
23 ¼		Thomas Lee (Tranmere)		1	Ormskirk		11 Jul
23.4	e	John Clegg (Sheffield FC)	15.06.50	2hc	Macclesfield		18 Jun
23.4	e	W. Page (LAC)		2	Walthamstow		1 Oct
23 ¾		Spencer Jackson (Oundle Gr Sch)	c52	1	Nottingham		23 Apr
23 ¾		Charles Pickering (Manchester AC)	22.02.48	1	Knutsford		30 Jul
24.0		John Cockerell (Brixton AC)	c46	1	London (BH)		2 May
24.0		Alfred Eames (Civil Service)	50	1	London (LB)		28 May
24.1	e	William Revis (Nottingham)	c48	2	Nottingham		23 Apr
24.1	e	Walter Eaton (Civil Service)	7.04.48	2	London (LB)		28 May
24.1	e	F. Robins (Buckhurst Hill CC)		3	Walthamstow		1 Oct
24.2	e	Arthur Wells (Blackheath FC)	9.04.50	2	London (BH)		2 May
24 ¼		Clegg		1	Manchester (Long)		25 Jun
24.3	e	Frederick Hartung (LAC)	29.05.46	3	London (BH)		2 May
24.3	e	Arthur Badcock (Civil Service)	12.07.47	3	London (LB)		28 May
24.3	e	Ernest Greenhalgh (Notts County FC)	c49	2hc	Nottingham		6 Jun

Notes
Estimates: Clegg ½y down on 23.25; Page 1½y down on 23.2; Robins 7½y down on 23.2; Wells 1½y down on 24.0; Hartung 2y down on 24.0; Revis 3y down on 23.75; Eaton ½y down on 24.0; Badcock 2y down on 24.0; Greenhalgh 2½y down on 24.0, possibly under distance.

440 Yards

50.7		Robert Somers-Smith (OU)	23.05.48	1	London (LB)	OvC	7 Apr
51.0		William Forsyth (Edinburgh U)	c49	1	Edinburgh		23 Jun
51.1	e p	Frank Hewitt (Millwall)	8.05.45	2hc	Ballarat, AUS		26 Mar
51.25	p	Hewitt		1	Melbourne, AUS		7 Mar
51.3	e	B. Flint (Edinburgh U)		2	Edinburgh		23 Jun
51.3		Abbot Upcher (CU)	19.10.49	2	London (LB)	OvC	7 Apr
51.5	p	Hewitt		1ht2hc	Ballarat, AUS		26 Mar
51.66		Upcher		1ht1hc	Cambridge		1 Mar
51.75	p	Harry Whitehead (Hyde)	26.04.47	1	Manchester (RO)		19 Feb
51.75		Richard Luck (CU)	14.09.47	1	Clapham		2 Apr
52.0		Upcher		1	Cambridge		29 Mar
52.0		William Clague (Stockport)	14.01.47	1	Bradford		23 Jul

52.0	Upcher		1	Oxford		12 Nov
52.0	George Templer (CU)	22.12.51	1	Cambridge		16 Nov
52.0	Robert Philpot (CU)	12.06.50	1	Cambridge		19 Nov
	(15/10)					
52.3 e p	James Nuttall (Manchester)	28.12.41	2hc	Manchester (RO)		19 Feb
52.4	Lewis Evans (CU)	9.07.51	1	Cambridge		21 Nov
52.5 e	Arthur Gwatkin (CU)	17.07.50	2	Clapham		2 Apr
52.5	Emanuel Goodhart (W. Kent FC)	c49	1hc	Chislehurst		14 May
52.6	Ernest Prothero (OU)	50	3	London (LB)	OvC	7 Apr
52.6	John Clegg (Sheffield FC)	15.06.50	1	Sheffield (BL)		2 May
52.6	Arthur Pollock (LAC)	c49	1	London (LB)		17 May

Short Course (approximately 10 yards under distance, equates to 52.2e, 52.5e and 52.6e for full distance)

51.0	Clegg		1	Nottingham	6 Jun
51.3 e	Benjamin Gardom (CU)	19.09.47	2	Nottingham	6 Jun
51.4 e	Arthur Walkden (Manchester AC)	45	3	Nottingham	6 Jun

Notes
Reports of the Oxford v Cambridge time differ. Somers-Smith is given 50.2 in *Fifty Years of Sport*; 50.7 in *Bell's Life*; 51.8 in *Athletics* (Shearman) and *Oxford v Cambridge* (Abrahams & Bruce-Kerr). Times here are as in BL, which used a Benson Marking Chronograph for 1st, 2nd and 3rd.
Estimates: Hewitt 3y down on 50.75; Flint 2y down on 51.0; Gardom 2¼y down on 51.0; Walkden 1ft behind Gardom; Nuttall 4y down on 51.75; Gwatkin 6y down on 51.75.
Philpot started 4y behind scratch in his 52.0 run.

880 Yards

1:58.7 e p	John Aspin (Rawtenstall)	44	2hc	Manchester (City)		12 Nov
1:59.0 p	Albert Bird (Sheffield)	15.08.46	1hc	Maitland, AUS		12 Jun
2:02.0	Robert Somers-Smith (OU)	23.05.48	1	London (LB)	AAC	9 Apr
2:02.3 e	Arthur Dowding (OU)	23.11.48	2	London (LB)	AAC	9 Apr
2:03.75	John Scott (LAC)	9.09.47	wo	London (LB)		22 Oct
2:04.0 e	Arthur Pelham (CU)	28.12.50	3	London (LB)	AAC	9 Apr
2:04.0 p	Frank Hewitt (Millwall)	8.05.45	1	Bathurst, AUS		7 May
2:04.0 p	Bird		1	Newcastle, AUS		4 Jun
2:04.2 e p	Bird		2	Bathurst, AUS		7 May
2:04.4	J. Parks (Charlton)		1	Woolwich		20 Aug
2:05.0	Somers-Smith		1	Oxford		24 Mar
2:05.0	John Harrison (QC Galway/IRL)		1	Galway, IRL		29 Mar
	(12/9)					
2:05.5 e	Thomas Nash (OU)	27.11.49	3	Oxford		24 Mar
2:05.6	John Brockbank (CU)	22.08.48	1	Cambridge		28 Mar
2:05.7 e	Thomas Hewitt (CU)	18.11.49	2	Cambridge		28 Mar
2:06.6 e	Archibald Michell (CU)	4.08.50	4	Cambridge		28 Mar
2:07.0	Hamlet Riley (Rugby School)	29.01.52	1	Rugby		5 Apr
2:07.0	James Becke (Northampton)	48	1	Northampton		24 May

Notes
Estimates: Aspin 3y down on 1:58.25; Dowding 1½y down on 2:02; Pelham 13½y down on 2:02; Bird "almost too close to call" down on 2:04.0; T. Hewitt 6in down on 2:05.6; Nash 3½y down on 2:05.0; Michell 5½y down on 2:05.6.

Mile

4:25.0 p	Stephen Ridley (Gateshead)	29.07.45	1hc	Edinburgh (Pow)		1 Jan
4:28.0 p	Albert Bird (Sheffield)	15.08.46	1hc	Newcastle, AUS		1 Jun
4:28.4 p	Edward Mills (Bethnal Green)	25.08.41	1	London (Star)		30 May
4:29.4 e p	Bob Rogers (Chelsea)	12.01.46	2	London (Star)		30 May
4:30.0 p	Ridley		1	Manchester (City)		9 Apr
4:30.5 p	Bird	15.08.46	1	Ballarat, AUS		14 Feb
4:30.5 p	Bird		1	L. Wendouree, AUS		29 Mar
4:31.0 p	Bird		2hc	Sydney, AUS		18 Apr
4:32.4	Robert Benson (OU)	24.09.50	1	London (LB)	OvC	7 Apr
4:33.0	Thomas Christie (OU)	15.10.49	2	London (LB)	OvC	7 Apr
4:33.2 e p	James Childerhouse (Deptford)	15.05.49	2	Manchester (City)		9 Apr
4:34.0 p	George Hazael (Deptford)	22.11.44	int	London (Bow)		15 Apr
	(12/8)					
4:35.0	John Scott (LAC)	9.09.47	1hc	London (LB)		7 May

4:36.4 e	Edward Hawtrey (CU)	10.10.47	3hc	Cambridge		1 Mar
4:37.0 p	Edward Golder (Canterbury)	1.07.43	1	London (Bow)		7 Mar
4:39.25	Walter Betts (Birmingham AC)	50	1	Birmingham (PR)		9 Jul
4:39.6 e	William Perrin (Birmingham Gym)	c45	2	Birmingham (PR)		9 Jul

Short course (approximately 30y under distance, equates to 4:31.2e and 4:34.3e for full distance)

4:26.5	Scott		1	Nottingham		6 Jun
4:29.6 e	James Becke (Northampton)	48	2	Nottingham		6 Jun

Notes
Estimates: Rogers 6y down on 4:28.4; Childerhouse 20y down on 4:30; Becke 20y down on 4:26.5; Hawtrey 17y down on 4:33.66; Perrin 2y down on 4:39.25.
Intermediate time in a 2 mile race [15/04].

2 Miles

9:32.5 p	George Hazael (Deptford)	22.11.44	1	London (Bow)		15 Apr
9:35.0 p	Edward Mills (Bethnal Green)	25.08.41	int	London (HW)		28 Nov
9:52.25 p	Hazael		1	London (HW)		19 Sep
10:00.4 p	Jack White (Gateshead)	1.03.37	int	London (Star)		11 Apr
10:00.8 e p	Edward Golder (Canterbury)	1.07.43	int	London (Star)		11 Apr
10:02.0 p	Hazael		int	Canterbury		4 Apr
10:02.4	John Scott (LAC)	9.09.47	1hc	London (LB)		19 Nov
10:04.6 e p	Hazael		2hc	London (HW)		14 Mar
10:06.0 p	Robert McKinstray (Ayr)	18.04.37	int	Edinburgh		31 Dec
10:08.0	John Morgan (OU)	19.08.47	int	London (LB)	OvC	7 Apr
10:08.2	Edward Hawtrey (CU)	10.10.47	int	London (LB)	OvC	7 Apr
10:09.0 p	Golder		inthc	Canterbury		3 Jan
10:09.0 p	Hazael		inthc	London (HW)		21 Feb

(13/8)

10:09.6	Francis Armitstead (OU)	20.03.49	int	London (LB)	OvC	7 Apr
10:12.5	Alfred Goodier (Macclesfield)	47	1	Congleton		?? Jul
10:14.5	James Edgar (IOM AC)	23.02.51	1	Douglas, IOM		9 Jun
10:17.0 p	William Virtue (Bedfordbury)	21.07.47	inthc	London (Bow)		19 Mar
10:22.2 p	John Fleet (Manchester)	6.04.45	int	Manchester (City)		17 Dec
10:23.4 e	James Warburton (Haslingden)	13.11.45	2	Douglas, IOM		9 Jun
10:23.5 p	G. Ross (Holloway)		c43	1	London (Bow)	30 Apr
10:24.3 e p	Henry Guy (Bow)	19.08.46	2	London (Bow)		12 Sep
10:25.0 p	Billy Mills (Bethnal Green)	09.43	int	London (HW)		20 Jun
10:26.8 e	John Dewyer (Dalton in Furness/IRL)	c41	2	Kirby, IOM		24 Aug
10:28.0	William Perrin (Birmingham Gym)	c45	1	Birmingham (PR)		23 Jul

Noteworthy foreign:

9:35.0 p	Daillebout (Canada)	46	int	London (HW)	28 Nov

Doubtful

9:40.0	Scott		1	Westward Ho!	25 Aug

Reported in the *Exeter Gazette*, (4:36 + 5:04) an amateur world best by some 19 sec if true.

Notes
Estimates: Golder 2y down on 10:00.4; Hazael 35y down on 9:58.5; Warburton 50y down on 10:14.5; Guy 30y down on 10:19.0; Dewyer 4y down on 10:26.0.
Intermediate times: in races at 3 miles [28/11, 31/12, 7/04, 21/02]; 4 miles [4/04; 3/01; 19/03]; 5 miles [11/04]; 10 miles [20/06, 17/12]
The Scotsman gives 10:03int for McKinstray on 31/12. The *Sporting Chronicle* gives 10:12.5 for Edgar at Douglas on 9/06.

3 Miles

15:02.3 e p	Edward Mills (Bethnal Green)	25.08.41	2	London (HW)	28 Nov
15:03.0 p	George Hazael (Deptford)	22.11.44	int	Manchester (City)	17 Dec
15:05.6 p	Jack White (Gateshead)	1.03.37	int	London (Star)	11 Apr
15:05.8 e p	Edward Golder (Canterbury)	1.07.43	int	London (Star)	11 Apr
15:10.0 p	Hazael		int	Canterbury	4 Apr
15:23.5	John Scott (LAC)	9.09.47	2hc	Northampton	24 May
15:25.0 p	Golder		inthc	Canterbury	3 Jan
15:25.0 p	Hazael		inthc	London (HW)	21 Feb
15:30.0	Edward Hawtrey (CU)	10.10.47	1	Cambridge	29 Mar

(9/6)

15:34.6	p	John Fleet (Manchester)	6.04.45	int	Manchester (City)		17 Dec
15:35.0	p	Billy Mills (Bethnal Green)	09.43	int	London (HW)		20 Jun
15:40.0		John Morgan (OU)	19.08.47	1	London (LB)	OvC	7 Apr
15:43.0		Frederick Shann (CU)	21.04.49	2	Cambridge		29 Mar
15:45.0		James Warburton (Haslingden)	13.11.45	1	Sheffield (BL)		2 May
15:48.2	p	William Virtue (Bedfordbury)	21.07.47	inthc	London (Bow)		19 Mar
15:52.3	e	George Stephenson (Norton AC)		2	Sheffield (BL)		2 May
16:02.0		Frederick Maitland (CU)	28.05.50	3	Cambridge		29 Mar
16:02.4		Francis Armitstead (OU)	20.03.49	3	London (LB)	OvC	7 Apr
16:13.0		Robert Benson (OU)	24.09.50	1	Oxford		23 Mar

Noteworthy foreign:

14:58.0	p	Daillebout (Canada)	46	1	London (HW)	28 Nov

Notes
Estimates: Mills 25y down on 14:58; Golder 1y down on 15:05.6; Stephenson 40y down on 15:45.0.
Intermediate times in races at 4 miles [21/02, 3/01, 19/03]; 5 miles [11/04, 4/04] and 10 miles [17/12, 20/06]

4 Miles

20:10.4	p	George Hazel (Deptford)	22.11.44	int	Manchester (City)		17 Dec
20:10.7	e p	Hazel		2hc	Canterbury		7 Jun
20:23.6	p	Jack White (Gateshead)	1.03.37	int	London (Star)		11 Apr
20:23.8	e p	Edward Golder (Canterbury)	1.07.43	int	London (Star)		11 Apr
20:30.0	p	Hazel		1	Canterbury		4 Apr
20:41.6	p	Hazel		1hc	London (HW)		21 Feb
20:48.2	p	John Fleet (Manchester)	6.04.45	int	Manchester (City)		17 Dec
20:51.0	p	Golder		1hc	Canterbury		3 Jan
			(8/4)				
21:04.2	p	Billy Mills (Bethnal Green)	09.43	int	London (HW)		20 Jun
21:11.0	p	William Virtue (Bedfordbury)	21.07.47	2hc	London (Bow)		19 Mar
21:24.0		Henry Riches (South Essex AC)	26.11.46	1	London (LB)	AAC	9 Apr
21:25.6		Edward Hawtrey (CU)	10.10.47	2	London (LB)	AAC	9 Apr
21:45.0	p	William Gentleman (Bethnal Green)	c41	inthc	London (Bow)		2 Apr
21:45.0	p	Harry Andrews (Monmouth)	28.05.31	1	London (LB)		12 Sep
22:10.8	p	John Brighton (Norwich)	14.07.32	1	London (Bow)		28 Feb
22:11.1	e p	Sam Barker (Billingsgate)	5.04.33	2	London (Bow)		28 Feb

Notes
Estimates: Hazel 20y down on 20:07.2; Golder 1y down on 20:23.6; Barker 1¾y down on 22:10.8
Intermediate times in races at 5 miles [11/04] and 10 miles [17/12, 20/06, 02/04]

6 Miles

30:37.0	p	George Hazel (Deptford)	22.11.44	int	Manchester (City)	17 Dec
31:30.4	p	John Fleet (Manchester)	6.04.45	int	Manchester (City)	17 Dec
32:32.4	p	Edward Golder (Canterbury)	1.07.43	int	Manchester (City)	17 Dec
33:20.6	p	William Gentleman (Bethnal Green)	c41	inthc	London (Bow)	2 Apr
35:25.0	p	Charles Mills (Aston)	15.05.46	int	Birmingham (AC)	1 Jan

Note: Intermediate times in races at 7½ miles [1/01] and 10 miles [17/12, 2/04 unfinished]

10 Miles

57:30.0	p	William Smith (Paisley)	27.12.46	1	Glasgow (Sto)	8 Oct

Note
Professional races were held in London (Bow) on 2/04, won by W. Gentleman, unfinished; (Hackney Wick) on 20/06, won by Hazel, unfinished; and Manchester (City) on 17/12, won by Hazel, unfinished at 8½ miles.

120 Yards Hurdles

16 1/5		John Stirling (CU)	5.11.49	1	Cambridge		29 Mar
16 2/5		Stirling		1ht1	Cambridge		26 Mar
16 3/5		Stirling		1	London (LB)	OvC	7 Apr
16 3/5		John Cockerell (Brixton AC)	c46	1	Richmond, Surrey		23 Apr
16.7	e	William Lindsay (Civil Service)	3.08.47	2	Richmond, Surrey		23 Apr
16 ¾		Stirling		1	Cambridge		12 Mar
17.0		Edward Garnier (OU)	5.04.50	1	Oxford		23 Mar
17.0		William Davies (CU)	7.10.48	1ht2	Cambridge		26 Mar
17.0	e	Davies		2	Cambridge		29 Mar

17.0		Stirling		1ht1	London (LB) AAC	9 Apr
17.0		Stirling		1	London (LB) AAC	9 Apr
17.0		G. Holden (Newark FC)		1r1	Newark	21 Apr
17.0		R.S.Smith (Sawley FC)		1r2	Newark	21 Apr
17.0 e		Ernest Toller (LAC)	11.11.47	3	Richmond, Surrey	23 Apr
17.0		Ernie Burney (3rd Dragoon Guards)	18.07.50	1	Aldershot	15 Jul
17.0		Abbot Upcher (CU)	19.10.49	1	Cambridge	25 Nov

Notes
Stirling's 16.2 & Davies' 17.0e were done in windy conditions.
Estimates: Davies 5y down on 16.2; Lindsay ½y down on 16.6; Toller 2½y down on 16.6.

220 Yards Hurdles

24.25		Charles Pickering (Manchester AC)	22.02.48	1	Manchester (Long)	25 Jun
26.8		Pickering		1	Manchester (Long)	13 Aug
28.8 e		William Clague (Burslem)	14.01.47	2	Manchester (Long)	13 Aug
30.0		Sidney Hermon (Preston Gym Soc)	30.01.49	1	Blackpool	20 Aug
30.3 e		Richard Luck (ex-CU)	14.09.47	3	Manchester (Long)	13 Aug
31.6		Rowland Mainwaring (RMC Sandhurst)	11.09.50	1	Camberley	16 Sep
32.0		Benjamin Sefton (Eccles)	5.07.45	1	Pendlebury	14 Aug
32.1 e		James St Clair (RMC Sandhurst)	16.10.50	2	Camberley	16 Sep
32.25		Hermon		1	Preston	29 Jul
32.8 e		Lambert Browne (RMC Sandhurst)	19.08.50	3	Camberley	16 Sep
33.0		Thomas Stretch (Ormskirk)	28.01.51	1	Ormskirk	21 May
		(11/9)				
33.2 e		Arthur Hornby (Blackburn AC)	10.02.47	2	Preston	29 Jul
34.3 e		Richard Mayor (Preston CC)	c40	2	Farnworth	27 Aug
35.5		John Sykes (Rochdale)	c48	1	Blackpool	29 Aug

12 flights						
28.8		H. Wilton (Upton Park FC)		1ht1hc	West Ham	2 Apr
29.0 e		Newton Nixon (Upton Park FC)	c48	2ht1hc	West Ham	2 Apr
29.0		Thomas Kitson (Upton Park FC)	c47	1hc	West Ham	2 Apr
29.3 e		Perry St Quintin (Upton Park FC)	17.12.51	2hc	West Ham	2 Apr
29.9 e		Wilton		3hc	West Ham	2 Apr
30.4		Kitson		1ht2	West Ham	2 Apr

Notes
Estimates: Clague 15y down on 26.8; Luck 25y down on 26.8; St Clair 3y down on 31.6; Browne 8y down on 31.6; Hornby 6y down on 32.25; Mayor 5y down on 33.5.
At West Ham Wilton actually ran 226y (worth 28.1e & 29.2e), Nixon 224y (worth 28.5e). Nixon 1y down on 28.8; St Quintin 2y and Wilton 6y down on 29.0.

440 Yards Hurdles

1:05.1 e p		J. Harris (Ashford)		2ht2hc	Smarden	20 Jun
1:05.5		Harry Beardsell (Huddersfield AC)	c48	1	Bradford	16 Jul
1:05.7 e		Rhys Jones (Northumberland CC)	48	2	Bradford	16 Jul
1:06.0		G. Burbery (Manchester FC)		1	Manchester (WR)	16 Jul
1:06.6		Walter Koch (University Coll Hosp)	19.03.48	1	London (LB)	9 Jun
1:06.75		Hubert Reynolds (Liverpool Gym)	20.02.49	1	Bury	1 Oct
1:06.8 e		Horatio Cross (King's College Hosp)	25.07.46	2	London (LB)	9 Jun
1:07.0 e		Jones		2	Bury	1 Oct
1:07.1 e		Charles Hartley (Charing Cross Hosp)	49	3	London (LB)	9 Jun
1:08.0		John Holway (Taunton)	c43	1rA	Exeter	10 Sep
1:09.75		L.E.Roberts (Exeter)		1	Exeter	20 May
1:10.0		Holway		1rB	Exeter	10 Sep
1:12.0		William Lucas (South Herts)	c47	1	South Herts	28 Jul

Notes
Estimates: Harris inches down on 1:05; Jones 1y down on 1:05.5 (16/07) and on 1:06.75 (1/10); Cross 1y down on 1:06.6; Hartley 3y down on 1:06.6.

12 flights						
1:01.6		Beardsell		1	Bradford	23 Jul
1:07.25		John Clegg (Sheffield FC)	15.06.50	1	Huddersfield	4 Jun
1:12.0		Alexander Mills (Manchester)	c45	1	Kirby, IOM	24 Aug

15 flights						
1:11.8		Shapland Newell (Dublin U/IRL)		1	Dublin (CP), IRL	18 Jun

16 flights						
1:07.0		Clegg		1	Manchester (Long)	25 Jun

20 flights						
1:12.0		Charles Wood (RMA Woolwich)	1.07.51	1	Woolwich	6 May

Note: Clegg's 1:07.25 was over 12 3ft flights and two water jumps.

High Jump

5'10	1.778	James Bland (Dublin U/IRL)	6.04.50	1	Sneem, IRL	15 Aug
5'9	1.753	Robert Mitchell (Manchester AC)	14.07.47	1	London (LB) AAC	9 Apr
5'9	1.753	Frederick Hargreaves (Haslingden)	5.09.50	1	Pendlebury	14 Aug
5'8½	1.740	Hargreaves		1	Burnley	6 Aug
5'8	1.727	Hargreaves		1hc	Liverpool	25 Jun
5'8	1.727	W. Hague (Worrall)		1	Worrall	11 Jul
5'7½	1.715	John Harwood (LAC)	22.06.45	1	Croydon	11 Jun
5'7½	1.715	Joseph Greaves (Manchester AC)	50	1	Rochdale	11 Jun
5'7½	1.715	Hargreaves		1	Haslingden	23 Jul
5'7	1.702	John Duckworth (Haslingden)	44	1	Nottingham	6 Jun
5'7	1.702	H. Howitt (Crick)		2	Worrall	11 Jul
5'7	1.702	Constable O'Connor (Castlebar/IRL)		1	Castlebar, IRL	17 Aug
		(12/9)				
5'6½	1.689	William Curteis (CU)	28.01.49	1	Tunbridge Wells	19 Apr
5'6½	1.689	P. Scott (Norwich)		1	Norwich	23 May
5'6	1.676	Alexander Allfrey (West Kent FC)	12.02.48	1hc	Chislehurst	14 May
5'6	1.676	John Peyton (Castlebar/IRL)		2	Castlebar, IRL	17 Aug
5'6	1.676	Rowland Money (RMC Sandhurst)	51	1	Camberley	16 Sep
5'6	1.676 i	Cox (Lancaster Gym Club)		ex	Lancaster Music Hall	2 Dec
5'6	1.676 i	David Marriage (Preston Gym Club)	52	ex	Lancaster Music Hall	2 Dec

Doubtful:

5'7½	1.715	Alfred Blaine (Brighton College)	3.04.53	1=	Brighton	29 Mar
5'7½	1.715	Arthur Soames (Brighton College)	30.11.52	1=	Brighton	29 Mar

[*The Field* made it 5'6½. A rope was believed to have been used between the standards. Although reported as a school record, the jumps were later disregarded, and 5'6¼ in 1898 was accepted]

Note
The Haslingden papers made the Haslingden result 5'9. The Burnley result is in the *Burnley Advertiser* as Hargreaves 5'8¼, with Edward Moore 2nd at 5'7½. However, *Bell's* gives 5'5 for Moore.

High Jump: Highland & Border

5'11	1.803 p	Andrew Milne (Forfar)	24.11.39	1	Birnam	25 Aug
5'9	1.753 p	James Rough (Kilbarchan)	c46	1	Barrhead	2 Jul
5'8½	1.740 p	Milne		1	Forfar	5 Aug
5'8	1.727 p	Samuel Muir (Stewarton)	c41	1	Greenock	11 Jun
5'8	1.727 p	Milne		1	Montrose	28 Jun
5'8	1.727 p	Milne		1=	Cupar	3 Aug
5'8	1.727 p	Muir		1=	Cupar	3 Aug
5'8	1.727 p	Muir		1=	Alloa	10 Aug
5'8	1.727 p	William Tait (Glendoch)	36	1=	Alloa	10 Aug
5'8	1.727 p	Muir		1=	Alexandria	20 Aug
5'8	1.727 p	Tait		1=	Alexandria	20 Aug
5'7½	1.715 p	Tait		1	Peebles	23 Jul
5'7½	1.715 p	Muir		2	Forfar	5 Aug
		(13/4)				
5'7	1.702 p	John Toy (Dundee)	c46	1	Blairgowrie	27 Jul
5'7	1.702 p	John Bell (Hawick)	c39	1	Kelso	13 Aug
5'6	1.676 p	Donald Dinnie (Aboyne)	8.06.37	1	Aberdeen	4 Jun
5'6	1.676 p	James Fleming (Ballinluig)	18.09.40	3	Greenock	11 Jun
5'6	1.676 p	Owen Toy (Forfar/IRL)	c46	1	Dundee	18 Jun
5'6	1.676 p	William Craig (Uddingston)		2=	Peebles	23 Jul
5'6	1.676 p	Neil McKay (Innerleithen)	6.01.46	2=	Peebles	23 Jul
5'6	1.676 p	Alexander Robson (Denholm)	c47	2=	Peebles	23 Jul
5'6	1.676 p	Moses Campbell (Forfar)	c43	1	Forfar (local)	5 Aug

5'6	1.676	p	Thomas Carruthers (Yetholm)	27.04.40	3	Alloa		10 Aug
5'6	1.676	p	Alexander Fleming (Glasgow)		3=	Alexandria		20 Aug
5'6	1.676	p	Malcolm McGregor (Bonhill)	c45	3=	Alexandria		20 Aug
5'6	1.676	p	Anthony Hall (Edinburgh)	c46	1=	Penicuik		20 Aug
5'6	1.676	p	Matthew Middlemist (Jedburgh)	c39	1=	Penicuik		20 Aug

Pole Vault

10'3	3.12	Robert Mitchell (Manchester AC)	14.07.47	1	London (LB)	AAC	9 Apr
10'3	3.12	Charles Leeds (Newark FC)	45	1	Nottingham		6 Jun
10'3	3.12	Arnold Graves (Civil Service/IRL)	17.11.47	1	Sneem, IRL		15 Aug
10'2	3.10	Edward Bergman (OU)	8.02.49	2	London (LB)	AAC	9 Apr
10'0	3.05	Spencer Jackson (Oundle Gr Sch)	c52	2	Nottingham		6 Jun
9'9	2.97	Frederick Barber (Sheffield United Gym)	c47	3	Nottingham		6 Jun
9'9	2.97	John Musgrave (Fritchley)	01.39	1	Chesterfield		7 Jun
9'8	2.95	John Howard (Beccles)	48	1	Norwich		23 May
9'8	2.95	Barber		2	Chesterfield		7 Jun
9'7	2.92	Barber		1=	Sheffield (BL)		2 May
9'7	2.92	John Whelan (Sheffield FC)	c48	1=	Sheffield (BL)		2 May

(11/9)

Pole Vault: Lakeland, Highland & Border

10'10	3.30	p	David Anderson (Alnwick)	c46	1	Bridge of Allan	6 Aug
10'6	3.20	p	Thomas Shevels (Durham)	c47	1	Bishop Auckland	28 Jun
10'6	3.20	p	Anderson		1	Alloa	10 Aug
10'5½	3.19	p	Anderson		1	Stirling	23 Jul
10'5	3.17	p	Anderson		1	Alva	11 Aug
10'3	3.12	p	Thomas Lawson (Bishop Auckland)		2	Bishop Auckland	28 Jun
10'2½	3.11	p	Anderson		1	Tillicoultry	12 Aug
10'2	3.10	p	Anderson		1	Otterburn	8 Apr
10'2	3.10	p	Mark Shearman (Keswick)	c49	1	Kendal	7 Jun
10'2	3.10	p	Anderson		1	Galashiels	16 Jul
10'1	3.07	p	Anderson		1	Glanton	2 Aug
10'1	3.07	p	William Ewing (Alexandria)	c47	2	Bridge of Allan	6 Aug
10'1	3.07	p	Anderson		1	Crieff	18 Aug
10'1	3.07	p	Anderson		1	Huntly	19 Aug

(14/5)

10'0	3.05	p	Philip Winder (Kendal)	13.12.47	1	Levens	12 May
10'0	3.05	p	William Little (Longtown)	c48	1=	Newcastle	7 Jun
10'0	3.05	p	Anthony Hall (Edinburgh)	c46	2	Galashiels	16 Jul
10'0	3.05	p	William Crichton (Brunty)	05.49	2	Crieff	18 Aug
9'11	3.02	p	David Milne (Forfar)	28.12.42	2	Blairgowrie	27 Jul
9'10	3.00	p	Archibald Mitchell (Alva)	51	2=	Stirling	23 Jul
9'10	3.00	p	A. Stewart		2=	Stirling	23 Jul
9'10	3.00	p	John Allison (Kendal)	8.02.43	2=	Liverpool	6 Jun
9'9	2.97	p	Henry James (Hutton Roof)	c46	1=	Kendal	8 Jun
9'9	2.97	p	Joseph Sedgwick (Lambrigg)	c41	1=	Kendal	8 Jun
9'9	2.97	p	Samuel Muir (Stewarton)	c41	3	Kirkintilloch	15 Jul
9'9	2.97	p	John Stewart (Alloa)	c47	2=	Alloa	10 Aug
9'9	2.97	p	William Tait (Glendoch)	36	2=	Alloa	10 Aug
9'9	2.97	p	William McCombie Smith (Lumphanan)	7.09.47	1=	Aberdeen	24 Sep
9'8	2.95	p	Duncan Ferguson (Alloa)	6.09.49	4	Alloa	10 Aug
9'8	2.95	p	W. Brown (Coupar Angus)		1	Perth	13 Aug
9'7	2.92	p	Andrew Ainslie (Galashiels)	6.04.51	3	Galashiels	16 Jul

Indoors

10'0	3.05 i p	Anderson		1	London (Ag Hall)	15 Apr
9'10	3.00 i p	Allison		2	London (Ag Hall)	15 Apr

Notes

Anderson's Bridge of Allan jump is shown as 10'1, not 10'10, in the *Dumbarton Herald*. *The Scotsman* gives 10'9. Little's jump of 10'0 was "after several futile attempts" (*Newcastle Courant*), but he shared the prize with Anderson, who cleared first time.

Long Jump

21'2½	6.46	Harold Ferguson (RMA Woolwich)	10.02.51	1	Woolwich		3 May
21'1½	6.44	Thomas Clerk (RMC Sandhurst)	c50	2	Woolwich		3 May
21'1	6.43	Charles Devis (Birmingham AC)	30.04.50	1	Atherstone		4 Jul
20'11	6.38	Percy Rivett-Carnac (Harrow School)	12.01.52	1	Harrow		9 Apr
20'10	6.35	Frederick Hargreaves (Haslingden AC)	5.09.50	1	Liverpool		25 Jun
20'10	6.35	Harry Sproston (Birmingham AC)	48	2	Atherstone		4 Jul
20'10	6.35	J. Maugham (Eccles)		1	Pendlebury		13 Aug
20'8	6.30	Edward Prior (Harrow School)	4.01.52	2	Harrow		9 Apr
20'7	6.27	John Ornsby (OU)	1.09.50	1	Oxford		28 Feb
20'7	6.27	Hargreaves		1	Accrington		30 Jul
20'6	6.25	Sidney Hermon (Preston Gym Club)	30.01.49	1	Preston		29 Jul
20'5	6.22	Charles Wood (RMA Woolwich)	1.07.51	3	Woolwich		3 May
20'5	6.22	Thomas Stretch (Ormskirk)	28.01.51	2	Liverpool		25 Jun
20'5	6.22	Thomas Seed (Preston Gym Club)	c50	2	Preston		29 Jul
		(14/13)					
20'3½	6.18	Henry Wilcox (CU)	14.10.49	2	London (LB)	OvC	7 Apr
20'2½	6.16	Edward Bergman (OU)	8.02.49	3	London (LB)	OvC	7 Apr
20'2	6.15	William Walker (OU)	14.12.48	1	Oxford		15 Nov
20'0	6.10	Augustus English (Wellington Coll)	26.09.51	1	Crowthorne		31 Mar
20'0	6.10	John Sykes (Rochdale)	c48	1	Todmorden		16 Jul
19'11¾	6.09	Robert Mitchell (Manchester AC)	14.07.47	1	London (LB)	AAC	9 Apr

Long Jump: Highland & Border

21'0	6.40	p	Samuel Muir (Stewarton)	c41	1	Alloa	10 Aug
20'9	6.32	p	Archibald Mitchell (Alva)	51	2	Alloa	10 Aug
20'7	6.27	p	Muir		1	Motherwell	19 Sep
20'6	6.25	p	Robert Knox (Newstead)	17.09.47	1	Milngavie	2 Jul
20'6	6.25	p	Knox		1	Whitburn	12 Jul
20'2½	6.16	p	Muir		1	Biggar	23 Jun
20'2	6.15	p	Thomas Carruthers (Yetholm)	27.04.40	2	Whitburn	12 Jul
20'2	6.15	p	William Craig (Uddingston)		2	Motherwell	19 Sep
20'0	6.10	p	Knox		1	Lenoxtown	25 Jun
20'0	6.10	p	Muir		1	Dalkeith	10 Sep

Note: The *Alloa Advertiser* gives Mitchell 20'0 at Alloa

Triple Jump

42'6	12.95	J.L.Power (QC Cork/IRL)		1	Cork, IRL	7 Apr
42'2	12.85	Edward Harding (QC Cork/IRL)		1	Cork, IRL	14 Oct
41'6	12.65	John Joyce (QC Cork/IRL)	4.07.49	2	Cork, IRL	7 Apr
41'6	12.65	Daniel Sheehan (Sneem/IRL)		1	Sneem, IRL	15 Aug
41'0	12.50	Power		2	Cork, IRL	14 Oct
39'6	12.04	F.T.Moore		1	Palermo, ARG	25 May
39'5	12.01	Cpl W. Barber (Scots Fusilier Guards)		1	Aldershot	15 Jul
39'4	11.99	James Elder (Derby AC)		1	Derby	8 Jun

Triple Jump: Highland & Border

48'7	14.81	p	Robert Knox (Newstead)	17.09.47	1	Lennoxtown	25 Jun
47'7	14.50	p	Knox		1	Leith	2 Aug
47'1	14.35	p	Knox		1	Biggar	23 Jun
46'10	14.27	p	Knox		1	Bridge of Allan	6 Aug
46'9	14.25	p	Samuel Muir (Stewarton)	c41	1	Alloa	10 Aug
46'6	14.17	p	Knox		1	Hawick	10 Jun
46'3	14.10	p	James Young (Alva)	c47	2	Bridge of Allan	6 Aug
46'2	14.07	p	Knox		1	Lochwinnoch	23 Jul
46'1	14.05	p	Knox		1	Barrhead	2 Jul
45'9½	13.96	p	Knox		1	Dalkeith	10 Sep
45'9	13.94	p	Knox		1	Whitburn	12 Jul
45'5	13.84	p	Muir		1	Kirkintilloch	15 Jul
45'5	13.84	p	Knox		2	Alloa	10 Aug
			(13/3)				
45'3	13.79	p	Peter Campbell (Alexandria)	c43	2	Greenock	11 Jun
45'2½	13.78	p	John Bell (Hawick)	c39	1	Galashiels	16 Jul
45'2	13.77	p	Owen Toy (Forfar/IRL)	c46	1	Dundee	18 Jun

45'2	13.77	p	William Craig (Uddingston)		1	Airdrie		26 Sep
45'1	13.74	p	Gavin Tait (Douglas)	34	2	Whitburn		12 Jul
45'1	13.74	p	Archibald Mitchell (Alva)	51	4	Bridge of Allan		6 Aug
45'0	13.72	p	Thomas Carruthers (Yetholm)	27.04.40	2	Linlithgow		17 Sep
44'10	13.67	p	Alexander Robson (Denholm)	c47	2	Hawick		10 Jun
44'3	13.49	p	P. Lee (Preston)		1	Preston		22 Jan
44'2	13.46	p	William Borland (Edinburgh)	c48	1	Paisley		23 Jun
43'10	13.36	p	Andrew Milne (Forfar)	24.11.39	1	Coupar Angus		21 Jul
43'9	13.33	p	James Rough (Kilbarchan)	c46	3	Greenock		11 Jun
43'7	13.28	p	William Murray (Leith)		3	Leith		2 Aug
43'6	13.26	p	P. Watson (Walton)		2	Preston		22 Jan
43'6	13.26	p	Malcolm McGregor (Bonhill)	c45	2	Paisley		23 Apr
43'4	13.21	p	David Milne (Forfar)	28.12.42	3	Dundee		18 Jun
42'7	12.98	p	Samuel Reid (Bridge of Allan)		1	Dunblane		25 Jun
41'10	12.75	p	James Gray (Craigton)		1	Milngavie		2 Jul

Note: At Bridge of Allan, Muir placed 3rd with over 45'1/13.74, but his mark was not reported. He also had a no-jump of 47'1½/14.36.

Shot

40'10	12.45	John Stone (Liverpool AC)	25.08.42	1	Warrington		20 Aug
38'9	11.81	William Bullock (Indian Civil Service)		1	London (LB)		28 May
38'0	11.58	Robert Mitchell (Manchester AC)	14.07.47	1	London (LB)	AAC	9 Apr
37'10	11.53	F. Batchelor (Peckham)		1	Peckham		11 Aug
37'4	11.38	Alexander Pringle (Edinburgh U)	c42	1	Edinburgh		23 Jun
37'1	11.30	Samuel Lucas (OU)	30.12.47	ex	London (LB)	OvC	7 Apr
36'11	11.25	Lucas		1	Oxford		23 Mar
36'2½	11.04	Lucas		1	London (LB)	OvC	7 Apr
36'0	10.97	Robert Irvine (Edinburgh U)	19.04.53	2	Edinburgh		23 Jun
35'9	10.90	Edmund Phelps (CU)	14.12.47	2	London (LB)	OvC	7 Apr
35'9	10.90	Edward Gittins (Leicester AC)	47	1	Leicester		9 Jun
35'4½	10.78	Henry Domvile (OU)	7.10.48	1hc	Oxford		7 Feb

18lb [with follow]

39'0	11.89	Edward Bor (RMA Woolwich/IRL)	25.08.50	1	Woolwich		3 May
37'7	11.46	Bor		1	Woolwich		6 May

Note: In the Oxford v Cambridge sports Lucas won with 36'2½ after 6 puts. His 37'1ex was an extra put.

Shot: Highland & Border

47'0	14.33	p	Donald Dinnie (Aboyne)	8.06.37	1	Montreal, CAN		11 Aug
43'7	13.28	p	Dinnie		1	Brooklyn, NY, USA		18 Aug
42'6	12.95	p	John George (Tarland)	46	1	Aboyne		9 Aug
42'3	12.88	p	George		1	Aboyne (prize)		9 Aug
41'2	12.55	p	David Donald (Newhills)		1	Easter Skene		25 Jun
41'1	12.52	p	Dinnie		1	Aberdeen		4 Jun
40'2	12.24	p	John Carmichael (Drumlee)	20.02.49	1	Balfron		16 Jul
				(7/4)				
39'2	11.94	p	John Moir (Aberdeen)	27.07.42	2	Aboyne		9 Sep
39'1*	11.91	p	Alexander Grant (Aboyne)		1	Ballater		27 Jul
38'9	11.81	p	William Tait (Douglas)	36	3	Aboyne		9 Sep
38'7	11.76	p	Joseph McHardy (Springburn)	c52	4	Aboyne		9 Sep
38'4	11.68	p	Peter McGregor (Dumdoig, Killearn)		2	Balfron		16 Jul
37'11	11.56	p	William Bremner (Glenbucket)	3.01.47	1	Lumphanan		6 Aug
37'6	11.43	p	James Walker (Skene)		2	Easter Skene		25 Jun
37'6*	11.43	p	George Mearns (Aberdeen)		2	Ballater		27 Jul
37'1	11.30	p	Francis Christie (Cluny)		3	Easter Skene		25 Jun
37'1	11.30	p	James Findlay (Craigiedhu)	c52	1	Colquhonnie		30 Aug
36'11¼*	11.26	p	Peter Bremner (Glenbucket)	20.01.42	3	Ballater		27 Jul
36'9*	11.20	p	James Russell (Huntly)	c48	1	Huntly		19 Aug
36'8	11.18	p	Charles Stewart (Blair Atholl)		4	Ballater		27 Jul
36'8	11.18	p	John Weir		1	Milngavie		27 Jul

Notes: *correct weight assumed from evidence of other years

Weight unstated

44'9	13.64	p	James Fleming (Ballinluig)	18.09.40	1	Dunkeld (prize)	30 Jul
39'0	11.89	p	John Anderson (Edinburgh)		1	Dalkeith	10 Sep
38'9	11.81	p	John Cameron (Leith)		2	Dalkeith	10 Sep

18lb

43'0	13.11	p	Dinnie		1	New York, USA	1 Sep
42'9	13.03	p	Dinnie		ex	Boston, Mass, USA	25 Aug
39'0	11.89	p	Anderson		1	Penicuik	20 Aug
38'5	11.71	p	Cameron		2	Penicuik	20 Aug

21lb

39'5	12.01	p	Fleming		1	Stirling	23 Jul
37'10	11.53	p	McDonald		2	Stirling	23 Jul

22lb by performer

44'4	13.51	p	Fleming		1	Balfron	16 Jul
41'5	12.62	p	Dinnie		1	Dundee	18 Jun
40'10	12.45	p	McDonald		2	Balfron	16 Jul
40'1	12.22	p	George		1	Bridge of Allan	6 Aug
39'2	11.94	p	Stewart		2	Kirkintilloch	15 Jul
38'0	11.58	p	John Scott (St Columbs)		2	Dunkeld	30 Jul
37'10	11.53	p	Anderson		3	Bridge of Allan	6 Aug
37'7	11.46	p	William Glen (93rd Highland Regt)		3	Dunkeld	30 Jul
37'6½	11.44	p	James Michie (Glenlivet)	20.10.46	2	Nairn	6 Aug
37'2½	11.34	p	John MacLagan (Dunfermline)		1	Tillicoultry	12 Aug

Doubtful (see 1868 note)

48'4	14.73	p	Dinnie		1	Greenock	11 Jun
47'0	14.33	p	Fleming		2	Greenock	11 Jun
45'6	13.87	p	Tait		3	Greenock	11 Jun

The *Greenock Advertiser* results are given. The *Dundee Advertiser* gives Fleming 47'2 and Tait 45'5.

Hammer

109'0	33.22		William A. Burgess (OU)	27.12.46	1hc	Oxford		8 Dec
107'2	32.66		Francis Waite (OU)	24.09.46	1	London (LB)	OvC	7 Apr
104'3	31.78		Henry Nicholl (OU)	9.05.49	2	London (LB)	OvC	7 Apr
104'0	31.70		Henry Leeke (CU)	6.02.46	1	Derby		8 Jun
102'5	31.22		Mortimer Shelton (CU)	14.09.48	2hc	Cambridge		26 Nov
102'0	31.09		Leeke		1	London (LB)	AAC	9 Apr
101'11	31.06		Waite		2	London (LB)	AAC	9 Apr
100'10	30.73		Leeke		1	Northampton		24 May
100'8½	30.70		Burgess		2	Northampton		24 May
100'5½	30.62		Burgess		1	Oxford		24 Mar
100'3	30.56		Waite		2	Oxford		24 Mar

(11/5)

96'0	29.26		Alaric Churchward (CU)	11.46	3	London (LB)	OvC	7 Apr
92'7	28.22		John Paterson (CU)	7.12.50	1	Cambridge		16 Nov
90'10	27.69		Cecil Hawkins (CU)	2.02.51	2	Cambridge		16 Nov
90'0	27.43		Francis Birley (OU)	14.03.50	1	Oxford		25 Feb

17lb

94'0	28.65		Matthew Stritch (RIC/IRL)	02.47	1	Castlebar, IRL	17 Aug

Hammer: Highland & Border

112'4	34.24	p	Joseph McHardy (Springburn)	c52	1	Balfron	16 Jul
112'0	34.14	p	Donald Dinnie (Aboyne)	8.06.37	1	New York, USA	1 Sep
108'9	33.15	p	James Fleming (Ballinluig)	18.09.40	2	Balfron	16 Jul
104'4	31.80	p	Donald McDonald (Murthly)		3	Balfron	16 Jul
102'6	31.24	p	Fleming		1	Coupar Angus	21 Jul
102'6*	31.24	p	Fleming		1	Dunkeld	30 Jul

(6/4)

94'0	28.65	p	James Paton (Murthly)	33	3	Coupar Angus	21 Jul
91'9	27.97	p	Alexander McLay (Bonhill)		1	Alexandria	20 Aug
91'6	27.89	p	William Bremner (Glenbucket)	3.01.47	2	Aboyne	9 Sep
91'4½*	27.85	p	John Scott (St Columbs)		2	Dunkeld	30 Jul
90'8*	27.64	p	Charles Stewart (Blair Atholl)		2	Barrhead	2 Jul

| 90'6 | 27.58 p | James Michie (Glenlivet) | 20.10.46 | 2 | Nairn | 6 Aug |

Note: *correct weight assumed from evidence of other years

Weight unstated

105'4	32.11 p	Dinnie		1	Greenock	11 Jun
100'7	30.66 p	John George (Tarland)	46	1	Brechin	10 Sep
100'6	30.63 p	Fleming		2	Greenock	11 Jun
100'5	30.61 p	Bremner		1	Craigievar	17 Aug
92'6	28.19 p	Alexander McLean		3	Greenock	11 Jun
92'6	28.19 p	Peter Ferris (Lumphanan)		2	Craigievar	17 Aug

17lb by performer

119'0	36.27 p	Dinnie		1	Dundee	18 Jun
112'2	34.19 p	Fleming		2	Dundee	18 Jun
96'8	29.46 p	Bremner		1	Lumphanan	6 Aug

18lb by performer

| 108'6 | 33.07 p | Dinnie | | 1 | Edinburgh | 15 Oct |
| 104'0 | 31.70 p | Fleming | | 2 | Edinburgh | 15 Oct |

Other Events

120 Yards

| 11.4 | | William Dawson (CU) | 3.12.50 | 1hthc | Cambridge | 10 Nov |
| 11.5 | | Dawson | | 1hc | Cambridge | 10 Nov |

Strong wind reported

150 Yards

| 15.1 e | | Alfred Eames (LAC) | 50 | 2hc | Belvedere | 18 Jun |

¾y down on 15.0

200 Yards

| 20.2 | | William Dawson (CU) | 3.12.50 | 1 | Cambridge | 15 Nov |

Note: *The Field* made it 20.66

300 Yards

| 30 ½ p | | Frank Hewitt (Millwall) | 8.05.45 | 1 | Melbourne, AUS | 25 Jun |

Straight course

| 31.8 e | | Robert Philpot (CU) | 12.06.50 | 3hc | Cambridge | 22 Nov |

3y down on 31.4

600 Yards

| 1:16.0 p | | Harry Whitehead (Hyde) | 26.04.47 | 1 | Manchester (RO) | 2 Jul |

1000 Yards

| 2:29.8 | | Herbert Wilson (Dublin U/IRL) | | 1 | Dublin (CP), IRL | 17 Jun |

1½ Miles

| 7:06.0 p | | George Hazael (Deptford) | 22.11.44 | int | London (Bow) | 15 Apr |

In a 2 miles race

1 Mile Walk

| 6:48.0 | | Thomas Griffith (South Essex AC) | c39 | int | Leeds | 6 Aug |

In a 2 miles walk

2 Miles Walk

| 14:20.0 p | | George Davison (Hoxton) | 2.09.44 | int | London (Bow) | 12 Feb |

In a 6 miles match

7 Miles Walk

| 55:46.0 | | Thomas Griffith (South Essex AC) | c39 | 1 | London (LB)   AAC | 9 Apr |

Cricket Ball

| 116y 0ft 0in   106.07 | Richard Osborne (Rochdale CC) | 4.11.48 | 1 | Rochdale | 11 Jun |

100 Yards

10.0		John Clegg (Sheffield FC)	15.06.50	1	Ormskirk	20 May
10.0		William Collett (LAC)	18.06.43	1	Dublin (CP), IRL	7 Jun
10.0		Henry Martin (Northampton)	49	1	Hitchin	5 Oct
10.1	e	John Tobin (Lismore AC/IRL)	29.11.47	2	Dublin (CP), IRL	7 Jun
10.1	e	William Dawson (CU)	3.12.50	1	Leeds	5 Aug
10.1	e	Collett		2	Hitchin	5 Oct
10 1/5		Richard Davis (CU)	6.07.49	1	Cambridge	23 Feb
10 1/5		Herman Krohn (CU/SA)	02.50	1	Cambridge	6 Mar
10 1/5		John Wilson (OU)	19.07.48	1	Oxford	11 Mar
10 1/5		Robert Philpot (CU)	12.06.50	1sf1	Cambridge	17 Mar
10 1/5		Philpot		1	Cambridge	18 Mar
10 1/5		Wilson		1	London (LB) OvC	31 Mar
10 1/5		Robert Clement (Red Rovers FC)	c48	1ht1hc	Tufnell Park	6 May
10 1/5		Clement		1hc	Tufnell Park	6 May
10 1/5		Clement		1ht1hc	Tufnell Park	6 May
10.2	e	Edwin Moore (Birkdale)	c46	2	Ormskirk	20 May
10 1/5		Collett		1	Belfast, IRL	9 Jun
10 1/5		Dawson		1	Douglas, IOM	9 Aug
10 1/5		George Johnstone (LAC)	c51	1	London (LB)	21 Oct
10 1/5		Francis Woods (OU)	22.05.50	1ht1	Oxford	10 Nov
10 1/5		Richard Milner (OU)	12.07.49	1	Oxford	11 Nov

School Sports

10 1/5	Richard Brunskill (Clifton Coll)	14.05.53	1	Clifton	24 Mar

Doubtful

10.0		Charles Monnington (Royal Agric Coll)	18.01.50	1	Cirencester	24 Oct
10.1	e	Charles Batters (Royal Agric Coll)	19.02.53	2	Cirencester	24 Oct

The winning time is as given in *Bell's Life*, but the *Athletic Almanack* gives 10 3/5. Batters inches down.

Notes

Estimates: Tobin 1ft down on 10.0; Dawson (5/08) "a shade over 10 sec, greatly helped by the wind";
Collett (5/10) ½y down on 10.0; Moore 1½y down on 10.0.
Clegg's 10.0 was said to have been slightly downhill. This also affects Moore's performance.
Collett (7/06) was given 10.0 by *Bell's*, 10 1/5 in *The Field*, the *Athletic Almanack* and *John Lawrence's Annual*.
Davis and Woods said to have been assisted by strong winds.
Clement's 10 1/5 timings were in separate handicap heats and one final in the members and open races.

220 Yards

23.9	e	William Palmer (Lewisham CC)	c47	2ht3hc	Croydon	17 Jun
24 ½		Arthur Badcock (Civil Service)	12.07.47	1	London (LB)	13 May
24 ¾		John McFarlane (Edinburgh U)	52	1	Edinburgh (GP)	21 Jun
24.9	e	Edmund Alpe (Civil Service)	48	2	London (LB)	13 May
25.0		Frederick Barff (Beaumont Lodge Sch)	54	1	Windsor	11 Apr
25.0	e	James Findlay (Edinburgh U)	8.04.52	2	Edinburgh (GP)	21 Jun
25.0		Edwin Moore (Southport CC)	c46	1	Bury	3 Jul
25 ¼		Henry Dalbiac (RMA)	30.06.50	1	Hertford	30 Aug
25.4	e	George Rayner (Edinburgh U)	50	3	Edinburgh (GP)	21 Jun

Doubtful

22.0	Arthur Malden (CU)	50	1	Ipswich ·	30 Mar

This, if true, would have been a world best, but Malden showed no such form at Cambridge.

23.0	John de Havilland (OU)	11.04.52	1	Oxford	11 Nov
23.7 e	Seymour Dolby (OU)	17.01.51	2	Oxford	11 Nov

Exeter College Sports Freshmen's Race (vide *Athletic Almanack*). *Bell's Life* listed no time and gave
T.A.Nutting second. Neither showed any form in the 100yds in the same sports, and neither competed
in the Oxford Freshmen's Sports a week later. Dolby 6y down.

Notes

Estimates: Palmer 1y down on 23.75 . Alpe 3y down on 24.5. Findlay 2y down on 24.75. Rayner 5y down on
24.75.
R. Hodge (Southport) recorded 22 3/4, and Cecil Eccles (Liverpool) 24.0 at St Helens on 15 Jul, but the course
was said by the *Athletic Almanack* to have been short.

440 Yards

49.75	Robert Philpot (CU)	12.06.50	1hc	Cambridge		7 Mar
49.9 e	Abbot Upcher (CU)	19.10.49	2hc	Cambridge		7 Mar
50.5	Philpot		1	London (LB)	OvC	31 Mar
50.5 e	Philpot		4hc	Cambridge		20 Nov
50.75 p	George Walsh (Royton)	3.02.44	1	Manchester (RO)		28 Jan
50.8 e	Upcher		2	London (LB)	OvC	31 Mar
51.0 e p	James Nuttall (Manchester)	28.12.41	2	Manchester (RO)		28 Jan
51.1 e	Robert Leach (OU)	18.12.49	3	London (LB)	OvC	31 Mar
51.2	Philpot		1	Cambridge		18 Mar
51.2 e	W. Page (LAC)		3=hc	London (LB)		18 Nov
		(10/6)				
52.0	Thomas Jones (Birmingham AC)	c49	1	Birmingham(PR)		29 Jul
52.1 e	Arthur Pelham (CU)	28.12.50	3	Cambridge		18 Mar
52.4 e	Charles Devis (Birmingham AC)	30.04.50	2	Birmingham (PR)		29 Jul
52.5 e	Arthur Dowding (OU)	23.11.48	2	Oxford		10 Mar
52.5	John Clegg (Sheffield FC)	15.06.50	1hc	Douglas, IOM		9 Aug
52.6	William Clague (Stockport)	14.01.47	1	Manchester (RO)		Dec
52.8 e	Walter Betts (Birmingham AC)	50	2	Birmingham (PR)		12 Aug
52.9 e	Henry Dalbiac (RMA)	30.06.50	3	London (LB)	AAC	3 Apr

Road run (see 880y below)

51.25 p	Frank Hewitt (Millwall)	8.05.45	int	Christchurch, NZL	23 Aug

Notes
Estimates: Upcher 1y down on 49.75; Philpot 4y down on 50.0; Upcher 2y down and Leach 5y down
on 50.5; Nuttall 1½y down on 50.75; Pelham 6y down on 51.2 (18/03); Dalbiac 9y down on 51.8 (3/04);
Dowding 4y down on 52.0; Devis 3y down on 52.0; Betts 2y down on 52.5; Page 6y 1ft down on 50.4 (18/11).
J.H.Stretch (Ormskirk) was given 50.5 at St Helens on 15/07 over a course said to be short.

880 Yards

1:58.0 p	Robert Hindle (Paisley)	46	1	Edinburgh	12 Aug
1:59.8 e p	James Nuttall (Manchester)	28.12.41	2hc	Manchester (RO)	1 Apr
2:01.5 e p	Hindle		1hc	Edinburgh	27 Aug
2:02.5	Charles Bryan (Liverpool)	c47	1	Leigh, Lancs	2 Sep
2:02.5 e	George Templer (CU)	22.12.51	3hc	Cambridge	18 Nov
2:03.4	Arthur Pelham (CU)	28.12.50	1	Cambridge	17 Mar
2:04.5	Robert Benson (OU)	24.09.50	1	Oxford	11 Nov
2:04.7 e	Thomas Vaughan (Manchester)	c49	2	Leigh, Lancs	2 Sep
2:04.9 e	Henry MacNaghten (CU)	24.01.50	2	Cambridge	17 Mar
2:05.0	Henry Bryden (Clapham Rovers)	3.05.54	1	Culworth	2 Aug
2:05.0	Walter Betts (Birmingham AC)	50	1	Birmingham (PR)	12 Aug
		(11/10)			
2:05.25	Joseph Moore (Birmingham AC)	3.04.52	1	Birmingham (PR)	5 Aug
2:05.3 e	Augustus Kirby (CU)	22.06.47	3	Cambridge	17 Mar
2:05.4 e	John Scott (LAC)	9.09.47	4hc	Leeds	5 Aug
2:05.6 e	Bernard Wareing (Birmingham AC)	52	2	Birmingham (PR)	5 Aug
2:05.5	William King (Douglas, IOM)	c47	1	Douglas, IOM	9 Aug
2:05.7 e	Thomas Hewitt (CU)	18.11.49	4	Cambridge	17 Mar
2:06.0 e	Sydenham Dixon (LAC)	4.05.48	2	Oxford	11 Nov

Noteworthy road run

1:53.5 p	Frank Hewitt (Millwall)	8.05.45	1	Christchurch, NZL	23 Aug

The time is given as 1:54.75 in some sources. A local newspaper, *The Star*, gave the time, by two official timekeepers, as 1:53.5. An independent timekeeper made it 1:53.75. In a £600 challenge to run under 1:55.75 he
covered the first 440 in 51.25 and was paced for the last 440 by J.G.Harris. The run was on the Riccarton Road,
near Christchurch, and the going was "all but level." The wind "a light but fitful breeze" was "almost direct across
the road."

Notes
Estimates: Nuttall 4y down on 1:59.25; Templer 2y down on 2:02.2; Moore 1½y down on 2:05.0;
MacNaghten 10y down on 2:03.4; Vaughan 15y down on 2:02.5; Scott 6y down on 2:04.5: Wareing 2y
down on 2:05.25; Kirby 13y down on 2:03.4; Hewitt 16y down on 2:03.4; Dixon 10y down on 2:04.5.
Jamieson's *Powderhall & Pedestrianism* (1943) gives Hindle a slower time of 2:02.0 on 12 Aug. The above
time is as given in *Bell's Life*.

Mile

4:20.0	p	Stephen Ridley (Gateshead)	29.07.45	1	Gateshead		11 Mar
4:30.1	e p	Ridley		2hc	London (LB)		7 Apr
4:31.0	p	Albert Bird (Sheffield)	15.08.46	1hc	Dunedin, NZL		24 May
4:31.4		Walter Chinnery (LAC)	19.08.43	1	London (LB)		15 Apr
4:31.8		Chinnery		1	London (LB)	AAC	3 Apr
4:32.0	p	Bird		1hc	Auckland, NZL		10 Apr
4:32.0		Patrick Madden (Kiltower/IRL)		1	Ballinasloe, IRL		28 Jul
4:32.25		John Scott (LAC)	9.09.47	4hc	London (LB)		13 May
4:32.5	p	George Hazael (Deptford)	22.11.44	1	London (Bow)		10 Apr
4:32.5		Scott		2	London (LB)		15 Apr
4:34.7	e	Thomas Christie (OU)	15.10.49	2	London (LB)	AAC	3 Apr
4:35.0		Scott		1	Nottingham		25 May
4:35.0		Pte A. Carson (Cheshire Rifle Vol)		1	Bromborough		5 Aug
4:35.2		Charles Gunton (CU)	26.06.50	1	Cambridge		6 Mar
4:35.2		Christie		1	London (LB)	OvC	31 Mar
		(15/9)					
4:36.0	e	Lewis Evans (CU)	9.07.51	2	Cambridge		6 Mar
4:36.4		Robert Benson (OU)	24.09.50	1hc	Oxford		18 Nov
4:36.7	e	George Urmson (OU)	11.02.51	3	London (LB)	OvC	31 Mar
4:36.9	e	William Haines (OU)	c48	4	London (LB)	OvC	31 Mar
4:37.9	e	Edward Hawtrey (CU)	10.10.47	3	Cambridge		6 Mar
4:39.0		James Edgar (Douglas, IOM)	23.02.51	1	Douglas, IOM		9 Aug
4:39.1	e	Henry MacNaghten (CU)	24.01.50	3	Cambridge		15 Mar
4:39.25		John Nairne (CU)	23.10.46	1	Cambridge		23 Nov

Estimates: Ridley 30y down on 4:25.4; Scott 7y down on 4:31.4 (15/04); Christie 20y down on 4:31.8 (3/04); Urmson 9y and Haines 10y down on 4:35.2 (31/03); Evans "4 or 5y" and Hawtrey 17y down on 4:35.2 (6/03); McNaghten 13y down on 4:37.0 (15/03).
Note: William Gilmour (Liverpool) was given 4:26.0 at St Helens on 15/07 over a short course.

2 Miles

9:49.0	p	Billy Mills (Bethnal Green)	09.43	inthc	London (LB)		30 Oct
9:54.0		John Scott (LAC)	9.09.47	1	London (LB)		21 Jun
10:03.0		Scott		inthc	London (LB)		25 Mar
10:06.0		Scott		int	London (LB)	AAC	3 Apr
10:10.5		Edward Hawtrey (CU)	10.10.47	wo	Cambridge		25 Feb
10:14.0	p	William Park (Glasgow)		1	Kelso		29 Jul
10:14.4	e p	Alexander McCleary (Alexandria)		2	Kelso		29 Jul
10:15.0	p	John Fleet (Manchester)	6.04.45	int	London (HW)		7 Apr
10:15.2	e p	George Hazael (Deptford)	22.11.44	int	London (HW)		7 Apr
10:15.8	e p	J. Hunter (Edinburgh)		3	Kelso		29 Jul
10:16.0	p	Hazael		int	London (HW)		10 Jul
10:16.2	p	Mills		int	London (HW)		10 Jul
10:18.4	p	Hazael		inthc	Canterbury		30 May
		(13/8)					
10:23.5		James Warburton (Haslingden)	13.11.45	1hc	Stoke-on-Trent		9 Aug
10:28.0		Frederick Shann (CU)	21.04.49	int	Cambridge		18 Mar
10:34.5		John Dewyer (Askam CC/IRL)	c41	1	Preston		17 Aug
10:35.0	p	Sam Barker (Billingsgate)	5.04.33	int	London (Bow)		21 Oct
10:35.2	e p	John Brighton (Norwich)	14.07.32	int	London (Bow)		21 Oct
10:36.0		Arthur Somerville (CU)	23.04.50	1	Cambridge		23 Feb
10:36.4	e	John Matthews (LAC)	50	2	Preston		17 Aug
10:37.9	e	William Izard (CU)	51	2	Cambridge		23 Feb
10:38.0		Henry Tytheridge (Civil Service)	26.06.47	1	London (LB)		13 May
10:38.25		Alfred Goodier (Macclesfield)	47	1	Knutsford		8 Jul

Doubtful

9:10.0	p	Albert Bird (Sheffield)	15.08.46	1hc	Auckland, NZL		10 Apr

Reported in the *Daily Southern Cross,* but clearly too fast for the standards of the period.

9:55.0		Henry McBride (Egremont)	50	1	Liverpool		24 Jun

In an amateur match with David Nesbitt (Egremont/IRL b 20.04.47) at Hoylake racecourse

Estimates: McLeary 2y and Hunter 10y down on 10:14.0 (29/07); Hazael 1y down (7/04); Mills 1y down (10/07); Brighton 1y down (21/10); Matthews 10y down (17/08); Izard 10y down (23/02).
Note: Intermediate times in races at 3 miles (18/03), (25/03), 4 miles (3/04), (7/04), (30/05), (10/07) & (30/10); 6 miles (21/10)

3 Miles

15:08.4		John Scott (LAC)	9.09.47	4hc	London (LB)			25 Mar
15:23.4		Arthur Clarke (OU)	22.12.48	1	London (LB)	OvC		31 Mar
15:25.0		Scott		int	London (LB)	AAC		3 Apr
15:27.0	p	George Hazael (Deptford)	22.11.44	int	London (HW)			10 Jul
15:27.0	p	Billy Mills (Bethnal Green)	09.43	int	London (HW)			10 Jul
15:37.0		Frederick Shann (CU)	21.04.49	1	Cambridge			18 Mar
15:37.5		Clarke		1	Oxford			11 Mar
15:39.6		Edward Hawtrey (CU)	10.10.47	3hc	Cambridge			2 Mar
15:43.0	p	John Fleet (Manchester)	6.04.45	int	London (HW)			7 Apr
15:43.1 e p		Hazael		int	London (HW)			7 Apr
15:44.2 e		Hawtrey		2	Cambridge			18 Mar
		(11/7)						
15:46.4 e		Walter Smith-Dorrien (OU)	13.06.51	2	Oxford			11 Mar
15:48.0		James Warburton (Haslingden)	13.11.45	1	Blackburn			25 Dec
15:49.2 e		William Haines (OU)	c48	3	Oxford			11 Mar
16:05.0	p	John Neary (IRL)	41	inthc	Melbourne, AUS			7 Oct
16:10.0	p	Sam Barker (Billingsgate)	5.04.33	int	London (Bow)			21 Oct
16:10.2 e p		John Brighton (Norwich)	14.07.32	int	London (Bow)			21 Oct
16:14.3 e		John Greaves (Wednesday FC)	c48	2	Sheffield (BL)			1 May
16:18.1 e		Frederick Smith (Chesterfield FC)		3	Sheffield (BL)			1 May

Estimates: Hazael "a trifle" down on 15:43.0 (7/04); Hawtrey 40y down on 15:37.0 (18/03); Smith-Dorrien 50y down and Haines 65y on 15:37.5 (11/03); Brighton 1y down on Barker; Greaves 30y and Smith 50y down on 16:08.75 (1/05).
Intermediate times in races at 4 miles (3/04), (7/04), (10/07); 6 miles (21/10); and 1 hour (7/10).
Note: Reports of the winning time by Clarke in the Oxford Sports (11 Mar) vary considerably, and this affects the estimates of times by Smith-Dorrien and Haines. *Bell's Life* made it 15:37.5, and said there were only two reliable watches and one made it 16:07.5. The *Athletic Almanack, The Field and The Times* 16:10.0. We have accepted *Bell's* time, taking into account Clarke's faster run three weeks later at Lillie Bridge.

4 Miles

20:38.0		John Scott (LAC)	9.09.47	1	London (LB)	AAC		3 Apr
20:46.6	p	George Hazael (Deptford)	22.11.44	1	London (HW)			10 Jul
20:52.0 e p		Billy Mills (Bethnal Green)	09.43	2	London (HW)			10 Jul
20:57.0	p	John Fleet (Manchester)	6.04.45	1	London (HW)			7 Apr
21:23.0	p	John Neary (IRL)	41	inthc	Melbourne, AUS			7 Oct
21:23.1 e p		Edward Mills (Bethnal Green)	25.08.41	3	London (HW)			10 Jul
22:02.0		Alfred Wheeler (London Gym S)		2	London (LB)	AAC		3 Apr
22:46.0	p	William Shrubsole (Croydon)	4.07.46	1	Crawley			29 Aug
22:53.0	p	Hazael		1hc	Cambridge			3 Jul
23:37.0		Frederick Rainsford (LAC)	16.09.46	3	London (LB)	AAC		3 Apr

Estimates: B. Mills 25y and E. Mills 200y down (10 Jul).
Note: Intermediate time in 1 hour race.

6 Miles

32:11.0	p	John Neary (IRL)	41	inthc	Melbourne, AUS	7 Oct

Note: Intermediate time in 1 hour race.

10 Miles

55:35.0	p	John Neary (IRL)	41	inthc	Melbourne, AUS	7 Oct
57:00.0	p	William Gentleman (Bethnal Green)	c41	1	London (HW)	26 Dec
64:05.0		Alfred Wheeler (London Gym S)		3hc	Tufnell Park	6 May

Note: Intermediate time in 1 hour race.

120 Yards Hurdles

16 ¼ w	Arnold Kirke-Smith (OU)	23.04.50	1	Leeds			5 Aug
16.4 e	William Davies (CU)	7.10.48	2ht1hc	Cambridge			1 Mar
16 ½	Edward Garnier (OU)	5.04.50	1	Oxford			10 Mar
16 3/5	Davies		1=	London (LB)	OvC		31 Mar
16 3/5	Garnier		1=	London (LB)	OvC		31 Mar
16 3/5	Garnier		1	London (LB)	AAC		3 Apr
16.9 ew	Thomas Kitson (Upton Park FC)	c47	2	Leeds			5 Aug
17.0	Everard Lempriere (OU)	11.01.51	1	Tunbridge Wells			11 Apr

17.0		Arthur Hornby (Brookhouse)	10.02.47	1	Blackburn	20 May
17.0	ew	William Clegg (Sheffield FC)	21.04.52	3	Leeds	5 Aug

School Sports

17.0		Edward Nash (Tonbridge Sch)	53	1	Tonbridge	30 Mar
17.0		Francis Fenwick (Eton College)		1	Eton	7 Nov

Notes
"A strong breeze helped the runners" at Leeds (5/08). Several sources give 17.0 for the OvC dead-heat, but the majority favour 16.6.
Estimates: Davies 2½y down on 16.0 (1 Mar); Kitson 4y and Clegg 4y 1ft down on 16.25 (5/08).

220 Yards Hurdles

29.5		Edwin Moore (Southport CC)	c46	1	Todmorden	15 Jul
29.8	e	James Moorhouse (Bury)	c45	2	Todmorden	15 Jul
30.0	e	Joseph Greaves (Stalybridge AC)	50	3	Todmorden	15 Jul
30.5		William Clague (Burslem)	14.01.47	1	Stoke-on-Trent	9 Aug
30.5		Frederick Hargreaves (Haslingden)	5.09.50	1	Burnley	23 Sep
31.0		John Cockerell (LAC)	c46	1	London (LB)	23 May
31.3	e	John Tickle (St Helens FC)	20.10.48	2	Stoke-on-Trent	9 Aug
31.6	e	Robert Clement (Carlton Hall FC)	c48	2=	London (LB)	23 May
31.6	e	Francis Lark (Ravenscourt Park)	c50	2=	London (LB)	23 May

Note: Estimates: Moorhouse 2y down and Greaves 3y on 29.5; Tickle 5y down on 30.5; Clement and Lark 4y down on 31.0.

440 Yards Hurdles

1:01.0		Charles Cranswick (Leeds)	c47	1	Malton	27 Jul
1:01.8	e	J. Hanson (Ouse RC)		2	Malton	27 Jul
1:04.0		Alfred Henderson (ex-Clifton Coll)	3.05.51	1	Clifton	24 Mar
1:04.0		J. Abbey (Derwent RC)		1	Malton	27 Jul

Notes: Estimate: Hanson 5y down. Abbey won the members-only event.

12 flights

1:05.75		William Clegg (Sheffield FC)	21.04.52	1	Leeds	5 Aug
1:06.6	e	Arnold Kirke-Smith (OU)	23.04.50	2=	Leeds	5 Aug
1:06.6	e	Harry Walker (Manningham AC)	30.10.46	2=	Leeds	5 Aug
1:09.0		Walker		1	Bradford	22 Jul
1:10.0		Alexander Mills (Bridgwater CC)	c45	1	Douglas, IOM	9 Aug

Note: Estimates: Walker and Kirke-Smith 5y down on 1:05.75

15 flights

1:08.5		G. Stevens (King's College Hosp)		1	London (LB)	1 Jun
1:08.9	e	Horatio Cross (King's College Hosp)	25.07.46	2	London (LB)	1 Jun
1:11.0		Russell Austin (S Herts AC)	31.08.46	1hc	Hertford	30 Aug

Notes
Estimate: Cross 2y down on 1:08.5.
Athletic Almanack states 16 flights at Hertford.

High Jump

5'9½	1.765	Robert Mitchell (Manchester AC)	14.07.47	1	London (LB)	AAC	3 Apr
5'9	1.753	Frederick Hargreaves (Haslingden)	5.09.50	1	Pendlebury		5 Aug
5'8	1.727	John Hurst (Louth AC)	1.07.47	1	Louth		7 Aug
5'7½	1.715	Thomas Brown (Edinburgh U)	c49	1	Edinburgh (ACG)		18 Mar
5'7½	1.715	William Curteis (CU)	28.01.49	1	Tunbridge Wells		11 Apr
5'7½	1.715	Joshua McCabe (Ranelagh AC/IRL)		1	Ballinasloe, IRL		28 Jul
5'7	1.702	John Graham (Rossall School)	1.05.51	1	Fleetwood		22 Mar
5'7	1.702	John Forbes (Edinburgh Inst FP)		1	Edinburgh		27 May
5'7	1.702	James Bland (Dublin U/IRL)	6.04.50	1	Dublin (CP), IRL		7 Jun
5'7	1.702	Hargreaves		1	St Helens		15 Jul
5'6½	1.689	R. Sieveright (Edinburgh U)		2	Edinburgh (ACG)		18 Mar
5'6½	1.689	John Gurney (CU)	19.06.49	1	London (LB)	OvC	31 Mar
5'6½	1.689	A. Charlton (Beaumont Lodge Sch)		1	Windsor		10 May
5'6½	1.689	C. Mason (Louth AC)		2	Louth		7 Aug

5'6¼	1.683	Arthur Court (Bebington CC)	c48	1=	Ormskirk		20 May
5'6¼	1.683	Hargreaves		1=	Ormskirk		20 May

Exhibition after winning at 5'6½

5'7	1.702	Gurney		ex	London (LB)	OvC	31 Mar

Doubtful

5'8	1.727	Samuel Burleigh (Hanover CC)	49	1	Peckham	29 Jul

Reported in the *Athletic Almanack*, but other reports suggest a misprint for 4'8

High Jump: Highland & Border

5'9½	1.765	p	Peter Milne (Forfar)		1	Perth	27 Jul
5'9	1.753	p	Donald Dinnie (Aboyne)	8.06.37	1	Perth	28 Jul
5'9	1.753	p	Samuel Muir (Stewarton)	c41	1=	Dalry	2 Aug
5'9	1.753	p	James Rough (Kilbarchan)	c46	1=	Dalry	2 Aug
5'9	1.753	p	Thomas Carruthers (Yetholm)	27.04.40	1=	Crofthead	25 Aug
5'9	1.753	p	Muir		1=	Crofthead	25 Aug
5'8½	1.740	p	Dinnie		2=	Perth	27 Jul
5'8½	1.740	p	Alexander Scott (Edinburgh)		2=	Perth	27 Jul
5'8	1.727	p	Dinnie		1	Wishaw	6 Jul
5'7	1.702	p	Dinnie		1	Peterhead	6 May
5'7	1.702	p	Carruthers		2	Wishaw	6 Jul
5'7	1.702	p	Carruthers		1	Whitburn	11 Jul
5'7	1.702	p	John Bell (Hawick)	c39	1=	Galashiels	15 Jul
5'7	1.702	p	Carruthers		1=	Galashiels	15 Jul
5'7	1.702	p	John Robson (Denholm)	c49	1=	Galashiels	15 Jul
5'7	1.702	p	Dinnie		1	Stirling	22 Jul
5'7	1.702	p	Neil McKay (Innerleithen)	6.01.46	1=	Peebles	22 Jul
5'7	1.702	p	William Tait (Douglas)	36	1=	Peebles	22 Jul
5'7	1.702	p	Muir		1	Alva	10 Aug
5'7	1.702	p	William Bremner (Strathdon)	3.01.47	1=	Strathdon	22 Aug
5'7	1.702	p	James Grant (Tomintoul)		1=	Strathdon	22 Aug
5'7	1.702	p	Alexander Milne (Forfar)		1	Aboyne	31 Aug

(22/13)

Notes

Aberdeen City Council's collection of medals won by Donald Dinnie includes one from Perth Highland Society engraved 'High Leaping 5'10½ Champion Medal, 1871'. No other details are known.

Peter Milne (27/07) and Alexander Milne may be errors for Andrew Milne, a well known jumper, but the names appear in several reports.

Pole Vault

10'4½	3.16	John Wigfull (Sheffield UGC)	2.12.51	1=	Douglas, IOM		9 Aug
10'4½	3.16	Edwin Woodburn (Ulverston)	19.04.50	1=	Douglas, IOM		9 Aug
10'1	3.07	Robert Mitchell (Manchester AC)	14.07.47	1	London (LB)	AAC	3 Apr
10'0	3.05	Wigfull		1	Chesterfield		29 May
10'0	3.05	Woodburn		1	Preston		17 Aug
9'11	3.02	John Musgrave (Fritchley)	01.39	2	Chesterfield		29 May
9'9	2.97	Shapland Newell (Dublin U/IRL)		1	Dublin (CP), IRL		7 Jun
9'9	2.97	Lupton Jackson (Manchester)	24.05.43	1	Pendlebury		5 Aug
9'9	2.97	Musgrave		1	Mansfield		23 Aug
9'8½	2.96	Henry Fullarton (Edinburgh)	22.05.48	1	Glasgow (Ac)		29 Apr
9'8	2.95	Wigfull		1	Sheffield (BL)		1 May
9'7	2.92	William Beever (Winchester Coll)	3.09.54	1=	Winchester		23 Mar
9'7	2.92	John Moyle (Winchester Coll)	19.12.52	1=	Winchester		23 Mar
9'7	2.92	William Powell Moore (LAC)	23.04.46	2	London (LB)	AAC	3 Apr

Pole Vault: Lakeland, Highland & Border

10'3	3.12	p	Thomas Jackson (Jarrow)	c48	1	Newcastle	30 May
10'2	3.10	p	Philip Winder (Kendal)	13.12.47	1	Kendal	2 Mar
10'2	3.10	p	David Anderson (Alnwick)	c46	1	Blairgowrie	31 Jul
10'1	3.07	p	Anderson		1	Coupar Angus	20 Jul
10'0	3.05	p	John Allison (Kendal)	8.02.43	2	Kendal	2 Mar
10'0	3.05	p	Allison		1	Kendal	7 Mar
10'0	3.05	p	John Richardson (Brampton)		2	Newcastle	30 May
10'0	3.05	p	William Borland (Kilbarchan)	c48	1	Whitburn	11 Jul
10'0	3.05	p	Anthony Hall (Edinburgh)	c46	1	West Linton	13 Jul

10'0	3.05	p	Anderson		1	Stirling	22 Jul
10'0	3.05	p	Anderson		1	Jedburgh	28 Jul
10'0	3.05	p	Anderson		1	Kelso	29 Jul
10'0	3.05	p`	Hall		2=	Blairgowrie	31 Jul
10'0	3.05	p	W. Muir (Kilmarnock)		2=	Blairgowrie	31 Jul
10'0	3.05	p	Anderson		1	Glanton	1 Aug
10'0	3.05	p	Borland		1	Leith	1 Aug
10'0	3.05	p	Borland		1=	Bridge of Allan	5 Aug
10'0	3.05	p	Hall		1=	Bridge of Allan	5 Aug
10'0	3.05	p	Borland		1	Tillicoultry	11 Aug
10'0	3.05	p	Borland		1	Crieff	19 Aug
				(20/8)			
9'10	3.00	p	John Wilson (Hutton Roof)	c46	1=	Liverpool	3 Aug
9'10	3.00	p	William Holme (Hutton Roof)	45	1=	Liverpool	3 Aug
9'9	2.97	p	William Crichton (Brunty)	05.49	2=	Coupar Angus	20 Jul
9'9	2.97	p	John Stewart (Alloa)	c47	2=	Coupar Angus	20 Jul
9'9	2.97	p	William Ewing (Bonhill)	c47	2=	Stirling	22 Jul
9'9	2.97	p	Thomas Shevels (Durham)	c47	1	Easington	14 Aug
9'8	2.95	p	Samuel Muir (Stewarton)	c41	1	Alexandria	24 Jun
9'8	2.95	p	P. Hailstones (West Calder)		3=	Whitburn	11 Jul
9'8	2.95	p	P. Thomson (Muirhead)		3=	Whitburn	11 Jul
9'8	2.95	p	Anderson Turner (Salsburgh)	17.03.38	3=	Whitburn	11 Jul
9'8	2.95	p	Andrew Ainslie (Galashiels)	6.04.51	3	Leith	1 Aug

Indoors

10'1	3.07	i p	Winder		1	London (Ag Hall)	7 Apr
10'0	3.05	i p	Anderson		2=	London (Ag Hall)	7 Apr
10'0	3.05	i p	Allison		2=	London (Ag Hall)	7 Apr

Notes
The *Islington Gazette* and other sources give Winder 11'0/3.35 at Ag Hall on 7/04, and 10'9/3.28 to Allison and Anderson. This was probably the official result, but is contradicted by other, more cautious reports, in line with the known form of the athletes.
The *Stirling Observer* gives Ewing 9'10/3.00 for 2= (with Borland) at Stirling.

Long Jump

21'0	6.40		John McFarlane (ex-Edinburgh Inst)	52	1	Edinburgh		27 May
20'11½	6.39		Edward Hodges (OU)	28.02.49	1	Oxford		11 Mar
20'9¼	6.33		Alick Tosswill (ex-OU)	21.01.45	1hc	Harrow		1 Apr
20'8	6.30		Charles Shepherd (RMC)	9.03.48	1	Sandhurst		30 May
20'7½	6.29		Richard Surtees (Malvern Coll)	8.04.53	1	Malvern		25 Mar
20'7	6.27		Bertram Brumell (Durham Sch)	c53	1	Durham		30 Mar
20'6	6.25		Stephen Gatty (OU)	9.10.49	2	Oxford		11 Mar
20'5	6.22		Harry Courtney (Highgate Sch)	23.05.52	1	Highgate		5 May
20'4½	6.21		Henry Griffith (OU)	23.07.50	1	Oxford		14 Nov
20'4	6.20		John Ornsby (OU)	1.09.50	3	Oxford		11 Mar
20'4	6.20		Robert Mitchell (Manchester AC)	14.07.47	1=	London (LB)	AAC	3 Apr
20'4	6.20		Jenner Davies (CU)	10.04.51	1=	London (LB)	AAC	3 Apr
20'4	6.20		Davies		1	Cambridge		30 Nov
				(13/12)				
20'3	6.17		Richard Glover (QC Galway/IRL)	c53	1	Cork. IRL		2 May
20'2½	6.16		Harry Sproston (Birmingham AC)	48	1	Stoke-on-Trent		9 Aug
20'1	6.12		Edward Prior (CU)	4.01.52	1	Cambridge		15 Mar
20'1	6.12		Frederick Hargreaves (Haslingden)	5.09.50	1	Ormskirk		20 May
20'1	6.12		Edward Waltham (Hornsea CC)	25.08.48	1	Hornsea		8 Jul
20'0½	6.11		Arthur Court (Bebington CC)	c48	2	Ormskirk		20 May
20'0½	6.11		John Tickle (St Helens CC)	20.10.48	2	Stoke-on-Trent		9 Aug
20'0	6.10		Hugh Upcher (Rossall School)	28.10.53	1	Fleetwood		20 Mar
20'0	6.10		Augustus English (Wellington Coll)	26.09.51	1	Crowthorne		23 Mar

Long Jump: Highland & Border

22'4	6.81	p	Thomas Carruthers (Yetholm)	27.04.40	1	Leven	5 Jul
21'3½	6.49	p	Robert Knox (Newstead)	17.09.47	1	Jedburgh	28 Jul
21'2	6.45	p	Knox		1	Leith	1 Aug
20'9	6.32	p	James Young (Alva)	c47	2	Leith	1 Aug
20'8	6.30	p	Carruthers		1	Whitburn	11 Jul

| 20'4 | 6.20 | | Carruthers | | 3 | Leith | 1 Aug |
| 20'3 | 6.17 | p | Knox | | 2 | Whitburn | 11 Jul |

Triple Jump

43'9	13.33		Edward Harding (Queens Coll Cork/IRL)		1	Cork, IRL	3 May
43'5	13.23		Joseph Walsh (Queens Coll Cork/IRL)		2	Cork, IRL	3 May
41'2	12.55		Richard Glover (QC Galway/IRL)	c53	1	Galway, IRL	30 Mar

Triple Jump: Highland & Border

48'0	14.63	p	James Young (Alva)	c47	1	Alva	10 Aug
47'8	14.53	p	Robert Knox (Newstead)	17.09.47	1	Leith	1 Aug
47'4	14.43	p	Young		1	Bridge of Allan	5 Aug
47'2	14.38	p	Young		1	Alloa	9 Aug
47'0	14.33	p	Knox		1	Kirkcaldy	8 Jul
46'10	14.27	p	Knox		2	Alloa	9 Aug
46'9	14.25	p	Knox		1	Whitburn	11 Jul
46'6	14.17	p	Knox		1	Galashiels	15 Jul
46'2½	14.08	p	Knox		1	Jedburgh	28 Jul
46'2	14.07	p	Knox		1	Peebles	22 Jul
			(10/2)				
46'0	14.02	p	Samuel Muir (Stewarton)	c41	3	Alloa	9 Aug
45'7	13.89	p	John Bell (Hawick)	c39	2	Jedburgh	28 Jul
44'8	13.61	p	Thomas Carruthers (Yetholm)	27.04.40	2	Whitburn	11 Jul
44'4	13.51	p	Alexander Robson (Denholm)	c47	3	Galashiels	15 Jul
44'0	13.41	p	Peter Campbell (Alexandria)	c43	1	Lennoxtown	8 Jul
43'7	13.28	p	James Rough (Kilbarchan)	c46	2	Pollokshaws	17 Jun
43'4	13.21	p	Donald Dinnie (Aboyne)	8.06.37	1	Leven	5 Jul
43'3	13.18	p	William Craig (Uddingston)		3	Lennoxtown	8 Jul
43'2	13.16	p	Alexander Scott (Swinton)		1	Dalkeith	23 Sep
43'0	13.11	p	Neil McKay (Innerleithen)	6.01.46	2	Peebles	22 Jul
42'8½	13.02	p	John Scott (Dunfermline)		2	Dunfermline	15 Jul
42'3	12.88	p	William Borland (Kilbarchan)	c48	3	Whitburn	11 Jul
42'0	12.80	p	Archibald Mitchell (Alva)	51	2	Stirling	22 Jul
41'10	12.75	p	William Murray (Leith)		2	Penicuik	19 Aug
41'9	12.73	p	John Robson (Buchanan)	c49	2	Balfron	15 Jul
41'9	12.73	p	John Campbell (Alexandria)		2	Dumbarton	12 Aug
41'3	12.57	p	Hugh Andrews (Glasgow)	c52	2=	Wishaw	6 Jul
41'3	12.57	p	Andrew Turnbull		1=	Holystone	c15 Jul
41'3	12.57	p	I. Turnbull		1=	Holystone	c15 Jul
41'0	12.50	p	Hugh Anderson		3	Milngavie	5 Aug
40'9	12.42	p	Thomas Dagg (Linbriggs)	51	2	Pennymuir	22 Mar
40'8	12.40	p	William Henderson		1	Dunblane	8 Jul
40'6	12.34	p	Richard Penny (Leeds)	53	1	Leeds	17 Jun
40'6	12.34	p	David Milne (Forfar)	28.12.42	1	Nairn	19 Aug
40'6	12.34	p	James Black (Glasgow)		2	Linlithgow	16 Sep

Note: Young is given 47'3/14.40 at Bridge of Allan on 5/08 by the *Stirling Observer*

Shot

41'0	12.50	David Lundie (St Andrews U)	23.11.46	1	Edinburgh (ACG)		18 Mar
40'5	12.32	William Forsyth (Edinburgh U)	c49	2	Edinburgh (ACG)		18 Mar
39'0	11.89	Forsyth		1	Edinburgh (GP)		21 Jun
38'11	11.86	Henry Foley (Park AC)	c48	1	Tottenham		8 Jul
38'8½	11.80	Robert Mitchell (Manchester AC)	14.07.47	1	London (LB)	AAC	3 Apr
38'7	11.76	Edward Bor (RMA Woolwich/IRL)	25.08.50	1	Woolwich		8 Jun
37'5½	11.42	Bor		2	London (LB)	AAC	3 Apr
37'3	11.35	Henry Domvile (OU)	7.10.48	1	Oxford		27 Nov
37'1	11.30	Charles Fraser (Met Police)	c39	1	London (LB)		13 Oct
37'0	11.28	George Power (Guy's Hosp)	49	1	London (LB)		1 Jun
35'11	10.95	Edward Tarleton (Birmingham AC)	4.02.47	1	Nottingham		25 May
35'11	10.95	Thomas Stone (Newton-le-Willows CC)	24.01.52	1	Great Harwood		23 Sep
35'10	10.92	William Powell Moore (LAC)	23.04.46	1	Hammersmith		6 May

Note: Shot was 4oz overweight for Forsyth's 39'0 throw.

Shot: Highland & Border
Includes putting the stone

48'5	14.76	p	Donald Dinnie (Aboyne)	8.06.37	2hc	Aberdeen	13 May
47'2	14.38	p	Dinnie		1	Peterhead	6 May
46'11	14.30	p	James Fleming (Ballinluig)	18.09.40	1hc	Aberdeen	13 May
46'9	14.25	p	Dinnie		1	Aberdeen	19 May
46'1	14.05	p	Fleming		2	Peterhead	6 May
46'0	14.02	p	Dinnie		1	Arbroath	29 Jul
45'3	13.79	p	Dinnie		1	Banff	24 Jun
44'6	13.56	p	Fleming		2	Aberdeen	19 May
44'6*	13.56	p	Dinnie		1	Udny	25 Jul
42'6	12.95	p	Fleming		1	Brooklyn, NY,USA	17 Aug
42'3	12.88	p	John George (Grangemouth)	46	1	Bridge of Allan	5 Aug
41'6	12.65	p	John Moir (Strathdon)	27.07.42	3	Aberdeen	19 May
41'4	12.60	p	George		1	Aboyne	31 Aug
41'4	12.60	p	Dinnie		ex	London (CP)	15 Aug
41'3	12.57	p	William Bremner (Glenbucket)	3.01.47	2	Banff	24 Jun
41'2	12.55	p	J. McPherson (Glenlivet)		2	Bridge of Allan	5 Aug
40'10	12.45	p	William Glen (93rd Highland Regt)		1	Edinburgh	8 Jul
40'8	12.40	p	Moir		2	Aboyne	31 Aug
40'1	12.22	p	Dinnie		1	Wishaw	6 Jul
			(19/7)				
39'10	12.14	p	John Anderson (Crieff)		2	Edinburgh	8 Jul
38'0	11.58	p	Charles Stewart (Glenlivet)		1	Ballater	25 Jul
37'3½	11.37	p	J. Murray (Anc Order of Foresters)		1	Edinburgh	8 Jul
37'2	11.33	p	William Drummond		1	Dunblane	8 Jul
36'10*	11.23	p	Lubin Dinnie (Aboyne)	10.08.44	2	Lumphanan	5 Aug
36'7½	11.16	p	William McCombie Smith (Lumphanan)	7.09.47	3	Banff	24 Jun
36'6	11.13	p	Lewis Smith (Speybridge)		1	Nairn	19 Aug
36'3	11.05	p	Peter Ferris (Lumphanan)		2	Aberdeen	20 May
36'3	11.05	p	James Begg (Boyndie)	c45	4	Banff	24 Jun
35'11	10.95	p	W. Brown (Anc Order of Foresters)		2	Edinburgh	8 Jul

Note: *correct weight assumed from evidence of other years

Weight unstated

45'7	13.89	p	D. Dinnie		1	Inverness	21 Sep
44'3	13.49	p	Moir		2	Inverness	21 Sep
42'0	12.80	p	James Smith (Torryburn)		1	Culcross	25 Jul
42'0	12.80	p	Fleming		1	Boston, Mass, USA	1 Sep
39'5	12.01	p	McCombie Smith		1	Leochel-Cushnie	17 Aug
38'8	11.79	p	Owen Duffy (Edinburgh/IRL)	c47	2	Dalkeith	23 Sep
38'6	11.73	p	Joseph McHardy (Springburn)	c52	1	Drymen	2 Jan
37'10½	11.54	p	Ferris		3	Leochel-Cushnie	17 Aug

17lb

40'8	12.40	p	D. Dinnie		1	Newcastle	30 May

18lb

41'4*	12.60	p	Anderson		1	Lasswade	2 Sep
37'0	11.28	p	John Carmichael (Drymen)	20.02.49	1	Balfron	15 Jul
36'3	11.05	p	Charles Mitchell (Corybrook)		1	Strathdon	22 Aug
35'11	10.95	p	Anderson		1	Penicuik	19 Aug

Note: *correct weight assumed from evidence of other years

22lb shot by performer

40'2	12.24	p	D. Dinnie		1	Stirling	22 Jul
38'0	11.58	p	George		2	Stirling	22 Jul
37'1½	11.32	p	John Scott (Kelso)		2	Blairgowrie	31 Jul
36'6	11.13	p	Stewart		2	Springburn	2 Sep
36'0	10.97	p	Moir		1	Aberdeen	22 Aug
35'10	10.92	p	Glen		2	Upper Strathearn	30 Aug

Notes
There were two competitions (open and closed) at the Ancient Order of Foresters meeting at Edinburgh (8/07).
Scottish papers give Dinnie 45'10 for his exhibition put at Crystal Palace on 5/08.
In a memoir in *Health & Strength* in 1912, Dinnie recalled meeting Duffy for the first time at Falkirk this year. After

three throws the result was Dinnie 49'9, Duffy 48'6, McRae 41'10, Anderson 41'8. Three further throws were then made by Dinnie and Duffy. Duffy put 50'0 and Dinnie then did 50'6. He claimed that the ball was 16lb and the ground level. Another account in *Men of Muscle* (1901) said that the ground was slightly downhill. We have not yet traced a contemporary report.

Hammer

105'5	32.13	Alaric Churchward (CU)	11.46	1	London (LB)	OvC	31 Mar
105'5	32.13	William A. Burgess (OU)	27.12.46	1	London (LB)	AAC	3 Apr
102'4	31.19	Burgess		3hc	Oxford		14 Nov
102'2	31.14	Churchward		2	London (LB)	AAC	3 Apr
102'0	31.09	Mortimer Shelton (CU)	14.09.48	1	Cambridge		15 Mar
101'2½	30.85	Henry Nicholl (OU)	9.05.49	2	London (LB)	OvC	31 Mar
100'4	30.58	Henry Leeke (CU)	6.02.46	3	London (LB)	AAC	3 Apr
99'8	30.38	Stephen Gatty (OU)	9.10.49	1	Oxford		9 Mar
99'3	30.25	Shelton		3	London (LB)	OvC	31 Mar
97'0	29.57	Churchward		2	Cambridge		15 Mar
96'0	29.26	Gatty		4	London (LB)	OvC	31 Mar
96'0	29.26	Stephen Brown (OU)	1.06.54	1	Oxford		25 Nov
95'6	29.11	Nicholl		2	Oxford		9 Mar
94'0	28.65	Edward Garnier (OU)	5.04.50	3	Oxford		9 Mar
92'0	28.04	Charles Thompson (CU)	5.12.49	1	Cambridge		18 Nov
91'3	27.81	Henry Domvile (OU)	7.10.48	1	Oxford		28 Nov

Notes
The Oxford v Cambridge result is given differently, with Gatty 2nd and Shelton 3rd in *50 years of Sport at Oxford & Cambridge* and also *Oxford versus Cambridge*, by Abrahams & Bruce-Kerr. Contemporary newspaper reports including *Bell's Life* give the result listed above.

Hammer: Highland & Border

134'2	40.89 p	Donald Dinnie (Aboyne)	8.06.37	1hc	Aberdeen	13 May
128'11	39.29 p	Dinnie		1hc	Dundee	11 Mar
128'1	39.04 p	Dinnie		1hc	Banff (challenge)	24 Jun
127'7	38.89 p	Dinnie		2hc	Aberdeen	25 Mar
126'4	38.51 p	Dinnie		1	Aberdeen	19 May
124'1	37.82 p	Dinnie		ex	London (CP)	15 Aug
123'7	37.67 p	Dinnie		1	Peterhead	6 May
122'8	37.39 p	Dinnie		1	Banff (open)	24 Jun
119'6	36.42 p	Dinnie		1	Arbroath (challenge)	29 Jul
116'8	35.56 p	Dinnie		1	Coupar Angus	20 Jul
116'3	35.43 p	James Fleming (Ballinluig)	18.09.40	2hc	Dundee	11 Mar
115'11½	35.34 p	Fleming		1hc	Aberdeen	25 Mar
114'0	34.75 p	Fleming		2	Aberdeen	19 May
112'6*	34.29 p	Dinnie		1	Glenisla	18 Aug
111'7	34.01 p	Fleming		2hc	Aberdeen	13 May
111'1	33.86 p	Fleming		2	Peterhead	6 May
109'10	33.48 p	William Glen (93rd Highland Regt)		1	London (CP)	15 Aug
		(17/3)				
105'9	32.23 p	John Moir (Strathdon)	27.07.42	1	Aberdeen	26 Aug
105'5	32.13 p	John George (Grangemouth)	46	1	Stirling	22 Jul
105'0	32.00 p	William McCombie Smith (Lumphanan)	7.09.47	4hc	Aberdeen	13 May
103'4	31.50 p	William Bremner (Leochel-Cushnie)	3.01.47	1	Inverness	21 Sep
97'5	29.69 p	Donald Mackintosh (Lochdu)		1	Nairn	19 Aug
96'8*	29.46 p	Peter McHardy (Glasgow)	c48	1	Dunkeld	22 Jul
95'4	29.06 p	James Michie (Corrie)	20.10.46	1	Tomintoul	30 Jul
93'7	28.52 p	Alexander McLay (Bonhill)		2	Stirling	22 Jul
92'5	28.17 p	Peter Ferris (Lumphanan)		2	Lumphanan	5 Aug
92'0	28.04 p	Alexander Roberts (Newtyle)		3	Coupar Angus	20 Jul
91'1	27.76 p	Kenneth McRae (Beauly)	50	3	Nairn	19 Aug

Note: *correct weight assumed from evidence of other years

Weight unstated

113'0	34.44 p	Dinnie		1	Udny	25 Jul
102'7	31.27 p	Dinnie		1	Perth	27 Jul
100'8	30.68 p	Dinnie		1	Inverarnan	1 Sep
98'2	29.92 p	Peter Stewart (Glenlivet)		2	Glenlivet	30 Aug

95'0	28.96 p	McLay		1	Dalry	2 Aug
93'2	28.40 p	Ferris		2	Leochel-Cushnie	17 Aug
19lb						
100'0	30.48 p	Dinnie		1	Perth	28 Jul
20lb						
96'2	29.31 p	Dinnie		1	Upper Strathearn	30 Aug
91'3	27.81 p	George		2	Upper Strathearn	30 Aug
22lb						
92'3	28.12 p	Dinnie		1	Stirling	22 Jul

Notes
This season Dinnie and Fleming used the US style hammer, with tapered handle 1'6" longer (ie 4'6), for their handicap matches, and probably some other Games. At Aberdeen on 25/03, Dinnie also had two throws of 123'0; Fleming's other throws included 114'2 and 115'9. At Crystal Palace on 15/08, Dinnie is given 125'10ex and Glen 110'0 by Scottish papers.

Other Events

110 Yards						
11.0		John Tennent (Leeds/AUS)	31.07.46	1	Leeds	5 Aug
120 Yards						
12.2		Jenner Davies (CU)	10.04.51	1	Cambridge	23 Nov
150 Yards						
14.75 p		John Clowry (Birmingham)	47	1hc	Edinburgh	20 May
200 Yards						
21.0		Charles Devis (Birmingham AC)	30.04.50	1	Much Wenlock	30 May
300 Yards						
32.0		Robert Philpot (CU)	12.06.50	1	Cambridge	22 Nov
straight course						
600 Yards						
1:15.5 p		Dick Buttery (Sheffield)	c50	1	Manchester (RO)	18 Dec
1000 Yards						
2:32.5		Brownlow Martin (Dublin U/IRL)	48	1	Dublin (CP), IRL	7 Jun
¾ Mile						
3:12.0 p		Stephen Ridley (Gateshead)	29.07.45	int	Gateshead	11 Mar
In 1 mile race.						
2000 Yards						
5:42.0 p		Robert Hindle (Paisley)	46	1	Edinburgh	7 Jan
1½ Miles						
7:14.0 p		George Hazael (Deptford)	22.11.44	1	London (Bow)	26 Dec
1 Hour						
10m 1170y		John Neary (IRL)	41	1hc	Melbourne, AUS	7 Oct
1 Mile Walk						
6:56.6 p		Joe Stockwell (Camberwell)	13.01.44	int	London (Star)	30 Jan
This, and the times below, in a 1 hour match v time.						
2 Miles Walk						
14:33.0 p		Joe Stockwell (Camberwell)	13.01.44	int	London (Star)	30 Jan
7 Miles Walk						
56:01.0 p		Joe Stockwell (Camberwell)	13.01.44	int	London (Star)	30 Jan
50 Miles Walk						
9:34:03.0 p		James Redfern (Shoreditch)	2.09.28	wo	London (Bow)	26 Jun

Cricket Ball
111y 0ft 6in 101.65 Frederick Bayer (Guy's Hosp)   14.08.50   1   London (LB)   1 Jun
Note: A. Shaw (AGC, Manchester) threw 112y/102.41 at Whitworth on 12 September, but the surface was said to have been 'situated on a hillside'.

1872 UK Year List

100 Yards

10.0	William Dawson (CU)	3.12.50	1	Sheffield (QG)	13 May
10.0	Brownlow Martin (Dublin U/IRL)	48	1	Dublin, IRL	25 May
10.0	William Clague (Stoke Victoria AC)	14.01.47	1ht1	Stoke-on-Trent	7 Aug
10.1 e	John McLean (QC Belfast/IRL)	19.09.51	2	Dublin, IRL	25 May
10 1/5	Hector Tennent (LAC)	6.04.42	1	London (LB)	23 Jan
10 1/5	Dawson		1	Cambridge	16 Mar
10 1/5	Martin		1	Dublin (CP), IRL	31 May
10 1/5	Martin		1ht1hc	Belfast, IRL	8 Jun
10 1/5	Martin		1hc	Belfast, IRL	8 Jun
10 1/5	Dawson		1ht2hc	Bradford	6 Jul
10 1/5	Dawson		1hc	Bradford	20 Jul
10 1/5	Clague		1	Douglas, IOM	1 Aug
10 1/5	Clague		1	Douglas. IOM	27 Aug
		(13/5)			
10 1/4	Arthur Brodie (CU)	9.05.51	1	Bournemouth	6 Apr
10.3 e	Robert Philpot (CU)	12.06.50	2	Cambridge	16 Mar
10.3 e	George Johnstone (LAC)	c51	2	Sheffield (BL)	13 May
10.3 e	John Tickle (St Helens FC)	20.10.48	2	Pendlebury	3 Aug

School Sports

10.0	A.G.Burn (Ilminster Gr Sch)	57	1	Ilminster	1 May
10 1/4	William Burridge (Epsom College)	54	1	Epsom	18 Oct
10 1/4	William Tomkin (Eton College)	56	1	Eton	8 Nov

Wind Assisted

10 1/5	Frederick Southam (OU)	17.05.50	1	Oxford	8 Mar
10.3 e	James Parsons (OU)	c50	2	Oxford	8 Mar
10.3 e	John Baines (OU)	10.12.47	3	Oxford	8 Mar

". . . with a strong rear wind" (*Oxford Journal*)

Doubtful

10.0	John McFarlane (Edinburgh U)	52	1	Glasgow (WSCG)	13 Apr

Bell's Life had doubts about the distance

Downhill

10.0	Clague		1	Ormskirk	18 May
10.0	Dawson		1	Huddersfield	22 Jun
10.1	Clague		1ht2	Ormskirk	18 May
10.2 e	James Hay Gordon (Liverpool CC)	9.11.49	2ht2	Ormskirk	18 May
10 1/5	Henry Crummack (Pendleton)	50	1ht3	Ormskirk	18 May
10.2 e	Clague		2	Huddersfield	22 Jun

Notes

Estimates: Philpot 'barely 6in' down on 10.2 (16/3); Johnstone 2y down on 10.0 (13/5); Parsons 6in down on 10.2;
Baines 1ft down on 10.2; McLean 2ft down (25/5); Tickle 1ft down on 10.25. Clague 1y down (22/6).
Gordon given second, but "breasted the tape together" with Clague (18/5).
Martin (25/5) variously reported as 10.0 (*The Field, Freeman's Journal* & *John Lawrence's Handbook*), 10.2 and
10.4. He was credited with 10.0 on three occasions in Ireland (25/5, 31/5 and 8/6), but *Bell's Life* doubted them.
However, Bell's remeasured the distance for his 10 1/5 on 31/5 and found it to have been 103y 2in "on good turf
with a slightly favouring breeze." Tennent (23/1) was given 10 2/5 in *Bell's Life*.
The *Isle of Man Times* gave Clague 10.0 at Douglas (1/8), with Sam Widdowson (Nottm Forest FC) 1y down
(10.2e). The *Irish Sportsman & Farmer* gives Martin 10.0 at Belfast on 8/06 and 10.4 in the heat.

220 Yards

23 2/5	George Johnstone (LAC)	c51	1	London (LB)	25 May
23 3/5	Richard Matthews (LAC)		1hc	London (CP)	20 Jul
23.7 e	R.C.Brown (Pirates FC)		2ht2hc	Northampton	5 Aug
23.9 e	Harry Tomlinson (Civil Service)	11.06.46	2	London (LB)	25 May
24.0 e	Brown		2hc	Northampton	5 Aug
24.1 e	Arthur Badcock (Civil Service)	12.07.47	3	London (LB)	25 May
24.5 e	Alexander Mills (Athenaeum Gym S)	c45	2hc	Preston	6 Apr
24 1/2	James Stephenson (Burnley)		1	Clough Fold	15 Jun
24 1/2	John Aston (Manchester)		1	Stalybridge	31 Aug
24 3/4	Sam Widdowson (Nottm Forest FC)	16.04.51	1	Hyde, Cheshire	3 Aug
24.8 e	N. Wright (Rawtenstall)		2	Clough Fold	15 Jun
25.0	John McFarlane (Edinburgh U)	52	1	Edinburgh	6 Apr

Notes
Brown 1ft down on 23.6 and 1½y down on 23.8; Tomlinson 4y and Badcock 6y down on 23.4; Mills 1½y down on 24.25; Wright 2y down on 24.5.

440 Yards

50.1	e	Robert Philpot (CU)	12.06.50	2hc	Cambridge		22 Feb
50.4		Arthur Brodie (CU)	9.05.51	1	Cambridge		16 Mar
50.5		L. Neville (Erith & Belvedere)		1	Erith		15 Jun
50.6	e	Philpot		2	Cambridge		16 Mar
50.8	e	George Templer (CU)	22.12.51	3	Cambridge		16 Mar
50.8	e	Templer		2hc	Cambridge		23 Nov
51.2	e	A.G.Clarke (South Essex AC)		2	Erith		15 Jun
51.2	e	George Urmson (OU)	11.02.51	3ht1hc	Oxford		29 Nov
51.4		Philpot		1	London (LB)	OvC	25 Mar
51.5	e	Arthur Pelham (CU)	28.12.50	4	Cambridge		16 Mar
51.6		Philpot		1ht1	Cambridge		14 Mar
51.7	e	Brodie		2ht1	Cambridge		14 Mar
51.7	e	Brodie		2	London (LB)	OvC	25 Mar
51.75	p	George Walsh (Oldham)	3.02.44	1	Manchester		25 May
51.8		Brodie		1	Sheffield (BL)		13 May
51.9	e	James Parsons (OU)	c50	3	London (LB)	OvC	25 Mar
		(16/9)					
52.0	p	James Davidson (Jarrow)	c48	1	Gateshead		23 Nov
52.1	e	Edmund Loder (CU)	7.08.49	3ht1	Cambridge		14 Mar
52.2		George Johnstone (LAC)	c51	1	London (LB)		15 Jun
52.2		John Potter (Whalley Range)	48	1hc	London (LB)		23 Nov
52.25	p	James Nuttall (Manchester)	28.12.41	1	Manchester (RO)		23 Mar
52.3	e p	James Talbot (Newcastle)	c46	2	Gateshead		23 Nov
52.4		Richard Geaves (CU)	6.05.54	1	Cambridge		16 Nov
52.5	e	Arthur Dalton (CU)	11.07.53	2	Cambridge		16 Nov
52.6		Arthur Dowding (OU)	23.11.48	1ht2	Oxford		7 Mar

School Sports

52.5		Edward Hamley (Uppingham Sch)	02.55	1	Uppingham		4 Mar
52.5		Hugh Hamilton (Marlborough Coll)	26.06.54	1	Marlborough		5 Apr

Doubtful

50.4		Potter		1	Tufnell Park		12 Sep

Said to have been downhill and aided by a strong wind along the straight (*Bell's Life*)

Notes
Philpot ½y down on 50.0 (22/2) and 1½y down on 50.4 (16/3); Templer 3y and Pelham 9y down on 50.4 (16/3); Templer 3-4y down on 50.4 (23/11); Clarke 6y down on 50.5; Urmson 3y down on 50.8; Brodie 6 to 8in down on 51.6 (14/3) and 2y on 51.4 (25/3); Parsons 3y down on 51.4 (25/3); Loder 3y 6in down on 51.6; Talbot 2½y down on 52.0; Dalton 1ft down on 52.4.
Dick Buttery (Sheffield) ran 50.5 in a professional match with Walsh at Manchester (RO) on 27 Jan, but on remeasurement the course was found to be 10y short (51.7e if full distance).

880 Yards

2:00.2	e	Walter Slade (LAC)	6.04.54	3hc	London (CP)		20 Jul
2:00.4		Thomas Christie (OU)	15.10.49	1=	London (LB)	AAC	27 Mar
2:00.4		George Templer (CU)	22.12.51	1=	London (LB)	AAC	27 Mar
2:01.4		Sydenham Dixon (LAC)	4.05.48	1	London (LB)		19 Oct
2:01.6	e	Arthur Pelham (CU)	28.12.50	3	London (LB)	AAC	27 Mar
2:01.6	e	Slade		2	London (LB)		19 Oct
2:01.75		David Watson (Glasgow Academicals)	7.01.54	1	Edinburgh (GP)		19 Jun
2:02.2		Christie		1	Oxford		9 Mar
2:02.8		Templer		1	Cambridge		14 Mar
2:03.0	e	Charles Michod (LAC)	9.10.49	3	London (LB)		19 Oct
2:03.3	e	Pelham		2	Cambridge		14 Mar
		(11/7)					
2:03.5	e	Cuthbert Mapleton (Edinburgh U)	18.08.54	2hc	Edinburgh (GP)		19 Jun
2:03.7	e	Lewis Evans (CU)	9.07.51	3	Cambridge		14 Mar
2:03.8	e	Thomas Hewitt (CU)	18.11.49	4	Cambridge		14 Mar
2:04.4	e	Arthur Dowding (OU)	23.11.48	2	Oxford		9 Mar
2:05.0		H. Illingworth (Chislehurst)		1	Chislehurst		11 May

2:05.0	A. Hepwell (Leicester)		1	Leicester	29 May
2:06.0	Joseph Moore (Birmingham AC)	3.04.52	1	Birmingham (PR)	3 Aug
2:06.0	Frederick Shapcott (Exeter)	c51	1	Chudleigh	1 Sep
2:06.0	Harry Courtney (OU)	23.05.52	1hc	Oxford	5 Nov

Notable performance from 3y start

1:59.8	Charles Mason (LAC)	3.06.51	1hc	London (CP)	20 Jul

Equates to 2:00.3e for full distance

Notes
Slade 3y down on 1:59.8 and 1y down on 2:01.4 (19/10); Pelham 8y down on 2:00.4 (27/03) and 3y down on 2:02.8 (14/03); Michod 11y down on 2:01.4; Evans 6y down on 2:02.8 and Hewitt 'almost level'; Dowding 15y down on 2:02.2; Mapleton 5y down on 2:02.75. *Bell's Life* suspected inaccuracy in measurement of Edinburgh course.

Mile

4:30.5	p	Frank Hewitt (Millwall)	8.05.45	1hc	Melbourne, AUS	2 Mar
4:31.5	p	Robert Hindle (Paisley)	46	1	Gateshead	30 Sep
4:32.5	e p	James McLeavy (Alexandria)	26.10.52	2	Gateshead	30 Sep
4:33.0	p	George Hazael (Deptford)	22.11.44	int	London (LB)	27 May
4:33.5	e p	McLeavy		int	London (LB)	27 May
4:33.5		John Scott (LAC)	9.09.47	1	London (LB)	8 Jun
4:33.6		Walter Slade (LAC)	6.04.54	3hc	London (LB)	13 Jul
4:34.0	e	Scott		3hc	London (LB)	25 May
4:34.4	e p	William Smith (Paisley)	27.12.46	3	Gateshead	30 Sep
4:34.5		Sydenham Dixon (LAC)	4.05.48	1	London (LB)	25 May
4:34.8	e	Dixon		2	London (LB)	8 Jun
4:37.0		Thomas Christie (OU)	15.10.49	3hc	Oxford	17 Feb
4:37.2	e p	McLeavy		inthc	London (LB)	12 Aug
		(13/9)				
4:37.6		Edward Hawtrey (CU)	10.10.47	4hc	Cambridge	17 Feb
4:38.0	e	Charles Mason (LAC)	3.06.51	3	London (LB)	8 Jun
4:38.6		Thomas Hewitt (CU)	18.11.49	1	Cambridge	13 Mar
4:38.8	e	Lewis Evans (CU)	9.07.51	2	Cambridge	13 Mar
4:39.3	e	Charles Michod (LAC)	9.10.49	2	London (LB)	25 May
4:39.4	e	George Templer (CU)	22.12.51	3	Cambridge	13 Mar
4:40.0	e	Charles Gunton (CU)	26.06.50	3	London (LB) OvC	25 Mar
4:41.0		Thomas Baker (ex-OU)	26.04.48	1	Lausanne, SUI	13 Apr
4:41.2	e	Percival Burt (LAC)	c47	4	London (LB)	8 Jun

Notes
McLeavy 6y and Smith 18y down on 4:31.5 (30/9); Hazael & 'McLeavy close at his heels' at 1m in a 4m race (27/5); Scott 10y down on 4:31.5 (25/5); Dixon 8y, Mason 28y & Burt 48y down on 4:33.5 (8/6); McLeavy 1y down on 4:37.0 (Hazael, 10y start, 12/08); Evans 2ft and Templer 4y 2ft down on 4:38.6 (13/3); Michod 30y down on 4:34.5; Gunton 10y down on 4:38.4.
Intermediate times in races at 2 miles (12/08); 4 miles (27/05).

2 Miles

9:26.7	i e p	Billy Mills (Bethnal Green)	09.43	2hc	London (Ag Hall)	3 Feb
9:31.0	p	George Hazael (Deptford)	22.11.44	int	London (LB)	27 May
9:31.4	e p	James McLeavy (Alexandria)	26.10.52	int	London (LB)	27 May
9:39.4	e p	McLeavy		2hc	London (LB)	12 Aug
9:44.5	i e p	Mills		3hc	London (Ag Hall)	10 Feb
9:44.9	i e p	Hazael		4hc	London (Ag Hall)	10 Feb
9:45.0	p	McLeavy		int	Edinburgh (Pow)	24 Aug
9:56.0		John Scott (LAC)	9.09.47	1	London (LB)	6 Sep
10:05.0		James Warburton (Haslingden)	13.11.45	1	Douglas, IOM	27 Aug
10:15.5	e	Charles Kenyon (West Derby)	18.11.48	2	Douglas, IOM	27 Aug
10:17.25		John Dewyer (Ireleth in Furness)	c41	1	Preston	24 Feb
10:18.2	e	Warburton		2	Preston	24 Feb
		(12/7)				
10:25.6		William Gilmour (Liverpool)		1	Knutsford	27 Jul
10:29.0		Charles Gunton (CU)	26.06.50	1hc	Cambridge	13 Feb
10:29.0		Charles Michod (LAC)	9.10.49	4hc	London (LB)	8 Jun
10:29.0		James Edgar (Douglas, IOM)	23.02.51	1	Douglas, IOM	1 Aug
10:30.0		Edward Hawtrey (CU)	10.10.47	int	Cambridge	16 Mar

10:34.0	Percival Burt (LAC)	c47	int	Sheffield (QG)		13 May
10:35.8	John Matthews (LAC)	50	1	Birmingham (PR)		5 Aug
10:36.4	Charles Mason (LAC)	3.06.51	2	Birmingham (PR)		5 Aug
10:36.6 e	S. Gibson (Chester)		2	Vale Royal		18 Jul
10:38.2 e	Lewis Evans (CU)	9.07.51	int	London (LB)	OvC	25 Mar
10:38.4 e	Robert Benson (OU)	24.09.50	int	London (LB)	OvC	25 Mar

Notes
Mills, indoors, 10y down on 9:25.0 (03/02) and 8y down on 9:43.2 (10/02); McLeavy 2y down on 9:31 (27/05) & 2y
down on 9:39 (Hazael, 10y start, 12/08); Hazael 10y down on 9:43.2 (10/02); Kenyon 60y down on 10:05.0 (27/8);
Warburton 5y down on 10:17.25 (24/02);Gibson 1y down on 10:36.4; Hawtrey 'just leading' Evans and Benson in
10:38.0 in 3m (25/03).
Intermediate times in races at 3 miles (16/03; 25/03); 4 miles (27/05;13/05;12/08); 6 miles (24/08).

3 Miles

14:40.0 p	Billy Mills (Bethnal Green)	09.43	int	London (Star)		6 Jul
14:45.0 p	George Hazael (Deptford)	22.11.44	int	London (LB)		27 May
14:45.4 e p	James McLeavy (Alexandria)	26.10.52	int	London (LB)		27 May
14:57.0 p	McLeavy		int	Edinburgh (Pow)		24 Aug
15:26.0	James Warburton (Haslingden)	13.11.45	1	Glossop		18 Sep
15:40.3 e	John Kenworthy (Rochdale)	52	2	Glossop		18 Sep
15:42.5 e	E. Turner (Sheffield PFBC)		3	Glossop		18 Sep
15:43.0i p	Hazael		1hc	London (Ag Hall)		29 Jan
15:44.4	Robert Benson (OU)	24.09.50	1=	London (LB)	OvC	25 Mar
15:44.4	Edward Hawtrey (CU)	10.10.47	1=	London (LB)	OvC	25 Mar
15:48.0	Hawtrey		3hc	Cambridge		27 Feb
15:49.8 e	Arthur Somerville (CU)	23.04.50	3	London (LB)	OvC	25 Mar
15:50.0	Walter Smith-Dorrien (OU)	13.06.51	1	Oxford		9 Mar
15:59.2 e	Percival Burt (LAC)	c47	1hc	London (CP)		20 Jul

Notes
McLeavy 2y down on 14:45.0; Kenworthy 80y and Turner 92y down on 15:26.0; Somerville 30y down on15:44.4;
Burt actually finished 2nd, 2y down on 15:28.8, from a 30sec start, but the winner was disqualified.
Intermediate times in races at 4 miles (27/05; 6/07); 6 miles (24/08).

4 Miles

19:52.0 p	James McLeavy (Alexandria)	26.10.52	1	London (LB)		27 May
21:13.0 p	McLeavy		1	London (LB)		29 Mar
21:31.25	James Edgar (Douglas, IOM)	23.02.51	1	London (LB)	AAC	27 Mar
21:40.8 e p	George Hazael (Deptford)	22.11.44	2	London (LB)		29 Mar
21:42.4 p	William Shrubsole (Croydon)	4.07.46	1	Crawley		27 Aug
21:44.0	Alfred Wheeler (German Gym Soc)		2	London (LB)	AAC	27 Mar
22:22.0	J. Powell (Barnes FC)		3	London (LB)	AAC	27 Mar
22:47.6 e	Henry Hill (LAC)	22.01.52	2hc	London (LB)		9 Mar
22:51.0	Percival Burt (LAC)	c47	1hc	London (LB)		9 Mar

Note
Estimates: Hazael 150y down on 21:13.0: Hill 8y down on 22:46.0.
Hill and Burt in a handicap based on times.

6 Miles

| 31:28.0 p | James McLeavy (Alexandria) | 26.10.52 | 1 | Edinburgh (Pow) | | 24 Aug |
| 32:32.8 e p | William Smith (Paisley) | 27.12.46 | 2 | Edinburgh (Pow) | | 24 Aug |

Notes
Smith 350y down on 31:28.0. No other Intermediate times after 3m were given for McLeavy.

Doubtful

| 29:27.0 p | Albert Bird (Sheffield) | 15.08.46 | ex | Moonta, AUS | | 28 Sep |

Billed as "the great feat of 6 miles within the half-hour" and over a 28-lap course

10 Miles
No recorded performances have been found. The professional, Albert Bird (Sheffield), ran 11 miles in 1:00.40.0 in
Moonta, near Adelaide, AUS on 25 Sep, claimed as 56:30 in the *Wallaroo Times*, but there are doubts about the
measurement of the course.

120 Yards Hurdles

16.4 e	Edward Rice (Northampton AC)	c51	2ht1hc	Hammersmith		4 May
16 2/5	Francis Lark (AAC)	c50	1	Worthing		10 Sep
16.5 e	John Reay (LAC)	9.07.53	2ht1hc	Hammersmith		4 May
16.6 e	Graham Willmore (Crystal Palace AC)	23.10.52	2	Worthing		10 Sep
16 4/5	Edward Garnier (OU)	5.04.50	1	London (LB)	OvC	25 Mar
16 4/5	John Stirling (LAC)	5.11.49	1	London (LB)	AAC	27 Mar
16 4/5	Reay		1	London (LB)		25 May
16 4/5	John Brockbank (AAC/CU)	22.08.48	1	Newark		27 May
16.9 e	Henry Beauchamp (CU)	25.12.51	2hc	Cambridge		27 Feb
16.9 e	Beauchamp		2	London (LB)	OvC	25 Mar
16.9 e	Garnier		2	London (LB)	AAC	27 Mar
17.0	Willmore		1ht2	Worthing		10 Sep
17.0 e	Beauchamp		3ht1hc	Cambridge		21 Nov
	(13/8)					
17 1/5	George Power (Guy's Hosp)	49	1	London (LB)		13 Jun
17 ¼	Henry Masters (St Bart's Hosp)	c52	1ht2	London (LB)		13 Jun
17.3 e	Edward Prior (CU)	4.01.52	3	London (LB)	OvC	25 Mar
17.5	Arthur Jervoise (Royal Agric Coll)	19.09.48	1	Cirencester		23 Oct

School Sports

17.0	Charles Smith (Tonbridge Sch)	51	1	Tonbridge	20 Mar
17.0	G.E.Davey (Christ's Coll)		1	Finchley	24 Apr
17.3 e	Walter Bicknell (Christ's Coll)	13.05.53	2	Finchley	24 Apr
17.5	William Robinson (Clifton Coll)	25.04.55	1	Clifton	1 Apr

Notes
Rice 1y down on 16.2; Reay 2ft down on 16.4; Willmore 1y down on 16.4; Beauchamp 4 or 5in down on 16.8 (27/2); 1ft down on 16.8 (25/3);and 1y and inches down on 16.8 on 21/11; Garnier ½y and Prior 3y down on 16.8 (27/3); Bicknell 1½y down on 17.0. Bell's Life reported the OvC race as 17.0, but other sources give 16.8. Bell's also reported Reay's time on 25/5 as 17 2/5.

220 Yards Hurdles

29.0	Sam Widdowson (Nottm Forest FC)	16.04.51	1	Stoke-on-Trent	7 Aug
29.6 e	William Clague (Stockport)	14.01.47	2	Stoke-on-Trent	7 Aug
30.8	John Aston (Manchester)		1	Southport	8 Jun
31.0 e	Clague		2	Southport	8 Jun
31.8	Henry Turner (Newton)	50	1	Hyde, Cheshire	3 Aug
32.0	Clague		1	Lurgan, IRL	7 Sep
32.5 e	David Rhodes (Huddersfield AC)	25.03.47	2hc	Blackley	10 Aug
32.8	Raymond Wickham (Bristol)	50	1	Clifton	20 Jul
33.2	Thomas Calvert (Huddersfield)	50	1	Huddersfield	22 Jun
33.25	W.W.Barcol (Owen's College)		1	Manchester	2 May
33.3 e	Alfred Hancock (Bath)	c49	2	Clifton	20 Jul
33.4	Clague		1ht	Southport	8 Jun
	(12/9)				
33.4	George Dunsmuir (Bowdon CC)	25.08.55	1hc	Sale	28 Sep
33.5 e	John Vickerman (Huddersfield)	17.01.52	2	Huddersfield	22 Jun
33.8 e	Henry Joliffe (Bristol)	c48	3	Clifton	20 Jul
34.0	John Hitchen (Stacksteads)	c53	1	Bacup	17 Aug
34.0	James Gorman (Lurgan AC/IRL)	31.10.50	1hc	Lurgan, IRL	7 Sep
34.0	R. Walker (Manchester CC)		1hthc	Sale	28 Sep

12 Flights

33.0	Widdowson		1	Preston	2 Aug

Notes
Clague 4y down on 29.0 (7/8) and 1y down on 30.8 (8/6); Rhodes 3y down on 32.0; Hancock 3y and Joliffe 6y down on 32.8 (20/7); Vickerman 1½y down on 33.2 (22/6).

440 Yards Hurdles

1:07.0	John Kinder (Chislehurst)	20.03.50	1	Chislehurst	11 May
1:07.0	William Clague (Stoke Victoria AC)	14.01.47	1hc	Douglas, IOM	27 Aug
1:09.0	Gunner Brunt (Royal Marines)		1	Portsmouth	28 Jun
1:10.0	James Warburton (Haslingden)	13.11.45	1	Clough Fold	15 Jun
1:10.0	Alexander Mills (Blackley CC)	c45	1	Glossop	18 Sep
1:10.2 e	James Royle (Manchester)	50	2	Glossop	18 Sep

1:10.5		Reginald Miller (Dublin U/IRL)	49	1	Dublin (CP), IRL	1 Jun
1:10.8		H.C.Mills (West Kent FC)		1	Bradford	20 Jul
1:11.0		Abram Abrams (Longsight CC)	c52	1	Compstall	15 Jun
1:12.2 e		William Hamilton (Dublin U/IRL)	1.07.50	2	Dublin (CP), IRL	1 Jun
1:13.0		Pte White (Royal Marines)		2	Portsmouth	28 Jun
1:13.2		Joseph Hadfield (Compstall)	17.02.49	1	Compstall (local)	15 Jun
1:14.4 e		John Vickerman (Huddersfield AC)	17.01.52	1	Compstall	15 Jun
1:15.0		Miller		1	Dublin (LCG), IRL	10 Sep
1:15.0 e		George Sherwin (Compstall FC)	c53	2	Compstall (local)	15 Jun

Notes
Royle 1y down on 1:10.0; Hamilton 10y down on 1:10.5; Vickerman 20y down on 1:11.0; Sherwin 10y down on 1:13.2.
Warburton's 1:10.0 reported as 1:01.0 in the *Sporting Chronicle*.

12 Flights
1:04.0		Clague		1hc	St Helens	20 Jul
1:05.0		David Rhodes (Huddersfield AC)	25.03.47	1	Shepley	31 Aug
1:08.8		Vickerman		1	Bradford	6 Jul
1:09.6 e		Thomas Calvert (Huddersfield)	50	2	Bradford	6 Jul
1:10.6 e		William Coulson (Manningham CC)	46	3	Bradford	6 Jul

Notes: Calvert 5y down and Coulson 11y down on 1:08.8.

12 Flights and twice over water
1:14.8		Charles Timms (Cheltenham Coll)	19.09.54	1	Cheltenham	6 Apr
1:14.8		Clague		1	Huddersfield	22 Jun
1:15.7 e		Charles Jenkins (Cheltenham Coll)	28.05.56	2	Cheltenham	6 Apr

Notes: Jenkins 5y down

16 Flights
| 1:14.6 | | Sam Widdowson (Nottm Forest FC) | 16.04.51 | 1 | Douglas, IOM | 1 Aug |

18 Flights
| 1:10.0 | | Charles Tylecote (Clifton) | 13.11.47 | 1 | Clifton | 2 Apr |

20 Flights
| 1:10.4 | | Clague | | 1hc | Lurgan, IRL | 7 Sep |
| 1:13.8 e | | Miller | | 2hc | Lurgan, IRL | 7 Sep |

Notes: Miller 20y down on 1:10.4 (7/09).

High Jump
5'8½	1.740	John Gurney (CU)	19.06.49	1	Cambridge	13 Mar
5'7¾	1.721	Robert Mitchell (Manchester AC)	14.07.47	1	Sheffield (QG)	13 May
5'7½	1.715	Edward Prior (CU)	4.01.52	2	Cambridge	13 Mar
5'7½	1.715	William Curteis (RMC)	28.01.49	1	Sandhurst	4 Oct
5'7¼	1.708	Michael Glazebrook (Dulwich Coll)	4.08.53	1	Dulwich	27 May
5'7	1.702	Francis Woods (OU)	22.05.50	1	Oxford	7 Mar
5'7	1.702	Thomas Davin (Carrick/IRL)	51	wo	Belfast, IRL	8 Jun
5'7	1.702	George Warren (Liverpool)	5.02.52	1=	Liverpool	24 Aug
5'7	1.702	Arthur Court (Bebington CC)	c48	1=	Liverpool	24 Aug
5'6¾	1.695	Pte Healy (1st Battn Royal Scots)		1	Warley	19 Apr
5'6½	1.689	Frederick Swanwick (CU)	28.05.51	3	Cambridge	13 Mar
5'6½	1.689	Warren		1	Bebington	20 Jul
5'6½	1.689	Alfred Pearson (Nottm Forest FC)	51	1	Ripley	23 Jul
		(13/12)				
5'6	1.676	John Graham (OU)	1.05.51	2	Oxford	7 Mar
5'6	1.676	James Green (QE School, Ipswich/IRL)	c54	1	Ipswich	9 Apr
5'6	1.676	James Bland (Dublin U/IRL)	6.04.50	1	Dublin (CP), IRL	3 Jun
5'6	1.676	Joseph Greaves (Stalybridge AC)	50	1	Southport	8 Jun
5'6	1.676	Lewis James (South Norwood AC)		1	Stroud Green	15 Jun
5'6	1.676	Thomas Brown (Edinburgh U)	c49	1	Edinburgh (GP)	19 Jun
5'6	1.676	Charles Grundy (Bebington CC)	c50	2	Bebington	20 Jul
5'6	1.676	John Harwood (LAC)	22.06.45	1	Douglas, IOM	1 Aug

Notes
The *Derby Mercury* report of Pearson's jump stated '…we understood he afterwards cleared 6ft.'

The *Rotherham Independent* of 14/05: 'Robert Mitchell did 5ft 10in some time since.'
Daniel Fraher (Dungarvan/IRL) is said to have cleared 5'8/1.727 this year in Ireland in an all-around match with Michael Branagan (date and venue uncertain).

High Jump: Highland & Border

5'9	1.753	p	Hugh Andrews (Glasgow)	c52	1	Lasswade	7 Sep
5'8	1.727	p	Samuel Muir (Stewarton)	c41	1	Stirling	20 Jul
5'8	1.727	p	Andrew Milne (Forfar)	24.11.39	1	Alloa	14 Aug
5'7	1.702	p	Andrews		1	Hawick	11 Jun
5'7	1.702	p	Muir		1	Pollokshaws	15 Jun
5'7	1.702	p	Muir		1	Ellon	17 Jun
5'7	1.702	p	John Robson (Denholm)	c49	2	Stirling	20 Jul
5'7	1.702	p	Andrews		1=	Falkirk	27 Jul
5'7	1.702	p	Muir		1=	Falkirk	27 Jul
5'7	1.702	p	Muir		1	Leith	6 Aug
5'7	1.702	p	Thomas Carruthers (Yetholm)	27.04.40	1=	Alva	15 Aug
5'7	1.702	p	Milne		1=	Alva	15 Aug
5'7	1.702	p	McAndrew (Hawick)		1=	Hawick	20 Sep
5'7	1.702	p	Muir		1=	Hawick	20 Sep
5'7	1.702	p	Andrews		1=	Paisley	31 Aug
5'7	1.702	p	Muir		1=	Paisley	31 Aug
				(16/6)			
5'6	1.676	p	Donald Dinnie (Aboyne)	8.06.37	1	Paterson, NY, USA	24 Jun
5'6	1.676	p	Andrew Crombie (Montrose)		1	Coupar Angus	18 Jul
5'6	1.676	p	John Wilson	c46	2	Lasswade	7 Sep

Pole Vault

10'3½	3.14		Edwin Woodburn (Ulverston)	19.04.50	1	Todmorden	20 Jul
10'3	3.12		Woodburn		1	Newton-le-Willows	31 Aug
10'1	3.07		Edwin Dawes (Highworth)	12.08.52	1	Frome	2 May
10'0	3.05		Gerald Onslow (RMC)	7.02.53	1	Chislehurst	11 May
10'0	3.05		Walter Kelsey (Hull CC)	04.51	1	Newark	27 May
9'11	3.02		Onslow		1	Woolwich	14 May
9'11	3.02		Dawes		ex	Clifton	20 Jul
9'11	3.02		Edward Mallard (Carlton C&AC)	49	ex	Clifton	20 Jul
9'10	3.00		John Wigfull (Sheffield FC)	2.12.51	1	Mansfield	11 Jul
9'9½	2.98		William Law (Stacksteads)	1.12.53	1	Bacup	17 Aug
9'9	2.97		Frederick Short (Wellington Coll)	28.04.55	1	Crowthorne	8 Mar
9'9	2.97		Mallard		1	Clifton	20 Jun
9'9	2.97		Woodburn		1	Lancaster	7 Aug
9'9	2.97		Mallard		1	Barnstaple	21 Aug
9'8	2.95		Arthur Penton (RMA)	6.10.54	2	Woolwich	14 May
9'8	2.95		William Lawes (Northallerton)	15.02.51	1	Northallerton	20 May
9'8	2.95		Onslow		1	Erith	15 Jun
9'8	2.95		Michael Ellison (Mansfield FC)	50	2	Mansfield	11 Jul
9'7½	2.93		John Trotter (Repton Sch)	8.04.54	1	Repton	6 Apr

Pole Vault: Highland, Lakeland & Border

10'9	3.28	p	William Crichton (Brunty)	05.49	1	Birnam	29 Aug
10'8	3.25	p	David Anderson (Alnwick)	c46	1=	Alva	15 Aug
10'8	3.25	p	Anthony Hall (Edinburgh)	c46	1=	Alva	15 Aug
10'7	3.23	p	James Lamond (Pitcur)		2	Birnam	29 Aug
10'6	3.20	p	Anderson		1	Blairgowrie	22 Jul
10'2	3.10	p	John Graham (Carlisle)	c51	1=	Hendon	20 May
10'2	3.10	p	John Musgrave (Fritchley)	01.39	1	Durham	20 May
10'2	3.10	p	Whitehead		1=	Hendon	20 May
10'2	3.10	p	J. Jackson (Sunderland)		1	Durham	27 May
10'2	3.10	p	William Borland (Kilbarchan)	c48	1=	Pollokshaws	15 Jun
10'2	3.10	p	Hall		1=	Pollokshaws	15 Jun
10'2	3.10	p	Anderson		1	Galashiels	20 Jul
				(12/9)			
10'1	3.07	p	David Milne (Forfar)	28.12.42	1	Forfar	9 Aug
10'0	3.05	p	John Kerss (Glasgow)	12.04.50	3	Alva	15 Aug
9'11½	3.04	p	C. Mason		1	Leithfield, NZL	6 Dec
9'11	3.02	p	John Richardson (Brampton)		1	Newcastle	21 May

9'10	3.00	p	John Allison (Kendal)	8.02.43	1	Musgrave	19 Jun
9'10	3.00	p	D. Kerr (Govan)		2	Galashiels	20 Jul
9'10	3.00	p	James Stewart (Dundee)		2=	Forfar	9 Aug
9'10	3.00	p	R. Wood (42nd Highlanders)		2	Kelso	17 Aug
9'9	2.97	p	Robert Jackson (Jarrow)		2	Newcastle	21 May
9'8	2.95	p	Jacob Field (Galashiels)		3=	Galashiels	20 Jul
9'8	2.95	p	William Bruce (Falkirk)		3	Falkirk	27 Jul
9'8	2.95	p	Philip Winder (Kendal)	13.12.47	1	Bolton	20 Jul
9'8	2.95	p	James Campbell (Calder)		2	Leith	6 Aug

Note
Graham and Whitehead were credited with 10'5 on 20/05 by *London Daily News*.

Long Jump

22'7	6.88		Jenner Davies (CU)	10.04.51	1	London (LB)	AAC	27 Mar
21'6	6.55		Thomas Stretch (Ormskirk AC)	28.01.51	1	Bebington		20 Jul
21'5	6.53		Davies		1	London (LB)	OvC	25 Mar
21'3	6.48		Arthur Court (Bebington CC)	c48	2	Bebington		20 Jul
21'2	6.45		John Tickle (St Helens)	20.10.48	1	Liverpool		24 Aug
21'0½	6.41		Davies		1	Cambridge		14 Mar
21'0	6.40		Stretch		2	Liverpool		24 Aug
				(7/4)				
20'11	6.38		John Gurney (CU)	19.06.49	2	Cambridge		14 Mar
20'9	6.32		Brownlow Martin (Dublin U/IRL)	48	1	Dublin (CP), IRL		3 Jun
20'8	6.30		Edward Harding (QC Cork/IRL)		1	Cork, IRL		25 Apr
20'8	6.30		Frederick Hargreaves (Haslingden)	5.09.50	1	Newton-le-Willows		31 Aug
20'6½	6.26		David Kennedy (QC Cork/IRL)		2	Cork, IRL		25 Apr
20'6	6.25		Hugh Upcher (OU)	28.10.53	2	London (LB)	OvC	25 Mar
20'6	6.25		Loftus Thornhill (ex-Eton Coll)	8.10.53	1	Lausanne, SUI		13 Apr
20'6	6.25		O'Brien (IRL)		1	Lahinch, IRL		nd
20'5	6.22		James Stephenson (Burnley)		1	Bacup		17 Aug
20'4	6.20		Edward Leggatt (Clapham Rovers FC)	c50	1	Clapham		13 Apr
20'4	6.20		James Wheble (RMA)	29.01.53	1	Woolwich		14 May
20'4	6.20		J. Darcy (Borris/IRL)		1	Borris, IRL		20 Sep
20'3	6.17		Ralph Dixon (CU)	51	3	Cambridge		14 Mar
20'3	6.17		Francis Cator (64th Regt)	7.06.51	2	Lausanne, SUI		13 Apr
20'3	6.17		Edward Nash (OU)	53	1	Oxford		13 Nov

Notes
Davies on 14/3: 20'6 - 20'11 - 20'4 - 20'7 - 21'0½ - 21'0; Gurney's 4th jump 20'8.
Davies on 25/3: 20'5½ - 21'4 - 20'9¾ - 20'11½ - 21'4 - 21'5.
Davies on 27/3 (AAC): 20'8½ - 21'5 - 22'7 - 21'9.
John Boyd (QC Belfast/IRL) did an exhibition of 21'2 after winning at 20'0 at Lurgan on 7 Sep, but the take-off was reported as downhill.

Long Jump: Highland & Border

20'7	6.27	p	Samuel Muir (Stewarton)	c41	1	Stirling	20 Jul
20'5	6.22	p	Archibald Mitchell (Alva)	51	1	Stirling (local)	20 Jul
20'4	6.20	p	Muir		1	Bridge of Allan	3 Aug
20'3	6.17	p	Robert Knox (Newstead)	17.09.47	1	Jedburgh	26 Jul
20'3	6.17	p	Knox		1	Dalkeith	10 Aug

Note
Muir's 20'4 on 3 Aug at Bridge of Allan was for "running distance leap over 3ft hurdle"

Triple Jump

45'0	13.72		Pte Healy (1st Battn Royal Scots)		1	Warley	19 Apr
44'0	13.41		Finucane (IRL)		1	Lahinch, IRL	nd
43'9	13.33		Edward Harding (QC Cork/IRL)		1	Cork, IRL	24 Apr
42'6	12.95		Richard Glover (QC Galway/IRL)	c53	1	Galway, IRL	20 Mar

Notable Junior:

| 39'6 | 12.04 | | Vernon Royle (Rossall School) | 29.01.54 | 1 | Fleetwood | 8 Mar |

Triple Jump: Highland & Border

48'1	14.66	p	Samuel Muir (Stewarton)		c41	1	Wishaw	1 Aug
47'10	14.58	p	Robert Knox (Newstead)		17.09.47	1	Jedburgh	26 Jul
47'0	14.33	p	Knox			1	Alloa	14 Aug
46'8	14.22	p	Knox			1	Hawick	8 Jun
46'7	14.20	p	Knox			1	Edinburgh	29 Jun
46'7	14.20	p	Alexander Robson (Denholm)		c47	2	Jedburgh	26 Jul
46'6	14.17	p	Knox			1	Alva	15 Aug
46'6	14.17	p	Knox			1	Tillicoultry	16 Aug
46'4	14.12	p	Muir			1	Falkirk	27 Jul
46'4	14.12	p	Muir			1	Hawick	20 Sep
46'3	14.10	p	Muir			1	Bridge of Allan	3 Aug
46'2	14.07	p	Peter Campbell (Alexandria)		c43	2	Wishaw	1 Aug
				(12/4)				
45'10	13.97	p	Charles Yeaman (Galashiels)		52	2	Galashiels	20 Jul
45'8	13.92	p	Archibald Mitchell (Alva)		51	2	Bridge of Allan	3 Aug
44'7	13.59	p	James Young (Alva)		c47	2	Leith	6 Aug
44'6	13.56	p	Hugh Andrews (Glasgow)		c52	2	Hawick	11 Jun
44'4	13.51	p	George Black (Dumfries)			3	Hawick	11 Jun
44'4	13.51	p	William Borland (Kilbarchan)		c48	3	Falkirk	27 Jul
44'0	13.41	p	John Leyland (Preston)		c47	1	Preston	30 Mar
44'0	13.41	p	Robert Rough (Kilbarchan)			2	Pollokshaws	15 Jun
44'0	13.41	p	John Don			1	Dunblane	13 Jul
43'7	13.28	p	W. Grass (Bamber Bridge)			2	Preston	30 Mar
43'4	13.21	p	Thomas Carruthers (Yetholm)		27.04.40	2	Biggar	26 Jun
43'3	13.18	p	Thomas Aitken (Walkerburn)		23.05.53	1	Innerleithen	10 Aug
42'9	13.03	p	Hugh Anderson			1	Blantyre	13 Jul
42'9	13.03	p	James Rough (Kilbarchan)		c46	2	Paisley	31 Aug
42'7	12.98	p	T. Finnie			2	Blantyre	13 Jul
42'6	12.95	p	D. Patterson			1	Stonehaven	31 Aug

Shot

42'6	12.95	David Kennedy (QC Cork/IRL)			1	Cork, IRL	25 Apr
42'5	12.93	Edward Bor (Royal Engineers/IRL)	25.08.50		1	London (LB) AAC	27 Mar
39'10	12.14	Edward Hunter (Crewe)			1	Daresbury	2 Sep
39'8	12.09	William Forsyth (Edinburgh U)	c49		1	Edinburgh	1 Jun
39'0	11.89	Charles Fraser (Met Police)	c39		1	London (LB)	27 Jun
38'9	11.81	Thomas Stone (Newton-le-Willows)	24.01.52		1	Sheffield	8 Jul
38'5½	11.72	Robert Mitchell (Manchester AC)	14.07.47		1	Sheffield	13 May
38'4½	11.70	Bor			2	Sheffield	13 May
38'4½	11.70	Stone			1	Newton-le-Willows	31 Aug
37'7	11.46	Nicholas Littleton (CU)	11.01.53		1	Cambridge	18 Nov
37'6	11.43	William Powell Moore (LAC)	23.04.46		1	London (LB)	20 Apr
37'6	11.43	Stone			2	Daresbury	2 Sep
37'5½	11.42	Henry Domvile (OU)	7.10.48		1	London (LB) OvC	25 Mar

Extra throw

42'11	13.08	Kennedy			ex	Dublin, IRL	22 May
39'9	12.12	Mitchell			ex	Sheffield	13 May
39'7	12.06	Bor			ex	Sheffield	13 May

'Slightly downhill'

43'4	13.21	Robert Irvine (Edinburgh U)	19.04.53		1	Edinburgh	19 Jun
42'0	12.80	Forsyth			2	Edinburgh	19 Jun

Shot: Highland, Border & Professional
Includes putting the 16lb stone

46'0*	14.02	p	Donald Dinnie (Aboyne)		8.06.37	1	Newcastle	20 May
44'9½	13.65	p	James Fleming (Ballinluig)		18.09.40	1	Brooklyn, NY, USA	22 Aug
43'3	13.18	p	Owen Duffy (Edinburgh/IRL)		c47	1	Edinburgh	29 Jun
42'3*	12.88	p	Charles Danford			1	Greenock	22 Jun
41'6	12.65	p	John Moir (Strathdon)		27.07.42	1	Insch	8 Jun
41'3	12.57	p	William Bremner (Glenbucket)		3.01.47	1	Aberdeen	20 Jul
41'2	12.55	p	G. Fraser (93rd Highlanders)			2	Edinburgh	29 Jun
40'6	12.34	p	Charles Lucas (Kirriemuir)			1	Forfar	9 Aug
40'3½	12.28	p	John Anderson (Edinburgh)			2	Brooklyn, NY, USA	22 Aug

40'0	12.19	p	Moir			1	Bon Accord	29 Jun
				(10/9)				
39'11	12.17	p	John Cameron (Leith)			3	Edinburgh	29 Jun
39'9	12.12	p	Dick Buttery (Sheffield)		c50	1=	Ripley	23 Jul
39'9	12.12	p	William Lievesley (Bampton)		c51	1=	Ripley	23 Jul
39'8½*	12.10	p	John George (Tarland)		46	2	Greenock	22 Jun
39'8	12.09	p	D. Leighton (Glentyrie)			2	Forfar	9 Aug
39'7	12.06	p	Donald McDonald (Lairg)			1	London (CP)	25 Jul
39'3½*	11.98	p	Alexander Ritchie (Greenock)			3	Greenock	22 Jun
39'2	11.94	p	Peter McHardy (Alexandria)		c48	1	Paisley	31 Aug
39'0	11.89	p	John Gray (Aberdeen)			2	Bon Accord	29 Jun
39'0	11.89	p	Charles Stewart (Glenmuick)			1	Glasgow	6 Sep
38'8	11.79	p	Hugh McKerracher (Strath Fillan)		47	1	Strath Fillan	28 Aug
38'6	11.73	p	John Sutherland (Aberdeen)			1	Stoneywood	13 Jul
38'5	11.71	p	Andrew Innes (Aberdeen)			1	Ellon	15 Jun
37'10	11.53	p	David Donald (Stoneywood)			2	Stoneywood	13 Jul
37'10	11.53	p	William McGregor (Park Villa)			2	Strathdon	20 Aug
37'9	11.51	p	James Russell (Forgue)		c48	2	Insch	8 Jun

Note: *correct weight assumed from evidence of other years
Dinnie and Fleming were touring America this year

Doubtful

44'1	13.44	p	J. Mackenzie		1	Golspie	22 Jul
43'6	13.26	p	J. Smith		2	Golspie	22 Jul
42'5	12.93	p	J. Macbeath		3	Golspie	22 Jul

Weight unstated

47'1	14.35	p	Dinnie		1	Paterson, NJ, USA	24 Jun
45'2	13.77	p	Fleming		2	Paterson, NJ, USA	24 Jun
41'10	12.75	p	McDonald		1	Bridge of Allan	3 Aug
40'6	12.34	p	Anderson		3	Paterson, NY, USA	24 Jun
40'6	12.34	p	R. Reid (Edinburgh)		1	Lasswade	7 Sep
40'4	12.29	p	William Graham (Dalkeith)		1	Dalkeith	10 Aug
40'3	12.27	p	Stewart		2	Bridge of Allan	3 Aug
				(7/7)			
39'7	12.06	p	John MacLagan (Dunkeld)		3	Bridge of Allan	3 Aug
39'6	12.04	p	A. Stewart		2	Dalkeith	10 Aug

17lb

43'0	13.11	p	Dinnie		1	Newcastle	20 May
42'6	12.95	p	Fleming		2	Newcastle	20 May

18lb

44'1	13.44	p	James Goodwin (Denny)		1	Stirling	20 Jul

Hammer

112'2	34.19		William A. Burgess (OU)	27.12.46	1hc	Oxford		2 Nov
111'7	34.01		Henry Leeke (ex-CU)	6.02.46	1	London (LB)	AAC	27 Mar
111'1	33.86		John Paterson (CU)	7.12.50	2	London (LB)	AAC	27 Mar
110'3	33.60		Burgess		1	Derby		19 Oct
109'0	33.22		Edward Garnier (OU)	5.04.50	1hc	Oxford		8 Feb
108'0	32.92		Stephen Brown (OU)	1.06.54	1	Oxford		16 Nov
107'6	32.77		Francis Birley (OU)	14.03.50	1	Oxford		8 Mar
107'3	32.69		Garnier		2	Oxford		8 Mar
105'6	32.16		Brown		3	Oxford		8 Mar
105'6	32.16		Charles Thompson (CU)	5.12.49	1	Cambridge		13 Mar
105'3	32.08		Burgess		3	London (LB)	AAC	27 Mar
105'2	32.05		Paterson		1	London (LB)	OvC	25 Mar
104'8	31.90		Garnier		4	London (LB)	AAC	27 Mar
				(13/7)				
104'0e	31.70		Thomas Todd (OU)	3.06.50	4	Oxford		8 Mar
101'2	30.84		Charles Fraser (Met Police)	c39	1	London (LB)		27 Aug
97'10	29.82		Maurice Davin (Suir RC/IRL)	29.06.42	1	Dublin, IRL		25 May
96'0	29.26	p	Edward Hunter (Crewe)		2	Derby		19 Oct

Notes
In the AAC championships, Leeke also had a throw of 108'0 and Paterson 110'5.

Estimated throw for Todd "only about three feet behind the first two."
Hunter was disqualified, when found to be a professional.

Hammer: Highland & Border

108'0	32.92	p	John Sutherland (Aberdeen)		1	Huntly (open)	23 Aug
106'4	32.41	p	Peter McHardy (Alexandria)	c48	1	Stirling	20 Jul
106'0	32.31	p	Joseph McHardy (Springburn)	c52	1	Balfron	13 Jul
106'0	32.31	p	John Moir (Strathdon)	27.07.42	2	Huntly (open)	23 Aug
104'10	31.95	p	John Scott (Dunkeld)		2	Stirling	20 Jul
103'10	31.65	p	Donald McDonald (Lairg)		3	Stirling	20 Jul
101'3	30.86	p	McDonald		1	London (CP)	25 Jul
100'11	30.76	p	William Bremner (Glenbucket)	3.01.47	1	Inverness	19 Sep
100'6½	30.65	p	Moir		2	Inverness	19 Sep
99'4	30.28	p	McDonald		2	Balfron	13 Jul
98'5	30.00	p	James Russell (Huntly)	c48	1	Huntly (local)	23 Aug

(11/8)

Weight unstated

119'0	36.27	p	J. McHardy		1	Milngavie	31 Aug
108'4	33.02	p	Donald Dinnie (Aboyne)	8.06.37	1	Paterson, NY, USA	24 Jun
107'10	32.87	p	Moir		1	Stonehaven	31 Aug
107'0	32.61	p	William McLay (Bonhill)		2	Milngavie	31 Aug
104'8	31.90	p	Sutherland		2	Stonehaven	31 Aug
104'0	31.70	p	J. Sim (Aberdeen)		3	Milngavie	31 Aug
101'2	30.84	p	J. Stewart (Portlethen)		3	Stonehaven	31 Aug

(8/7)

Note: The Crystal Palace result on 25/7 is as given in the *Perthshire Courier*. *Bell's Life* made it 108'9 (indistinct) and 99'0. Dinnie and Fleming were touring America this year and Dinnie injured his arm early in the tour.

Other Events

120 Yards

12.0	William Palmer (LAC)	c47	1	London (CP)	20 Jul

150 Yards

15 1/3	Archibald Hamilton (CU)	22.12.47	1	Cambridge	20 Feb

200 Yards

20.5 e	Arthur Brodie (CU)	9.05.51	2hc	Cambridge	25 Nov
[6y down on 19.8]					

300 Yards

31.8 e	Robert Philpot (CU)	12.06.50	3hc	Cambridge	19 Nov
[5ft down on 31.6]					

600 Yards

1:15.5 p	James Davidson (Jarrow)	c48	1	Gateshead	6 Jul

1000 Yards

2:19.2 e p	James Nuttall (Manchester)	28.12.41	2hc	London (LB)	4 Mar
[10y down on 2:17.8]					
2:19.75 p	Nuttall		1	Manchester (RO)	13 Jan

1½ Miles

7:08.4	Sydenham Dixon (LAC)	4.05.48	1	London (LB)	13 Jul

1 Mile Walk

6:45.0 p	Joe Stockwell (Camberwell)	13.01.44	int	London (LB)	22 Apr
in a 4 miles match, unfinished					

2 Miles Walk

13:50.0 p	Joe Stockwell (Camberwell)	13.01.44	int	London (LB)	22 Apr
in a 4 miles match, unfinished					

7 Miles Walk

56:30.0	Henry Steib (Preston Gym Soc)	27.08.52	1	Preston	4 May

Cricket Ball

120y 1ft 0in 110.03	Charles Hodges (OU)	6.10.53	1	Oxford	2 Nov

100 Yards

10.0	George Urmson (OU)	11.02.51	1	London (LB)	OvC	31 Mar
10.0	John Tennent (WSCC/AUS)	31.07.46	1	Glasgow (WSCG)		19 Apr
10.0	Marceline Chabrile (QC Cork/IRL)	c51	1	Cork, IRL		23 Apr
10.0	R. Tucker (Bridport)		1	Crewkerne		23 Jun
10 1/5	Robert Philpot (CU)	12.06.50	1ht1	Cambridge		25 Mar
10 1/5	Henry Crummack (Western CC)	50	1	Rochdale		5 Jul
10 1/5	Reginald Miller (Dublin U/IRL)	49	1	Dublin (CP) IRL ICAC		7 Jul
10 ¼	Edward Nash (OU)	53	1	Oxford		10 Feb
10 ¼	Richard Surtees (OU)	8.04.53	1	Oxford		13 Feb
10 ¼	Arthur Riddle (OU)	c53	1	Oxford		17 Feb
10 ¼	Edward Monck (OU)	24.09.51	1ht1	Oxford		13 Mar
10 ¼	Charles Barrett (OU)	50	1ht3	Oxford		13 Mar
10 ¼	Philpot		1	Cambridge		26 Mar
10 ¼	T. Hazel (Witney)		1	Witney		14 Apr
10 ¼	Alfred Pearson (Nottm Forest FC)	51	1	Nottingham		26 Apr
10 ¼	John McLean (NICC/IRL)	19.09.51	1	Cork, IRL		19 May
10 ¼	George Blaxter (Derby)	11.03.56	1	Hyde		19 Jul
10.3 e	Jenner Davies (CU)	10.04.51	2	London (LB)	OvC	31 Mar
10.3 e	Robert Summerhayes (Somerset)	14.04.53	2	Montreal, CAN		20 Sep

School sports

10 ¼	Thomas Lang (Clifton Coll)	22.06.54	1	Clifton	28 Mar

Downhill

9 4/5	John Clegg (Sheffield FC)	15.06.50	1	Leicester	26 Jun

Doubtful

10.0	John Curtis (Leeds AC)	22.07.51	1	Burley-in-Wharfedale	26 Apr

"Distances were not exactly as represented on the card." (*Yorkshire Post*)

10.0	R. Dent (New College, Southsea)		1	Southsea	19 Jun

All timings rounded to nearest second.

10.1 e	William Coulson (Manningham)	46	2	Burley-in-Wharfedale	26 Apr

Notes
Estimates: Davies 2y down on 10.0;
Coulson 2ft down on 10.0; Summerhayes
6in down on 10¼.
Urmson's 10.0 as in *Bell's Life,* Shearman's
Athletics and *Fifty Years of Sport* and
Oxford versus Cambridge, by Abrahams
and Bruce-Kerr. Others made it slower.
Bell's Life regarded Crummack's time as
dubious. Nash said by *The Field* to have
been assisted by a strong wind.
Chabrile's country of origin uncertain. The
name is also spelt Chabrel/Chatrell in other
sources.

220 Yards

22 4/5	John Reay (Civil Service)	9.07.53	1	London (LB)	17 May
23.1 e	George Johnstone (Civil Service)	c51	2	London (LB)	17 May
23.2 e	Henry Tobin (Indian CS)	18.09.51	3	London (LB)	17 May
23.9 e	Alfred Oldfield (Birmingham AC)	2.10.53	2hc	Birmingham (PR)	27 Sep
24 ¼	William Blaxter (Derwent RC)	29.03.54	1ht2	Knutsford	2 Aug
24 2/5	William Clague (Civil Service)	14.01.47	1	Manchester	20 Sep
24.6 e	Harry De Moist (SLH)	28.10.50	2h2t	Knutsford	2 Aug
24 ¾	George Gower (St Albans)	6.11.49	1	St Albans	24 May
24 4/5	Blaxter		1	Southport	7 Jun

Doubtful

24.4 e	Wogan (Guildford GS)		2hc	Guildford	3 Apr

1y down on 24.25 in school sports.

Notes
Estimates: Johnstone 2y down on 22.8; Oldfield ½y down on 23.8; Tobin 3½y down on 22.8; De Moist 3y down
on 24.25. The Lillie Bridge race on 17/05 was described by the *London Standard* as "very fast with a wind behind"
but it was partly around a turn.

440 Yards

48.25 p	Dick Buttery (Sheffield)		c50	1hc	Gateshead	4 Oct
51.0 e	John Potter (LAC)		48	2hc	Tufnell Park	20 Oct
51.25	Thomas Snow (OU)		11.09.52	3hc	Oxford	20 Nov
51.4	George Templer (CU)		22.12.51	1	Cambridge	25 Mar
51.4	George Urmson (OU)		11.02.51	1	London (LB) OvC	31 Mar
51.4 e	Snow			2hc	Oxford	8 Nov
51.5	John Clegg (Sheffield FC)		15.06.50	1	Stoke-on-Trent	5 Aug
51.6	Reginald Miller (Dublin U/IRL)		49	1	Dublin (CP) IRL ICAC	7 Jul
51.6	George Grasett (CU/CAN)		16.09.49	1	Cambridge	12 Nov
51.7 e	Richard Bell (NICC/IRL)			2	Dublin (CP) IRL ICAC	7 Jul
51.7 e	John McLean (NICC/IRL)		19.09.51	3	Dublin (CP) IRL ICAC	7 Jul
51.75	Clegg			1	London (LB)	28 Jun
51.8 e	Arthur Brodie (CU)		9.05.51	2	Cambridge	25 Mar
51.8	George Gower (GWR)		6.11.49	1hc	Ealing	20 Sep
		(14/12)				
51.9 e	Arthur Pelham (CU)		28.12.50	3	Cambridge	25 Mar
52.0 e	Sam Widdowson (Nottm Forest FC)		16.04.51	2	Stoke-on-Trent	5 Aug

School sports

50.75	Edward Hamley (Uppingham Sch)		02.55	1	Uppingham	?? Mar

Doubtful

50.0	Frederick Shapcott (Exeter)		c51	1	Exmouth	18 Sep
50.2 e	Harry Shapley (Torquay)		5.02.52	2	Exmouth	18 Sep

Several timings at Exmouth were impossible, including 150y (under 14) in 13.0. Shapley 1y down.

Notes
Estimates: Potter 8y down on 50.0; Snow 'rather over a yd' down on 51.2 (8/11; Brodie 3y & Pelham 3½y down on 51.4 (25/3); Bell ½y down on 51.6; McLean 2ft 6 down on 51.6; Widdowson 4y down on 51.5. Gower (51.8) was put back 1y for going over his mark so probably ran 51.7.

880 Yards

1:59.75	Arthur Pelham (CU)		28.12.50	1	Cambridge	26 Mar
2:00.0 e	George Templer (CU)		22.12.51	2	Cambridge	26 Mar
2:00.0	Walter Slade (LAC)		6.04.54	4hc	London (LB)	21 Jun
2:01.25	Edward Sandford (OU)		11.05.51	4hc	Oxford	13 Nov
2:02.0	Slade			1	London (LB)	4 Oct
2:02.0 p	J. Dyson (Outlane)		c45	1	Manchester (RO)	6 Dec
2:02.5 p	James Davidson (Jarrow)		c48	1	Gateshead	7 Jun
2:02.6 e p	J. Hopper (Fairfield)		c46	2	Manchester (RO)	6 Dec
2:02.8 e p	Stephen Ridley (Gateshead)		29.07.45	2	Gateshead	7 Jun
2:02.8	George Gower (GWR)		6.11.49	1	Ealing	20 Sep
2:03.5	Alfred Courtney (Dublin U/IRL)		02.53	1	Dublin (CP) IRL ICAC	7 Jul
2:03.75	Joseph Moore (Birmingham AC)		3.04.52	1=	London (LB)	28 Jun
2:03.75	F.W.Todd (GWR)			1=	London (LB)	28 Jun
2:04.0	Sandford			1	Oxford	15 Mar
2:04.0	Moore			1	Birmingham (ALG)	16 Aug
		(15/12)				
2:04.3 e	Robert Benson (OU)		24.09.50	2	Oxford	15 Mar
2:04.5 e	Henry Bryden (LAC)		3.05.54	3	London (LB)	28 Jun
2:04.5	James Edgar (Douglas, IOM)		23.02.51	1	Douglas, IOM	15 Jul
2:05.0	D. McEneiry (Kilmacomina/IRL)			1	Powerstown, IRL	25 Jun
2:05.0 p	William Baglin (London)		c47	1	Manchester (City)	22 Nov

Notable handicap performance (875y)

1:59.1 e p	Robert Hindle (Paisley)		46	2hc	London (LB)	3 Feb

5y down (from 5y start) on 1:58.4. Equates to 1:59.8e for full distance

Doubtful

2:03.5	Robert Bailey (Leeds AC)		c52	1	Burley-in-Wharfedale	26 Apr
2:03.8 e	G.B.Walker (Bradford)			2	Burley-in-Wharfedale	26 Apr

"Distances not exactly as represented on the card" (*Yorkshire Post*). Walker 2y down.

Notes:
Estimates: Templer 1¾y down on 1:59.75; Hopper 4y down on 2:02.0; Ridley 2y down on 2:02.5; Benson 1½y down on 2:04.0; Bryden 5y down on 2:03.75.

Mile

4:21.0	p	James McLeavy (Alexandria)	26.10.52	1	Gateshead	11 Oct
4:21.5	e p	Stephen Ridley (Gateshead)	29.07.45	2	Gateshead	11 Oct
4:28.6		Charles Gunton (CU)	26.06.50	1	London (LB) OvC	31 Mar
4:29.6		Walter Slade (LAC)	6.04.54	1	Oxford	19 Nov
4:30.2	e	Edward Sandford (OU)	11.05.51	2	London (LB) OvC	31 Mar
4:30.5		Slade		1	London (LB)	28 Jun
4:31.0	e	Lewis Evans (CU)	9.07.51	3	London (LB) OvC	31 Mar
4:31.2		Slade		1hc	London (LB)	17 May
4:31.25		Walter Smith-Dorrien (OU)	13.06.51	1	Oxford	13 Mar
4:31.5	e	Sandford		2	Oxford	13 Mar
4:32.0	p	Bob Rogers (Chelsea)	12.01.46	1	Manchester (RO)	22 Feb
4:32.6		Slade		1	London (LB) AAC	5 Apr
		(12/8)				
4:33.1	e	Thomas Bush (OU)	8.04.51	3	Oxford	13 Mar
4:33.4	e	Robert Benson (OU)	24.09.50	4	Oxford	13 Mar
4:35.0		Joseph Moore (Birmingham AC)	3.04.52	1	Birmingham (PR)	27 Sep
4:35.0		H. or J. Stimpson (OU servant)		1	Oxford	14 Nov
4:35.5	e	J. Richmond (OU servant)		2	Oxford	14 Nov
4:38.0	p	Albert Bird (Sheffield)	15.08.46	1hc	Melbourne, AUS	13 May
4:39.0		Bernard Marshall (Levenshulme FC)	26.05.53	1	Huddersfield	21 Jun
4:39.0		C.P.Nash (Seavington)		1	Langport	8 Aug
4:39.0	p	James Sanderson (Whitworth)	28.12.37	1	Manchester (RO)	18 Oct
4:39.25	p	J. Richmond (Manchester)		1	Eccleshill	28 Jun
4:39.2		Alfred Courtney (Dublin U/IRL)	02.53	1	Dublin (CP) IRL ICAC	7 Jul
4:40.0		M. Bryan (Borris/IRL)		1	Borris, IRL	9 Aug
4:40.2	e	W. Kidd (Borris/IRL)		2	Borris, IRL	9 Aug
4:40.2	e p	Robert Hindle (Paisley)	46	2	Glasgow	2 Sep
4:40.6	e	John North (Huddersfield AC)	52	2	Huddersfield	21 Jun
4:41.4		William Izard (CU)	51	3hc	Cambridge	1 Dec

Notes

Estimates: Ridley 3y down on McLeavy; Sandford 10y and Evans 15y down on 4:28.6 (31/03); Sandford 1½y and Bush 11½y down on 4:31.25 (13/03); Benson "close to Bush" (13/03); Richmond 3y down on 4:35.0; Kidd 1y down on 4:40.0; Hindle 1y down on 4:40.0 (02/09); North 10y down on 4:39.0.
Gunton's time in the Oxford v Cambridge Sports is given as 4:29.6 in *Fifty Years of Sport* and 4:29.4 in *Bell's Life*; the time here is from Shearman's *Athletics* and Lupton's *The Pedestrian's Record*.
Courtney was credited with 4:29.4 in the Dublin University Sports on 9/06 by *John Lawrence's Handbook* but *Bell's Life* made it 4:49.2 and the *Freeman's Journal* and *Irish Sportsman* 4:49.4.
J. Richmond at Eccleshill on 28/06 was said by *Bell's Life* to have been a professional. No connection has been established with the Oxford servant of the same name.

2 Miles

9:54.0		Walter Slade (LAC)	6.04.54	5hc	London (LB)	15 Nov
10:09.0	p	William Shrubsole (Bromley)	4.07.46	1	East London	2 Jun
10:10.4	e p	Henry Hescott (Mile End)	6.11.51	2	East London	2 Jun
10:11.4		James Warburton (Haslingden)	13.11.45	1	Stoke-on-Trent	6 Aug
10:15.0		Warburton		int	London (LB)	28 Jun
10:15.9	e	John Scott (LAC)	9.09.47	int	London (LB)	28 Jun
10:16.4		Warburton		1	Southport	7 Jun
10:17.4		Warburton		1	Widnes	5 Jul
10:17.4		Alfred Wheeler (London)		2	Stoke-on-Trent	6 Aug
10:18.0		Scott		inthc	London (LB)	21 Jun
10:18.4		William Gilmour (Liverpool AC)		2	Southport	7 Jun
		(11/7)				
10:21.0		Arthur Somerville (CU)	23.04.50	int	London (LB) OvC	31 Mar
10:21.5	e	Walter Smith-Dorrien (OU)	13.06.51	int	London (LB) OvC	31 Mar
10:21.8		John Kenworthy (Rochdale RC)	52	3	Southport	7 Jun
10:29.0		Alfred Courtney (Dublin U/IRL)	02.53	1	Dublin, IRL	12 Jun
10:30.0	e	Frederick Smith (Chesterfield)		3	Stoke-on-Trent	6 Aug
10:30.8		Thomas Duckett (Liverpool)	5.12.52	2	Widnes	5 Jul
10:31.0		W. Watson (Thames H&H)		inthc	London (LB)	21 Jun

Notes

Estimates: Hescott 8y down on 10:09.0; Scott 'a couple of yards' down on 10:15.0; Smith-Dorrien close up to Somerville 10:21.0; Smith 70y down on 10:17.4.

Intermediate times at 3 miles (31/03; 21/06; 28/06)
Corrie Jackson (CU) ran 10:32.4 for 2m 80y at Cambridge on 25 Nov. Alfred Courtney was given 10:29.0 in the
Dublin University Sports on 12/06, but *Bell's Life* stated that the course was short through the removal of a flag.

3 Miles
14:55.0 p	Billy Mills (Bethnal Green)	09.43	1	Manchester (City)		7 Jun
15:12.3 e p	Joseph Mellor (Gorton)	c52	2	Manchester (City)		7 Jun
15:18.6	Walter Smith-Dorrien (OU)	13.06.51	1	London (LB)	OvC	31 Mar
15:34.5	John Scott (LAC)	9.09.47	1	London (LB)		28 Jun
15:46.0	Scott		5hc	London (LB)		21 Jun
15:48.4	Somerville		1	Cambridge		26 Mar
15:48.5	Arthur Somerville (CU)	23.04.50	2	London (LB)	OvC	31 Mar
15:59.0	Smith-Dorrien		1	Oxford		17 Mar
16:01.2	James Warburton (Haslingden)	13.11.45	1	Sheffield (BL)		7 Jul
16:06.2 e	George Armitstead (OU)	24.04.53	3	London (LB)	OvC	31 Mar
16:10.1 e	Herbert Russell (OU)	17.10.52	2	Oxford		17 Mar
16:10.4	Percy Stenning (Clevedon FC)	31.08.54	4hc	London (LB)		21 Jun
16:15.0	W. Watson (Thames H&H)		1hc	London (LB)		21 Jun
16:23.6 e	John Greaves (Wednesday FC)	c48	2	Sheffield (BL)		7 Jul
16:25.8 e	Corrie Jackson (CU)	19.10.53	2	Cambridge		26 Mar

Notes
Estimates: Mellor 100y down on 14:55.0; Armitstead 260y down on 15:18.6; Greaves 120y down on 16:01.2;
Jackson 200y down on 15:48.4; Russell 60y down on 15:59.0. Scott reported as 15:39.4 by *Sporting Chronicle*
(28/06).

4 Miles
20:11.0 p	Billy Mills (Bethnal Green)	09.43	2hc	London (Bow)		19 May
21:38.0	Arthur Somerville (CU)	23.04.50	1	London (LB)	AAC	5 Apr
21:47.3 e	Alfred Wheeler (Stoke-on-Trent)		2	London (LB)	AAC	5 Apr
21:53.75	James Warburton (Haslingden)	13.11.45	1	Hyde		19 Jul
22:12.7 e	John Kenworthy (Rochdale)	52	2	Hyde		19 Jul
22:39.0	William Fuller (LAC)	7.06.51	inthc	London (LB)		14 Jul

Notes
Estimates: Wheeler 50y down on 21:38.0; Kenworthy 100y down on 21:53.75
Intermediate time in a 10 mile race (14/07)

6 Miles
34:42.0	William Fuller (Thames H&H)	7.06.51	inthc	London (LB)	14 Jul
36:31.0 p	Albert Bird (Sheffield)	15.08.46	intex	Mount Gambier, AUS	24 Feb
36:34.0	Sydney Weall (LAC)	54	1	Feltham	7 Jun

Note
Fuller in a 10 mile race; Bird in a one-hour solo run against time, uncompleted.

10 Miles
58:25.0 p	John Brighton (Norwich)	14.07.32	1	Norwich	13 Oct
58:58.0	William Fuller (Thames H&H)	7.06.51	3hc	London (LB)	14 Jul

Doubtful
57:15.0 p	Albert Bird (Sheffield)	15.08.46	ex	Burra, AUS	8 Feb

Said to be 11 miles, in an attempt to run the distance within the hour. Laps of "approximately 400y".

120 Yards Hurdles
16 2/5	Hugh Upcher (OU)	28.10.53	1	London (LB)	AAC	5 Apr
16 ½	Edward Garnier (OU)	5.04.50	1	Oxford		17 Mar
16.5 e	Garnier		2=	London (LB)	AAC	5 Apr
16.5 e	John Reay (AAC)	9.07.53	2=	London (LB)	AAC	5 Apr
16 ½	Reay		1	Dulwich		3 May
16 ½	Reay		1	London (LB)		28 Jun
16.6 e	Upcher		2	Oxford		17 Mar
16 4/5	Jenner Davies (CU)	10.04.51	1	Cambridge		25 Mar
16.9 e	Henry Beauchamp (CU)	25.12.51	2	Cambridge		25 Mar
17.0	Davies		1ht2	Cambridge		22 Mar
17.0 e	Samuel Roberts (CU)	30.04.52	3	Cambridge		25 Mar

17.0	Charles Spencer (Nottm Forest FC)	48	1	Sheffield (BL)	7 Jul
	(12/7)				
17.2 e	Edward Prior (CU)	4.01.52	4	Cambridge	25 Mar
17 ¼	Michael Glazebrook (OU)	4.08.53	1	Dulwich	3 May
17 ¼	Gerald Onslow (RMA)	7.02.53	1	Woolwich	16 May

Doubtful

16.0	W.R.John (Cork/IRL)		1	Cork, IRL	21 Sep

Notes
The Oxford U Sports race was run on cinders (17/03); Upcher 'almost dead level' but 2nd to 16.5 (17/03).
Estimates: Garnier & Reay ½y down on 16.4 (5/04); Beauchamp 2ft and Roberts 2ft and inches down on 16.8;
Prior 'close up' (25/03)

220 Yards Hurdles

29.4	John Bennett (Bicester AC)	c50	1	Bicester	18 Sep
29.6 e	Harold Littledale (ICAC/IRL)	10.10.53	3hc	Dublin (LCG), IRL	11 Aug
31.1 e	S. Holmes (Bicester AC)		2	Bicester	18 Sep
31.75	John Vickerman (Huddersfield AC)	17.01.52	1	Huddersfield	21 Jun
33.2	Frank Preston (Cheetham Hill CC)	51	1hc	Cheetham Hill	20 Sep
34.0	Arthur Ward (Sale FC)	c50	1	Wigan	4 Jun
34.1 e	Thomas Calvert (Huddersfield AC)	50	2	Huddersfield	21 Jun

Irregular

33.0	Samuel Roberts (CU)	30.04.52	1	Cambridge	21 Feb

Hurdles arranged in ten flights over the last 120y

Notes
Estimates: Littledale 5y 1ft down on 28.8; Holmes 12y down on 29.4; Calvert 15y down on 31.75

440 Yards Hurdles

1:02.5	William Lomas (Grappenhall)	c47	1hc	Newton-le-Willows	30 Aug
1:03.6	Harold Littledale (ICAC/IRL)	10.10.53	1	Powerscourt, IRL	14 Aug
1:06.6	Lomas		1	Stockport	9 Aug
1:06.8 e	Charles Bryan (Liverpool)	c47	2	Stockport	9 Aug

Over 12 flights:

1:02.75	John Vickerman (Huddersfield AC)	17.01.52	1	Eccleshill	28 Jun
1:04.3 e	John Curtis (Leeds AC)	22.07.51	2	Eccleshill	28 Jun
1:05.4	Vickerman		1	Bradford	19 Jul
1:05.8 e	J.M.Howson (Keighley AC)		3	Eccleshill	28 Jun
1:07.7 e	Curtis		2	Bradford	19 Jul
1:08.6 e	Howson		3	Bradford	19 Jul
1:09.8	Sam Widdowson (Nottm Forest FC)	16.04.51	1	Compstall	31 May
1:12.3 e	J. Davies (Mersey H&H)		2	Compstall	31 May
1:13.2 e	J.F.Harrison (Good Templers CC)		3	Compstall	31 May
1:15.0	William Carver (Marple)	55	1	Compstall	31 May

Over 12 flights and twice over water:

1:05.0	Samuel Roberts (Sheffield FC)	30.04.52	1	Huddersfield	21 Jun

Over 20 flights:

1:12.2 e	Alexander Mills (Manchester)	c45	2hc	Lurgan, IRL	6 Sep
1:16.2	James Gorman (Lurgan/IRL)	31.10.50	1hc	Dublin, IRL	13 Sep

Short course (400y)

1:00.4	Reginald Miller (Dublin U/IRL)	49	1	Dublin (CP), IRL	10 Jun
1:01.9 e	William Hamilton (Dublin U/IRL)	1.07.50	2	Dublin (CP), IRL	10 Jun
1:02.5 e	Littledale		3	Dublin (CP), IRL	10 Jun

(We have listed this because it is a well known performance, but the *Irish Sportsman & Farmer* report invalidates
it: Hamilton 10y & Littledale 14y down on 1:00.4)

Notes
Estimates: Bryan 1y down on 1:06.6; Curtis 10y and Howson 20y down on 1:02.75 (28/06); Curtis 15y and
Howson 20y down on 1:05.4 (19/07); Davies 15y and Harrison 20y down on 1:09.8; Mills 1y down on 1:12.0.
Widdowson ran 1:00.75 over 12 flights at Leeds on 2 Aug, but the course was said by *Bell's Life* to have been
'palpably incorrect'.

High Jump

5'10¼	1.784	Thomas Davin (Suir RC/IRL)	51	1	Dublin (CP) IRL ICAC	7 Jul
5'9½	1.765	William Morton (Crewkerne)	49	1	Weston-super-Mare	15 Sep
5'9	1.753	John Gurney (CU)	19.06.49	1	Cambridge	26 Mar
5'9	1.753	James Bland (Dublin U/IRL)	6.04.50	2	Weston-super-Mare	15 Sep
5'8	1.727	P.L.O'Connell (Milford/IRL)		1	Freemount, IRL	6 Aug
5'7½	1.715	Davin		1	Dublin (EG) IRL	2 Jun
5'7	1.702	John Graham (OU)	1.05.51	1=	Oxford	13 Mar
5'7	1.702	Francis Woods (OU)	22.05.50	1=	Oxford	13 Mar
5'7	1.702	John Hurst (Louth AC)	1.07.47	1	Nottingham	26 Apr
5'7	1.702	Marshall Brooks (OU)	30.05.55	1	Oxford	10 Nov

(10/9)

5'6½	1.689	Joseph Watson (German Gym Soc)	15.10.51	1	London (LB)	28 Jun
5'6¼	1.683	Percy Johnston (QC Cork/IRL)	13.07.51	1	Cork, IRL	17 May
5'6¼	1.683	Walter Scott (Victoria Coll)	c52	1	St Helier	23 May
5'6	1.676	Edward Prior (CU)	4.01.52	2	Cambridge	26 Mar
5'6	1.676	Henry Armstrong (Oundle Gr Sch)	c50	2	Nottingham	26 Apr
5'6	1.676	Daniel Fraher (Dungarvan/IRL)	18.11.52	1	Powerstown, IRL	25 Jun
5'6	1.676	Charles Grundy (Liverpool)	c50	1	Ormskirk	28 Jun
5'6	1.676	Henry Batterbury (Tollington Park Sch)	c48	1	Alexandra Palace	19 Jul
5'6	1.676	Thomas Stretch (Ormskirk)	28.01.51	1	Leigh	23 Aug
5'6	1.676	A Patient (Richmond Lunatic Asylum/IRL)		1	Dublin, IRL	9 Sep
5'6	1.676	Michael Glazebrook (OU)	4.08.53	1	Oxford	2 Dec

Note
Armstrong and Batterbury were not juniors, but assistant masters at their respective schools.
Michael Brannagan (Ballymahon/IRL) is said to have jumped 5'9 at Ballynakill this year.

High Jump: Highland & Border

5'9	1.753	p	John Hunter (Galashiels)		1	Galashiels	26 Jul
5'9	1.753	p	Hunter		1	St Boswells	9 Aug
5'8	1.727	p	Hugh Andrews (Glasgow)	c52	1=	Johnstone	19 Jul
5'8	1.727	p	Samuel Muir (Stewarton)	c41	1=	Johnstone	19 Jul
5'8	1.727	p	Neil McKay (Innerleithen)	6.01.46	2=	Galashiels	26 Jul
5'8	1.727	p	Anthony Hall (Edinburgh)	c46	2=	Galashiels	26 Jul
5'8	1.727	p	Andrews		1	West Wemyss	8 Aug
5'8	1.727	p	Thomas McDougall (Galashiels)	c53	2	St Boswells	9 Aug
5'7½	1.715	p	Andrews		1	Wishaw	31 Jul
5'7½	1.715	p	Andrews		1=	Dalkeith	30 Aug
5'7½	1.715	p	Muir		1=	Dalkeith	30 Aug
5'7	1.702	p	Andrews		1	Pollokshaws	21 Jun
5'7	1.702	p	Andrews		1	Cupar	6 Aug
5'7	1.702	p	Muir		1	Leith	12 Aug

(14/6)

5'6	1.676	p	Donald Dinnie (Aboyne)	8.06.37	1	Alexandra Palace	28 Jun
5'6	1.676	p	William McDonald		1=	Dunblane	12 Jul
5'6	1.676	p	William Henderson		1=	Dunblane	12 Jul
5'6	1.676	p	William Borland (Tillicoultry)	c48	3	Johnstone	19 Jul
5'6	1.676	p	Alexander Scott (Edinburgh)		2=	Leith	12 Aug
5'6	1.676	p	William McDuff (Dunkeld)	c51	1	Inverness	26 Sep

Pole Vault

10'7	3.23	Edwin Woodburn (Ulverston CC)	19.04.50	1	Lancaster	2 Jun
10'7	3.23	Walter Kelsey (Hull CC)	04.51	1=	Sheffield (BL)	7 Jul
10'7	3.23	John Wigfull (Sheffield FC)	2.12.51	1=	Sheffield (BL)	7 Jul
10'6	3.20	Kelsey		1	London (LB) AAC	5 Apr
10'5	3.17	Arthur Lermit (Dedham Gr Sch)	10.07.54	1	Dedham	26 May
10'4½	3.16	Gerald Onslow (RMA)	7.02.53	1	Woolwich	16 May
10'4½	3.16	Kelsey		1	Newark	2 Jun
10'4	3.15	Kelsey		1	Barnes	5 Apr
10'4	3.15	Kelsey		1	Hull	17 Jul
10'2½	3.11	Arthur Penton (RMA)	6.10.54	2	Woolwich	16 May
10'2	3.10	Charles Leeds (AAC)	45	2	London (LB) AAC	5 Apr
10'2	3.10	Robert Sabin (Culworth)	52	2hc	Culworth	23 Jul
10'1	3.07	Woodburn		1	Cheetham Hill	20 Sep

			(13/8)				
10'0	3.05		John Trotter (CU)	8.04.54	1	Cambridge	26 Mar
10'0	3.05		Edwin Dawes (Highworth)	12.08.52	1	Wells	10 Sep
9'10	3.00		Lupton Jackson (Hull Town FC)	24.05.43	1	Louth	4 Aug
9'9	2.97		Kenneth Kemp (CU)	21.04.53	1=	Cambridge	25 Mar

Pole Vault: Highland, Lakeland & Border

10'6	3.20	p	David Anderson (Alnwick)	c46	1	Bolton	26 Jul
10'4	3.15	p	David Milne (Forfar)	28.12.42	1	Forfar	8 Aug
10'3	3.12	p	Marcellus Thompson (Kendal)	19.01.55	1	Kendal	3 Jun
10'3	3.12	p	Peter Cameron (Kincardine O'Neil)	8.12.52	2	Forfar	8 Aug
10'2	3.10	p	James Lamond (Pitcur)		3	Forfar	8 Aug
10'2	3.10	p	Anderson		1	Leith	12 Aug
10'2	3.10	p	Anderson		1	Alloa	13 Aug
10'1	3.07	p	Anderson		1	Alva	14 Aug
10'0	3.05	p	Anderson		1=	Newcastle	3 Jun
10'0	3.05	p	Joseph Milburn (Hayton)		1=	Newcastle	3 Jun
10'0	3.05	p	William Crichton (Brunty)	05.49	1	Newburgh	20 Jun
10'0	3.05	p	Anderson		1	Tillicoultry	15 Aug
10'0	3.05	p	Anderson		1=	Springburn	16 Aug
10'0	3.05	p	William Borland (Tillicoultry)	c48	1=	Springburn	16 Aug
10'0	3.05	p	George Brymer (Manchester)	25.09.49	1	New York, USA	4 Sep
			(15/9)				
9'10	3.00	p	Anthony Hall (Edinburgh)	c46	1	Galashiels	26 Jul
9'10	3.00	p	Thomas Newby (Ulverston)	c52	1	Grasmere	21 Aug
9'9	2.97	p	J. Wilson (Pennington)		1	Lancaster	2 Jun
9'9	2.97	p	Jacob Field (Galashiels)		2	Galashiels	26 Jul

Indoors

10'6	3.20	i p	John Richardson (Brampton)		1	London (Ag Hall)	12 Apr
9'10	3.00	i p	John Allison (Kendal)	8.02.43	1=	Manchester	29 Apr
9'10	3.00	i p	T. Clifton (Weaste)		1=	Manchester	29 Apr
9'9	2.97	i p	John Graham (Carlisle)	c51	2	London (Ag Hall)	12 Apr

Note: The bar was at 10'3 for Brymer's NY jump, but sagged 3 inches (*Spirit of the Times*)

Long Jump

22'3	6.78	Jenner Davies (CU)	10.04.51	1	Cambridge	22 Mar
21'9	6.63	Davies		1	Cambridge	19 Nov
21'4	6.50	John Lane (ICAC/IRL)	53	1	Dublin (CP) IRL ICAC	7 Jul
21'4	6.50	Alfred Monnington (Bitteswell)	29.05.53	1	Market Harborough	14 Jul
21'4	6.50	Charles Lockton (LAC)	2.07.56	1	Alexandra Palace	9 Aug
21'3½	6.49	Bryan Scott (Liverpool)	c51	1	St Helens	19 Jul
21'3	6.48	Edward Nash (OU)	53	1	Oxford	17 Mar
21'3	6.48	Lane		1	Dublin (CP) IRL	10 Jun
21'3	6.48	Davies		1	London (LB) OvC	31 Mar
21'2	6.45	Scott		1	Daresbury	26 Aug
21'1	6.43	Thomas Davin (Suir RC/IRL)	51	2	Dublin (CP) IRL ICAC	7 Jul
21'0	6.40	James Kough (Dublin U/IRL)	30.03.51	2	Dublin (CP) IRL	10 Jun
21'0	6.40	Kough		3	Dublin (CP) IRL ICAC	7 Jul
		(13/8)				
20'11½	6.39	Thomas Stretch (Ormskirk)	28.01.51	2	St Helens	19 Jul
20'10	6.35	William Lucas (AAC)	c47	2	Alexandra Palace	9 Aug
20'8	6.30	Edward Hodges (OU)	28.02.49	1	Oxford	13 Nov
20'7	6.27	Hugh Upcher (OU)	28.10.53	2	Oxford	17 Mar
20'7	6.27	Frederick Warde (Mote Park CC)	18.03.52	3	Alexandra Palace	9 Aug
20'6½	6.26	J. Barker (104th Bengal Fusiliers)		1	Aldershot	21 Aug
20'6	6.25	James Wheble (RMA)	29.01.53	1	Woolwich	16 May
20'5½	6.24	James Daly (QC Cork/IRL)	c54	1	Cork, IRL	19 May
20'4	6.20	Henry Armstrong (Oundle Gr Sch)	c50	2	Market Harborough	14 Jul
20'4	6.20	T. Fielding (Cloughfold)		1	Lowerhouse	23 Aug
20'4	6.20	William Lyon (Mersey H&H)	c50	3	Daresbury	26 Aug

Doubtful

21'0	6.40	Stretch	1	Douglas, IOM	15 Jul
20'9	6.32	Lyon	2	Douglas, IOM	15 Jul

'The way it was measured gives the jumper a great advantage, viz, the competitors are allowed to take off where they like and are not obliged to start behind a mark.' (*Bell's Life*)

Note: Davies at Cambridge (on 22/3) 21'6½ - 22'3; (on 19/11) 20'11½ - 21'2 – 21'3½ - 21'9

Long Jump: Highland & Border

20'5	6.22	Samuel Muir (Stewarton)	c41	1	Alloa	13 Aug
20'4	6.20	Archibald Mitchell (Alva)	51	2	Alloa	13 Aug

Triple Jump

45'4	13.82	James Daly (QC Cork/IRL)	c54	1	Cork, IRL	22 Apr
44'6	13.56	J.J.O'Flynn (Castletownroche/IRL)		2	Cork, IRL	22 Apr
43'0	13.11	J. Murphy (Charleville/IRL)		1	Freemount, IRL	7 Aug
42'2½	12.87	Murphy		1	Buttervant, IRL	26 Dec
41'5½	12.64	Henry Dick (St Andrews U)	5.08.53	1	St Andrews	15 Mar
41'1	12.52	Pte Healy (1st Regt)		1	Aldershot	2 Jul
40'8	12.40	E. Gaynor (IRL)		1	Dublin, IRL	16 Apr
40'0	12.19	P. Walsh (Shandram/IRL)		2	Freemount, IRL	7 Aug
40'0	12.19	John Wolstenholme (100th Regt)	c52	1	Portsmouth	2 Oct
39'9	12.12	Francis Atkins (Cheltenham)	12.05.52	1	Cheltenham	8 May
39'8½	12.10	Peter Lyall (St Andrews U)	c53	2	St Andrews	15 Mar
39'8	12.09	John Walsh (Bandon/IRL)		1	Milford, IRL	22 May
39'8	12.09	J. Merritt (100th Regt)		2	Portsmouth	2 Oct
39'6	12.04	Albert Neale	c51	2	Cheltenham	8 May
39'4	11.99	C.W.Plummer (Newcastle/IRL)		2	Milford, IRL	22 May
39'0	11.89	M. Murphy (Charleville/IRL)		1	Kanturk, IRl	5 Jul
38'11	11.86	Dick		1	St Andrews	1 Mar
38'0	11.58	D. Smith (Kanturk/IRL)		2	Kanturk, IRL	5 Jul
37'6	11.43	Francis Scott (St Andrews U)	c57	1	St Andrews	17 May
37'0	11.28	George Cran (Aberdeen U)	7.06.52	1	Aberdeen	8 Mar
36'7	11.15	William McCombie Smith (Aberdeen U)	7.09.47	2	Aberdeen	8 Mar

Notes
Some sources give J.C.Smythe as the winner of the Queen's College, Cork, Sports with 45'4, but this was probably a pseudonym used by Daly; H.F.Wilkinson cites *The Irish Sportsman*, 10.05.73. There is also a query about the name of the second-placed jumper, (O'Flynn) reported by *Sport* as T. Bourke (Glanworth, Co. Cork).

Triple Jump: Highland & Border

47'3	14.40	p	Robert Knox (Newstead)	17.09.47	1	Jedburgh	25 Jul
47'1	14.35	p	Samuel Muir (Stewarton)	c41	1	Alloa	13 Aug
47'0	14.33	p	Knox		1	Galashiels	26 Jul
47'0	14.33	p	James Young (Alva)	c47	1	Bridge of Allan	2 Aug
46'9½	14.26	p	Knox		1	Hawick	6 Jun
46'3	14.10	p	Muir		2	Bridge of Allan	2 Aug
46'3	14.10	p	Young		2	Alloa	13 Aug
45'11½	14.01	p	Young		1	West Wemyss	8 Aug
45'10½	13.98	p	James Stewart (Dumfries)		2	Hawick	6 Jun
45'10	13.97	p	Stewart		2	Galashiels	26 Jul
45'10	13.97	p	Adam Scott (Edinburgh)	15.08.52	3	Bridge of Allan	2 Aug
45'9	13.94	p	Thomas Aitken (Walkerburn)	23.05.53	1	Peebles	9 Aug
				(12/6)			
45'0	13.72	p	Hugh Andrews (Glasgow)	c52	2	Kirkcaldy	7 Aug
44'9	13.64	p	James Rough (Kilbarchan)	c46	1	Dalry	2 Aug
43'6	13.26	p	John Hunter (Galashiels)		2	Innerleithen	23 Aug
43'4	13.21	p	Peter Cameron (Kincardine O'Neil)	8.12.52	1	Aberdeen	19 Jul
43'3	13.18	p	Alexander Hume (Greenock)		2	Kelso	26 Jul
43'3	13.18	p	William Borland (Tillicoultry)	c48	1	Lochwinnoch	27 Sep
43'1	13.13	p	William Millar (Balfron)		2	Pollokshaws	21 Jun
42'10	13.06	p	Charles Yeaman (Galashiels)	52	3	Galashiels	26 Jul
42'9	13.03	p	John Toy (Dundee)	c46	2	Aberdeen (HSL)	21 Jul
42'9	13.03	p	William Bruce (Falkirk)		2	Dalry	2 Aug
42'6	12.95	p	William McDonald		1	Dunblane	12 Jul
42'5	12.93	p	Owen Toy (Forfarshire/IRL)		2	Aberdeen (HHL)	21 Jul
42'4	12.90	p	Neil McKay (Innerleithen)	6.01.46	2	Peebles	9 Aug
42'3	12.88	p	George Hutcheson (Aberdeen)		3	Aberdeen (HSL)	21 Jul
42'2	12.85	p	Andrew Innes (Aberdeen)		2	Aberdeen	19 Jul

42'2	12.85	p	Daniel Lamont (Kilbarchan)		c55	3	Dalry	2 Aug
42'0	12.80	p	Robert Millar (Kilbarchan)			1	Johnstone	19 Jul
42'0	12.80	p	J. Neary (Leeds)			1	Leeds	26 Jul

Notes
The Souvenir Programme of the 150th St Ronan's Border Games, 1977, mentioned a 49'1 mark by Tom Aitken at the 1873 Games at Innerleithen, but contemporary reports give his winning effort as 45'2.
There were separate competitions at Aberdeen on 21/07 for hop, step & leap and hop, hop & leap.

Shot

41'8	12.70	R. Montgomery (Edinburgh U)		1	Edinburgh		18 Jun
41'5	12.62	Edward Bor (LAC/IRL)	25.08.50	1	London (LB)		28 Jun
40'6	12.34	Francis Power (Farington)	52	1	Newton-le-Willows		30 Aug
40'3½	12.28	Charles Wadsworth (QC Belfast/IRL)	c50	1	Dublin (CP) IRL ICAC		7 Jul
40'0	12.19	Bor		1	London (LB)	AAC	5 Apr
39'11	12.17	Thomas Ashley (IRL)	c55	1	Dublin (LCG) IRL		11 Aug
39'9	12.12	Edward Hodges (OU)	28.02.49	1	Oxford		12 Nov
39'0	11.89	Matthew Stritch (RIC/IRL)	02.47	1	Dublin (EG) IRL		2 Jun
39'0	11.89	J. Curtis (Upper Clapton CC)		1	Clapton		12 Jul
38'8	11.79	Wadsworth		1	Cork, IRL		19 May
38'7	11.76	Thomas Stone (Newton-le-Willows)	24.01.52	2	London (LB)	AAC	5 Apr
38'3	11.66	Bor		1	London (LB)		22 Mar
38'2	11.63	William Powell Moore (LAC)	23.04.46	2	London (LB)		28 Jun
38'1	11.61	Wadsworth		1	Belfast, IRL		2 May
		(13/9)					
37'6	11.43	J. Wallace (Newcastle-under-Lyme CC)		1	Leicester		26 Jun
37'5½	11.42	Edward Gittins (Leicester AC)	47	2	Leicester		26 Jun
37'3	11.35	James Daly (QC Cork/IRL)	c54	2	Cork, IRL		19 May
36'8	11.18	Nicholas Littleton (CU)	11.01.53	1	Cambridge		22 Mar

Note: John Lawrence's Handbook gives Stritch's throw at Dublin on 2/06 as 37'4; Bell's Life gives 37'7, noting that "afterwards the winner putted 39'0".

Shot: Highland & Border
Includes putting the 16lb stone

48'6	14.78	p	Donald Dinnie (Aboyne)	8.06.37	1	Falkirk	19 May
48'5	14.76	p	Dinnie		1	Dundee	23 Jun
46'6	14.17	p	James Fleming (Ballinluig)	18.09.40	2	Falkirk	19 May
45'1	13.74	p	Fleming		2	Dundee	23 Jun
45'1*	13.74	p	Dinnie		1	Forfar	8 Aug
45'0	13.72	p	Dinnie		1hc	Aberdeen	3 May
44'11	13.69	p	Dinnie		1	Aberdeen	14 Jun
43'11*	13.39	p	Dinnie		1	Milngavie	30 Aug
42'9	13.03	p	Dinnie		1	Aberdeen	21 Jul
42'4	12.90	p	Dinnie		1	Aboyne	9 Sep
42'4	12.90	p	James Brown (Edinburgh)		1	Lasswade	13 Sep
42'3	12.88	p	Fleming		2	Aboyne	9 Sep
42'2	12.85	p	Fleming		2	Aberdeen	14 Jun
42'0*	12.80	p	Dinnie		1	Ballater	29 Jul
42'0*	12.80	p	Fleming		2	Forfar	8 Aug
42'0	12.80	p	Birkett (Royal Artillery)		2	Lasswade	13 Sep
			(16/4)				
41'10	12.75	p	William Bremner (Strathdon)	3.01.47	1	Udny	6 Aug
41'9	12.73	p	William Fleming (Dundee)	22.08.42	3	Dundee	23 Jun
41'7	12.67	p	George Mearns (Aberdeen)		2	Aberdeen	21 Jul
41'6*	12.65	p	Owen Duffy (Edinburgh/IRL)	c47	1	Edinburgh	30 Aug
40'3	12.27	p	John Gray (Aberdeen)		3	Aberdeen	14 Jun
39'8	12.09	p	John Moir (Strathdon)	27.07.42	1	Aberdeen	19 Jul
39'0	11.89	p	William McGregor		1	Rinloan	14 Jul
39'0	11.89	p	J. Grieve (Grandholm)		1	Parkhill	23 Aug
39'0	11.89	p	Charles Stewart (Glenmuick)		1	Glasgow (local)	6 Sep
38'5	11.71	p	James Finlan (Strathdon)		2	Rinloan	14 Jul
38'5	11.71	p	G. McLeod (Grandholm)		2	Parkhill	23 Aug
38'0	11.58	p	Ebenezer McElroy (Glasgow)	24.02.50	2	Glasgow (local)	6 Sep
37'5	11.40	p	John Anderson (Edinburgh)		2	Udny	6 Aug
37'0	11.28	p	C. Greig (Parkhill)		3	Parkhill	23 Aug

36'10	11.23	p	R. Sherrard		3	Udny	6 Aug
36'9	11.20	p	Charles Leys (Glengairn)		3	Rinloan	14 Jul

Note: *correct weight assumed from evidence of other years

Weight unstated

42'0	12.80	p	William Graham (Dalkeith)		1	Dalkeith	30 Aug

22lb by performer

41'9	12.73	p	Dinnie		1hc	Dundee	19 Jul
37'9	11.51	p	J. Fleming		2	Forfar	8 Aug
36'8	11.18	p	Duffy		1	Leith	12 Aug

22lb doubtful

37'11	11.56	p	John Scott (Dunkeld)		2	Bridge of Allan	2 Aug

Weight unstated and doubtful

55'2	16.81	p	Dinnie		1	Bridge of Allan	2 Aug
53'7	16.33	p	Dinnie		1	Inverness	25 Sep
52'8	16.05	p	J. Fleming		2	Bridge of Allan	2 Aug
50'9	15.47	p	Scott		3	Bridge of Allan	2 Aug
50'4	15.34	p	J. Fleming		2	Inverness	25 Sep
47'10	14.58	p	J. Fleming		1	Greenock	7 Jun
43'1	13.13	p	Peter McHardy (Aberdeen)	c48	2	Greenock	7 Jun
41'0	12.50	p	Alexander Ritchie (Greenock)		3	Greenock	7 Jun

Note: The ground at Bridge of Allan had a notorious slope.

Hammer

122'6	37.34	Stephen Brown (OU)	1.06.54	1	London (LB)	OvC	31 Mar
122'4	37.29	Brown		1	Oxford		17 Mar
120'6	36.73	John Todd (OU)	19.09.52	1	Oxford		8 Nov
116'7	35.53	William A. Burgess (ex-OU)	27.12.46	1	Derby		19 Jul
116'0	35.36	John Paterson (CU)	7.12.50	1	Cambridge		25 Mar
111'8	34.04	Paterson		2	London (LB)	OvC	31 Mar
111'6	33.99	Todd		1	Sleaford		3 Sep
110'8	33.73	Brown		2hc	Oxford		20 Nov
110'3	33.60	Todd		3	London (LB)	OvC	31 Mar
110'2	33.58	Matthew Stritch (RIC/IRL)	02.47	1	Dublin (CP) IRL ICAC		7 Jul
109'7	33.40	Paterson		2hc	Cambridge		20 Nov
109'4	33.32	Stritch		1	Dublin, IRL		31 May
108'0	32.92	Paterson		1	London (LB)	AAC	5 Apr
			(13/5)				
107'7	32.79	George Hales (CU)	20.05.54	1hc	Cambridge		20 Nov
107'3	32.69	Arthur Pelham (CU)	28.12.50	2	Cambridge		25 Mar
105'8	32.21	J. Wallace (Newcastle-under-Lyme CC)		1	Wigan		4 Jun
104'0	31.70	Edward Garnier (OU)	5.04.50	1hc	Oxford		12 Feb
100'10½	30.75	Maurice Davin (Suir RC/IRL)	29.06.42	2	Dublin (CP) IRL ICAC		7 Jul
100'0+	30.48+	Nicholas Littleton (CU)	11.01.53	3	Cambridge		25 Mar
100'0+	30.48+	William Winthrop (CU)	15.06.52	4	Cambridge		25 Mar

Note: Littleton and Winthrop 'also reached' 100' in the Cambridge University Sports, but the precise distances were not reported.

Hammer: Highland & Border

135'11	41.43	p	Donald Dinnie (Aboyne)	8.06.37	1	Falkirk	19 May
129'9	39.55	p	Dinnie		1hc	Dundee	23 Jun
123'10	37.74	p	James Fleming (Ballinluig)	18.09.40	2	Falkirk	19 May
123'2	37.54	p	Dinnie		1hc	Aberdeen	3 May
122'0	37.19	p	Dinnie		2hc	Dundee	19 Jul
119'0	36.27	p	Dinnie		1	Cupar	6 Aug
118'4	36.07	p	Fleming		2hc	Dundee	23 Jun
118'0	35.97	p	Dinnie		1	Aberdeen	14 Jun
118'0*	35.97	p	Dinnie		1	Forfar	8 Aug
116'7	35.53	p	Dinnie		1	Kildrummy	20 Aug
114'5	34.87	p	Dinnie		1	Glasgow (Alex)	6 Sep
112'0	34.14	p	Dinnie		1	Alexandra Palace	28 Jun
110'0	33.53	p	William McCombie Smith (Blairgowrie)	7.09.47	3	Falkirk	19 May

110'0	33.53	p	Dinnie			1	Springburn	16 Aug
109'3	33.30	p	Fleming			2hc	Aberdeen	3 May
109'0	33.22	p	William Fleming (Dundee)		22.08.42	1hc	Dundee	19 Jul
				(16/4)				
103'2	31.45	p	John McHattie (Aberdeen)			1	Parkhill	23 Aug
102'0	31.09	p	John Gray (Aberdeen)			3	Aberdeen	14 Jun
101'5	30.91	p	William McDuff (Dunkeld)		c51	2	Inverness	25 Sep
101'1	30.81	p	William Bremner (Strathdon)		3.01.47	1	Udny	6 Aug

Note: *correct weight assumed from evidence of other years

Weight unstated

116'6	35.51	p	Dinnie			1	Nairn (light)	9 Aug
109'4	33.32	p	McHattie			1	Stonehaven	9 Aug

20lb sledge

111'0	33.83	p	Dinnie			1	Crieff	23 Aug

Note
Dinnie threw 138'3/42.14 at Coupar Angus on 1/08, but the handle measured 4'8", compared to the 3'6" then in use by amateurs. His Springburn throw was with 17¼lb hammer.

Other Events

120 Yards

12.0		Robert Philpot (CU)	12.06.50	1	Cambridge	27 Mar

150 Yards

15.0		George Urmson (OU)	11.02.51	1	Oxford	17 Mar

250 Yards

26.8		R.C.Brown (Pirates FC)		1	Tufnell Park	26 Apr

300 Yards

34.0		Thomas Snow (OU)	11.09.52	1hc	Oxford	13 Feb

600 Yards

1:15.0		John Clegg (Sheffield FC)	15.06.50	1hc	Sheffield (BL)	7 Jul

1000 Yards

2:23.6		Alfred Courtney (Dublin U/IRL)	02.53	1	Dublin (CP), IRL	9 Jun

1½ Miles

7:43.0		James Warburton (Haslingden)	13.11.45	inthc	Douglas, IOM	15 Jul

In a 2 mile race

1 Hour

10 miles		William Fuller (Thames H&H)	7.06.51	3hc	London (LB)	14 Jul

In a 10 mile race
Doubtful

11 miles		Albert Bird (Sheffield)	15.08.46	ex	Burra, AUS	8 Feb

See note for 10 miles

1 Mile Walk

6:25.0	p	Joe Stockwell (Camberwell)	13.01.44	int	London (Star)	26 May

In a 2 mile match which he finished alone, 'at leisure'

2 Miles Walk

14:38.0		William Morgan (Atalanta RC)	45	int	London (LB)	AAC	5 Apr

In a 7 mile walk

7 Miles Walk

54:56.0		William Morgan (Atalanta RC)	45	1	London (LB)	AAC	5 Apr

Cricket Ball

123y	112.47	William Game (OU)	2.10.53	1hc	Oxford	1 Nov
127y 1ft 3in	116.51	Game		1	Oxford	15 Mar

Regarded as the best on record, but thrown "in a perfect gale".

1874 UK Year List

100 Yards

10.0	John Clegg (Sheffield FC)	15.06.50	1	Huddersfield		20 Jun
10 1/5	Charles Barrett (OU)		50	1ht1	Oxford	18 Mar
10 1/5	William Gordon (OU)	9.09.52	1=ht3	Oxford		18 Mar
10 1/5	Edward Nash (OU)	53	1=ht3	Oxford		18 Mar
10 1/5	Nash			1	Oxford	20 Mar
10 1/5	Jenner Davies (CU)	10.04.51	1=	London (LB)	OvC	27 Mar
10 1/5	Michael Glazebrook (OU)	4.08.53	1=	London (LB)	OvC	27 Mar
10 1/5	George Templer (CU)	22.12.51	1=	London (LB)	OvC	27 Mar
10 1/5	James Heron (Lurgan AC/IRL)	c55	1	Belfast, IRL		2 May
10 1/5	William Blaxter (Derwent RC)	29.03.54	1	Nottingham		23 May
10 1/5	Douglas Ogilby (Dublin U/IRL)	16.02.53	1ht2	Dublin (CP) IRL open		11 Jun
10 1/5	Ogilby		1	Dublin (CP) IRL open		11 Jun
10 1/5	Ogilby		1hthc	Belfast, IRL		20 Jun
		(13/10)				
10 ¼	Clement Woodland (CU)	13.06.51	1ht2	Cambridge		16 Mar

Downhill

10 1/5	Alfred Oldfield (Birmingham AC)	2.10.53	1	Much Wenlock	26 May

Doubtful

10.0	Robert Thomson (Glasgow U)	24.11.54	1ht2	Glasgow (WSCG)	18 Apr
10.0	John Tennent (ex-OU/AUS)	31.07.46	1ht3	Glasgow (WSCG)	18 Apr
10.0	Thomas Hambridge (Eynsham)	5.03.54	1	Eynsham	27 May
10.0	John Langstaff (Richmond)	c50	1	Richmond, Yorks	25 Aug

Note: The triple dead heat in the Oxford v Cambridge match was run off, and Davies won.

220 Yards

23 ½	George Blaxter (Derby)	11.03.56	1	Hyde	25 Jul
23.7 e	George Gower (GWR)	6.11.49	3hc	Ealing	2 May
23 ¾	Thomas Wraith (N. Durham CC)	13.09.54	1	Gateshead	15 Aug
24.0	Francis Woods (ex-OU)	22.05.50	1ht1	Stowmarket	13 Apr
24.0	Woods		1	Stowmarket	13 Apr
24.0	G.F.Griffin (Post Office)		1	London (LB)	30 May
24.0 e	Frederick Finch (Bayswater Hornets FC)	55	3hc	Northampton	3 Aug
24.2 e	Edward Robinson (St Helens)	8.06.52	2	Hyde	25 Jul
24 ¼	T. Sanderson (Manchester)		1ht1	Hyde	25 Jul
24 ½	William Mather (Sale)	57	1	Hyde	25 Jul
24 ½	Wraith		1ht2	Gateshead	15 Aug
24 ½	Ralph Dowson (Leeds)	13.01.54	1	Horsforth	24 Aug
		(12/10)			
24.6 e	Harry Milner (Salford)	57	2	Hyde	25 Jul
24.7 e	Alfred Powles (Peckham AC)	15.06.53	2ht1hc	London (Oval)	18 Apr
24.7 e	Ernest Prentice (Stowmarket)	50	2ht1	Stowmarket	13 Apr
24 4/5	George Simpson (Lincoln FC)	53	1hc	Lincoln	1 Aug

Notes
Estimates: Gower 6y down on 23.0; Finch 1y down on 23.8; Robinson 6y down on 23.5; Powles 1y down on 24.5;
Milner ½y down on 24.5; Prentice 6y down on 24.0.
Mather and Milner were in the under 18 race at Hyde.
Powles was put back 1y for the final at the Oval, but won in 24¾.

440 Yards

50.5	John Clegg (Sheffield FC)	15.06.50	1	Sheffield (BL)		6 Jul
51.25	John Potter (LAC)	48	1	Manchester (CH)		20 Jun
51.25 p	Dick Buttery (Norton)	c50	1	Manchester (RO)		4 Jul
51.4	George Templer (CU)	22.12.51	1	Cambridge		24 Feb
51.4 e p	George Walsh (Royton)	3.02.44	2	Manchester (RO)		4 Jul
51.5	Templer		1	Cambridge		16 Mar
51.6	Templer		1	Cambridge		24 Feb
51.8	Alfred Lewis (CU)	10.08.54	1hc	Cambridge		19 Nov
52.0	G.F.Griffin (Post Office)		1	London (LB)		30 May
52.0	Lewis		1	Cambridge		12 Nov
52.0	Templer		1	London (LB)	OvC	27 Mar
		(11/7)				
52.4 e	John Batten (CU)	28.02.53	3	Cambridge		16 Mar

52.4 e	Charles Barrett (OU)	50	2	London (LB) OvC	27 Mar
52.4	F.W.Todd (GWR CC)		1	London (LB)	4 Jul
52.4	William Blaxter (Derwent RC)	29.03.54	1	Lincoln	1 Aug
52.4	Frederick Elborough (Ino RC)	30.07.52	1	Hove	23 Sep
52.5	George Gower (GWR CC)	6.11.49	1	Ealing	2 May
52.5 e	Galfred Congreve (Civil Service)	16.07.49	2	London (LB)	30 May
52.5 e	William Clague (Civil Service)	14.01.47	2	Manchester (CH)	20Jun
52.5	Francis Jones (OU)	3.09.53	1	Oxford	7 Nov

Road run
51.0 p	Philip Keohane (Cheltenham/IRL)	30.04.41	1	Nunhead, Surrey	10 Jun

Notes
Estimates: Walsh 1¼y down on 51.25; Batten 7y down on 51.5; Barrett 3y down on 52.0; Congreve 4y down on 52.0; Clague 10y down on 51.25
Clegg's time is as given in *The Field*. Bell's made it 51.2

880 Yards
2:00.5	F.W.Todd (GWR CC)		1	Willesden	5 Sep
2:01.2 e	Edward Sandford (OU)	11.05.51	3hc	Oxford	3 Dec
2:01.3 e	Sandford		2hc	Cambridge	14 Nov
2:01.4 e	Galfred Congreve (Civil Service)	16.07.49	2hc	London (LB)	20 Apr
2:01.75 p	George Walsh (Royton)	3.02.44	1	Manchester (RO)	9 May
2:02.1 e p	Joe Bailey (Manchester)		2	Manchester (RO)	9 May
2:02.25	Henry Hill (LAC)	22.01.52	1	London (LB)	10 Oct
2:02.9 e	Walter Slade (LAC)	6.04.54	2	London (LB)	10 Oct
2:02.9 e	Henry Bryden (LAC)	3.05.54	3	London (LB)	10 Oct
2:03.0 e	Sandford		3hc	Oxford	9 Nov
2:03.2	Sandford		1	Oxford	20 Mar
		(11/8)			
2:03.3 e	John Clegg (Sheffield FC)	15.06.50	2hc	Bradford	18 Jul
2:04.0	Joseph Moore (Birmingham AC)	3.04.52	1	Southport	5 Jun
2:04.1 e	Guy Power (OU)	4.11.52	2	Oxford	20 Mar

Notes
Estimates: Sandford 1½y down 2:01.0 (14/11) and 2 2/3y down on 2:00.75 (3/12) and 7y down on 2:02.0 (9/11); Bailey 2y down on 2:01.75; Congreve 15y down on 1:59.25; Slade 4y and Bryden 4y1ft down on 2:02.25; Clegg 1½y down on 2:03.0; Power 6y down on 2:03.2.

Mile
4:26.0	Walter Slade (LAC)	6.04.54	1hc	London (LB)	30 May
4:26.8 e p	James McLeavy (Alexandria)	26.10.52	3hc	Edinburgh	1 Jan
4:34.4	Slade		1hc	Blackheath	19 Sep
4:35.6	Edward Sandford (OU)	11.05.51	1	Oxford	18 Mar
4:36.25	James Warburton (Haslingden)	13.11.45	1	Manchester (CH)	20 Jun
4:36.6 e	William Stevenson (OU)	22.12.53	2	Oxford	18 Mar
4:38.0 p	George Waddell (SCO)		1	Auchinbegg	12 Sep
4:38.4	Alfred Wheeler (NLH)		1hc	London (LB)	26 Sep
4:38.5 e	Reginald Winter (OU)	54	3	Oxford	18 Mar
4:38.75 p	Henry Hescott (Mile End)	6.11.51	1	Weston-super-Mare	28 Jul
4:39.0	Sandford		1	London (LB) OvC	27 Mar
4:39.5 e	Bernard Marshall (Levenshulme FC)	26.05.53	2	Manchester (CH)	20 Jun
4:39.5	Slade		1	Lurgan, IRL	12 Sep
		(13/10)			
4:40.0	William Snell (Chudleigh)	54	1	Torquay	29 Aug
4:40.5	Alfred Courtney (ICAC/IRL)	02.53	1	Dublin (CP), IRL	10 Jun
4:40.6 e	John Chester (OU)	15.05.52	2	London (LB) OvC	27 Mar
4:41.4 e	Thomas Fairbairn (CU)	26.05.54	3	London (LB) OvC	27 Mar
4:41.6	William Seary (Oxford City AC)	52	1	Widnes	4 Jul
4:41.8	George Gower (GWR)	6.11.49	1	Nottingham	23 May
4:42.0	John North (Huddersfield)	52	1	Lancaster	25 May
4:42.66	Corrie Jackson (CU)	19.10.53	1	Cambridge	14 Mar
4:43.0	Thomas Duckett (Liverpool)	5.12.52	1	Grappenhall	22 Aug

Notes
Estimates: McLeavy 5y down on 4:26.0; Stevenson 6y and Winter 18y down on 4:35.6; Marshall 20y down on 4:36.25; Chester 10y and Fairbairn 15y down on 4:39.0. Stevenson ran 1m 40y (handicapped), winning in 4:44.5

at Oxford on 12 Nov, which equates to 4:38.2.

2 Miles

9:51.0	James Warburton (Haslingden)	13.11.45	1hc	Southport	6 Jun
9:57.8	Warburton		1hc	Blackburn	27 Jun
10:07.2	Warburton		int	Sheffield (BL)	6 Jul
10:07.4	Warburton		1hc	Lurgan, IRL	12 Sep
10:09.8	Warburton		2hc	Douglas, IOM	25 Aug
10:10.4	Warburton		1	Stoke-on-Trent	4 Aug
10:15.0	G.J.Stoddart (West of Scotland CC)		1	Glasgow (Alex)	2 May
10:19.25	John Bateman (Birmingham AC)	18.02.55	1	Birmingham(ALG)	25 Jul
10:19.4 e	Charles Larrette (SLH)	23.02.44	2	Birmingham (ALG)	25 Jul
10:19.5 e	Joseph Moore (Birmingham AC)	3.04.52	3	Birmingham (ALG)	25 Jul
		(10/5)			
10:28.3 e	Thomas Duckett (Liverpool)	5.12.52	2	Stoke-on-Trent	4 Aug
10:29.8	Alfred Courtney (Dublin U/IRL)	02.53	1	Dublin (LR) IRL	6 Jun
10:32.0	William Edwards (Birmingham AC)	24.05.53	1hc	Birmingham	4 Jul
10:35.0	William Stevenson (OU)	22.12.53	int	London (LB) OvC	27 Mar
10:35.3 e	Corrie Jackson (CU)	19.10.53	int	London (LB) OvC	27 Mar
10:36.25	Alfred Wheeler (NLH)		int	London (LB) AAC	30 Mar
10:36.4 e	Walter Slade (LAC)	6.04.54	int	London (LB) AAC	30 Mar
10:38.1 e	Herbert Russell (OU)	17.10.52	int	London (LB) OvC	27 Mar
10:38.9 e	J.J.Nunns (Dublin/IRL)		2	Dublin (LR) IRL	6 Jun
10:43.8	John Yardley (CU)	14.10.53	1	Cambridge	24 Nov
10:45.0	William Izard (CU)	51	int	Cambridge	17 Mar

Notes
Estimates: Larrette 1ft and Moore 4ft down on 10:19.25; Duckett 'nearly 100y' down on 10:10.4: Jackson 1½y and Russell 17y down on 10:35.0; Slade 'close up' on 10:36.25; Nunns 50y down on 10:29.8.
Intermediate times in races at 3 miles (17/03; 20/03; 27/03; 6/07) and 4 miles (30/03)

3 Miles

15:40.4	James Warburton (Haslingden)	13.11.45	1	Sheffield (BL)	6 Jul
15:47.5	William Stevenson (OU)	22.12.53	1	London (LB) OvC	27 Mar
15:48.0	Stevenson		1	Oxford	20 Mar
15:54.0	Alfred Wheeler (NLH)		int	London (LB) AAC	30 Mar
15:54.2 e	Walter Slade (LAC)	6.04.54	int	London (LB) AAC	30 Mar
16:01.4	Corrie Jackson (CU)	19.10.53	1	Cambridge	17 Mar
16:10.6 e	William Izard (CU)	51	2	Cambridge	17 Mar
16:12.0 e	Reginald Winter (OU)	54	2	Oxford	20 Mar
16:13.4 e	John Yardley (CU)	14.10.53	3	Cambridge	17 Mar
16:21.0 e	Frederick Shann (CU)	21.04.49	4	Cambridge	17 Mar
16:21.0	Herbert Russell (OU)	17.10.52	2	London (LB) OvC	27 Mar
16:21.5 e	Russell		3	Oxford	20 Mar
		(12/10)			
16:25.4 e	Henry Tylecote (OU)	24.07.53	4	Oxford	20 Mar
16:29.8 e	Thomas Duckett (Liverpool)	5.12.52	int	Stoke-on-Trent	5 Aug

Notes
Estimates: Slade 1y down on 15:54.0; Izard 50y, Yardley 65y and Shann 105y down on 16:01.4;
Winter 130y, Russell 180y and Tylecote 200y down on 15:48.0; Duckett 18y down on 16:26.4.
Intermediate times in races at 4 miles.

4 Miles

20:52.0	Walter Slade (LAC)	6.04.54	1	London (LB) AAC	30 Mar
20:57.4 e	James Warburton (Haslingden)	13.11.45	2	London (LB) AAC	30 Mar
21:51.2	Warburton		1	Stoke-on-Trent	5 Aug
22:05.4 e	Thomas Duckett (Liverpool)	5.12.52	2	Stoke-on-Trent	5 Aug
22:17.5 e	Augustus Micklefield (CU)	12.07.46	3	London (LB) AAC	30 Mar
23:21.25	Duckett		1	Hyde	25 Jul

Notes
Estimates: Warburton 30y & Micklefield 450y down on 20:52.0; Duckett 75y down on 21:51.2

6 Miles

38:37.0	p	J. Baker (Bethnal Green)		int	London (Bow)		3 Oct

Note
Intermediate time in a match against time to run 9 miles in 1 hour.

10 Miles
no reported times

120 Yards Hurdles

16 1/5	Hugh Upcher (OU)	28.10.53	1	London (LB)	OvC	27 Mar
16 1/5	Jenner Davies (CU)	10.04.51	1	Belfast, IRL		19 Jun
16 ½	Upcher		1	London (LB)	AAC	30 Mar
16 ½	Charles Bayly (OU/IRL)	26.02.52	1	Leeds		15 Jun
16 3/5	Upcher		1ht1	London (LB)	AAC	30 Mar
16 3/5	Sam Widdowson (Nottm Forest FC)	16.04.51	1	Nottingham		23 May
16 3/5	Samuel Roberts (CU)	30.04.52	1hc	Sheffield (BL)		6 Jul
16 3/5	Charles Spencer (Nottm Forest FC)	48	1	Sheffield (BL)		6 Jul
16.7 e	Roberts		2	London (LB)	OvC	27 Mar
16.7 e	Bayly		3	London (LB)	OvC	27 Mar
16.7 e	Spencer		2	Nottingham		23 May
16 4/5	Henry Beauchamp (CU)	25.12.51	1=ht2	London (LB)	AAC	30 Mar
16 4/5	John Reay (LAC)	9.07.53	1=ht2	London (LB)	AAC	30 Mar
16 4/5	Davies		1	Dublin (LR), IRL		6 Jun
16 4/5	Charles Lockton (Thames H&H)	2.07.56	1ht2	Worthing		2 Sep
16 4/5	Lockton		1	Worthing		2 Sep
16 4/5	Roberts		1hc	Cambridge		10 Nov
		(17/9)				
16.9 e	John Graveley (Guy's Hosp)	4.04.53	2	Worthing		2 Sep
17.0	William Tomkin (ex-Eton Coll)	56	1	Lewes		7 Sep

125y
17.0	Bayly		1hc	Oxford		7 Nov

126y
17.0	Reay		1hc	London (LB)		30 May

Doubtful
16 ¼	Spencer		1	Nottingham	25 Apr
16.9 e	Samuel Bestow (Nottm Forest FC)	3.03.52	2	Nottingham	25 Apr

The hurdles 'averaged 3ft 2in in height' (*Bell's Life*)

Notes
Estimates: Roberts 3y and Bayly 3y 6in down on 16.2 (27/03); Spencer 6in down on 16.6 (23/05); Graveley ½y down on 16.8; Bestow 4y down on 16.25.
Bell's Life this year made the times slower at the OvC and AAC meetings: Upcher 16½ (27/03); Beauchamp & Reay 17.0ht (30/03). *John Lawrence's Handbook* credited Davies with 16.2 in Dublin on 6/06.

220 Yards Hurdles

31.8	Charles Gardiner (Stow-on-the-Wold)	52	1	Bicester	24 Aug
32.0 e	W. Read (Northampton AC)		2	Bicester	24 Aug
32.4	Sam Widdowson (Nottm Forest FC)	16.04.51	1	Clifton	5 Sep
32.6 e	Robert Weaving (Drayton)	53	3	Bicester	24 Aug
33.4 e	H.V.Thomas (Hereford)		2	Clifton	5 Sep

Notes
Estimates: Read 1y and Weaving 5y down on 31.8; Thomas 6y down on 32.4.

440 Yards Hurdles

1:03.25	Sam Widdowson (Nottm Forest FC)	16.04.51	1	Douglas, IOM	28 Jul
1:03.8 e	James Gorman (Lurgan AC/IRL)	31.10.50	2	Douglas, IOM	28 Jul
1:06.2	John Curtis (Leeds AC)	22.07.51	1hc	Halifax	11 Jul
1:06.2 e	Samuel Bestow (Nottm Forest FC)	3.03.52	2hc	Lurgan, IRL	12 Sep
1:06.2	Widdowson		1	Douglas, IOM	25 Aug
1:06.5	George Blaxter (Derwent FC)	11.03.56	1	Compstall	23 May
1:06.5	Jenner Davies (CU)	10.04.51	1	Dublin (CP), IRL	11 Jun
1:07.2 e	William Lomas (Grappenhall)	c47	2	Douglas, IOM	25 Aug
1:08.1 e	Reginald Miller (Dublin U/IRL)	49	2	Dublin (CP), IRL	11 Jun

12 Hurdles

1:06.3 e	Thomas Bennett (Wakefield Trinity CC)	2.04.52	3hc	Wakefield		27 Jun
1:06.4	R.R.Robson (Sigglesthorne CC)		1	Bradford		18 Jul
1:06.5	John Vickerman (Huddersfield)	17.01.52	1	Malton		15 Jul
1:07.2 e	William Jefferson (Northallerton CC)	30.05.55	2	Bradford		18 Jul
1:07.5	T. Rolf (WECC School)	c56	1hc	Kilburn		29 Aug

12 hurdles + twice over water

1:01.75	Samuel Roberts (CU)	30.04.52	1	Huddersfield		20 Jun

Notes
Estimates: Bestow 10y down on 64.6; Lomas 6y down on 66.2; Miller 10y down on 66.5; Bennett 5y 6in down on 65.5; Jefferson 5y down on 66.4.

High Jump

5'11	1.803	Marshall Brooks (OU)	30.05.55	1	London (LB)	AAC	30 Mar
5'10	1.778	Brooks		1	London (LB)	OvC	27 Mar
5'10	1.778	Thomas Davin (ICAC/IRL)	51	2	London (LB)	AAC	30 Mar
5'9½	1.765	Brooks		1	Oxford		20 Mar
5'8½	1.740	John Graham (OU)	1.05.51	2	London (LB)	OvC	27 Mar
5'7	1.702	Graham		2	Oxford		20 Mar
5'7	1.702	Joseph Watson (LAC)	15.10.51	1	Barnes		28 Mar
5'7	1.702	Watson		3	London (LB)	AAC	30 Mar
5'7	1.702	Michael Glazebrook (OU)	4.08.53	1	Oxford		28 Nov
5'6½	1.689	Watson		1	Uxbridge		6 May
		(10/5)					
5'6	1.676	Frederick Swanwick (CU)	28.05.51	1	Cambridge		28 Feb
5'6	1.676	M. Kelly (QC Galway/IRL)		1	Galway, IRL		24 Mar
5'6	1.676	Alfred Oldfield (Birmingham AC)	2.10.53	1	Much Wenlock		26 May
5'6	1.676	Frederick Nott Bower (Civil Service)	15.08.54	1hc	London (LB)		30 May
5'6	1.676	Alfred Monnington (Bitteswell)	29.05.53	1	Market Harborough		13 Jul
5'6	1.676	Fred Mallinson (Gawthorpe)	c52	1	Kirkburton		25 Jul
5'6	1.676	Charles Oldfield (Birmingham AC)	28.10.55	1	Birmingham (ALG)		25 Jul
5'6	1.676	Henry King (Salisbury CC)	c55	1	Salisbury		17 Aug

Doubtful

5'10	1.778	John Bell (Cardiff)		1	Neath	6 Apr
5'8	1.727	Isaac Brown (Mountain Ash CC)		2=	Neath	6 Apr
5'8	1.727	John Morgan		2=	Neath	6 Apr

Three performances of this quality by little-known athletes suggests the conditions were irregular.

High Jump: Highland & Border

5'11	1.803	p	Hugh Andrews (Glasgow)	c52	1	Wishaw	23 Jul
5'11	1.803	p	F.T.H.Dixon (Morpeth)		1	Morpeth	15 Aug
5'9	1.753	p	Andrews		1	Alloa	12 Aug
5'8	1.727	p	Samuel Muir (Stewarton)	c41	1	Glasgow (QP)	9 May
5'8	1.727	p	Andrews		1=	Pollokshaws	20 Jun
5'8	1.727	p	Muir		1=	Pollokshaws	20 Jun
5'8	1.727	p	Peter Cameron (Kincardine O'Neil)	8.12.52	1	Coupar Angus	16 Jul
5'8	1.727	p	Andrews		1	Alva	13 Aug
5'8	1.727	p	Muir		1	Forfar	7 Aug
5'7½	1.715	p	Andrews		1	Springburn	19 Sep
5'7	1.702	p	Andrews		2	Glasgow (QP)	9 May
5'7	1.702	p	Andrews		1=	Hawick	5 Jun
5'7	1.702	p	John Robson (Denholm)	c49	1=	Hawick	5 Jun
5'7	1.702	p	Robert Easton (Barrhead)		3	Pollokshaws	20 Jun
5'7	1.702	p	Muir		2	Alva	13 Aug
5'7	1.702	p	Andrew Milne (Forfar)	24.11.39	2	Forfar	7 Aug
5'7	1.702	p	Cameron		3	Forfar	7 Aug
			(17/7)				
5'6	1.676	p	James Rough (Kilbarchan)	c46	3	Glasgow (QP)	9 May
5'6	1.676	p	Donald Dinnie (Stonehaven)	8.06.37	2	Coupar Angus	16 Ju

Pole Vault

10'7	3.23		Edwin Woodburn (Ulverston CC)	19.04.50	1	London (LB)	AAC	30 Mar
10'6	3.20		Charles Gaskin (Wisbech Fen)	56	1	Market Harborough		13 Jul
10'6	3.20		Gaskin		1=	Northampton		3 Aug
10'6	3.20		Robert Sabin (Culworth)	52	1=	Northampton		3 Aug
10'5	3.17		Walter Kelsey (Hull CC)	04.51	1	Ilkley		8 Aug
10'4	3.15		Hugh Fyffe (SLH)	23.10.52	2=	London (LB)	AAC	30 Mar
10'4	3.15		Kelsey		2=	London (LB)	AAC	30 Mar
10'4	3.15		Sabin		2=	London (LB)	AAC	30 Mar
10'4	3.15		Sabin		2	Market Harborough		13 Jul
10'3	3.12		Joseph Turnbull (Ernest NSCC)	c50	2	Ilkley		8 Aug
10'2	3.10		Edwin Dawes (Long Sutton)	12.08.52	1	Lincoln		1 Aug
10'2	3.10		John Gorham (Tonbridge)	53	2	Lincoln		1 Aug
10'2	3.10		Gaskin		1	Hinckley		3 Sep
10'2	3.10		Thomas Done (Northwich)	54	1	Stretford		12 Sep
			(14/9)					
10'0	3.05		James Symington (Market Harborough)	c53	1	Nottingham		25 Apr
10'0	3.05		Robert Mole (Stafford)	4.05.56	1=	Much Wenlock		26 May
10'0	3.05		George Wilson (Brentwood, Flint)		1=	Much Wenlock		26 May
10'0	3.05		Gerald Onslow (RMA)	7.02.53	1	Erith		20 Jun
10'0	3.05		John Peyton (Balla/IRL)		1	Castlebar, IRL		12 Aug
10'0	3.05		Henry King (Salisbury CC)	c55	1	Salisbury		17 Aug

Note
Dawes was awarded first prize at Lincoln because he "cleared it better".

Pole Vault: Highland, Lakeland & Border

11'0	3.35	p	David Anderson (Alnwick)	c46	1=	Bolton		11 Jul
11'0	3.35	p	Thomas Newby (Ulverston)	c52	1=	Bolton		11 Jul
10'9	3.28	p	William Borland (Edinburgh)	c48	1	Kilbarchan		11 Jul
10'9	3.28	p	Anderson		1	Bridge of Allan		6 Aug
10'7	3.23	p	David Milne (Forfar)	28.12.42	1	Forfar		7 Aug
10'6	3.20	p	Borland		1	Johnstone		18 Jul
10'6	3.20	p	Anderson		1	Leith		4 Aug
10'4	3.15	p	Borland		1=	Milngavie		29 Aug
10'4	3.15	p	John Kerss (Glasgow)	12.04.50	1=	Milngavie		29 Aug
10'3	3.12	p	Anderson		1	Bolton		13 Jul
10'3	3.12	p	Anthony Hall (Edinburgh)	c46	1=	Dundee		25 Jul
10'3	3.12	p	James Stewart (Dundee)		1=	Dundee		25 Jul
			(12/7)					
10'2	3.10	p	Samuel Muir (Stewarton)	c41	2	Johnstone		18 Jul
10'2	3.10	p	Peter Cameron (Kincardine O'Neil)	8.12.52	2	Forfar		7 Aug
10'1	3.07	p	William Ewing (Alexandria)	c47	2	Bridge of Allan		6 Aug
10'0	3.05	p	Marcellus Thompson (Kendal)	19.01.55	2	Bolton		13 Jul
10'0	3.05	p	William Crichton (Coupar Angus)	05.49	3	Forfar		7 Aug

Indoors

10'10	3.30 i p		Newby		1	Manchester (Cir)	1 Apr

Note
Another source gives the Milngavie result as 10'0/3.05.

Long Jump

23'1½	7.05		John Lane (Dublin U/IRL)	53	1	Dublin (CP), IRL		11 Jun
22'10½	6.97		Jenner Davies (CU)	10.04.51	1	London (LB)	OvC	27 Mar
22'10¼	6.97		Davies		2	Dublin (CP), IRL		11 Jun
22'8½	6.92		Charles Lockton (Merchant Taylors' Sch)	2.07.56	1	London		27 Apr
22'5	6.83		Davies		1	London (LB)	AAC	30 Mar
22'0½	6.72		Davies		1	Cambridge		16 Mar
22'0	6.71		Frederick Capps (ex-King's Coll Sch)	17.03.52	1	London		Mar
21'10½	6.67		Lockton		1	Louth		3 Aug
21'9	6.63		Hugh Upcher (OU)	28.10.53	2	London (LB)	OvC	27 Mar
21'6	6.55		Capps		1	Birmingham (ALG)		25 Jul
21'4	6.50		Lockton		1	London (LB)		20 Apr
21'4	6.50		Edwin Woodburn (Ulverston)	19.04.50	1	Lancaster		25 May
21'3	6.48		James Stephenson (Burnley)		2	Lancaster		25 May

21'1	6.43	Davies		1=	Dublin (LR), IRL	6 Jun
21'1	6.43	Lane		1=	Dublin (LR), IRL	6 Jun
			(13/5)			
21'0	6.40	Aaron Adshead (Durham Sch)	57	1	Durham	28 Mar
21'0	6.40	Edward Stocks (CU)	27.05.56	1	Whitstable	24 Apr
21'0	6.40	William Tilley (Widnes)	c56	1	Liverpool	1 Oct
20'11	6.38	Edward Nash (OU)	53	1	Oxford	18 Mar
20'8	6.30	H. Lee (Richmond FC)		1	Worthing	2 Sep
20'8	6.30	James Bird (Liverpool)		2	Liverpool	1 Oct
20'7	6.27	Harry Sproston (Birmingham AC)	48	2	Birmingham (ALG)	25 Jul
20'6¾	6.27	William Morton (Crewkerne)		1	Crewkerne	30 Jun
20'6	6.25	John Archdall (CU/IRL)	3.04.55	1	Charlbury	25 May

Notes
According to *Bell's Life,* the Dublin jumps on 11 June were aided by a strong wind and a slight decline, though over rather indifferent ground. The event was a decider after they tied at the Irish Civil Service sports on 6 June, and the terms were that they could take as many tries as they liked. Davies jumped his best with his fourth. Lane "after numerous attempts" bettered it.

Long Jump: Highland & Border

22'3	6.78	Samuel Muir (Stewarton)	c41	1	Milngavie	29 Aug
21'10	6.65	Muir		1	Alva	12 Aug
21'3	6.48	James Rough (Kilbarchan)	c46	2	Alva	12 Aug
20'11	6.38	Rough		2	Milngavie	29 Aug

Triple Jump

42'2	12.85	E. Egan (Kenmare/IRL)		1	Kenmare, IRL	14 Oct
42'0	12.80	Richard Glover (QC Galway/IRL)	c53	1	Galway, IRL	19 Mar
41'5	12.62	Thomas Wraith (N. Durham CC)	13.09.54	1	Newcastle	17 Oct
40'0	12.19	Michael Cannon (Tuam/IRL)		1	Tuam, IRL	24 Sep
38'11	11.86	Patrick Nally (Balla/IRL)	56	2	Tuam, IRL	24 Sep
37'6	11.43	Cpl W. Forrest (93rd Regt)		1	Woolwich	18 Aug
36'10	11.23	J.G.Dixon (Northern AC)		2	Newcastle	17 Oct
36'9	11.20	J.F.Williams (Merchiston Castle Sch)	c56	1	Merchiston	17 Apr
36'0	10.97	Magnus Sandison (St Andrews U)	6.09.57	1	St Andrews	25 Apr
35'8	10.87	Maxwell Wright (St Andrews U)	9.09.57	2	St Andrews	25 Apr
35'0	10.67	Pte Mulholland (E. Norfolk Regt)		1	Dover	29 May
34'2	10.41	Pte Flemming (E. Norfolk Regt)		2	Dover	29 May

Triple Jump: Highland & Border

48'0	14.63 p	Thomas Aitken (Walkerburn)	23.05.53	1	Dalkeith	5 Sep
47'10	14.58 p	Robert Knox (Newstead)	17.09.47	1	Galashiels	25 Jul
47'9	14.55 p	Aitken		2	Galashiels	25 Jul
47'3	14.40 p	Samuel Muir (Stewarton)	c41	1	Milngavie	29 Aug
46'4	14.12 p	Muir		1	Alva	13 Aug
46'3	14.10 p	James Rough (Kilbarchan)	c46	2=	Milngavie	29 Aug
46'3	14.10 p	James Young (Alva)	c47	2=	Milngavie	29 Aug
46'2	14.07 p	Rough		2	Alva	13 Aug
46'0	14.02 p	Peter Cameron (Kincardine O'Neil)	8.12.52	1	Aberdeen	18 Jul
46'0	14.02 p	Muir		1	Alloa	12 Aug
45'11½	14.01 p	Young		3	Alva	13 Aug
45'7	13.89 p	Muir		1	Bridge of Allan	1 Aug
45'7	13.89 p	Young		2	Alloa	12 Aug
			(13/6)			
45'2	13.77 p	Hugh Andrews (Glasgow)	c52	2	Dalkeith	5 Sep
45'0	13.72 p	Archibald Mitchell (Alva)	51	3=	Alloa	12 Aug
45'0	13.72 p	William Rough		3=	Alloa	12 Aug
44'6	13.56 p	William Borland (Kilbarchan)	c48	3	Bridge of Allan	1 Aug
44'4	13.51 p	Adam Scott (Edinburgh)	15.08.52	2	Jedburgh	31 Jul
44'2	13.46 p	James Stewart (Dumfries)		2	Hawick	5 Jun
44'1	13.44 p	John Hunter (Tillicoultry)		1	Clackmannan	26 Jun
43'6	13.26 p	John Wilson (Edinburgh)	c46	1	Carlops	8 Aug
43'5	13.23 p	Alexander Hume (Govan)		1	Dalry	1 Aug
43'2	13.16 p	J. Murray		3	Dalkeith	5 Sep
42'8	13.00 p	James Aitken (Walkerburn)		2	Innerleithen	15 Aug

42'6	12.95 p	J. Hume (Greenock)		3=	Glasgow (QP)		9 May
42'5	12.93 p	Daniel Lamont (Kilbarchan)	c55	2	Lochwinnoch		19 Sep
42'2	12.85 p	John McIntosh (Dunblane)		1	Dunblane (local)		11 Jul
42'0	12.80 p	John Campbell (Alexandria)		2	Balfron		18 Jul
42'0	12.80 p	James Weir (Innerleithen)	c56	1	Peebles		8 Aug

Shot

40'8¾	12.41	Edward Bor (LAC/IRL)	25.08.50	1	Dublin (LR) IRL ICAC		27 Jun
40'8½	12.41	Charles Wadsworth (QC Belfast/IRL)	c50	2	Dublin (LR) IRL ICAC		27 Jun
40'5	12.32	Maurice Davin (Suir/IRL)	29.06.42	1	Dublin (LR), IRL		6 Jun
40'2	12.24	Wadsworth		1	Belfast, IRL		16 May
39'11	12.17	William Powell Moore (LAC)	23.04.46	1	London (LB)	AAC	30 Mar
39'9	12.12	Robert Irvine (Edinburgh U)	19.04.53	1	Edinburgh (ACG)		17 Jun
39'7	12.06	David Kennedy (QC Cork/IRL)		2	Belfast, IRL		16 May
39'6	12.04	Wadsworth		2	Dublin (LR), IRL		6 Jun
39'4	11.99	Wadsworth		wo	Belfast, IRL		20 Jun
39'3	11.96	Thomas Stone (Liverpool)	24.01.52	2	London (LB)	AAC	30 Mar
39'2	11.94	Wadsworth		1hc	Belfast, IRL		2 May
		(11/7)					
38'5	11.71	J. Wallace (Newcastle-under-Lyme)		1	Newcastle-und-Lyme		21 Aug
38'11½	11.62	Nicholas Littleton (CU)	11.01.53	3	London (LB)	AAC	30 Mar
37'11	11.56	Stephen Brown (OU)	1.06.54	1	London (LB)	OvC	27 Mar
37'8	11.48	James Daly (QC Cork/IRL)	c54	1	Cork, IRL		22 Apr
37'7½	11.47	Frederick Coxhead (ex-OU)	10.10.48	1	Bournemouth		6 Apr
37'6	11.43	Peter Anton (St Andrews U)	25.06.50	1	St Andrews		28 Feb
37'4	11.38	Jackson (Trent College)		1	Nottingham		16 Apr

Note
42'0 by T. Stone and 40'9 by F. Power at Southport on 6 June with a shot reweighed at 14¼lb.

Shot: Highland & Border
Includes putting 16lb stone

44'11*	13.69 p	Donald Dinnie (Stonehaven)	8.06.37	1	Huntly		1 Aug
44'11	13.69 p	Dinnie		1	Stonehaven		15 Aug
44'1	13.44 p	Dinnie		1	Aboyne		11 Sep
44'0*	13.41 p	Dinnie		1	Forfar		7 Aug
43'9*	13.33 p	James Fleming (Tullymet)	18.09.40	1	Lumphanan		18 Jul
43'2	13.16 p	John George (Edinburgh)	46	1	Johnstone		18 Jul
43'1*	13.13 p	Dinnie		2	Lumphanan		18 Jul
43'0	13.11 p	Fleming		2	Aboyne		11 Sep
42'6*	12.95 p	William Bremner (Glenbucket)	3.01.47	1	Udny		6 Aug
42'0	12.80 p	Bremner		1	Ballater		28 Jul
41'10*	12.75 p	Fleming		2	Forfar		7 Aug
41'5*	12.62 p	Bremner		3	Lumphanan		18 Jul
		(12/4)					
40'10	12.45 p	George Mearns (Aberdeen)		3	Aboyne		11 Sep
40'2	12.24 p	John McHattie (Aberdeen)		1	Aberdeen		18 Jul
38'10	11.84 p	Charles Stewart (Glenmuick)		2	Ballater		28 Jul
38'3*	11.66 p	John Brown (Dalkeith)		1	Tranent		18 Jun
38'2*	11.63 p	John Dewar		2	Comrie		26 Aug
37'7	11.46 p	James Shedden (Johnstone)		2	Johnstone		18 Jul

Note
The stone at Ballater was 16½lb.
*correct weight assumed from evidence of other years

Weight unstated

43'7	13.28 p	William Graham (Dalkeith)		1	Dalkeith	5 Sep
40'9	12.42 p	Fleming		1	Nairn	8 Aug
40'2	12.24 p	Bremner		2	Nairn	8 Aug
40'0	12.19 p	John Anderson (Edinburgh)		2	Dalkeith	5 Sep
38'0	11.58 p	W. Henderson		1	Carlops	8 Aug

22lb stone by performer

40'2	12.24 p	Dinnie		1	Birnam	27 Aug
40'0	12.19 p	Fleming		2hc	Dundee	11 Jul
38'6	11.73 p	Duffy		1	Bridge of Allan	1 Aug

36'2	11.02	p	Mearns		3	Aberdeen		20 Jul

Doubtful

54'6	16.61	p	Owen Duffy (Edinburgh/IRL)	c47	1	Bridge of Allan		1 Aug
51'4	15.65	p	Fleming		1	Inverness		17 Sep
49'9	15.16	p	George		2	Bridge of Allan		1 Aug
48'8	14.83	p	Dinnie		1	Montrose		8 Aug
47'6	14.48	p	Peter McCowan (Comrie)		3	Bridge of Allan		1 Aug
47'6	14.48	p	Dinnie		1	Milngavie		29 Aug
47'0	14.33	p	Dinnie		1	Greenock		6 Jun
47'3½	14.41	p	Bremner		2	Inverness		17 Sep
45'10	13.97	p	Fleming		2	Greenock		6 Jun
45'1	13.74	p	Fleming		2	Milngavie		29 Aug
37'10	11.53	p	Alexander Ritchie (Glasgow)		3	Greenock		6 Jun

Note
Donald Dinnie's biography lists a medal inscription for putting the 20lb stone 41'4/12.60 at Aberdeen.

Hammer

126'9	38.63		George Hales (CU)	20.05.54	1	London (LB)	OvC	27 Mar
126'0	38.40		John Todd (OU)	19.09.52	1hc	Oxford		7 Nov
120'0	36.58		Todd		2	London (LB)	OvC	27 Mar
120'0	36.58		Stephen Brown (OU)	1.06.54	1	London (LB)	AAC	30 Mar
119'8	36.47		William A. Burgess (ex-OU)	27.12.46	2	London (LB)	AAC	30 Mar
119'6½	36.44		Brown		3	London (LB)	OvC	27 Mar
119'2	36.32		Hales		1	Cambridge		28 Feb
118'10	36.22		John Paterson (CU)	7.12.50	4	London (LB)	OvC	27 Mar
117'0	35.66		Todd		1	Sleaford		3 Sep
116'10	35.61		Hales		1	Cambridge		17 Mar
116'10	35.61		Paterson		3	London (LB)	AAC	30 Mar
115'8	35.26		Todd		1	Oxford		20 Mar
114'3	34.82		Brown		2	Oxford		20 Mar

(13/5)

110'8	33.73		M. Lawler (Borris/IRL)		1	Borris, IRL		22 Jul
110'6	33.68		P. Barron (Borris/IRL)		2	Borris, IRL		22 Jul
108'7½	33.11		Maurice Davin (Suir/IRL)	29.06.42	1	Dublin (LR), IRL		6 Jun
108'0	32.92		Matthew Stritch (RIC/IRL)	02.47	1	Dublin (LR) IRL ICAC		27 Jun
105'0	32.00		John Galwey Foley (RIC/IRL)	50	2	Dublin (LR), IRL		6 Jun
100'5	30.61		Orlando Coote (Malvern Coll)	14.03.55	1	Malvern		6 Apr
100'0+	30.48		Henry Leeke (ex-CU)	6.02.46	4	London (LB)	AAC	30 Mar
98'6	30.02		James Daly (QC Cork/IRL)	c54	1	Cork, IRL		21 Apr
98'5	30.00		Joseph Moxley (QC Belfast/IRL)	c44	1	Belfast, IRL		2 May
98'4	29.97		George Cartland (OU)	30.01.53	1hc	Oxford		14 Nov
96'0	29.26		J. Wallace (N. Staffs CC)		1	Manchester (CH)		20 Jun
94'6	28.80		Charles Wadsworth (QC Belfast/IRL)	c50	2	Belfast, IRL		2 May
93'5	28.47		Charles Bayly (OU/IRL)	26.02.52	2hc	Oxford		7 Nov
92'9	28.27		William Cloete (OU)	5.07.51	1hc	Oxford		9 Nov

Hammer: Highland & Border

117'9*	35.89	p	Donald Dinnie (Stonehaven)	8.06.37	1	Forfar	7 Aug
114'3	34.82	p	Dinnie		1	Dundee	25 Jul
113'5*	34.57	p	James Fleming (Ballinluig)	18.09.40	2	Forfar	7 Aug
111'10	34.09	p	Dinnie		1	Aberfeldy	8 Sep
110'6*	33.68	p	Dinnie		1	Lumphanan	18 Jul
110'0	33.53	p	Dinnie		1	Milngavie	29 Aug

(6/2)

102'1	31.11	p	William Bremner (Glenbucket)	3.01.47	1	Aberdeen	20 Jul
99'5½	30.31	p	William Fleming (Dundee)	22.08.42	1	Inverness	17 Sep
92'2	28.09	p	John McHattie (Aberdeen)		2	Inverness	17 Sep

Note: *correct weight assumed from evidence of other years

Weight unstated

127'3	38.79	p	Dinnie		1	Sheffield (BL)	22 Jun
118'9	36.19	p	Dinnie		1hc	Stonehaven	15 Aug
117'8	35.86	p	Alexander Robertson (New Craig)		1	Udny (local)	6 Aug
113'10	34.70	p	Dinnie		1	Greenock (heavy)	6 Jun

112'10	34.39	p	J. Fleming		2	Sheffield (BL)	22 Jun
				(5/3)			
109'5	33.35	p	George Yeats (Udny)		2	Udny (local)	6 Aug
103'0	31.39	p	James Shedden (Johnstone)		1	Dalry	1 Aug
101'7	30.96	p	John McCurrach (Gartly)	2.06.52	1	Huntly (local)	31 Jul
100'11	30.76	p	James Russell (Gartly)	c48	2	Huntly (local)	31 Jul
100'0	30.48	p	William Brown (Elderslie)		2	Dalry	1 Aug
95'6	29.11	p	William McGregor (Drumdelgie)		3	Huntly (local)	31 Jul
94'2	28.70	p	Peter McHardy (Glasgow)	c48	3	Greenock (heavy)	6 Jun
93'6	28.50	p	J. Smith (Edinburgh)		1	Tranent	18 Jun
93'6	28.50	p	A.C.Joiner		1	Arbibolt	8 Aug

Other Events

150 Yards

15.5		Charles Chappell (Buxton CC)	c52	1	Buxton	19 Sep
15.5	p	Philip Keohane (Cheltenham/IRL)	30.04.41	1	Dulwich	24 Aug

Note
William Clague (Civil Service) ran 14.8 from scratch in a handicap at Douglas, IOM on 25 Aug, but on remeasurement the course was found to be short.

200 Yards

21.1	e	Samuel Roberts (CU)	30.04.52	3hc	Cambridge	18 Nov

'Won by 1ft, (21.0), with Roberts close up.'

250 Yards

27.0		Tom Mantell (Brighton AC)	53	1hc	Hove	23 Sep

300 Yards

32.25	p	Mungo Waterston (Edinburgh)	12.10.54	1	Manchester (RO)	16 May

500 Yards

1:00.75	p	George Walsh (Royton)	3.02.44	1	Manchester (RO)	23 May

Best on record

600 Yards

1:14.1	e p	Dick Buttery (Norton)	c50	2hc	Manchester (RO)	7 Nov

4y down on 1:13.6

1000 Yards

2:36.5		Alfred Courtney (Dublin U/IRL)	02.53	1	Dublin (CP), IRL	10 Jun

1 Mile Walk

6:23.0	p	William Perkins (Old Kent Road)	16.09.52	int	London (LB)	1 Jun

2 Miles Walk

13:30.0	p	William Perkins (Old Kent Road)	16.09.52	int	London (LB)	1 Jun

Each of the above walks was in a 3 mile match.

7 Miles Walk

55:26.75		William Morgan (Atalanta RC)	45	1	London (LB) AAC	30 Mar

50 Miles Walk

9:24:16.5	p	Alexander Clarke (Bethnal Green)	49	1	London (Star)	11 Oct

Cricket Ball

121y 0ft 0in	110.64	William Game (OU)	2.10.53	1	Oxford	18 Mar

1875 UK Year List

100 Yards

10.0	Edward Salmon (CU)	29.10.54	1		Bury St Edmunds	15 Apr
10 1/5	Clement Woodland (CU)	13.06.51	1		London (LB) OvC	19 Mar
10 1/5	John Potter (SLH)	48	1ht2hc		Belfast, IRL	12 Jun
10 ¼	William Blaxter (Derwent FC)	29.03.54	1		Newark	17 May
10 ¼	H. Simpkin (Bury)		1		Lancaster	17 May
10 ¼	Frederick Elborough (LAC)	30.07.52	1		Sheffield (BL)	5 Jul
10.3 e	Blaxter		2		Sheffield (BL)	5 Jul
10 2/5	Cornwallis Martin (OU)	19.03.55	1		Oxford	1 Feb
10 2/5	Edward Evans (OU)	54	1ht2		Oxford	6 Mar
10.4 e	Evans		2		London (LB) OvC	19 Mar
10 2/5	R.B.Stewart (Eton House)		1		Tonbridge	23 Mar
10 2/5	James Heron (Lurgan AC/IRL)	c55	1ht2hc		Belfast, IRL	1 May
10 2/5	Douglas Ogilby (NICC/IRL)	16.02.53	1hc		Belfast, IRL	1 May
10 2/5	Ogilby		1ht1		Dublin (LR), IRL	17 May
10 2/5	Ogilby		1		Dublin (LR), IRL	17 May
10.4 e	Robert Shaw (Liverpool)		2		Lancaster	17 May
10 2/5	Ogilby		1ht1		Dublin (CP), IRL	8 Jun
10 2/5	Abraham Cronyn (Dublin U/IRL)	3.09.55	1ht2		Dublin (CP), IRL	8 Jun
10 2/5	Potter		1		Belfast, IRL	11 Jun
10 2/5	George Kenny (Clongowes Coll/IRL)	7.06.55	1ht		Dublin, IRL	7 Aug
10 2/5	Alfred Scott (OU)	53	1ht2		Oxford	13 Nov
	(21/15)					

School Sports

10.0	Edgar Storey (Fettes College)	6.02.59	1		Edinburgh	6 Apr
10.2 e	James Nicol (Fettes College)		2		Edinburgh	6 Apr

"This can hardly be accepted as correct" (*The Scotsman*). Nicol 1y down.

10 2/5	Charles Lockton (Merchant Taylors' Sch)	2.07.56	1		London (LB)	17 Apr

Reported wind-assisted

10 1/5	Ogilby		1		Dublin (LR) IRL ICAC	22 May
10 1/5	Kenny		1		Dublin (LR), IRL	26 Jun
10 1/5	Ogilby		1ht2		Dublin (LR), IRL	26 Jun
10 2/5	Kenny		1ht1		Dublin (LR), IRL	26 Jun
10.4 e	Ogilby		2		Dublin (LR), IRL	26 Jun

Doubtful

9 ¾	Charles Davis (Witney)	c51	1		Witney	29 Mar
10 1/5	Heron		1		Belfast, IRL	1 May

' …got about a yard the best of the pistol' *Irish Sportsman & Farmer.*

Downhill

10 ¼	W. Blaxter		1		Widnes	10 Jul

Estimates: Blaxter 6in down on 10.25 (5/07); Evans 'nearly 2y down' on 10.2 (19/03); Shaw 1y down on 10.25 (17/05).

220 Yards

23.0	David Watson (Glasgow Academicals)	7.01.54	1		Glasgow (Ac)	8 May
23.0	Richard Coombes (Paignton)	53	1		Crewkerne	22 Jun
23.2 e	Robert Thomson (Glasgow U)	24.11.54	2		Glasgow (Ac)	8 May
23 1/5	Alfred Powles (SLH)	15.06.53	1		Dublin, IRL	3 Jun
23 1/5	Douglas Ogilby (Dublin U/IRL)	16.02.53	1ht2hc		Dublin (CP), IRL	8 Jun
23 ¼	Frederick Elborough (LAC)	30.07.52	1		London (LB)	13 Mar
23.3 e	Woodford Woodforde (Crewkerne)	c54	2		Crewkerne	22 Jun
23.3 e	George Blaxter (Derwent FC)	11.03.56	2hc		Sale	26 Jun
23.3 e	Arthur Tindall (LAC)	26.12.53	2ht1hc		Northampton	2 Aug
23.7 e	Edward Singer (Frome)	c51	3		Crewkerne	22 Jun
23 4/5	James Heron (Lurgan AC/IRL)	c55	1		Belfast, IRL	11 Jun
23.8 e	John Potter (SLH)	48	2		Belfast, IRL	11 Jun
	(12/12)					
24 1/5	Alexander Brash (Pendleton)	c51	1hc		Manchester (CH)	7 Aug
24 ½	John Reay (LAC)	9.07.53	1		London (LB)	22 May
24.5 e	Alfred Courtney (Dublin U/IRL)	02.53	4		Belfast, IRL	11 Jun
24 ½	Thomas Bartens (Peckham AC)	54	1		Brighton	22 Sep
24.6 e	Samuel Hornidge (Peckham AC)	51	2		Brighton	22 Sep
24.8 e	G.F.Griffin (Civil Service)		2		London (LB)	22 May

Estimates: Thomson 1y down on 23.0; Woodforde 2y and Singer 5½y down on 23.0; Blaxter 1ft down on 23.25; Tindall 6in down on 23.25; 'we thought Potter had won' (23.8); Ogilby 5y and Courtney 6y down on 23.8 (11/06); Hornidge 'just shot on the post' (24.5); Griffin 2y down on 24.5.

440 Yards

50.7	Frederick Elborough (LAC)	30.07.52	1	Sheffield (BL)		5 Jul
51.0	Elborough		1	London (LB)	AAC	22 Mar
51.0	George Blaxter (Derwent FC)	11.03.56	1	Blackley		31 Jul
51.2 e	J. Taylor (Blackley)		2	Blackley		31 Jul
51.25	Elborough		1	London (LB)		19 Jun
51.4 e	Elborough		3hc	London (LB)		22May
51.5	William Seary (Oxford City AC)	52	1	Oadby		21 Jun
51.6	Thomas Snow (OU)	11.09.52	1	London (LB)	OvC	19 Mar
51.6 e	Alfred Lewis (CU)	10.08.54	2	London (LB)	AAC	22 Mar
51.7 e	John Potter (SLH)	48	3	London (LB)	AAC	22 Mar
51.8 e	Lewis		2	London (LB)	OvC	19 Mar
52.0	Lewis		1	Cambridge		2 Mar
		(12/7)				
52.3 e	F.W.Todd (GWR)		2hc	Ealing		24 Jul
52.5 e	William Blaxter (Derwent FC)	29.03.54	2	Sheffield (BL)		5 Jul
52.6 e	Wilfred Grant (CU)	7.04.54	2	Cambridge		2 Mar
52.7 e	G.F.Griffin (LAC)		2	London (LB)		19 Jun
52.8 e	Edward Salmon (CU)	29.10.54	3	Cambridge		2 Mar
52.9 e	Alfred Powles (LAC)	15.06.53	3hc	London (Oval)		11 Sep

Downhill

49.6 e	Powles		3hc	Tufnell Park	16 Oct
49.9 e	Powles		2ht2hc	Tufnell Park	16 Oct

"Tufnell Park is nearly all downhill" (*Bell's Life*).

Estimates: Taylor 1y down on 51.0; Elborough 3y 1ft down on 51.0; Lewis 5y and Potter 5y 1ft down on 51.0 (22/03); Lewis 1y down on 51.6 (19/03); Griffin 12y down on 51.25; Grant 5y and Salmon 6½y down on 52.0 (02/03); Blaxter 15y down on 50.7 (05/07); Todd 2y down on 52.0 (24/07); Powles 7y down on 52.0 (11/09); Powles 4½y down on 49.0 (16/10) and 3y down on 49.5 in ht.
The Field gave Lewis 51.8 in the CU sports on 2/03. Grant would get 52.4e and Salmon 52.6e.
The *Sheffield Telegraph* gives 50¾ for Elborough (05/07).

880 Yards

2:00.4	Henry Hill (LAC)	22.01.52	1	London (LB)		23 Oct
2:00.6	Hill		1	Oxford		9 Nov
2:01.2 e	Charles Bryan (Liverpool)	c47	2hc	Hanley		17 May
2:01.2	Alfred Courtney (Dublin U/IRL)	02.53	1	Dublin (CP), IRL		9 Jun
2:01.3 e	Llewellyn Burt (LAC)	c54	2	London (LB)		23 Oct
2:01.5 e	Arthur Pelham (CU)	28.12.50	2	Oxford		9 Nov
2:01.7 e	Walter Slade (LAC)	6.04.54	2	Dublin (CP), IRL		9 Jun
2:02.0	Slade		1	London (LB)		8 May
2:02.2	Courtney		3hc	Belfast, IRL		12 Jun
2:02.4	Edward Sandford (OU)	11.05.51	1	Oxford		8 Mar
2:02.6 e	John Chester (OU)	15.05.52	2	Oxford		8 Mar
2:03.2 e	William Seary (Oxford City AC)	52	2hc	Manchester (Pom)		19 Jun
2:03.5	Slade		int	London (LB)		19 Jun
		(13/9)				
2:03.6 e	Charles Metcalfe (OU)	8.09.53	3	Oxford		8 Mar
2:03.75	John Ferguson (NICC/IRL)	52	1	Lurgan, IRL		4 Sep
2:04.0	Charles Cumberbatch (CU)	22.04.55	1	Cambridge		4 Mar
2:04.2 e	John Smith (Bury AC)	13.04.55	3hc	Manchester (Pom)		28 Aug
2:04.4 e	Henry Bryden (LAC)	3.05.54	2	London (LB)	AAC	22 Mar
2:04.8 e	F.W.Todd (GWR)		3	London (LB)	AAC	22 Mar

Doubtful

1:59.0	James Harris (5th Warwickshire Volunteers)	1	Stratford-on-Avon	29 Mar

Another little-known runner, A.C.Child, "a good second".

Estimates: Bryan 1y down on 2:01.0; Burt 6y down on 2:00.4; Pelham 6y down on 2:00.6 (9/11); Slade 3½y down on 2:01.2 (9/06); Chester 1y and Metcalfe 8y down on 2:02.4 (8/03); Seary 3y down on 2:02.75 (19/06); Smith 4½y down on 2:03.5 (28/08); Bryden 1y and Todd 4y down on 2:04.2 (22/03).
Intermediate time in 1 mile race.

Mile

4:24.5	Walter Slade (LAC)	6.04.54	1	London (LB)		19 Jun
4:25.6 e p	James McLeavy (Alexandria)	26.10.52	3hc	Glasgow (Spr)		4 Sep
4:26.75	Slade		1	Sheffield (BL)		5 Jul
4:28.5	Henry Bryden (LAC)	3.05.54	2	London (LB)		19 Jun
4:28.8	Slade		1	Dublin (CP), IRL		8 Jun
4:29.5	Llewellyn Burt (LAC)	c54	3	London (LB)		19 Jun
4:31.5	Alfred Courtney (Dublin U/IRL)	02.53	1	Belfast, IRL		1 May
4:33.0	Courtney		2	Dublin (CP), IRL		8 Jun
4:33.75	William Seary (Oxford City AC)	52	1	Manchester (Pom)		18 Jun
4:34.0	Slade		1	Belfast, IRL		11 Jun
4:34.5	Thomas Duckett (Liverpool)	5.12.52	1	St Helens		17 Jul
		(11/7)				
4:34.7 e	James Gibb (LAC)	11.12.53	2	Manchester (Pom)		18 Jun
4:34.75	Edward Sandford (OU)	11.05.51	1	London (LB)	OvC	19 Mar
4:34.8	Henry Sandford (OU)	27.07.52	1	Oxford		12 Nov
4:34.9 e	Edward Nicolls (OU)	27.02.54	2	London (LB)	OvC	19 Mar
4:35.5 e	John Smith (Bury AC)	13.04.55	3	Manchester (Pom)		18 Jun

Estimates: McLeavy 5y down on 4:24.75; Nicolls ½y down on 4:34.75; Gibb 6y, Smith 11y on 4:33.75 (18/6).
The *Sheffield Telegraph* gives Slade 4:27.5 (05/07).

2 Miles

9:41.75 p	James Sanderson (Whitworth)	28.12.37	1	Manchester (RO)		4 Sep
9:46.5	Thomas Duckett (Liverpool)	5.12.52	1hc	St Helens		17 Jul
9:50.0	Walter Slade (LAC)	6.04.54	1hc	Belfast, IRL		11 Jun
9:50.75	Duckett		1	Burley-in-Wharfedale		22 May
9:51.0	James Warburton (Haslingden)	13.11.45	1	Belfast, IRL		1 May
9:56.6	Warburton		1	Belfast, IRL		29 Mar
9:57.25	Duckett		1	Southport		21 Aug
9:58.0 p	George Hazael (Deptford)	22.11.44	int	London (LB)		15 Feb
9:59.0	Duckett		1	Stoke-on-Trent		4 Aug
9:59.9 e	Duckett		2hc	Manchester (Pom)		19 Jun
10:02.5	George Philips (Rangers FC)		1	Glasgow (Alex)		24 Apr
		(11/6)				
10:03.0	James Gibb (LAC)	11.12.53	int	London (LB)		26 Apr
10:03.6 e	John Finlayson (Clydesdale FC)	27.07.54	2	Glasgow (Alex)		24 Apr
10:08.3 e	J.F.G.Gordon (NICC/IRL)		2	Belfast, IRL		1 May
10:12.5	Percy Stenning (LAC)	31.08.54	inthc	London (LB)		13 Mar
10:13.0 e	John Bateman (Birmingham AC)	18.02.55	2	Southport		21 Aug
10:20.0	William Stevenson (OU)	22.12.53	int	London (LB)	OvC	19 Mar
10:20.2 e	Charles Bulpett (OU)	18.08.52	int	London (LB)	OvC	19 Mar
10:23.0	Charles Mason (LAC)	3.06.51	int	London (LB)		20 Nov

Estimates: Duckett 40y down on 9:53.0 (19/06); Finlayson 6y down on 10:02.5; Gordon nearly 100y down on 9:51
(1/05); Bateman 90y down on 9:57.25 (21/08); Bulpett 'together' with Stevenson (19/03).
Intermediate times in races at 3 miles (19/03; 20/11); 4 miles (15/02; 13/03; 26/04)
Note: Hazael passed 2 miles in 9:38.0 from a 50y start in a 4 mile handicap at Hackney Wick on 2 Aug. This
would equate to 9:46.4e.

3 Miles

15:20.0	James Gibb (LAC)	11.12.53	int	London (LB)		26 Apr
15:21.0	Walter Slade (LAC)	6.04.54	int	London (LB)		26 Apr
15:30.4	William Stevenson (OU)	22.12.53	1	London (LB)	OvC	19 Mar
15:32.0	Thomas Duckett (Liverpool)	5.12.52	int	Stoke-on-Trent		4 Aug
15:33.5	Gibb		int	London (LB)	AAC	22 Mar
15:36.5	Charles Bulpett (OU)	18.08.52	2	London (LB)	OvC	19 Mar
15:37.0	Gibb		int	London (LB)		13 Mar
15:44.0	Charles Mason (LAC)	3.06.51	2hc	London (LB)		20 Nov
15:46.0 p	George Hazael (Deptford)	22.11.44	int	Glasgow (Spr)		2 Oct
15:50.0	Percy Stenning (LAC)	31.08.54	int	London (LB)		13 Mar
15:59.25	Bulpett		1	Oxford		9 Mar
16:04.0	Frederick Jefferson (CU)	25.04.54	1	Cambridge		4 Mar
		(12/9)				
16:10.0	John Bateman (Birmingham AC)	18.02.55	inthc	Birmingham (ALG)		26 Jul

All Intermediate times in 4 mile races.

Hazael passed 3 miles in 14:28 from a 50y start in a 4 mile handicap at Hackney Wick on 2 Aug. This equates to 14:36.3e. *The Field* gave Bulpett 15:15.0 in the OU sports on 9/03; however, *Bell's Life* gave times for first and second as above, and seems the more reliable.

4 Miles

20:17.3	e p	James McLeavy (Alexandria)	26.10.52	2hc	London (HW)		2 Aug
20:22.0		Walter Slade (LAC)	6.04.54	1	London (LB)		26 Apr
20:30.8	e	James Gibb (LAC)	11.12.53	2	London (LB)		26 Apr
20:48.25		Thomas Duckett (Liverpool)	5.12.52	1	Stoke-on-Trent		4 Aug
20:56.75		Gibb		2hc	London (LB)		13 Mar
21:09.4		Gibb		1	London (LB)	AAC	22 Mar
21:11.0	p	George Hazael (Deptford)	22.11.44	1	Glasgow (Spr)		2 Oct
21:12.2		Charles Mason (LAC)	3.06.51	1	Dublin (IRL)		5 Jun
21:26.7	e p	Hazael		2hc	Canterbury		18 May
21:36.75		Percy Stenning (LAC)	31.08.54	1hc	London (LB)		13 Mar
		(10/7)					
21:37.0		John Bateman (Birmingham AC)	18.02.55	2hc	Birmingham (ALG)		26 Jul
21:55.0		J.J.Nunns (ICAC/IRL)		1	Dublin (LR) IRL		13 May
22:11.0		William Fuller (LAC)	7.06.51	int	London (LB)		25 Sep
22:26.0	p	William Shrubsole (Bromley)	4.07.46	int	London (LB)		3 Jul
22:28.5		John Ferguson (NICC/IRL)	52	1	Belfast, IRL		22 Sep
22:57.5		Charles Ford (Dublin U/IRL)	54	1	Dublin (LR)	ICAC	22 May

Estimates: McLeavy 100y down on 20:00.0; Gibb 50y down on 20:22.0; Hazael, starting 50y behind scratch, 10y down on 21:34.0 (18/5).
Intermediate times in races at 10 miles (25/09) and 20 miles (3/07).
Hazael 20:00.0 from a 50y start to win a handicap at Hackney Wick on 2 Aug [20:08.6e].
The placings of Gibb and Stenning on 13/3 were in a handicap based on timing.

6 Miles

30:55.5	p	James Sanderson (Whitworth)	28.12.37	1	Manchester (RO)	24 Jul
33:57.0	p	William Shrubsole (Bromley)	4.07.46	int	London (LB)	3 Jul
33:58.0		William Fuller (LAC)	7.06.51	int	London (LB)	25 Sep
35:03.0	p	Charles Rowell (Cambridge)	12.08.52	int	London (LB)	3 Jul

Intermediate times in races at 10 miles (25/09) and 20 miles (3/07).

10 Miles

56:07.0		William Fuller (LAC)	7.06.51	2hc	London (LB)	16 Oct
57:41.6		Fuller		1	London (LB)	25 Sep
57:42.8	e	Charles Dicker (LAC)	18.03.55	2	London (LB)	25 Sep
57:58.5	p	William Beavan (Camberwell)	c54	1hc	London (LB)	27 Dec
58:27.0	p	Alfred Markham (Marylebone)	c48	3hc	London (LB)	27 Dec
58:34.0	p	William Shrubsole (Bromley)	4.07.46	int	London (LB)	3 Jul
58:41.0	p	J. Burnley (Paddington)		2hc	London (LB)	27 Dec
59:00.0	p	Charles Rowell (Cambridge)	12.08.52	int	London (LB)	3 Jul
59:36.0		Henry Oliver (Spartan H)	28.02.55	7hc	London (LB)	16 Oct
59:55.0		Henry Thomas (Peckham AC)	c52	11hc	London (LB)	16 Oct

Estimate: Dicker 6y down on 57:41.6.
Intermediate times in a 20 mile race.

Right: Lillie Bridge stadium, the venue for the majority of performances on this double-page, was the home of the Amateur Athletic Club from 1869. The illustration shows the aftermath of a riot and fire in 1887, triggered by the cancellation of a professional sprint match.

120 Yards Hurdles

16 ¾	Alfred Loder (CU)	25.03.55	1	London (LB)	OvC	19 Mar
16 ¾	Charles Spencer (Nottm Forest FC)	48	1	Sheffield (BL)		5 Jul
16.8 e	Hugh Upcher (OU)	28.10.53	2	London (LB)	OvC	19 Mar
16 4/5	Upcher		1	London (LB)	AAC	22 Mar
16.8 e	Arthur Barker (LAC)	c55	2	Sheffield (BL)		5 Jul
16.9 e	Loder		2	London (LB)	AAC	22 Mar
17.0 e	Charles Bayly (OU/IRL)	26.02.52	3	London (LB)	AAC	22 Mar
17.0	Spencer		1	Blackburn		26 Jun
17.0 e	Samuel Bestow (Nottm Forest FC)	3.03.52	3	Sheffield (BL)		5 Jul
17.1 e	William Bedford (OU)	29.05.52	4	London (LB)	AAC	22 Mar
		(10/7)				
17 2/5	James Gorman (Lurgan AC/IRL)	31.10.50	1	Belfast, IRL		11 Jun
17 ½	D.L.D.Jones (Watford)		1	Watford		5 Jul
17 ½	Henry Macdougall (Stamford FC)	c52	1	Worthing		8 Sep

Height of hurdles unknown

16 ¼	F. Brett (Horsham)		1	Crawley	31 Aug
16 ¾	William Edgar (Dartford FC)	27.09.53	1	Erith	3 Jul
16 ¾	Henry Norris (Cirencester)	55	1	Cirencester	14 Oct
16.9 e	Alfred Anscombe (Cuckfield)	c57	2	Crawley	31 Aug
17.0	George Morphew (Sevenoaks)	54	1	Sevenoaks	8 May

School Sports

17.0	Charles Jephson (Tonbridge Sch)	15.02.57	1	Tonbridge	13 Mar

Notes
Estimates: Upcher 1ft down on 16.75; Barker 6in down on 16.75; Loder 1ft down on 16.8; Bayly 4ft down on 16.8; Bestow 5ft down on 16.75; Bedford 'close' to Bayly; Anscombe 4y down on 16.25.

220 Yards Hurdles

30.5	Raymond Wickham (Ariel RC)	50	1	Bristol	4 Sep
30.7 e	A. Harrison (Nottm Forest FC)		2	Bristol	4 Sep
30.8 e	H. Williams (Cambridge)		3	Bristol	4 Sep
31.25	James Gorman (Lurgan AC/IRL)	31.10.50	1	Blackley	31 Jul
31.4	H.O.Mackay (Vale of Aylesbury CC)		1hc	Aylesbury	6 May
31.5 e	Hubert Heron (Vale of Aylesbury CC)	30.01.52	2hc	Aylesbury	6 May
32.0	Williams		1ht1	Bristol	4 Sep
32.2 e	Harrison		2ht1	Bristol	4 Sep
32.3 e	W.H.Brown (Ariel RC)		3ht1	Bristol	4 Sep
33.0	John Fowler (Aylesbury)	50	1	Bicester	13 Sep
33.5 e	Robert Weaving (Abingdon)	53	2	Bicester	13 Sep
33.75	J.L.Watts (Bath RC)		1ht2	Bristol	4 Sep

Notes
Estimates: Harrison 6in and Williams 1y 6in down on 30.5; Heron 1ft down on 31.4; Harrison 1y and Brown 1½y down on 32.0 (ht); Weaving 3y down on 33.0.

440 Yards Hurdles

1:04.5	James Gorman (Lurgan AC/IRL)	31.10.50	1hc	Lurgan, IRL	4 Sep
1:06.0	George Dobell (Northwich)	14.11.54	1hc	Lymm, Cheshire	9 Aug

12 Hurdles

1:03.9 e	George Blaxter (Derwent FC)	11.03.56	2hc	Derby	7 Aug
1:05.0	Frederick Heath (RMA)	21.02.58	1	Woolwich	3 Jun
1:05.5	Blaxter		1hc	St Helens	17 Jul
1:05.8 e	Reginald Boothby (RMA)	18.01.55	2	Woolwich	3 Jun

Note: Estimates: Blaxter 6y down on 63.0; Boothby 5y down on 65.0.

14 Hurdles (3ft 3)

1:05.4	William Hamilton (Dublin U/IRL)	1.07.50	1	Dublin (CP), IRL	9 Jun

16 Hurdles

1:05.9 e	Charles Spencer (Nottm Forest FC)	48	3hc	Manchester (Pom)	17 Jun
1:06.0 e	William Lomas (Grappenhall)	c47	4hc	Manchester (Pom)	17 Jun

Note: Estimates: Spencer 4y and Lomas 'only just beaten for 3rd place' down on 65.25.

High Jump

5'11	1.803	Michael Glazebrook (OU)	4.08.53	1	London (LB)	AAC	22 Mar
5'10½	1.791	George Kenny (Clongowes Coll/IRL)	7.06.55	1	Dublin (LR), IRL		26 Jun
5'9	1.753	Samuel Walker (CU)	15.02.55	1	Torquay		30 Aug
5'8½	1.740	Marshall Brooks (OU)	30.05.55	1	Oxford		9 Mar
5'8½	1.740	Edward Prior (ex-CU)	4.01.52	1	Stanmore		17 May
5'8¼	1.734	Glazebrook		1	London (LB)	OvC	19 Mar
5'8	1.727	William Tomkin (ex-Eton Coll)	56	1	Lewes		28 Apr
5'8	1.727	Robert Thomas (Liverpool)	22.11.56	1	St Helens		17 Jul
5'8	1.727	Tomkin		1	Sudbury		2 Aug
5'8	1.727	Tomkin		1	Lincoln		18 Sep
5'7½	1.715	Tomkin		1	Uxbridge		8 May
5'7½	1.715	John Hargreaves (Cheadle Hulme)		1	Farnworth		7 Aug
5'7½	1.715	Frank Jones (RMC Sandhurst)	5.08.56	1	Camberley		15 Oct
		(13/9)					
5'7	1.702	Frederick Warde (Mote Park CC)	18.03.52	2	Lewes		28 Apr
5'7	1.702	M. Roseingrave (French Coll/IRL)	c57	1	Blackrock, IRL		23 Jun
5'7	1.702	Patrick Nally (Balla/IRL)	56	1	Claremorris, IRL		19 Aug
5'7	1.702	Charles Gaskin (Wisbech CC)	56	2=	Lincoln		18 Sep
5'7	1.702	Thomas Tomlinson (Gosforth CC)	c55	2=	Lincoln		18 Sep
5'6½	1.689	Charles Lockton (LAC)	2.07.56	1	Worthing		8 Sep

Doubtful

5'10	1.778	William Milner (Liverpool)	c55	1	Liverpool		27 May

Probably from a springboard.

High Jump: Highland & Border

5'10	1.778	p	David Milne (Forfar)	28.12.42	1	Dundee	17 Jul
5'9	1.753	p	Peter Cameron (Kincardine O'Neil)	8.12.52	1	Nairn	7 Aug
5'9	1.753	p	Daniel Lamont (Kilbarchan)	c55	1	Milngavie	28 Aug
5'8½	1.740	p	John Toy (Dundee)	c46	2	Dundee	17 Jul
5'8	1.727	p	Hugh Andrews (Glasgow)	c52	1	Coupar Angus	15 Jul
5'8	1.727	p	Cameron		2	Coupar Angus	15 Jul
5'8	1.727	p	Andrews		1	Blairgowrie	22 Jul
5'8	1.727	p	Adam Scott (Swinton)	15.08.52	1=	Kelso	31 Jul
5'8	1.727	p	Lamont		1=	Kelso	31 Jul
5'8	1.727	p	Andrews		2	Milngavie	28 Aug
5'8	1.727	p	Andrews		1	Rosewell	4 Sep
5'8	1.727	p	Alexander Edington (Edinburgh)	17.11.57	1	Stenhousemuir	18 Sep
			(12/7)				
5'7	1.702	p	Andrew Milne (Forfar)	24.11.39	2	Blairgowrie	22 Jul
5'7	1.702	p	Thomas McDougall (Galashiels)	c53	1	Lauder	7 Aug

Note
Cameron at Nairn is credited with 5'9 in the report and 5'8 in the results in the *Nairnshire Telegraph*.

Pole Vault

10'7	3.23	William Law (Stacksteads)	1.12.53	1	Manchester (Pom)	16 Jun
10'7	3.23	John Wigfull (Sheffield FC)	2.12.51	1	Sheffield (BL)	5 Jul
10'6	3.20	Charles Gaskin (Wisbech)	56	1	Northampton	2 Aug
10'6	3.20	Gaskin		1	Olney	2 Aug
10'6	3.20	Joseph Turnbull (Hetton Colliery)	c50	1	Liverton	14 Aug
10'4½	3.16	Robert Sabin (Culworth CC)	52	1	Reading	7 Jul
10'4	3.15	Sabin		2=	Olney	2 Aug
10'4	3.15	Horace Strachan (LAC)	21.09.55	2=	Olney	2 Aug
10'4	3.15	Strachan		1	Bicester	13 Sep
10'3	3.12	Charles Leeds (ex-OU)	45	1=	London (LB)	22 May
10'3	3.12	Sabin		1=	London (LB)	22 May
10'3	3.12	Sabin		2=	Northampton	2 Aug
10'3	3.12	Strachan		2=	Northampton	2 Aug
10'3	3.12	William Bracegirdle (Winsford)		1	Crewe	21 Aug
		(14/8)				
10'2	3.10	Samuel Ratcliffe (Ashby FC)	53	2	Sheffield (BL)	5 Jul
10'2	3.10	Henry Johnson (Fawsley Park CC)	51	1	Husbands Bosworth	29 Jul
10'1½	3.09	Joseph Bracegirdle (Winsford)		1	Manchester (Pom)	28 Aug
10'0	3.05	C. Wright (Leicester & Cotesbach)		2	Husbands Bosworth	29 Jul

10'0	3.05		George Barker (Bacup)	c55	2=	Manchester (Pom)	28 Aug
9'11	3.02		Thomas Done (Northwich)	54	1	Hanley	17 May
9'11	3.02		Wildon Thompson (Hedon)	56	1	Market Weighton	26 Jul

Note
Wigfull is credited with 10'7⅛ and Ratcliffe with 10'3 at Sheffield on 5/07 in the *Sheffield Telegraph*.

Pole Vault: Highland, Lakeland & Border

10'9	3.28	p	Alexander MacGregor (42nd Highlanders)		1	Dundee	17 Jul
10'8	3.25	p	David Anderson (Alnwick)	c46	1=	Morpeth	21 Aug
10'8	3.25	p	F.T.H.Dixon (Morpeth)		1=	Morpeth	21 Aug
10'6	3.20	p	Dixon		1	Ashington	15 May
10'6	3.20	p	David Milne (Forfar)	28.12.42	2	Dundee	17 Jul
10'6	3.20	p	MacGregor		1	Crieff	21 Aug
10'4	3.15	p	William Barron (Keswick)	c56	1	Grasmere	19 Aug
10'3	3.12	p	Anderson		2	Ashington	15 May
10'2	3.10	p	MacGregor		1	Milnathort	3 Aug
10'1	3.07	p	MacGregor		1	Inverness	24 Sep
10'0	3.05	p	William Borland (Kilbarchan)	c48	1	Alexandria	26 Jun
10'0	3.05	p	MacGregor		1	Coupar Angus	15 Jul
10'0	3.05	p	William Speedie (Dundee)	c52	3	Dundee	17 Jul
10'0	3.05	p	MacGregor		1	Coupar Angus	29 Jul
10'0	3.05	p	Peter Cameron (Kincardine O'Neil)	8.12.52	1	Nairn	7 Aug
10'0	3.05	p	MacGregor		1	Alloa	11 Aug
10'0	3.05	p	MacGregor		1	Tillicoultry	13 Aug
			(17/8)				
9'11	3.02	p	Marcellus Thompson (Kendal)	19.01.55	1	Bolton	17 Jul

Indoors

9'11	3.02	i p	John Allison (Kendal)	8.02.43	1=	Manchester (Cir)	20 Mar
9'11	3.02	i p	Thomas Newby (Ulverston)	c52	1=	Manchester (Cir)	20 Mar

Long Jump

22'5	6.83	John Alkin (Nuneaton CC)	10.07.55	1	Hinckley	28 Aug
22'2	6.76	Charles Lockton (LAC)	2.07.56	1	Nuneaton	2 Aug
21'10	6.65	Lockton		1	London (LB)	17 Apr
21'9	6.63	J.R.Harper (Tadcaster CC)		1	Market Weighton	26 Jul
21'6	6.55	George Kenny (Clongowes Coll/IRL)	7.06.55	1	Dublin (LR) IRL ICAC	22 May
21'6	6.55	Hugh Upcher (OU)	28.10.53	1	Hadleigh	7 Jul
21'6	6.55	Lockton		1	Worthing	8 Sep
21'4	6.50	Upcher		1	Oxford	8 Mar
21'3	6.48	William Tomkin (ex-Eton Coll)	56	2	Hadleigh	7 Jul
21'2	6.45	Tomkin		1	Uxbridge	12 May
21'2	6.45	John Lane (Dublin U/IRL)	53	2	Dublin (LR) IRL ICAC	22 May
21'2	6.45	Alkin		2	Nuneaton	2 Aug
21'1	6.43	Edward Prior (ex-CU)	4.01.52	2	Stanmore	17 May
21'1	6.43	M.J.McN.Nally (Balla/IRL)		1	Headford, IRL	22 Sep
		(14/9)				
21'0	6.40	Richard Walsh (IRL)		1	Tuam, IRL	25 Mar
20'11	6.38	Wildon Thompson (Hedon)	56	1	Market Weighton	26 Jul
20'9½	6.34	Richard Surtees (OU)	8.04.53	2	Oxford	8 Mar
20'9	6.32	Thomas Stretch (Ormskirk)	28.01.51	1	Bebington	8 May
20'8½	6.31	Edward Stocks (CU)	27.05.56	1	Cambridge	26 Feb
20'7	6.27	Horace Strachan (LAC)	21.09.55	1	Bicester	13 Sep
20'6½	6.26	Edwin Woodburn (Ulverston)	19.04.50	1	Lancaster	17 May
20'6¼	6.25	John Graveley (Guy's Hosp)	4.04.53	1	Brighton	22 Sep
20'6	6.25	Dominick O'Connor (86th Regt/IRL)		1	Ballymote, IRL	19 Aug
20'6	6.25	John Fowler (Aylesbury)	50	2	Bicester	13 Sep

Measured from heelmark to heelmark and said to be downhill

21'1	6.43	Prior		1	Lurgan, IRL	4 Sep

Downhill

22'0	6.71	J. Johnson (Lymm)		1	Lymm	9 Aug
21'6	6.55	J. Brookes (Lymm)		2	Lymm	9 Aug

Note: Upcher in the OU sports: 20'8 – 21'4 – 20'3 – 20'5 – 21'3.

Long Jump: Highland & Border

22'0	6.71	p	D. McGillivray (Dunblane)		1	Dunblane	10 Jul
22'0	6.71	p	Robert Knox (Newstead)	17.09.47	1=	Alva	12 Aug
22'0	6.71	p	Archibald Mitchell (Alva)	51	1=	Alva	12 Aug
21'9	6.63	p	James Young (Alva)	c47	3	Alva	12 Aug
21'0	6.40	p	George Robertson (Aberdeen)		1	Inverness	24 Sep
20'9	6.32	p	Peter Cameron (Kincardine O'Neil)	8.12.52	1	Aboyne	8 Sep
20'8	6.30	p	Mitchell		1	Alloa	11 Aug
20'7	6.27	p	Cameron		1	Kildrummy	11 Aug
20'6	6.25	p	Cameron		1	Culter	31 Jul

Triple Jump

42'0	12.80	M. Maloney (Claremorris/IRL)		1	Claremorris, IRL	19 Aug
41'11	12.78	Henry Dick (St Andrews U)	5.08.53	1	Edinburgh (ACG)	27 Mar
41'11	12.78	James Dwyer (Graigue/IRL)		1	Graigue, IRL	2 Sep
41'7	12.67	P. O'Shea (Graigue/IRL)		2	Graigue, IRL	2 Sep
41'7	12.67	Maloney		1	Headford, IRL	22 Sep
41'1	12.52	John Smith (Edinburgh)		2	Edinburgh (ACG)	27 Mar
41'0	12.50	Thomas Vicars (Liverpool)	22.12.52	1	Manchester (Pom)	28 Aug
40'8	12.40	P. Maher (Drangan/IRL)		1	Drangan, IRL	17 Sep
40'6	12.34	M.J.McN.Nally (Balla/IRL)		1	Swineford, IRL	26 Aug
40'5½	12.33	John Hargreaves (Cheadle Hulme)		2	Manchester (Pom)	28 Aug

Triple Jump: Highland & Border

47'8	14.53	p	Robert Knox (Newstead)	17.09.47	1	Alloa	11 Aug
47'0	14.33	p	Knox		1	Alva	12 Aug
46'9	14.25	p	Archibald Mitchell (Alva)	51	1	Bridge of Allan	7 Aug
46'4	14.12	p	Knox		1	Dalkeith	18 Sep
46'0	14.02	p	Mitchell		2	Alva	12 Aug
45'7	13.89	p	Knox		1	Jedburgh	24 Jul
45'7	13.89	p	Thomas Aitken (Walkerburn)	23.05.53	1	Milnathort	3 Aug
45'7	13.89	p	James Young (Alva)	c47	2	Bridge of Allan	7 Aug
45'6	13.87	p	Mitchell		2	Alloa	11 Aug
45'5	13.84	p	John Wilson (Edinburgh)	c46	2	Jedburgh	24 Jul
45'5	13.84	p	R. Thompson		3	Alloa	11 Aug
45'5	13.84	p	Aitken		1	Innerleithen	14 Aug
			(12/6)				
44'4	13.51	p	Peter Cameron (Kincardine O'Neil)	8.12.52	1	Huntly	6 Aug
44'2	13.46	p	George Walsh (Royton)	3.02.44	1	Glasgow	11 Sep
44'0	13.41	p	James Duncan (Blackford)		1	Dunblane	10 Jul
44'0	13.41	p	James Rush (Addiewell)	c52	1	Blackburn	13 Aug
44'0	13.41	p	James Weir (Innerleithen)	c56	2	Innerleithen	14 Aug
43'10	13.36	p	James Rough (Kilbarchan)	c46	1	Dalry	31 Jul
43'10	13.36	p	Hugh Andrews (Glasgow)	c52	1	Armadale	10 Sep
43'7	13.28	p	Alexander Edington (Edinburgh)	17.11.57	1	Stenhousemuir	18 Sep
43'4	13.21	p	John McAllister (Alloa)		1	Alloa	25 Jun
43'3	13.18	p	William Borland (Kilbarchan)	c48	2	Dalry	31 Jul
43'0	13.11	p	James Stewart (Dumfries)		2	Hawick	11 Jun
43'0	13.11	p	William McCleaver		3	Dalry	31 Jul
42'10	13.06	p	James Fox		1	Alloa (extra prize)	11 Aug
42'6	12.95	p	William McCombie Smith (Lumphanan)	7.09.47	1	Aberdeen CC	19 Jul
42'6	12.95	p	James Aitken (Walkerburn)		1	Peebles	31 Jul
42'4	12.90	p	William Croag (Blackford)		2	Dunblane	10 Jul
42'4	12.90	p	James Hunter (Galashiels)		2	Balfron	17 Jul

Shot

42'7	12.98	Patrick Nally (Balla/IRL)	56	1	Swineford, IRL	26 Aug
41'6	12.65	M. MacGrath (Longford/IRL)		1	Ballymahon, IRL	2 Aug
40'10	12.45	Maurice Davin (Suir/IRL)	29.06.42	1	Dublin (LR) IRL ICAC	22 May
40'3	12.27	T. Deniston (Longford/IRL)		2	Ballymahon, IRL	2 Aug
39'11½	12.18	David Kennedy (QC Cork/IRL)		2	Dublin (LR) IRL ICAC	22 May
39'10	12.14	Thomas Stone (Liverpool)	24.01.52	1	London (LB) AAC	22 Mar
39'10	12.14	Michael Cusack (Dublin/IRL)	20.09.47	1	Dublin (LR), IRL	26 Jun
39'8	12.09	Stone		1	Sheffield (BL)	5 Jul
38'5	11.71	Francis Power (Manchester BC)	52	1	Manchester (Pom)	15 Jun

38'1	11.61	Kennedy		1	Cork, IRL	10 May
38'0	11.58	Wyndham Evanson (Civil Service)	51	1	London (LB)	22 May
38'0	11.58	John McDowell (Enfield/IRL)	c56	1	Belfast, IRL	29 May
		(12/10)				
37'8	11.48	William Forsyth (Edinburgh U)	c49	1	Edinburgh (ACG)	22 Jun
37'4	11.38	G. Fraser (93rd Highlanders)		1	London (LB)	26 Mar
37'0	11.28	D. Mackenzie (Hanley)		1	Hanley	18 May
37'0	11.28	Patrick Hickey (QC Cork/IRL)	18.12.54	2	Cork, IRL	10 May
36'10	11.23	William Winthrop (LAC)	15.06.52	2hc	London (LB)	19 Jun
36'9	11.20	Stephen Brown (OU)	1.06.54	1	Oxford	6 Mar
36'8½	11.19	Nicholas Littleton (CU)	11.01.53	1	Cambridge	1 Mar
36'0	10.97	W. Robertson (St Andrews U)		1	St Andrews	20 Mar
36'0	10.97	R. Wilson (Glasgow U)		2hc	Glasgow	29 Apr
36'0	10.97	W. Wakeleigh (Liverpool)		1	Bebington	8 May
35'11	10.95	Henry Davidson (CU)	23.04.54	2	Cambridge	1 Mar

Note: Fraser used a 17lb shot. This was an amateur contest. In 1872 he had competed as a professional.

Extra throw

42'11	13.08	Kennedy		Dublin (LR) IRL ICAC	22 May
41'4	12.60	Davin		Dublin (LR) IRL ICAC	22 May

18lb stand at mark and follow

39'5	12.01	M. Tobin (Mullinahone/IRL)	1	Drangan, IRL	17 Sep
39'0	11.89	T. Kennedy (Mullinahone/IRL)	2	Drangan, IRL	17 Sep

Shot: Highland & Border
Includes putting 16lb stone

47'0	14.33	p	Donald Dinnie (Aboyne)	8.06.37	1	Aberdeen CC (a)	19 Jul
46'9	14.25	p	Dinnie		1	Manchester (Pom)	28 Aug
44'2	13.46	p	James Fleming (Ballinluig)	18.09.40	2	Manchester (Pom)	28 Aug
43'11	13.39	p	Fleming		1	Aberdeen CC (b)	19 Jul
43'9	13.33	p	Fleming		2	Aberdeen CC (a)	19 Jul
43'3	13.18	p	George Mearns (Aberdeen)		3	Aberdeen CC (a)	19 Jul
41'9	12.73	p	Mearns		1	Aboyne	8 Sep
41'5*	12.62	p	Dinnie		1	Forfar	6 Aug
41'4	12.60	p	John McHattie (Aberdeen)		1	Aberdeen CC	17 Jul
41'4	12.60	p	Mearns		2	Aberdeen CC (b)	19 Jul
41'3*	12.57	p	Dinnie		1	Cupar	4 Aug
			(11/4)			
40'9	12.42	p	Peter McCowan (Comrie)		1	Lochearnhead	25 Aug
40'0	12.19	p	George Davidson (Drumoak)	19.11.54	2	Aberdeen CC	17 Jul
39'10*	12.14	p	John Dow (Thornhill)		1	Dunblane	10 Jul
39'10	12.14	p	William Bremner (Glenbucket)	3.01.47	2	Aboyne	8 Sep
39'9	12.12	p	Charles Laing (Aberdeen)		3	Aberdeen CC	17 Jul
38'10	11.84	p	Lewis Smith (Speybridge)		1	Castle Grant	18 Aug
38'5*	11.71	p	Peter Adam (Coupar Angus)		3	Forfar	6 Aug
38'2	11.63	p	William Fleming (Dundee)	22.08.42	3	Manchester (Pom)	28 Aug
37'7	11.46	p	James Watt (Glasgow)		2	Kildrummy	11 Aug
37'6	11.43	p	David Anderson (Alnwick)	c46	1	Morpeth	21 Aug

Note
There were two competitions at Aberdeen Cricket Club on 19/07 marked (a) and (b).
*correct weight assumed from evidence of other years.

Weight unstated

47'5	14.45	p	Dinnie		1	Sheffield (BL)	21 Jun
45'11	14.00	p	J. Fleming		2	Sheffield (BL)	21 Jun
44'8	13.61	p	Dinnie		1	Nairn	7 Aug
44'7	13.59	p	J. Brown (Penicuik)		1	Dalkeith	18 Sep
42'0	12.80	p	Davidson		1	Culter	31 Jul
41'10	12.75	p	J. Smith (Dalkeith)		2	Dalkeith	18 Sep
39'8	12.09	p	William McCombie Smith (Lumphanan)	7.09.47	2	Culter	31 Jul
39'4	11.99	p	David Milne (Forfar)	28.12.42	1	Durris	7 Aug
38'10	11.84	p	William Stewart (Tomintoul)		2	Nairn	7 Aug
37'2	11.33	p	A. Robson		1	Inverurie	24 Jul
37'0	11.28	p	William Machray (Skene)	13.05.54	2	Culter (local)	31 Jul

17lb

39'9	12.12	p	James Walker		1	Muchalls	31 Jul

21lb

40'0	12.19	p	Dinnie		1	Jedburgh	30 Jul
39'10	12.14	p	John Brown (Edinburgh)		1	Falkirk	28 Aug
36'9	11.20	p	John Anderson (Edinburgh)		1	Jersey City, USA	5 Jul
36'7	11.15	p	Anderson		1	New York, USA	2 Sep
36'5	11.10	p	John George (Edinburgh)	46	2	Falkirk	28 Aug

22lb (by performer)

39'5	12.01	p	Owen Duffy (Edinburgh/IRL)	c47	2	Bridge of Allan	7 Aug
37'9	11.51	p	George		3	Bridge of Allan	7 Aug
36'11	11.25	p	J. Lander		1	Milngavie	28 Aug
36'5	11.10	p	Bremner		1	Kildrummy	11 Aug
36'0	10.97	p	Watt		1	Glasgow	31 Jul

Doubtful

48'9	14.86	p	J. Fleming		1	Inverness	23 Sep
48'5	14.76	p	John Cameron (Leith)		2	Inverness	23 Sep
45'3	13.79	p	J. Fleming		1	Bridge of Allan	7 Aug
43'8	13.31	p	Duffy		2	Bridge of Allan	7 Aug
40'10	12.45	p	George		3	Bridge of Allan	7 Aug
40'7	12.37	p	Angus McLaughlan (Greenock)		1	Greenock	19 Jun
40'3	12.27	p	Alexander Ritchie (Greenock)		2	Greenock	19 Jun

22lb Doubtful

44'8	13.61	p	Dinnie		1	Alloa	11 Aug
43'8	13.31	p	J. Fleming		2	Alloa	11 Aug
41'9	12.73	p	Alexander McGregor (Strathbraan)		1	Birnam (local)	26 Aug
40'2	12.24	p	J. Stewart (Glasgow)		3	Alloa	11 Aug

Hammer

132'11	40.51	George Hales (CU)	20.05.54	1	Cambridge		24 Nov
129'3	39.40	Hales		ex	Cambridge		22 Nov
127'0	38.71	Hales		1	London (LB)	OvC	19 Mar
123'3	37.57	Hales		1	Cambridge		16 Nov
121'4	36.98	John Todd (OU)	19.09.52	2	London (LB)	OvC	19 Mar
119'1	36.30	Hales		ex	Cambridge		1 Mar
117'6	35.81	Stephen Brown (OU)	1.06.54	3	London (LB)	OvC	19 Mar
116'7	35.53	Brown		1	Oxford		9 Mar
116'6	35.51	Hales		1	Cambridge		1 Mar
113'6	34.59	Maurice Davin (Suir/IRL)	29.06.42	1	Dublin (LR) IRL ICAC		22 May
108'6	33.07	Matthew Stritch (RIC/IRL)	02.47	1	Dublin (LR) IRL		26 Jun
104'7	31.88	M. Tobin (Mullinahone/IRL)		2hc	Mullinahone, IRL		20 Jul
104'4	31.80	Tobin		1	Drangan, IRL		17 Sep

(13/6)

103'9	31.62	William A. Burgess (ex-OU)	27.12.46	1	London (LB)	AAC	22 Mar
103'5	31.52	Thomas Snow (OU)	11.09.52	2	Oxford		9 Mar
102'2	31.14	Nicholas Littleton (CU)	11.01.53	2	Cambridge		1 Mar
101'0	30.78	H.R.Malley (Balla/IRL)		1	Swineford, IRL		26 Aug
100'9	30.71	Alfred Lyttelton (CU)	7.02.57	2	Cambridge		24 Nov
99'0	30.18	John Peyton (Balla/IRL)		2	Swineford, IRL		26 Aug
98'6	30.02	M. Whelan (IRL)		2	Drangan, IRL		17 Sep
97'8	29.77	Edward Fraser (OU)	26.04.53	1	Oxford		29 Nov
97'4	29.67	J. Tobin (Ballytwogill/IRL)		1	Carrick-on-Suir, IRL		23 Sep
96'2	29.31	John Galwey Foley (RIC/IRL)	50	1	Ballymahon, IRL		2 Aug
95'10	29.21	Edmund Baddeley (CU)	9.04.57	1	Cambridge		26 Nov
94'8	28.85	J. Muir (Ballymahon/IRL)		2	Ballymahon, IRL		2 Aug
94'4	28.75	Hugh Upcher (OU)	28.10.53	3	Oxford		9 Mar
92'6	28.19	Thomas Huggins (Glenalmond Coll)	7.12.57	1	Edinburgh		6 Apr
92'0	28.04	A. Comrie (Civil Service)		1	London (LB)		22 May

Notes
Hales in CU sports: 115'2 – 110'5 – 109'0 – 108'6 – 116'6 – 110'7. He was permitted extra throws to attempt the standard of 120ft. With his eleventh he reached 119'1.
Brown in OU sports: 109'10 – 114'0 – 109'10 – 115'5 – 115'6 – 116'7.

Hales in OvC 118'11½ – 113'10 – 114'11 – 120'4½ - 124'2 – 127'0.
Todd in OvC 112'8 – 121'3½ – 121'4 – 115'11 – 120'0½ – 109'0.
Brown in OvC 108'8½ – 113'10½ – 116'9 – 117'6 – 114'10½ – 114'11.

Hammer: Highland & Border

127'5*	38.84	p	Donald Dinnie (Aboyne)	8.06.37	1	Aberfeldy	10 Sep
126'9*	38.63	p	Dinnie		1	Forfar	6 Aug
125'3*	38.18	p	Dinnie		1	Manchester (Pom)	28 Aug
121'10*	37.13	p	Dinnie		1	Sheffield (BL)	21 Jun
119'2*	36.32	p	John Dempster (Coupar Angus)		2	Forfar	6 Aug
118'0*	35.97		James Fleming (Blair Atholl)	18.09.40	3	Forfar	6 Aug
115'0*	35.05	p	Dinnie		1	Cupar	4 Aug
114'8*	34.95	p	Fleming		2	Aberfeldy	10 Sep
113'3	34.52	p	Dinnie		1	Alexandria	26 Jun
112'0	34.14	p	Dinnie		1hc	Coupar Angus	15 Jul
108'11*	33.20		Fleming		2	Manchester (Pom)	28 Aug
107'6*	32.77	p	William McDuff (Dunkeld)	c51	3	Aberfeldy	10 Sep
107'4	32.72	p	Dinnie		1	Aberdeen CC	19 Jul
107'0*	32.61	p	Dinnie		1	Birnam	26 Aug
			(14/4)				
106'11	32.59	p	John McHattie (Aberdeen)		1	Braes of Gight (open)	29 Jul
106'9*	32.54	p	William Fleming (Dundee)	22.08.42	3	Manchester (Pom)	28 Aug
103'3	31.47	p	Peter McHardy (Aberdeenshire)	c48	3	Alexandria	26 Jun
98'9	30.10	p	William Bremner (Leochel-Cushnie)	3.01.47	1	Aboyne	8 Sep
96'9	29.49	p	George Davidson (Drumoak)	19.11.54	1	Culter	31 Jul
95'6	29.11	p	William McCombie Smith (Lumphanan)	7.09.47	1	Lumphanan	17 Jul
94'10	28.91	p	Alexander Robertson (New Craig)		1	Braes of Gight (local)	29 Jul
94'9	28.88	p	John Gray (Ayr)		2	Braes of Gight (open)	29 Jul
94'8	28.85	p	John Anderson (Edinburgh)		1	New York, USA	5 Jul
94'6	28.80	p	James Wilson (Aberdeen)		2	New Deer	24 Jul
94'4	28.75	p	G. Walton (Aberdeen)		2	Culter	31 Jul
92'8	28.24	p	James Melrose (Innerleithen)	17.04.47	1	Boston, USA	26 Aug
92'7	28.22	p	James Dempster (Coupar Angus)		2hc	Coupar Angus	15 Jul
92'7*	28.22	p	David Annand (Glenisla)	54	1	Glenisla (local)	20 Aug
92'4	28.14	p	James Watt (Glasgow)		3	Kildrummy	11 Aug
92'2*	28.09	p	George Innes		3	Lumphanan	17 Jul

Doubtful

120'0	36.58	p	James Muir (Overtown)		1	Overtown	13 Sep
98'0	29.88	p	R. McRae (Overtown)		2	Overtown	13 Sep

Note
*correct weight assumed from evidence of other years.

Weight unstated

120'3	36.65	p	Dinnie		2hc	Glasgow	11 Sep
119'6	36.42	p	Dinnie		1	Nairn	7 Aug
118'0	35.97	p	Dinnie		1	Glenisla (heavy)	20 Aug
117'5	35.79	p	Davidson		1	Durris (local)	7 Aug
115'0	35.05	p	Dinnie		1	Edzell	31 Jul
113'10	34.70	p	David Milne (Forfar)	28.12.42	1	Durris (open a)	7 Aug
112'11	34.42	p	Davidson		1	Durris (open b)	7 Aug
112'8	34.34	p	William Machray (Skene)	13.05.54	2	Durris (open b)	7 Aug
112'3	34.21	p	J. Fleming		1hc	Glasgow	11 Sep
111'3	33.91	p	Milne		2	Durris (local)	7 Aug
111'0	33.83	p	John George (Edinburgh)	46	1	Milnathort	3 Aug
110'10	33.78	p	James Thomson (Culter)		3	Durris (open b)	7 Aug
108'10	33.17	p	J. Fleming		2	Sheffield	21 Jun
106'0	32.31	p	J. Black		3	Durris (local)	7 Aug
104'4	31.80	p	John McCurrach (Rothiemay)	2.06.52	1	Huntly	6 Aug
100'0	30.48	p	Alexander Fraser		2	Durris (open a)	7 Aug
100'0	30.48	p	Robertson		1	Birse	20 Aug
97'8	29.77	p	James Russell (Gartly)	c48	2	Huntly	6 Aug
97'6	29.72	p	Stewart Adams (Skene)		2	Skene (light)	26 Jun
96'4	29.36	p	J. Simpson		2	Luss	4 Sep
93'6	28.50	p	John McLaine (Oban)		1	Oban	8 Sep
93'4½	28.46	p	William McGregor (Drumdelgie)		3	Huntly	6 Aug

93'0	28.35 p	William Rust (Drumoak)	1.01.55	3	Skene (light)	26 Jun

Weight unstated and doubtful
97'0	29.57 p	McCombie Smith		1	Greenock	19 Jun

18lb by performer
112'10	34.39 p	Dinnie		1	Manchester (Pom)	28 Aug
100'0	30.48 p	J. Fleming		2	Manchester (Pom)	28 Aug
95'9	29.18 p	W. Fleming		3	Manchester (Pom)	28 Aug

20lb by performer
104'0	31.70 p	Dinnie		1	Crieff	21 Aug

22lb by performer
96'1	29.29 p	McHattie		1	Aberdeen (CC)	17 Jul

Other Events

150 Yards
15¼		Arthur Tindall (LAC)	26.12.53	1ht1hc	Northampton	2 Aug

200 Yards
20.6 p		Robert Watson (IRL)	11.06.54	1	Maitland, NSW, AUS	22 May
21.0		William Blaxter (Derwent FC)	29.03.54	1hc	Castle Donington	3 Jun

300 Yards
31.8		Frederick Elborough (LAC)	30.07.52	1ht1hc	Cambridge	17 Nov

The Cambridge track had a slope.

600 Yards
1:14.8 e		Henry Hill (LAC)	22.01.52	2hc	London (LB)	25 Sep

Estimate: 3y down on 1:14.4

1000 Yards
2:22.75		Henry Hill (LAC)	22.01.52	1hc	Northampton	2 Aug

¾ Mile
3:15.0		Walter Slade (LAC)	6.04.54	int	London (LB)	19 Jun

Intermediate time in 1 mile race.

5 Miles
28:02.0		William Fuller (LAC)	7.06.51	int	London (LB)	25 Sep

World amateur record

1 Mile Walk
6:46.0 p		William Perkins (Old Kent Road)	16.09.52	int	London (LB)	20 Sep

This and walks below in an 8 mile match.

2 Miles Walk
14:13.0 p		William Perkins (Old Kent Road)	16.09.52	int	London (LB)	20 Sep

7 Miles Walk
51:51.0 p		William Perkins (Old Kent Road)	16.09.52	int	London (LB)	20 Sep

50 Miles Walk
9:24:16.5 p		Alexander Clarke (Bethnal Green)	49	1	London (Star)	11 Oct

Cricket Ball
126y	115.21	John Hargreaves (Cheadle Hulme)		1	Crewe	21 Aug

Noteworthy junior exhibition throw:
122y 1ft 9in	112.09	Walter Forbes (Eton College)	20.01.58	ex	Eton	10 Mar

1876 UK Year List

100 Yards

9 ½	p	Frank Hewitt (Millwall)	8.05.45	1		Sydney, AUS	1 May
10.0		Edward Salmon (CU)	29.10.54	1ht1hc		Bury St Edmunds	30 Mar
10 1/5		Montague Shearman (OU)	7.04.57	1		London (LB) OvC	7 Apr
10 1/5		Shearman		1ht1		London (LB)	10 Apr
10 1/5		Douglas Ogilby (Dublin U/IRL)	16.02.53	1ht1		Dublin (LR) IRL ICAC	27 May
10 ¼		George Blaxter (Derwent FC)	11.03.56	1		Manchester	17 Jun
10 ¼		Charles Gardiner (Stow-on-the-Wold)	52	1ht1		Stow-on-the-Wold	2 Aug
10 ¼		Gardiner		1		Stow-on-the-Wold	2 Aug
10 ¼		Herbert Booth (Wigston/SA)	59	1ht3		Hinckley	2 Sep
10 ¼		Richard Coombes (Paignton)	53	1		Budleigh Salterton	7 Sep
10 ¼	p	Hewitt		1		Melbourne, AUS	5 Nov
10.3	e	William Blaxter (Derwent RC)	29.03.54	2hc		Derby	22 Jul
10.3	e	W. Massey (Budleigh Salterton CC)		2		Budleigh Salterton	7 Sep
			(13/10)				
10 2/5		Clement Woodland (CU)	13.06.51	1ht1		Cambridge	22 Mar
10 2/5		J. Taylor (QTFC)		1=ht3		Glasgow (WSCG)	15 Apr
10 2/5		Alexander Broadfoot (QTFC)	29.02.52	1=ht3		Glasgow (WSCG)	15 Apr
10.4	e	William Barter (ICAC/IRL)	c55	2ht1		Dublin (LR) IRL ICAC	27 May
10 2/5		Henry Macdougall (LAC)	c52	1=		Belfast, IRL	9 Jun
10 2/5		C.F.Young (IRL)		1		Belfast, IRL	25 Jun
10.4	e	John Reay (LAC)	9.07.53	3		Manchester	17 Jun
10.4	e	T. Wheeler (Cirencester)		2ht1		Stow-on-the-Wold	2 Aug
10 2/5		Henry Hodges (Hereford CC)	53	1		Worthing	12 Sep
10 2/5		Arthur Pelham (Royal Agric Coll)	28.12.50	1		Cirencester	12 Oct
10 2/5		Frederick Eden (CU)	3.09.57	1		Cambridge	29 Nov

Downhill

10.0		Ogilby		1	Belfast, IRL	6 May
10.0		Ogilby		1hc	Belfast, IRL	6 May
10.1 e		Abraham Cronyn (Dublin U/IRL)	3.09.55	2	Belfast, IRL	6 May

[downhill and stiffish breeze in favour for each]

10 ¼		Godfrey Lyons (Wood Green CC)	23,05.53	1	Wood Green	24 Jun

Foreign Competitor

10.4 e		F. Goodfellow (Adelaide/AUS)		2	Manchester	17 Jun

Notes

In Hewitt's professional race the men "started themselves" (*Sydney Morning Herald*).
Shearman's run in the OvC match (7/04) started by word of mouth and possibly wind assisted.
Estimates: W. Blaxter a few inches down on 10.25; Massey 1ft down on 10.25; Barter 1½y down on 10.2;
Reay 2ft 6in down on 10.25 (17/06) [actually penalised 1y for false start, but this has not been taken into account];
Wheeler 1y down on 10.25; Cronyn 1½ft down on 10.0; Goodfellow 1½ft down on 1.25.

220 Yards

22 3/5		Frederick Elborough (LAC)	30.07.52	1	London (LB)	7 Oct
22.7 e		Charles Lockton (LAC)	2.07.56	2hc	Northampton	7 Aug
23 1/5		Alfred Powles (LAC)	15.06.53	1	Dublin (LR) IRL IrlvEng	5 Jun
23 2/5		Abraham Cronyn (Dublin U/IRL)	3.09.55	1	Belfast, IRL	6 May
23 2/5		Lockton		1ht3hc	Northampton	7 Aug
23.5 e		James Pinion (Ulster CC/IRL)	c52	2	Belfast, IRL	6 May
23.5 e		Douglas Ogilby (Dublin U/IRL)	16.02.53	3	Belfast, IRL	6 May
23.6 e		Ogilby		2	Dublin (LR) IRL IrlvEng	5 Jun
23 3/5		Ogilby		1	Belfast, IRL	10 Jun
23.7 e		Richard Dudgeon (LAC/USA)	c54	2	Belfast, IRL	10 Jun
23.7 e		Powles		2	London (LB)	7 Oct
			(11/7)			
23.8 e		Arthur Smith (Birkenhead)	c55	3ht1hc	Newcastle-und-Lyme	25 Aug
23 4/5		Philip Cronhelm (ICAC/IRL)	c56	1	Dublin (LR), IRL	26 Aug
23.9 e		John Warren (Northampton AC)	c55	2	Dublin (LR), IRL	26 Aug
24.0 e		William Barter (Dublin U/IRL)	c55	3	Dublin (LR), IRL	26 Aug
24 ¾		John Reay (LAC)	9.07.53	1	London (LB)	20 May
25.0		J.R.Trayer (Borris/IRL)		1	Borris, IRL	5 Jul
25.0 e		Albert Twigg (Hanley CC)	c54	3ht1hc	St Helens	15 Jul

Notes

Lockton ½y down on 22.6 (07/08): Pinion 1ft and Ogilby 1ft 6in down on 23.4 (6/05); Ogilby 3y down on 23.2

(05/06); Dudgeon 'almost 1y' down on 23.6 (10/06); Smith 2½y down on 23.5 (25/08); Warren ½y down on 23.8, Barter 'close'; Powles 10y down on 22.6; Twigg 2y down on 24.75

440 Yards

50.8		Alfred Lewis (CU)	10.08.54	1	Cambridge	8 Mar
50.8		Alfred Powles (LAC)	15.06.53	1	Dublin (LR), IRL	6 Jun
51.0		Herbert Flockton (Snettisham)	56	1	Spalding	7 Aug
51.3	e	Abraham Cronyn (Dublin U/IRL)	3.09.55	2	Dublin (LR), IRL	6 Jun
51.4		Lewis		1	Cambridge	21 Mar
51.5		William Barter (Dublin U/IRL)	c55	1	Dublin (LR), IRL	18 Apr
51.7	e	Richard Dudgeon (LAC/USA)	c54	3	Dublin (LR), IRL	6 Jun
51.75		Henry Hill (LAC)	22.01.52	1	Sheffield (BL)	3 Jul
51.8		Hill		1	Dublin (LR) IRL IrlvEng	5 Jun
51.8		Cronyn		1	Belfast, IRL	9 Jun
51.8	e	George Blaxter (Derwent FC)	11.03.56	2	Sheffield (BL)	3 Jul
51.9	e	John Lonsdale (CU)	25.06.55	2	Cambridge	21 Mar
		(12/9)				
52.0	e	Edward Salmon (CU)	29.10.54	3	Cambridge	21 Mar
52.0		James Pinion (Ulster CC/IRL)	c52	1	Belfast, IRL	6 May
52.2	e	James Heron (Lurgan AC/IRL)	c55	2	Belfast, IRL	9 Jun
52.25		Albert Twigg (Hanley CC)	c54	1	Scarborough	18 Aug
52.3	e	Raymond Wickham (Bristol Ariel RC)	50	3	Sheffield (BL)	3 Jul
52.4		George Solly (OU)	27.03.55	1ht	Oxford	16 Mar
52.4		Frederick Elborough (LAC)	30.07.52	1	London (LB) AAC	10 Apr
52.5		Paul Springmann (Craigmount Sch)	11.12.56	1	Musselburgh	20 Apr
52.6		F.W.Todd (GWR)		1	Dublin(LR), IRL	26 Aug
52.6		William Churchill (CU)	9.04.55	1	Cambridge	14 Nov
52.7	e	Charles Metcalfe (OU)	8.09.53	2ht	Oxford	16 Mar

Doubtful

51.75		Oswald Daniell (OU)	9.07.56	1	Brighton	4 April
52.25		Henry Davidson (CU)	23.04.54	1	Brighton	4 April

Brighton College Sports Old Boys' and Strangers' races respectively, reported in *The Field*. Neither showed such form at university.

Notes

Blaxter 1ft down on 51.75 (03/07); Cronyn 4y down and Dudgeon 7y down on 50.8 (06/06); Lonsdale 4y & Salmon 5y down on 51.4 (21/03); Heron 3y down on 51.8 (09/06); Wickham 4y down on 51.8e; Metcalfe 2y down on 52.4 (16/03).

880 Yards

1:57.5		Frederick Elborough (LAC)	30.07.52	1	London (LB)	7 Oct
1:58.1	e	Henry Hill (LAC)	22.01.52	2	London (LB)	7 Oct
1:58.2		Walter Slade (LAC)	6.04.54	1hc	Belfast, IRL	10 Jun
1:58.8		Slade		1	Dublin (LR), IRL	6 Jun
1:58.9	e	Slade		3	London (LB)	7 Oct
1:59.5		Slade		1	Dublin (LR) IRL IrlvEng	5 Jun
1:59.7	e	Arthur Pelham (Cirencester Ag Coll)	28.12.50	4	London (LB)	7 Oct
2:00.9	e	Henry Moore (Dublin U/IRL)	48	2	Dublin (LR) IRL IrlvEng	5 Jun
2:01.3	e	Moore		2	Dublin (LR) IRL	6 Jun
2:01.5	e	John Ferguson (NICC/IRL)	52	3hc	Belfast, IRL	9 Jun
2:01.5		Charles Hazen Wood (Chester)	c56	1	Newcastle-und-Lyme	25 Aug
2:01.5	p	Alexander Clark (Glasgow)	c53	1=	Glasgow	31 Dec
2:01.5	p	Robert Hindle (Paisley)	46	1=	Glasgow	31 Dec
		(13/9)				
2:02.2		Walter Cunliffe (CU)	4.12.55	1	Cambridge	22 Mar
2:02.7	e	James Gibb (LAC)	11.12.53	2hc	Olney	7 Aug
2:03.3	e	Henry Bryden (LAC)	3.05.54	3	London (LB) AAC	10 Apr
2:04.8	e	Alfred Lewis (CU)	10.08.54	2	Cambridge	22 Mar
2:04.9	e	Charles Mason (LAC)	3.06.51	2	Dublin (LR), IRL	6 Jun
2:05.0		James Eden (Durham FC)	52	1hc	Durham	7 Oct

Notes

Hill 4y, Slade 10y & Pelham 16y down on 1:57.5; Moore 18y down on 1:58.8 (06/06) and 10y down on 1:59.5 (05/06); Ferguson 4½y down on 2:00.8 (09/06); Gibb 1½y down on 2:02.4 (07/08); Bryden 2y down on 2:03.0 (10/04); Lewis 20y down on 2:02.2; Mason 20y down on 2:02.0.

Gibb's 2:02.7 was on an uneven course that had 3 downhill stretches to 2 uphill.
The Field stated that Eden's performance must be treated with reserve, owing to the system of measurement.

Mile

4:25.25	p	James McLeavy (Alexandria)	26.10.52	1	Glasgow (Spr)		4 Nov
4:27.2		Edward Nicolls (OU)	27.02.54	1	London (LB)	OvC	7 Apr
4:28.5 e		Walter Cunliffe (CU)	4.12.55	2	London (LB)	OvC	7 Apr
4:28.6	p	McLeavy		1	London (LB)		1 Apr
4:31.0		E. Whittaker		1	Hemel Hempstead		20 May
4:31.6		Walter Slade (LAC)	6.04.54	1	London (LB)		23 May
4:32.0		James Eden (Durham FC)	52	1hc	Sunderland		6 Jun
4:33.0		Adam Campbell (ex-Edinburgh Acad)	3.04.57	1	Edinburgh (ACG)		21 Jun
4:33.0 e		Thomas Duckett (Stoke Victoria AC)	5.12.52	2hc	Leeds		1 Jul
4:35.0		Nicolls		1	Oxford		16 Mar
4:35.0		A. Feltham (Swindon)		1	Swindon		16 May
4:35.2		Cunliffe		1	Cambridge		21 Mar
4:35.2		Slade		1	London (LB)	AAC	10 Apr
4:35.5 e p		McLeavy		2hc	Glasgow (Spr)		18 Mar
4:35.6		Slade		1	Dublin (LR) IRL IrlvEng		5 Jun
4:36.0		George Philips (Rangers FC)		1	Glasgow		15 Apr
		(16/10)					
4:36.6		Arthur Smith (LAC)	21.03.52	1hc	London (LB)		15 Jul
4:37.0		James Warburton (Haslingden)	13.11.45	1	Widnes		24 Jun
4:37.5	p	Alexander Clark (Glasgow)	c53	1	Glasgow (Spr)		27 May
4:37.75		John Smith (Bury)	13.04.55	1	Wigan		26 Aug
4:38.2 e		Arthur Maddock (Notts County FC)	c56	2hc	Hinckley		2 Sep
4:39.0		George Mawby (Bourn)	17.07.57	1	Spalding		7 Aug
4:39.2 e		William Collier (CU)	56	2	Cambridge		21 Mar
4:39.2		James Gibb (LAC)	11.12.53	1	Olney		7 Aug
4:39.5 e		Lewis Evans (ex-CU)	9.07.51	2	London (LB)	AAC	10 Apr
4:39.8 e		Alfred Goodwin (OU)	57	2	Oxford		16 Mar

Doubtful measurement

4:33.0	Warburton		1	Belfast, IRL		6 May
4:35.4 e	John Ferguson (NICC/IRL)	52	2	Belfast, IRL		6 May

Reported by *Bell's Life* as 8 yards under distance, equating to 4:34.3e and 4:36.7e for the full mile.

Notes
Cunliffe 8y down on 4:27.2 (07/04); Duckett 5y down on 4:32.2 (01/07); McLeavy 1y down on 4:35.25 (18/03); Ferguson 15y down on 4:33 (06/05); Collier 25y down on 4:35.2; Evans 27y down on 4:35.2; Goodwin 30y down on 4:35.0; Maddock 1y down on 4:38.0. *Bell's Life* made Nicoll's time in the OvC sports 4:28.0.

2 Miles

9:42.0	p	George Hazael (Deptford)	22.11.44	int	Glasgow (Spr)		13 May
9:42.0		Walter Slade (LAC)	6.04.54	3hc	Belfast, IRL		10 Jun
9:44.5	p	James McLeavy (Alexandria)	26.10.52	int	Glasgow (Shaw)		10 Jun
9:45.0	p	Hazael		int	London (LB)		19 Jun
9:45.2 e p		James Sanderson (Whitworth)	28.12.37	int	London (LB)		19 Jun
9:48.0		Slade		1	London (Oval)		21 Jun
9:52.5		Thomas Duckett (Liverpool)	5.12.52	1	St Helens		15 Jul
9:53.75		Duckett		1=	Stoke-on-Trent		8 Aug
9:53.75		James Warburton (Haslingden)	13.11.45	1=	Stoke-on-Trent		8 Aug
9:55.0		Warburton		1hc	Blackburn		15 Jul
9:55.25		Warburton		1	Blackburn		9 Dec
9:55.4 e		Duckett		2	Blackburn		9 Dec
		(12/6)					
10:05.0		William Grenfell (OU)	30.10.55	int	London (LB)	OvC	7 Apr
10:06.0 e		Alfred Goodwin (OU)	57	int	London (LB)	OvC	7 Apr
10:12.0		Charles Mason (LAC)	3.06.51	inthc	London (LB)		11 Nov
10:18.4 e		Edward Winter (OU)	6.03.53	2hc	Cambridge		18 Feb
10:19.0		James Gibb (LAC)	11.12.53	1hc	London (Oval)		30 Sep
10:25.0 e		Frank Bullock-Webster (OU)	21.12.54	int	Oxford		18 Mar
10:29.75		H.I.Armitage (Leeds AC)		1	Burley-in-Wharfedale		13 May
10:30.0		Lees Knowles (CU)	16.02.57	int	Cambridge		23 Mar
10:30.0		John Penrose (CU)	12.11.53	int	Cambridge		23 Mar

Doubtful measurement
9:49.5   Warburton   1   Belfast, IRL   6 May
Said to have been 16y under distance. Equates to 9:52.2e for the full distance.

Notes
Sanderson 'slightly behind' (19/06); Goodwin in close contact (07/04); Winter 12y down on 10:16.2 (18/02);
Bullock-Webster in close attendance (18/03). *Bell's Life* made the Blackburn race on 9/12 slower, at 9:55.75.
Duckett ½y down. *The Field* gave Armitage 10:24.5 on 13/5.
Intermediate times in races at 3 miles (18/03; 23/03; 7/04; 10/06; 11/11); 4 miles (19/06); and 10 miles (13/05).

3 Miles
14:42.25	p	James McLeavy (Alexandria)	26.10.52	1	Glasgow (Shaw)			10 Jun
14:49.5	p	George Hazael (Deptford)	22.11.44	int	Glasgow (Spr)			13 May
15:10.6	e p	William Shrubsole (Wellingborough)	4.07.46	inthc	London (LB)			11 Dec
15:12.0	p	Hazael		int	London (LB)			6 Mar
15:12.4		Alfred Goodwin (OU)	57	1	London (LB)	OvC		7 Apr
15:15.0		James Gibb (LAC)	11.12.53	2hc	London (LB)			11 Nov
15:17.7	e	William Grenfell (OU)	30.10.55	2	London (LB)	OvC		7 Apr
15:24.8	e p	James Bailey (Sittingbourne)	2.05.52	inthc	London (LB)			11 Dec
15:30.0		Charles Mason (LAC)	3.06.51	1hc	London (LB)			11 Nov
15:31.0	p	McLeavy		1hc	Glasgow			9 Sep
15:33.8	e p	Alexander Clark (Glasgow)	c53	1	Glasgow (Spr)			13 May
15:36.0	p	McLeavy		2hc	Manchester (RO)			22 Jan
		(12/9)						
15:41.0		Lees Knowles (CU)	16.02.57	1	Cambridge			23 Mar
15:46.4	e	John Penrose (CU)	12.11.53	2	Cambridge			23 Mar
15:47.1	e	Frank Bullock-Webster (OU)	21.12.54	3	Oxford			18 Mar
16:00.0		Julius Bendixen (SLH)	51	int	London (LB)	AAC		10 Apr

Notes
Grenfell 30y down on 15:12.4 (07/04); Shrubsole 80y and Bailey 160y down on 14:56.75; Clark 250y down on
14:49.5; Bullock-Webster 30y 9in down on 15:41.6 (18/03); Penrose 30y down on 15:41.0. James Sanderson
must have recorded times of around 15 min in his 4 mile runs at Oldham (20:12 on 23/09), Glasgow (20:15.3e on
11/11) and London (20:43.5 on 19/06), but no details are available. McLeavy must also have got inside 15 min in
Glasgow on 11/11.
Intermediate times in races at 4 miles (10/04), 5 miles (11/12) and 10 miles (6/03; 13/05)

4 Miles
19:58.0	p	James McLeavy (Alexandria)	26.10.52	1	Glasgow (Spr)			11 Nov
20:00.5	p	George Hazael (Deptford)	22.11.44	int	Glasgow (Spr)			13 May
20:12.0	p	James Sanderson (Whitworth)	28.12.37	1	Oldham			23 Sep
20:15.3	e p	Sanderson		2	Glasgow (Spr)			11 Nov
20:20.7	e p	Hazael		2hc	Canterbury			6 Jun
20:29.0	p	Hazael		int	London (LB)			6 Mar
20:35.0	i p	Hazael		1	London (Ag Hall)			12 Feb
20:40.0	p	Hazael		3hc	London (LB)			7 Feb
20:41.9	e p	William Shrubsole (Wellingborough)	4.07.46	2inthc	London (LB)			11 Dec
20:43.5	p	Sanderson		1	London (LB)			19 Jun
20:56.4	e p	James Bailey (Sittingbourne)	2.05.52	3inthc	London (LB			11 Dec
		(11/5)						
21:05.0	p	Charles Price (Kennington)	17.05.53	1hc	London (LB)			7 Feb
21:12.2		Charles Mason (LAC)	3.06.51	1	Dublin (LR) IRL	IrlvEng		5 Jun
21:17.0	p	A. Tucker (Notting Hill)		2hc	London (LB)			7 Feb
21:17.2		Alfred Goodwin (OU)	57	1	London (LB)	AAC		10 Apr
21:44.75		James Warburton (Haslingden)	13.11.45	1hc	Manchester			19 Jun
22:03.5	e p	William Smith (Paisley)	27.12.46	2hc	Edinburgh			23 Sep
22:08.5		Laurence Nunns (ICAC/IRL)	03.55	int	Dublin (LR) IRL	ICAC		27 May

Notes
Hazael 4y down on 20:20.0 (06/06); Sanderson 100y down on 19:58.0; Shrubsole 80y and Bailey 160y down
on 20:27.75 (11/12); Smith 2sec and 20-30y down on 21:56.
Some reports give the AAC result as 21:16.0. *The Sporting Annual, 1878-9* gives 19:52.0 for McLeavy in
Glasgow in October [could be a confusion with the 11 Nov run].
Intermediate times in races at 5 miles (11/12); and 10 miles (6/03; 13/05).

6 Miles

30:36.25	p	George Hazael (Deptford)	22.11.44	int	Glasgow (Spr)		13 May
31:03.0	p	Hazael		int	London (LB)		6 Mar
31:44.0	p	Hazael		1	Glasgow		23 Dec

Note: Intermediate times in races at 10 miles.

10 Miles

52:05.0	p	George Hazael (Deptford)	22.11.44	1	Glasgow (Spr)		13 May
52:21.6	p	Hazael		wo	London (LB)		6 Mar
53:22.0	p	William Smith (Paisley)	27.12.46	1hc	London (LB)		26 Dec
55:41.0	p	Smith		1hc	Glasgow (Spr)		29 Apr
56:40.0	p	H. Baker (Harrow)		6hc	London (LB)		26 Dec
56:45.0	p	Arthur Flaunty (Deptford)	54	4hc	London (LB)		26 Dec
56:54.0	p	James Tester (Billingsgate)	2.05.49	2hc	London (LB)		26 Dec
57:34.0	p	Robert Sammon (Bow)	c44	5hc	London (LB)		26 Dec
57:55.0	p	John Beavan (Camberwell)	c54	7hc	London (LB)		26 Dec
58:05.0	p	Charles Price (Kennington)	17.05.53	8hc	London (LB)		26 Dec
58:45.0	p	Joseph Rowe (Bethnal Green)	c46	wo	London (Bow)		20 Jun
59:34.0	p	Henry Brown (Fulham)	16.01.43	3hc	London (LB)		26 Dec

120 Yards Hurdles

16.0		Alfred Loder (CU)	25.03.55	1	Bury St Edmunds	30 Mar
16 ¼		Hugh Upcher (ex-OU)	28.10.53	1	Woodbridge	17 Apr
16 2/5		Loder		1	London (LB) AAC	10 Apr
16 3/5		Loder		1	London (LB) OvC	7 Apr
16 3/5		Henry Macdougall (LAC)	c52	1	Belfast, IRL	10 Jun
16 ¾		Henry Kayll (Sunderland)	16.07.55	1hc	Sunderland	5 Jun
16 ¾		W. Spalton (Leeds)		1	Horsforth	24 Jun
16 4/5		Loder		1	Cambridge	22 Mar
16.9 e		James Gorman (Lurgan AC/IRL)	31.10.50	2	Belfast, IRL	10 Jun
16.9 e		John Reay (LAC)	9.07.53	2	London (LB) AAC	10 Apr
17.0		Alfred Peterkin (Glasgow U)	2.10.54	1	Glasgow (WSCG)	1 Apr
17.0		J.R.Harper (Tadcaster)		1ht2	Ilkley	5 Aug
17.0		Richard Coombes (Paignton)	53	1	Exmouth	12 Sep
		(13/10)				
17.1 e		William Anderson (RBA Inst/IRL)		3	Belfast, IRL	10 Jun
17.2 e		Ernest Wood (LAC)	25.01.57	2	Bury St Edmunds	30 Mar
17 1/5		George Turner (St George's Hosp)	22.10.55	1	London (LB)	1 Jul
17 1/5		Samuel Bestow (Nottm Forest FC)	3.03.52	1ht1	Ilkley	5 Aug
17.3 e		Francis Wood (ex-Harrow Sch)	28.09.55	3	London (LB) AAC	10 Apr
17 2/5		Charles Lockton (LAC)	2.07.56	1	Dublin (LR) IRL IrlvEng	5 Jun
17 ½		Richard Kelly (RMA)	24.09.57	1	Woolwich	7 Jun
17 ½		Patrick Davin (Suir RC/IRL)	4.06.57	1ht1	Limerick, IRL	14 Sep

School Sports

17.0		Charles Theobald (Tonbridge Sch)	60	1	Tonbridge	1 Apr

Doubtful

16 ¾		C. Davis (Eastbourne)		1	Eastbourne	22 Aug

"Starting was with the almost obsolete flag, rendering the times taken virtually valueless." (*The Field*)

17 1/5		Leonard Armstrong (Epsom College)	58	1	Epsom	17 Apr
17.4 e		Frederick Baylis (Epsom College)	57	2	Epsom	17 Apr

Downhill

17.0		William Edgar (Dartford FC)	27.09.53	1	Erith	8 Jul

Notes
Gorman 2y & Anderson 3y down on 16.6 (10/06); Reay 3y down on 16.4 (10/04); E.R.Wood 8y down on 16.0;
F.J.W.Wood 6y down on 16.4 in AAC; Baylis 1y down on 17.2.

220 Yards Hurdles

28.8 e	George Dobell (Northwich FC)	14.11.54	2hc	Newcastle-und-Lyme	25 Aug
31.0	George Hingeston (Railway Clearing HAC)	c50	1ht2	London (LB)	9 Sep
31.2	Raymond Wickham (Bristol Ariel RC)	50	1	Bicester	11 Sep
31.5	Wickham		1	Clifton	2 Sep
31.6 e	Carlyle Bernhardt (Lancaster)	53	2hc	Preston	29 Jul
32.0 e	Walter Singer (Frome)	53	2	Clifton	2 Sep
32.0 e	Horace Strachan (LAC)	21.09.55	3	Clifton	2 Sep

12 flights

32.0	Richard Coombes (Paignton)	53	1	Exmouth	12 Sep

13 flights

30.0	G. Perrin (Dalkey/IRL)		1	Dalkey, IRL	18 Jul
30.2 e	E. Dunbar (Dublin AC/IRL)		2	Dalkey, IRL	18 Jul
30.3 e	A.J.Newell (Dalkey/IRL)		3	Dalkey, IRL	18 Jul

Notes
Dunbar 1y & Newell 2y down on 30.0; Dobell 6y down on 28.0; Bernhardt 4y down on 31.0; Singer 3y & Strachan 3y 1ft down on 31.5

440 Yards Hurdles

1:07.6 e	George Dobell (Northwich FC)	14.11.54	2hc	Grappenhall	8 Jul
1:09.0	C. Barret (IRL)		1	Tullamore, IRL	17 Apr
1:09.5	John Edwards (Birmingham AC)	55	1	Birmingham	6 May
1:09.6 e	J.C.Flynn (Derby AC)		2hc	Buxton	26 Aug
1:10.0	E. Casey (Littleton/IRL)		1	Littleton, IRL	27 Sep
1:10.3 e	Grady (Littleton/IRL)		2	Littleton, IRL	27 Sep
1:10.4	Thomas Kelly (Clonmel/IRL)		1	Crague, IRL	14 Sep
1:11.0	E. Morris (IRL)		1	Drangan, IRL	Sep
1:11.75	Alfred Cowin (Douglas, IOM)	c54	1	Douglas, IOM	30 Aug

12 flights

1:05.0	Dobell		1hc	Wakefield	2 Sep

13 flights

1:11.0	Charles Hamilton (Dublin U/IRL)	9.10.53	1	Dublin (CP), IRL	15 Jun
1:11.1 e	William Hamilton (Dublin U/IRL)	1.07.50	2	Dublin (CP), IRL	15 Jun

20 flights

1:09.0	C. Hamilton		1	Borris, IRL	5 Jul

Notes
Dobell 12y down on 65.75; Flynn 5y down on 68.75; Hamilton 1ft down on 1:11.0. Dobell also recorded 65.2 at Compstall on 27/05, but *Bell's Life* reported that the course was short.

High Jump

6'2½	1.892	Marshall Brooks (OU)	30.05.55	1	London (LB)	OvC	7 Apr
6'0⅛	1.832	Brooks		1	Oxford		17 Mar
6'0	1.829	Brooks		1	London (LB)	AAC	10 Apr
5'10½	1.791	William Kelly (QC Cork/IRL)		1	Cork, IRL		17 May
5'9¼	1.759	Ernest Wood (LAC)	25.01.57	1	Woodbridge		17 Apr
5'9¼	1.759	Kelly		1	Cork, IRL		2 May
5'8¾	1.746	Gerard Blathwayt (CU)	27.06.55	2	London (LB)	OvC	7 Apr
5'8½	1.740	George Kenny (Clongowes Coll/IRL)	7.06.55	1	Dublin (CP), IRL		16 Jun
5'8½	1.740	Thomas Tomlinson (Gosforth CC)	c55	1	Durham		14 Jul
5'8¼	1.734	Francis Wood (LAC)	28.09.55	2	Woodbridge		17 Apr
5'8¼	1.734	D. Lehane (QC Cork/IRL)		1	Kanturk, IRL		4 Oct
5'8	1.727	William Fitzgerald (QC Cork/IRL)		2	Cork, IRL		17 May
5'8	1.727	Tomlinson		1	Leeds		1 Jul
5'8	1.727	Wildon Thompson (Burton Pidsea)	56	2hc	Beverley		19 Jul
5'8	1.727	John Alkin (Nuneaton CC)	10.07.55	1	Caernarvon		11 Aug
5'8	1.727	Tomlinson		1	Hinckley		2 Sep
		(16/11)					
5'7½	1.715	Charles Lucas (OU)	7.08.53	3	London (LB)	OvC	7 Apr
5'7½	1.715	Patrick Davin (Suir RC/IRL)	4.06.57	1=	Dublin (LR) IRL IrlvEng	5 Jun
5'7½	1.715	Thomas Davin (Suir RC/IRL)	51	1=	Dublin (LR) IRL IrlvEng	5 Jun
5'7¼	1.708	Lt. Newington (Royal Marines)		1	Gosport		3 Jul

5'7	1.702	Henry Kayll (Sunderland FC)	16.07.55	1	Darlington	13 May
5'7	1.702	Joseph Watson (LAC)	15.10.51	1	London (LB)	23 May
5'7	1.702	Horace Strachan (LAC)	21.09.55	1=	London (LB)	29 May
5'7	1.702	Charles Lockton (LAC)	2.07.56	1=	London (LB)	29 May
5'7	1.702	Edwin Smith (Leeds)		1	Lancaster	5 Jun
5'7	1.702	William Anderson (RBA Inst/IRL)		1	Belfast, IRL	9 Jun
5'7	1.702	Fielding Chevallier (Ipswich)	53	1	Hadleigh	26 Jul
5'7	1.702	Charles Cross (Hadleigh)	56	2	Hadleigh	26 Jul
5'7	1.702	John Hargreaves (Manchester AC)		1	Stoke-on-Trent	8 Aug

Indoors Doubtful (rope/springboard)

6'0	1.829 i	Robert Thomas (Liverpool)	22.11.56	1	Liverpool Gym	21 Dec
5'11	1.803 i	William Milner (Everton)	c55	2	Liverpool Gym	21 Dec

Note: Tom Davin was reported to have jumped 5'11 in a trial at Dublin on 1 June, whilst training for the Ireland v England match. Chevallier and Cross tied at 5'7 and Chevallier won the jump-off.

High Jump: Highland & Border

6'0	1.829 p	Hugh Andrews (Glasgow)	c52	1	Crofthead	25 Aug
5'11	1.803 p	Thomas McDougall (Galashiels)	c53	1	Galashiels	22 Jul
5'10½	1.791 p	E. Andrews (Edinburgh)		1=	Kelso	29 Jul
5'10½	1.791 p	H. Andrews		1=	Kelso	29 Jul
5'10	1.778 p	H. Andrews		1	Alexandria	24 Jun
5'10	1.778 p	Thomas Aitken (Walkerburn)	23.05.53	2	Galashiels	22 Jul
5'9	1.753 p	Peter Cameron (Banchory)	8.12.52	1	Lumphanan	15 Jul
5'8	1.727 p	H. Andrews		1	Tranent	15 Jun
5'8	1.727 p	William Borland (Kilbarchan)	c48	2=	Alexandria	24 Jun
5'8	1.727 p	Daniel Lamont (Kilbarchan)	c55	2=	Alexandria	24 Jun
5'8	1.727 p	Cameron		1	Nairn	5 Aug
		(11/7)				
5'7	1.702 p	Alexander Edington (Edinburgh)	17.11.57	2	Tranent	15 Jun
5'7	1.702 p	George Mearns (Aberdeen)		2	Lumphanan	15 Jul

Note
The *Falkirk Herald* reported Hugh Andrews' 6'0 as "the highest known".

Pole Vault

11'1	3.38	Edwin Woodburn (Ulverston)	19.04.50	1	Ulverston	21 Jul
10'10¾	3.32	Charles Gaskin (Wisbech CC)	56	1	Sheffield (BL)	3 Jul
10'9	3.28	Horace Strachan (LAC)	21.09.55	1	Olney	7 Aug
10'8½	3.26	Gaskin		1	Newark	5 Jun
10'8	3.25	Henry Johnson (Daventry)	51	2	Olney	7 Aug
10'7	3.23	Henry Kayll (Sunderland)	16.07.55	1	Sunderland	5 Jun
10'6	3.20	Robert Sabin (Culworth AC)	52	1	Birmingham	6 May
10'6	3.20	Strachan		wo	London (LB)	20 May
10'6	3.20	Strachan		2	Newark	5 Jun
10'6	3.20	Gaskin		1=	Northampton	7 Aug
10'6	3.20	Strachan		1=	Northampton	7 Aug
10'5	3.17	Samuel Ratcliffe (Ashby FC)	53	1	Nuneaton	7 Aug
10'4	3.15	Ernest Edwards (Birmingham AC)	21.03.59	2	Birmingham	6 May
10'4	3.15	Kayll		1	Durham	6 Oct
		(14/8)				
10'3	3.12	J. Power (Tullahea/IRL)		1	Crague, IRL	14 Sep
10'2¼	3.11	John Gorham (Lincoln FC)	53	3	Newark	5 Jun
10'2	3.10	Kendal Wilkinson (Urswick)	54	2	Ulverston	21 Jul
10'1	3.07	Charles Hamilton (Dublin U/IRL)	9.10.53	1	Dublin (CP), IRL	15 Jun
10'0	3.05	Thomas Bellamy (Mortomley)	c53	2	Sheffield (BL)	3 Jul
10'0	3.05	Walter Kelsey (Hull CC)	04.51	1	Selby	27 Jul
10'0	3.05	John Crockford (Crusaders FC)	57	1	Birmingham	19 Aug

Exhibition

11'2	3.40	Woodburn		ex	Ulverston	14 Jul

Note
Woodburn's jumps at Ulverston on 21/07 were 10'5, 10'8½ and 11'1.
The bar was at 11'0 for Gaskin's 10'10¾, measured. T. Bellamy was second, given 10'0, which would be 9'10¾ with a similar adjustment.

Pole Vault: Highland, Lakeland & Border

10'6	3.20	p	Joseph Hewitson (Keswick)	c55	1	Grasmere	17 Aug
10'5	3.17	p	David Milne (Forfar)	28.12.42	1	Forfar	4 Aug
10'4	3.15	p	William Barron (Keswick)	c56	1	Keswick	24 May
10'4	3.15	p	George Barker (Bacup)	c55	1	Altrincham	24 Jun
10'4	3.15	p	Anthony Hall (Edinburgh)	c46	1	Stenhousemuir	15 Jul
10'4	3.15	p	William Borland (Kilbarchan)	c48	1	Birnam	24 Aug
10'3	3.12	p	Barker		1	Hanley	22 May
10'3	3.12	p	Joseph Milburn (Hayton)		1	Newcastle	6 Jun
10'3	3.12	p	Barker		1	Burnley	1 Jul
10'3	3.12	p	David Anderson (Alnwick)	c46	1	Whittingham	24 Aug
			(10/8)				
10'2½	3.11	p	William Bracegirdle (Warrington)		1=	Manchester (WR)	29 Jul
10'2	3.10	p	John Thwaites (Keswick)	c57	2	Keswick	24 May
10'2	3.10	p	Thomas Stark (East Calder)	c56	2	Birnam	24 Aug
10'2	3.10	p	James Rush (Addiewell)	c52	1	Linlithgow	2 Sep
10'0	3.05	p	Peter Cameron (Banchory)	8.12.52	1	Lumphanan	15 Jul
10'0	3.05	p	William Ferguson (Alloa)		2	Stenhousemuir	15 Jul
10'0	3.05	p	Thomas Milne (Dundee)	c52	2=	Dundee	15 Jul
10'0	3.05	p	John Toy (Montrose)	c46	2=	Dundee	15 Jul

Indoors

10'8	3.25	i p	Hewitson		1	Manchester (Cir)	18 Apr
10'4	3.15	i p	Richard Bagot (Fleetwood)	52	2	Manchester (Cir)	18 Apr
10'1	3.07	i p	Marcellus Thompson (Kendal)	19.01.55	3	Manchester (Cir)	18 Apr

Long Jump

22'6	6.86	Frederick Hargreaves (Manchester)	5.09.50	1	Douglas, IOM		30 Aug
21'11	6.68	Marshall Brooks (OU)	30.05.55	1	Oxford		18 Mar
21'9½	6.64	Henry Macdougall (LAC)	c52	2	Douglas, IOM		30 Aug
21'8½	6.62	Richard Surtees (OU)	8.04.53	2	Oxford		18 Mar
21'8½	6.62	Brooks		1	London (LB)	OvC	7 Apr
21'7	6.58	John Alkin (Nuneaton CC)	10.07.55	1	Hinckley		2 Sep
21'6½	6.57	Charles Lockton (LAC)	2.07.56	1	Dublin (LR) IRL IrlvEng		5 Jun
21'5½	6.54	Edmund Baddeley (CU)	9.04.57	1	Cambridge		23 Nov
21'5	6.53	Lockton		1	Worthing		12 Sep
21'4½	6.52	Brooks		1	Oxford		6 Mar
21'4	6.50	Herbert Flockton (Snettisham)	56	1	Spalding		7 Aug
21'3	6.48	Alkin		1	London (LB)	AAC	10 Apr
21'3	6.48	Lockton		1	London (LB)		29 May
21'3	6.48	Alkin		1	Stoke-on-Trent		8 Aug
		(14/8)					
21'2¼	6.46	Patrick Davin (Suir RC/IRL)	4.06.57	2	Dublin (LR) IRL IrlvEng		5 Jun
21'1½	6.44	Alfred Clunies-Ross (Edinburgh Institution)	46	1=	Edinburgh		10 Jun
21'1½	6.44	George Gaukroger (Edinburgh Institution)		1=	Edinburgh		10 Jun
21'1	6.43	Charles Hamilton (Dublin U/IRL)	9.10.53	1	Borris, IRL		5 Jul
21'1	6.43	Gerard Fowler (Birmingham)	57	2	Hinckley		2 Sep
21'0	6.40	William Tomkin (ex-Eton Coll)	56	2	London (LB)	AAC	10 Apr
20'11½	6.39	William Kelly (Cork AC/IRL)		1	Cork, IRL		17 May
20'11	6.38	Charles Scott-Chad (Eton College)	23.03.57	1	Eton		16 Mar
20'11	6.38	Hugh Upcher (ex-OU)	28.10.53	1	Woodbridge		17 Apr
20'10½	6.36	Claude Bayley (CU)	25.11.55	2	London (LB)	OvC	7 Apr
20'10	6.35	Alfred Stevens (KCLAC)		3	Douglas, IOM		30 Aug
20'10	6.35	William Tilley (Widnes)	c56	1	Great Crosby		9 Sep
20'10	6.35	Thomas Wraith (Berwick AC)	13.09.54	1	Durham		6 Oct

Favourable take-off

21'6	6.55	Alkin		1	Caernarvon	11 Aug

Long Jump: Highland & Border

20'10	6.35	p	Archibald Mitchell (Alva)	51	1	Alloa	9 Aug

Triple Jump

43'5	13.23	James Daly (QC Cork/IRL)		c54	1	Cork, IRL	2 May
43'0	13.11	D. Lehane (QC Cork/IRL)			1	Kanturk, IRL	4 Oct
42'7	12.98	William Kelly (QC Cork/IRL)			2	Cork, IRL	2 May
41'8	12.70	Arthur Boucher (Edinburgh U)		c55	1	Edinburgh (ACG)	21 Jun
41'6	12.65	P.J.Tobin (Tullahea/IRL)			1	Tullahea, IRL	14 Aug
41'0	12.50	J.K.O'Connor (Cahirciveen/IRL)			1	Cahirciveen, IRL	3 Aug
40'9½	12.43	J.J.O'Flynn (Castletownroche/IRL)			1	Brisbane,AUS	11 Sep
40'8½	12.41	John Smith (Edinburgh U)			2	Edinburgh (ACG)	21 Jun
40'7	12.37	John Hargreaves (Caledonian Assoc)			1	Manchester (WR)	29 Jul
40'6	12.34	Michael Anglin (Tullahea/IRL)			2	Tullahea, IRL	14 Aug
40'2	12.24	Edward Smith (Cowling)			2	Manchester (WR)	29 Jul
40'1	12.22	C.H.Conway (Cahirciveen/IRL)			2	Cahirciveen, IRL	3 Aug
40'0	12.19	Thomas Stretch (Ormskirk AC)	28.01.51		1	Ormskirk	10 Jun
40'0	12.19	Michael Brannagan (Ballymahon/IRL)			1	Ballymahon, IRL	7 Aug
		(14/14)					
39'10½	12.15	Gunner J. Bell (Dep RHA)			1	Woolwich	8 Aug
39'9	12.12	T. Cook (Garston)			2	Ormskirk	10 Jun
39'8	12.09	Thomas Farrington (QC Cork/IRL)			3	Cork, IRL	2 May
39'5½	12.03	Duncan Brunton (Glasgow U)	5.02.52		2	Glasgow (WSCG)	1 Apr

Notes

Some reports give D.C.James as the winner of the Queen's College,Cork, Sports (2/05), but this was a
pseudonym used by James C. Daly. The *Irish Sportsman & Farmer* gives Kelly 43'2½/13.17 on 2/05.

Triple Jump: Highland & Border

47'4	14.43	p	Robert Knox (Newstead)	17.09.47		1	Alloa	9 Aug
47'1	14.35	p	Archibald Mitchell (Alva)	51		2	Alloa	9 Aug
47'0	14.33	p	R. Thompson			3	Alloa	9 Aug
46'9	14.25	p	Knox			1	Hawick	10 Jun
46'7	14.20	p	Knox			1	Jedburgh	28 Jul
46'4	14.12	p	Knox			1	Alva	10 Aug
46'0	14.02	p	E. Andrews (Edinburgh)			1	Kelso	29 Jul
45'9	13.94	p	Mitchell			1	Motherwell	3 Jun
45'7	13.89	p	Knox			2	Kelso	29 Jul
45'6	13.87	p	G. Ferguson (Edinburgh)			2	Jedburgh	28 Jul
45'6	13.87	p	James Young (Alva)		c47	1	South Queensferry	11 Aug
45'4	13.82	p	John Wilson (Edinburgh)		c46	2	South Queensferry	11 Aug
45'2	13.77	p	Alexander Edington (Edinburgh)	17.11.57		1	Tranent	15 Jun
45'1	13.74	p	Wilson			1	Stenhousemuir	15 Jul
45'0	13.72	p	Knox			1	Tillicoultry	11 Aug
			(15/8)					
44'11	13.69	p	George Walsh (Royton)	3.02.44		2	Stenhousemuir	15 Jul
44'7	13.59	p	Thomas Aitken (Walkerburn)	23.05.53		1	Govan	27 May
44'5	13.54	p	Daniel Lamont (Kilbarchan)		c55	1	Dalkeith	16 Sep
44'1	13.44	p	James Weir (Innerleithen)		c56	2	Innerleithen	12 Aug
43'7	13.28	p	William McLiver (Stewarton)		c57	1	Pollokshaws	10 Jun
43'5	13.23	p	R. Trainer (Glasgow)			3	Govan	27 May
43'4	13.21	p	James Rush (Barrhead)		c52	2=	Pollokshaws	10 Jun
43'3	13.18	p	John Toy (Montrose)		c46	1	Lochee	29 Jul
43'2	13.16	p	James Fox (Alloa)			1	Alloa (local)	9 Aug
42'7	12.98	p	Peter Cameron (Banchory)	8.12.52		1	Aberdeen CC	24 Jul
42'7	12.98	p	John McAllister (Alloa)			2	Alloa (local)	9 Aug
42'4	12.90	p	James Hunter (Galashiels)			2	Balfron	17 Jul
42'3½	12.89	p	John Campbell (Alexandria)			3	Balfron	17 Jul
42'3	12.88	p	Hugh Andrews (Glasgow)		c52	2	Alexandria	24 Jun
42'3	12.88	p	William Murray			2	Dalkeith	16 Sep

Shot

41'5	12.62	James Daly (QC Cork/IRL)		c54	1	Dublin (LR) IRL ICAC	27 May
40'5	12.32	Maurice Davin (Suir RC/IRL)	29.06.42		2	Dublin (LR) IRL ICAC	27 May
40'2	12.24	Davin			1	Dublin (LR) IRL IrlvEng	5 Jun
40'0	12.19	Thomas Stone (Newton-le-Willows)	24.01.52		2	Dublin (LR) IRL IrlvEng	5 Jun
40'0	12.19	Stone			1	Manchester (WR)	19 Jun
39'7	12.06	Stone			2hc	Widnes	24 Jun

39'6	12.04		Patrick Nally (Ballinrobe/IRL)		56	1	Ballinrobe, IRL	31 Aug
39'5	12.01		Stone			1	Bebington	27 May
38'9	11.81		Stone			1	Wigan	26 Aug
38'8	11.79		William Orr (QC Belfast/IRL)		c55	1	Belfast, IRL	6 May

(10/5)

38'5	11.71	William Winthrop (LAC)	15.06.52	1	London (LB)	24 Jun
38'2½	11.65	Patrick Hickey (QC Cork/IRL)	18.12.54	1	Cork, IRL	25 Apr
38'0	11.58	Richard Garnons-Williams (RMC S'hurst)	15.06.56	1	Camberley	13 Oct
37'9	11.51	Charles Peake (Barnsley FC)		1	Barnsley	21 Aug
37'7	11.46	C. Hogan (French Coll/IRL)	c59	1	Blackrock, IRL	26 Jun
37'6	11.43	Alexander Inglis (Manchester Caledn Ass)	c53	1	Manchr (WR) (local)	29 Jul
36'10	11.23	George Kenny (Dublin U/IRL)	7.06.55	1	Dublin (CP), IRL	16 Jun
36'6	11.13	Charles Hodges (OU)	6.10.53	1	Oxford	17 Mar
36'6	11.13	Wyndham Evanson (Civil Service)	51	1	London (LB)	20 May
36'3	11.05	Arthur Kelly (RMA)	1.05.57	1	Woolwich	7 Jun
36'1	11.00	R. Wilson (Glasgow U)		1	Partick	1 Apr

Shot: Highland & Border
Includes 16lb stone

47'5	14.45	p	Donald Dinnie (Stonehaven)	8.06.37	1	Govan	27 May
47'0	14.33	p	Dinnie		1	Aberdeen CC	24 Jul
46'9½	14.26	p	Dinnie		1	Aboyne	12 Sep
45'2	13.77	p	Dinnie		1	Manchester (WR)	29 Jul
44'9*	13.64	p	James Fleming (Ballinluig)	18.09.40	1	Forfar (light)	4 Aug
43'10½	13.37	p	Fleming		2	Aboyne	12 Sep
43'9	13.33	p	Fleming		2	Aberdeen CC	24 Jul
43'3	13.18	p	George Mearns (Aberdeen)		3	Aberdeen CC	24 Jul
43'2*	13.16	p	John George (Edinburgh)	46	2	Forfar (light)	4 Aug
43'2	13.16	p	Dinnie		1	Wigan	26 Aug
43'0	13.11	p	W. Smith (Glasgow)		1	Stenhousemuir	15 Jul
42'10½	13.07	p	Mearns		3	Aboyne	12 Sep

(12/5)

42'7	12.98	p	George Davidson (Drumoak)	19.11.54	1	Aberdeen CC	22 Jul
41'6*	12.65	p	William Fleming (Dundee)	22.08.42	3	Forfar (light)	4 Aug
41'0*	12.50	p	Owen Duffy (Edinburgh/IRL)	c47	1	Edinburgh	7 Aug
40'5	12.32	p	J. Smith (Glasgow)		2	Stenhousemuir	15 Jul
39'4*	11.99	p	William Bremner (Leochel-Cushnie)	3.01.47	1	Ballater (light)	23 Aug
38'6	11.73	p	Robert McGregor (Perthshire RV)		1	Perth	30 Sep
38'5*	11.71	p	John Smith (Kildrummy)		1	Kildrummy	8 Aug
37'4*	11.38	p	John Robertson (Aberdeen)		3	Ballater (light)	23 Aug
37'0*	11.28	p	John Brown (Edinburgh)		1	Tranent	15 Jun
37'0	11.28	p	Peter McCowan (Perthshire RV)		2	Perth	30 Sep
36'7*	11.15	p	James Russell (Gartly)	c48	1	Huntly (local)	4 Aug
36'4*	11.07	p	Kenneth McRae (Wishaw)	50	1	Milngavie (light)	26 Aug
36'3*	11.05	p	John Wilson		3	Lumphanan	15 Jul

Note
*correct weight assumed from evidence of other years
46'9½ by Dinnie at Aboyne said to have been on a slope (*Aberdeen Journal*, 8.09.1904)

Weight unstated

44'2	13.46	p	George		1	Newburgh	23 Jun
43'6½	13.27	p	Dinnie		1	Nairn	5 Aug
38'11	11.86	p	McCowan		2	Newburgh	23 Jun
37'6	11.43	p	Peter Adam (Perth)		3	Newburgh	23 Jun

17lb

44'0	13.41	p	William Graham (Dalkeith)		1	Dalkeith	16 Sep
41'0	12.50	p	George		2	Dalkeith	16 Sep

22lb by performer

40'11	12.47	p	Dinnie		1	Dundee	15 Jul
39'10	12.14	p	J. Fleming		2	Dundee	15 Jul
38'5	11.71	p	Mearns		2	Aberdeen	24 Jul
37'4	11.38	p	Duffy		1	Leith	8 Aug
37'1	11.30	p	George		3	Blairgowrie	25 Jul

36'9	11.20	p	W. Fleming		3	Dundee	15 Jul

Doubtful

51'6	15.70	p	John Cameron (Leith)		1	Inverness (light)	21 Sep
50'9	15.47	p	Dinnie		1	Greenock (light)	17 Jun
49'9	15.16	p	Mearns		2	Inverness (light)	21 Sep
47'1	14.35	p	J. Fleming		2	Greenock (light)	17 Jun
46'2	14.07	p	Duffy		1	Bridge of Allan (light)	5 Aug
44'9	13.64	p	J. Fleming		2	Bridge of Allan (light)	5 Aug
43'9	13.33	p	George		3	Greenock (light)	17 Jun
42'8	13.00	p	George		3	Bridge of Allan (light)	5 Aug
37'10	11.53	p	Alexander Ritchie (Greenock)		1	Greenock (light/local)	17 Jun
37'4	11.38	p	Robert Lindsay (Bridge of Allan)	c55	4	Bridge of Allan (light)	5 Aug

Hammer
All styles

138'3	42.14		George Hales (CU)	20.05.54	1	London (LB)	OvC	7 Apr
136'8	41.66		Hales		1hc	Cambridge		21 Nov
135'9	41.38		Hales		1	Cambridge		24 Feb
131'10	40.18		Hales		1	Cambridge		23 Mar
131'6	40.08		Maurice Davin (Suir RC/IRL)	29.06.42	1	Dublin (LR) IRL IrlvEng		5 Jun
129'0	39.32		Hales		1	Cambridge		8 Mar
128'10	39.27		Davin		1	Dublin (LR) IRL ICAC		27 May
117'0½	35.67		James Daly (QC Cork/IRL)	c54	1	Cork, IRL		2 May
116'0	35.36		John Tobin (Ninemilehouse/IRL)		1	Mullinahone, IRL		11 Jul
110'11½	33.82		Patrick Hickey (QC Cork/IRL)	18.12.54	2	Cork, IRL		2 May
			(10/5)					
109'8	33.43		M.D.Ambrose (QC Cork/IRL)		3	Cork, IRL		2 May
109'0	33.22		William A. Burgess (ex-OU)	27.12.46	1	Derby		22 Jul
107'7	32.79		Alfred Lyttelton (CU)	7.02.57	2	London (LB)	OvC	7 Apr
104'0	31.70		Matthew Stritch (RIC/IRL)	02.47	1	Belfast, IRL		10 Jun
102'6	31.24		Neil McDonald (Glasgow Alexandra AC)	c54	1	Glasgow (HP)		9 Sep
101'4	30.89		George Kenny (Dublin U/IRL)	7.06.55	1	Dublin (CP), IRL		15 Jun
100'11	30.76		Edmund Baddeley (CU)	9.04.57	1	Cambridge		23 Nov
99'11	30.45		Alexander Inglis (Manchester AC)	c53	1	Sheffield (BL)		7 Aug
99'2	30.23		Hugh Holme (OU)	4.11.53	1	Oxford		16 Mar
97'11	29.84		John McNiven (Manchester)	c54	1	Manchester (WR)		29 Jul
94'8	28.85		Arthur Soames (CU)	30.11.52	4	Cambridge		23 Mar
94'5	28.78		Charles Lewis (OU)	20.08.53	2	Oxford		16 Mar

Notes
This year the AAC introduced the 7ft run and 3ft 6in maximum length of handle for the Championship meeting. Elsewhere, including Ireland, the run was unlimited. The length of the wooden hammer handles varied considerably. Daly used one of 4ft 9½ in. Holme achieved practice throws of 120ft with a 4ft 1in handle, but had it shortened to 3ft 8in for the OU standard competition on 06/03. Davin used a 3ft 6in handle and threw one-handed.
Bell's Life reported that Hales threw 137'6 a few days previous to 8 March, but this may have been in practice. In the CU sports (23/03) Hales also threw 131'4 – 131'4 – 129'9 – 127'4½ - 127'4. Lyttelton also threw 100'3 – 101'4. In the Irish Champion AC Sports, Davin's first throw was 124'6.

Hammer: Highland & Border

127'6	38.86	p	Donald Dinnie (Stonehaven)	8.06.37	1	London (Alex Palace)	1 Jul
123'10	37.74	p	Dinnie		1	Aboyne	12 Sep
118'2	36.02	p	Dinnie		1	New Deer	21 Jul
116'0	35.36	p	Dinnie		1	Manchester (WR)	29 Jul
115'2*	35.10	p	William Fleming (Dundee)	22.08.42	1	Forfar (light)	4 Aug
114'0	34.75	p	Dinnie		1	Coupar Angus	20 Jul
112'9	34.37	p	Dinnie		1	Govan	27 May
112'0*	34.14	p	Dinnie		1	Glenisla (prize)	18 Aug
112'0*	34.14	p	Dinnie		1	Luss	25 Aug
111'1*	33.86	p	Dinnie		1	Birnam	24 Aug
110'0	33.53	p	W. Fleming		1	Burrelton	4 Jul
108'0	32.92	p	John George (Edinburgh)	46	2	Forfar (light)	4 Aug
107'4	32.72	p	Dinnie		1	Aberdeen (CC)	24 Jul
			(13/3)				
104'4	31.80	p	George Davidson (Drumoak)	19.11.54	2	New Deer	21 Jul

101'5*	30.91	p	William McDuff (Dunkeld)	c51	1	Inverness (light)	21 Sep
106'5	32.44	p	James Fleming (Ballinluig)	18.09.40	3	Forfar (light)	4 Aug
99'2*	30.23	p	Kenneth McRae (Wishaw)	50	2	Inverness (light)	21 Sep
98'3	29.95	p	John Ogg (Banff/NZL)	7.08.47	2	Dunedin., NZL	1 Jan
98'2	29.92	p	John Dempster (Stamford)		3	Manchester (WR)	29 Jul
96'3*	29.34	p	John Moir (Strathdon)	27.07.42	3	Inverness (light)	21 Sep
96'2	29.31	p	James Thomson (Culter)		3	New Deer	21 Jul
96'2	29.31	p	William Bremner (Glenbucket)	3.01.47	2	Aboyne	12 Sep
96'1	29.29	p	Stewart Adams (Skene)		1	Culter (local)	5 Aug
96'0*	29.26	p	John Cameron (Leith)		1	Leith	8 Aug

Note: *correct weight assumed from evidence of other years

Weight unstated

113'9	34.67	p	Dinnie		1	Greenock	17 Jun
111'0	33.83	p	William Stewart		1	Glenlivet	26 Aug
110'10	33.78	p	Dinnie		1	Nairn	5 Aug
				(3/2)			
107'10	32.87	p	James Mackie (Tillygreig)		1	Udny (local)	9 Aug
106'10	32.56	p	James Proctor (Hillbrae)		2	Udny (local)	9 Aug
105'9	32.23	p	James Smith (Cragganmore)		2	Glenlivet	26 Aug
102'9	31.32	p	Thomas Murison (Pettymuck)		3	Udny (local)	9 Aug
101'5	30.91	p	R. Scott (Dalkeith)		1	Tranent	15 Jun
101'2	30.84	p	John Brown (Edinburgh)		2	Tranent	15 Jun
101'0	30.78	p	J. Smith (Edinburgh)		3	Tranent	15 Jun
98'10	30.12	p	J. Turner		3	Glenlivet	26 Aug
98'0	29.87	p	Alexander Ritchie (Glasgow)		1	Greenock (local)	17 Jun
97'5	29.69	p	George Bowie (Newmachar)	1.09.56	1	Udny (open)	9 Aug
95'0	28.96	p	William Rust (Kintore)	1.01.55	2	Udny (open)	9 Aug
94'6	28.80	p	W. Forbes		1	Mugiemore (light)	10 Jun

19lb

118'0	35.97	p	Dinnie		1	Dundee	15 Jul
102'0	31.09	p	W. Fleming		2	Dundee	15 Jul
100'0	30.48	p	J. Fleming		3	Dundee	15 Jul

22lb

94'8	28.85	p	Dinnie		1	Manchester (WR)	29 Jul

Other Events

120 Yards

12 1/5	James Pinion (Ulster CC/IRL)	c53	1ht1	Belfast, IRL	17 Apr

150 Yards

14 5/8 p	Frank Hewitt (Millwall)	8.05.45	1	Sydney, AUS	1 May
14 ¾	Richard Dudgeon (LAC/USA)	c54	1	Marlow	18 Apr

200 Yards

20.2 e p	Frank Hewitt (Millwall)	8.05.45	2	Maitland, NSW, AUS	8 May
21 2/5	Alfred Lewis (CU)	10.08.54	1hc	Cambridge	14 Nov

Note: Hewitt "nearly 1y down" on Robert F. Watson (AUS/IRL, b, Londonderry 11.06.54), 20 1/10.

300 Yards

31.5 p	Daniel Wight (Jedburgh)	c51	1	Glasgow (Shaw)	5 Aug

600 Yards

1:20.0	Abraham Cronyn (Dublin U/IRL)	3.09.55	1	Dublin (CP) IRL	16 Jun
1:20.0	W.S.Richardson (N. Durham CC)		1	Durham	15 Jul
Doubtful					
1:14.0	Adam Marshall (Dundee)	c52	1	Nairn	5 Aug

1000 Yards

2:31.6	Henry Hill (LAC)	22.01.52	1	Birmingham	29 Jul

¾ Mile

3:17.0	Walter Slade (LAC)	6.04.54	int	London (LB)	23 May
In 1 mile race					

5 Miles

25:17.5 p	George Hazael (Deptford)	22.11.44	int	Glasgow (Spr)	13 May

1 Mile Walk
6:20.0 p   William Perkins (London)   16.09.52   int   Brighton   29 Jul
in a match to walk 8 miles in 1 hour.

2 Miles Walk
14:02.0 p   James Miles (Brixton)   24.07.40   1   Fulham   17 Apr

7 Miles Walk
53:07.0 p   William Perkins (London)   16.09.52   int   Edinburgh   1 Jul
in a match to walk 8 miles in 1 hour.

50 Miles Walk
8:48:28.0 i p   James Miles (Brixton)   24.07.40   int   London (Ag Hall)   8/9 May
[In a 24 hours race, indoors]
9:04:52.5   Charles Ford (Dublin U/IRL)   54   1   Dublin (LR) IRL   7 Oct

100 Miles Walk
18:51:35.0 i p   Harry Vaughan (Chester)   23.08.47   int   London (Ag Hall)   8/9 May
[In a 24 hours race, indoors]

Cricket Ball
119y 0ft 0in 108.81   John Chappell (Manchester)   c54   1   Bamford   1 Jul
Exhibition
132y 1ft 0in 121.01   Walter Forbes (Eton College)   20.01.58 ex   Eton   16 Mar

50 mile professional walking match at Lillie Bridge, 14 August, 1876. In excessive heat William
Perkins, the favourite, was forced to retire after 24 miles. William Howes finished in 9 hrs 37 min
35sec. Two years later at the Agricultural Hall, Islington, he set a world best of 7 hrs 57 min 44sec.

1877 UK Year List

100 Yards

10.0 p	Thomas Wadeson (Preston)	56	1=hc	Lancaster		21 May
10 1/5	Ernest Trepplin (OU)	56	1	London (LB)	OvC	23 Mar
10 1/5	Douglas Ogilby (Dublin U/IRL)	16.02.53	1	Dublin (LR) IRL ICAC		19 May
10 1/5	William McCord (QC Belfast/IRL)	c56	1	Belfast, IRL		9 Jun
10 1/5 p	A. Edwards (London)		1	Dublin, IRL		16 Jul
10 1/5	Arthur Smith (Birkenhead)	c55	1	Southport		18 Aug
10 ¼	John Tennent (ex-OU/AUS)	31.07.46	1	Edinburgh		21 Apr
10 ¼	Henry Macdougall (LAC)	c52	1	London (LB)		28 Apr
10 ¼	Robert Stratton (Cirencester)	22.09.56	1	Cirencester		16 May
10 ¼	J.E.White (NECC)		1	Newcastle		7 Jul
10 ¼	Montague Betty (Bridgwater)	59	1	Taunton		13 Sep
10.3 e	Frederick Elborough (LAC)	30.07.52	2	London (LB)		28 Apr
10.3 e	McCord		2	Dublin (LR) IRL ICAC		19 May
10.3 e	William Barter (ICAC/IRL)	c55	3	Dublin (LR) IRL ICAC		19 May
		(14/13)				
10 2/5	Edward Salmon (CU)	29.10.54	1	Cambridge		17 Mar
10 2/5	John Bruce Williamson (Glasgow Ac)	28.01.59	1	Glasgow (Ac)		28 Apr
10 2/5	Herbert Bent (Bury St Edmunds)	57	1	Bury St Edmunds		24 May
10 2/5	Charles Lockton (LAC)	2.07.56	1	London (SB)		2 Jun
10 2/5	Lionel Walker (Dewsbury CC)	14.06.56	1hc	Huddersfield		16 Jun
10 2/5	Richard Bond		1	Burnley		30 Jun
10.4 e	Horace Crossley (Leyton FC)	2.10.55	3hc	Leyton		30 Jun
10 2/5	Anthony Bowlby (St Bart's Hosp)	10.05.55	1ht4	London (LB)		4 Jul
10.4 e p	T. Pollitt (Manchester)		2	Dublin, IRL		16 Jul
10 2/5	James Stewart (Dublin AC/IRL)	10.02.51	1	Dublin (LR), IRL		21 Jul
10 2/5	Sgt Hopkinson (RA)		1	Aldershot		25 Jul
10 2/5	John Shearman (LAC)	6.08.55	1	Birmingham (PR)		28 Jul
10 2/5	George Kirk (Exeter)	21.12.56	1	Exmouth		17 Sep
10 2/5	Paul Springmann (OU)	11.12.56	1	Oxford		13 Nov
10 2/5	Edmund Baddeley (CU)	9.04.57	1	Cambridge		17 Nov
10 2/5	Charles Scott-Chad (CU)	23.03.57	1	Cambridge		21 Nov
10 2/5	Sir Savile Crossley (OU)	14.06.57	1	Oxford		6 Dec

Foreign competitor:

10 1/5	Louis Junker (LAC/RUS)	20.11.54	1	London (SB)	6 Oct

School Sports

10 1/5	Charles Milvain (Cheltenham Coll)	28.07.58	1	Cheltenham	26 Mar
10 ¼	Stewart Bruce (King William's Coll/IRL)	17.11.58	1	Castletown, IOM	8 May

Said to be unreliable

10 2/5	Henry Dunn (Wellington Coll)	58	1	Wellington	15 Mar

Doubtful

10.0	McCord		1ht1hc	Belfast, IRL	9 Jun
10 1/5	McCord		1hc	Belfast, IRL	9 Jun

Strong wind in favour in heat. Slight wind in final.

10.4 e	Philip Cronhelm (ICAC/IRL)	c56	2ht2hc	Belfast, IRL	9 Jun

Notes

Elborough 1ft down on 10.25 (28/04); Crossley 1ft 6in down on 10.25 (30/06); McCord 1ft & Barter 1ft 6in down on 10.2 (19/05); Pollitt 'quite a yd' down on Edwards (16/07); Cronhelm 1y down on 10 1/5.
Trepplin was credited with 10 1/5 by *The Field* in the OU sports on 10 May, but *Bell's* made it 10¾ and wrote an editorial piece about the difference between local clockers and the 'crucial test of a London timekeeper'. The race was started by word of mouth. In the OvC match *The Field* credited Trepplin with 10 1/5 and most results lists follow this, but *Bell's* had it as 10½. There seems to have been wind assistance and the start was again by word of mouth.

220 Yards

22.8 e	William Barter (Dublin U/IRL)	c55	2hc	Dublin (CP), IRL		16 Jun
22.9 e	Horace Crossley (Leyton FC)	2.10.55	2hc	London (SB)		7 Jul
23 1/5	Charles Lockton (LAC)	2.07.56	1	London (SB)		27 Oct
23.4 e	John Shearman (LAC)	6.08.55	2ht1hc	London (SB)		8 May
23 2/5	Herbert Sturt (LAC)	24.07.56	1	London (SB) EngvIrl		26 May
23 2/5	William Piers (RMC Sandhurst)	14.04.59	1ht3	Camberley		5 Oct
23.6 e	William Phillips (LAC)	5.08.58	2	London (SB) EngvIrl		26 May
23 3/5	Piers		1	Camberley		6 Oct

23.6 e	Sturt		2	London (SB)	27 Oct
23.7 e	Lestock Reid (RMC Sandhurst)	22.07.57	2ht3	Camberley	5 Oct
	(10/8)				
23.8 e	William McCord (QC Belfast/IRL)	c56	3	London (SB) Engvlrl	26 May
23.8 e	John Alkin (Stoke Victoria AC)	10.07.55	3ht1hc	Northampton	6 Aug
23.8 e	Robert Garrett (RMC Sandhurst)	25.11.55	2	Camberley	6 Oct
24.0	John Reay (LAC)	9.07.53	1	London (SB)	2 Jun
24.0 e	Saumarez Grosvenor (RMC Sandhurst)	5.12.57	3ht3	Camberley	5 Oct
24.0 e	Alfred Puttick (LAC)	51	3	London (SB)	27 Oct

Notes
Barter 1y down on 22.6 (16/06); Crossley 1ft down on 22.8 (7/07); Shearman 1½y down on 23.2 (8/05);
Phillips 1½y and McCord 3¼y down on 23.4 (26/05); Reid 2y & Grosvenor 5y down on 23.4 (5/10);
Garrett 1½y down on 23.6 (6/10); Alkin 3y 6in down on 23.4 (6/08); Sturt 3½y & Puttick 7y down on 23.2 (27/10).
There must be some doubt about the Sandhurst performances.

440 Yards

50.4	John Shearman (LAC)	6.08.55	1	London (LB)	6 Jun
50.7 e	Herbert Sturt (LAC)	24.07.56	2	London (LB)	6 Jun
51.2	William Churchill (CU)	9.04.55	1	Cambridge	16 Mar
51.2	Shearman		1	London (LB)	5 May
51.3 e	Churchill		3hc	Cambridge	15 Feb
51.4	Frederick Elborough (LAC)	30.07.52	1	London (LB) AAC	26 Mar
51.4	Shearman		1	London (SB) Engvlrl	26 May
51.4	Horace Crossley (Leyton FC)	2.10.55	1hc	Sheffield (BL)	6 Aug
51.8	Frederick Warren (Northampton)	c57	1=hc	Olney	6 Aug
52.0 e	Richard Leach (CU)	56	2	Cambridge	16 Mar
52.0 e	Churchill		2	London (LB) AAC	26 Mar
52.0	William McCord (QC Belfast/IRL)	c56	1	Dublin (LR) IRL ICAC	19 May
	(12/8)				
52.2 e	John Belcher (QC Cork/IRL)	28.06.55	2=	Dublin (LR) IRL ICAC	19 May
52.2 e	James Pinion (Windsor FC/IRL)	c53	2=	Dublin (LR) IRL ICAC	19 May
52.25	Robert Belcher (Irish CS/IRL)	3.10.53	1	Dublin (LR)	26 May
52.4	George Hoffmeister (CU)	10.10.58	1	Cambridge	10 Nov
52.5 e	Henry Hill (LAC)	22.01.52	3	London (LB) AAC	26 Mar
52.6	William Bruce (OU)	15.01.58	1	Oxford	9 Mar
52.8 e	James Hough (Widnes AC)	14.05.56	2hc	Widnes	16 Jun
52.8 e	Robert Allen (OU)	11.05.57	2	Oxford	9 Mar
52.9 e	Henry Whately (OU)	6.04.55	3	Oxford	9 Mar

Estimates: Sturt 2y down on 50.4 (06/06); Churchill 4y down on 50.8 (15/02); Leach 6y down on 51.2 (16/03);
Churchill 5y & Hill 9y down on 51.4 (26/03); Pinion & Belcher 1y down on 52.0 (19/05); Hough 6y down on 52.0
(16/06); Allen 1y & Whately 2y down on 52.6 (09/03).

880 Yards

2:00.0	Frederick Elborough (LAC)	30.07.52	1	London (LB) AAC	26 Mar
2:00.2	Charles Hazen Wood (Chester)	c56	1	Southport	18 Aug
2:00.2	Hazen Wood		1	London (SB)	6 Oct
2:00.2 e p	Robert Hindle (Paisley)	46	2	Boston, USA	13 Oct
2:00.5 e	Arthur Pelham (AAC)	28.12.50	2	London (LB) AAC	26 Mar
2:00.8	Walter Cunliffe (CU)	4.12.55	1	Cambridge	17 Mar
2:00.8 e	James Gibb (SLH)	11.12.53	2	Southport	18 Aug
2:00.9 e	Richard Andrews (Warrington)	c58	3	Southport	18 Aug
2:01.0 e p	Hindle		4hc	Glasgow (Spr)	17 Feb
2:01.2 e	Hazen Wood		2hc	Shrewsbury	15 Aug
2:01.6	Henry Hill (LAC)	22.01.52	1	London (SB) Engvlrl	26 May
2:02.0	Cunliffe		1hc	Cambridge	13 Feb
2:02.0	Hazen Wood		int	Birmingham (PR)	28 Jul
2:02.0	Henry Whately (OU)	6.04.55	1	Oxford	21 Nov
	(14/9)				
2:02.2 e	James Pinion (Windsor FC/IRL)	c53	2	London (SB) Engvlrl	26 May
2:02.5	Henry Tylecote (OU)	24.07.53	1	Oxford	10 Mar
2:03.2 e	Ernest Escott (OU)	20.08.57	2	Oxford	21 Nov
2:03.3 e	John Ferguson (NICC/IRL)	52	2	Belfast, IRL	9 Jun
2:03.5 e	William Edwards (Birmingham AC)	24.05.53	3hc	Birmingham (ALG)	3 Sep
2:03.9 e	Francis Humphrey (OU)	10.03.54	3	Oxford	21 Nov

2:04.8	Edgar Dickerson (RA)	7.04.54	1	Aldershot	25 Jul
2:05.0	Harold Davison (Andover)	c53	1	Torquay	21 May
2:05.0	Walter Dickson (Birkenhead)	54	1hc	St Helens	21 Jul
2:05.0	T. Wild (Redditch)		1	Halifax	28 Jul
2:05.2 e	Arnold Hills (OU)	12.03.57	2	Oxford	9 Feb

Doubtful
| 1:59.4 | John Sadler (LAC) | 14.04.55 | 1hc | Windsor | 15 Sep |

Bell's Life says course was about 20y short
| 2:00.0 | James Eden (Darlington) | 52 | 1 | Durham | 6 Oct |

Bell's Life says 'obviously incorrect'

Notes
Bell's Life gave Elborough's AAC time as 1:59.8, but most other sources preferred 2:00.0.
Pelham 3y down on 2:00.0 (26/03); Gibb 4 y and Andrews 4½y down on 2:00.2 (18/08); Hindle 1y down on 2:00.0 by J. Manning (USA) (13/10); and 3y 6in down on 2:00.5 (17/02); Hazen Wood 30y down on 1:57.0 (15/08); Pinion 4y down on 2:01.6 (26/05); Edwards 16y down on 2:01.2 (03/09); Escott 8y & Humphrey 13y down on 2:02.0 (21/11); Ferguson 6y down on 2:02.4 (9/06); Hills 5½y down on 2:04.4 (09/02).
Intermediate times in races at 1000y.

Mile

4:28.5	p	William Cummings (Paisley)	10.06.58	1	Glasgow (Spr)		9 Jun
4:28.75	p	James McLeavy (Alexandria)	26.10.52	1	Glasgow (Spr)		17 Nov
4:29.1 e p		James Wood (Tranent)	c53	2	Glasgow (Spr)		17 Nov
4:29.2		Walter Slade (LAC)	6.04.54	wo	London (LB)	AAC	26 Mar
4:29.3 e p		Henry Hescott (Mile End)	6.11.51	2	Glasgow (Spr)		9 Jun
4:29.4 e p		Robert Hindle (Paisley)	46	3	Glasgow (Spr)		9 Jun
4:30.0	p	Wood		1	Glasgow (Shaw)		29 Sep
4:30.0 e p		Alexander Clark (Glasgow)	c53	3	Glasgow (Spr)		17 Nov
4:30.25	p	Wood		1	Glasgow (Spr)		31 Mar
4:31.0 e p		McLeavy		2	Glasgow (Shaw)		29 Sep
4:31.1 e p		McLeavy		2	Glasgow (Spr)		31 Mar
4:33.0		Walter Cunliffe (CU)	4.12.55	1	London (LB)	OvC	23 Mar
4:33.5 e		Henry Tylecote (OU)	24.07.53	2	London (LB)	OvC	23 Mar
4:34.0		Lees Knowles (CU)	16.02.57	1	Cambridge		15 Mar
4:34.0		James Gibb (SLH)	11.12.53	1hc	Olney		6 Aug
		(15/11)					
4:35.25		W. Butler (St Helens CC)		1	St Helens		6 Aug
4:35.6 e		John Plant (CU)	5.08.55	2	Cambridge		15 Mar
4:36.4		Edward Nicolls (OU)	27.02.54	1	Oxford		8 Mar
4:39.0		John Smith (Bury)	13.04.55	1	Sheffield (BL)		16 Jul
4:41.0		Harry Mudd (Stoke-by-Nayland)	06.54	1	Mistley, Suffolk		20 Jun
4:41.1 e		Charles O'Malley (LAC/IRL)	53	2	London (SB)	EngvIrl	26 May
4:41.2 e		Arnold Hills (OU)	12.03.57	3	Oxford		8 Mar
4:41.7 e		George Thirlwell (Rotherham)	c57	2hc	Sheffield (BL)		6 Aug
4:41.8		George Philips (Glasgow Alexandra AC)		1	Glasgow (Ac)		5 May
4:41.8		Walter Walters (St George's Hosp)	c59	1	London (LB)		4 Jul

Notes
In *Powderhall & Pedestrianism*, Wood is reported as running 4:27.0 at Glasgow on 29 Dec, 10y ahead of McLeavy. However, *Bell's Life* reported it as 4:49.0 with Clark ¾y down and McLeavy a further 10y down, remarking that those who expected to see champion form were sadly disappointed.
Wood 2y & Clark 8y down on 4:28.75 (17/11); Hescott 5y & Hindle 5½y down on 4:28.5 (9/06); McLeavy 6y down on 4:30.0 (29/09) and 5y down on 4:30.25 (31/03);Tylecote 3y down on 4:33.0 (23/03); Plant 10y down on 4:34.0 (15/03); Hills 30y down on 4:36.4 (8/03); O'Malley 23y down on 4:37.4 (26/05); Thirlwell 3y down on 4:41.2.

2 Miles

9:48.0		James Gibb (SLH)	11.12.53	int	Cambridge	3 Mar
9:52.0		Gibb		int	London (SB)	30 Apr
9:52.0		Gibb		1	Belfast, IRL	5 May
10:05.0		Gibb		inthc	London (SB)	3 Nov
10:07.0		Thomas Duckett (Liverpool)	5.12.52	1	Blackburn	30 Jun
10:07.0	p	James McLeavy (Alexandria)	26.10.52	1	Glasgow (Shaw)	3 Nov
10:08.5 e		Duckett		2hc	Blackburn	11 Aug
10:10.0		Gibb		int	London (SB)	17 Nov
10:11.5		Charles Rooke (Spartan H)	19.05.53	1hc	Beckenham	23 Jun

10:11.6		John Bateman (Birmingham AC)	18.02.55	3hc	Birmingham (PR)	28 Jul
10:15.0		Gibb		int	London (LB)　AAC	26 Mar
10:15.6		Duckett		2hc	Stoke-on-Trent	7 Jul
		(12/5)				
10:16.0		William Stevenson (OU)	22.12.53	int	London (LB)　OvC	23 Mar
10:19.0		William Collier (CU)	56	1hc	Cambridge	26 Nov
10:21.5	e p	James Tester (Billingsgate)	2.05.49	int	London (LB)	5 Feb
10:22.0	p	W. Salter (West Brompton)		int	London (LB)	5 Feb
10:33.0		Laurence Nunns (ICAC/IRL)	03.55	int	Dublin (LR) IRL ICAC	19 May
10:33.0		Harold Lee-Evans (CU)	12.05.57	3hc	Cambridge	26 Nov
10:37.0		Edward Nicolls (OU)	27.02.54	int	Oxford	17 Nov
10:39.0		Leonard Strange (Civil Service)	06.57	1	London (SB)	2 Jun

Notes

McLeavy's time on 3 Nov is variously reported as 9:45.0, 9:52.0 and 10:07. We have followed the *Glasgow Herald*. Duckett 20y down on 10:05 (11/08); Tester leading, but about to be overtaken by Salter timed at 10:22 (05/02). At Beckenham, in a timed handicap, Rooke, the scratch man, was mistakenly sent off 12 secs early, recording 9:59.5, amended to 10:11.5. However, *The Field* made it 10:48.2.
Intermediate times in races at 3 miles (5/02; 3/03; 23/03; 17/11, Oxford), 4 miles (26/03; 30/04;19/05) 5 miles (3/11) and 10 miles (17/11 London [SB]).

3 Miles

14:46.0		James Gibb (SLH)	11.12.53	2hc	Cambridge	3 Mar
15:14.0		Gibb		int	London (SB)	30 Apr
15:16.0	p	Charles Price (Kennington)	17.05.53	inthc	London (Star)	16 Jun
15:24.0		Frank Bullock-Webster (OU)	21.12.54	1	Oxford	10 Mar
15:24.8	e	William Stevenson (OU)	22.12.53	2	Oxford	10 Mar
15:30.0	p	W. Salter (West Brompton)		1	London (LB)	5 Feb
15:35.0		Gibb		int	London (SB)	17 Nov
15:36.0		Gibb		inthc	London (SB)	3 Nov
15:37.1	e p	James Tester (Billingsgate)	2.05.49	2	London (LB)	5 Feb
15:38.0		Stevenson		1	London (LB)　OvC	23 Mar
15:48.0		Gibb		int	London (SB) Engvlrl	26 May
15:53.0		Charles Rooke (Spartan H)	19.05.53	1hc	Edmonton	7 Jul
15:57.5		Lees Knowles (CU)	16.02.57	1	Cambridge	17 Mar
15:58.0	p	George Hazael (Deptford)	22.11.44	inthc	Glasgow (Shaw)	1 Dec
15:59.4	e	William Collier (CU)	56	2	Cambridge	17 Mar

Note: Stevenson 4y down on 15:24.0; Collier 10y down on 15:57.5; Tester 40y down on 15:30 (05/02).
Intermediate times in races at 4 miles (30/04; 26/05; 16/06), 5 miles (3/11) and 10 miles (17/11; 1/12).

4 Miles

20:01.0	p	George Hazael (Deptford)	22.11.44	1	Glasgow (VC)	3 Feb
20:38.0		James Gibb (SLH)	11.12.53	1	London (SB)	30 Apr
20:58.0	p	William Smith (Paisley)	27.12.46	1	Glasgow (Shaw)	2 Jun
21:00.0		Thomas Duckett (Liverpool)	5.12.52	1	Heywood	9 Aug
21:00.5	p	P. Simpson (Edinburgh)		2	Glasgow (Shaw)	2 Jun
21:02.5		Gibb		int	London (SB)	17 Nov
21:02.75	p	James Bailey (Sittingbourne)	2.05.52	1hc	Glasgow (Shaw)	1 Sep
21:03.0		Gibb		1	London (SB) Engvlrl	26 May
21:13.0	e p	Charles Price (Kennington)	17.05.53	2hc	Glasgow (Shaw)	1 Sep
21:13.0		Gibb		inthc	London (SB)	3 Nov
21:33.4		Laurence Nunns (ICAC/IRL)	03.55	1	Dublin (LR) IRL ICAC	19 May
21:42.0		Percy Stenning (LAC)	31.08.54	2hc	London (SB)	8 Dec
21:45.4		Arthur Smith (LAC)	21.03.52	2	London (SB) Engvlrl	26 May

Intermediate times in races at 5 miles (3/11) and 10 miles (17/11).

6 Miles

32:07.0		James Gibb (SLH)	11.12.53	int	London (SB)	17 Nov
32:16.5	p	James McLeavy (Alexandria)	26.10.52	1	Glasgow (Shaw)	6 Oct
32:25.0	p	George Hazael (Deptford)	22.11.44	inthc	Glasgow (Shaw)	1 Dec
32:42.0	p	J. Simpson (Cambridge)		int	London (LB)	26 Dec
32:53.9	e p	Hazael		2	Glasgow (Shaw)	6 Oct
34:28.0	p	Hazael		int	London (LB)	10 Dec
34:47.0		William Fuller (LAC)	7.06.51	nt	London (LB)	27 Apr

34:47.0	Charles Larrette (SLH)	23.02.44	int	London (LB)	27 Apr

Note: Hazael 200y down on 32:16.5 (6/10).
Intermediate times in races at 10 miles (27/04, 17/11, 1/12, 26/12) and 20 miles (10/12).

10 Miles

54:32.0	p	George Hazael (Deptford)	22.11.44	1hc	Glasgow (Shaw)	1 Dec
54:49.0		James Gibb (SLH)	11.12.53	1	London (SB)	17 Nov
56:10.0	p	James McLeavy (Alexandria)	26.10.52	1	Glasgow (Shaw)	30 Jun
56:11.2	e p	William Smith (Paisley)	27.12.46	2	Glasgow (Shaw)	30 Jun
57:10.0		Percy Stenning (LAC)	31.08.54	2	London (SB)	17 Nov
57:24.0	p	J. Simpson (Cambridge)		1	London (LB)	26 Dec
57:39.0	p	Hazael		int	London (LB)	10 Dec
58:43.0		Walter Tyler (LAC)	15.11.57	3	London (SB)	17 Nov
58:45.0	p	Arthur Flaunty (Woolwich)	54	2	London (LB)	26 Dec
59:05.0		William Fuller (LAC)	7.06.51	4	London (SB)	17 Nov
59:16.0	p	Charles Price (Kennington)	17.05.53	3	London (LB)	26 Dec
59:39.0		Fuller		1=	London (LB)	27 Apr
59:39.0		Charles Larrette (SLH)	23.02.44	1=	London (LB)	27 Apr

Note: *Powderhall & Pedestrianism* gives 52:05.5 for Hazael on 1/12. Smith 6y down on 56:10.0 (30/06).
Intermediate time in a 20 mile match.

120 Yards Hurdles

16 1/5	Herbert Bevington (Clapham Rovers FC)	15.12.52	1	Rochester		20 Jun
16 1/5	John Graveley (Guy's Hosp)	4.04.53	1	London (LB)		4 Jul
16.3 e	James Lane (St Mary's H)	24.07.57	2	London (LB)		4 Jul
16.5 e	Frederick Warde (Rochester FC)	18.03.52	2	Rochester		20 Jun
16 4/5	Charles Lockton (LAC)	2.07.56	1	London (SB)	EngvIrl	26 May
16.9 e	Henry Macdougall (LAC)	c52	2	London (SB)	EngvIrl	26 May
17.0	Sydney Jackson (OU)	2.10.56	1	London (LB)	OvC	23 Mar
17.0	John Twining (Appleby)	56	1	Walthamstow		28 Apr
17.0	Charles Bayly (ex-OU/IRL)	26.02.52	1	Sydney, AUS		6 Oct
17.0	Spencer Colvile (Royal Agric Coll)	13.11.56	1	Cirencester		11 Oct
17.2 e	Lewis Jarvis (CU)	3.08.57	2	London (LB)	OvC	23 Mar
17 1/5	John Reay (LAC)	9.07.53	1ht1	London (LB)	AAC	26 Mar
17 1/5	Reay		1	London (LB)	AAC	26 Mar
17 1/5	Lane		1ht2	London (LB)		4 Jul
17 1/5	Henry Allan (Highbury CC)	c56	1	Eastbourne		22 Aug
		(16/14)				
17 ¼	John Wylie (LAC)	54	1	Worthing		20 Sep
17.4 e	Edward Salmon (CU)	29.10.54	2ht1	London (LB)	AAC	26 Mar
17 2/5	Patrick Davin (Suir/IRL)	4.06.57	1	Limerick, IRL		21 Jun
17 2/5	Sam Widdowson (Nottm Forest FC)	16.04.51	1	Ilkley		11 Aug
17 2/5	James Hynes (Clare/IRL)	c53	1	Ennis. IRL		18 Sep
17.5 e	Charles Kemp (OU)	26.04.56	3	London (LB)	OvC	23 Mar
17.5 e	Charles Gilbert (LAC)	9.01.55	3ht1	London (LB)	AAC	26 Mar

Doubtful

15 ½	Ernest Wood (Woodbridge)	25.01.57	1	Bury St Edmunds	24 May

Said by the *Bury and Norwich Post* to be "not only unprecedented, but impossible. We really must refer our correspondents to the rev gentleman who acted as timekeeper. It is his time, not ours, and is doubtless too good to be true."

Notes

Bell's Life gave Reay 16 3/5 for the AAC final on 26/03, with Jackson 3y back, but others made it 17 1/5.
Lane 1ft down on 16.2 (04/07); Warde 2y down on 16.2 (20/06); Macdougall inches down on 16.8 (26/05);
Jarvis 1y and Kemp 3y down on 17.0 (23/03); Salmon 1y and Gilbert 1½y down on 17.2 (26/03).

220 Yards Hurdles

30.5	Thomas Ham (SLH)	c55	1	Clifton	11 Aug
32.0 e	John Banwell (Weston-super-Mare)	3.07.55	2	Clifton	11 Aug
32.1 e	Edward Strachan (Cheltenham)	16.08.58	3	Clifton	11 Aug
34.2	Horace Crossley (Leyton FC)	2.10.55	1	Stoke on Trent	8 Aug
34.4 e	Sam Widdowson (Nottm Forest FC)	16.04.51	2	Stoke on Trent	8 Aug
34.6 e	John Alkin (Nuneaton CC)	10.07.55	3	Stoke on Trent	8 Aug
34.8	Edward Carpenter (Kempston CC)	c52	1ht1hc	Olney	6 Aug

12 flights					
34.0	George Kirk (Exeter)	21.12.56	1	Exmouth	17 Sep

Notes: Banwell 10y & Strachan 10y and "inches" down on 30.5; Widdowson 1y & Alkin 2½y down on 34.2.

440 Yards Hurdles

1:02.0	Alfred Stevens (Douglas, IOM)		1	Douglas, IOM	21 May
1:05.2	Horace Crossley (Leyton FC)	2.10.55	1	Shrewsbury	16 Aug
1:07.5 e	Charles Bryan (Liverpool)	c47	2hc	Middleton	22 Sep
1:07.75	George Bradley (Wigan CC)		1hc	Crewe	23 Jun
1:08.0	Robert Vassall (RMA Woolwich)	4.04.58	1	Woolwich	20 Jun
1:08.4 e	Sydney Weall (LAC)	54	2	Shrewsbury	16 Aug
1:08.6 e	John Harvey (RMA Woolwich)	28.10.59	2	Woolwich	20 Jun
1:08.8 e	Wellesley Paget (RMA Woolwich)	2.03.58	3	Woolwich	20 Jun
1:13.0	Alexander Thompson (Dublin U/IRL)		1	Dublin (CP), IRL	15 Jun
3'6 hurdles					
1:08.25	Robert Summerhayes (Somerset)	14.04.53	1	Montreal, CAN	6 Oct
12 flights					
1:06.3 e	George Dobell (Northwich)	14.11.54	2hc	Blackburn	11 Aug
Doubtful (School sports/number of flights unknown)					
1:00.0	Alfred Evans (Clifton Coll)	14.06.58	1	Clifton	22 Mar
1:01.7 e	Carleton Haynes (Clifton Coll)	7.02.58	2	Clifton	22 Mar
1:02.2 e	John King (Clifton Coll)	10.07.58	3	Clifton	22 Mar

Notes: Bryan 1y down on 1:07.25; Dobell 5y down on 1:05.5; Weall 20y down on 1:05.2; Harvey 4y and Paget 5y down on 1:08.0; Haynes 12y and King 15y down on 1:00.0.
Summerhayes emigrated in 1869 and became a Canadian national.

High Jump

5'10	1.778	Patrick Davin (Suir RC/IRL)	4.06.57	1	Dublin (LR), IRL	21 Jul
5'9	1.753	Thomas Tomlinson (Gosforth CC)	c55	1	Ilkley	11 Aug
5'9	1.753	William Kelly (QC Cork/IRL)		1	Cork. IRL	15 May
5'8½	1.740	Charles Gaskin (Wisbech CC)	56	2	Ilkley	11 Aug
5'8	1.727	George Kenny (Dublin U/IRL)	7.06.55	1	Dublin (CP), IRL	15 Jun
5'8	1.727	Gerard Blathwayt (CU)	27.06.55	1	Market Harborough	9 Jul
5'8	1.727	Tomlinson		1	Hinckley	1 Sep
5'8	1.727	Arthur Shaw (Manchester FC)		1=	Glasgow (HP)	8 Sep
5'8	1.727	Andrew Watson (Parkgrove FC)	24.05.56	1=	Glasgow (HP)	8 Sep
5'8	1.727	Tomlinson		1	Lincoln	22 Sep
5'8	1.727	John Hobson (OU)	6.07.58	1	Oxford	29 Nov
5'7½	1.715	Kelly		1	Cork, IRL	8 May
5'7½	1.715	Horace Strachan (LAC)	21.09.55	1	London (SB) Engvlrl	26 May
5'7½	1.715	Davin		1	Limerick, IRL	21 Jun
5'7½	1.715	John Dee (Dungarvan/IRL)		1	Mullinahone, IRL	24 Jul
		(15/11)				
5'7¼	1.708	John Hargreaves (Manchester)		1	Compstall	9 Jun
5'7	1.702	Charles Lockton (LAC)	2.07.56	1	London (SB)	2 Jun
5'7	1.702	Robert Thomas (Liverpool Gym)	22.11.56	1	Widnes	16 Jun
5'7	1.702	Samuel Ratcliffe (Ashby FC)	53	1	Leamington	21 Jul
5'7	1.702	William Hayter (OU)	30.08.58	1	Oxford	14 Nov
Indoors (possibly springboard)						
5'11	1.803 i	G. Burgess (Chester)		1=	Chester Gym	1 Mar
5'11	1.803 i	William Milner (Everton)	c55	1=	Chester Gym	1 Mar
5'10	1.778 i	Hargreaves		1	Manchester	25 Oct
At the Athenaeum, Manchester.						
5'5	1.651 i	Peter Hyman (German Gym Soc/GER)	c53	2	London (St Pancras)	5 Dec

Achieved in a jump-off for 2nd place. The winner, F.G.Nott Bower, did 5'4.

Doubtful						
5'11	1.803	Lt. Carden (Military)		1	Maryborough, IRL	Jul
5'10	1.778	George Kirk (Exeter)	21.12.56	1	Cleve	6 Aug
5'9	1.753	J. Davis		2	Cleve	6 Aug

Note: Some sources give Kelly 5'11 at Ennis on 18/09. The *Irish Sportsman & Farmer* has 5'7.

High Jump: Highland & Border

5'10	1.778	p	Thomas McDougall (Galashiels)	c53	1=	Galashiels	21 Jul
5'10	1.778	p	Adam Scott (Swinton)	15.08.52	1=	Galashiels	21 Jul
5'10	1.778	p	E. Andrews (Edinburgh)		1=	Kelso	28 Jul
5'10	1.778	p	Daniel Lamont (Kilbarchan)	c55	1=	Kelso	28 Jul
5'9½	1.765	p	Peter Cameron (Banchory)	8.12.52	1	Forfar	10 Aug
5'9	1.753	p	Scott		3	Kelso	28 Jul
5'8	1.727	p	E. Andrews		1=	Stenhousemuir	21 Jul
5'8	1.727	p	Lamont		1=	Stenhousemuir	21 Jul
5'8	1.727	p	Cameron		1	Bridge of Allan	4 Aug
5'7½	1.715	p	Hugh Andrews (Glasgow)	c52	1	Glasgow (Spr)	26 May
5'7	1.702	p	Lamont		2=	Glasgow (Spr)	26 May
5'7	1.702	p	William McLiver (Stewarton)	c57	2=	Glasgow (Spr)	26 May
5'7	1.702	p	Cameron		1	Aberdeen (CC)	21 Jul
5'7	1.702	p	George Davidson (Aberdeen)	19.11.54	1	Nairn	11 Aug
5'7	1.702	p	Davidson		1	Glasgow (VC)	29 Sep

Pole Vault

11'0¾	3.37	Henry Kayll (Sunderland FC)	16.07.55	1	Ilkley		11 Aug
11'0	3.35	Charles Gaskin (Wisbech CC)	56	2	Ilkley		11 Aug
10'10	3.30	Robert Sabin (Culworth AC)	52	1	Olney		6 Aug
10'9	3.28	Kayll		1	London (LB)	AAC	26 Mar
10'9	3.28	Sabin		wo	Reading		29 Aug
10'8	3.25	Horace Strachan (LAC)	21.09.55	2	Olney		6 Aug
10'7	3.23	Gaskin		1	Newark		21 May
10'6	3.20	Strachan		2	London (LB)	AAC	26 Mar
10'6	3.20	Sabin		1	Rothwell		29 May
10'6	3.20	Gaskin		1	Kings Lynn		6 Jul
10'6	3.20	Gaskin		1	Wisbech		6 Jul
10'6	3.20	Strachan		1	Northampton		6 Aug
10'5	3.17	Kayll		wo	Darlington		26 May
10'4	3.15	Ernest Edwards (Birmingham AC)	21.03.59	1	Much Wenlock		22 May
10'4	3.15	W. Miller (Bacup)		1	Manchester		30 Jul
10'4	3.15	Gaskin		1	Hinckley		1 Sep
			(16/6)				
10'2	3.10	Frederic Robinson (Beccles)	14.09.56	2	Kings Lynn		6 Jul
10'2	3.10	John Culhane (Vipers FC/IRL)	c53	2	Erith		14 Jul
10'1	3.07	Thomas Bellamy (Sheffield)	15.02.54	1	Huddersfield		16 Jun
10'0	3.05	John Crockford (Crusaders FC)	57	2	Much Wenlock		22 May
10'0	3.05	John Dean (Northwich)	c54	2	Compstall		9 Jun

Notable youth performance

9'9	2.97	Tom Ray (Ulverston)	5.02.62	1=	Milnthorpe	21 May

Notes
The Field gave Sabin 10'10 at Reading
(29/08). George Barker competed at a
number of amateur meetings as well as
professional, all listed below. One report
gave Bellamy 10'11 at Huddersfield, but
The Field gave 10'1 and this seems
more likely.

**Right: rudimentary technique in
the high jump, from *Athletics and
Football* by Montague Shearman.**

Pole Vault: Highland, Lakeland, Border and Professional

10'7½	3.24	p	George Barker (Bacup)	c55	1	Manchester	30 Jul
10'6	3.20	p	David Milne (Forfar)	28.12.42	1	Dundee	21 Jul
10'5	3.17	p	Barker		1	Clayton-le-Moors	22 Sep
10'4	3.15	p	Peter Cameron (Banchory)	8.12.52	1	Bridge of Allan	4 Aug
10'3	3.12	p	Barker		1	Hanley	22 May
10'3	3.12	p	Barker		1	Compstall	9 Jun
10'3	3.12	p	Barker		1	Burnley	30 Jun
10'3	3.12	p	Barker		1	Blackburn	11 Aug
10'2½	3.11	p	Barker		1	Cobridge	21 May
10'2	3.10	p	Thomas Milne (Dundee)	c52	2	Dundee	21 Jul
10'2	3.10	p	Barker		1	Rotherham	23 Jul
10'1	3.07	p	William Barron (Keswick)	c56	2	Bridge of Allan	4 Aug
10'1	3.07	p	Cameron		1=	Forfar	10 Aug
10'1	3.07	p	D. Milne		1=	Forfar	10 Aug
			(14/5)				
10'0	3.05	p	James Rush (Barrhead)	c52	1	Glasgow (VC)	23 Jun
10'0	3.05	p	David Anderson (Alnwick)	c46	1=	Jedburgh	27 Jul
10'0	3.05	p	J. Austin (Addiewell)		1=	Jedburgh	27 Jul
10'0	3.05	p	L. Baxter (Carlisle)		3	Bridge of Allan	4 Aug
10'0	3.05	p	John Thwaites (Keswick)	c57	1=	Keswick	20 Aug
10'0	3.05	p	Joseph Hewitson (Keswick)	c55	1=	Grasmere	23 Aug
10'0	3.05	p	William Borland (Kilbarchan)	c48	1	Milngavie	25 Aug

Long Jump

22'10	6.96	Gerard Fowler (Birmingham AC)	57	1	Birmingham (PR)	28 Jul
22'10	6.96	John Alkin (Nuneaton CC)	10.07.55	2	Birmingham (PR)	28 Jul
22'1	6.73	Laurence Gjers (W. Kent FC)	58	1	Chislehurst	2 Jun
22'0	6.71	Alkin		ex	Husbands Bosworth	1 Aug
21'9	6.63	Alkin		1	Stoke-on-Trent	7 Aug
21'7½	6.59	Patrick Davin (Suir RC/IRL)	4.06.57	1	Dublin (LR), IRL	21 Jul
21'7	6.58	William Kelly (QC Cork/IRL)		1	Cork, IRL	29 May
21'6	6.55	Davin		1	Limerick, IRL	21 Jun
21'5	6.53	Alkin		1	Northampton	6 Jul
21'5	6.53	Pte Hill (Coldstream Guards)		1	Warley	13 Oct
21'4	6.50	Alkin		1	Husbands Bosworth	1 Aug
21'3	6.48	Frank Richardson (St Bart's Hosp)	c58	2	Chislehurst	2 Jun
21'3	6.48	Alkin		1	Market Harborough	9 Jul
21'2¾	6.47	Robert Longe (36th Regt, Devonport)	c57	ex	Torquay	21 May
21'1¾	6.45	Charles Kemp (OU)	26.04.56	1	Oxford	15 Mar
		(15/9)				
21'1	6.43	Thomas Stretch (Ormskirk)	28.01.51	1	Bebington	2 Jun
21'1	6.43	George Kenny (Dublin U/IRL)	7.06.55	1	Dublin (CP), IRL	16 Jun
21'0	6.40	James Kough (Torquay/IRL)	30.03.51	ex	Torquay	21 May
21'0	6.40	Edmund Baddeley (CU)	9.04.57	1	Cambridge	17 Nov
20'11	6.38	C. Neilson (Oakham CC)		2	Husbands Bosworth	1 Aug
20'8½	6.31	William Garforth (ex-Uppingham Sch)	08.56	1	Storrington	16 Mar
20'8½	6.31	Stewart Bruce (King William's Coll/IRL)	17.11.58	1	Belfast, IRL	4 May
20'8½	6.31	Charles Lockton (LAC)	2.07.56	2	London (SB) Engvlrl	26 May
20'8	6.30	Algernon Haskett-Smith (OU)	4.07.56	1	Oxford	10 Mar
20'8	6.30	J. Ryan (Borris/IRL)		1	Carlow, IRL	11 Jul
20'7	6.27	Thomas Parrington (Wavertree)	c55	1	Bebington	26 May
20'7	6.27	A. Baldwin (Carlow/IRL)		2	Carlow, IRL	11 Jul
20'6	6.25	Frederick Fellowes (Burton on Trent)	12.02.58	3	Husbands Bosworth	1 Aug
20'6	6.25	Patrick Nally (Balla/IRL)	56	1	Claremorris, IRL	23 Aug
20'5¼	6.23	John Graveley (Worthing)	4.04.53	1	Woodbridge	2 Apr
20'5	6.22	Graham Sowerby (Louth)	57	1	Spalding	6 Aug

School Sports

21'8	6.60	Stewart Bruce (King William's Coll/IRL)	17.11.58	1	Castletown, IOM	8 May

Notes

At Birmingham, Fowler won the jump-off for first, doing 22'6/6.86 to Alkin's 22'0/6.71.

The Field reported Lockton's wo jump at the Civil Service Sports (02/06) as 22'3½/6.79.

J.H.Burke (53rd Regt/IRL) was misreported as jumping 22'2/6.76 in the Irish Championships this year but his winning jump was 20'0¼/6.10.

Long Jump: Highland & Border

21'6	6.55	p	Archibald Mitchell (Alva)		51	1	Bridge of Allan	4 Aug
21'5	6.53	p	Peter Cameron (Banchory)		8.12.52	2	Bridge of Allan	4 Aug
20'9	6.32	p	David Johnstone (Alva)		1.05.57	1	Alloa	8 Aug
20'9	6.32	p	Cameron			1	Alva	9 Aug
20'8	6.30	p	Johnstone			2	Alva	9 Aug
20'6	6.25	p	John Hutchison (Glasgow)			1	Parkhill	14 Jul
20'4+	6.20	p	Robert Knox (Jedburgh)		17.09.47	2	Alloa	8 Aug
20'4	6.20	p	Mitchell			3	Alloa	8 Aug

Note
Bridge of Allan event was a running distance leap over a 3'0 hurdle.
At Alloa, Knox was 2nd, but his jump was omitted in the several reports checked.

Triple Jump

44'6	13.56	p	John Hargreaves (Caledonian Assoc)			1	Manchester (WR)	30 Jul
44'4	13.51		Patrick Nally (Balla/IRL)	56		1	Castlebar, IRL	21 Sep
43'5	13.23		Nally			1	Claremorris, IRL	23 Aug
43'0	13.11		Cpl Rooney (16th Regt/IRL)			1	Curragh, IRL	1 Aug
42'0	12.80	p	Alexander Inglis (Caledonian Assoc)		c53	2	Manchester (WR)	30 Jul
41'7	12.67		Henry Dick (St Andrews U)		5.08.53	1	St Andrews	17 Mar
41'6½	12.66		J.M.Parnell (Knockraha/IRL)			1	Glounthaune, IRL	18 Aug
41'2	12.55		William Kelly (QC Cork/IRL)			1	Cork, IRL	24 Apr
41'1	12.52		Henry Johnston (Edinburgh U)		13.09.56	1	Kirkwall	8 Sep
41'0	12.50		M. Quinn (IRL)			1	Hollymount, IRL	5 Jul
41'0	12.50		M. Mullowney (Claremorris/IRL)			2	Claremorris, IRL	23 Aug
40'10½	12.46		Orlando Coote (OU)		14.03.55	1	Dublin (LR), IRL	21 Jul
			(12/11)					
40'8½	12.41		J. Ryan (Kingsbridge FC/IRL)			2	Dublin (LR), IRL	21 Jul
40'6	12.34		T. Bourke (QC Cork/IRL)			1	Kanturk, IRL	9 Sep
40'1	12.22		James Crombie (St Andrews U)		18.09.55	2	St Andrews	17 Mar

Triple Jump: Highland & Border

48'8	14.83	p	Thomas Aitken (Walkerburn)		23.05.53	1	Jedburgh	27 Jul
47'10	14.58	p	Robert Knox (Jedburgh)		17.09.47	2	Jedburgh	27 Jul
47'6	14.48	p	David Johnstone (Alva)		1.05.57	1	Alva	9 Aug
47'1½	14.36	p	Knox			2	Alva	9 Aug
47'0	14.33	p	Aitken			1	Galashiels	21 Jul
46'11	14.30	p	Archibald Mitchell (Alva)		51	1	Bridge of Allan	4 Aug
46'6	14.17	p	Daniel Lamont (Kilbarchan)		c55	1	Milngavie	25 Aug
46'3	14.10	p	Knox			2	Galashiels	21 Jul
46'3	14.10	p	E. Andrews (Edinburgh)			2	Bridge of Allan	4 Aug
46'2	14.07	p	James Fox (Stirling)			3	Bridge of Allan	4 Aug
45'9	13.94	p	Knox			1	Alloa	8 Aug
45'6	13.87	p	Knox			1	Hawick	8 Jun
45'6	13.87	p	William McLiver (Stewarton)		c57	1	Kilbirnie	28 Jul
45'6	13.87	p	Johnstone			2	Alloa	8 Aug
			(14/8)					
45'2	13.77	p	James Rush (Barrhead)		c52	2	Milngavie	25 Aug
45'0	13.72	p	John Lucas (Forfar)			1	Dundee	21 Jul
44'11	13.69	p	G. Fox (Alloa)			3	Alva	9 Aug
44'10	13.67	p	William Young (Alva)		c53	2	Clackmannan	26 Jun
44'6	13.56	p	Adam Scott (Swinton)		15.08.52	3	Kelso	28 Jul
44'3	13.49	p	C. Ferguson (Jedburgh)			3	Milngavie	25 Aug
43'10	13.36	p	William Borland (Kilbarchan)		c48	2	Kilbirnie	28 Jul
43'8	13.31	p	R. Trainer (Glasgow)			3	Glasgow (Spr)	26 May
43'7	13.28	p	Adam Marshall (Dundee)		c52	2	Dundee	21 Jul
43'6	13.26	p	John Low (Forfar)		19.01.57	2	Falkirk	11 Aug
43'5	13.23	p	W. Fox (Alva)			3	Falkirk	11 Aug
43'2	13.16	p	Frank Harrison (Morpeth)			1	Embleton	28 May
43'1	13.13	p	James Wilson (Aberdeen)			1	Campfield	30 Jun
43'1	13.13	p	A. McMillan (Alva)			2	Milnathort	23 Jul

Note
The *Border Advertiser* has Aitken's Jedburgh jump on 27/07 as 48'0; the *Southern Reporter* gives 48'8.

Shot

41'9	12.73		Thomas Stone (Newton-le-Willows)	24.01.52	1	London (SB) EngvIrl	26 May
41'6	12.65		Maurice Davin (Suir RC/IRL)	29.06.42	2	London (SB) EngvIrl	26 May
41'3	12.57		Stone		2hc	Widnes	16 Jun
40'9	12.42		Davin		1	Dublin (LR), IRL	21 Jul
40'4	12.29		Stone		1	St Helens	6 Aug
40'3½	12.28		Albert Cotterill (Ashton-in-Makerfield)	c52	2	St Helens	6 Aug
40'2	12.24		Patrick Hickey (QC Cork/IRL)	18.12.54	1	Cork, IRL	24 Apr
39'9	12.12		Alexander Inglis (Manchester)	c53	1hc	Widnes	16 Jun
38'9	11.81		Inglis		1	Rotherham	23 Jul
38'5	11.71		Davin		1	Dublin (LR) IRL ICAC	19 May
38'5	11.71		Richard Glover (Rainhill)	c53	1	Walton, Lancs	25 Aug
38'4	11.68		Wyndham Evanson (Civil Service)	51	1hc	London (LB)	2 Jun
38'4	11.68		Wilfred Hirst (Rotherham)	56	2	Rotherham	23 Jul
38'3	11.66		John Tobin (Ninemilehouse/IRL)		1	Kilkenny, IRL	29 Aug
			(14/9)				
37'11	11.56		William Kelly (QC Cork/IRL)		2	Cork, IRL	24 Apr
37'7	11.46		John Albright (Sch of Engineering)	15.04.57	1	London (CP)	16 Mar
37'7	11.46		William Peterkin (LAC)	2.01.58	1	Catford Bridge	28 Jul
37'0	11.28		Pte Murphy (16th Regt/IRL)		1	Curragh, IRL	1 Aug
36'7	11.15		Pte Lanigan (16th Regt/IRL)		2	Curragh, IRL	1 Aug
36'6	11.13		Pte Fraser (95th Horse/IRL)		1	Curragh, IRL	9 Aug
36'5	11.10		Walter Tyndale (Sch of Engineering)	26.07.53	1	London (CP)	16 Mar
36'5	11.10		M. Tobin (Drangan/IRL)		1	Drangan, IRL	27 Sep
36'4	11.07		Claude Corfield (ex-Trent Coll/IRL)	30.01.57	1	Nottingham	12 Apr
36'3	11.05		George Kenny (Dublin U/IRL)	7.06.55	1	Dublin (CP), IRL	16 Jun
36'3	11.05		Patrick Davin (Suir RC/IRL)	4.06.57	2	Dublin (LR), IRL	21 Jul
36'3	11.05		E. Purchase (Bridgnorth FC)		1	Shrewsbury	15 Aug
36'2½	11.04		R. Wilson (Glasgow U)		1	Edinburgh (ACG)	24 Mar
36'2	11.02		William Winthrop (LAC)	15.06.52	2	London (LB) AAC	26 Mar

Extra trial

39'10	12.14		Hickey		ex	Dublin (LR) IRL ICAC	19 May

Shot: Highland & Border
Includes 16lb stone

47'6	14.48	p	Donald Dinnie (Aboyne)	8.06.37	1	Glasgow (VC)	29 Sep
46'6	14.17	p	William McDuff (Dunkeld)	c51	1	Glasgow (Spr)	26 May
46'6	14.17	p	Dinnie		ex	Manchester (WR)	30 Jul
45'9	13.94	p	George Davidson (Drumoak)	19.11.54	1	Manchester (WR)	30 Jul
45'4	13.82	p	Dinnie		1hc	Glasgow (VC)	23 Jun
45'4	13.82	p	Davidson		2	Glasgow (VC)	29 Sep
45'0	13.72	p	Kenneth McRae (Wishaw)	50	2	Glasgow (Spr)	26 May
44'8	13.61	p	John George (Cromar)	46	3	Glasgow (Spr)	26 May
44'6	13.56	p	J. Smith (Edinburgh)		1	Stenhousemuir	21 Jul
43'0	13.11	p	Dinnie		1	Dumfries	26 Jul
43'0	13.11	p	James Fleming (Ballinluig)	18.09.40	2	Manchester (WR)	30 Jul
42'0*	12.80	p	Dinnie		1	Vale of Leven	1 Sep
41'8	12.70	p	Duncan Ross (Glasgow/CAN)	16.03.55	1	Elizabeth, NJ, USA	23 Aug
41'4	12.60	p	McRae		3	Manchester (WR)	30 Jul
41'0	12.50	p	McRae		3	Glasgow (VC)	29 Sep
			(15/8)				
40'10	12.45	p	George Mearns (Aberdeen)		1	Aboyne	11 Sep
40'3	12.27	p	Peter McCowan (Comrie)		1	Comrie (open)	31 Aug
39'8	12.09	p	John Hutchison (Glasgow)		1	Parkhill	14 Jul
39'5*	12.01	p	George Bowie (Tulchan)	1.09.56	1	Castle Grant (light)	21 Aug
39'4*	11.99	p	Robert McGregor (Perthshire RV)		1	Perth	3 Nov
38'7*	11.76	p	John Smith (Speybridge)		2	Castle Grant (light)	21 Aug
38'5½	11.72	p	William Bremner (Leochel-Cushnie)	3.01.47	3	Aboyne	12 Sep
37'11*	11.56	p	Hugh McLaughlan (Perth)		2	Perth	3 Nov
37'10	11.53	p	William Monro (Aberdeen)		2	Aberdeen (CC)	21 Jul
37'10	11.53	p	James Ferguson (Glenartney)		3	Comrie (open)	31 Aug
37'9	11.51	p	William Rust (Drumoak)	1.01.55	3	Aberdeen (CC)	21 Jul
37'9	11.51	p	George Topp (Glasgow)		2	Parkhill	14 Jul
37'7*	11.46	p	A. Taylor (Perth)		3	Perth	3 Nov
37'4½	11.39	p	John Dewar (Glenalmond)		2	Comrie (local)	31 Aug

37'4	11.38	p	William Innes (Edinburgh)		4	Aboyne	12 Sep
36'8*	11.18	p	James Wilson (Aberdeen)		2	Lumphanan (light)	21 Jul
36'7	11.15	p	William Jamieson		1	Huntly	25 Aug

Note: * correct weight assumed from evidence of other years.

Weight unstated

44'2	13.46	p	Dinnie		1	Fochabers	26 Sep
43'8	13.31	p	Dinnie		1	Saline	7 Aug
42'3	12.88	p	Davidson		1	Nairn	11 Aug
42'2	12.85	p	Rust		1	Culter (local)	28 Jul
41'6	12.65	p	Rust		1	Culter (open)	28 Jul
41'6	12.65	p	McRae		1	Milngavie (light)	25 Aug
41'3	12.57	p	John Hutcheon (Dyce)		2	Culter (open)	28 Jul
41'3	12.57	p	Davidson		2	Fochabers	26 Sep
41'0	12.50	p	George Reid (Newhills)		2	Culter (local)	28 Jul
40'10	12.45	p	Owen Duffy (Edinburgh/IRL)	c47	1	Bridge of Allan (heavy)	4 Aug
40'10	12.45	p	William Stewart (Tomintoul)		2	Nairn	11 Aug
40'7	12.37	p	James Thomson (Aberdeen)		3	Culter (open)	28 Jul
40'5	12.32	p	Simon Wilson		1	Rothesay (light)	4 Aug
40'0	12.19	p	Archibald Macfie		2	Rothesay (light)	4 Aug
39'0	11.89	p	John Carmichael (Drymen)	20.02.49	2	Milngavie (light)	25 Aug
38'11	11.86	p	George Stewart (79th Regt)		3	Nairn	11 Aug
38'0	11.58	p	A. Robertson (Skene)		3	Culter (local)	28 Jul
37'8	11.48	p	Peter Adam (Perth)		1	Newburgh	11 Jun
37'5	11.40	p	Andrew Scobbie		2	Newburgh	11 Jun
36'9	11.20	p	George Anderson (Edinburgh)		3	Bridge of Allan (heavy)	4 Aug

18lb

43'4	13.21	p	John Brown (Edinburgh)		1	Burnfoot	28 Jul
40'6	12.34	p	John Anderson (Edinburgh)		2	Burnfoot	28 Jul
36'3	11.05	p	William Ferguson (Alloa)		1	Alloa	8 Aug

22lb by performer

45'6	13.87	p	Dinnie		1	Milnathort	23 Jul
42'1	12.83	p	J. Fleming		2	Milnathort	23 Jul
40'10*	12.45	p	Duffy		1	Alva (heavy)	9 Aug
40'3	12.27	p	McRae		3	Milnathort	23 Jul
39'4	11.99	p	Davidson		1	Alloa	8 Aug
39'2	11.94	p	Duffy		2	Alloa	8 Aug

Note: *correct weight assumed from evidence of other years.

Doubtful

51'7	15.72	p	Dinnie		1	Campfield	30 Jun
50'4	15.34	p	Smith		2	Campfield	30 Jun
49'2	14.99	p	Duffy		1	Bridge of Allan (light)	4 Aug
47'9	14.55	p	Dinnie		1	Greenock (light)	18 Aug
47'0	14.33	p	Davidson		1	Inverness (light)	20 Sep
46'7	14.20	p	G. Sanderson		3	Campfield	30 Jun
45'4	13.82	p	Davidson		2	Greenock (light)	18 Sep
43'7	13.28	p	Davidson		2	Bridge of Allan (light)	4 Aug
43'4	13.21	p	John Cameron (Leith)		2	Inverness (light)	20 Sep
42'3	12.88	p	J. Anderson		3	Bridge of Allan (light)	4 Aug
40'9	12.42	p	Cameron		4	Bridge of Allan (light)	4 Aug
39'10	12.14	p	H. McLeod		3	Greenock (light)	18 Aug
39'3	11.96	p	Alexander Ritchie (Greenock)		1	Greenock (local)	18 Aug

Hammer
All Styles

138'0	42.06		George Hales (CU)	20.05.54	1	London (LB) OvC	23 Mar
134'0	40.84		Hales		1	Cambridge	17 Mar
125'4	38.20		Maurice Davin (Suir RC/IRL)	29.06.42	1	London (SB) EngvIrl	26 May
123'0	37.49		Davin		1	Dublin (LR) IRL ICAC	19 May
113'0	34.44		Patrick Hickey (QC Cork/IRL)	18.12.54	2	Dublin (LR) IRL ICAC	19 May
111'4	33.93		Edmund Baddeley (CU)	9.04.57	1	Cambridge	16 Nov
110'0	33.53		Hugh Holme (OU)	4.11.53	1	Oxford	8 Mar
110'0	33.53		Hales		wo	London (LB) AAC	26 Mar

107'9	32.84	John Tobin (Ninemilehouse/IRL)			1	Drangan, IRL	27 Sep
106'4	32.41	Hickey			1	Cork, IRL	15 May
105'10	32.26	Alexander Inglis (Manchester)		c53	1	Sheffield (BL)	6 Aug
103'7	31.57	Baddeley			2	London (LB) OvC	23 Mar
103'7	31.57	M. Tobin (Drangan/IRL)			2	Drangan, IRL	27 Sep
		(13/8)					
102'4	31.19	Lindsay Bury (CU)	8.07.57		1	Cambridge	20 Nov
102'2	31.14	A.G.Williams (Lichfield FC)			1	Lichfield	21 Apr
101'11	31.06	Duncan Ross (Glasgow/CAN)	16.03.55		1	Elizabeth, NJ, USA	23 Aug
101'0	30.78	Walter Pattison (Gypsies FC)	27.08.54		2	London (SB) Engvlrl	26 May
99'3	30.25	J. O'Donoghue (Inniscarra/IRL)			1	Inniscarra, IRL	9 Sep
99'0	30.18	Pte Fraser (93rd Regt)			1	Dublin, IRL	12 May
99'0	30.18	Cpl Martin (Cupar)			1	Kilconquhar	4 Sep
98'9	30.10	C. Holland (Kanturk/IRL)			1	Kanturk, IRL	10 Sep
98'2	29.92	Benedict Jones (CU)	29.04.55		2hc	Cambridge	16 Nov
98'0	29.87	W. Delaney (Mullinahone/IRL)			3	Drangan, IRL	27 Sep
97'6	29.72	Patrick Nally (Balla/IRL)		56	1	Claremorris, IRL	23 Aug
97'4½	29.68	Neil McDonald (Glasgow Alexandra AC)		c54	1	Glasgow (Alex)	12 May
96'6	29.41	J. Murphy (Claremorris/IRL)			2	Claremorris, IRL	23 Aug
94'6	28.80	Edmund Wilkinson (CU)	15.09.57		4	Cambridge	17 Mar

Exhibition

105'10	32.26	Inglis		ex	Sheffield (BL)	6 Aug

Notes

In the AAC Championship, throws were from a 7ft square using a 3ft 6in handle, but most other meetings allowed an unlimited run.

Davin's series in the England v Ireland Match: 125'4 - 118'5 – 119'0 –118'8 – 120'8

In practice at Cambridge on 21 Feb Hales achieved 141'7/43.15, smashing a fence and breaking the hammer handle.

Hammer: Highland & Border

123'6	37.64	p	Donald Dinnie (Aboyne)	8.06.37		1	Milnathort	23 Jul
122'3	37.26	p	Dinnie			1	Dumfries	26 Jul
120'10	36.83	p	Dinnie			1	Glasgow (VC)	23 Jun
120'3	36.65	p	Dinnie			1	Glasgow (VC)	29 Sep
116'2	35.41	p	Dinnie			1	Glasgow (Shaw)	7 Apr
115'7	35.23	p	Dinnie			ex	Manchester (WR)	30 Jul
112'4*	34.24	p	Dinnie			1	Cupar	8 Aug
112'3	34.21	p	George Davidson (Drumoak)	19.11.54		2	Dumfries	26 Jul
112'0	34.14	p	Dinnie			1	Campfield	30 Jun
111'10	34.09	p	Kenneth McRae (Wishaw)		50	2	Milnathort	23 Jul
111'4	33.93	p	John Hutchison (Glasgow)			1	Parkhill	14 Jul
110'8	33.73	p	McRae			1	Manchester (WR)	30 Jul
110'4	33.63	p	Davidson			2	Glasgow (VC)	29 Sep
110'1	33.55	p	McRae			3	Glasgow (VC)	29 Sep
109'10	33.48	p	Dinnie			1	Coupar Angus	19 Jul
109'0	33.22	p	John Ogg (Banff/NZL)	7.08.47		2	Dunedin, NZL	1 Jan
			(16/5)					
104'5	31.83	p	Francis Christie (Dunecht)			2	Parkhill	14 Jul
103'0	31.39	p	William Fleming (Dundee)	22.08.42		1	Edzell	28 Jul
102'0	31.09	p	Alexander Ross (Ardgay)			2	Inverness	20 Sep
101'8	30.99	p	James Fleming (Ballinluig)	18.09.40		3	Manchester (WR)	30 Jul
100'7*	30.66	p	John Mcgregor (Glasgow)			2	Birnam	30 Aug
99'11	30.45	p	William Rust (Drumoak)	1.01.55		1	Culter (open)	28 Jul
99'6	30.33	p	William Innes (Edinburgh)			3	Inverness	20 Sep
98'5	30.00	p	John George (Tarland)		46	2	Glasgow (Shaw)	7 Apr
98'2	29.92	p	James Ferguson (Glenartney)			1	Comrie (local)	31 Aug
97'8	29.77	p	James Thomson (Aberdeen)			2	Culter (open)	28 Jul
97'4*	29.67	p	Henry Michie (Strathardle)			1	Glenisla	24 Aug
96'10	29.51	p	William Balfour (Savoch)			2	Gight	3 Aug
96'9	29.49	p	William McDuff (Dunkeld)		c51	1	Comrie (open)	31 Aug
96'7	29.44	p	George Topp (Glasgow)			3	Parkhill	14 Jul
95'0	28.96	p	John Smith (Speybridge)			3	Campfield	30 Jun
95'0	28.96	p	William Bremner (Strathdon)	3.01.47		2	Aboyne (light)	12 Sep
93'10½	28.61	p	William McCombie Smith (Lumphanan)	7.09.47		3	Aboyne (light)	12 Sep

93'4	28.45 p	Alexander Robertson (Denmore)		3	Gight	3 Aug
93'0	28.35 p	George Cheyne (East Lodge)		4	Gight	3 Aug
92'10	28.30 p	William Leslie (Insch)		3	Culter (open)	28 Jul

Note: *correct weight assumed from evidence of other years.

18lb

| 109'0* | 33.22 p | Dinnie | | 1 | Fochabers (heavy) | 26 Sep |

Notes
*correct weight assumed from evidence of other years. Dinnie is given 138'8 by the *Aberdeen Journal*.
We have followed the *Daily Free Press*.

20lb

| 100'0 | 30.48 p | Dinnie | | 1 | Crieff | 25 Aug |
| 93'6 | 28.50 p | Davidson | | 2 | Crieff | 25 Aug |

22lb

| 94'0 | 28.65 p | Hutchison | | 1 | Parkhill | 14 Jul |

Weight unstated

133'0	40.54 p	Dinnie		1	Glasgow (Spr)	20 Oct
126'0	38.40 p	Davidson		2	Glasgow (Spr)	20 Oct
115'10	35.31 p	Dinnie		1	Saline (light)	7 Aug
114'1	34.77 p	George Bowie (Tulchan)	1.09.56	1	Castle Grant (light)	?? Aug
113'3	34.52 p	Robertson		1	Udny (local)	15 Aug
111'5	33.96 p	McRae		1	Nairn	11 Aug
111'4	33.93 p	George Yeats (Udny)		2	Udny (local)	15 Aug
109'0	33.22 p	George Grant (Tomintoul)		1	Murtie	16 Jun
108'0	32.92 p	Alexander Birnie (Bogfechel)		3	Udny (local)	15 Aug
106'7	32.49 p	William Maclennan (Grantown)		2	Castle Grant (light)	?? Aug
106'0	32.31 p	J. Clark		1	Mugiemoss (light)	16 Jun
106'0	32.31 p	James Elmslie (Rayne)	c59	2	Murtie	16 Jun
100'0	30.48 p	J. Grant (Glenlivet)		3	Nairn	11 Aug
99'8	30.38 p	W. Forbes		2	Mugiemoss (light)	16 Jun
99'7	30.35 p	Alexander Ritchie (Greenock)		1	Greenock (heavy)	18 Aug
98'0	29.87 p	John Elmslie (Rayne)	c53	3	Murtie	16 Jun
94'2	28.70 p	Peter Adam (Coupar Angus)		1	Newburgh	11 Jun
94'2	28.70 p	W. Mathieson		3	Mugiemoss (light)	16 Jun
93'5	28.47 p	Alexander Campbell (Aberfeldy)		1	Aberfeldy (light/local)	29 Aug
93'3	28.42 p	Charles Dewar (Dunfallandy)		1	Blair Castle (prize)	5 Sep

Other Events

120 Yards

| 12.0 | | James Hough (Widnes) | 14.05.56 | 1hc | Widnes | 16 Jun |

150 Yards

| 14¼ p | | Daniel Wight (Jedburgh) | c51 | 1=hc | Edinburgh | 3 Jan |

Foreign competitor

| 15.0 | | Louis Junker (LAC/RUS) | 20.11.54 | 1ht6hc | London (SB) | 6 Oct |

200 Yards

| 20 2/5 | | John Shearman (LAC) | 6.08.55 | 1ht1hc | London (LB) | 2 Jun |

"A slight wind behind him" (*Bell's Life*)

300 Yards

| 33.0 e | | Wyndham Evanson (Civil Service) | 51 | 2hc | London (LB) | 2 Jun |

3y down on 32.6

600 Yards

| 1:14.6 | | Frederick Elborough (LAC) | 30.07.52 | 1hc | London (SB) | 28 Apr |

1000 Yards

| 2:20.8 | | Charles Hazen Wood (Manchester AC) | c56 | 1 | Birmingham (PR) | 28 Jul |

Given as 2:19.4 in the *Sporting Gazette*

¾ Mile

| 3:14.6 | | Walter Slade (LAC) | 6.04.54 | int | London (LB) | AAC | 26 Mar |

In 1 mile race.

5 Miles

26:06.0	p	James McLeavy (Alexandria)	26.10.52	1	Glasgow (Shaw)	10 Mar
26:27.0		James Gibb (LAC)	11.12.53	int	London (SB)	17 Nov

20 Miles

1:57:27.0	p	George Hazael (Deptford)	22.11.44	1	London (LB)	10 Dec

1 Mile Walk

6:52.0	Harry Webster (Knotty Ash)	14.05.54	1	Stoke on Trent	7 Aug

2 Miles Walk

13:47.25	Harry Webster (Knotty Ash)	14.05.54	1	Heywood	4 Aug

7 Miles Walk

53:55.0	p	William Perkins (Old Kent Road)	16.09.52	int	London (LB)	28 May

In 15 mile match against time.

50 Miles Walk

8:29:36.5	Charles Ford (Dublin U/IRL)	54	1	Dublin (LR), IRL	13 Oct

100 Miles Walk

20:36:08.0	John Dixon (Mars FC)	3.09.50	1	London (LB)	21 Aug

Cricket Ball

116y 0ft 0in	106.08	H. Harris (York)	1	Malton	21 Jun
116y 0ft 0in	106.08	John Hargreaves (Manchester)	1	Hinckley	1 Sep

4 miles amateur match for a gold medal, 1877. James Gibb (left) and Walter Slade round the lone apple tree on the new ground at Stamford Bridge, formerly a market garden and orchard. The two set many records in the 1870s, but Gibb (South London Harriers) was the better stayer and won in 20 min 38.0 sec after Slade pulled up ten yards short of 2 miles. Gibb is said to have invented the game of table tennis.

1878 UK Year List

100 Yards

10.1 e	George Hoffmeister (CU)	10.10.58	1	Cambridge		28 Nov
10 1/5	Ernest Trepplin (OU)	56	1	London (LB)	OvC	12 Apr
10 1/5	William McCord (QC Belfast/IRL)	c56	1	Belfast, IRL		22 Apr
10 1/5	McCord		1hc	Belfast, IRL		4 May
10 1/5	James Stewart (ICAC/IRL)	10.02.51	1hc	Dublin (LR), IRL		11 May
10 1/5	Thomas Malone (Tradaree AC/IRL)	26.12.59	1hc	Ennis, IRL		19 Jun
10 1/5	Henry Kayll (Sunderland FC)	16.07.55	1sf1hc	Sunderland		22 Jun
10 1/5	J.R.Walker (Dewsbury AC)		1	Bingley		13 Jul
10 ¼	John Wylie (LAC)	54	1hc	Bournemouth		22 Apr
10 ¼	Richard Bond (King's Coll Hosp/IRL)	c56	1	London (LB)		29 Jun
10 ¼	Robert Summerhayes (Somerset)	14.04.53	1hc	Montreal, CAN		5 Oct
10.3 e	Stewart		3hc	Belfast, IRL		4 May
10.3 e	Wylie (LAC)		2hthc	Walsall		8 Jun
10.3 e	Harry Massey (St Thomas's H)	c57	2	London (LB)		29 Jun
		(14/11)				
10 2/5	George Dodd (CU)	14.06.57	1	Cambridge		30 Mar
10.4 e	Montague Shearman (OU)	7.04.57	2	London (LB)	OvC	12 Apr
10 2/5	F. Davis (Pershore CC)		1=	Oxford		22 Apr
10 2/5	William Packford (OU)	c58	1=	Oxford		22 Apr
10 2/5	Horace Crossley (LAC)	2.10.55	1	Widnes		22 Jun
10 2/5	George Fishbourne (Carlow/IRL)	3.10.55	1	Carlow, IRL		2 Jul
10 2/5	Edward Lucas (CU)	15.02.60	1	Cambridge		15 Nov
10 2/5	Melville Portal (OU)	9.12.56	1hc	Oxford		30 Nov
10.4 e	Sir Savile Crossley (OU)	14.06.57	2hc	Oxford		30 Nov

Foreign competitor

10.1 e	Louis Junker (LAC/RUS)	20.11.54	3hc	Belfast, IRL		15 Jun
10 1/5	Junker		1	London (LB)	AAC	15 Apr
10 1/5	Junker		1	Belfast, IRL		14 Jun
10 1/5	Junker		1hthc	Belfast, IRL		15 Jun
10 1/5	Junker		1	Dublin (CP), IRL		18 Jun
10 ¼	Junker		1	Woodbridge		20 Apr

School Sports

10 2/5	Charles Melvill (Highgate Sch)	21.10.59	1	Highgate		6 Apr
10 2/5	James Cotterell (Q. Mary Sch)	59	1hc	Walsall		21 Sep

Notes
Hoffmeister was penalised 3y and ran 10 2/5; Stewart 6 inches down on 10 1/5 (4/05); Wylie ½y down on 10¼ (8/06); Massey 1ft down on 10¼; Shearman 1½y down on 10 1/5 (12/04); Sir Savile Crossley penalised 1y and finished 1ft down on 10 2/5. Junker 2ft down on 10.0.
Athletic News reported "a cross wind blowing in favour of a good time" in Trepplin's 10 1/5 (12/04).

220 Yards

22.0	William Phillips (LAC)	5.08.58	1hc	London (SB)		25 May
22 2/5	Phillips		1hc	London (SB)		28 Sep
22.8 e	John Shearman (LAC)	6.08.55	2=hc	London (SB)		30 Mar
22.8 e	Montague Shearman (LAC)	7.04.57	2=hc	London (SB)		30 Mar
23.0 e	Horace Crossley (LAC)	2.10.55	3hc	Bradford		24 Aug
23.0	Thomas Malone (Tradaree AC/IRL)	26.12.59	1	Miltown Malbay, IRL		25 Sep
23.0	Phillips		1	London (SB)		26 Oct
23.1 e	Herbert Sturt (LAC)	24.07.56	2	London (SB)		26 Oct
23.2 e	Herbert Booth (Bedford/SA)	59	2hc	Wigston		24 Jun
23 1/5	Crossley		1ht2hc	Bradford		24 Aug
23.3 e	Sturt		2hc	London (SB)		27 Apr
23 1/5	Charles Lockton (LAC)	2.07.56	1	London (LB)		1 Jun
23 1/5	Sturt		1hc	London (SB)		29 Jun
		(13/8)				
23 2/5	Percy Livingston (RMC Sandhurst)	21.01.60	1ht2	Camberley		11 Oct
23.7 e	William Wickham (RMC Sandhurst)	22.01.60	2ht2	Camberley		11 Oct
23 4/5	William McCord (QC Belfast/IRL)	c56	1	Belfast, IRL		4 May
23 4/5	Amand Routh (University Coll Hosp)	10.11.53	1	London (SB)		30 May
23 4/5	Charles Groome (Railway Clearing HAC)	c58	1ht	London (LB)		7 Sep
23.8 e	Edward McSwiney (RMC Sandhurst)	25.02.58	3ht	Camberley		11 Oct
24.0	Robert Burke (QC Cork/IRL)		1	Cork, IRL		26 Jun

24.0	J. Smith (Romiley AC)		1	Romiley, Cheshire	10 Aug

Foreign competitor

23 3/5	Louis Junker (LAC/RUS)	20.11.54	1	Belfast, IRL	14 Jun

Notes
Bell's Life made Phillips' time on 25 May 22½, but *The Field* and official timekeeper made it 22.0, and the latter was the time ratified as the inaugural British Record.
Both Shearmans 1½y down on 22.6 (30/03); Crossley 4ft down on 22.8 (24/08); Booth 1y down on 23.0 (24/06); Sturt 3/4y down on 23.0 (26/10) and 4y down on 22.8 (27/04); Wickham 2y and McSwiney 3y down on 23.4 (11/10).
The Stamford Bridge marks were on the straight track.

440 Yards

50.4	William Churchill (CU)	9.04.55	1hc	Cambridge	19 Nov
50.8 e	Churchill		2hc	Cambridge	9 Nov
50.9 e	Churchill		4hc	Cambridge	9 Mar
51.4	John Shearman (LAC)	6.08.55	1hc	Oxford	19 Mar
51.6	Horace Crossley (LAC)	2.10.55	1	London (SB)	5 Oct
51.7 e	Crossley		2hc	Birmingham (ALG)	7 Sep
51.75	Crossley		1	Widnes	22 Jun
51.8	Churchill		1	London (LB) OvC	12 Apr
51.8	Crossley		1	Stoke-on-Trent	6 Aug
51.8	Churchill		1hthc	Cambridge	18 Nov
52.0	Lennard Stokes (Guy's Hosp)	12.02.56	1	London (LB)	29 Jun
52.0	William Bruce (OU)	15.01.58	1hc	Oxford	30 Nov
		(12/5)			
52.2	Montague Shearman (OU)	7.04.57	1	Oxford	18 Mar
52.2	William Packford (OU)	c58	1	Oxford	16 Nov
52.4 p	Robert Hindle (Paisley)	46	1	Liverpool	2 Nov
52.5 e	William Beverley (OU)	18.04.59	2	Oxford	16 Nov
52.6 e	Melville Portal (OU)	9.12.56	2	Oxford	18 Mar
52.6 e	James Hough (Widnes)	14.05.56	2	Stoke-on-Trent	6 Aug
52.7 e	Graeme Cox (OU)	26.09.58	3	Oxford	18 Mar
52.7 e p	George Walsh (Royton)	3.02.44	2	Liverpool	2 Nov
52.75	John Belcher (QC Cork/IRL)	28.06.55	1	Dublin (LR) IRL ICAC	10 Jun
52.8 e	Frederick Fellowes (Burton AC)	12.02.58	2hthc	Walsall	8 Jun
52.8	Herbert Sturt (LAC)	24.07.56	1	London (SB)	30 Nov

School Sports

51.0	George Harris (Uppingham Sch)	21.06.60	1	Uppingham	Mar
51.2	Harry Shearburn (Wellington Coll)	3.07.59	1	Crowthorne	6 Apr
51.7 e	William Wickham (Wellington Coll)	22.01.60	2	Crowthorne	6 Apr

Notes
Churchill 3½y down on 50.4 (09/03) and 5y down on 50.2 (09/11); Crossley 1y down on 51.5 (07/09); Hough 6y down on 51.8 (06/08); Portal 3y & Cox 4y down on 52.2 (18/03); Fellowes 15y down on 51.0 (8/06); Walsh 2y down on 52.4 (02/11); Beverley 2y down on 52.2 (16/11); Wickham 4y down on 51.2.

880 Yards

2:00.2	Charles Hazen Wood (LAC)	c56	1	Northampton	5 Aug
2:01.3 e	Richard Andrews (Warrington)	c58	2hc	St Helens	20 Jul
2:02.0	Henry Whately (OU)	6.04.55	1	Oxford	20 Mar
2:02.5	Andrews		1hc	Heywood	3 Aug
2:02.5	Andrews		1hc	Rochdale	21 Aug
2:02.9 e	Alfred Jones (OU)	57	2	Oxford	20 Mar
2:03.0	Hazen Wood		1	Widnes	22 Jun
2:03.0 e	Herbert Sturt (LAC)	24.07.56	2hc	London (SB)	29 Jun
2:03.0	Samuel Holman (Belsize FC)	29.01.53	1	Newport, Mon	5 Aug
2:03.0 p	David Livingstone (Tranent)	10.11.55	int	Glasgow (Spr)	5 Oct
2:03.2 e	Arnold Hills (OU)	12.03.57	3	Oxford	20 Mar
2:03.2 e p	William Cummings (Paisley)	10.06.58	int	Glasgow (Spr)	5 Oct
		(12/9)			
2:03.4	Lees Knowles (CU)	16.02.57	1=	London (LB) AAC	15 Apr
2:03.4	Henry Dwyer (ICAC/IRL)	c57	1	Dublin (LR), IRL	22 Jun
2:03.6 e	Walter George (Worcester FC)	9.09.58	2	Newport, Mon	5 Aug
2:04.0	William Bolton (CU)	3.07.58	1	Cambridge	30 Mar

2:04.0 e	John Sadler (LAC)	14.04.55	3	London (LB)	AAC	15 Apr
2:04.0	Thomas Sloggett	22.10.54	1	Cardiff		19 Jun
2:04.2 e	James Christian (ICAC/IRL)	3.12.58	2	Dublin (LR), IRL		22 Jun
2:04.25	James Eden (Darlington FC)	52	1hc	Leeds		15 Jun
2:04.4 e	Charles Ford (ICAC/IRL)	54	3	Dublin (LR), IRL		22 Jun
2:04.5	James Pinion (QC Belfast/IRL)	c53	1	Dublin (LR) IRL ICAC		10 Jun
2:04.8 e	John Smith (Bury AC)	13.04.55	3	Widnes		22 Jun
2:04.9 e	Charles Johnstone (CU)	16.06.57	2	Cambridge		30 Mar

Downhill finish

1:55.8	Sturt		1	Edmonton	2 May

Notes
Andrews 5y down on 2:00.6 (20/07); Jones 6y & Hills 8y down on 2:02.0 (20/03); Cummings 1y down on 2:03.0 (05/10); George 4y down on 2:03.0 (05/08); Sadler 4y down on 2:03.4 (15/04); Christian 5y & Ford 7y down on 2:03.4; Sturt 20y down on 2:00.2 (29/06);Johnstone 6y down on 2:04.0 (30/03); Smith 12y down on 2:03.0 (22/06).
All Intermediate times made in 1 mile races.

Mile

4:19.5 p	William Cummings (Paisley)	10.06.58	1	Glasgow (Spr)		5 Oct
4:25.0 p	David Livingstone (Tranent)	10.11.55	1	Glasgow (Shaw)		25 May
4:25.0 p	Cummings		1=	Glasgow (Spr)		28 Sep
4:25.0 p	Livingstone		1=	Glasgow (Spr)		28 Sep
4:25.1 e p	Cummings		2	Glasgow (Shaw)		25 May
4:28.0 p	Cummings		1	London (LB)		1 Jul
4:28.8	Arnold Hills (OU)	12.03.57	1	London (LB)	AAC	15 Apr
4:29.2 e	James Gibb (LAC)	11.12.53	2	London (LB)	AAC	15 Apr
4:29.5	Gibb		1	Widnes		22 Jun

(9/4)

4:30.3 e	John Smith (Bury AC)	13.04.55	2	Widnes		22 Jun
4:31.0	Percival Stockdale (Bourne FC)	c56	1	Bradford		24 Aug
4:31.0 p	Daniel Houldsworth (Middleton)	58	1	Manchester (WR)		23 Nov
4:31.2 e	William La Touche (Ulverston/IRL)	c54	2	Bradford		24 Aug
4:31.2 e p	William Duddle (Preston)	14.03.58	2	Manchester (WR)		23 Nov
4:31.4	Denison Clarke (OU)	21.10.54	1	London (LB)	OvC	12 Apr
4:31.4 e p	James McLeavy (Alexandria)	26.10.52	int	Glasgow (Shaw)		21 Dec
4:31.8 e	Henry Jenkins (OU)	13.02.56	3	London (LB)	OvC	12 Apr
4:35.0	George Philips (Rangers FC)		1	Glasgow (WSCG)		27 Apr
4:35.7 e	William Bolton (CU)	3.07.58	4	London (LB)	OvC	12 Apr
4:37.4 e	Samuel Holman (Belsize FC)	29.01.53	2hc	London (LB)		27 Jul
4:38.7 e	Harold Lee-Evans (CU)	12.05.57	3	London (LB)	AAC	15 Apr
4:39.0 e	Alfred Jones (OU)	57	4	Oxford		18 Mar
4:39.25	T.K.Dwyer (Thurles/IRL)	02.52	1	Dublin (LR) IRL ICAC		10 Jun
4:40.0	Arthur Parsons	61	1	Dulwich		18 May
4:40.9 e	Henry Oliver (LAC)	28.02.55	2hc	London (SB)		28 Sep
4:41.0	J. May (RNC Greenwich)		1	Greenwich		5 Apr
4:41.0	George Adey (Reading)	58	1	Pewsey		17 Sep
4:41.7 e	Henry Dwyer (ICAC/IRL)	c57	2	Dublin (LR) IRL ICAC		10 Jun
4:41.7 e	John Denning (Trinity Coll Dublin/IRL)	54	3	Dublin (LR) IRL ICAC		10 Jun
4:42.6 e	Lees Knowles (CU)	16.02.57	3	Cambridge		28 Mar
4:43.1 e	Charles Ford (ICAC/IRL)	54	4	Dublin (LR) IRL ICAC		10 Jun
4:43.4	Thomas Bailey (Birchfield H)		1hc	Coventry		21 Sep
4:44.5	Walter George (Worcester FC)	9.09.58	1	Chesterfield		10 Jun

Doubtful

4:18.5 p	Cummings		1hc	Glasgow (Spr)		21 Sep

Bell's Life made it 4:21.0 and said he was 20-30y on his way when the gun was fired.

Notes
Cummings ½y down on 4:25.0 (25/05); Gibb 2½y down & Evans 60y down on 4:28.8 (15/04); Duddle ¾y down on 4:31.0 (23/11); McLeavy 2y down on 4:31.0 (21/12); Smith 5y on 4:29.5 (22/06); Jenkins 2¼y & Bolton 27¼y down on 4:31.4 (12/04); La Touche 1y down on 4:31.0 (24/08); Holman 2y down on 4:37.0 (27/07); Jones 20½y down on 4:33.4 (18/03); Knowles 12y down on 4:40.6 (28/03); Oliver 8y down on 4:39.6 (28/09); Dwyer 15y, Denning 15y 6in, Ford 23y 6in down on 4:39.25 (10/06).
Intermediate time in 2 mile race (21/12).

2 Miles

9:20.5	p	William Cummings (Paisley)	10.06.58	1	Glasgow (Spr)		1 Jun
9:33.0	p	David Livingstone (Tranent)	10.11.55	1	Glasgow (Spr)		19 Oct
9:33.5	p	Cummings		2	Glasgow (Spr)		19 Oct
9:44.0	p	Cummings		1	Glasgow (Shaw)		21 Dec
9:50.0		James Gibb (LAC)	11.12.53	2hc	Belfast, IRL		3 May
9:50.4	e p	Cummings		3hc	Glasgow (Shaw)		9 Feb
9:50.8	e p	James McLeavy (Alexandria)	26.10.52	2	Glasgow (Shaw)		21 Dec
9:56.0	p	William Smith (Paisley)	27.12.46	int	London (LB)		17 Jun
10:00.0	p	James Bailey (Sittingbourne)	2.05.52	int	London (LB)		17 Jun
10:00.0	p	Charles Price (Kennington)	17.05.53	int	London (LB)		17 Jun
		(10/7)					
10:07.2		Harold Lee-Evans (CU)	12.05.57	1hc	Cambridge		25 Nov
10:08.0		William Houghton (Widnes)	c56	1	St Helens		10 Jun
10:25.0	p	George Hazael (Deptford)	22.11.44	int	London (LB)		17 Jun
10:25.8		T.K.Dwyer (Thurles/IRL)	02.52	1hc	Belfast, IRL		15 Jun
10:28.0		James Warburton (Haslingden)	13.11.45	int	Ilkley		10 Aug
10:29.0		William Collier (CU)	56	inthc	Cambridge		9 Mar
10:30.0	p	William Shrubsole (Croydon)	4.07.46	int	London (LB)		17 Jun
10:30.0		M.A.Sheehan (Tradaree AAC/IRL)		1hc	Tradaree, IRL		25 Jul
10:38.0		John Steele (Wellington Coll)	c59	1	Crowthorne		5 Apr
10:39.0		Ben Parkin (CU)	2.03.56	int	London (LB)	OvC	12 Apr

Notes
Cummings 32y down on 9:45.0 (09/02); McLeavy 40y down on 9:44.0 (21/12).
Intermediate times in races at 3 miles (9/03; 12/04), 6 miles (10/08) and 10 miles (17/06).

3 Miles

15:13.5	p	William Smith (Paisley)	27.12.46	int	London (LB)		17 Jun
15:21.0	p	Charles Price (Kennington)	17.05.53	int	London (LB)		17 Jun
15:24.0		James Gibb (LAC)	11.12.53	int	London (LB)	AAC	15 Apr
15:27.0	p	David Livingstone (Tranent)	10.11.55	int	Glasgow (Spr)		12 Oct
15:46.0		Henry Oliver (LAC)	28.02.55	1hc	Edmonton		20 Jul
15:48.0		James Warburton (Haslingden)	13.11.45	int	Heywood		5 Aug
15:50.0		Ernest Nunns (Civil Service/IRL)	17.04.59	1	Dublin (LR), IRL		22 Jun
15:50.4		Alfred Goodwin (OU)	57	1	London (LB)	OvC	12 Apr
15:54.1	e	Harold Lee-Evans (CU)	12.05.57	2	London (LB)	OvC	12 Apr
15:55.0		George Mawby (Spartan H)	17.07.57	2hc	Edmonton		20 Jul
15:55.5	e	Laurence Nunns (Civil Service/IRL)	03.55	2	Dublin (LR), IRL		22 Jun
15:58.1	e	John Wills (OU)	01.58	3	London (LB)	OvC	12 Apr

Doubtful
| 15:02.0 | p | Smith | | 1 | Comrie | | 23 Aug |

Notes
Lee-Evans 20y and Wills 'rather more' (say 20+22y) down on 15:50.4; L. Nunns 30y down on 15:50.0.
Intermediate times in races at 4 miles (15/04; 5/08), 6 miles (12/10) and 10 miles (17/06).

4 Miles

20:29.8		James Gibb (LAC)	11.12.53	1	London (LB)	AAC	15 Apr
20:35.4	e p	Charles Price (Kennington)	17.05.53	2hc	London (LB)		19 Jan
20:41.0	p	William Smith (Paisley)	27.12.46	int	Glasgow (Spr)		13 May
20:45.0	p	Smith		int	London (LB)		17 Jun
20:45.2	e p	Price		int	London (LB)		17 Jun
20:46.0		James Warburton (Haslingden)	13.11.45	1	Heywood		5 Aug
20:49.9	e p	James McLeavy (Alexandria)	26.10.52	int	Glasgow (Spr)		13 May
20:53.0	p	David Livingstone (Tranent)	10.11.55	int	Glasgow (Spr)		12 Oct
21:13.2	e	William Davies (Chester)	52	2	Heywood		5 Aug
21:34.0		Warburton		int	Ilkley		10 Aug
21:49.5		Laurence Nunns (ICAC/IRL)	03.55	1	Dublin (LR) IRL	ICAC	10 Jun
21:53.25		Ernest Nunns (ICAC/IRL)	17.04.59	2	Dublin (LR) IRL	ICAC	10 Jun

Notes
Price 50y down on 20:26.6 (19/01) & 1y down on 20:45.0 (17/06); McLeavy 50y down on 20:41.0 (13/05);
Davies 150y down on 20:46.0.
Intermediate times in races at 6 miles (13/05; 10/08;12/10) and 10 miles (17/06).

6 Miles

31:29.25	p	William Smith (Paisley)	27.12.46	1	Glasgow (Spr)		13 May
31:34.5	p	James McLeavy (Alexandria)	26.10.52	1	Glasgow (Spr)		8 Jun
31:35.6 e p		Smith		2	Glasgow (Spr)		8 Jun
31:38.0	p	Charles Price (Kennington)	17.05.53	int	London (LB)		17 Jun
31:38.2 e p		Smith		int	London (LB)		17 Jun
31:50.5	p	David Livingstone (Tranent)	10.11.55	1	Glasgow (Spr)		12 Oct
32:10.0	p	McLeavy		1	Glasgow (Shaw)		23 Nov
33:07.0		James Warburton (Haslingden)	13.11.45	1	Ilkley		10 Aug
33:35.0		James Gibb (LAC)	11.12.53	2	Ilkley		10 Aug
34:37.0		Walter Stevenson (LAC)		int	London (LB)		26 Oct

Notes
Smith 1y down on 31:38.0 (17/06) & 6y down on 31:34.5 (08/06).
Intermediate times in 10 mile races.

10 Miles

53:42.5	p	William Smith (Paisley)	27.12.46	1	London (LB)		17 Jun
53:53.0	p	James Bailey (Sittingbourne)	2.05.52	2	London (LB)		17 Jun
53:58.0	p	Charles Price (Kennington)	17.05.53	3	London (LB)		17 Jun
54:22.8 e		James Warburton (Haslingden)	13.11.45	wo	Blackburn		27 Apr
54:42.0	p	Smith		1	Glasgow (Spr)		2 Feb
54:57.0	p	James McLeavy (Alexandria)	26.10.52	1hc	Dundee		20 Jul
55:34.0		James Gibb (LAC)	11.12.53	1	London (SB)		30 Mar
57:11.0		John Bateman (LAC)	18.02.55	2	London (SB)		30 Mar
57:40.0	p	George Hazael (Deptford)	22.11.44	1	Rotherhithe		13 Apr
57:56.0		George Mawby (Spartan H)	17.07.57	1	London (LB)		2 Nov
58:55.0		Henry Oliver (Moseley H)	28.02.55	4hc	Birmingham (PR)		23 Feb
59:02.0		E.W.Parker (Spartan H)		2	London (LB)		2 Nov
59:16.0		Walter Stevenson (LAC)		1	London (SB)		26 Oct
59:22.0		Hugh Spong (Moseley H)	c56	1hc	Birmingham (PR)		23 Feb
59:28.0		Walter Tyler (Spartan H)	15.11.57	3	London (LB)		2 Nov
59:54.0		Thomas Prime (Moseley H)	c56	3hc	Birmingham (PR)		23 Feb
59:56.0 e		H.C.Howard (LAC)		2	London (SB)		26 Oct
59:58.0		M. Smith (Spartan H)		4	London (LB)		2 Nov

Note
Howard 200y down on 59:16.0.
Warburton ran against time in a match to cover 10¾ miles in the hour. He finished in 55:29.5 (or 55:06.0 or 55:20.5 in other accounts), but on remeasurement the distance covered was only 10 miles 360 yards.

120 Yards Hurdles

16.0		Samuel Palmer (CU)	15.12.54	1	London (LB)		15 Apr
16 1/5		James Lane (St Mary's H)	24.07.57	1	London (LB)		29 Jun
16 ¼		Francis Wood (Woodbridge FC)	28.09.55	1	Woodbridge		20 Apr
16 2/5		Palmer		1	Cambridge		30 Mar
16 2/5		Palmer		1	London (LB)	OvC	12 Apr
16 2/5		Sydney Jackson (OU)	2.10.56	1ht2	London (LB)	AAC	15 Apr
16.5 e		Jackson		2	London (LB)	OvC	12 Apr
16.5 e		Palmer		2ht2	London (LB)	AAC	15 Apr
16.5 e		Jackson		2=	London (LB)	AAC	15 Apr
16.5 e		Charles Lockton (LAC)	2.07.56	2=	London (LB)	AAC	15 Apr
16.5 e		William Pollock (St George's Hosp)	2.02.59	2	London (LB)		29 Jun
		(11/6)					
16.6 e		Lewis Jarvis (CU)	3.08.57	2	Cambridge		30 Mar
16.7 e		Henry Macdougall (LAC)	c52	2	Woodbridge		20 Apr
16.9 e		Charles Kemp (OU)	26.04.56	3	London (LB)	OvC	12 Apr
16.9 e		Alfred Loder (ex-CU)	25.03.55	2	Worthing		31 Aug
17.0		Samuel Bestow (Stoke Victoria AC)	c51	1	Leeds		15 Jun
17.0		William Crossland (S. Milford)	c58	1	Horsforth		22 Jun
17.0		Archibald Farmer (Private Banks)	c52	1hc	Catford Bridge		22 Jun
17.0		William Edgar (Dartford FC)	27.09.53	1	Rochester		3 Jul
17.0		Henry Allan (LAC)	c56	1	Windsor		7 Sep
17.0		Charles Gilbert (OU)	9.01.55	1	Langport		12 Sep
17.1 e		Arthur Barker (LAC)	c55	2ht1	London (LB)	AAC	15 Apr
17.1 e		Herbert Bevington (Clapham Rovers FC)	15.12.52	2hc	Catford Bridge		22 Jun

Notes
The official time for Palmer in the AAC Championship was 16 1/5, yet *Bell's Life* made it 'a fraction inside 16.0'
and it was later ratified by the AAA as an inaugural British record at 16.0.
Farmer's 17.0 was from a start 7y behind the line.
Jackson & Lockton 3y down on 16.0 (AAC final); Jackson 1ft, Kemp 3y 1ft down on 16.4 (12/04);
Pollock 2y down on 16.2 (29/06); Jarvis ¾y down on 16.4 (30/03); Palmer ½y down on 16.4 (AACht2);
Barker 2y down on 16.8 (AAC ht1); Macdougall 3y down on 16.25 (20/04); Loder 2y down on 16.6 (31/08);
Bevington 6in down on 17.0 (22/06).
Lockton recorded 16.0 at Uppingham on 16 Jul, but it was over 6 flights only.

220 Yards Hurdles

29.5		Wildon Thompson (Burton Pidsea CC)	56	1	Scarborough	15 Aug
30.4		G. Adams (Bladon)		1	Bicester	16 Sep
30.5 e		George Dodd (Wallingford)	14.06.57	2	Bicester	16 Sep
30.5		George Bradley (Wigan CC)		1	Southport	29 Jun
31.3 e		Thomas Shonksmith (York)	56	2	Scarborough	15 Aug
32.0		Charles Croker (ICAC/IRL)	3.11.56	1	Borris, IRL	26 Jun
32.0		John Banwell (Weston-super-Mare)		1	Wootton-under-Edge	4 Sep
32.3 e		A.W.Smith (London)		2	Wootton-under-Edge	4 Sep
33.0		Frederick Schofield (Wigan CC)	56	1	Newtown, Wales	20 Jul
33.2 e		Charles Danby (Brigg)	c59	3	Scarborough	15 Aug

Notes
The Scarborough and Borris races were over 12 flights.
Dodd ½y down on 30.4; Shonksmith 12y and Danby 24y down on 29.5: Smith 1½y down on 32.0.

440 Yards Hurdles

1:01.2		James Gorman (Lurgan AC/IRL)	31.10.50	1=hc	Lurgan, IRL	31 Aug
1:01.3 e		George Bradley (Wigan CC)		2hc	St Helens	20 Jul
1:01.4		Richard Cole (Lutterworth FC)	54	1hthc	Coventry	21 Sep
1:02.5		George Dobell (Stoke Victoria AC)	14.11.54	1hc	Crewe	29 Jun
1:04.6		Dobell		1	Ulverston	13 Sep
1:08.0		John Harvey (RMA Woolwich)	28.10.59	1	Woolwich	12 Jun
1:08.5 e		Charles Watkins (RMA Woolwich)	13.08.59	2	Woolwich	12 Jun
1:08.8 e		Henry Oldfield (RMA Woolwich)	14.07.58	3	Woolwich	12 Jun
1:10.6		Arthur Archer (Dublin U/IRL)	c56	1	Dublin (CP), IRL	17 Jun
1:10.75		Patrick Nally (Balla/IRL)	56	1	Ballaghadareen, IRL	3 Aug
1:12.3 e		Richard Power (Dublin U/IRL)	c55	2	Dublin (CP), IRL	17 Jun

Notes
Bradley 1½y down on 61.0 (20/07); Watkins 3y and Oldfield 5y down on 1:08.0 (12/06); Power 10y down
on 1:10.6 (17/06).

High Jump

5'11	1.803	Charles Power (Callan/IRL)	56	1	Carlow, IRL		2 Jul
5'11	1.803	Patrick Davin (Suir RC/IRL)	4.06.57	1	Kilkenny, IRL		19 Aug
5'11	1.803	Thomas Tomlinson (Gosforth CC)	c55	1	Windsor		7 Sep
5'10½	1.791	William Kelly (QC Cork/IRL)		1	Cork, IRL		29 May
5'10½	1.791	Davin		1	Limerick, IRL		3 Jul
5'10¼	1.784	Tomlinson		1	London (LB)	AAC	15 Apr
5'10	1.778	William Hall (Wootton-under-Edge)	57	1	Newport, Mon		5 Aug
5'9	1.753	Gerard Blathwayt (CU)	27.06.55	2	London (LB)	AAC	15 Apr
5'9	1.753	Robert Thomas (Liverpool Gym)	22.11.56	1	Chester		10 Jun
5'9	1.753	Wildon Thompson (Burton Pidsea CC)	56	1	Newark		10 Jun
5'9	1.753	Isaac Wright (Emberton)	20.02.50	1	Newport Pagnell		10 Jun
5'9	1.753	Power		1	New Ross, IRL		24 Jun
5'9	1.753	Blathwayt		1	Shrewsbury		11 Jul
		(13/9)					
5'8	1.727	Harold Wilson (Cheltenham Coll)	20.06.60	1	Cheltenham		12 Apr
5'8	1.727	Graham Sowerby (Louth AC)	57	2	Newark		10 Jun
5'8	1.727	Ernest Edwards (Birmingham AC)	21.03.59	1	Birmingham		29 Jun
5'8	1.727	John Dee (Dungarvan/IRL)		2	Kilkenny, IRL		19 Aug
5'8	1.727	Andrew Watson (Parkgrove FC)	24.05.56	1	Glasgow (HP)		7 Sep
5'7¾	1.721	John Hargreaves (Manchester)		1	Pendleton		27 Apr
5'7½	1.715	Francis Wood (Woodbridge FC)	28.09.55	1	Woodbridge		22 Apr
5'7½	1.715	Horace Strachan (LAC)	21.09.55	1	Erith		6 Jul

5'7½	1.715	Reginald Macaulay (CU)	24.08.58	1	Cambridge		4 Nov
5'7	1.702	Charles Rees-Mogg (OU)	27.11.57	2	London (LB)	OvC	12 Apr
5'7	1.702	R. Pack (Independent Coll)	c61	1	Taunton		30 Apr
5'7	1.702	G. Burgess (Routh)		2	Chester		10 Jun
5'7	1.702	Thomas Malone (Tradaree AC/IRL)	26.12.59	1	Ennis, IRL		19 Jun
5'7	1.702	J.M.Parker (Shrivenham)		2	Clifton		22 Jun
5'7	1.702	Harry Luke (Axbridge)	59	2hc	Langport		12 Sep

Exhibition jump

5'8	1.727	Macaulay		ex	Eton	15 Mar

Indoors

5'11	1.803 i	Thomas		1	Liverpool Gym	22 May
5'10	1.778 i	Thomas		1	Chester	19 Mar
5'8	1.727 i	Burgess		2	Chester	19 Mar

Notes

The AAC results sometimes list G. Tomlinson (Northumberland) as the winner, but this was certainly Thomas Tomlinson.
Wilson's 5'8 at Cheltenham College stood as a school record for over seventy years.

High Jump: Highland, Lakeland & Border

5'9	1.753	p	Hugh Andrews (Glasgow)	c52	1	Forfar	9 Aug
5'8½	1.740	p	Andrews		1	Thornhill	?? Jul
5'8	1.727	p	Andrews		1	Barrhead	29 Jun
5'8	1.727	p	Andrews		1	Cupar	7 Aug
5'8	1.727	p	Peter Cameron (Kincardine)	8.12.52	2	Forfar	9 Aug
5'8	1.727	p	Andrews		1	Birnam	29 Aug
5'7½	1.715	p	Andrews		1	Alva	15 Aug
5'7	1.702	p	Andrews		1	Stenhousemuir	22 Jul
5'7	1.702	p	Adam Scott (Swinton)	15.08.52	1	Swinton	21 Jun
5'7	1.702	p	James Hunter (Tillicoultry)		1=	Clackmannan	26 Jun
5'7	1.702	p	David Johnstone (Alva)	1.05.57	1=	Clackmannan	26 Jun
5'7	1.702	p	Daniel Lamont (Kilbarchan)	c55	3	Forfar	9 Aug
5'7	1.702	p	Andrews		1	Alloa	14 Aug
5'7	1.702	p	Thomas McDougall (Galashiels)	53	2=	Alva	15 Aug
5'7	1.702	p	E. Andrews (Edinburgh)		2=	Alva	15 Aug
5'7	1.702	p	Lamont		2=	Alva	15 Aug
5'7	1.702	p	George Davidson (Aberdeen)	19.11.54	2	Birnam	29 Aug
5'7	1.702	p	H. Andrews		1=	Alexandria	31 Aug
5'7	1.702	p	Lamont		1=	Alexandria	31 Aug
5'7	1.702	p	H. Andrews		1	Dalkeith	28 Sep

(20/9)

Pole Vault

10'10½	3.31	George Barker (Bacup)	c55	1=	Huddersfield	22 Jun
10'10½	3.31	Horace Strachan (LAC)	21.09.55	1=	Huddersfield	22 Jun
10'7	3.23	Ernest Edwards (Birmingham AC)	21.03.59	2hc	Birmingham (ALG)	6 Jul
10'7	3.23	Charles Gaskin (Wisbech)	56	1	Sheffield (BL)	21 Jul
10'6½	3.21	Barker		1	Nelson	24 Aug
10'6	3.20	Frederic Robinson (Beccles)	14.09.56	1	Woodbridge	22 Apr
10'6	3.20	Strachan		1	London (LB)	1 Jun
10'6	3.20	Barker		1	Leeds	15 Jun
10'6	3.20	Samuel Parrington (Cark in Cartmel)	c52	1	Wigan	15 Jun
10'6	3.20	Thomas Bellamy (Sheffield)	15.02.54	3	Huddersfield	22 Jun
10'6	3.20	Strachan		1	Erith	6 Jul
10'6	3.20	Strachan		1	Olney	5 Aug
10'6	3.20	Robinson		1	Beccles	9 Jul
10'6	3.20	Frederick Wrinch (Ipswich FC)	58	2	Beccles	9 Jul

(14/8)

10'5	3.17	Herbert Gaye (Ipswich FC)	56	2	Woodbridge	22 Apr
10'5	3.17	Robert Sabin (Culworth)	52	wo	Banbury	30 Jul
10'4½	3.16	George Callow (Peterborough CC)	c60	1	Long Buckly	5 Aug
10'3	3.12	Edward Strachan (LAC)	16.08.58	3hc	Market Harborough	15 Jul
10'2	3.10	Kendal Wilkinson (Ulverston)	54	1	Settle	24 Aug
10'0	3.05	Thomas Cannon (Bexleyheath FC)	30.11.58	2	Erith	6 Jul
10'0	3.05	Walter Kelsey (Scarborough)	04.51	1=	Hunmanby	30 Jul

10'0	3.05	George Robinson (Hunmanby)		1=	Hunmanby	30 Jul
10'0	3.05	T. Horwood (East Haddon)		3=	Olney	5 Aug

Junior

9'11	3.02	Gunning Campbell (Wellington Coll)	6.01.63	1	Crowthorne	6 May
9'10	3.00	William Tonge (Cheltenham Coll)	14.04.62	1	Cheltenham	13 Apr
9'8¾	2.97	Tom Ray (Ulverston)	5.02.62	1	Ulverston	10 Jun

Pole Vault: Highland, Lakeland & Border

10'11	3.33	p	William Steel (Canonbie)		1	Glasgow	8 Sep
10'9	3.28	p	Richard Bagot (Sea Dyke)	52	1	Stockton	23 Apr
10'8	3.25	p	J. Harrison (Carlisle)		2	Glasgow	8 Sep
10'6	3.20	p	Anthony Hall (Edinburgh)	c46	1	Edinburgh	14 Sep

(4/4)

10'5	3.17	p	John Thwaites (Keswick)	c57	2	Stockton	22 Apr
10'4	3.15	p	William Barron (Keswick)	c56	1	Grasmere	22 Aug
10'3	3.12	p	William Borland (Kilbarchan)	c48	1=	Alva	15 Aug
10'3	3.12	p	Thomas Milne (Edinburgh)	c52	2=	Edinburgh	14 Sep
10'3	3.12	p	James Rush (Addiewell)	c52	2=	Edinburgh	14 Sep
10'0	3.05	p	George Bird (Stockton)	55	1	Hexham	24 Apr
10'0	3.05	p	Robert Musgrave (Cockermouth)	11.10.41	1	Durham	10 Jun
10'0	3.05	p	George Davidson (Drumoak)	19.11.54	1	Kirkcaldy	18 Jul
10'0	3.05	p	Adam Anderson (Alnwick)	c55	1	Whittingham	21 Aug

Long Jump

22'8½	6.92	Charles Lockton (LAC)	2.07.56	1	London (LB)		27 Apr
22'8	6.91	Edmund Baddeley (CU)	9.04.57	1	London (LB)	AAC	15 Apr
22'4½	6.82	Baddeley		1	Cambridge		30 Mar
22'4½	6.82	Patrick Davin (Suir RC/IRL)	4.06.57	1	Limerick, IRL		3 Jul
22'3½	6.79	Lockton		1hc	London (LB)		1 Jun
22'2¾	6.78	Charles Kemp (OU)	26.04.56	1	London (LB)	OvC	12 Apr
22'2	6.76	Gerard Fowler (Birmingham AC)	57	2	London (LB)	AAC	15 Apr
22'0½	6.72	Baddeley		2	London (LB)	OvC	12 Apr
22'0	6.71	Davin		1	Dublin (LR) IRL ICAC		10 Jun
22'0	6.71	Lockton		1	Uppingham		16 Jul

(10/5)

21'9	6.63	Charles Power (Callan/IRL)	56	1	Callan, IRL	1 Jun
21'8	6.60	Horace Crossley (LAC)	2.10.55	1	Norwich	10 Jun
21'7	6.58	William Kelly (QC Cork/IRL)		wo	Cork, IRL	29 May
21'5	6.53	Wildon Thompson (Burton Pidsea CC)	56	1hc	Beverley	21 Aug
21'4	6.50	Ernest Wood (Woodbridge FC)	25.01.57	1	Woodbridge	22 Apr
21'3½	6.49	Samuel Palmer (CU)	15.12.54	2	Cambridge	30 Mar
21'3½	6.49	Thomas Malone (Tradaree AC/IRL)	26.12.59	1	Miltown Malbay, IRL	25 Sep
21'3	6.48	Harry Luke (Axbridge)	59	2hc	Crewkerne	27 Jun
21'3	6.48	Laurence Gjers (Middlesbrough)	58	1	Middlesbrough	17 Aug
21'2	6.45	Thomas Vallance (Rangers FC)	27.05.56	1	Glasgow (HP)	7 Sep
21'1	6.43	Thomas Stretch (Ormskirk)	28.01.51	1	Bebington	1 Jun
21'0	6.40	Joseph Cussen (French Coll)		1	Blackrock, IRL	22 May
21'0	6.40	Mulligan (Loughglinn/IRL)		1	Loughglinn, IRL	22 Aug
20'11½	6.39	William Fletcher (IRL)		1hc	Liverpool	12 Jun
20'11	6.38	R. Pack (Independent Coll)	c61	1	Taunton	30 Apr
20'10	6.35	Henry Macdougall (LAC)	c52	2	Woodbridge	22 Apr
20'10	6.35	William Dance (N. Durham CC)	c60	1	N. Durham	5 Aug
20'8½	6.31	Stewart Bruce (King William's Coll/IRL)	17.11.58	1	Belfast, IRL	4 May
20'8	6.30	Cecil Hunt (Marlborough Coll)	6.05.60	1	Marlborough	2 Apr
20'8	6.30	Cpl Delaney (90th Light Infantry)		1	Camp Utrecht, SA	Nov

Extra Jump

22'1	6.73	Davin		ex	Kilkenny, IRL	19 Aug

Downhill

20'10½	6.36	James Dwyer (Carrick-on-Suir/IRL)		2	Kilsheelan, IRL	19 Sep

Notes
Baddeley's series in the CU sports (30/03): 21'7½ – 22'0½ – 21'11– 22'4½ (disallowed) – 22'3 – 22'4½.
Peerless Tom Malone by Kieran Sheedy gives 21'11½/6.69 for Malone at Miltown-Malbay (25/09).

Long Jump: Highland, Lakeland & Border

21'3	6.48	David Johnstone (Alva)	1.05.57	1	Thornhill	?? Jul
21'2	6.45	Archibald Mitchell (Alva)	51	2	Thornhill	?? Jul
20'6	6.25	Johnstone		1	Clackmannan	26 Jun

Triple Jump

46'11	14.30	Daniel Looney (Cork/IRL)		1	Cork, IRL	nd
42'8	13.00	Thomas Maloney (Ballina/IRL)		1	Balla, IRL	13 Sep
42'6	12.95	Alexander Inglis (6th Brigade, RA)	c53	1	Woolwich	27 Aug
42'6	12.95	Tom Phillips (Ballina/IRL)		2	Balla, IRL	13 Sep
41'11	12.78	Daniel Galvin (Mallow/IRL)	30.09.60	1	Mallow, IRL	10 Oct
41'0	12.50	Thomas Malone (Tradaree AC/IRL)	26.12.59	1	Ennis, IRL	19 Jun
41'0	12.50	John Smith (Edinburgh U)		1	Edinburgh (ACG)	5 Jul
41'0	12.50	J. McCarthy (Mallow/IRL)		2	Mallow, IRL	10 Oct
40'4	12.29	George Ross (Skibbereen/IRL)		1	Skibbereen, IRL	4 Jun
40'0	12.19	German Woodhead (Edinburgh U)	29.04.55	1	Glasgow (WSCG)	16 Mar
40'0	12.19	W. Sumner (RA Dis Staff)		2	Woolwich	27 Aug
40'0	12.19	William Hall (Wootton-under-Edge)	57	1	Wootton-under-Edge	4 Sep
39'11¾	12.19	Phillips		1	Ballavary, IRL	22 Aug
39'10	12.14	William Reid (Edinburgh U)	c60	2	Glasgow (WSCG)	16 Mar

Triple Jump: Highland, Border & Lancashire Professional

48'7	14.81	p	Thomas Aitken (Walkerburn)	23.05.53	1	Alva	15 Aug
47'5	14.45	p	Aitken		1=	Bridge of Allan	3 Aug
47'5	14.45	p	Archibald Mitchell (Alva)	51	1=	Bridge of Allan	3 Aug
47'0	14.33	p	Aitken		1	Galashiels	20 Jul
46'5	14.15	p	John Low (Forfar)	19.01.57	1	Bo'Ness	13 Jul
46'1	14.05	p	Mitchell		2	Bo'Ness	13 Jul
46'1	14.05	p	David Johnstone (Alva)	1.05.57	1	Thornhill	?? Jul
46'1	14.05	p	Robert Knox (Jedburgh)	17.09.47	2	Galashiels	20 Jul
46'1	14.05	p	Aitken		1	Alloa	14 Aug
46'0	14.02	p	Johnstone		1	Stenhousemuir	20 Jul
45'10	13.97	p	Knox		1	Hawick	7 Jun
45'8½	13.93	p	Knox		1	Kelso	27 Jul
			(12/5)				
45'6	13.87	p	Adam Scott (Swinton)	15.08.52	2	Dalkeith	28 Sep
45'3	13.79	p	James Fox (Alloa)		3	Bridge of Allan	3 Aug
44'6	13.56	p	Daniel Lamont (Kilbarchan)	c55	1	Alexandria	31 Aug
44'2	13.46	p	John Rennie (Alva)		3	Bo'Ness	13 Jul
44'0	13.41	p	C. Ferguson (Jedburgh)		4	Bridge of Allan	3 Aug
43'8	13.31	p	William McGuire (Dunblane)	c58	1	East Boreland	17 Aug
43'7	13.28	p	William Young (Alva)	c53	3	Stenhousemuir	22 Jul
43'3	13.18	p	James Hunter (Tillicoultry)		1	Edinburgh	18 May
43'2	13.16	p	J. Hughes		1	Daley	3 Aug
42'11	13.08	p	A. McLeavie		2	Daley	3 Aug
42'10	13.06	p	James Ballantyne (Glasgow)		2	Balfron	13 Jul
42'9	13.03	p	D. McLiver		1	Barrhead	29 Jun
42'9	13.03	p	Peter Cameron (Banchory)	8.12.52	1	Aberdeen (CC)	20 Jul
42'8	13.00	p	J. Smith (Edinburgh)		2	Edinburgh	18 May
42'7	12.98	p	James Thomson (Culter)		2	Skene	29 Jun
42'4	12.90	p	J. Stewart		1	Peebles	27 Jul
42'2	12.85	p	John Hunter (Galashiels)		1	Perth	10 Aug
42'1	12.83	p	T. Barlow (Oldham)		1	Barnsley	1 Jan
42'0	12.80	p	J. Stirling (Walkerburn)		2	Innerleithen	17 Aug
42'0	12.80	p	Frank Harrison (Morpeth)		1	Whittingham	24 Aug

Shot

42'7	12.98	Patrick Hickey (QC Cork/IRL)	18.12.54	1	Cork, IRL	2 May
42'0	12.80	William Kelly (QC Cork/IRL)		2	Cork, IRL	2 May
41'9	12.73	Thomas Stone (Newton-le-Willows)	24.01.52	1hc	Liverpool	12 Jun
41'5	12.62	"P.J.McCarthy" (QC Cork/IRL)		1	Galway, IRL	4 Apr
41'0	12.50	Thomas Malone (Tradaree AC/IRL)	26.12.59	1	Ennis, IRL	19Jun
40'6½	12.36	Maurice Davin (Suir RC/IRL)	29.06.42	wo	Dublin (LR) IRL ICAC	10 Jun
40'6	12.34	Hickey		1	Cork, IRL	9 May

(7/6)

39'6	12.04		Edward O'Grady (Limerick/IRL)	c52	1	Hospital, IRL	28 Sep
38'10	11.84		William Winthrop (LAC)	15.06.52	wo	London (LB) AAC	15 Apr
38'8	11.79		J.C.Cannon (Killadysert/IRL)		1	Killadysert, IRL	1 Sep
38'0	11.58		George Sweeney (Tradaree AC/IRL)		2	Ennis, IRL	19 Jun
37'11½	11.57		Robert Thomas (Liverpool Gym)	22.11.56	2hc	Widnes	22 Jun
37'10	11.53		J. Brown (Noag/IRL)		1	Noag, IRL	21 Aug
37'6	11.43		Alexander Inglis (Manchester)	c53	1	Manchester (WR)	7 Sep
37'2	11.33		Wyndham Evanson (Civil Service)	51	1hc	London (LB)	1 Jun
36'9	11.20		Henry Johnston (Edinburgh U)	13.09.56	1	Edinburgh (ACG)	5 Jul
36'8	11.18		Patrick Davin (Suir RC/IRL)	4.06.57	1	Kilkenny, IRL	19 Aug
36'7½	11.16		Arthur East (CU)	3.11.57	1	London (LB) OvC	12 Apr
36'5	11.10		W.A.Black (Birkenhead)		1hc	Widnes	22 Jun
36'4	11.07		Alfred Orford (Royal Naval C)	c59	1	Greenwich	5 Apr
36'4	11.07		M. Lawler (Borris/IRL)		1	Borris, IRL	26 Jun
36'4	11.07		G. Scott (Rochester)		1	Rochester	3 Jul

Note
Inglis was credited with 39'6 by *Athletic News* on 7 Sep.
"P.J.McCarthy" (41'5 on 4/04) was a pseudonym for a QC Cork athlete, believed to be Kelly.

Shot: Highland & Border
Includes 16lb stone

47'0	14.33	p	W. Smith (Edinburgh)		1	Stenhousemuir	22 Jul
46'5	14.15	p	Donald Dinnie (Aboyne)	8.06.37	1	Comrie	23 Aug
45'5	13.84	p	George Davidson (Drumoak)	19.11.54	1	Aberdeen (CC)	20 Jul
45'2	13.77	p	Dinnie		1	Glasgow	6 Apr
44'9	13.64	p	Dinnie		1	Manchester (WR)	31 Aug
44'0	13.41	p	Dinnie		1	Aberdeen	22 Jul
44'0	13.41	p	Smith		1	Falkirk	27 Jul
43'7	13.28	p	John Cameron (Leith)		1	Inverness	19 Sep
43'7	13.28	p	Davidson		2	Inverness	19 Sep
43'0	13.11	p	Davidson		2	Glasgow	6 Apr
42'10	13.06	p	Dinnie		1	Errol	31 Jul
42'10	13.06	p	Duncan Ross (Glasgow/CAN)		1	Guelph, Ont, CAN	1 Oct
42'8	13.00	p	John Anderson (Crieff)		1	Comrie (local)	23 Aug
42'8	13.00	p	Davidson		2	Manchester (WR)	31 Aug

(14/6)

42'5*	12.93	p	William Bremner (Glenbucket)	3.01.47	1	Kildrummy	23 Aug
40'9*	12.42	p	William Innes (Edinburgh)		1	Johnstone	13 Jul
40'0	12.19	p	George Mearns (Aberdeen)		3	Aberdeen	22 Jul
39'6	12.04	p	George Bowie (Newmachar)	1.09.56	1	Glasgow	3 Aug
39'0	11.89	p	Kenneth McRae (Nairn)	50	3	Manchester (WR)	31 Aug
38'11½	11.87	p	James Fleming (Ballinluig)	18.09.40	2	Aboyne	11 Sep
38'11	11.86	p	Andrew Ross (Glenlivet)		1	Elgin	20 Jul
38'4	11.68	p	Adam Scott (Swinton)	15.08.52	1	Swinton	21 Jun
38'3*	11.66	p	John Smith (Kildrummy)		2	Kildrummy	23 Aug
38'1	11.61	p	William Fleming (Dundee)	22.08.42	2	Errol	31 Jul
38'0	11.58	p	John McGregor (Glasgow)		3	Falkirk	27 Jul
37'4*	11.38	p	Francis Christie (Cluny)		1	Skene	29 Jun
37'3	11.35	p	James Ferguson (Meigar)		2	Comrie (local)	23 Aug
37'1	11.30	p	D. McLaren (Balquhidder)		3	Comrie (local)	23 Aug
36'11*	11.25	p	William Rust (Drumoak)	1.01.55	2	Skene	29 Jun
36'11	11.25	p	James McArthur (Brodie)		2	Elgin	20 Jul
36'9*	11.20	p	James Smith (Kildrummy)		3	Kildrummy	23 Aug
36'5	11.10	p	Thomas McDougall (Galashiels)	53	2	Swinton	21 Jun
35'8	10.87	p	Evan Clayton (Nairn)	17.03.52	3	Elgin	20 Jul

Note: *correct weight assumed from evidence of other years.

Exhibition

49'9	15.16	p	Dinnie		ex	Manchester (WR)	31 Aug
47'9	14.55	p	Davidson		ex	Manchester (WR)	31 Aug

Reported as "afterwards" in *Athletic News*. Competition result as in list.

Weight unstated

49'1	14.96	p	Dinnie		1	Kingussie (light)	6 Sep
47'3½	14.41	p	Davidson		2	Kingussie (light)	6 Sep

43'1½	13.14	p	McRae		3	Kingussie (light)	6 Sep
42'6	12.95	p	Bowie		1	Fintray	27 Jul
37'5	11.40	p	George Reid (Newhills)		2	Fintray	27 Jul
37'2	11.33	p	John Hutcheon (Dyce)		3	Fintray	27 Jul
36'5	11.10	p	William Ferguson (Alloa)		1	Clackmannan	26 Jun
36'2	11.02	p	John McGilchrist (Alloa)		2	Clackmannan	26 Jun
35'8	10.87	p	James Ross (Fochabers)		1	Fochabers (local)	21 Sep

18lb by performer

45'0	13.72	p	John Dow (Thornhill)		1	Thornhill	?? Jul
41'4	12.60	p	Owen Duffy (Edinburgh/IRL)	c47	1	Edinburgh	14 Sep
40'8	12.40	p	John Dewar (Crieff)		2	Thornhill	?? Jul
40'6	12.34	p	R. McLaren		3	Thornhill	?? Jul

22lb by performer

46'0	14.02	p	Dinnie		1	Glasgow (Shaw)	29 Jun
39'8	12.09	p	Duffy		1	Cupar	7 Aug
39'7	12.06	p	J. Fleming		2	Dundee	20 Jul
39'2	11.94	p	Davidson		2	Birnam	29 Aug
38'1	11.61	p	W. Fleming		3	Dundee	20 Jul
36'9	11.20	p	R. Johnstone (Alva)		1	Alva	15 Aug
36'3½	11.06	p	Anderson		3	Crieff	24 Aug
36'0	10.97	p	McRae		1	Tomintoul	22 Aug

Doubtful

48'2	14.68	p	Davidson		1	Bridge of Allan (light)	3 Aug
47'5	14.45	p	Duffy		2	Bridge of Allan (light)	3 Aug
46'10	14.27	p	Dinnie		1	Greenock	14 Sep
45'8	13.92	p	Anderson		3	Bridge of Allan (light)	3 Aug
44'4	13.51	p	Davidson		2	Greenock	14 Sep
43'7	13.28	p	McRae		3	Greenock	14 Sep
42'6	12.95	p	McRae		4	Bridge of Allan (light)	3 Aug

Note
Dinnie is said to have thrown 50'9/15.47 at Alexandra Park, North London, on 1 Jul. This may have been an exhibition throw (*The Sporting Annual, 1878-9*).

Hammer

All Styles. The 7ft circle was introduced at the AAC Championships this year (see note), but most meetings allowed an unlimited run and follow.

123'2	37.54	Maurice Davin (Suir RC/IRL)	29.06.42	1	Dublin (LR) IRL ICAC	10 Jun
118'0	35.97	James Tobin (Mullinahone/IRL)		1	Killadysert, IRL	17 Sep
116'3	35.43	McKennion (78th Highlanders)		1	Curragh, IRL	31 Aug
107'1	32.64	Edmund Baddeley (CU)	9.04.57	1	Cambridge	29 Mar
107'0	32.61	Alexander Inglis (Manchester)	c53	1	Manchester (WR)	7 Sep
106'2	32.36	Baddeley		1	London (LB) OvC	12 Apr
106'2	32.36	M. Tobin (Drangan/IRL)		1	Kilsheelan, IRL	19 Sep
106'2	32.36	M. Tobin		1	Clonmel, IRL	23 Sep
105'10	32.26	Baddeley		1	Cambridge	9 Mar
105'7	32.18	Patrick Hickey (QC Cork/IRL)	18.12.54	1	Cork, IRL	9 May
104'4½	31.81	Lindsay Bury (CU)	8.07.57	1	Cambridge	19 Nov
102'6	31.24	Arthur East (CU)	3.11.57	1	Cambridge	14 Nov
		(12/9)				
102'3	31.17	Patrick Nally (Balla/IRL)	56	1	Miltown Malbay, IRL	25 Sep
100'9	30.71	William A. Burgess (ex-OU)	27.12.46	1	London (SB)	27 Apr
99'6	30.33	T. Murphy (Kilmallock/IRL)		1	Kilmallock, IRL	2 Nov
99'1	30.20	Charles Coote (RMC Sandhurst)	5.08.59	1	Camberley	11 Oct
98'10	30.12	Henry Otter (OU)	4.02.56	2	London (LB) OvC	12 Apr
98'10	30.12	William Kelly (QC Cork/IRL)		2	Cork, IRL	9 May
98'6	30.02	J. Brown (Noag/IRL)		1	Noag, IRL	21 Aug
97'2	29.62	Henry Macaulay (OU)	20.01.57	1	Oxford	22 Mar
96'7	29.44	Richard Jones (CU)	14.03.57	2	Cambridge	14 Nov
96'0	29.26	C. Lyons (Kilfinane/IRL)		1	Kilfinane, IRL	15 Aug
94'4	28.75	Francis Goodman (Skibbereen/IRL)	c54	1	Skibbereen, IRL	4 Jun

Exhibition

112'0	34.14	Burgess		ex	London (SB)	27 Apr

Notes
Davin's throw was from an unlimited run. On the same day he threw 104'4/31.80 from a 7ft circle.
The AAC title (7ft circle) was won with a world best for this new limited style by Baddeley 98'10/30.12 from
Burgess 88'7/27.00 at LB on 15/04.

Hammer: Highland & Border

123'6	37.64	p	Donald Dinnie (Aboyne)	8.06.37	1	Dundee	20 Jul
116'4	35.46	p	George Davidson (Drumoak)	19.11.54	1	Inverness	19 Sep
116'3	35.43	p	Kenneth McRae (Nairn)	50	2	Dundee	20 Jul
115'0*	35.05	p	Dinnie		1	Luss	30 Aug
112'5	34.26	p	Dinnie		1	Kirkcaldy	18 Jul
112'3	34.21	p	John Ogg (Banff/NZL)	7.08.47	2	Dunedin, NZL	1 Jan
112'2	34.19	p	McRae		2	Inverness	19 Sep
111'9*	34.06	p	Davidson		1	Edzell (open)	27 Jul
110'7*	33.71	p	Davidson		2	Luss	30 Aug
110'6*	33.68	p	Dinnie		2	Edzell (open)	27 Jul
110'0	33.53	p	Davidson		1	Braes O'Gight	26 Jul
109'0*	33.22	p	McRae		3	Luss	30 Aug
108'2*	32.97	p	Dinnie		1	Blairgowrie	23 Jul
107'8*	32.82	p	Dinnie		1	Birnam	29 Aug
107'7	32.79	p	Dinnie		1	Aberfeldy	28 Aug
107'6	32.77	p	Dinnie		1	Pitcairngreen	10 Aug
107'0	32.61	p	James Fleming (Ballinluig)	18.09.40	3=	Dundee	20 Jul
107'0	32.61	p	William Fleming (Dundee)	22.08.42	3=	Dundee	20 Jul
			(18/6)				
100'0	30.48	p	John Cameron (Leith)		3	Inverness	19 Sep
98'7	30.05	p	William McDuff (Ballinluig)	c51	1	Aberfeldy (local)	28 Aug
98'3	29.95	p	George Bowie (Strathdon)	1.09.56	1	New Deer	20 Jul
97'9	29.79	p	William Innes (Lumphanan)		1	Lumphanan	20 Jul
97'2	29.62	p	William Meldrum (Pitmedden)		2	Braes O'Gight	26 Jul
96'10	29.51	p	J. Ness (Perth)		2hc	Perth	19 Oct
96'8	29.46	p	Duncan Ross (Glasgow/CAN)	16.03.55	1	Newark, NJ, USA	5 Jul
96'6	29.41	p	William McCombie Smith (Blairgowrie)	7.09.47	2	Lumphanan	20 Jul
95'7*	29.13	p	William Bremner (Leochel-Cushnie)	3.01.47	1	Kildrummy	23 Aug
94'4	28.75	p	William Balfour (Savoch)		2	New Deer	20 Jul

Notes: *correct weight assumed from evidence of other years. Ross's 96'8 was with a 17¾lb hammer.

Extra trial

113'6*	34.59	p	Dinnie		ex	Edzell	27 Jul

Weight unstated

121'1	36.91	p	G. Bowie		1	Glasgow (light)	3 Aug
117'6	35.81	p	John Hutcheon (Dyce)		2	Glasgow (light)	3 Aug
116'3	35.43	p	Francis Christie (Skene)		1	Skene (light)	29 Jun
113'0	34.44	p	Peter Bowie (Strathdon)	54	3	Glasgow (light)	3 Aug
113'0	34.44	p	Dinnie		1	Oban (heavy)	10 Sep
112'10	34.39	p	Davidson		1	Nairn	10 Aug
111'8	34.04	p	Dinnie		1	Kingussie (light)	6 Sep
110'8½	33.74	p	Davidson		2	Kingussie (light)	6 Sep
110'8	33.73	p	McRae		2	Oban (heavy)	10 Sep
108'6	33.07	p	Davidson		1	Oban (heavy)	11 Sep
107'7	32.79	p	Davidson		3	Oban (heavy)	10 Sep
107'6½	32.78	p	McRae		3	Kingussie (light)	6 Sep
107'0	32.61	p	McRae		2	Oban (heavy)	11 Sep
106'4	32.41	p	William Rust (Drumoak)	1.01.55	2	Skene (light)	29 Jun
105'7	32.18	p	William Machray (Skene)	13.05.54	3	Skene (light)	29 Jun
101'2	30.84	p	George Topp (Glasgow)		3	Glasgow (heavy)	3 Aug
95'10	29.21	p	Alexander Fraser (East Mulloch)		1	Durris	17 Aug

18lb

107'7	32.79	p	Dinnie		1	Aberfeldy	28 Aug
107'3	32.69	p	Davidson		1	Glenisla	23 Aug
105'4*	32.11	p	Dinnie		1	Fochabers (heavy)	21 Sep
104'4	31.80	p	Davidson		2	Aberfeldy	28 Aug
101'4*	30.89	p	Davidson		2	Fochabers (heavy)	21 Sep
99'8	30.38	p	McRae		3	Aberfeldy	28 Aug

Note: *correct weight assumed from evidence of other years.

20lb
104'1	31.72	p	Dinnie	1	Crieff	24 Aug
98'7	30.05	p	McRae	2	Crieff	24 Aug
95'2	29.01	p	Davidson	3	Crieff	24 Aug

Other Events

120 Yards
12.0	Thomas Malone (Tradaree AC/IRL)	26.12.59	1	Dublin (LR) IRL	31 May

Foreign performer
12.0	Louis Junker (LAC/RUS)	20.11.54	1=hc	London (SB)	25 May

150 Yards
15.8	George Hoffmeister (CU)	10.10.58	1hthc	Cambridge	27 Nov

200 Yards
21.0	Amos Booth (Hyde)	c54	1	Compstall	8 Jun
21.0	William Young (Private Banks)	c55	1	Catford	22 Jun

Foreign performer
20.0	Louis Junker (LAC/RUS)	20.11.54	1	Woodbridge	22 Apr

250 Yards
27.5	Lennard Stokes (Guy's Hosp)	12.02.56	1	London (LB)	29 Jun

300 Yards
33.0	Melville Portal (OU)	9.12.56	1hc	Oxford	19 Nov

600 Yards
1:17.8 e	J.J.Stephens (LAC)		2hc	London (SB)	25 May

1y down on 1:17.6

1000 Yards
2:19.8	William Bolton (CU)	3.07.58	1hc	Cambridge	26 Nov

¾ Mile
3:14.0 p	William Cummings (Paisley)	10.06.58	int	Glasgow (Spr)	5 Oct

In a 1 mile race

1½ Miles
6:56.2 p	William Cummings (Paisley)	10.06.58	1	Edinburgh (Pow)	31 Dec

25 Miles
2:53:20.0 p	William Smith (Paisley)	27.12.46	int	London (LB)	15 Jul

in a 50 miles race

50 Miles
7:15:23.0 p	George Hazael (Deptford)	22.11.44	1	London (LB)	15 Jul

100 Miles
17:03:06 i p	George Hazael (Deptford)	22.11.44	int	London (Ag Hall)	4 Nov

In a 6 day race, indoors

1 Hour run
10m 440y/16,495m p	William Smith (Paisley)	27.12.46	1	Forfar	9 Aug
10m 360y/16,422m	James Warburton (Haslingden)	13.11.45	wo	Blackburn	27 Apr

1 Mile Walk
6:37.0 p	William Perkins (Camberwell)	16.09.52	1	London (LB)	24 Jun

2 Miles Walk
14:13.0	Henry Venn (LAC)	57	int	London (LB)	AAC	15 Apr

In a 7 miles race

7 Miles Walk
52:25.0	Henry Venn (LAC)	57	1	London (LB)	AAC	15 Apr

Cricket Ball
119y 2ft 0in 109.42	Charles Gilbert (OU)	9.01.55	1	Oxford	18 Mar

Dating from 1815, the Braemar Gathering became the most famous of highland games after Queen Victoria began patronising the event in 1844. This illustration is from 1878. The caber and the hammer were won by William McCombie Smith, who wrote the definitive book *The Athletes and Athletic Sports of Scotland.*

100 Yards

10 1/5	George Hoffmeister (CU)	10.10.58	1	Cambridge		21 Mar
10 1/5	Ernest Trepplin (OU)	56	1	London (LB)	OvC	4 Apr
10 1/5	William McCord (QC Belfast/IRL)	c56	1	Belfast, IRL		14 Apr
10 1/5	McCord		1	Belfast, IRL		8 May
10 1/5	Charles Lockton (LAC)	2.07.56	1	London (SB)	LAC	14 Jun
10 1/5	Horace Crossley (LAC)	2.10.55	1	Walsall		19 Jul
10 1/5	Lockton		1	London (SB)		4 Oct
10.2 e	Lockton		2hc	London (SB)		1 Nov
10.3 e	Melville Portal (OU)	9.12.56	1ro	Oxford		15 Mar
10.3 e	Portal		2	London (LB)	OvC	4 Apr
10.3 e	James Stewart (ICAC/IRL)	10.02.51	2	Belfast, IRL		14 Apr
10.3 e	Stewart		2	Belfast, IRL		8 May
		(12/7)				
10 2/5	Henry Allan (LAC)	c56	1	Woodbridge		14 Apr
10 2/5 p	John Jones		1ht1	Swansea		2 Jun
10 2/5	Thomas Malone (Tradaree AC/IRL)	26.12.59	1	Dublin (LR) IRL ICAC		2 Jun
10 2/5 p	A. Nicholls (Tenby)		1	Swansea		2 Jun
10 2/5	Richard Shaw (Hereford FC)	18.02.59	1	Leeds		14 Jun
10.4 e	Sidney Sheppard (Rushall Rovers)	c59	2	Walsall		19 Jul
10 2/5	Tom Pank (Birmingham City FC)	59	1ht1hc	Birmingham (ALG)		16 Aug
10 2/5	Harry Luke (Axbridge)	59	1ht1	Taunton		18 Sep
10 2/5	Edward Growse (OU)	8.07.60	1	Oxford		11 Nov

Wind assisted

10.0	Allan		1	Birmingham (ALG)		9 Jun
10.1 e	Lockton		2hthc	London (SB)		28 Jun
10.1 e	Shaw		2	Birmingham (ALG)		9 Jun
10.2 e	Frederick Fellowes (Burton FC)	12.02.58	3	Birmingham (ALG)		9 Jun

Birmingham race said to be slightly downhill and with the wind at their backs; in the 100y handicap.
H.H.Sturt twice did 9.8 from a 3y start. In Lockton's race: "From the direction and force of the wind it was apparent that fast times would be the order of the day." Lockton ¾y down on 10.0.

Doubtful

10.0	Samuel Sherwood (Anc Order of Foresters)	54	1	Halesworth	4 Aug

Timing rounded to seconds only

10.0	William Beveridge (Edinburgh U)	27.11.58	1	Edinburgh (ACG)	nd

Mentioned in the history of the University AC as "credited in 1879"

10.0	Charles Gilbert (LAC)	9.01.55	1	Langport	28 Aug

Time reported in *The Field* but ignored in *Bell's Life*.

10.1 e	J. Cross (Tottenham House CC)		2hc	Willesden	13 Sep

6in down on 10.0, but timekeeping said to be 'atrocious'.

10 1/5	Harry Massey (United Hospitals AC)	c57	1	Birmingham (PR)	26 Jul

Said to have poached half a dozen yards and ducked under the tape at the finish.

Notes: Hoffmeister's race in the CU sports was started by word of mouth.
Lockton 1½y down on 10.0 (1/11); Stewart ½y down (14/04) and inches (8/05); Portal 'a shade outside 10.2' (ro 15/03); Portal 1ft down on 10.2 (04/04); Sheppard 1y down on 10.2 (19/07); Shaw 1ft and Fellowes 4ft down on 10.0 (09/06).

220 Yards

22 4/5	Lennard Stokes (Guy's Hosp)	12.02.56	1	London (SB)		2 Jul
23.0 e	Harry Massey (St Thomas's H)	c57	2	London (SB)		2 Jul
23.0 e	H. England (LAC)		2hc	London (SB)		5 Jul
23.0	E. Parker (Stratford BC)		1	Birmingham		12 Jul
24 1/5	Duncan Kemp (Liverpool)	c55	1	Belfast, IRL		2 May
24 1/5	Kemp		1hc	Belfast, IRL		3 May
24 1/5	Sydney Stoneham (Beckenham)	c57	1	Beckenham		5 Jul
24 1/5	W.J.Bull (Rotherham CC)		1	Rotherham		25 Aug
24 ¼	H.W.Yates (St Mary's H)		1hc	Ealing		17 Jun
24 ¼	Charles Lockton (LAC)	2.07.56	1ht1hc	Catford Bridge		21 Jun
24.5 e	Richard Gwillim (St Mary's H)	57	2hc	Ealing		17 Jun
24 3/5	Thomas Guinness (King's Coll Hosp/IRL)	15.03.59	1	London (SB)		7 Jun
24.6 e	Thomas McMorland (Beckenham)	54	2	Beckenham		5 Jul
24 4/5	Thomas Lynch (ICAC/IRL)	25.03.59	1	Belfast, IRL		13 Jun
24.9 e	J. Cummings (Ballyclare CC/IRL)		2	Belfast, IRL		13 Jun

Doubtful

22.0 or less	Henry Allan (LAC)		c56	3hc	Birmingham (ALG)	9 Jun

Downhill, with wind and in rain, so "palpably erroneous" (*Bell's Life*).

Notes: Massey 1y down on 22.8 (02/07); England 1y down on 22.8 (05/07); Gwillim 2y down on 24.25; McMorland 3y down on 24.2; Cummings ½y down on 24.8.

440 Yards

50.4 e	Melville Portal (OU)	9.12.56	2hc	Cambridge		8 Mar
50.7 e	Henry Ball (LAC)	10.04.59	4hc	London (SB)		2 Sep
51.2	Thomas Malone (Tradaree AC/IRL)	26.12.59	1	Dublin (LR)	IRL ICAC	2 Jun
51.2	William Beverley (OU)	18.04.59	1	Oxford		13 Nov
51.3 e	Thomas Lynch (ICAC/IRL)	25.03.59	2	Dublin (LR)	IRL ICAC	2 Jun
51.4	Portal		1	Oxford		13 Mar
51.4	Edgar Storey (CU)	6.02.59	1	London (LB)	AAC	7 Apr
51.5 e	Portal		2	London (LB)	AAC	7 Apr
51.5 e	George Christian (ICAC/IRL)	6.09.57	3	Dublin (LR)	IRL ICAC	2 Jun
51.6	Portal		1	Oxford		22 Feb
51.6	Sidney Baker (LAC)	17.06.58	1	Oxford		27 Nov
51.7 e	Edward Growse (OU)	8.07.60	2	Oxford		27 Nov
51.7 e	Beverley		3	Oxford		27 Nov
		(13/9)				
51.8	George Hoffmeister (CU)	10.10.58	1	Cambridge		22 Mar
51.8	Herbert Sturt (LAC)	24.07.56	1hc	London (SB)		1 Nov
51.9 e	Thomas Pawson (Ilkley)		2hc	Ilkley		8 Aug
52.0 e	Lees Knowles (CU)	16.02.57	2	Cambridge		22 Mar

Notes: Portal 12y down on 49.0 (08/03); Ball 2½y down on 50.4 (02/09); Lynch ½y & Christian 2½y down on 51.2 (02/06); Portal 1ft down on 51.4 (07/04); Growse ½y down and Beverley inches more on 51.6 (27/11); Knowles 1y down on 51.8 (22/03); Pawson 2½y down on 51.6 (08/08).

880 Yards

1:59.2	Charles Hazen Wood (LAC)		c56	1	London (LB)		4 Oct
2:00.0	Walter George (Worcester BC)	9.09.58	1	Stoke-on-Trent		6 Aug
2:00.4	William Bolton (CU)	3.07.58	1	Cambridge		21 Mar
2:01.0 e	Henry Ball (LAC)	10.04.59	2	London (LB)		4 Oct
2:01.2	Hazen Wood		1	London (SB)	LAC	14 Jun
2:01.2 e	Richard Andrews (Warrington)	c58	2	Stoke-on-Trent		6 Aug
2:01.3 e	Lees Knowles (CU)	16.02.57	2	Cambridge		21 Mar
2:01.4	Hazen Wood		1	London (SB)		19 Apr
2:01.9 e	Neville Turner (LAC)	4.04.55	2	London (SB)	LAC	14 Jun
2:02.0 e	Charles Johnstone (CU)	16.06.57	3	Cambridge		21 Mar
2:03.6	Bolton		1	London (LB)	AAC	7 Apr
2:03.8	George Searight (ICAC/IRL)	15.01.59	1	Dublin (LR)	IRL ICAC	2 Jun
2:03.8	Samuel Holman (LAC)	29.01.53	1	Newport, Mon		4 Aug
		(13/10)				
2:04.0 p	William Cummings (Paisley)	10.06.58	int	London (LB)		6 Dec
2:04.1 e	James Pinion (QC Belfast/IRL)	c53	2	Dublin (LR)	IRL ICAC	2 Jun
2:04.1 e	William Pedley (Royal Indian Eng Coll)	16.06.58	3	London (SB)	LAC	14 Jun
2:04.2	Bernhard Wise (OU)	10.02.58	1	Oxford		21 Nov
2:04.3 e	Henry Dwyer (Leicester CC/IRL)	c57	3hc	Northampton		2 Aug
2:04.4 p	Edgar Dickerson (Ipswich)	7.04.54	int	London (LB)		6 Dec
2:04.9 e	Edward Growse (OU)	8.07.60	2	Oxford		20 Nov

Notes: Knowles 6y and Johnstone 10½y down on 2:00.4; Andrews 8y down on 2:00.0; Ball 13y down on 1:59.2; Turner 5y down on 2:01.2; Pinion 2y down on 2:03.8; Dwyer 12y down on 2:02.6; Growse 3y down on 2:04.4; Pedley 20y down on 2:01.2.

Mile

4:19.5 e p	William Cummings (Paisley)	10.06.58	2hc	Moston Pk, Manchr		8 Nov
4:20.8 p	Edgar Dickerson (Ipswich)	7.04.54	1	London (LB)		6 Dec
4:21.7 e p	Cummings		2	London (LB)		6 Dec
4:21.8 e p	Cummings		2hc	Preston		19 Jul
4:25.4 e p	Cummings		4hc	Audenshaw		26 Apr
4:26.6	Walter George (Worcester BC)	9.09.58	1	London (SB)	LAC	14 Jun
4:29.0	Bernhard Wise (OU)	10.02.58	1	London (LB)	AAC	7 Apr

4:29.2		George		1	Birmingham (ALG)		10 May
4:29.7 e		George		3hc	Pershore		14 Aug
4:30.5	p	Thomas Herbert (Barrow-in-Furness)	c53	1	Sheffield (QG)		30 Aug
4:30.5		Henry Thomas (Blackheath H)	c52	3hc	London (SB)		4 Oct
4:31.2	p	David Livingstone (Tranent)	10.11.55	wo	London (LB)		29 Mar

(12/7)

4:31.4 e		Henry Jenkins (OU)	13.02.56	2	London (LB)	AAC	7 Apr
4:31.4		Charles Hazen Wood (LAC)	c56	1	London (SB)		1 Nov
4:32.4		Arnold Hills (OU)	12.03.57	1	Oxford		13 Mar
4:33.6		Thomas Bailey (Birchfield H)		1	Birmingham (ALG)		6 Sep
4:33.7 e p		Robert Needham (Sheffield)	13.12.57	2	Sheffield (QG)		30 Aug
4:35.0		Richard Andrews (Warrington)	c58	1hc	Heywood		2 Aug

Notes: Cummings 10y down on 4:18.0 (8/11); 6y down on 4:20.8 (6/12); 12y down on 4:20.0 (19/07); 22y down on 4:22.0 (26/04); George 24y down on 4:26.0 (14/08); Jenkins 15y down on 4:29.0 (07/04); Needham 20y down on 4:30.5 (30/08).

2 Miles

9:33.0	p	William Cummings (Paisley)	10.06.58	int	Preston		11 Oct
9:33.5	p	Cummings		int	Glasgow (Spr)		30 Aug
9:45.0	p	David Livingstone (Tranent)	10.11.55	1	Jedburgh		12 Jul
9:55.0	p	Livingstone		int	London (LB)		9 Jun
9:55.4 e p		Charles Price (Kennington)	17.05.53	int	London (LB)		9 Jun
9:57.4	p	Livingstone		1	London (Bow)		17 Feb
9:57.7 e p		Cummings		2	London (Bow)		17 Feb

(7/3)

10:01.0		Walter George (Worcester BC)	9.09.58	3hc	Oxford		26 Nov
10:03.0		James Warburton (Stoke Victoria AC)	13.11.45	int	London (LB)	AAC	7 Apr
10:08.6		George Mawby (Spartan H)	17.07.57	1	Barnes		5 Apr
10:10.0		Arnold Hills (OU)	12.03.57	int	London (LB)	OvC	4 Apr
10:15.4 e		Charles Mason (LAC)	3.06.51	int	London (SB)	LAC	14 Jun
10:15.6 e		M.A.Sheehan (Tradaree AC/IRL)		2hc	Limerick, IRL		5 Jun
10:17.0		J. Nolan (Borris/IRL)		1	Leighlinbridge, IRL		15 Jul
10:20.0		Ernest Nunns (ICAC/IRL)	17.04.59	int	Dublin (LR) IRL ICAC		2 Jun
10:34.2		Thomas Crellin (Liverpool AC)	1.01.58	1	Belfast, IRL		3 May
10:35.4 e		Frank Benson (OU)	4.11.58	int	Oxford		15 Mar
10:37.3 e		George Stanley (Spartan H)	58	int	London (SB)		2 May
10:37.4		Harold Lee-Evans (CU)	12.05.57	2hc	Cambridge		17 Nov

Note: Cummings 1½y down on 9:57.4 (17/02); Sheehan 3y down on 10:15.0 (5/06).
Intermediate times in races at 3 miles (15/03; 4/04), 4 miles (7/04; 2/06; 14/06; 30/08; 11/10), 6 miles (9/06), 10 miles (02/05). Intermediate estimated times are for runners tracking the leader within one or two yards.

3 Miles

14:42.0	p	William Cummings (Paisley)	10.06.58	int	Preston		11 Oct
14:50.5	p	Cummings		int	Glasgow (Spr)		30 Aug
15:12.0		George Mawby (LAC)	17.07.57	int	London (SB)		19 Apr
15:14.6		Arnold Hills (OU)	12.03.57	1	London (LB)	OvC	4 Apr
15:21.0		James Warburton (Stoke Victoria AC)	13.11.45	int	London (LB)	AAC	7 Apr
15:24.5	p	Charles Price (Kennington)	17.05.53	int	London (LB)		10 May
15:24.9 e p		David Livingstone (Tranent)	10.11.55	int	London (LB)		10 May
15:25.0	p	Livingstone		int	London (LB)		26 Apr
15:25.4 e p		Price		int	London (LB)		26 Apr
15:26.0		Warburton		int	Heywood		4 Aug
15:29.1 e		Warburton		2hc	Blackburn		31 May

(11/6)

15:36.0		Walter George (Worcester BC)	9.09.58	int	London (SB)	LAC	14 Jun
15:43.2 e		Harold Lee-Evans (CU)	12.05.57	2	London (LB)	OvC	4 Apr
15:45.4 e		Frank Benson (OU)	4.11.58	3	London (LB)	OvC	4 Apr
15:53.3 e		William Hamilton (OU)	4.05.59	2	Oxford		15 Mar
15:53.5		George Dunning (Clapton Beagles)	15.07.55	1	Walthamstow		13 Sep

Notes: Intermediate estimated times are for runners tracking the leader within one or two yards.
Warburton 50y down on 15:20.2 (31/05); Lee-Evans 160y down on 15:14.6 (04/04); Benson 172y down on 15:14.6 (04/04); Hamilton 90y down on 15:37.0 (15/03);
Intermediate times in races at 4 miles (7/04; 14/06; 30/08; 11/10), 6 miles (4/08) & 10 miles (19/04; 26/04; 10/05).

4 Miles

19:57.0	p	William Cummings (Paisley)	10.06.58	1	Preston		11 Oct
19:58.0	p	Cummings		1	Preston		16 Aug
20:22.0	p	Cummings		1hc	Glasgow (Spr)		30 Aug
20:39.25	p	Charles Price (Kennington)	17.05.53	int	London (LB)		10 May
20:39.7	e p	David Livingstone (Tranent)	10.11.55	int	London (LB)		10 May
20:41.6		James Warburton (Stoke Victoria AC)	13.11.45	1	London (LB)	AAC	7 Apr
20:44.0	p	Price		int	London (LB)		26 Apr
20:44.4	e p	Livingstone		int	London (LB)		26 Apr
20:50.0	p	Livingstone		int	London (LB)		9 Jun
20:50.4	e p	Price		int	London (LB)		9 Jun
20:52.2		Walter George (Worcester BC)	9.09.58	1	London (SB)	LAC	14 Jun
		(11/5)					
21:30.0		George Mawby (LAC)	17.07.57	int	London (SB)		19 Apr
21:57.8	e	George Stanley (Spartan H)	58	int	London (SB)		2 May
22:03.0		Charles Mason (LAC)	3.06.51	int	London (LB)		4 Oct
22:04.2		M.A.Sheehan (Tradaree AC/IRL)		1	Dublin (LR) IRL ICAC		2 Jun
22:07.1	e	George Gibson (Ulster CC/IRL)		2	Dublin (LR) IRL ICAC		2 Jun
22:15.6		James Harris (Middlesbrough BC)		2	London (LB)	AAC	7 Apr

Notes: Intermediate estimated times are for runners tracking the leader within one or two yards.
Stanley 100y down on 21:39.0 (02/05); Gibson 15y down on 22:04.2 (02/06).
George also ran 20:17.8 from a 25y start at Birmingham on 27/09, equivalent to 20:22.5e.
The *Sporting Chronicle* gave Warburton 20:45.0 at Radcliffe on 11/10, but other sources made it 21:11.
Intermediate times in races at 6 miles (9/06) and 10 miles (19/04; 26/04; 2/05; 10/05; 4/10).

6 Miles

31:12.5		James Warburton (Stoke Victoria AC)	13.11.45	wo	Heywood		4 Aug
31:20.5	p	Charles Price (Kennington)	17.05.53	int	London (LB)		10 May
31:20.9	e p	David Livingstone (Tranent)	10.11.55	int	London (LB)		10 May
31:30.0	i p	James McLeavy (Alexandria)	26.10.52	int	New York, USA		20 Oct
31:27.5	p	Price		int	London (LB)		26 Apr
31:27.9	e p	Livingstone		int	London (LB)		26 Apr
31:40.0	p	Price		1	London (LB)		9 Jun
32:02.0		Warburton		int	Radcliffe		11 Oct
33:07.0		Warburton		1	Ilkley		9 Aug
33:14.0		George Mawby (LAC)	17.07.57	int	London (SB)		2 May
33:31.8	e	Walter George (Worcester BC)	9.09.58	2	Ilkley		9 Aug
33:33.1	e	George Stanley (Spartan H)	58	int	London (SB)		2 May
33:53.0		Stanley		int	London (SB)	LAC	16 Jun
33:56.9	e	Charles Mason (LAC)	3.06.51	int	London (SB)	LAC	16 Jun

Notes: Intermediate estimated times are for runners tracking the leader within one or two yards.
George 130y down on 33:07.0; Stanley 100y down on 33:14.0 (02/05); Mason 20y down on 33:53.0.
Sporting Chronicle gave 33:14.6 for Warburton at Ilkley (9/08).
Intermediate times in races at 10 miles, except McLeavy, who stopped at 10 miles in a 20 mile indoor race.

10 Miles

52:36.0	p	Charles Price (Kennington)	17.05.53	1	London (LB)		10 May
53:17.25	p	Price		1	London (LB)		26 Apr
54:06.5		James Warburton (Stoke Victoria AC)	13.11.45	wo	Radcliffe		11 Oct
55:00.0	p	William Stedman (Lenham)	13.07.51	1hc	Sittingbourne		21 Jul
55:17.0	i p	Price		3hc	London (Ag Hall)		28 Jun
55:55.0	i p	Price		int	New York, USA		20 Oct
56:31.6		Charles Mason (LAC)	3.06.51	1	London (SB)	LAC	16 Jun
57:18.0	i p	James McLeavy (Alexandria)	26.10.52	int	New York, USA		20 Oct
57:40.0		George Mawby (LAC)	17.07.57	1	London (SB)		2 May
57:51.5	p	James Bailey (Sittingbourne)	2.05.52	3hc	Sittingbourne		21 Jul
57:51.8		George Stanley (Spartan H)	58	2	London (SB)	LAC	16 Jun
57:54.0		Stanley		2	London (SB)		2 May
58:27.0		Charles Turner (Spartan H)	c56	3	London (SB)		2 May
59:17.0		Edmund Hobson (Spartan H)	c53	4	London (SB)		2 May

Note: Intermediate times for Price and McLeavy in a 20 mile indoor race, completed by Price (see note above).

120 Yards Hurdles

16 2/5	Thomas Lynch (ICAC/IRL)	25.03.59	1hc	Borris, IRL		9 Jul
16 3/5	Lewis Jarvis (CU)	3.08.57	1	Cambridge		22 Mar
16 3/5	Jarvis		1	London (LB)	OvC	4 Apr
16 3/5	Charles Lockton (LAC)	2.07.56	1	London (SB)	LAC	14 Jun
16 4/5	William Pollock (St George's Hosp)	2.02.59	1	London (SB)		2 Jul
16.9 e	George Lawrence (OU)	17.03.59	2	London (LB)	OvC	4 Apr
16.9 e	Henry Allan (LAC)	c56	2	London (SB)	LAC	14 Jun
	(7/6)					
17.0	Francis Wood (LAC)	28.09.55	1	Woodbridge		14 Apr
17.0	Alfred Foers (Whiston CC)	56	1	Huddersfield		28 Jun
17.1 e	Richard Brown (CU)	26.07.56	2	Cambridge		22 Mar
17 1/5	C.C.Clarke (LAC)		1	Godalming		14 Apr
17.3 e	Greville Livett (CU)	3.03.59	2	Cambridge		20 Mar
17.3 e	William Garlick (Leeds AC)	c56	2ht2	Huddersfield		28 Jun
17.3 e	George Dobell (Stoke Victoria AC)	14.11.54	2	Huddersfield		28 Jun
17.4 e	Edward Clarke (CU)	3.05.59	3	Cambridge		22 Mar
17 2/5	William Pedley (Royal Indian Eng Coll)	16.06.58	1	Barnes		5 Apr
17 2/5	Samuel Palmer (CU)	15.12.54	1	London (LB)	AAC	7 Apr
17 2/5	James Gorman (Lurgan/IRL)	31.10.50	1	Belfast, IRL		28 Jun
17 2/5	Richard Mallett (Darlington CC)	14.10.58	1	Ilkley		9 Aug

Doubtful
17.0	Charles Gilbert (LAC)	9.01.55	1	Langport		28 Aug

Timing rounded to nearest second

Notes
Thomas A Lynch ran under a pseudonym as A. Thomas.
Lawrence 2y down on 16.6; Allan 2y down on 16.6 (14/06); Brown 3y down on 16.6; Clarke 5y down on 16.6;
Livett & Dobell 2y down on 17.0; Garlick 1ft down on 17¼.
Some of the above marks were made from starts behind the line: Foers was owed 3y (28/06); Dobell 5y (28/06);
and Pedley 5y (05/04).

220 Yards Hurdles

28.0	George Dobell (Stoke Victoria AC)	14.11.54	1	Southport	14 Jun
30.0	G. Clark (Halesworth)		1	Halesworth	4 Aug
31.0	Arthur Porter (Leicester)	59	1	Newtown, Wales	12 Jul
31.7 e	Dobell		2hc	Preston	12 Jul
32.0	E. Haines (Farringdon)		1	Bristol	21 Jun
32.5 e	John Banwell (Weston-super-Mare)	3.07.55	2	Bristol	21 Jun
32.5	Thomas Prentice (Leicester)	10.07.55	1	Leicester	4 Aug
33.0	Haines		1ht2	Bristol	21 Jun
33.5 e	Raymond Wickham (Bristol)	50	2ht2	Bristol	21 Jun

Notes: Dobell 2y down on 31.4 (12/07); Banwell 3y down on 32.0; Wickham 3y down on 33.0

440 Yards Hurdles

1:01.0	George Dobell (Stoke Victoria AC)	14.11.54	1hc	Crewe	5 Jul
1:02.0	Arthur Mullins (RMA Woolwich)	1.02.61	1	Woolwich	5 Jun
1:02.3 e	William Vidal (RMA Woolwich)	13.11.60	2	Woolwich	5 Jun
1:03.1 e	Archibald Crawford	14.06.61	3	Woolwich	5 Jun
1:03.8 e	Dobell		2hc	Widnes	20 Jun
1:05.0	James Horrocks (Leigh)	7.09.57	1	Leigh	9 Aug
1:05.5	Dobell		1	Dunchurch	16 Jul

Notes: Vidal 2y and Crawford 7y down on 1:02.0; Dobell 5y down on 1:03.0 (20/06, after falling).

High Jump

6'1½	1.867	Patrick Davin (Suir RC/IRL)	4.06.57	1	Kilkenny		16 Jul
6'0	1.829	Davin		1	Thurles, IRL		26 Jun
5'10	1.778	William Hall (Ariel RC)	57	1	Newport, Mon		?? May
5'9½	1.765	Reginald Macaulay (CU)	24.08.58	1	London (LB)	AAC	7 Apr
5'9½	1.765	Davin		1	Callan, IRL		14 Jun
5'9	1.753	Charles Hammond (ex-CU)	6.12.56	1	Bury St Edmunds		27 Mar
5'9	1.753	William Kelly (QC Cork/IRL)		1	Cork, IRL		22 Apr
5'9	1.753	Hall		1=	London (SB)	LAC	14 Jun

5'9	1.753	Robert Thomas (Liverpool Gym)	22.11.56	1=	London (SB)	LAC	14 Jun
5'8¾	1.746	Macaulay		1	London (LB)	OvC	4 Apr
5'8½	1.740	John Dee (Dungarvan/IRL)		1	Lismore, IRL		2 Jun
5'8½	1.740	Dee		1	Limerick, IRL		5 Jun
		(12/7)					
5'8	1.727	John Parsons (Edinburgh U)	10.07.59	1	Glasgow (WSCG)		12 Apr
5'8	1.727	William Reid (Edinburgh U)	c60	1=	Edinburgh (ACG)		5 Jul
5'7	1.702	James Housam (Normanby)	c52	1	Boosbeck, Yorks		2 Aug
5'7	1.702	Harry Luke (Axbridge)	59	1	Axbridge		12 Aug
5'7	1.702	Henry Cooke (CU)	4.02.59	1	Cambridge		18 Nov

Indoors

5'6	1.676 i	Charles Poland (German Gym Soc)	12.02.59	1	London (KC)	10 Dec
5'5	1.651 i	H. Harris (German Gym Soc)		2	London (KC)	10 Dec

Notes
A *Sporting Mirror* biography of Francis Wood (LAC) claimed that he jumped 5'7½/1.715 at Woodbridge on 14 Apr, but *The Field* and *Suffolk Times* made it 5'5¾ and *Bell's* did not report the meeting.
Thomas Malone was credited with 5'9 at Ennis this year, but his biographer, Kieran Sheedy, reported that Kelly won at Ennis on 29 July with 5'6 and Malone was injured.

High Jump: Highland & Border

5'9	1.753	p	Hugh Andrews (Glasgow)	c52	1	Pollokshaws	21 Jun
5'9	1.753	p	Andrews		1	Cupar	6 Aug
5'9	1.753	p	Andrews		1	Forfar	8 Aug
5'9	1.753	p	Andrews		1	Stenhousemuir	16 Aug
5'9	1.753	p	George Davidson (Drumoak)	19.11.54	1	Boston, USA	28 Aug
5'8	1.727	p	Daniel Lamont (Kilbarchan)	c55	2=	Pollokshaws	21 Jun
5'8	1.727	p	J. McLeaver		2=	Pollokshaws	21 Jun
5'7½	1.715	p	Andrews		1	Birnam	28 Aug
5'7½	1.715	p	Andrews		1	Alexandria	30 Aug
5'7	1.702	p	Andrews		1	Greenock	14 Jun
5'7	1.702	p	Thomas Aitken (Walkerburn)	23.05.53	1=	Milnathort	28 Jul
5'7	1.702	p	James Rush (Addiewell)	c52	1=	Milnathort	28 Jul
5'7	1.702	p	Lamont		2	Cupar	6 Aug
5'7	1.702	p	Lamont		2	Forfar	8 Aug
5'7	1.702	p	Andrews		1	Alloa	13 Aug
			(15/6)				

Note
The Scotsman gives Andrews 5'8 at Alloa. J. McLeaver may be a reporting error for William McLiver (Stewarton).

Pole Vault

11'2¾	3.42	Tom Ray (Ulverston)	5.02.62	1	Ulverston	19 Sep
10'9	3.28	George Callow (Peterborough CC)	c60	1	Husbands Bosworth	6 Aug
10'6	3.20	Callow		1	Northampton	4 Aug
10'6	3.20	Callow		1	Olney	4 Aug
10'6	3.20	Ernest Edwards (Birmingham AC)	21.03.59	2=	Husbands Bosworth	6 Aug
10'6	3.20	Robert Sabin (ex-Culworth AC)	52	2=	Husbands Bosworth	6 Aug
10'6	3.20	Callow		1	Hinckley	30 Aug
		(7/4)				
10'5½	3.19	Horace Strachan (LAC)	21.09.55	1	London (LB)	24 May
10'5	3.17	George Barker (Bacup)	c55	1	Mytholmroyd, Yorks	9 Aug
10'4	3.15	Richard Bagot (Fleetwood)	52	1	Blackburn	31 May
10'4	3.15	Henry Kayll (Sunderland FC)	16.07.55	1	Ilkley	9 Aug
10'4	3.15	Edward Strachan (108th Regt)	16.08.58	1	Fareham	9 Aug
10'1	3.07	Kendal Wilkinson (Urswick)	54	1	Ulverston	2 Jun
10'1	3.07	Frederic Robinson (Beccles AC)	14.09.56	wo	Lowestoft	14 Aug
10'1	3.07	Horace Hamilton (Dublin U/IRL)	16.11.54	1	CANADA	nd
10'0	3.05	William Tonge (Cheltenham Coll)	14.04.62	1	Cheltenham	7 Apr
10'0	3.05	William Caldwell (CU)	7.04.59	1	Glasgow (WSCG)	12 Apr
10'0	3.05	George Gill (Carnforth)	c51	1	Carnforth	2 Aug
10'0	3.05	Henry Johnson (Warwick)	51	4	Husbands Bosworth	6 Aug

Note
In Ray's record jump (aged 17), the bar was set at 11'4½ and measured at 11'2¾ at the centre.
The 10'1 by Hamilton is quoted in *The Bold Collegians*, by Trevor West. The best we have found is 9'11½ at

Toronto on 11/10. Johnson is credited with 10'3 at Husbands Bosworth by H. Berry in *A History of the Pole Vault*, but the *Leicester Journal* states that he failed at this height.

Pole Vault: Highland, Lakeland & Border

10'7	3.23	p	Samuel Parrington (Cark in Cartmel)	c52	1=	Carnforth	23 Aug
10'7	3.23	p	John Simpson (Ulverston)		1=	Carnforth	23 Aug
10'5½	3.19	p	Thomas Aitken (Innerleithen)	23.05.53	1=	Crieff	23 Aug
10'5½	3.19	p	James Rush (Addiewell)	c52	1=	Crieff	23 Aug
10'5	3.17	p	Rush		1	Crossford	20 Sep
10'4	3.15	p	Anthony Hall (Edinburgh)	c46	1=	Kelso	26 Jul
10'4	3.15	p	William Irvine (Hawick)	c57	1=	Kelso	26 Jul
10'3½	3.14	p	Rush		1	Milngavie	6 Sep
10'2	3.10	p	Thomas Milne (Forfar)	c52	1	Dundee	19 Jul
10'2	3.10	p	Peter Cameron (Kincardine O'Neil)	8.12.52	1	Blairgowrie	23 Jul
10'2	3.10	p	Hall		1	Cupar	6 Aug
10'2	3.10	p	Irvine		1	Edinburgh	9 Aug
			(12/8)				
10'1½	3.09	p	William Borland (Kilbarchan)	c48	2=	Milngavie	6 Sep
10'1	3.07	p	Duncan Ferguson (Alloa)		1=	Alva	14 Aug
10'0	3.05	p	David Milne (Forfar)	28.12.42	2	Dundee	19 Jul
10'0	3.05	p	Joseph Hewitson (Askam)	c55	1=	Ulverston	9 Aug

Indoors
10'5	3.17	i p	William Barron (Keswick)	c56	1=	London (Ag Hall)	14 Apr
10'5	3.17	i p	John Thwaites (Keswick)	c57	1=	London (Ag Hall)	14 Apr

Long Jump

22'7	6.88	Patrick Davin (Suir RC/IRL)	4.06.57	1	Dublin (LR) IRL ICAC	2 Jun
22'6	6.86	Charles Lockton (LAC)	2.07.56	1hc	London (LB)	24 May
22'5½	6.85	Harry Massey (St Thomas's H)	c57	1	Birmingham (PR)	26 Jul
22'3½	6.79	Robert Coll (Bruree/IRL)	54	1	Thurles, IRL	26 Jun
22'1½	6.74	Lockton		1	London (SB) LAC	14 Jun
22'1½	6.74	Davin		2	Thurles, IRL	26 Jun
21'6	6.55	Lockton		1	Northampton	4 Aug
21'4	6.50	Thomas Malone (Tradaree AC/IRL)	26.12.59	2	Dublin (LR) IRL ICAC	2 Jun
21'4	6.50	Dominick Tully (Dunmore/IRL)	59	1	Dunmore, IRL early Jun
21'4	6.50	James Dwyer (Carrick-on-Suir/IRL)		1	Ballymacarbry. IRL ?? Aug
		(10/7)				
21'3½	6.49	Gerard Fowler (Birmingham AC)	57	2	Birmingham (PR)	26 Jul
21'3	6.48	Francis Wood (LAC)	28.09.55	1	Market Harborough	14 Jul
21'2	6.45	Thomas Vallance (Rangers FC)	27.05.56	1	Glasgow (HP)	6 Sep
20'11	6.38	Henry Allan (LAC)	c56	1	Woodbridge	14 Apr
20'10¾	6.37	Edmund Baddeley (CU)	9.04.57	1	London (LB) OvC	4 Apr
20'10½	6.36	William Elliott (CU)	9.11.58	1	London (LB) AAC	7 Apr
20'10½	6.36	William Kelly (QC Cork/IRL)		1	Cork, IRL	6 May
20'10	6.35	William Fletcher (Liverpool Gym/IRL)		1	Bebington	24 May
20'10	6.35	H. Whiteman (Kimbolton)		2	Market Harborough	14 Jul
20'10	6.35	M.J.Ryan (Limerick/IRL)		1	Limerick, IRL	16 Jul
20'10	6.35	Horace Strachan (LAC)	21.09.55	2=	Northampton	4 Aug
20'10	6.35	W. McPherson (Arthurlee)		1	Govan	23 Aug
20'10	6.35	Frederick Betty (Weston-super-Mare)	57	2	Taunton	18 Sep

Exhibition Jumps
22'9	6.93	Lockton		ex	London (LB)	24 May
21'4½	6.52	Elliott		ex	London (LB) AAC	7 Apr

Long Jump: Highland & Border

21'4	6.50	p	John Low (Monymusk)	19.01.57	1	Craigevar	11 Aug
21'3	6.48	p	William Young (Alva)	c53	1	Thornhill	28 Jun
21'1	6.43	p	David Johnstone (Alva)	1.05.57	2	Thornhill	28 Jun
21'0	6.40	p	Daniel Lamont (Kilbarchan)	c55	3	Thornhill	28 Jun

Triple Jump

46'0	14.02		Robert Coll (Bruree/IRL)	54	1	Ardpatrick, IRL	Aug
44'6	13.56		Dominick Tully (Dunmore/IRL)	59	1	Dunmore, IRL	early Jun
44'0	13.41		Coll		1	Bruff, IRL	25 Feb
41'10¾	12.77		William Kelly (QC Cork/IRL)		1	Cork, IRL	22 Apr
41'6½	12.66		J. O'Connor (Limerick/IRL)		1	Kilfinane, IRL	3 Jul
41'5	12.62		John Parsons (Edinburgh U)	10.07.59	1	St Andrews	22 Mar
41'5	12.62		Thomas Ashley (IRL)	c55	1	Campbelltown	10 May
41'0	12.50		Adam McLeod		2	Campbelltown	10 May
40'11½	12.48		R. Kent (Limerick/IRL)		2	Kilfinane, IRL	3 Jul

Triple Jump: Highland & Border

49'1	14.96	p	Thomas Aitken (Walkerburn)	23.05.53	1	Bridge of Allan	2 Aug
48'10	14.88	p	David Johnstone (Alva)	1.05.57	2	Bridge of Allan	2 Aug
48'8	14.83	p	William Young (Alva)	c53	3	Bridge of Allan	2 Aug
48'7	14.81	p	Daniel Lamont (Kilbarchan)	c55	4	Bridge of Allan	2 Aug
48'3	14.71	p	Aitken		1	Rothesay	22 Aug
47'2	14.38	p	Lamont		2	Rothesay	22 Aug
46'11	14.30	p	Aitken		1	Innerleithen	30 Aug
46'6	14.17	p	John Low (Monymusk)	19.01.57	1	Craigevar	11 Aug
46'5½	14.16	p	Johnstone		1	Thornhill	28 Jun
46'4	14.12	p	Johnstone		1	Milnathort	28 Jul
46'3	14.10	p	Aitken		1	Milngavie	6 Sep
46'2	14.07	p	Lamont		2	Thornhill	28 Jun
46'2	14.07	p	Aitken		2	Milnathort	28 Jul
46'0	14.02	p	Lamont		1	Birnam	28 Aug
45'11	14.00	p	Lamont		1	Balfron	19 Jul
			(15/5)				
45'10	13.97	p	Adam Scott (Swinton)	15.08.52	1	Swinton	20 Jun
45'6	13.87	p	Robert Knox (Newstead)	17.09.47	1	Hawick	6 Jun
45'5	13.84	p	E. Andrews (Edinburgh)		2	Innerleithen	30 Aug
45'2	13.77	p	William McGuire (Dunblane)	c58	2	Balfron	19 Jul
44'8	13.61	p	Thomas Webster (Dundee)		3	Milnathort	28 Jul
44'6½	13.58	p	George Black (Dumfries)		2	Dumfries	24 Jul
44'6	13.56	p	John Wilson (Edinburgh)	c46	1	Dalkeith	11 Oct
44'3	13.49	p	Peter Cameron (Kincardine O'Neil)	8.12.52	1	Aberdeen (CC)	19 Jul
43'10	13.36	p	James Rush (Barrhead)	c52	3	Birnam	28 Aug
43'5	13.23	p	James Millar (Bridge of Allan)		1	Bridge of Allan (local)	2 Aug
43'5	13.23	p	Adam Marshall (Dundee)	c52	2=	Renton	13 Sep
43'5	13.23	p	J. Watson		2=	Renton	13 Sep
43'1	13.13	p	Robert Borland (Kilbarchan)	19.01.58	3	Milngavie	6 Sep
42'0	12.80	p	James Thomson (Culter)		2	Craigevar	11 Aug
41'10	12.75	p	David Suttie (Alyth)	c51	1	Glenisla	22 Aug
41'7	12.67	p	James Ballantyne (Glasgow)		3	Balfron	19 Jul
41'7	12.67	p	P. McDonald (Bonhill)		2	Alexandria	30 Aug
41'5	12.62	p	James Lundin (Kirriemuir)		2	Glenisla	22 Aug

Note: The Bridge of Allan jumps must be regarded with reserve. Reports speak of a sloping field.

Shot

41'3	12.57		Maurice Davin (Suir RC/IRL)	29.06.42	1	Dublin (LR) IRL ICAC	2 Jun
39'8	12.09		B. Finn (Balla/IRL)		1	Balla, IRL	19 Sep
39'5	12.01		William Winthrop (LAC)	15.06.52	1	London (SB) LAC	14 Jun
39'4	11.99		M. McCaulay (Ballyclare CC/IRL)		1	Ballymena, IRL	24 Sep
39'2	11.94		Tom Phillips (Balla/IRL)		2	Balla, IRL	19 Sep
39'0	11.89		Robert Coll (Bruree/IRL)	54	1	Bruff, IRL	25 Feb
39'0	11.89		T. Smith (Mountmellick/IRL)		1	Mountmellick, IRL	23 Jun
39'0	11.89		J. Carruth (Ballymena CC/IRL)		2	Ballymena, IRL	24 Sep
			(8/8)				
38'11	11.86		M. Lawler (Borris/IRL)		1	Borris, IRL	9 Jul
38'8	11.79		Arthur East (CU)	3.11.57	1	Cambridge	21 Mar
38'7	11.76		J.M.Cole (QC Belfast/IRL)		1	Belfast, IRL	2 May
38'5½	11.72		William Kelly (QC Cork/IRL)		1	Ennis, IRL	29 Jul
38'3	11.66		Patrick Davin (Suir RC/IRL)	4.06.57	1	Kilkenny, IRL	16 Jul
37'10	11.53		Patrick Nally (Balla/IRL)	56	2hc	Ballina, IRL	24 Jul

37'9	11.51		D. Browning (IRL)			1	Limerick, IRL	5 Jun
37'6½	11.44		George Ross (Patricroft)		2.03.59	1	Widnes	20 Jun
37'0	11.28		John Orford (St Thomas's H)		57	1	London (SB)	2 Jul
36'8½	11.19		Lindsay Bury (CU)		8.07.57	2	Cambridge	7 Mar
36'8	11.18		T. Boyle (Royal Irish Const/IRL)			1hc	Ballina, IRL	24 Jul
36'5	11.10		W.M.Massey jun.			1	Weston-super-Mare	7 Jul
36'1	11.00		T. Healy (Callan/IRL)			2	Kilkenny, IRL	16 Jul
36'0	10.97		Wyndham Evanson (Civil Service)		51	1	London (LB)	24 May

With follow:

41'11	12.78		W. Kelly			1	Cork, IRL	22 Apr
41'7	12.67		M.P.Kelly (QC Cork/IRL)			2	Cork, IRL	22 Apr

Shot: Highland & Border
Includes 16lb stone

48'0	14.63	p	Donald Dinnie (Stonehaven)		8.06.37	1	Milngavie	6 Sep
45'7	13.89	p	Owen Duffy (Edinburgh/IRL)		c47	2	Milngavie	6 Sep
45'2	13.77	p	Dinnie			1	Birmingham ALG)	2 Aug
45'0	13.72	p	Kenneth McRae (Nairn)		50	1	Errol	29 Aug
44'8	13.61	p	Dinnie			1hc	Forfar (heavy)	8 Aug
44'6	13.56	p	Dinnie			1	Aberdeen (CC)	21 Jul
43'10	13.36	p	John Anderson (Edinburgh)			1	Comrie (local)	22 Aug
43'8	13.31	p	Dinnie			1	Aboyne	3 Sep
43'3	13.18	p	Anderson			1	Comrie	22 Aug
43'3	13.18	p	McRae			3	Milngavie	6 Sep
43'1	13.13	p	William McDuff (Dunkeld)		c51	2	Comrie	22 Aug
42'6*	12.95	p	Francis Boyne (Disblane)		c59	1	Udny	20 Aug
41'10	12.75	p	Dinnie			1	Falkirk	26 Jul
41'8	12.70	p	James Fleming (Blair Atholl)		18.09.40	2	Aberdeen (CC)	21 Jul
41'8	12.70	p	Anderson			2	Falkirk	26 Jul
41'6*	12.65	p	Dinnie			1	Perth	4 Oct
40'1	12.22	p	George Mearns (Aberdeen)			3	Aberdeen (CC)	21 Jul
				(17/8)				
39'2	11.94	p	William Bremner (Leochel-Cushnie)		3.01.47	1	Kildrummy	28 Aug
39'0	11.89	p	Alexander Grant (Lyngarrie)			1	Grantown	29 Aug
39'0	11.89	p	David Milne (Forfar)		28.12.42	1	Mearns	30 Aug
38'9	11.81	p	George Bowie (Newmachar)		1.09.56	2	Aberdeen (RG)	21 Jul
37'11*	11.56	p	William McInnes (Edinburgh)			1	Johnstone	19 Jul
37'7	11.46	p	D. McLaren (Balquhidder)			2	Comrie (local)	22 Aug
37'3	11.35	p	Adam Scott (Coldstream)		15.08.52	1	Swinton	20 Jun
36'11	11.25	p	Adam Hay (Glenbucket)			2	Ballater	20 Aug
36'10	11.23	p	John McHattie (Aberdeen)			3	Aberdeen (RG)	21 Jul
36'8	11.18	p	William Rust (Drumoak)		1.01.55	3	Ballater	20 Aug
36'7*	11.15	p	Robert Gray (Udny)			2	Udny	20 Aug
36'4	11.07	p	James Smith (Kildrummy)			2=	Kildrummy	28 Aug
36'4	11.07	p	John Smith (Speybridge)			2=	Kildrummy	28 Aug
36'2*	11.02	p	William Stables (Udny)		1.08.59	3	Udny	20 Aug

Note: * correct weight assumed from evidence of other years.

Exhibition

43'1	13.13	p	Dinnie			ex	London (LB)	AAC	7 Apr

Weight unstated

49'7	15.11	p	Dinnie			1	Rothesay (light)	22 Aug
48'7	14.81	p	Duffy			2	Rothesay (light)	22 Aug
47'7	14.50	p	Duffy			1	Alexandria (heavy)	30 Aug
46'8	14.22	p	Duffy			1	Renton (heavy)	13 Sep
46'6	14.17	p	Dinnie			2	Alexandria (heavy)	30 Aug
42'3	12.88	p	Alexander McKay (Taynuilt)			1	Oban (local/light)	9 Sep
41'9	12.73	p	McRae			1	Fochabers	26 Sep
40'10	12.45	p	James C. Thomson (Fochabers)		7.06.61	1	Fochabers (local)	26 Sep
40'3	12.27	p	Dugald Sinclair (Oban)			2	Oban (local/light)	9Sep
40'2	12.24	p	Donald Mackenzie (Braes)			1	Portree (light)	3 Sep
40'2	12.24	p	John McGregor (Glasgow)			3	Alexandria (heavy)	30 Aug
				(11/8)				
39'3	11.96	p	R. Johnstone (Alva)			1	Clackmannan	26 Jun

39'2	11.94	p	R. Scott (Crossford)		1	Crossford	20 Sep
39'1	11.91	p	William McLean (Fochabers)		2	Fochabers (local)	26 Sep
39'0	11.89	p	John Robertson (Aberdeen)		1	Culter (heavy)	9 Aug
38'6	11.73	p	Alexander Brown (Elgin)		1	Elgin	1 Jan
38'6	11.73	p	James Thomson (Fochabers)	22.07.56	3	Fochabers (local)	26 Sep
37'1	11.30	p	William Meldrum (Pitmedden)		3	Inverness (heavy)	18 Sep
36'10	11.23	p	Duncan McRae		2	Clackmannan	26 Jun
36'10	11.23	p	Rust		2	Culter (heavy)	9 Aug
36'8	11.18	p	James Walker (Muchalls)		1	Muchalls (light)	26 Jul

17½lb

38'7	11.76	p	J. Douglas (Stonehaven)		1	Aberdeen (RG)	19 Jul

19lb

40'8	12.40		George Davidson (Drumoak)	19.11.54	1	Providence, RI, USA	27 Aug

22lb by performer

44'2	13.46	p	Duffy		1	Leith	9 Aug
41'0	12.50	p	Dinnie		1=hc	Dundee	19 Jul
39'0	11.89	p	K. McRae		1=hc	Dundee	19 Jul
37'6	11.43	p	Anderson		2	Crieff	23 Aug

Doubtful

54'0	16.46	p	Dinnie		1	Elgin	20 Sep
51'0	15.54	p	K. McRae		2	Elgin	20 Sep
49'0	14.94	p	Joseph McHardy (Glenlivet)		3	Elgin	20 Sep
48'9	14.86	p	Duffy		1	Bridge of Allan	2 Aug
47'5	14.45	p	Dinnie		2hc	Greenock	14 Jun
45'9	13.94	p	Anderson		2	Bridge of Allan	2 Aug
44'9	13.64	p	K. McRae		3	Bridge of Allan	2 Aug
44'5½	13.55	p	Duffy		1	Inverness	18 Sep
44'2	13.46	p	K. McRae		2	Inverness	18 Sep
43'7	13.28	p	Davidson		1hc	Greenock	14 Jun
43'0	13.11	p	McGregor		3hc	Greenock	14 Jun
41'6	12.65	p	John Cameron (Leith)		4	Bridge of Allan	2 Aug
36'6	11.13	p	Donald White (Greenock)		1	Greenock (local)	14 Jun

Hammer

117'1½	35.70		Arthur East (CU)	3.11.57	1	London (LB) OvC	4 Apr
110'3	33.60		Bertram Latter (OU)	11.08.58	2	London (LB) OvC	4 Apr
110'0	33.53		James Tobin (Mullinahone/IRL)		1	Thurles, IRL	26 Jun
106'0	32.31		James Slattery (Carrick-on Suir/IRL)		2	Thurles, IRL	26 Jun
105'9	32.23		East		1	Cambridge	21 Mar
105'5	32.13		Lindsay Bury (CU)	8.07.57	2	Cambridge	21 Mar
102'0	31.09		Bury		1	Cambridge	18 Nov
101'10	31.04		Neil McDonald (Glasgow Alexandra AC)	c54	1	Glasgow (Alex)	7 Jun
101'10	31.04		P. Kennedy (Tybroughney/IRL)		1	Tybroughney, IRL	18 Nov
100'6	30.63		Maurice Davin (Suir RC/IRL)	29.06.42	wo	Dublin (LR) IRL ICAC	2 Jun
100'0	30.48		Bury		3	London (LB) OvC	4 Apr
			(11/8)				
99'0	30.18		G. Bailey (Mountmellick/IRL)		1	Mountmellick, IRL	23 Jun
97'3	29.64		William Winthrop (LAC)	15.06.52	1	London (SB)	28 Jun
96'9	29.49		William A. Burgess (ex-OU)	27.12.46	1	London (SB) LAC	14 Jun
96'0	29.26		E.S.Reeves (Mountmellick/IRL)		2	Mountmellick, IRL	23 Jun
94'10	28.91		Walter Lawrence (OU)	20.05.59	1	Oxford	3 Mar
93'6	28.50		Henry Johnston (Edinburgh U)	13.09.56	1	Edinburgh (ACG)	5 Jul

Exhibition

116'7½	35.55		Davin		ex	Dublin (LR) IRL ICAC	2 Jun

One-handed, with hammer of unrestricted length, with follow.

Hammer: Highland & Border

120'6	36.73	p	Kenneth McRae (Beauly)	50	1	Inverness	18 Sep
117'6*	35.81	p	Donald Dinnie (Stonehaven)	8.06.37	1	Aberfeldy	16 Aug
116'8½	35.57	p	John Ogg (Banff/NZL)	7.08.47	3hc	Dunedin, NZL	2 Jan
116'3	35.43	p	Dinnie		1	Birmingham (ALG)	2 Aug
115'3*	35.13	p	Dinnie		1	Perth	4 Oct

113'4	34.54	p	Dinnie		2hc	Dundee	19 Jul
112'8*	34.34	p	McRae		2	Aberfeldy	16 Aug
112'2*	34.19	p	Dinnie		1	Birnam	28 Aug
110'7	33.71	p	Dinnie		1	Pitcairngreen	9 Aug
110'3*	33.60	p	Dinnie		1	Luss	29 Aug
109'9	33.45	p	Duncan Ross (Glasgow/CAN)	16.03.55	1	Philadelphia, USA	28 Jul
109'6*	33.38	p	William McInnes (Edinburgh)		1	Johnstone	19 Jul
109'4	33.32	p	Dinnie		1	Oban	10 Sep
109'1*	33.25	p	McRae		2	Birnam	28 Aug
109'0*	33.22	p	McRae		1	Edzell	26 Jul
108'6	33.07	p	McRae		1hc	Dundee	19 Jul
108'0	32.92	p	George Davidson (Drumoak)	19.11.54	2	Philadelphia, USA	28 Jul
107'7	32.79	p	Dinnie		1	Milngavie	6 Sep
107'1	32.64	p	Dinnie		1	Aboyne	3 Sep
107'0	32.61	p	David Milne (Forfar)	28.12.42	1	Mearns	30 Aug
			(20/7)				
104'10*	31.95	p	William Fleming (Aberdeen)	22.08.42	3	Aberfeldy	16 Aug
103'5	31.52	p	Alexander McKay (Taynuilt)		1	Oban (local)	9 Sep
102'0*	31.09	p	John Christie (Coupar Angus)		3hc	Forfar (heavy)	8 Aug
101'0*	30.78	p	D. Burness (Mains of Letham)		1hc	Forfar (heavy)	8 Aug
100'6*	30.63	p	James Fleming (Ballinluig)	18.09.40	2	Edzell	26 Jul
100'4	30.58	p	William Meldrum (Pitmedden)		2	Inverness	18 Sep
100'0	30.48	p	John Grant (Mearns)		2	Mearns	30 Aug
99'11	30.45	p	James Melrose (Peebles/USA)	17.04.47	3	Philadelphia, USA	28 Jul
99'6*	30.33	p	J. Horn (Glasgow)		2	Johnstone	19 Jul
99'6*	30.33	p	Alexander Stewart (Dumbarrow)		2hc	Forfar (heavy)	8 Aug
99'1*	30.20	p	William McDuff (Strathbraan)	c51	4	Aberfeldy	16 Aug
98'10	30.12	p	William Bremner (Leochel-Cushnie)	3.01.47	1	Lumphanan	19 Jul
98'3	29.95	p	John McLean (Oban)		2	Oban (local)	9 Sep
97'10	29.82	p	Harry Macdonald (Viewfield)		1	Portree (light)	3 Sep
96'8*	29.46	p	W. Stewart (Glasgow)		3	Johnstone	19 Jul
96'6	29.41	p	John McCall (Oban)		3	Oban (local)	9 Sep
96'6	29.41	p	Owen Duffy (Edinburgh/IRL)	c47	3	Inverness	18 Sep
96'0	29.26	p	John Robertson (Mearns)		3	Mearns	30 Aug
95'10*	29.21	p	T. Stewart (Mountboy)		1	Edzell (local)	26 Jul
95'9	29.18	p	Francis Boyne (Disblane)	c59	2	Lumphanan	19 Jul
95'9	29.18	p	John Anderson (Edinburgh)		1	Comrie	22 Aug

Note: *correct weight assumed from evidence of other years.

Weight unstated

124'2	37.85	p	Dinnie		1	Alexandria (heavy)	30 Aug
122'0	37.19	p	McRae		2	Alexandria (heavy)	30 Aug
116'6	35.51	p	Dinnie		1	Rothesay (light)	22 Aug
116'0	35.36	p	A. McKay		3	Alexandria (heavy)	30 Aug
115'11	35.33	p	McRae		1	Tomintoul	20 Aug
114'10	35.00	p	McRae		1	Nairn	9 Aug
114'10	35.00	p	McRae		2	Rothesay (light)	22 Aug
111'0	33.83	p	Dinnie		1	Errol	31 Jul
108'10	33.17	p	W. Fleming		2	Tomintoul	20 Aug
108'5	33.05	p	Bremner		1	Colquhonnie	19 Aug
107'3	32.69	p	Davidson		2	Errol	31 Jul
107'1½	32.65	p	Robert Smith (Gragganmore)		1	Lossiemouth	14 Jun
106'2	32.36	p	Fleming Miller (Rothesay)	23.12.58	1	Rothesay (local/light)	22 Aug
103'3	31.47	p	A. McKinnon (Moyness)		2	Nairn	9 Aug
102'10	31.34	p	John Gruer (Innes House)	19.03.57	2	Lossiemouth	14 Jun
102'2	31.14	p	John McHattie (Aberdeen)		3	Nairn	9 Aug
100'8	30.68	p	R. Scott (Crossford)		1	Crossford	20 Sep
100'6	30.63	p	William McCombie Smith (Blairgowrie)	7.09.47	3	Tomintoul	20 Aug
100'4	30.58	p	J. Taylor (Birnie)		3	Lossiemouth	14 Jun
97'0	29.57	p	J.D.Eaton		1	Jarrow	7 Jun
96'9	29.49	p	George Calder (Stonehaven)		1	Muchalls (heavy)	26 Jul

17lb

105'0	32.00	p	Dinnie		1	Blairgowrie	23 Jul
101'0	30.78	p	McRae		2	Blairgowrie	23 Jul

94'0	28.65	p	William Shaw		3	Blairgowrie	23 Jul

18lb

107'4	32.72	p	Dinnie		1	Aberdeen (CC)	21 Jul
102'6	31.24	p	McRae		1	Fochabers	26 Sep

20lb

101'8	30.99	p	Dinnie		1	Crieff	23 Aug
98'8	30.07	p	McRae		2	Crieff	23 Aug

Light hammer doubtful

115'11	35.33	p	Calder		1	Muchalls (light)	26 Jul
110'6	33.68	p	James Walker (Muchalls)		2	Muchalls (light)	26 Jul
106'10	32.56	p	James Black (Netherley)		3	Muchalls (light)	26 Jul

Other Events

120 Yards

12.0		Charles Lockton (LAC)	2.07.56	1hc	London (SB)	4 Oct

150 Yards

15.2		Charles Lockton (LAC)	2.07.56	1hc	London (SB)	10 May

300 Yards

32.8		Frederick Fellowes (Burton FC)	12.02.58	1	Burton-on-Trent	17 May

600 Yards

1:18.0		Walter George (Worcester BC)	9.09.58	1	Birmingham (ALG)	10 May

¾ Mile

3:15.0	p	William Cummings (Paisley)	10.06.58	int	London (LB)	6 Dec
In 1 mile race						

1½ Miles

7:00.6	p	William Cummings (Paisley)	10.06.58	1hc	Gorton, Manchr	31 May

20 Miles

2:01.09.4	p	David Livingstone (Tranent)	10.11.55	1	Swansea	2 Jun
2:08:18.0		Percy Stenning (LAC)	31.08.54	int	London (SB)	5 Apr
In a 60 miles race.						

25 Miles

2:37:28.0	p	Thomas Herbert (Barrow-in-Furness)	c53	int	London (LB)	20 Oct
2:48:42.0		Percy Stenning (LAC)	31.08.54	int	London (SB)	26 Dec
Each in a 50 mile race						

30 Miles

3:18:17.0	p	James Bailey (Sittingbourne)	2.05.52	1	London (LB)	20 Oct
3:25:37.0		Percy Stenning (LAC)	31.08.54	int	London (SB)	26 Dec
Each in a 50 mile race						

40 Miles

4:50:12.0		George Dunning (Clapton Beagles)	15.07.55	int	London (SB)	26 Dec
In a 50 mile race						

50 Miles

6:14:47.0 i p		George Hazael (Deptford)	22.11.44	int	London (Ag Hall)	21 Apr
In a 6 day race, indoors						
6:38:41.0		Francis Firminger (LAC)	56	1	London (SB)	26 Dec

100 Miles

15:35:31.0 i p		George Hazael (Deptford)	22.11.44	int	London (Ag Hall)	21/22 Apr
In a 6 day race, indoors						

1 Mile Walk

7:00.75	p	Charles Baynard (Bloomsbury)	48	1	London (LB)	13 Oct

2 Miles Walk

13:54.8		Harry Webster (Stoke Victoria AC)	14.05.54	1hc	Preston	12 Jul

7 Miles Walk

52:02.0	p	Henry Thatcher (Henley-on-Thames)	13.04.53	int	London (LB)	6 Oct
In a 3 hour race regarded as unfair walking by *Bell's Life*						

52:34.5	Harry Webster (Stoke Victoria AC)	14.05.54	wo	London (LB)	AAC	7 Apr

50 Miles Walk

8:25:25.5	Archibald Sinclair (North London AC)	c50	wo	London (LB)	17 Nov

100 Miles Walk

18:08:20.0 p   William Howes (Felthorpe)   03.39   int   London (Ag Hall) 22/23 Feb
In a 26 hour race, indoors

Cricket Ball

117y 2ft 7in 107.77   George Ashburner (Barrow-in-Furness)   12.60   1   Barrow-in-Furness   5 Jul

Left: Walter Goodall George, arguably the greatest distance runner of the nineteenth century, was at the start of his career in the years we have covered. In 1879 he did the double of winning the mile and 4 miles in the rival LAC Championships and then repeated the feat in 1880 at the first-ever AAA Championships.

Right: Donald Dinnie, with 345 listings, is by far the most featured athlete in the lists, including shot and hammer in every year, yet his entire career had a much wider span. He started in 1853 at 16 and was still winning as a veteran at Nairn in 1910 when 73. He won over 11,000 prizes. The surge in popularity of the games in Scotland and abroad was due in large measure to Dinnie. Not only was he supreme in all the throwing events, including the caber, but he was also a fine wrestler, runner and jumper. He claimed to have high jumped 6ft 1in at Turriff Games in September, 1860, but the only report so far discovered, in the Banffshire Journal, had it as 5ft 11in.

1880 UK Year List

100 Yards

10.0		Edward Lucas (CU)	15.02.60	1	Cambridge	9 Mar
10.0		Melville Portal (RMC Sandhurst)	9.12.56	1	Camberley	15 May
10.0	p	H. Russell (Bristol)		1h2hcp	Taunton	15 Jul
10 1/5		Lucas		1ht2	Cambridge	8 Mar
10 1/5		Lucas		1	London (LB) OvC	19 Mar
10 1/5		Patrick Davin (Carrick AAC/IRL)	4.06.57	1	Dublin (LR) IRL ICAC	17 May
10 1/5		Harry Massey (LAC)	c57	1	Birmingham (ALG)	22 May
10 1/5		Thomas Malone (Tradaree AC/IRL)	26.12.59	1hc	Limerick, IRL	15 Jun
10 1/5		Malone		1	Limerick, IRL	15 Jun
10 1/5		Charles Lockton (LAC)	2.07.56	1	London (SB)	26 Jun
10 1/5		Lockton		1ht7hc	London (SB)	26 Jun
10 1/5		William Phillips (LAC)	5.08.58	1	London (LB) AAA	3 Jul
10 1/5		James Cowie (LAC)	21.09.59	1hc	London (LB)	10 Jul
10 1/5		W. Garbutt (N. Durham CC)		1ht	Gateshead	12 Jul
10 1/5		Garbutt		1	Gateshead	12 Jul
10 1/5		Montague Shearman (OU)	7.04.57	1	Stoke-on-Trent	3 Aug
10 1/5		Lucas		1	Cambridge	13 Nov
10 1/5		George Hoffmeister (CU)	10.10.58	1	Cambridge	26 Nov
		(18/12)				
10 ¼		William Beveridge (Edinburgh U)	27.11.58	1	Glasgow (Alex)	1 May
10 ¼		Robert Climie (Ayr FC)	4.11.58	1	Kilmarnock	26 Jun
10 ¼		Edward Chalk (Linton)	61	1ht2	Saffron Walden	2 Aug
10.3	e	Sir Savile Crossley (OU)	14.06.57	2	London (LB) OvC	19 Mar
10 2/5		Allan Steel (CU)	24.09.58	1	Cambridge	21 Feb
10 2/5		Charles Cave (OU)	17.03.61	1ht1	Oxford	6 Mar
10 2/5		Wilfred Bayley (CU)	1.06.59	1ht1	Cambridge	8 Mar
10 2/5		Thomas Clulee (Stourbridge FC)	c57	1hc	Coleshill	29 Mar
10 2/5		Arthur Smith (Birkenhead)	c55	1=	Belfast, IRL	29 Mar
10 2/5		J. Cummins (IRL)		1=	Belfast, IRL	29 Mar
10 2/5		George Mackay (St Andrews U)		1	St Andrews	3 Apr
10 2/5		John Parsons (Edinburgh U)	10.07.59	1	Glasgow (Ac)	1 May
10.4	e	J. Mitchell (Glasgow Alexandra AC)		2	Glasgow (Alex)	1 May
10.4	e	Thomas Lynch (ICAC/IRL)	25.03.59	2	Dublin (LR) IRL ICAC	17 May
10 2/5		Tom Pank (Moseley H)	59	1	Birmingham (ALG)	5 Jun
10 2/5		Francis Cleaver (Nottm Forest FC)	58	1	Huddersfield	26 Jun
10 2/5		George Christian (ICAC/IRL)	6.09.57	1	Carlow, IRL	27 Jul
10 2/5		John Belcher (ex-QC Cork/IRL)	28.06.55	1hc	San Francisco, USA	7 Aug
10 2/5		John Saxton (Broughton FC)		1=	Southport NCAA	14 Aug
10.4	e	Francis Ware (CU)	25.04.58	2	Cambridge	13 Nov

School Sports

10 1/5		Green (Bedford County Sch)		1	Bedford	10 Apr
10 ¼		David Simson (Fettes Coll)	21.01.61	1	Edinburgh	nd

"… seems to be almost too good for a grass course" (*Fettes College Register*)

10 2/5		A.G.Edwards (Friars Sch)		1	Bangor, Gwynedd	14 Apr

Doubtful

10.0		Phillips		1	Woodbridge	29 Mar

Windy and downhill

10.0		T. Smith (HMS St Vincent)		1	Portsmouth	13 Aug
10.0		R. Fryer (Royal Artillery)		1	Portsmouth	14 Aug

Timing apparently to nearest second

10.0		Francis Lucas (CU)	16.05.62	1	Cambridge	16 Nov

'Had the best of the start and a strong rear wind'

10 1/5		F. Lucas		1	Cambridge	3 Nov

'A gale of a wind behind them'

10 2/5		Frederic Searight (Lansdowne FC/IRL)	c59	1hthc	Dungannon, IRL	31 Aug

Irish Sportsman & Farmer reports it with a (?)

10.4	e	Edgar Storey (CU)	6.02.59	2	Cambridge	16 Nov

'Strong rear wind'

Notes

Crossley 2ft down on 10.2; Mitchell 1¼y down on 10.2; Ware 1y down on 10.2; Lynch 1½y down on 10.2; Storey 3y down on 10.0. Russell on 15/07 was afterwards disqualified as a professional.

220 Yards

22 3/5	Thomas Clulee (Stourbridge FC)	c57	1ht4hc	Birmingham (ALG)	12 Jun
23.0	Melville Portal (RMC Sandhurst)	9.12.56	1	Camberley	14 May
23.0	Clulee		1ht1hc	Northampton	2 Aug
23.0 e	Clulee		2hc	Northampton	2 Aug
23.1 e	John Belcher (ex-QC Cork/IRL)	28.06.55	2	Oakland, Ca, USA	9 Oct
23 1/5	Harry Massey (St Thomas's H)	c57	1	London (SB)	30 Jun
23 2/5	Arthur Smith (LAC/Birkenhead)	c55	1	Belfast, IRL	7 May
23 ½	Edward Wolfe (Armagh/IRL)	c59	1	Lurgan, IRL	21 Aug
23 ½	J. Douglas (Northampton AC)		1ht3hc	Blisworth	6 Sep
23.5 e	Belcher		2	San Francisco, USA	11 Sep
23.6 e	Thomas Guinness (King's Coll Hosp/IRL)	15.03.59	2	London (SB)	30 Jun
23.7 e	George Dodd (St Thomas's H)	14.06.57	3	London (SB)	30 Jun
23 4/5	Portal		1	London (LB)	27 May
24.0 e	Thomas Lynch (Dublin/IRL)	25.03.59	2	Belfast, IRL	7 May
24.0 e	Arthur Lavers (University Coll, London)	19.01.60	3hc	London (SB)	15 May
24.0	C. Caufield (Fareham)		1	Fareham	14 Jul
24.0 e	Herbert Sturt (LAC)	24.07.56	2ht1hc	London (SB)	31 Jul

School sports

23.0	Rev Foulkes		1	Bath	25 Sep

Invitation race at Grosvenor School sports.

Downhill

23 ½	Belcher		1hc	San Francisco, USA	6 Mar

Notes: Clulee 2y down on 22.75; Belcher 2ft down on 23.0 (9/10) & 4y down on 23.0 (11/09); Guinness 3y down on 23.2; Dodd 4y down on 23.2; Lynch 3y down on 23.6; Lavers 1½y down on 23.8; Sturt 3y down on 23.6.

440 Yards

50.2	Melville Portal (RMC Sandhurst)	9.12.56	1	Camberley		15 May
50.6	John Belcher (ex-QC Cork/IRL)	28.06.55	1	Oakland, Ca, USA		9 Oct
50.75	Walter Lovegrove (Maidenhead FC)	57	1hc	Maidenhead		5 Jun
51.0	Edward Growse (OU)	8.07.60	1	Oxford		6 Mar
51.0	Montague Shearman (LAC)	7.04.57	1	London (SB)		26 Jun
51.0	William Phillips (LAC)	5.08.58	1ht2	London (LB)	AAA	3 Jul
51.2	Reginald Macaulay (CU)	24.08.58	1	Cambridge		10 Mar
51.2 e	John Goodliffe (Huntingdon)		3hc	Market Harborough		12 Jul
51.3 e	William Bruce (OU)	15.01.58	2	Oxford		6 Mar
51.3 e	Sidney Baker (LAC)	17.06.58	2	London (SB)		26 Jun
51.3 e	Baker		2=ht2	London (LB)	AAA	3 Jul
51.3 e	Henry Ball (LAC)	10.04.59	2=ht2	London (LB)	AAA	3 Jul
	(12/11)					
51.4 e	William Beverley (OU)	18.04.59	3	Oxford		6 Mar
51.4	Arthur Smith (LAC/Birkenhead)	c55	1	London (SB)		6 Nov
51.6 e	Herbert Sturt (LAC)	24.07.56	3	London (SB)		26 Jun
51.6	Thomas Lynch (ICAC/IRL)	25.03.59	1ht1	London (LB)	AAA	3 Jul
51.8	Thomas Guinness (King's Coll Hosp/IRL)	15.03.59	1	London (SB)		30 Jun
52.1 e	William Parry (Moseley H)	c59	2hc	Birmingham (ALG)		26 Jun
52.4 e	James Gregory (CU)	5.08.59	2	Cambridge		10 Mar
52.5 e	Harold Smith (CU)	16.03.58	3hc	Cambridge		14 Feb
52.5 p	Robert Cooper (Birmingham)		1hc	London (Bermondsey)		21 Sep

Notes: Bruce 2y & Beverley 2½y down on 51.0 (06/03); Baker 2½y & Sturt 5y down on 51.0 (26/06); Baker & Ball 2y down on 51.0 (03/07); Goodliffe 3y 6in down on 50.8(12/07); Parry 1ft down on 52.0 (26/06); Gregory 10y down on 51.2 (10/03); H. Smith 14y down on 50.8 (14/02).

880 Yards

2:00.4		Samuel Holman (LAC)	29.01.53	1	London (LB)	AAA	3 Jul
2:00.4		John Sadler (LAC)	14.04.55	1	London (SB)		2 Oct
2:00.6		Sadler		1	London (SB)		30 Apr
2:00.7	e	Sidney Baker (LAC)	17.06.58	2	London (SB)		2 Oct
2:01.0		Walter George (Moseley H)	9.09.58	int	Birmingham (PR)		31 Jul
2:01.3	e	Sadler		2	London (LB)	AAA	3 Jul
2:01.6	e	Holman		3	London (LB)	AAA	3 Jul
2:01.8		George		1hc	Lewes		21 Jul
2:02.0		John Bradshaw (CU)	27.05.60	1	Cambridge		9 Mar
2:02.2		Sadler		1hc	London (SB)		19 May
2:02.2		Thomas Wells (OU)	15.06.61	1	Oxford		8 Mar
2:02.4		Edwin Etheridge (Joint Stock Banks)	59	1	London (Ladywell)		27 Aug
2:02.7	e	Holman		2	London (SB)		30 Apr
2:03.0		Baker		1	Witham		17 May
2:03.0		Henry Uniacke (Newton Abbot)	13.09.62	1	Fareham		14 Jul
2:03.0		Robert Whalley (Widnes AC)	c55	1	Bangor		31 Aug
		(16/9)					
2:03.2	e	William Harvey (CU)	27.01.58	2	Cambridge		9 Mar
2:03.2	e p	Thomas Herbert (Barrow-in-Furness)	c53	3hc	Glasgow (Shaw)		13 Nov
2:03.5	e	John Crewdson (Longsight H)		2=	Bangor		31 Aug
2:03.5	e	C. Spencer Thorn (Wrexham H&H)		2=	Bangor		31 Aug
2:03.5	e p	William Duddle (Preston)	14.03.58	int	Manchester		20 Dec
2:03.9	e	Samuel Hewitt (Newton-le-Willows)	c58	3	Southport	NCAA	14 Aug
2:04.0		Walter Slade (ex-LAC)	6.04.54	int	Melbourne, AUS		9 Nov
2:04.4	e	Bertram Latter (OU)	11.08.58	2	Oxford		8 Mar
2:05.0		Richardson (Spottiswoode's AC)		1	London (Rotherhithe)		13 Nov

800m (i.e. 5y start in 880y handicap)

2:01.6	John Smith (Bury AC)	13.04.55	1	Blackburn		21 Aug

Equates to 2:02.3e for 880y.

Doubtful

1:59.2		Holman		1	Beckenham	10 Jul
1:59.9	e	Baker		2	Beckenham	10 Jul
1:59.9	e	Henry Thomas (Blackheath H)	c52	3	Beckenham	10 Jul

[The Beckenham track was remeasured and found to be 870y. Equates to Holman 2:00.6e, Baker & Thomas 2:01.3e].

2:00.7 e	Arthur Liddal (Clapton Beagles)	c59	2hc	Alexandra Park	25 Sep

['We cannot vouch for the accuracy of the measurement' – *Bell's Life*]

Notes
Baker 2y down on 2:00.4 (02/10); Sadler 6y and Holman 8y down on 2:00.4 (3/07); Harvey 8y down on 2:02.0 (09/03); Holman 15y down on 2:00.6 (30/04); Herbert 8y down on 2:00.75; Crewdson & Thorn 3y down on 2:03.0 Hewitt rather less than 3y down on 2:03.4; Latter 15y down on 2:02.2. Baker & Thomas passed the post 'almost simultaneously' 5y down on 1:59.2 (doubtful 10/07); Liddal 3y down on 2:00.2 (doubtful 25/09). Intermediate times in 1000y (31/07); and mile races.

Mile

4:19.5	p	William Duddle (Preston)	14.03.58	1	Moston Pk, Manchr		20 Dec
4:20.3	e p	Robert Cummins (Cardiff)	c61	2	Moston Pk, Manchr		20 Dec
4:22.6	p	William Cummings (Paisley)	10.06.58	1	London (LB)		10 May
4:23.2		Walter George (Moseley H)	9.09.58	1hc	London (SB)		16 Aug
4:25.25	p	James McLeavy (Alexandria)	26.10.52	1	Glasgow (Shaw)		4 Nov
4:26.25	p	Cummings		1hc	Liverpool		4 Oct
4:27.2		George		1hc	Lewes		21 Jul
4:27.4		Bernhard Wise (OU)	10.02.58	1	Oxford		6 Mar
4:28.0		George		wo	London (LB)	AAA	3 Jul
4:28.8		Wise		1	London (LB)	OvC	19 Mar
4:29.0	p	Cummings		1hc	Swansea		17 May
		(11/6)					
4:30.2		William Hough (CU)	19.12.59	1hc	Cambridge		21 Feb
4:31.0	e	Edward Wright (Widnes FBC)	c57	2hc	Ashbourne		25 Aug
4:32.0		Walter Slade (ex-LAC)	6.04.54	3hc	Melbourne, AUS		9 Nov
4:32.1	e	Alfred Jones (OU)	57	2	Oxford		6 Mar
4:32.8		Samuel Holman (LAC)	29.01.53	1	London (SB)		6 Nov

4:33.4	e p	James Bailey (Sittingbourne)	2.05.52	3hc	Sittingbourne		17 May
4:33.5	e	Thomas Wells (OU)	15.06.61	2	London (LB)	OvC	19 Mar
4:35.0	p	David Livingstone (Tranent)	10.11.55	int	Preston		17 Apr
4:35.2	e	John Bradshaw (CU)	27.05.60	2	Cambridge		8 Mar
4:35.5	e	Robert Norton (Ilminster)	c55	2hc	Taunton		15 Jul
4:36.0		Thomas Bailey (Birchfield H)		1hc	Coleshill		29 Mar
4:36.3	e	Robert Benson (Royal Sch of Mines)	19.10.58	3hc	London (SB)		30 Jun
4:36.8		Frederick Chattaway (LAC)	c57	1	London (SB)		29 May
4:37.1	e	Thomas Shann (CU)	21.09.58	3	Cambridge		8 Mar
4:37.2		John Finlayson (Queen's Park FC)	27.07.54	1hc	Glasgow (Alex)		1 May
4:39.0	e	William Snook (Moseley H)	3.02.61	2	Widnes		19 Jun
4:39.4		Frank Impey (Moseley H)	31.12.58	1	Birmingham (ALG)		22 May
4:39.8		Thomas Crellin (Liverpool AC)	1.01.58	1	Southport	NCAA	14 Aug
4:40.0		James Carmody (Carrick AAC/IRL)		1	Dublin (LR)	IRL ICAC	17 May
4:40.0		George Harris (Stratford-on-Avon)	21.06.60	1hc	Tewkesbury		7 Aug
4:40.0		J.L.Read (Hull AC)		1hc	Hull		21 Aug

Notes
Cummins 5y down on 4:19.5; Wright 1½y down on 4:30.75; Jones 30y down on 4:27.4; Bailey 9y down on 4:32.0; Benson 40y down on 4:30.0 (30/06); Wells 30y down on 4:28.8; Bradshaw 11y & Shann 23y down on 4:33.4; Norton 3y down on 4:35.0; Snook 10y down on 4:37.4.
Intermediate time at 1½ miles (17/04)

2 Miles

9:35.25	p	William Duddle (Preston)	14.03.58	1	Oldham		4 Sep
9:36.0	e p	Nicholas Cox (Bristol)	c56	2	Oldham		4 Sep
9:40.0	p	David Livingstone (Tranent)	10.11.55	int	Preston		12 Jun
9:43.0	p	Livingstone		int	London (LB)		31 May
9:43.2	e p	William Cummings (Paisley)	10.06.58	int	London (LB)		31 May
9:48.0		Walter George (Moseley H)	9.09.58	inthc	London (SB)		6 Sep
9:48.0	p	Cummings		int	London (LB)		25 Oct
9:48.3	e p	Thomas Herbert (Barrow-in-Furness)	c53	int	London (LB)		31 May
9:54.0	p	Robert Sharples (Preston)	22.06.53	1	Darwen		31 Jul
9:57.0		Frank Benson (OU)	4.11.58	int	Oxford		8 Mar
9:59.0	p	Livingstone		1	Manchester (Pom)		2 Jun
			(11/8)				
10:04.0		William Hough (CU)	19.12.59	int	London (LB)	OvC	19 Mar
10:04.0	p	James Bailey (Sittingbourne)	2.05.52	1hc	Sittingbourne		2 Aug
10:04.0	p	William Young (Gloucester)	c54	int	London (LB)		25 Oct
10:10.0		George Dunning (Clapton Beagles)	15.07.55	int	London (SB)		6 Nov
10:12.0		J. Jackson (Holcombe)		1	Darwen		31 Jul
10:17.4		P. Noonan (Rathkeale/IRL)		1	Belfast, IRL		7 May
10:19.0		Percy Stenning (LAC)	31.08.54	int	London (SB)		30 Apr
10:21.7	e	Howard Chesshire (OU)	14.06.57	int	London (LB)	OvC	19 Mar
10:24.0		William Suffell (Clapton Beagles)	59	1hc	London (Barnes)		20 Mar
10:24.0		Charles Rooke (Spartan H)	19.05.53	inthc	Edmonton		17 Jul
10:32.6		A.H.Davies (Blackheath H)		1	Exmouth		20 Sep
10:36.0		William Snook (Moseley H)	3.02.61	1	Southport	NCAA	14 Aug
10:40.0		Reginald Hall (CU)	22.02.60	int	Cambridge		10 Mar

Notes
Cummings must have done under 10:00 (int) running second to Livingstone at Preston (12/06).
Cox 4y down on 9:35.25 (04/09); Cummings 1y (31/05); Herbert 30y down on 9:43.2e; Chesshire 100y down on 10:04.0 (19/03).
Intermediate times in races at 3 (8/03; 10/03; 19/03: 17/07), 4 (12/06; 6/09; 6/11) and 10 miles (30/04; 31/05; 25/10).

3 Miles

14:21.0	p	William Cummings (Paisley)	10.06.58	int	Preston		12 Jun
14:50.0		Walter George (Moseley H)	9.09.58	int	London (SB)		6 Sep
14:53.0	p	David Livingstone (Tranent)	10.11.55	int	London (LB)		31 May
14:53.0	p	Cummings		int	London (LB)		31 May
15:01.0	p	Cummings		int	London (LB)		25 Oct
15:01.2		William Hough (CU)	19.12.59	1	London (LB)	OvC	19 Mar
15:14.0	p	Livingstone		int	Glasgow (Shaw)		26 Jun
15:14.4	e p	Cummings		int	Glasgow (Shaw)		26 Jun

15:15.6 e p	Thomas Herbert (Barrow-in-Furness)	c53	int	London (LB)	31 May
15:16.9 e	Frank Benson (OU)	4.11.58	2	London (LB) OvC	19 Mar
15:20.2	Hough		1hc	Cambridge	27 Feb
15:21.0 p	William Young (Gloucester)	c54	int	London (LB)	25 Oct
15:29.0	George Dunning (Clapton Beagles)	15.07.55	inthc	London (SB)	6 Nov
(13/8)					
15:45.0	Charles Rooke (Spartan H)	19.05.53	1hc	Edmonton	17 Jul
15:48.0	Percy Stenning (LAC)	31.08.54	int	London (SB)	30 Apr
16:01.5 i p	Charles Price (ex-Kennington)	17.05.53	1	New York (MSG) USA	4 Mar
16:02.4	John Walker (CU)	3.12.57	2	Cambridge	10 Mar

Notes
Herbert 130y down on 14:53.0; Benson 90y down on 15:01.2.
Intermediate times in races at 4 (12/06; 6/09; 6/11), 6 (26/06) and 10 miles (30/04; 31/05; 25/10).

4 Miles

19:48.5 p	William Cummings (Paisley)	10.06.58	1	Preston	12 Jun
19:49.6	Walter George (Moseley H)	9.09.58	1hc	London (SB)	6 Sep
19:58.0 p	James McLeavy (Alexandria)	26.10.52	1	Glasgow (Shaw)	11 Nov
19:59.0 p	Cummings		int	London (LB)	31 May
20:09.4 e p	David Livingstone (Tranent)	10.11.55	int	London (LB)	31 May
20:15.3 e p	James Sanderson (Whitworth)	28.12.37	2	Glasgow (Shaw)	11 Nov
20:18.0 p	Cummings		int	London (LB)	25 Oct
20:30.0 p	Cummings		int	Glasgow (Shaw)	26 Jun
20:31.4	George Dunning (Clapton Beagles)	15.07.55	1hc	London (SB)	6 Nov
20:41.0 p	William Young (Gloucester)	c54	int	London (LB)	25 Oct
20:45.8	George		1	London (LB) AAA	3 Jul
(11/7)					
20:52.1 e p	Thomas Herbert (Barrow-in-Furness)	c53	int	London (LB)	31 May
21:05.6 p	Thomas Guy (Whitechapel)	c56	2hc	London (Bow)	18 Oct
21:12.2 e	Charles Cattlin (Blackheath H)	18.04.59	2hc	London (SB)	6 Nov
21:15.0	A.H.Davies (Blackheath H)		2	London (LB) AAA	3 Jul
21:21.0	Percy Stenning (LAC)	31.08.54	int	London (SB)	30 Apr
21:53.0	Harry Burrows (SLH)	c61	int	London (LB)	7 Jul
21:56.0	William Suffell (Clapton Beagles)	59	3	London (LB) AAA	3 Jul
22:09.0 p	James Warburton (Blackburn)	13.11.45	int	Blackburn	29 May
22:21.0	P. Noonan (Rathkeale/IRL)		1	Dublin (LR) IRL ICAC	17 May
22:28.75	William Snook (Pengwern BC)	3.02.61	1hc	Ilkley	7 Aug
22:41.0	John Voelcker (LAC)	24.06.54	int	London (SB)	30 Apr

Notes
Livingstone 60y down on 19:59.0; Sanderson 100y down on 19:58.0; Herbert 240y down on 20:09.4e;
Cattlin 4y down on 20:31.4 from 40sec start.
Intermediate times in races at 6 (26/06),10 (30/04; 31/05; 7/07; 25/10) and 20 miles (29/05).

6 Miles

30:31.0 p	William Cummings (Paisley)	10.06.58	int	London (LB)	31 May
30:37.0 e p	David Livingstone (Tranent)	10.11.55	int	London (LB)	31 May
31:01.0 p	Cummings		1	Glasgow (Shaw)	26 Jun
31:07.0 p	Cummings		int	London (LB)	25 Oct
31:32.0 e p	Thomas Herbert (Barrow-in-Furness)	c53	int	London (LB)	31 May
31:44.0 p	William Young (Gloucester)	c54	int	London (LB)	25 Oct
32:50.0	Percy Stenning (LAC)	31.08.54	int	London (SB)	30 Apr
33:13.0	William Suffell (Clapton Beagles)	59	int	London (LB) AAA	7 Jul
33:13.2 e	Charles Mason (LAC)	3.06.51	int	London (LB) AAA	7 Jul
33:13.8 e	William Snook (Pengwern BC)	3.02.61	int	London (LB) AAA	7 Jul
33:19.5 e	Stenning		int	London (LB) AAA	7 Jul
33:42.5 e	A.H.Davies (Blackheath H)		int	London (LB) AAA	7 Jul

6¼ Miles [10,000m approx]

34:28.0	Stenning		int	London (SB)	30 Apr

Notes
Livingstone 40y & Herbert 340y down on 30:31.0 (31/05); Mason 1y, Snook 4y, Stenning 34y & Davies
154y down on 33:13.0 (07/07).
Intermediate times all in 10 mile races.

10 Miles

Time		Name		Pos	Venue		Date
51:44.8	p	William Cummings (Paisley)	10.06.58	1	London (LB)		31 May
52:53.5	p	David Livingstone (Tranent)	10.11.55	2	London (LB)		31 May
53:07.5	p	Thomas Herbert (Barrow-in-Furness)	c53	3	London (LB)		31 May
53:10.6	p	Cummings		1	London (LB)		25 Oct
54:25.4	p	William Young (Gloucester)	c54	2	London (LB)		25 Oct
56:07.0		Charles Mason (LAC)	3.06.51	1	London (LB)	AAA	7 Jul
56:18.5		William Snook (Pengwern BC)	3.02.61	2	London (LB)	AAA	7 Jul
56:32.0	p	James Warburton (Blackburn)	13.11.45	1	Milford, Mass, USA		24 Jul
56:34.5		Percy Stenning (LAC)	31.08.54	3	London (LB)	AAA	7 Jul
57:05.5	p	Warburton		int	Blackburn		29 May
57:13.2		William Suffell (Clapton Beagles)	59	4	London (LB)	AAA	7 Jul
57:30.0	p	Herbert		int	Newcastle		25 Dec
57:39.4	p	Charles Price (ex-Kennington)	17.05.53	1	Providence, RI, USA		2 Aug
57:43.0	p	Herbert		int	Preston		7 Feb
58:07.0	p	Warburton		int	Radcliffe		17 Apr
58:08.6 e	p	James Bailey (Sittingbourne)	2.05.52	int	Radcliffe		17 Apr

Notes
The *Sporting Chronicle* gave Cummings 51:47.5 on 31/05 and provided the times for Livingstone and Herbert.
Bell's Life used a Benson's chronograph, but gave only the winning time, as shown.
Bailey (17/04) 8y down on 58:07.0.
Intermediate times in 20 mile races.

120 Yards Hurdles

Time		Name		Pos	Venue		Date
16 2/5		George Lawrence (OU)	17.03.59	1	London (LB)	OvC	19 Mar
16 2/5		Lawrence		1	London (LB)	AAA	3 Jul
16.6 e		Charles Gilbert (OU)	9.01.55	2	London (LB)	OvC	19 Mar
16.6 e		Samuel Palmer (ex-CU)	15.12.54	2	London (LB)	AAA	3 Jul
16 3/5		Richard Mallett (Stoke Victoria AC)	14.10.58	1	Ilkley		7 Aug
16 3/5		Frederick Shapley (Exeter)	28.08.55	1	Exmouth		20 Sep
16.8 e		Lewis Jarvis (CU)	3.08.57	3	London (LB)	OvC	19 Mar
16 4/5		Herbert Dugdale (RMC Sandhurst)	3.04.60	1	Camberley		15 May
16 4/5*		Wyndham Evanson (Civil Service)	51	1hc	London (LB)		22 May
16 4/5		William Pollock (St George's Hosp)	2.02.59	1	London (SB)		30 Jun
16.9 e		Wilfred Bayley (CU)	1.06.59	4	London (LB)	OvC	19 Mar
16.9 e		John Reay (LAC)	9.07.53	2hc	London (LB)		22 May
16.9** e		Charles Lockton (LAC)	2.07.56	3hc	London (LB)		22 May
		(13/12)					
17.0		Joseph Orford (Ipswich AFC)	16.08.62	1	Bury St Edmunds		29 Apr
17.0		J.F.Murphy (QC Cork/IRL)		1	Cork, IRL		20 May
17.0		W.H.Darby (Royal Artillery)		1	Portsmouth		14 Aug
17.1 e		George Dodd (St Thomas's H)	14.06.57	2	London (SB)		30 Jun
17.1 e		Francis Cleaver (Nottm Forest FC)	58	2	Ilkley		7 Aug
17.3 e		John Fellowes (OU)	29.04.59	2	Oxford		6 Mar
17 2/5		Patrick Davin (Suir RC/IRL)	4.06.57	1	Dublin (LR) IRL ICAC		17 May

Doubtful
16.3** e Lockton 2ht Norwood 12 Jun
[Doubt over measurement of course, so "palpably absurd" *Bell's Life*]
16 2/5 Lawrence 1 Woodbridge 29 Mar
[Downhill, according to *Bell's Life*]
17.0 R. Fryer (Royal Artillery) 1 Portsmouth 1 Aug
[Times rounded to nearest second]

Notes
* Owed 1y, so ran 121y.
** Ran 136y.
Gilbert 1y, Jarvis 2¼y & Bayley 3¼y down on 16.4: Palmer ¾y down on 16.4 (03/07); Reay ½y & Lockton 2ft
down on 16.8 (22/05); Dodd 1½y down on 16.8 (30/06); Cleaver 3y down on 16.6; Fellowes 2y down on 17.0
(06/03); Lockton 1½y down on 16.0 (12/06).

220 Yards Hurdles

31.0	Patrick Davin (Suir RC/IRL)	4.06.57	1	Monasterevin, IRL	21 Sep
32.0	Richard Power (Ballylaneen/IRL)	c55	1	Ballylaneen, IRL	9 Oct
32.6	W. O'Shea (Tybroughney/IRL)		1	Tybroughney, IRL	29 Oct
33.0	H.H.Green (ex-Bedford)		1hc	Willesden	11 Sep

440 Yards Hurdles

1:03.3		M. Ryan (Nenagh/IRL)		1	Nenagh, IRL	14 Jul
1:03.3 e		P. Burke (QC Cork/IRL)		2	Nenagh, IRL	14 Jul
1:07.0		Arthur Mullins (RMA Woolwich)	1.02.61	1	Woolwich	21 May
1:08.0 e		Joseph Hanwell (RMA Woolwich)	c61	2=	Woolwich	21 May
1:08.0 e		Charles Cowie (RMA Woolwich)	20.04.61	2=	Woolwich	21 May
1:08.75 p		Thomas Aitken (ex-Walkerburn)	23.05.53	1	Brooklyn, NY, USA	6 Aug

Described as a 440y steeplechase in *Bell's Life*

1:04.6		James Concannon (Widnes)	c56	1	Belfast, IRL	7 May
1:05.4 e		James Neill (Ulster CC/IRL)		2	Belfast, IRL	7 May
1:06.4		Edward Wolfe (Armagh/IRL)	c59	1hc	Belfast, IRL	4 Jun
1:06.8 e		James Ferguson (NICC/IRL)	c56	2hc	Belfast, IRL	4 Jun

Doubtful (school sports)

1:03.0		W. Lambert (Ampleforth Coll)		1	Ampleforth	7 Apr

Notes
Burke inches down; Hanwell & Cowie 6y down on 1:07.0; Neill 5y down on 1:04.6; Ferguson 2y down on 1:06.4. Aitken over ten 3'6 hurdles.

High Jump

6'2¾	1.899	Patrick Davin (Carrick AAC/IRL)	4.06.57	1	Carrick-on-Suir, IRL	5 Jul
6'0	1.829	Davin		1	Monasterevin, IRL	21 Sep
5'11	1.803	Davin		1	Dublin (LR) IRL ICAC	17 May
5'11	1.803	John Parsons (Edinburgh U)	10.07.59	1	Edinburgh (ACG)	10 Jul
5'10	1.778	Parsons		1	Glasgow (Ac)	1 May
5'9¾	1.772	Parsons		1	London (LB) AAA	3 Jul
5'9	1.753	Reginald Macaulay (CU)	24.08.58	1	Cambridge	9 Mar
5'9	1.753	Macaulay		1	London (LB) OvC	19 Mar
5'9	1.753	Parsons		1	Glasgow (WSCG)	17 Apr
5'8½	1.740	John Dee (Carrick AAC/IRL)		2	Carrick-on-Suir, IRL	5 Jul
		(10/4)				
5'8	1.727	George Lawrence (OU)	17.03.59	2	London (LB) OvC	19 Mar
5'8	1.727	Francis Bell (Dulwich Coll)	14.04.62	1	Dulwich	1 May
5'8	1.727	T.J.Hanrahan (Carrick AAC/IRL)		1	Kilkenny, IRL	20 Jul
5'8	1.727	William Kelly (QC Cork/IRL)		1	Leighlinbridge, IRL	12 Aug
5'8	1.727	Sgt C. Dearing (3rd King's Own Hussars)		1	Colchester	5 Oct
5'7¾	1.721	P. Noonan (Cork AC/IRL)		1	Mitchelstown, IRL	18 Sep
5'7½	1.715	H.G.Roberts (Birmingham AC)		1	Birmingham (PR)	31 Jul
5'7½	1.715	Harry Luke (Castle Cary)	59	1hc	Axminster	8 Sep
5'7	1.702	Albert Sorby (CU)	27.06.59	1	Cambridge	20 Feb
5'7	1.702	Henry Cooke (CU)	4.02.59	2	Cambridge	9 Mar
5'7	1.702	Charles Gilbert (LAC)	9.01.55	1=hc	Faringdon	17 May
5'7	1.702	J. Keating (Lismore/IRL)		1	Lismore, IRL	17 May
5'7	1.702	Francis Wood (LAC)	28.09.55	1	Leighton Buzzard	17 May
5'7	1.702	William Clarke (West Haddon)		1	West Haddon	20 May
5'7	1.702	Robert Thomas (Liverpool Gym)	22.11.56	2=	Birmingham (PR)	31 Jul
5'7	1.702	E.J.Wade (Crownfield CC)		2=	Birmingham (PR)	31 Jul
5'7	1.702	Douglas Brownfield (Stoke Victoria AC)	30.03.56	2=	Birmingham (PR)	31 Jul

Indoors

5'7	1.702 i	Charles Poland (German Gym Soc)	12.02.59	1	London (KC)	8 Dec

Notes
Davin also cleared 6'1¾/1.873 prior to his winning jump at Carrick on 5/07.
The Sporting Mirror gives 5'7½ for Wood at Leighton Buzzard on 17/05.
Bell's Life for 6 March states, "R.H.Macaulay has jumped 5'10". Presumably this was in training.

High Jump: Highland & Border

6'1	1.854	p	Hugh Andrews (Glasgow)	c52	1	Alva	12 Aug
5'11	1.803	p	Thomas Aitken (ex-Walkerburn)	23.05.53	1=	Boston, USA	17 Jun
5'10	1.778	p	H. Andrews		1	Forfar	6 Aug
5'9	1.753	p	H. Andrews		1	Cupar	4 Aug
5'9	1.753	p	E. Andrews (Edinburgh)		2	Forfar	6 Aug
5'9	1.753	p	William McLiver (Stewarton)	c57	1	Mearns	7 Aug
5'9	1.753	p	William McGuire (Dunblane)	c58	1	Blackford	14 Aug
5'9	1.753	p	H. Andrews		1	Alexandria	28 Aug
5'9	1.753	p	Daniel Lamont (Kilbarchan)	c55	2	Alexandria	28 Aug
5'8½	1.740	p	Lamont		1=	Dalry	26 Jul
5'8½	1.740	p	McLiver		1=	Dalry	26 Jul
			(11/6)				
5'8	1.727	p	George Davidson (Drumoak)	19.11.54	3	Alexandria	28 Aug
5'7	1.702	p	Robert Borland (Kilbarchan)	19.01.58	2=	Mearns	7 Aug
5'7	1.702	p	W. McAdam (Newton)		2=	Mearns	7 Aug

Doubtful

5'10	1.778	p	Charles McHardy (Durris)	1.07.60	1	Durris	14 Aug
5'8	1.727	p	D. Watson (Durris)		2	Durris	14 Aug

At a picnic event. Neither are known as jumpers.

Note: The 6'1 by Andrews is from the *Stirling Journal*.
Donald Dinnie was said to have cleared 6'1/1.854 at Turriff this year (*Scottish Highland Games,* by David Webster, 1973), but this was a misprint. His best at Turriff was 5'11 in 1860.

Pole Vault

11'0	3.35		Tom Ray (Ulverston)	5.02.62	1	Widnes		19 Jun
10'9	3.28		Edward Strachan (103rd Regt)	16.08.58	wo	Clifton		19 Jun
10'8½	3.26		Ray		1	Ulverston		6 Aug
10'8	3.25		William Tonge (Cheltenham Coll)	14.04.62	1	Cheltenham		17 Mar
10'7	3.23		Strachan		1	Newark		17 May
10'7	3.23		George Barker (Bacup)	c55	2	Widnes		19 Jun
10'6	3.20		Edwin Woodburn (Ulverston CC)	19.04.50	1	Ulverston		29 Mar
10'6	3.20		George Callow (Peterborough CC)	c60	1	Burton-on-Trent		8 May
10'6	3.20		Ray		1	Darwen		31 Jul
10'6	3.20		Kendal Wilkinson (Urswick)	54	2	Ulverston		6 Aug
10'6	3.20		Ray		wo	Southport	NCAA	14 Aug
10'4½	3.16		Ray		2	Ulverston		29 Mar
			(12/7)					
10'4	3.15		Samuel Parrington (Cark in Cartmel)	c52	1	Preston		4 Sep
10'3	3.12		Herbert Gaye (Ipswich FC)	56	1	Hadleigh		2 Aug
10'1	3.07		Frederic Robinson (Beccles AC)	14.09.56	2	London (LB)	AAA	3 Jul
10'1	3.07		Horace Strachan (Cheltenham)	21.09.55	1	Hinckley		28 Aug
10'0	3.05		David McFarlane (Loretto Sch)	1.03.62	1	Glasgow (WSCG)		17 Apr
10'0	3.05		Herbert Dugdale (RMC Sandhurst)	3.04.60	1	Camberley		15 May
10'0	3.05		W. Miller (Bolton)		1=	Bolton		26 Jun
10'0	3.05		George Gill (Carnforth)	c51	1=	Bolton		26 Jun
10'0	3.05		Charles Squier (West Horndon)	58	2	Hadleigh		2 Aug
10'0	3.05		John Kellett (Ulverston)	6.01.57	3	Ulverston		6 Aug
10'0	3.05		Harry Reading (Market Harborough)	24.05.58	ex	Loughborough		25 Sep

Pole Vault: Highland, Lakeland & Border

11'0	3.35	p	James Rush (Barrhead)	c52	1	Linlithgow	21 Aug
10'11	3.33	p	Piper M. Martin (71st Highlanders)		1	Dundee	21 Aug
10'8	3.25	p	John Simpson (Ulverston)		1	Preston	24 Jul
10'8	3.25	p	William Barron (Keswick)	c56	1	Keswick	18 Aug
10'7	3.23	p	Rush		1	Bridge of Allan	7 Aug
10'7	3.23	p	William Dick (Forfar)	c57	2	Dundee	21 Aug
10'6	3.20	p	Rush		1	Dalry	26 Jul
10'6	3.20	p	George Davidson (Drumoak)	19.11.54	1	Saline	12 Aug
10'6	3.20	p	Simpson		2	Keswick	18 Aug
10'5	3.17	p	William Borland (Guisaghan)	c48	1=	Johnstone	17 Jul
10'5	3.17	p	Rush		1=	Johnstone	17 Jul
			(11/7)				
10'4	3.15	p	William Milne (Forfar)		1=	Dundee	24 Jul

10'4	3.15	p	David Milne (Forfar)	28.12.42	3	Dundee	21 Aug
10'3	3.12	p	William Ferguson (Alloa)		2	Bridge of Allan	7 Aug
10'3	3.12	p	Thomas Aitken (ex-Walkerburn)	23.05.53	1	Philadelphia, USA	18 Sep
10'2	3.10	p	John Thwaites (Keswick)	c57	3	Keswick	18 Aug
10'1	3.07	p	Joseph Thwaites (Keswick)	c60	3=	Grasmere	19 Aug
10'1	3.07	p	J. Hutchinson		3=	Grasmere	19 Aug
10'1	3.07	p	Peter Cameron (Kincardine O'Neil)	8.12.52	1	Inverness	24 Sep
10'0	3.05	p	P. Kerr (Aboyne)		1	Aberdeen (CC)	19 Jul
10'0	3.05	p	J. Black (Fetteresso)		1	Culter	7 Aug

Long Jump

23'0	7.01	Stewart Bruce (Lurgan/IRL)	17.11.58	1	Moneymore, IRL	27 Aug
22'9	6.93	Patrick Davin (Carrick AAC/IRL)	4.06.57	1	Kilkenny, IRL	20 Jul
22'2	6.76	William Fletcher (Liverpool Gym)	c62	1	Bebington	29 May
22'2	6.76	Charles Lockton (LAC)	2.07.56	1	London (LB) AAA	3 Jul
21'11	6.68	Davin		1	Dublin (LR) IRL ICAC	17 May
21'9	6.63	Herbert Flockton (Snettisham)	56	1	Fakenham	29 Mar
21'7	6.58	John Fellowes (OU)	29.04.59	1	Oxford	6 Mar
21'7	6.58	Davin		1	Monasterevin, IRL	21 Sep
21'6	6.55	Pte Dillon (13th Regt)		1	Aldershot	29 Jun
21'6	6.55	Harry Luke (Castle Cary)	59	1hc	Weston-super-Mare	5 Jul
		(10/8)				
21'5	6.53	Thomas Malone (Tradaree AC/IRL)	26.12.59	4hc	Limerick, IRL	15 Jun
21'5	6.53	Douglas Brownfield (Stoke Victoria AC)	30.03.56	1	Birmingham (PR)	31 Jul
21'5	6.53	William Kelly (QC Cork/IRL)		1	Leighlinbridge, IRL	12 Aug
21'3	6.48	George Lawrence (OU)	17.03.59	2	Oxford	6 Mar
21'3	6.48	Henry Graham (RMC)	30.11.60	1	London (LB)	27 May
21'3	6.48	Philip Clifford (Walthamstow FC)	16.02.56	1	Walthamstow	5 Jun
21'3	6.48	P. Shelly (Callan/IRL)		1	Castlecomer, IRL	7 Jul
21'3	6.48	Thomas Vallance (Rangers FC)	27.05.56	1	Glasgow (HP)	4 Sep
21'2½	6.46	Herbert Wood (OU)	29.08.55	3	Oxford	6 Mar
21'2	6.45	Herbert Dugdale (RMC Sandhurst)	3.04.60	1	Camberley	14 May
21'1½	6.44	John Parsons (Edinburgh U)	10.07.59	2	London (LB) AAA	3 Jul
21'1	6.43	Frederick Betty (Weston-super-Mare)	57	2hc	Weston-super-Mare	5 Jul
21'0	6.40	Harry Massey (LAC)	c57	3	London (LB) AAA	3 Jul

Note: "The jumping of Davin (at Kilkenny) was certainly a brilliant performance as the ground was very indifferent, besides being somewhat up an incline. His first jump was 21'7, second 21'8 and he finally cleared the distance given above." (*Irish Sportsman & Farmer*). Other sources give Davin 22'8¾/6.93.

Long Jump: Highland & Border

21'2	6.45	p	James Kerr (Aboyne)		1	Craigievar	5 Aug
21'1½	6.44	p	Thomas Aitken (ex-Walkerburn)	23.05.53	1	Montreal, CAN	22 Sep
20'9	6.32	p	Adam Marshall (Dundee)	c52	2	Craigievar	5 Aug
20'9	6.32	p	Peter Cameron (Kincardine O'Neil)	8.12.52	1	Inverness	24 Sep
20'6	6.25	p	William Young (Alva)	c53	1	Bridge of Allan	7 Aug
20'6	6.25	p	Young		1	Alva	12 Aug

Triple Jump

46'0	14.02	Daniel Looney (Cork/IRL)	c59	1	Kilfinane, IRL	2 Aug
44'8	13.61	W.R.Nally (IRL)		1	St Louis, USA	23 Aug
44'0	13.41	T. Burke (QC Cork/IRL)		2	Kilfinane, IRL	2 Aug
43'9	13.33	David Suttie (Glasgow)	c51	1	Glenisla	20 Aug
41'8½	12.71	George Russell (St Andrews U)	2.04.60	1	St Andrews	3 Apr
40'0	12.19	Dominick O'Connor (Mountmellick/IRL)		1	Mountmellick, IRL	17 Jun
40'0	12.19	D. Mulcahy (IRL)		1	Conna, IRL	23 Nov
38'0	11.58	Gunner Anderson (Royal Marine Artillery)		1	Portsmouth	16 Jul
37'5	11.40	R. Gilson (Working Men's Club)		1	London (SB)	29 Mar

Doubtful

43'0	13.11	Burke		1	Mitchelstown, IRL	18 Sep
42'0	12.80	T.J.Hanrahan (Carrick AAC/IRL)		2	Mitchelstown, IRL	18 Sep

Said to have been "slightly downhill"

41'7	12.67	John O'Neill (New Ross/IRL)		1	New Ross, IRL	28 Jul
39'5	12.01	Edward Wolfe (Armagh/IRL)	c59	2	New Ross, IRL	28 Jul

Downhill, according to the *Irish Sportsman & Farmer*

Notes
The jumps by Looney and Burke are also reported in the *Dublin Daily Express* as at Cork in a fete on 3/08.
Suttie was in an amateur competition at the Glenisla Games. He had competed elsewhere for money prizes. We
give the result from the *Dundee Advertiser*; the *Dundee Courier* had 42'9.

Triple Jump: Highland, Border & Lancashire Professional

48'10	14.88	p	Thomas Aitken (ex-Walkerburn)	23.05.53	1	Philadelphia, USA	18 Sep
48'1	14.66	p	William Young (Alva)	c53	1	Bridge of Allan (open)	7 Aug
47'10	14.58	p	Daniel Lamont (Kilbarchan)	c55	1	Rothesay	19 Aug
47'5	14.45	p	William McGuire (Dunblane)	c58	2	Bridge of Allan (open)	7 Aug
47'2	14.38	p	E. Andrews (Edinburgh)		3	Bridge of Allan (open)	7 Aug
46'11	14.30	p	Young		1	Alva	12 Aug
46'10	14.27	p	David Johnstone (Alva)	1.05.57	2	Rothesay	19 Aug
46'8	14.22	p	Andrews		1	Saline	12 Aug
46'7	14.20	p	Johnstone		1	Culross	27 Jul
46'7	14.20	p	Young		3	Rothesay	19 Aug
46'5	14.15	p	Andrews		1	Alloa	11 Aug
46'2	14.07	p	Young		1	Inverkeithing	6 Aug
46'1	14.05	p	Johnstone		2	Alva	12 Aug
46'0	14.02	p	Johnstone		1	Milnathort	26 Jul
46'0	14.02	p	A. McMillan (Alva)		3	Alva	12 Aug
			(15/7)				
45'11	14.00	p	Adam Scott (Swinton)	15.08.52	2	Inverkeithing	6 Aug
45'6½	13.88	p	Robert Knox (Jedburgh)	17.09.47	1	Hawick	11 Jun
45'6	13.87	p	C. Webster (Dundee)		4	Bridge of Allan (open)	7 Aug
45'6	13.87	p	George Black (Dumfries)		1	Milngavie	28 Aug
45'4	13.82	p	James Fox (Stirling)		3	Culross	27 Jul
44'6	13.56	p	Hugh Andrews (Glasgow)	c52	2	Hawick	11 Jun
44'6	13.56	p	H. Templeton (Darlington)		2	Saline	12 Aug
44'4	13.51	p	James Rush (Barrhead)	c52	3	Saline	12 Aug
43'10	13.36	p	George Bowie (Parkhill)	1.09.56	1	Kildrummy	10 Aug
43'7	13.28	p	Thomas Webster (Dundee)		3	Balfron	17 Jul
43'5	13.23	p	John Campbell		1	West Wemyss	13 Jul
43'1	13.13	p	James Kerr (Aboyne)		1	Craigevar	5 Aug
43'0	13.11	p	P. McDonald (Bonhill)		2	Alexandria	28 Aug
42'11½	13.09	p	James Thomson (Culter)		2	Craigevar	5 Aug
42'1	12.83	p	Adam Marshall (Dundee)	c52	2	Aberdeen (CC)	19 Jul
42'1	12.83	p	Peter Cameron (Kincardine O'Neil)	8.12.52	2	Kildrummy	10 Aug
42'0	12.80	p	William McLiver (Stewarton)	c57	1	Mearns	7 Aug
41'10	12.75	p	P. Kerr (Aboyne)		1	Ballater	17 Aug
41'9	12.73	p	Robert Craig (West Kilbride)		1	West Kilbride	17 Jul
41'8	12.70	p	John Graham (Upper Kidston)		1	Peebles	10 Jul
41'7	12.67	p	Andrew Johnstone (Alva)		2	Peebles	10 Jul
41'6	12.65	p	Richard Gledhill (Ovenden)	c58	1	Halifax	15 May

Note: Two meetings were held at Aberdeen on 17 and 19 July, at the cricket ground and the recreation ground
(marked CC and RG). Suttie competed in an amateur event at the Glenisla games, but generally entered
professional events.

Shot

40'3	12.27	Thomas Stone (Newton-le-Willows)	24.01.52	2hc	Newton-le-Willows		25 Sep
39'6	12.04	H. Gubbins (Kilsheeban/IRL)		1	Callan, IRL		2 Aug
39'6	12.04	William Winthrop (LAC)	15.06.52	1	Southport	NCAA	14 Aug
39'4½	12.00	M. Lawler (Borris/IRL)		1	Borris, IRL		4 Aug
39'0	11.89	Walter Dinnie (Met Police)	26.12.50	1hc	London (LB)		24 Jun
39'0	11.89	Arthur Reynolds (Childwall)	c55	2	Southport	NCAA	14 Aug
38'10½	11.85	F. Scott (Rochester FC)		1	Rochester		26 Jun
38'9½	11.82	James Slattery (Carrick AAC/IRL)		1	Carrick-on-Suir, IRL		29 Mar
38'8	11.79	Wyndham Evanson (Civil Service)	51	1hc	London (LB)		22 May
38'6	11.73	T. O'Brien (Clare/IRL)		1	Bunratty, IRL		26 Jul
38'3	11.66	J. Courtenay (Kilkenny/IRL)		1	Kilkenny, IRL		20 Jul
37'6½	11.44	L.P.McDonnell (IRL)		1	Montreal, CAN		2 Oct
		(12/12)					
37'6	11.43	J. Sheely (Carrick/IRL)		2	Carrick-on-Suir, IRL		29 Mar
37'6	11.43	Alexander Duguid (Working Men's Club)		1	London (SB)		29 Mar
37'5	11.40	Arthur East (CU)	3.11.57	1	London (LB)	OvC	19 Mar

37'2	11.33		William Peterkin (Edinburgh U)	2.01.58	1	Edinburgh	10 Jul
37'0	11.28		John Orford (St Thomas's H)	57	1	London (SB)	30 Jun
37'0	11.28		Patrick Davin (Carrick AAC/IRL)	4.06.57	1	Monasterevin, IRL	21 Sep
36'10	11.23		Thomas Malone (Tradaree AC/IRL)	26.12.59	2hc	Limerick, IRL	15 Jun
36'8	11.18		G.H.St George (QC Cork/IRL)		1	Cork, IRL	24 Apr
36'7	11.15		C.M.O'Connor (Tralee/IRL)		1	Tralee, IRL	17 Jun

Shot: Highland & Border
Includes 16lb stone

48'8	14.83	p	Donald Dinnie (Stonehaven)	8.06.37	1	Aberdeen (RG)	19 Jul
46'10	14.27	p	Owen Duffy (Edinburgh/IRL)	c47	1	Falkirk	4 Sep
46'7	14.20	p	George Davidson (Drumoak)	19.11.54	1	Craigievar	5 Aug
45'8	13.92	p	Dinnie		1hc	Tranent	17 Jun
45'5	13.84	p	Davidson		1	Aberdeen (CC)	17 Jul
45'3	13.79	p	Dinnie		1	Aberdeen (RG)	17 Jul
44'10	13.67	p	Davidson		1	Aberdeen (CC)	19 Jul
44'10	13.67	p	Davidson		1	Errol	28 Jul
44'10	13.67	p	William Bremner (Leochel-Cushnie)	3.01.47	2	Craigievar	5 Aug
43'11*	13.39	p	Alexander Robertson (Bridge of Dee)		1	Culter (heavy)	7 Aug
43'11	13.39	p	Kenneth McRae (Nairn)	50	2	Falkirk	4 Sep
43'7	13.28	p	John Anderson (Edinburgh)		3	Falkirk	4 Sep
43'6*	13.26	p	William Innes (Edinburgh)		2	Culter (heavy)	7 Aug
43'3	13.18	p	Dinnie		1	London (LB)	24 May
43'0	13.11	p	Davidson		2hc	Tranent	17 Jun
42'11	13.08	p	Innes		3	Craigievar	5 Aug
42'9	13.03	p	Davidson		2	London (LB)	24 May
42'9*	13.03	p	Davidson		1	Ballater (light)	17 Aug
42'6	12.95	p	Dinnie		1	Milngavie	28 Aug
			(19/8)				
42'1	12.83	p	Richard Ingram (Tillyfourie)		4	Craigievar	5 Aug
41'9	12.73	p	George Bowie (Parkhill)	1.09.56	1	Kildrummy	10 Aug
41'8	12.70	p	William Machray (Skene)	13.05.54	3	Culter (heavy)	7 Aug
41'7*	12.67	p	John Hatrick (Johnstone)		1	Johnstone	17 Jul
40'9*	12.42	p	A. Robinson		1	Lumphanan	12 Jul
40'9	12.42	p	James Fleming (Ballinluig)	18.09.40	2	Aberdeen (CC)	19 Jul
40'6	12.34	p	A. Ingram (Kemnay)		2	Aberdeen (CC)	17 Jul
40'0	12.19	p	William Pullar (Cargill)	14.04.55	1	Burrelton	6 Jul
39'8	12.09	p	John Robertson (Heughhead)		2	Aberdeen (RG)	19 Jul
39'7*	12.06	p	Hugh Gillespie (Glasgow)		2	Johnstone	17 Jul
39'0	11.89	p	John McGregor (Glasgow)		2	Milngavie	28 Aug
38'8	11.79	p	Thomas Murison (Fyvie)	25.05.55	1	Fingask	26 Jun
38'6	11.73	p	John Smith (Speybridge)		1	Abernethy	2 Sep
37'11	11.56	p	James Smith (Kildrummy)		1	Kildrummy (local)	10 Aug
37'5	11.40	p	E. Pelham (Grantown)		2	Abernethy	2 Sep
37'4	11.38	p	W. Lindsay		1	Banchory (light)	24 Jul
36'11	11.25	p	Alexander Grant (Lyngarrie)		3	Abernethy	2 Sep
36'8	11.18	p	James Wilson (Aberdeen)		2	Aberdeen (RG)	17 Jul

Note: *correct weight assumed from evidence of other years.

Weight unstated

47'3	14.40	p	Duffy		1	Rothesay (light)	19 Aug
46'11	14.30	p	Dinnie		2	Rothesay (light)	19 Aug
44'5	13.54	p	John McHardy (Glenlivet)		1	Keith (light)	12 Jun
44'2	13.46	p	Davidson		1	Crossford	4 Sep
44'0	13.41	p	Duffy		ex	Alexandria (heavy)	28 Aug
44'0	13.41	p	Dinnie		1	Fochabers	25 Sep
43'11	13.39	p	Davidson		3	Rothesay (light)	19 Aug
43'5½	13.25	p	Dinnie		1	Dundee	10 Apr
43'4	13.21	p	Davidson		1	Alexandria (heavy)	28 Aug
43'3	13.18	p	Evan Clayton (Forres)	17.03.52	2	Keith (light)	12 Jun
43'2	13.16	p	Duffy		2	Alexandria (heavy)	28 Aug
43'0	13.11	p	John Cameron (Leith)		1	Leith (open)	7 Aug
43'0	13.11	p	Cameron		1	Leith (local)	7 Aug
42'8	13.00	p	Machray		1	Kinnellar	17 Jul
42'6	12.95	p	Bowie		1	Newmill	26 Jun

41'6	12.65	p	James Thomson (Fochabers)	22.07.56	3	Keith (light)	12 Jun
41'0	12.50	p	G. Stewart (Leith)		2	Leith (open)	7 Aug
40'9	12.42	p	Hector Fraser (Dyce)		2	Kinnellar	17 Jul
40'3	12.27	p	Theodore Campbell (Leith)		3	Leith (open)	7 Aug
40'0	12.19	p	John Dowell (Dyce)		3	Kinnellar	17 Jul
40'0	12.19	p	John Reid (Aberdeen)		1	Strathdon (local light)	24 Aug
40'0	12.19	p	John Smith		1	Grantown	31 Aug
39'9	12.12	p	Cpl Craigmile (Deeside Highlanders)		1	Banchory (heavy)	21 Aug
38'10	11.84	p	G. Ross		1	Crathes (light)	24 Jul
38'8	11.79	p	William Fleming (Dundee)	22.08.42	3	Dundee	10 Apr
38'4	11.68	p	A. Laing		2	Crathes (light)	24 Jul
38'4	11.68	p	D. Cameron (Nairn)		2	Elgin	21 Aug
38'0	11.58	p	Robertson		2	Strathdon (local light)	24 Aug
37'10	11.53	p	James Stewart (Stonehaven)		2	Auchinblae	5 Jan
37'1	11.30	p	Charles McHardy (Durris)	1.07.60	1	Strathdon	24 Aug

Extra trial

44'0	13.41	p	Duffy		ex	Alexandria (heavy)	28 Aug

17lb

47'3	14.40	p	Dinnie		1	Manchester (Pom)	3 Jun
47'2	14.38	p	Davidson		2	Manchester (Pom)	3 Jun
44'0	13.41	p	George Ross (Patricroft)	2.03.59	3	Manchester (Pom)	3 Jun

18lb by performer

36'9	11.20	p	J. Stewart		1	Fetteresso (heavy)	30 Jul

22lb by performer

39'3	11.96	p	Dinnie		1	Dunkeld	26 Aug
38'5	11.71	p	McRae		1	Dundee	21 Aug
37'1	11.30	p	Davidson		1=	Aberfeldy	25 Aug
36'8	11.18	p	Bremner		1	Kildrummy	10 Aug

Doubtful

50'2	15.29	p	Dinnie		1	Kingussie	3 Sep
48'0	14.63	p	Duffy		1	Bridge of Allan (light)	7 Aug
47'9	14.55	p	Davidson		2	Kingussie	3 Sep
46'0	14.02	p	Davidson		2	Bridge of Allan (light)	7 Aug
45'8	13.92	p	McRae		3	Kingussie	3 Sep
44'7½	13.60	p	Davidson		1	Inverness (light)	23 Sep
44'3	13.49	p	Fleming		3	Bridge of Allan (light)	7 Aug
43'7	13.28	p	Anderson		4	Bridge of Allan (light)	7 Aug
42'11	13.08	p	Pelham		4	Kingussie	3 Sep
38'5	11.71	p	William Mackintosh (Kingussie)		1	Kingussie (local)	3 Sep
37'3	11.35	p	Ewen Campbell (Kingussie)	18.11.56	2	Kingussie (local)	3 Sep

Hammer

119'0	36.27	Walter Lawrence (OU)	20.05.59	1	Oxford	8 Mar
116'0	35.36	Arthur East (CU)	3.11.57	1	London (LB) OvC	19 Mar
113'6	34.59	John Tobin (Carrick AAC/IRL)		1	Carrick-on-Suir, IRL	5 Jul
113'0	34.44	James Slattery (Carrick AAC/IRL)		2	Carrick-on-Suir, IRL	5 Jul
112'10	34.39	East		1	Cambridge	9 Mar
109'6	33.38	Bertram Latter (OU)	11.08.58	2	London (LB) OvC	19 Mar
108'4	33.02	Lawrence		3	London (LB) OvC	19 Mar
104'7	31.88	East		1	Cambridge	27 Feb
104'0	31.70	Latter		2	Oxford	8 Mar
100'0	30.73	Lindsay Bury (CU)	8.07.57	2	Cambridge	9 Mar
100'7	30.66	Lawrence		1	Oxford	23 Feb
100'0	30.48	Bury		4	London (LB) OvC	19 Mar
		(12/6)				
96'6	29.41	Neil McDonald (Glasgow Alexandra AC)	c54	1	Glasgow (Alex)	1 May
95'9	29.18	Norman Campbell (CU)	14.08.54	3	Cambridge	9 Mar
92'6	28.19	Montague Shearman (OU)	7.04.57	1hc	Oxford	17 Feb
91'10	27.99	Stephen Moxley (QC Cork/IRL)	c57	1	Cork, IRL	24 Apr

Weight unstated

94'0	28.65	A. England		1	Culter (light)	7 Aug

Amateur competition in the Scottish Games.

Hammer: Highland & Border

130'0	39.62	p	Donald Dinnie (Stonehaven)	8.06.37	1	Sheffield (BL)	1 Jun
130'0	39.62	p	Dinnie		1	Manchester (Pom)	3 Jun
129'2	39.37	p	Dinnie		1	Manchester (Pom)	2 Jun
127'0	38.71	p	George Davidson (Drumoak)	19.11.54	2	Manchester (Pom)	3 Jun
124'9	38.02	p	John Ogg (Banff/NZL)	7.08.47	1	Dunedin, NZL	1 Jan
122'5	37.31	p	Davidson		2	Manchester (Pom)	2 Jun
120'7	36.75	p	Dinnie		1	London (LB)	24 May
119'0	36.27	p	Davidson		2	Sheffield (BL)	1 Jun
116'4	35.46	p	Davidson		2	London (LB)	24 May
115'0	35.05	p	Dinnie		1	Milnathort	26 Jul
113'11+	34.72	p	Kenneth McRae (Nairn)	50	1	Inverness	23 Sep
112'0*	34.14	p	Dinnie		1hc	Glenisla	20 Aug
111'1*	33.86	p	Dinnie		1	Cupar (light)	4 Aug
111'0	33.83	p	Dinnie		1	Edzell	31 Jul
110'10	33.78	p	William Machray (Skene)	13.05.54	3to	Craigievar	5 Aug
109'8	33.43	p	William Bremner (Leochel-Cushnie)	3.01.47	1	Craigievar	5 Aug
109'6	33.38	p	James Stewart (Stonehaven)		1	Fetteresso	30 Jul
109'6+	33.38	p	Davidson		2	Inverness	23 Sep
			(18/7)				
108'0	32.92	p	J. Horn (Glasgow)		1	Mearns	7 Aug
107'0	32.61	p	A. Cameron (Thornliebank)		2	Mearns	7 Aug
102'6	31.24	p	Alexander Murray (Stonehaven)		2	Fetteresso	30 Jul
102'4+	31.19	p	William Innes (Edinburgh)		3	Inverness	23 Sep
101'4	30.89	p	Duncan Ross (Glasgow/CAN)	16.03.55	1	Boston, USA	29 Sep
100'0	30.48	p	George Grant (Curr)		1	Abernethy	4 Sep
99'0	30.18	p	Alexander McDonald (Abernethy)		2	Abernethy	4 Sep
98'5+	30.00	p	James Grey (Dorbshill)		1	Dudwick	17 Jul
98'3	29.95	p	John Robertson (Alloa)		1	Johnstone	17 Jul
97'11	29.84	p	David Cramb (Logiealmond)	13.12.59	1	Almondbank	28 Aug
97'8	29.77	p	James Fleming (Ballinluig)	18.09.40	2	Dundee	21 Aug
96'11	29.54	p	John Anderson (Edinburgh)		2	Falkirk	4 Sep
96'5	29.39	p	James Melrose (Peebles/Hartford USA)	17.04.47	1	Peebles	10 Jul
95'11	29.24	p	R. Stewart (Broughty Ferry)		3	Dundee	21 Aug
95'6	29.11	p	James Walker (Muchalls)		3	Fetteresso	30 Jul
95'0	28.96	p	Owen Duffy (Leith/IRL)	c47	3	Falkirk	4 Sep
94'4*	28.75	p	A. Robinson		2	Lumphanan	17 Jul
93'10	28.60	p	Archibald Robertson (Percie)		1	Strachan	23 Jul
93'2	28.40	p	Francis Boyne (Andrewsford)	25.11.57	1	Braes of Gight	12 Aug
93'0*	28.35	p	William Mackintosh (Kingussie)		4	Aberfeldy	25 Aug

Notes
*correct weight assumed from evidence of other years.
+ The Inverness hammer was 16½lb, the Blairgowrie and Dudwick hammers 17lb.
There was a throw-off for 3rd place at Craigievar.

Weight unstated

123'9	37.72	p	Dinnie		1	Nairn	7 Aug
118'5½	36.11	p	Dinnie		1hc	Dundee	24 Jul
115'0	35.05	p	Dinnie		1	Rothesay	19 Aug
114'0	34.75	p	Dinnie		1	Saline	12 Aug
113'6½	34.61	p	McRae		2	Nairn	7 Aug
113'4	34.54	p	Dinnie		1	Kingussie (light)	3 Sep
112'0	34.14	p	Machray		1	Culter	7 Aug
111'2	33.88	p	Dinnie		1	Oban	15 Sep
111'1	33.86	p	Machray		1	Kinnellar	17 Jul
111'0	33.83	p	Dinnie		1	Edzell	31 Jul
110'11	33.81	p	Davidson		2hc	Dundee	24 Jul
110'9	33.76	p	Davidson		2	Oban	15 Sep
109'6	33.38	p	Davidson		2	Kingussie (light)	3 Sep
109'0	33.22	p	J. Fleming		1	Auchinblae	5 Jan
104'8	31.90	p	W. Angus		1	Garmond	22 Jul
104'7	31.88	p	William Rust (Drumoak)	1.01.55	2	Culter	7 Aug
104'7	31.88	p	John Robertson (Aberdeen)		1	Strathdon (confined)	24 Aug
103'0	31.39	p	George Calder (Stonehaven)		3	Auchinblae	5 Jan

101'10	31.04	p	John Reid (Aberdeen)		2	Strathdon (confined)	24 Aug
101'3	30.86	p	Charles McHardy (Durris)	1.07.60	3	Strathdon (confined)	24 Aug
101'0	30.78	p	John Rose (Cromdale)		1	Grantown (local light)	31 Aug
98'9	30.10	p	Alexander McKay (Lochgilphead)		1	Oban (light)	14 Sep
98'5	30.00	p	John Stuart (Dufftown)		1	Cabrach (light)	17 Jul
98'2	29.92	p	J. Scott		1	Crossgates (heavy)	15 Jul
96'8½	29.48	p	A. McKinnon (Moyness)		3	Nairn	7 Aug
96'4	29.36	p	Hector Fraser (Dyce)		2	Kinnellar	17 Jul
96'4	29.36	p	James Duguid (Strathdon)		2	Glenbucket	24 Jul
96'0	29.26	p	T. Fraser		2	Crathes	24 Jul
95'8	29.16	p	William McCombie Smith (Blairgowrie)	7.09.47	2	Glenisla (heavy)	20 Aug
94'4	28.75	p	J. Maitland (Scotsmill)		3	Kinnellar	17 Jul
94'2	28.70	p	John McGregor (Glasgow)		3	Crossford	4 Sep
94'1	28.68	p	George Bowie (Parkhill)	1.09.56	3	Udny	4 Aug
92'8	28.24	p	George Milne		1	Newburgh (light)	26 Jul
92'5	28.17	p	Francis Wood		2	Newburgh (light)	26 Jul

18lb by performer

114'7	34.92	p	Dinnie		1	Fochabers	25 Sep
105'3	32.08	p	McRae		2	Fochabers	25 Sep
95'0	28.96	p	James Thomson (Fochabers)	22.07.56	3	Fochabers	25 Sep

20lb by performer

98'10	30.12	p	Dinnie		1	Crieff	21 Aug
91'11	28.02	p	Davidson		2	Crieff	21 Aug

22lb by performer

114'0*	34.75	p	Davidson		1	Alexandria (heavy)	28 Aug
100'6	30.63	p	Dinnie		1	Manchester (Pom)	2 Jun
100'2*	30.53	p	Duffy		2	Alexandria (heavy)	28 Aug
98'9*	30.10	p	G. Read (Dumbarton)		3	Alexandria (heavy)	28 Aug
96'2	29.31	p	Davidson		2	Manchester (Pom)	2 Jun

Note: *correct weight assumed from evidence of other years

Other Events

120 Yards

12.0	William Phillips (LAC)	5.08.58	1ht2hc	London (SB)	22 May
12.0	Phillips		1hc	London (SB)	22 May
Doubtful					
11.6	Montague Shearman (OU)	7.04.57	1ht2hc	Oxford	4 Mar

Reported in *The Field*. *Bell's Life* declined to print the sprint times as "too fast to be of any value".

150 Yards

15.0	William Phillips (LAC)	5.08.58	1hc	London (LB)	22 May

200 Yards

20.2 w	Edward Lucas (CU)	15.02.60	1	Cambridge	13 Nov

300 Yards

31.8	William Beverley (OU)	18.04.59	1ht1hc	Oxford	16 Feb

500 Yards

56.25	John Belcher (ex-QC Cork/IRL)	28.06.55	1	Hartford, Conn, USA	4 Aug

600 Yards

1:16.2	George Dobell (Stoke Victoria AC)	14.11.54	1	Birmingham (ALG)	1 May
1:16.2	John Sadler (LAC)	14.04.55	1	London (LB)	22 May

1000 Yards

2:19.4	Walter George (Moseley H)	9.09.58	1	Birmingham (PR)	31 Jul

¾ Mile

3:14.0	Walter George (Moseley H)	9.09.58	inthc	London (SB)	16 Aug
In a 1 mile race					

1½ Miles

6:43.5 p	William Cummings (Paisley)	10.06.58	1	Preston	17 Apr

5 Miles

25:19.0 p	William Cummings (Paisley)	10.06.58	int	London (LB)	31 May

20 Miles

1:56:38.0 p	James Warburton (Haslingden)	13.11.45	1	Blackburn	29 May

25 Miles

2:41:36.0 p	James Bailey (Sittingbourne)	2.05.52	int	London (LB)	30 Mar

In a 50 mile race.

30 Miles

3:18:17.0 p	James Bailey (Sittingbourne)	2.05.52	int	London (LB)	30 Mar

In a 50 mile race.

40 Miles

4:49:09.0 p	James Bailey (Sittingbourne)	2.05.52	int	London (LB)	30 Mar

In a 50 mile challenge race, which he won after 42¼ miles.

1 Mile Walk

6:30.0	Harry Webster (Stoke AC)	14.05.54	1	Stoke-on-Trent	31 Jul

7 Miles Walk

54:45.0 p	Henry Thatcher (Southwark)	13.04.53	1	London (LB)	16 Aug

100 Miles Walk

18:08:15.0 i p	William Howes (Felthorpe)	03.39	int	London (Ag Hall)	14/15 May

In a 26 hour race, indoors.

Cricket Ball

122y 0ft 0in 111.56 Andrew Don Wauchope (Fettes Coll) 29.04.61 1 Edinburgh nd
Fettes College sports. Remained the school record until 1929, when the event was discontinued.

Cambridge University Handicaps, 1878. W.Westmacott (Oxford U) wins the 440yds from a 20yds start in 50.4. Handicap running was popular by this time. In this open event at Fenners 'strangers' were admitted without having to run heats. Seven Oxford men started and dominated the race. W.H.Churchill (Cambridge), the scratch runner, was unable to get through in the blanket finish (a handicapper's job well done) and was fifth.

INDEX

Note: AAC/LAC results include LAC placings with the designation 79L.
Where an athlete may have a double-barrelled surname without a hyphen, e.g. William McCombie Smith, they are generally indexed under the second surname

A BBEY, J.
440H 1871
ABBOTT, Sydney Wells (c1843 – 02.04.1887)
HJ 1868
ABRAMS, Abram (c1852 – 25.01.1934)
440H 1872
ABSOLOM, Charles Alfred (07.06.1846 – 30.07.1889)
100 1868; LJ 1866-68; SP 1866, 68
ADAM, Peter M.
SP 1875-77; HT 1877
ADAMS, G.
220H 1878
ADAMS, Stewart
HT 1875-76
ADEY, George (1858 – 1930)
1M 1878
ADSHEAD, Aaron Edward (1857 – 10.02.1895)
LJ 1874
AINSCOW, William (c1845)
440 1869
AINSLIE, Andrew (06.04.1851)
PV 1870-71
AITKEN, James
TJ 1874-75
AITKEN, Thomas (23.05.1853 – 07.1923)
440H 1880; HJ 1876, 79-80; PV 1879-80;
LJ 1880; TJ 1872-80
AKROYD, Swainson Howden (13.11.1848 –
05.12.1925) 120H 1867
ALBISON, Siah (26.04.1840 – 1891)
440 1867
ALBRIGHT, John Francis (15.04.1857)
SP 1877
ALKIN, John Griffith (10.07.1855 – 1901)
220 1877; 220H 1877; HJ 1876; LJ 1875-77
AAC: 100 77/3h; HJ 73/ac, 77/2=; LJ 76/1, 77/1,
78/ac
ALLAN, Henry (c1856)
100 1879; 220 1879; 120H 1877-79; LJ 1879
AAC/LAC: 100 79L/2; 120H 78/3h, 79L/2
ALLAN, John
TJ 1866, 69
ALLANSON, James Audus (1843 – 24.12.1903)
2M 1867
AAC: 4M 67/dnf
ALLEN, Robert Thomas (11.05.1857 – 22.11.1885)
440 1877
ALLEN, W.
PV 1866
ALLEN, William (c1847 – 10.06.1886)
100 1866
ALLFREY, Alexander (12.02.1848 – 06.1920)
100 1869; HJ 1870
ALLINGHAM, Thomas (31.03.1843)
220 1867
ALLISON, John (08.02.1843)
HJ 1868; PV 1866-73, 75
ALPE, Edmund Nicholas (1848 – 17.12.1897)
220 1871
AMBROSE, M.D.
HT 1876

ANDERSON, Gunner
TJ 1880
ANDERSON, Adam
PV 1878
ANDERSON, David (c1846)
HJ 1869; PV 1866-77; SP 1875
ANDERSON, George
SP 1877
ANDERSON, Hugh
TJ 1871-72
ANDERSON, James
HT 1869
ANDERSON, John (– 29.07.1938)
SP 1869-73, 74-75, 77-80; HT 1875, 79-80
ANDERSON, William J.
120H 1876; HJ 1876
ANDREWS, E.
HJ 1876-78, 80; TJ 1876-77, 79-80
ANDREWS, Harry (28.05.1831 – 07.03.1885)
2M 1866; 3M 1866; 4M 1866, 70
ANDREWS, Hugh (c1852)
HJ 1872-80; TJ 1871-76, 80
ANDREWS, Richard (c1858)
880 1877-79; 1M 1879
ANGELL, Arthur (1844 – 03.02.1930)
PV 1867
ANGLIN, Michael James (1852)
TJ 1876
ANGUS, W.
HT 1880
ANNAND, David (1854 – 1941)
HT 1875
ANSCOMBE, Alfred (c1857 – 06.07.1928)
120H 1875
ANTON, Peter A. (25.06.1850)
SP 1874
ARCHDALL, John P. (03.04.1855)
LJ 1874
ARCHER, Sergeant
100 1867
ARCHER, Arthur Montford (c1856 – 17.09.1930)
440H 1878
ARMITAGE, C.C.
AAC: 880 72/dnf
ARMITAGE, H.I.
2M 1876
ARMITSTEAD, Francis Edward (20.03.1849 –
13.04.1907)
2M 1870; 3M 1870
ARMITSTEAD, George Henry (24.04.1853 –
23.12.1911) 3M 1873
ARMSTRONG, Henry Wylde (c1850 – 19.01.1924)
HJ 1873; LJ 1873
ARMSTRONG, Leonard Henry (1858 – 17.01.1942)
120H 1876
ARMSTRONG, William
100 1869
ARTHUR, George (19.01.1851)
120H 1868
ASHBURNER, George Banks (12.1860 – 05.10.1889)
CB 1879

BARTLETT, Ellis Ashmead (24.08.1849 – 18.01.1902)
880 1869
AAC: 1M 70/2
BARTLEY, Arthur Harrison (16.03.1848 – 29.12.1891)
120H 1866
BATCHELOR, F.
SP 1870
BATCHELOR, William Jesse (14.11.1846 –
19.11.1917) 1M 1867
BATEMAN, John Joseph (18.02.1855 – 27.04.1886)
2M 1874-75, 77; 3M 1875; 4M 1875; 10M 1878
BATSON, Thomas (18.05.1846 – 11.01.1928)
SP 1867-68; HT 1868-69
AAC: HT 69/4
BATTEN, John Maxwell (28.02.1853 – 15.10.1917)
440 1874
BATTERBURY, Henry Charles (bapt. 01.04.1849 –
26.07.1915) HJ 1873
BATTERS, Charles James (19.02.1853 – 14.02.1918)
100 1871
BAUCHOPE, Charles Robertson (1843 – 19.12.1888)
220 1866, 68; SP 1867
BAXTER, L.
PV 1877
BAYER, Frederick Benjamin (14.08.1850 - 03.10.1895)
CB 1871
BAYLEY, Claude Villiers Emilius [later LAURIE]
(25.11.1855 – 19.02.1930) LJ 1876
BAYLEY, George Adam (1845 – 19.04.1876)
PV 1866; LJ 1866
BAYLEY, Wilfred Emilius (01.06.1859 – 15.12.1936)
100 1880; 120H 1880
BAYLIS, Frederick (1857)
120H 1876
BAYLY, Charles Algernon (26.02.1852 – 10.03.1904)
120H 1874-75, 77; HT 1874
AAC: 120H 75/3
BAYNARD, Charles (1848 – 01.09.1897)
1MW 1879
BEARDSELL, Charles William (18.10.1845 -
03.06.1928)
AAC: 440 66/3; 4M 66/dnf
BEARDSELL, Harry (c1848)
440H 1870
BEAUCHAMP, Henry Woodrooffe (25.12.1851 –
16.07.1915)
120H 1872-74
AAC: 120H 71/4, 72/3, 74/3
BEAVAN, John (c1854)
10M 1876
BEAVAN, William (c1854)
10M 1876
BECKE, James Henry (1848 – 11.10.1910)
880 1869-70; 1M 1870
AAC: 7MW 75/dnf
BEDFORD, William Campbell Riland (29.05.1852 –
15.08.1922) 120H 1875
AAC: 100 75/3; 120H 74/3h, 75/4
BEEVER, William Frederick Holt (03.09.1854 –
11.06.1945) PV 1871
BEGG, James
SP 1871
BELCHER, John Tresilian (28.06.1855 – 26.01.1930)
100 1880; 220 1880; 440 1877-78, 80; 500 1880
BELCHER, Robert Tresilian (03.10.1853 – 1936)
440 1877

BELL, Francis Henry Augustus (14.04.1862 –
25.08.1935) HJ 1880
BELL, Gunner J.
TJ 1876
BELL, John [Hawick] (c1839)
HJ 1866-67, 70-71; LJ 1866-67; TJ 1866-71
BELL, John [Army]
880 1867
BELL, John [Cardiff]
HJ 1874
BELL, Richard
440 1873
BELL, Thomas
PV 1869
BELL, William
1M 1866; 2M 1867; 3M 1867; 4M 1867
BELLAMY, Thomas (15.02.1854 – 1924)
PV 1876-78
BENDIXEN, Julius Carl (1851 – 24.02.1924)
3M 1876
AAC: 4M 76/3
BENNETT, Adam
TJ 1867
BENNETT, John H. (c1850)
220H 1873
BENNETT, Thomas Oliver (02.04.1852 – 08.08.1905)
440H 1874
BENSON, Francis (Frank) Robert (04.11.1858 –
31.12.1939) 2M 1879-80; 3M 1879-80
BENSON, Robert Henry (24.09.1850 – 07.04.1929)
880 1871, 73; 1M 1870-71, 73; 2M 1872;
3M 1870, 72
AAC: 1M 70/1
BENSON, Robert Seymour (19.10.1858 – 2.03.1938)
1M 1880
AAC/LAC: SC 79L/3
BENT, Herbert (1857)
100 1877
BENTLEY, J.E.
AAC: 7MW 70/3, 71/dsq
BENTON, P.
220H 1868
BENWELL, C.
600 1869
BENZIES, Samuel
SP 1867; HT 1867
BERGMAN, Edward (08.02.1849 – 12.1871)
HJ 1867-68; PV 1867-68, 70; LJ 1869-70
AAC: HJ 70/2=; PV 70/2; LJ 70/5
BERKELEY, J.K.
440H 1868
BERNHARDT, Carlyle Washington W. (1853 – 1884)
220H 1876
BEST, J.
PV 1869
BESTOW, Samuel Frederick (03.03.1852 – 1915)
120H 1874-76, 78; 440H 1874
BETHUNE, David (18.04.1832 – 26.05.1919)
HT 1867
BETHUNE, Walter Ross Munro (19.02.1845)
880 1868
AAC: 880 68/3
BETTS, Walter (1850 – 1928)
440 1871; 880 1871; 1M 1870
BETTS, William Hammond (25.08.1846 – 14.06.1884)
AAC: 100 68/3h; 120H 68/4; LJ 68/ac

BETTY, Frederick William (1857 – 25.05.1935)
LJ 1879-80
BETTY, Montague (1859)
100 1877
BEVERIDGE, William Wightman (27.11.1858 –
20.04.1941) 100 1879-80
BEVERLEY, William Le Vane Robert Roxby
(18.04.1859 – c1896) 300 1880; 440 1878-80
BEVINGTON, Herbert Shelley (15.12.1852 –
09.08.1926) 120H 1877-78
BEVIR, Edward Lawrence (02.06.1847 – 29.10.1923)
1M 1867
BICKNELL, Walter Lionel (13.05.1853 – 13.12.1895)
120H 1872
BINNS, David (20.08.1841 – 1876)
440 1869; 880 1868
BIRD, Albert Edward (15.08.1846 – 14.02.1916)
880 1868-70; 1M 1869-71, 73; 2M 1871;
6M 1872-73; 10M 1872-73; 1Hr 1873
BIRD, George Oliver (21.06.1860 – 15.08.1932)
PV 1878
BIRD, James
LJ 1874
BIRKETT
SP 1873
BIRLEY, Francis Hornby (14.03.1850 – 01.08.1910)
HT 1870, 72
BIRNIE, Alexander
HT 1877
BLACK, A.
SP 1866
BLACK, George
TJ 1872, 79-80
BLACK, J.
PV 1880
BLACK, J.
HT 1875
BLACK, James [Glasgow]
HJ 1869; TJ 1869, 71
BLACK, James [Netherley]
HT 1879
BLACK, John
HJ 1869
BLACK, W.A.
SP 1878
BLAINE, Alfred Edmund Bousfield (03.04.1853)
HJ 1870
BLAIR, James
SP 1869
BLAND, James Franklin McMahon (06.04.1850 –
16.09.1927) HJ 1869-73
AAC: HJ 72/3
BLATHWAYT, Gerard Wynter (27.06.1855 –
07.08.1943) HJ 1876-78
AAC: HJ 77/1, 78/2
BLAXTER, George Henry (11.03.1856 – 03.05.1927)
100 1873, 76; 220 1874-75; 440 1875-76;
440H 1874-75
BLAXTER, William Foulkes (29.03.1854 – 14.12.1932)
100 1874-76; 200 1875; 220 1873; 440 1874-75
BODINGTON, Herbert (23.07.1849)
120H 1868
BOLTON, John (07.07.1852)
AAC: 880 73/dnf
BOLTON, T.
AAC: SP 71/ac

BOLTON, William Washington (03.07.1858 –
09.07.1946)
880 1878-79; 1000 1878; 1M 1878
AAC: 880 78/ac, 79/1
BOND, Richard
100 1877
BOND, Richard Pratt (c1856 – 02.12.1935)
100 1878
BOOTH, Amos (c1854 – 1922)
200 1878
BOOTH, Herbert A. (1859)
100 1876; 220 1878
BOOTHBY, Reginald Evelyn (18.01.1855 –
25.02.1915)
440H 1875
BOR, Edward John (25.08.1850 – 15.04.1929)
SP 1869-74
AAC: SP 71/2, 72/1, 73/1
BORLAND, Robert (19.01.1858)
HJ 1880; TJ 1879
BORLAND, William (c1848)
HJ 1873, 76; PV 1869, 71-80; TJ 1869-75, 77
BOUCHER, Arthur Henry (c1855 – 13.11.1907)
TJ 1876
BOURKE, T.
TJ 1873, 77
BOWER see NOTT BOWER
BOWIE, Alexander (1844 – 19.01.1892)
SP 1868-69
BOWIE, George (01.09.1856)
TJ 1880; SP 1877-80; HT 1876-78, 80
BOWIE, Peter (1854)
HT 1878
BOWLBY, Anthony Alfred (10.05.1855 – 07.04.1929)
100 1877
BOWMAN, William Paget (25.09.1845 – 07.01.1917)
880 1867-68; 1M 1866-68; 2M 1866
AAC: 1M 66/2
BOYD, John
LJ 1872
BOYD, William (c1845)
SP 1866
BOYLE, Joseph Barnes Swift (22.06.1844 – 1919)
AAC: LJ 66/4
BOYLE, T.
SP 1879
BOYNE, Francis (25.11.1857)
SP 1879; HT 1879-80
BRACEGIRDLE, Joseph
PV 1875
BRACEGIRDLE, William
PV 1875-76
BRADBURY, H. (c1850)
220 1869
BRADLEY, George
220H 1878; 440H 1877-78
BRADSHAW, John Gerald (27.05.1860 – 05.09.1931)
880 1880; 1M 1880
BRAMELD, Godfrey (10.09.1848)
100 1867
BRANNAGAN, Michael
HJ 1872-73; TJ 1876
BRASH, Alexander (c1851 – 17.09.1911)
220 1875
BREMNER, Peter (20.01.1842 – 1881)
SP 1866, 68-70; HT 1868-69

BREMNER, William (03.01.1847 – 30.10.1934)
HJ 1871; SP 1867-768, 70-80; HT 1867, 69-80
BRETT, F.
120H 1875
BRIGHTON, John (14.07.1832 – 1896)
2M 1866-67, 69, 71; 3M 1866-67, 71; 4M 1866-67,
70; 6M 1866-67, 69; 10M 1866-67, 73; 1HR 1866
BRINDLEY, P.A.
LJ 1867
BROAD, C.E.
AAC: 7MW 69/2
BROADFOOT, Alexander Primrose (29.02.1852)
100 1876
BROCKBANK, John (22.08.1848 – 29.01.1904)
880 1867, 70; 120H 1872
AAC: 120H 72/3h
BRODIE, Arthur William Lawson (09.05.1851 –
13.06.1874)
100 1872; 200 1872; 440 1872-73
AAC: 100 72/4; 440 72/2
BROOKE, Henry William (07.1848 – 23.01.1929)
HJ 1866
BROOKE, Joshua (06.06.1846 – 01.01.1934)
220 1866
BROOKE, Sir Victor Alexander (bapt. 05.01.1843 –
23.11.1891) HJ 1867
BROOKES, J.
LJ 1875
BROOKES, James (1847)
LJ 1869
BROOKS, Hon. Marshall Jones (30.05.1855 –
05.01.1944) HJ 1873-76; LJ 1876
AAC: HJ 74/1, 76/1
BROWN, Alexander
SP 1879
BROWN, Henry (16.01.1843 – 09.03.1884)
10M 1876
BROWN, Isaac
HJ 1874
BROWN, J. [Penicuik]
SP 1875
BROWN, J. [Noag/IRL]
SP 1878; HT 1878
BROWN, James [Leith]
SP 1866
BROWN, James [Edinburgh]
SP 1873
BROWN, John [Edinburgh]
SP 1875-77; HT 1876
BROWN, John [Dalkeith]
SP 1874
BROWN, R.C.
220 1872; 250 1873
BROWN, Richard Howel (27.06.1856 – 14.05.1928)
120H 1879
BROWN, Stephen Stawell (01.06.1854 – 01.06.1909)
SP 1874-75; HT 1871-75
AAC: SP 74/4; HT 74/1, 75/3
BROWN, Thomas S. (c1849)
HJ 1871-72
BROWN, W.
PV 1870
BROWN, W. [Ancient Order of Foresters]
SP 1871
BROWN, W.H.
220H 1875

BROWN, William
HT 1874
BROWNE, Lambert John (19.08.1850 – 16.05.1916)
220H 1870
BROWNFIELD, Douglas Harold (30.03.1856 –
05.08.1917) HJ 1880; LJ 1880
BROWNING, D.
SP 1879
BRUCE, J.
PV 1869
BRUCE, Stewart Armit Macdonald (17.11.1858 –
06.04.1937) 100 1877; LJ 1877-78, 80
BRUCE, William.
PV 1872; TJ 1873
BRUCE, William Napier (15.01.1858 – 20.03.1936)
440 1877-78, 80
BRUMELL, Bertram (c1853 – 14.05.1905)
LJ 1871
BRUNSKILL, Richard Fothergill (14.05.1853 –
27.09.1900) 100 1871
BRUNT, Gunner
440H 1872
BRUNTON, Duncan Macnaughten (05.02.1852 –
14.11.1876) TJ 1876
BRYAN, Charles (c1847 – 24.10.1892)
880 1871, 75; 440H 1873, 77
BRYAN, M.
1M 1873
BRYDEN, Henry Anderson (03.05.1854 – 23.09.1937)
880 1871, 73-76; 1M 1875
AAC: 880 75/2, 76/3
BRYMER, George (25.09.1849)
PV 1873
BULL, W.J.
220 1879
BULLOCK, William
SP 1870
BULLOCK-WEBSTER, Frank (21.12.1854 –
21.09.1942) 2M 1876; 3M 1876-77
BULPETT, Charles William Lloyd (18.08.1852 –
11.07.1939) 2M 1875; 3M 1875
AAC: 4M 75/dnf
BURBERY, G.
440H 1870
BURGESS, G.
HJ 1877-78
BURGESS, John Francis Chassereau (22.09.1848 –
08.06.1919) SP 1869
BURGESS, William Arnold (27.12.1846 – 13.12.1919)
HT 1866, 68-76, 78-79
AAC/LAC: HT 69/1, 70/3, 71/1, 72/3, 74/2, 75/1,
78/2, 79L/1
BURGESS, William Ralph (bapt. 14.05.1845 –
02.12.1910) SP 1868
BURKE, J.H.
LJ 1877
BURKE, P.
440H 1880
BURKE, Robert B.
220 1878
BURKE, T.
TJ 1880
BURLEIGH, Samuel Charles (1849 – 1918)
HJ 1871
BURN, A.G. (1857)
100 1872

ELLIOTT, J.
SP 1869
ELLIOTT, J. Garratt
AAC: 120H 69/4
ELLIOTT, William Gerald (09.11.1858 – 30.08.1930)
LJ 1879
AAC: LJ 79/1
ELLISON, Michael (1850 – 14.04.1899)
PV 1872
ELMSLIE, James (c1859)
HT 1877
ELMSLIE, John (c1853)
HT 1877
EMERY, Charles George (c1843 – 1911)
220 1866-67
AAC: 100 66/4, 67/2h; 120H 66/5, 67/3h
EMSLIE, Charles
SP 1866, 68-69; HT 1866, 68
ENGLAND, A.
HT 1880
ENGLAND, H.
220 1879
ENGLISH, Augustus John (26.09.1851 – 18.11.1909)
LJ 1870-71
ESCOTT, Ernest Birkham Sweet (20.08.1857 –
09.04.1941) 880 1877 [aka SWEET-ESCOTT]
ESSON, James
SP 1868-69; HT 1867
ETHERIDGE, Edwin John Charles (1859 - 10.07.1912)
880 1880
EVANS, Alfred Henry (14.06.1858 – 26.03.1934)
440H 1877
EVANS, Edward Cecil Middleton (1854 – 26.01.1902)
100 1875
EVANS, Lewis (09.07.1851 – 08.12.1939)
100 1868; 440 1870; 880 1872; 1M 1871-73, 76;
2M 1872
EVANSON, Wyndham Alleyn Daubeny (1851 –
30.10.1934) 300 1877; 120H 1880; SP 1875-80
EWBANK, Christopher Cooper (10.03.1845 –
09.07.1933) PV 1866
AAC: PV 66/2
EWING, James
PV 1869
EWING, William (c1847)
PV 1867-71, 74
EYRE, John Rashdall (29.01.1845 – 12.06.1902)
HT 1867-68
AAC: HT 67/2

FAIRBAIRN, Thomas Gordon (26.05.1854 –
19.12.1931) 1M 1874
FAIRLIE, James Ogilvy Reginald (28.12.1848 –
20.09.1916) 100 1866, 68
FARMER, Archibald Sidney (c1852 – 06.05.1929)
120H 1878
FARRAN, Edmond Chomley (27.08.1847 – 1881)
1M 1867
FARNWORTH, Thomas Hodson (1844 – 1887)
AAC: 7MW 67/1
FARRAN, Charles Frederick (1840 – 10.09.1898)
AAC: 4M 66/dnf
FARRINGTON, Thomas Hudson
TJ 1876
FELL, Charles Yates (NZ) (05.08.1844 – 09.06.1918)
440 1866; 120H 1866

FELLOWES, Frederick William (12.02.1858 –
20.08.1928)
100 1879; 300 1879; 440 1878; LJ 1877
AAC: 440 79/3
FELLOWES, Henry Cecil (22.11.1851 – 10.10.1915)
LJ 1868-69
AAC: PV 72/1; LJ 72/4
FELLOWES, John Adolphus Liddell (29.04.1859 –
04.04.1939) 120H 1880; LJ 1880
FELLOWS, Private
HJ 1867
FELTHAM, A.
1M 1876
FENWICK, Francis
120H 1871
FERGUSON, B.
AAC: 7MW 72/dsq
FERGUSON, C.
TJ 1877-78
FERGUSON, Duncan (06.09.1849)
PV 1870, 79
FERGUSON, G.
TJ 1876
FERGUSON, Harold Stuart (10.02.1851 – 05.01.1921)
LJ 1870
AAC: LJ 71/4
FERGUSON, James
SP 1877-78; HT 1877
FERGUSON, James Shiels (c1856 – 14.07.1934)
440H 1880
FERGUSON, John Burnside (1852 – 19.10.1906)
880 1875-77; 1M 1876; 4M 1875
FITZGERALD, John Vesey (25.02.1848 – 24.04.1929)
AAC: 100 70/4sf
FERGUSON, William
PV 1876, 80; SP 1877-78
FERRIS, Peter
SP 1871; HT 1870-71
FIELD, Jacob
PV 1867-68, 72-73
FIELDING, T.
LJ 1873
FINCH, Frederick John (1855)
220 1874
FINDLAY, James [Edinburgh Univ] (08.04.1852)
220 1871
FINDLAY, James [Craigiedhu] (c1852)
SP 1868, 70
FINLAN, James
SP 1873
FINLAY, Alexander Kirkman (24.09.1844 - 29.07.1883)
440 1868
FINLAYSON, John Donald (27.07.1854 – 10.02.1910)
1M 1880; 2M 1875
FINN, B.
SP 1879
FINNIE, T.
TJ 1872
FINUCANE
TJ 1872
FIRMINGER, Francis Waldemar (1856 – 01.11.1931)
50M 1879
FISHBOURNE, George (03.10.1855 – 30.12.1907)
100 1878
FITZGERALD, Dudley R. (c1848)
TJ 1869

HACKINGLEY, W.
  100 1869
HADFIELD, Joseph (17.02.1849 – 13.11.1904)
  440H 1872
HAGGARD, William Henry Doveton (25.06.1846 –
  22.01.1926)
  AAC: 120H 66/3h
HAGUE, John H. (c1847)
  AAC: 100 69/2=; LJ 69/2
HAGUE, W.
  HJ 1870
HAILSTONES, P.
  PV 1871
HAINE
  1M 1869
HAINES, E.
  220H 1879
HAINES, John Pleydell Wilton (23.03.1850)
  TJ 1867
HAINES, William (c1848)
  1M 1871; 3M 1871
HALES, George Henry (20.05.1854 – 22.11.1922)
  HT 1873-77
  AAC: HT 74/5, 76/1, 77/1
HALKETT, Patrick (02.04.1837 – 1886)
  SP 1867-68; HT 1867-68
  AAC: SP 67/ac; HT 67/1, 68/3
HALL, Anthony (c1846 – 09.06.1901)
  HJ 1869-70, 73; PV 1868-74, 76, 78-79
HALL, Reginald (22.02.1860)
  2M 1880
HALL, William
  PV 1866, 68
HALL, William (1857)
  HJ 1878-79; TJ 1878
  AAC/LAC: HJ 79L/1=
HALLETT, Henry (1841)
  SP 1866
HALLILEY, William George (16.09.1851 – c1915)
  HJ 1867
HAM, Thomas Goodman (c1855)
  220H 1877
HAMBRIDGE, Thomas (05.03.1854)
  100 1874
HAMILTON, Archibald Henry (22.12.1847 –
  21.08.1900) 150 1872
HAMILTON, Charles Pollock (09.10.1853)
  440H 1876; PV 1876; LJ 1876
HAMILTON, Horace George Pollock (16.11.1854 –
  17.01.1891) PV 1879
HAMILTON, Hugh Montgomery (26.06.1854 –
  11.08.1930) 440 1872
HAMILTON, William Drummond (04.05.1859 –
  04.03.1914) 3M 1879
HAMILTON, William Joseph (01.07.1850 - 22.05.1931)
  440H 1872-73, 75-76
HAMLEY, Edward Charles (02.1855 – 25.06.1926)
  440 1872-73
HAMMOND, Charles Edward (06.12.1856 – 1926)
  HJ 1879
HANCOCK, Alfred (c1849)
  220H 1872
HANRAHAN, T.J.
  HJ 1880; TJ 1880
HANSON, J.
  440H 1871

HANWELL, Joseph (c1861 – 30.10.1900)
  440H 1880
HARDING, Edward
  LJ 1872; TJ 1870-72
HARDY, A.
  AAC: 4M 70/3
HARGREAVES, Frederick (05.09.1850 – 04.1907)
  220H 1871; HJ 1870-71; LJ 1870-72, 76
HARGREAVES, John
  HJ 1875-78; TJ 1875-77; CB 1875, 77
HARPER, J.R.
  120H 1876; LJ 1875
HARRINGTON, Sergeant
  HT 1867
HARRIS, George Stanley (21.06.1860 – 15.08.1932)
  440 1878; 1M 1880
HARRIS, H. [York]
  CB 1877
HARRIS, H. [German Gymnastic Society]
  HJ 1879
HARRIS, J. [Ashford]
  440H 1870
HARRIS, James [Army]
  1M 1875
HARRIS, James [Middlesbrough BC]
  4M 1879
  AAC: 4M 79/2
HARRIS, John Gregory (AUS) (– 14.06.1912)
  440 1868
HARRIS, R.E.
  2M 1868
HARRISON, A.
  220H 1875
HARRISON, Frank
  TJ 1877-78
HARRISON, J.
  PV 1878
HARRISON, J.F.
  440H 1873
HARRISON, John (22.03.1851) [Wellington Coll]
  100 1868
HARRISON, John [QC Galway]
  100 1870; 880 1870
HART, Horatio Holt (09.08.1850 – 1915)
  440H 1868
HARTLEY, Charles (1849 – 15.07.1909)
  440H 1870
HARTLEY, J.R.
  SP 1867
HARTUNG, Frederick Morris (29.05.1846 – 1909)
  220 1869-70
HARVEY, John Edward (28.10.1859)
  440H 1877-78
HARVEY, William Morton (27.01.1858 – 27.01.1939)
  880 1879
HARWOOD, John Augustus (22.06.1845 - 19.02.1929)
  HJ 1866-68, 70, 72
  AAC: HJ 69/2, 70/2=, 71/2, 72/4, 73/2=
HASKETT-SMITH, Algernon (04.07.1856 - 21.11.1887)
  LJ 1877
HASSARD, Fairfax Norman Fielding (13.10.1848 –
  07.05.1875) 880 1869
HATFIELD, Alexander (7.09.1857 – 24.07.1890)
  AAC: 100 73/3h
HATRICK, John
  SP 1880

KIRK, George Henry (21.12.1856 – 28.10.1938)
100 1877; 220H 1877; HJ 1877
KIRKE-SMITH, Arnold (23.04.1850 – 08.10.1927)
120H 1867, 71; 440H 1871
KITCHEN, C.
100 1870
KITSON, Thomas (c1847)
120H 1871; 220H 1870
AAC: 120H 72/4h
KNIGHT, Montagu George (26.10.1844 – 11.07.1914)
440 1867; 880 1867
KNOT, J.
TJ 1868
KNOWLES, Lees (16.02.1857 – 07.10.1928)
440 1879; 880 1878-79; 1M 1877-78; 2M 1876;
3M 1876-77
AAC: 880 78/1=, 79/2
KNOX, Henry (1841)
PV 1866
KNOX, Robert (17.09.1847 – 13.02.1911)
LJ 1867-72, 75, 77; TJ 1866-80
KOCH, Walter Edward (19.03.1848 – 25.05.1916)
440H 1870
KOUGH, James Thomas (30.03.1851 – 27.06.1927)
LJ 1873, 77
KROHN, Hermann Alexander (SA) (02.1850 –
01.02.1929) 100 1871

LAING, A.
SP 1880
LAING, Charles
SP 1875
LAING, John William (01.04.1846)
440 1866; 880 1866; 1M 1866-69; 2M 1866-67;
120H 1868
LAMBERDON, A.
TJ 1869
LAMBERT, Arthur William (17.01.1847 – 06.1873)
440 1868; 880 1868; 120H 1868
LAMBERT, Richard Eyre (14.07.1827 – 06.06.1898)
AAC: PV 66/3
LAMBERT, W.
440H 1880
LAMOND, James
PV 1872-73
LAMONT, Daniel (c1855 – 15.02.1886)
HJ 1875-80; LJ 1879; TJ 1873-74, 76-80
LANDER, J.
SP 1875
LANE, James Ernest (24.07.1857 – 04.11.1926)
120H 1877-78
LANE, John Godwin (1853 – 05.07.1918)
LJ 1873-75
LANG, William (22.12.1838 – 29.07.1905)
2M 1867-68; 3M 1867-68; 4M 1867-68;
6M 1867-68; 10M 1867-68
LANG, William Thomas (22.06.1854 – 1902)
100 1873
LANGALL, Private W.
100 1867
LANGSTAFF, John (c1850)
100 1874
LANIGAN, Private
SP 1877
LARK, Francis Bothamley (c1850 – 1928)
120H 1872; 220H 1871

LARRETTE, Charles Henry (23.02.1844 – 09.05.1913)
2M 1874; 6M 1877; 10M 1877
AAC: 4M 73/dnf, 74/dnf
LA TOUCHE, William Martin Diques (c1854 –
14.08.1926) 1M 1878
LATTER, Bertram Henry (11.08.1858 – 07.10.1919)
880 1880; HT 1879-80
LAVERS, Arthur Charles (19.01.1860 – 29.05.1908)
220 1880
LAW, Arthur James (21.03.1844 – 28.06.1920)
LJ 1866
AAC: 120H 67/1
LAW, William
SP 1869
LAW, William (01.12.1853 – 12.02.1932)
PV 1872, 75
LAWES, Charles Bennet (03.10.1843 – 06.10.1911)
[Assumed additional name of WITTEWRONGE by
Royal Licence in 1902]
880 1866; 1M 1866
AAC: 1M 66/1; SP 67/ac
LAWES, William Pattison (15.02.1851 – 23.06.1894)
PV 1872
LAWLER, M.
SP 1878-80; HT 1874
LAWRENCE, George Patrick Charles (17.03.1859 –
18.04.1908)
120H 1879-80; HJ 1880; LJ 1880
LAWRENCE, Walter (20.05.1859)
HT 1879-80
LAWRENCE, Wyndham (11.01.1851 – 03.10.1886)
HJ 1868
LAWSON, Thomas
PV 1870
LAWSON, W.
PV 1866-67
LEACH, Richard Ernest (1856 – 02.02.1929)
440 1877
LEACH, Robert (18.12.1849 – 10.09.1939)
440 1871
LEAK, John William (1851)
120H 1868
LEE, H.
LJ 1874
LEE, P.
TJ 1870
LEE, Thomas
220 1870; 440H 1869
LEE-EVANS, Harold James (12.05.1857 – 18.09.1893)
1M 1878; 2M 1877-79; 3M 1878-79
AAC: 1M 76/2, 78/3
LEEDS, Charles Edward (1845 – 07.03.1905)
PV 1868, 70, 73, 75
AAC: PV 73/2
LEEKE, Henry A. (06.02.1846 – 21.02.1922)
HT 1866-72, 74
AAC: SP 69/1, 70/ac, 71/ac; HT 68/1, 69/2, 70/1,
71/3, 72/1, 74/4
LEGGATT, Edward Colebrook (c1850 – 12.01.1911)
LJ 1872
LEHANE, D
HJ 1876; TJ 1876
LEIGHTON, D.
SP 1872
LEIGHTON, James
SP 1866, 68

McSWINEY, Edward Frederick Henry (25.02.1858 –
  21.01.1907) 220 1878
MADDEN, Patrick
  1M 1871
MADDOCK, Arthur L. (c1856)
  1M 1876
MAHER, P.
  TJ 1875
MAINWARING, Rowland Broughton (11.09.1850 –
  22.11.1926) 220H 1870
MAITLAND, Frederick William (28.05.1850 –
  21.12.1906)
  3M 1870
MAITLAND, J.
  HT 1880
MAITLAND, William Fuller (06.05.1844 – 15.11.1932)
  100 1866; 440 1867; LJ 1866-67
  AAC: 100 66/3h
MALDEN, Arthur Russell (1850 – 22.10.1913)
  100 1869; 220 1871; 120H 1869
MALLARD, Edward Christopher (1849 – 01.06.1892)
  PV 1872
MALLETT, Richard Henry (14.10.1858 – 29.11.1939)
  120H 1879-80
MALLEY, H.R.
  HT 1875
MALLINSON, Fred (c1852 – 1915)
  HJ 1874
MALONE, Thomas Michael (26.12.1859 – 12.1919)
  100 1878-80; 120 1878; 220 1878; 440 1879;
  HJ 1878-79; LJ 1878-80; TJ 1878; SP 1878, 80
MALONEY, M.
  TJ 1875
MALONEY, Tom
  TJ 1878
MANN, William Woodham (17.11.1849 – 10.05.1915)
  LJ 1869
  AAC: LJ 71/ac
MANNING, J. (USA)
  880 1877
MANTELL, Tom (1853 – 11.02.1928)
  250 1874
MAPLETON, Cuthbert Walter (18.08.1854 –
  12.12.1916) 880 1872
MAPPLEBECK, Edward (06.04.1845 – 1937)
  1M 1867-68; 2M 1868-69
MARKHAM, Alfred (c1848)
  2M 1869; 3M 1869; 10M 1875
MARRIAGE, David (1852 – 07.10.1922)
  HJ 1870
MARRYAT, F.
  100 1870
MARSDEN, Reginald Godfrey (15.07.1845 –
  11.05.1927) HT 1866
MARSHALL, Adam (c1852 – 14.04.1896)
  600 1876; LJ 1880; TJ 1877, 79-80
MARSHALL, Bernard (26.05.1853 – 16.02.1912)
  1M 1873-74
MARSHALL, W.
  SP 1867
MARTIN, Corporal
  HT 1877
MARTIN, Brownlow Rudinge (1848 – 13.02.1923)
  100 1872; 1000 1871; LJ 1872
MARTIN, Cornwallis Philip Wykeham (19.03.1855 –
  23.02.1924) 100 1875

MARTIN, Henry (1849)
  100 1871
MARTIN, John Biddulph (10.06.1841 – 20.03.1897)
  440 1866; 1M 1867; 120H 1866
  AAC: 120H 66/3, 67/5
MARTIN, Piper M.
  PV 1868, 80
MARTIN, Robert Jasper (17.06.1846 – 13.09.1905)
  HT 1866
MASON, C.
  HJ 1871; PV 1872
  AAC: HJ 71/3
MASON, Charles Henry (03.06.1851 – 29.12.1902)
  880 1872, 76 1M 1872; 2M 1872, 75-76, 79;
  3M 1875-76; 4M 1875-76, 79; 6M 1879-80;
  10M 1879-80
  AAC/LAC: 1M 72/1; 4M 73/dnf, 76/2, 79L/dnf; 10M
  79L/1
MASSEY, Harry M. (c1857)
  100 1878-80; 220 1879-80; LJ 1879-80
  AAC/LAC: 100 79L/4
MASSEY, W.
  100 1876
MASSEY, W.M. jun.
  SP 1879
MASTERS, Henry H. (c1852)
  120H 1872
MATHER, Allan
  SP 1866
MATHER, William (1857 – 05.07.1934)
  220 1874
MATHIESON, W.
  HT 1877
MATTHEWS, John Ernest (1850 – 28.04.1930)
  2M 1871-72
  AAC: 4M 72/dnf, 74/dnf
MATTHEWS, Richard.
  220 1872
  AAC: 100 70/4sf
MATTHEWS, Thomas (1845)
  100 1868
MAUGHAM, J.
  LJ 1870
MAWBY, George Turnell (17.07.1857 – 1900)
  1M 1876; 2M 1879; 3M 1878-79; 4M 1879;
  6M 1879; 10M 1878-79
MAXWELL-LYTE, John Walker (20.06.1850 –
  28.01.1887) LJ 1869
MAY, J.
  1M 1878
MAY, John R. (c1842)
  1M 1869
MAYOR, Richard (c1840 – 22.12.1891)
  220H 1870; HJ 1867-68
MEARNS, George
  HJ 1876; SP 1869-70, 73-79
MELDRUM, William
  SP 1879; HT 1878-79
MELLOR, Joseph (c1852)
  3M 1873
MELROSE, James (17.04.1847 – 04.10.1899)
  SP 1869, 79; HT 1875, 79-80
MELVILL, Charles Curling (21.10.1859 – 17.12.1931)
  100 1878
MENZIES, Archibald
  HT 1867

MONEY, Rowland Fearnley Kyrle (1851 – 22.03.1903)
   HJ 1870
MONNINGTON, Alfred (29.05.1853 – 01.02.1945)
   HJ 1874; LJ 1873
MONNINGTON, Charles Jones (18.01.1850 –
   19.12.1931)
   100 1871
MONRO, William
   SP 1877
MONTGOMERIE, Hon. George Arnulph (23.02.1848 –
   10.08.1918)
   AAC: 4M 66/dnf
MONTGOMERY, Hugh de Fellenberg (14.08.1844 –
   08.10.1924)
   AAC: 7MW 66/dnf
MONTGOMERY, R.
   SP 1873
MOON, James
   SP 1868
MOONEY, Private J.
   SP 1868
MOORE, Edward
   HJ 1870
MOORE, Edwin (c1846 – c1904)
   100 1871; 220 1871; 220H 1871
MOORE, F.T.
   TJ 1870
MOORE, Henry Ogle (1848 – 06.09.1903)
   880 1876
MOORE, Joseph Westwood (03.04.1852 - 05.02.1895)
   880 1871-74; 1M 1873; 2M 1874
   AAC: 880 73/3, 74/3; 1M 73/3
MOORE, W.F.P. – see POWELL MOORE, W.F.
MOORHOUSE, James Henry (c1845 – 22.03.1918)
   220H 1871; 440H 1869
MORGAN, David Parker (1843 – 26.09.1915)
   120H 1866; SP 1866; HT 1866
   AAC: 120H 66/dnf; HT 66/2
MORGAN, John
   HJ 1874
MORGAN, John Hammond (19.08.1847 – 11.10.1924)
   2M 1867-70; 3M 1867-70
MORGAN, W.J.F.
   AAC: 100 69/4h
MORGAN, William James (1845)
   2MW 1873; 7MW 1873-74
   AAC: 7MW 73/1, 74/1, 75/1, 76/dnf, 77/2
MORPHEW, George Edward (1854 – 13.10.1942)
   120H 1875
MORRIS, E.
   440H 1876
MORRIS, William G.
   440H 1866-68
MORTON, William (1849)
   HJ 1873; LJ 1874
'MOSQUITO, Jimmy' (AUS) – see GROUGARRONG
MOXLEY, Joseph Henry Sutton (c1844)
   HT 1874
MOXLEY, Stephen Emanuel M. (c1857 – 1893)
   HT 1880
MOYLE, John Baron (19.12.1852 – 25.02.1930)
   PV 1871
MUDD, Harry Thomas (06.1854 – 01.08.1891)
   1M 1877
MUGGERIDGE, John (07.07.1846 – 01.06.1876)
   440 1867

MUIR, J. [Ballymahon]
   HT 1875
MUIR, James [Overtown]
   HT 1875
MUIR, Samuel (c1841)
   HJ 1866-74; PV 1869-71, 74; LJ 1866-70, 72-74;
   TJ 1866-74; SP 1869
MUIR, W.
   PV 1871
MULCAHY, D.
   TJ 1880
MULES, Philip Henry (1843 – 01.09.1905)
   SP 1867
MULHOLLAND, Private
   TJ 1874
MULLIGAN
   LJ 1878
MULLINS, Arthur John (01.02.1861 – 1938)
   440H 1879-80
MULLOWNEY, M.
   TJ 1877
MURISON, Thomas (25.05.1855)
   SP 1880; HT 1876
MURPHY, Dr.
   TJ 1869
MURPHY, Private
   SP 1877
MURPHY, J. [Charleville/IRL]
   TJ 1873
MURPHY, J. [Claremorris/IRL]
   HT 1877
MURPHY, J.F.
   120H 1880
MURPHY, M.
   TJ 1873
MURPHY, T.
   HT 1878
MURRAY, Alexander
   HT 1880
MURRAY, Harry W.
   AAC: 880 73/dnf
MURRAY, J. [Ancient Order of Foresters]
   SP 1871
MURRAY, J.
   TJ 1874
MURRAY, James [Greenock]
   SP 1869
MURRAY, William [Dublin Univ]
   440H 1867
MURRAY, William [Leith]
   TJ 1870-71
MURRAY, William
   TJ 1876
MUSGRAVE, John (01.1839 – 08.03.1919)
   PV 1870-72
MUSGRAVE, Robert (11.10.1841 – 19.03.1901)
   PV 1866-69, 78

NAIRNE, John Domett (23.10.1846 – 15.01.1929)
   1M 1871
NALLY, M.J. McNeeve
   LJ 1875; TJ 1875
NALLY, Patrick W. (1856)
   440H 1878; HJ 1875; LJ 1877; TJ 1874, 77; SP
   1875-76, 79; HT 1877-78

INDEX SPENCER - 239

SINGER, Edward William (c1851)
220 1875
SINGER, Walter Herbert John (1853 – 27.01.1922)
220H 1876
SLADE, Frederick (1849 – 06.10.1929)
440H 1868-69
SLADE, Walter (06.04.1854 – 13.06.1919)
880 1872-76, 80; ¾M 1875-77; 1M 1872-77, 80;
2M 1873-76; 3M 1874-75; 4M 1874-75
AAC: 1M 73/1, 74/1, 75/1, 76/1, 77/1; 4M 74/1,
75/dnf
SLATTERY, James
SP 1880; HT 1879-80
SLOGGETT, Thomas John Picton (22.10.1854 –
05.10.1925) 880 1878
SMALL, Tom (11.03.1843)
880 1868
SMALLEY, Henry Alfred (18.02.1832 – 10.1874)
25M 1868
SMITH, A.W.
220H 1878
SMITH, Arthur Parkyn (21.03.1852)
1M 1876; 4M 1877
AAC: 4M 76/dnf, 78/dnf
SMITH, Arthur S. (c1855)
100 1877, 80; 220 1876, 80; 440 1880
SMITH, Charles Mollett Sundius [afterwards SMITH-
SUNDIUS] (1851 – 1903) 120H 1872
SMITH, D.
TJ 1873
SMITH, Edward
TJ 1876
SMITH, Edwin
HJ 1876
SMITH, Frederick [Chesterfield FC]
2M 1873; 3M 1871
SMITH, Frederick W. [Dublin U]
440H 1866-67
SMITH, Harold (16.03.1858 – 11.09.1938)
440 1880
SMITH, J. [Edinburgh]
TJ 1878; SP 1877; HT 1874, 76
SMITH, J. [Dalkeith]
SP 1875
SMITH, J. [Glasgow]
SP 1876
SMITH, J.
SP 1872
SMITH, J. [Romiley AC]
220 1878
SMITH, James [Kildrummy]
SP 1869, 71, 78-80; HT 1869
SMITH, James [Cragganmore]
HT 1876
SMITH, John [Bury AC] (13.04.1855)
880 1875, 78, 80; 1M 1875-78
SMITH, John [Edinburgh]
TJ 1875
SMITH, John [Edinburgh Univ]
TJ 1876, 78
SMITH, John [Kildrummy, Speybridge]
SP 1876-80; HT 1877
SMITH, John Thornton [OUAC] (1845 – 18.03.1871)
100 1866; 120H 1866
SMITH, Lewis
SP 1871, 75

SMITH, M.
10M 1878
SMITH, R.S.
120H 1870
SMITH, Robert
HT 1879
SMITH, Robert W.
HJ 1867
AAC: 100 66/ac-h; 120H 66/3h; HJ 66/4; LJ 66/3
SMITH, T. [Mountmellick, IRL]
SP 1879
SMITH, T. [HMS St Vincent]
100 1880
SMITH, W. [Glasgow]
SP 1876
SMITH, W. [Edinburgh]
SP 1878
SMITH, William (27.12.1846 – 31.12.1907)
1M 1872; 2M 1878; 3M 1878; 4M 1876-78; 6M
1872, 78; 10M 1870, 76-78; 1Hr 1878; 25M 1878
SMITH, William McCombie (07.09.1847 - 29.06.1905)
PV 1870; TJ 1873, 75; SP 1871, 75;
HT 1869, 71, 73, 75, 77-80
SMITH-DORRIEN, Walter Montgomery (13.06.1851 –
17.12.1924)
1M 1870; 2M 1873; 3M 1871-73
SMYTHE, J.C.
TJ 1873
SNELL, William James (1854)
1M 1874
SNOOK, William (03.02.1861 – 09.12.1916)
1M 1880; 2M 1880; 4M 1880; 6M 1880; 10M 1880
SNOW, Joseph (c1846)
880 1866; 2M 1868-69
AAC: 4M 68/2
SNOW, Thomas (11.09.1852 – 07.06.1927)
300 1873; 440 1873, 75; HT 1875
SOAMES, Arthur Wellesley (30.11.1852 – 02.11.1934)
HJ 1870; HT 1876
SODEN, Frederick Brewer (20.03.1846 – 13.04.1877)
AAC: SP 70/ac, 71/ac
SOLLY, George Edward (27.03.1855 – 10.03.1930)
440 1876
SOMERS-SMITH, Robert Vernon (23.05.1848 –
31.03.1934)
440 1869-70; 880 1868-70; 1M 1869
AAC: 880 69/1, 70/1
SOMERVELL, James (19.09.1845 – 10.02.1924)
AAC: 100 67/2h
SOMERVILLE, Arthur Fownes (23.04.1850 –
21.11.1942)
2M 1871, 73; 3M 1872-73; 4M 1873
AAC: 4M 72/dnf, 73/1
SORBY, Albert Ernest (27.06.1859 – 01.10.1934)
HJ 1880
SOUTHAM, Frederick Armitage (17.05.1850 –
09.03.1927) 100 1872
SOWERBY, John Graham (1857)
HJ 1878; LJ 1877
SPALTON, W.
120H 1876
SPEEDIE, William (c1852)
PV 1875
SPENCER, Charles James (1848 – 17.07.1907)
120H 1873-75; 440H 1875
AAC: 120H 74/dnf

STONEHAM, Sydney Dick Allen (c1857 – 27.05.1901)
220 1879
AAC/LAC: 440 79L/4
STOREY, Edgar (06.02.1859 – 16.03.1909)
100 1875, 80; 440 1879
AAC: 100 79/2; 440 79/1
STOREY, J.
TJ 1868
STRACHAN, Edward Aubrey (16.08.1858 –
18.04.1853) 220H 1877; PV 1878-80
STRACHAN, Francis (c1837)
SP 1866
STRACHAN, Horace Ward (21.09.1855 – 13.06.1894)
220H 1876; HJ 1876-78; PV 1875-80; LJ 1875, 79
AAC/LAC: 120H 79L/4; HJ 77/2=, 79L/3=;
PV 76/1, 77/2, 78/1; LJ 76/ac, 77/2, 78/ac
STRAFFORD, H.
2M 1869
STRANG, James (c1850)
SP 1869
STRANG, William (c1848)
SP 1869
STRANGE, Leonard (06.1857)
2M 1877
STRATTON, Robert Mansell (22.09.1856)
100 1877
STRETCH, Edmund Chalmer (13.08.1849 –
15.01.1915) 220H 1869
STRETCH, J.H.
440 1871
STRETCH, Thomas Herbert (28.01.1851 - 25.12.1929)
220 1868; 220H 1870; HJ 1873; LJ 1870, 72-73,
75, 77-78; TJ 1876
STRITCH, John Russell (1844 – 22.09.1933)
HT 1867-68
STRITCH, Matthew Michael (02.1847)
SP 1873; HT 1870, 73-76
STUART, F. – see PACE, Frederick
STUART, John
HT 1880
STURGEON, T.
100 1868
STURT, Herbert Halse (24.07.1856 – 1922)
220 1877-78, 80; 440 1877-80; 880 1878
AAC/LAC: 100 77/4; 440 78/4, 79L/3
STYLES, Sidney (23.11.1848)
1M 1868
SUFFELL, William Spenceley (1859 – 12.12.1933)
2M 1880; 4M 1880; 6M 1880; 10M 1880
SUMMERHAYES, Robert Edmund Jefferies
(14.04.1853 – 19.12.1929)
100 1873, 78; 440H 1877
SUMNER, W.
TJ 1878
SURTEES, Richard Villiers (08.04.1853 – 26.04.1938)
100 1873; LJ 1871, 75-76
SUTHERLAND, John
SP 1872; HT 1872
SUTTIE, David McDonald (c1851 – 04.05.1925)
TJ 1879-80
SUTTON, Samuel (1842)
2M 1868
SWAILES, Henry (c1840)
TJ 1867
SWANWICK, Frederick Tertius (28.05.1851 –
27.07.1931) HJ 1872, 74

SWEENEY, George
SP 1878
SWIFT, J.
AAC: 4M 75/dnf
SYKES, John Thomas (c1848 – 08.07.1890)
220H 1869-70; 440H 1869; LJ 1870
SYMINGTON, James Lindsey (c1853 – 23.04.1911)
PV 1874

TAIT, Gavin (1834)
220 1869; HJ 1866-69; LJ 1866-67; TJ 1866-70;
SP 1867
TAIT, William (1836 – 09.12.1899)
HJ 1866-67, 69-71; PV 1870; TJ 1866-67, 69;
SP 1866-67, 69-70; HT 1866-67, 69
TALBOT, James (c1846 – 1900)
440 1872
TARLETON, Edward Eustace (04.02.1847 –
29.06.1888) SP 1871
TAYLOR, A.
SP 1877
TAYLOR, J. [Blackley]
440 1875
TAYLOR, J. [QTFC]
100 1876
TAYLOR, J. [Birnie]
HT 1879
TAYLOR, Joseph
HJ 1866
TAYLOR, Robert
PV 1866-67
TAYLOR, W.
220H 1869
TELFORD, William (1845)
PV 1866
TEMPLER, Frederick Gordon (12.06.1849-28.08.1918)
AAC: 100 68/3h
TEMPLER, George Anson (22.12.1851 – 07.10.1913)
100 1874; 440 1870, 72-74; 880 1871-73; 1M 1872
AAC: 100 74/3h; 440 74/1; 880 70/4, 72/1=, 73/2;
1M 69/2
TEMPLETON, H.
TJ 1880
TEMPLETON, Mitchell (23.07.1846 – 25.01.1925)
100 1867
TENNENT, Hector Norman (06.04.1842 – 19.04.1904)
100 1872
AAC: 100 72/3h; 120H 72/dnf-h
TENNENT, John Pattison (AUS) (31.07.1846 –
31.10.1893) 100 1868, 73-74, 77; 110 1871
TENNENT, William Middleton (06.10.1845 –
05.07.1883)
100 1867-68; 120H 1868
AAC: 100 68/1; 120H 68/1; LJ 68/ac
TESTER, James Alexander (02.05.1849 – 31.01.1878)
2M 1877; 3M 1877; 10M 1876
THATCHER, Henry (13.04.1853)
7MW 1879-80
THEOBALD, Charles Henry Gordon Eyre (1860 –
21.05.1924) 120H 1876
THIRLWELL, George William (c1857)
1M 1877
THOMAS, H.V.
220H 1874
THOMAS, Henry David (c1852)
880 1880; 1M 1879; 10M 1875

WELLS, Thomas Edward (15.06.1861 – 09.03.1934)
880 1880; 1M 1880
WESTELL, James
AAC: 7MW 67/ac
WETHERALL, Henry (bapt. 17.05.1849 – 1905)
2M 1868
WHALLEY, Robert Walter (c1855 – 04.08.1916)
880 1880
WHATELY, Henry Arthur (06.04.1855 – 02.05.1957)
440 1877; 880 1877-78
AAC: 880 78/1=
WHEBLE, James William St. Lawrence (29.01.1853 –
01.04.1925) LJ 1872-73
WHEELER, Alfred
1M 1874; 2M 1873-74; 3M 1874; 4M 1871-73;
10M 1871
AAC: 4M 71/2, 72/2, 73/2, 74/dnf
WHEELER, F. or J.
PV 1866
AAC: PV 66/1
WHEELER, T.
100 1876
WHELAN, Francis (Frank) Joseph (1847 – 04.10.1920)
120H 1869; PV 1868-69
WHELAN, John Mary (c1848)
100 1869; PV 1870
WHELAN, M.
HT 1875
WHITE, Private
440H 1872
WHITE, Donald
SP 1879
WHITE, Edwin (09.06.1845)
100 1868
WHITE, J.E.
100 1877
WHITE, Jack (01.03.1837 – 18.11.1910)
2M 1868-70; 3M 1868-70; 4M 1868-70; 6M 1868;
10M 1868
WHITEHEAD
PV 1872
WHITEHEAD, Harry (26.04.1847)
220 1869; 300 1869; 440 1868-70; 600 1870;
880 1867
WHITEMAN, H.
LJ 1879
WHITTAKER, E.
1M 1876
WICKHAM, Raymond Hugh (1850 – 15.04.1923)
440 1876; 220H 1872, 75-76, 79
WICKHAM, William James Richard (22.01.1860 –
08.06.1932)
220 1878; 440 1878
WIDDETT, G.
HJ 1869
WIDDOWSON, Sam Weller (16.04.1851 – 09.05.1927)
100 1872; 220 1872; 440 1873; 120H 1874, 77;
220H 1872, 74, 77; 440H 1872-74
WIGFULL, John (02.12.1851 – 1892)
PV 1871-73, 75
WIGHT, Daniel (c1851 – 1937)
150 1877; 300 1876
WILCOX, Henry Augustus Mortimer (14.10.1849 –
12.12.1908) LJ 1868, 70
WILD, T.
880 1877

WILKINSON, Anthony John Anstruther (28.05.1935 –
11.12.1905)
AAC: 100 66/5; 440 66/2
WILKINSON, Edmund (15.09.1857)
HT 1877
WILKINSON, Henry Fazakerley (1845 – 1888)
AAC: 7MW 68/3
WILKINSON, Kendal (1854)
PV 1876, 78-80
WILLIAMS, A.G.
HT 1877
WILLIAMS, H.
220H 1875
WILLIAMS, J.F. (c1856)
TJ 1874
WILLIAMS, Robert Manners Howard (27.04.1846 –
31.10.1916)
AAC: 7MW 67/dnf
WILLIAMSON, Frederick Clements (1846 –
29.11.1899) 120H 1869
WILLIAMSON, John Bruce (28.01.1859 – 07.07.1938)
100 1877
WILLIS, Reginald Charles Bruce (1848 – 21.01.1935)
SP 1866
WILLMORE, Graham (23.10.1852 – 22.03.1900)
120H 1872
AAC: 120H 75/3h
WILLS, John Tayler (01.1858 – 18.03.1922)
3M 1878
WILMOT, Arthur Alfred (14.02.1845 – 12.05.1876)
120H 1866
WILSON, George [Leochel-Cushnie]
SP 1867, 69; HT 1867
WILSON, George [Brentwood, Flint]
PV 1874
WILSON, Harold Charles (20.06.1860 – 14.07.1940)
HJ 1878
WILSON, Herbert
1000 1870
WILSON, J. [Glasgow]
SP 1869
WILSON, J. [Pennington]
PV 1873
WILSON, James, jun. [Tillyfourie]
HT 1867
WILSON, James, sen. [Tillyfourie]
SP 1867; HT 1867
WILSON, James [Aberdeen]
TJ 1877; SP 1877, 80; HT 1875
WILSON, John
TJ 1866
WILSON, John [Hutton Roof] (c1846)
PV 1869, 71
WILSON, John [Edinburgh] (c1846)
TJ 1874-76, 79
WILSON, John (c1846)
HJ 1872
WILSON, John
SP 1876
WILSON, John George (19.07.1848 – 23.06.1929)
100 1869-71; 440 1869; LJ 1866-67
AAC: 100 69/1, 71/1
WILSON, R.
SP 1875-77
WILSON, Simon
SP 1877

Oxford v Cambridge at Lillie Bridge, 1875. Stephen Brown (Oxford), winner of the shot for the third year in a row, was also a fine hammer thrower, topping the UK list in 1873 and winning the AAC championship in 1874. Students from Oxford or Cambridge won every AAC title except one in the hammer between 1866 and 1880, but not a single one in the shot.

Steeplechase courses could be testing. The cadets at the Royal Military Academy in 1867 had to clear a 15ft water jump, a 10ft brook and 'ever so many hurdles at intervals of 40 yards'.

Famous In Other Spheres

Charles Absolom (long jump and shot, 1866), nicknamed 'the navvy', played cricket for Cambridge University, Kent and England. Appearing for Lord Harris's team in the one test match of the Australian tour in 1878/9, he came in to bat at number nine after the 'demon bowler' Spofforth had done the hat trick and reduced England to 26 for 7. Absolom scored 52, but wasn't able to save the match. After 1880 he 'simply disappeared off the face of the earth' (Benny Green: *The Curious Affair of Charlie Absolom*). It emerged later that he had been at sea as a ship's purser and died in a bizarre accident in Port of Spain. Accounts vary. He was either buried under a load of sugar or floored by a crane hoisting bananas. He was 43.

Francis Robert Benson, later **Sir Frank Benson** (2M and 3M, 1879/80) became interested in the theatre at Oxford and produced the first performance there of a classic Greek play, *Agamemnon*. He joined Henry Irving's company at the Lyceum and in 1883 became a successful actor-manager himself. The Benson company specialised in Shakespeare and led the Stratford-on-Avon Festival season from 1886 until the outbreak of war in 1914. He was ultimately knighted and his contribution to Stratford is commemorated by the huge Benson stained glass window in the original Memorial Theatre.

John Graham Chambers (AAC 7 mile walk champion, 1866), the great codifier of sport, is most famous for devising the Queensberry Rules for boxing (1867). At Cambridge he was in at the start of inter-university athletics and had much to do with the programme that became the template for modern track and field. His main sport was rowing and he was in the Cambridge eight in 1862 and 1863 and coached the crews from 1871-5. After founding the AAC and opening the Lillie Bridge sports complex, he initiated championships there for boxing, billiards, rackets and cycling. As editor of the weekly newspaper *Land & Water*, he sponsored Captain Webb's pioneering Channel swim. He was said to have worked himself to death and didn't recover from a short illness when only 40.

Charles Gordon Lennox Fraser (AAC shot put champion, 1866), a farrier by trade, competed in highland games before coming south in 1858 to join the Metropolitan Police. He rose to the rank of superintendent and was appointed head of Queen Victoria's royal household police. This entitled him to live in the Norman Tower at Windsor Castle, and he also travelled extensively with the Queen's retinue. He was a great supporter of the police sports.

James Gibb (AAC 4 miles champion 1875, 77 and 78) dominated distance running for a few years in the mid-seventies. An engineer, he is often credited with the invention of table tennis, using cigar-box lids and celluloid balls he brought back from a business trip to America, but the history of the game is complex and he seems to have been just one of several people who influenced it. He may well have coined the name ping-pong.

William Gilbert Grace (150y, 440y, 880y, triple jump and cricket ball, 1869), better known as WG, is a legend of cricket so well known that we shall concentrate on his athletics. Between 1866 and 1870, before he became the formidable size familiar in photographs, he competed regularly in many events from the sprints to 1 mile. As well as those already listed, he was a high jumper, long jumper and pole vaulter. On July 30 and 31 1866, in a match between Surrey and an England XI, Grace scored 224 not out. Surrey were dismissed cheaply on August 1, but Grace wasn't involved. He was at Crystal Palace, where the National Olympian Association sports were under way. He ran the 440y hurdles, the event sometimes called the 'man-killer' - and this was over 20 hurdles - and won his Olympic honours in 1:10.0. He was that kind of man.

William Henry Grenfell, later **Lord Desborough** (2M and 3M 1876) won the Harrow school mile in 4:37.0, a record that lasted 60 years, and ran second for Oxford against Cambridge in the 1876 3 miles. President of Oxford athletics and boats, he twice rowed in the boat race. He stroked an eight across the Channel, won the punting championship of the Thames three times, climbed the Matterhorn three times and twice swam Niagara below the falls. For twenty years an MP, he was created a peer in 1905 and uniquely held office as president of five national sports associations, including the AAA and MCC. As President of the British Olympic Council and the moving spirit behind the 1908 Olympics, he got the White City stadium built at no cost to the Olympic organisers.

Edmund Gurney (pole vault, 1867 and 69), the subject of a biography *The Strange Case of Edmund Gurney* (Trevor H Hall, 1964*)*, was a promising pole vaulter at Cambridge who became interested in psychic investigation and was one of the founders and secretary of the Society for Psychical Research and author of *Phantasms of the Living*. He sat in on numerous spiritualist séances – 'an alien formidable figure' – and eventually wrote of the 'inherent rottenness of the evidence on which the huge fabric of modern spiritualism has principally rested'. A manic-depressive, he committed suicide with chloroform in a Brighton hotel room in 1888.

Arthur Neilson Hornby (120y hurdles, 1871 and 220y hurdles, 1870) captained the England cricket team that lost to Australia and gave rise to the ashes. Known as 'Monkey' Hornby because of his vitality and small stature, he captained England at rugby and cricket. He also played a few games of soccer for Blackburn Rovers. As a cricketer, he played for Lancashire for 33 years.

John Stanislaus Joyce (triple jump, 1869-70) was the father of ten surviving children of whom the writer James Joyce, born 1882, was the eldest. John Joyce inherited properties in Cork and did his triple jumping (as well as high and long jumps) in the Queen's College sports. After moving to Dublin he was employed in a distillery and ultimately became a dedicated imbiber of the product. He was said to be partly the inspiration for two of his son's main characters, Stephen Dedalus, in *A Portrait of the Artist as a Young Man* and *Ulysses*, and Humphrey Chimpden Earwicker in *Finnegan's Wake*.

Maurice Kingsley (120y hurdles, 1866) was the son of Charles Kingsley, writer of *The Water Babies*. After Cambridge University, he became a railway engineer and emigrated to the US and was for many years in the US engineering corps. He died at New Rochelle, New York, in 1910.

Charles Bennet Lawes, later *Sir C.B.Lawes-Wittewronge* (AAC mile champion, 1866) had an incredibly long career in sport. He dominated the sports at Eton (1860-3) and was the first winner of the Inter-Varsity 1 mile (1864). He stroked the Cambridge eight in 1865 and was supreme as a skuller, winning the Colquhoun, Diamond and Wingfield Skulls. He became a successful sculptor, but in 1882 was sued for libel by Richard Belt, another sculptor. The case was heard in Westminster Hall, lasted 43 days and Lawes lost, was required to pay £5000 in damages and was bankrupted. But the man was irrepressible and in 1898-9, aged 55, he took up paced speed cycling and set a series of English amateur records at distances ranging from 440yds to 25 miles. In 1900 he inherited the baronetcy and paid off his debts. When he died of appendicitis in 1911 he left a 33-page will, but there was no money left to divide.

Alfred Lyttelton (hammer, 1875-6) threw for Cambridge against Oxford in 1876, finishing second to the world record holder, 'Hammer' Hales. He was a Blue in five sports and went on to play cricket for Middlesex and for England against Australia in 1880, 1882 and 1884. In one test match in the latter year, the Australians scored 500 for 6 and in desperation Lord Harris asked Lyttelton, his wicket-keeper, to bowl. He proceeded to take 4 for 19 with underarm lobs. At soccer he was in the Old Etonians team in the 1876 Cup Final and went on to play for England in 1877. He won the real tennis championship twelve times. In 1899 he became President of the MCC. Somehow he fitted in a legal career, rising to Attorney-General in 1882-6.

James Lynam Molloy (2 miles, 1866), born near Rahan in Co. Offaly, Ireland, attended the Catholic University, Dublin, graduating in 1858. After studies in London, Paris and Bonn, he settled in London and became a private secretary to the Attorney-General. In 1866 he joined a group of Oxbridge friends for a trip to St Servan, Brittany, where he ran a respectable time for 2 miles in a minor meeting. He became a poet and composer and is most famous for *Love's Old Sweet Song* (*Just a Song at Twilight*), 1884, immortalised in Joyce's *Ulysses*, and *Kerry Dance* (1879).

Montague Shearman (AAC 440y Champion, 1876), besides being author of *Athletics and Football* in the Badminton Library series, was the judge who controversially passed the death sentence in 1922 on the lovers Frederick Bywaters & Edith Thompson for the murder of Thompson's husband. He was also a co-founder of the AAA and an astute collector of contemporary art (Picasso, Dali, Matisse, Utrillo, Sisley, Monet, Lautrec)

Sam Weller Widdowson (all sprints and hurdles between 1872 and 1877) was an international footballer, centre forward for Nottingham Forest and England. He also played one county cricket match for Nottinghamshire, but his main claim to fame was the invention of shin guards in football

Among those immortalised in biographies or autobiographies are Albert Bird, George Pallant Butcher, Thomas Carruthers, Maurice Davin, Patrick Davin, Donald Dinnie, Walter Goodall George, William Gilbert Grace, Edmund Gurney, Thomas Michael Malone, Edward Mills, Walter Rye, William Snook, Percy Melville Thornton, James Warburton, Richard Everard Webster and Jack White.

Internationals In Other Sports

Charles Alfred Absolom, test cricket
Arthur Montfort Archer, Ireland rugby
Thomas Batson, England rugby
William Wightman Beveridge, Scotland soccer
Francis Birley, England soccer
Marshall Jones Brooks, England rugby
Stewart Armit Macdonald Bruce, Ireland rugby
Lindsay Bury, England soccer
Henry Anderson Bryden, England rugby
John Charles Clegg, England soccer
William Edwin Clegg, England soccer
Abraham Prim Cronyn, Ireland rugby
William Cross, Scotland rugby
Wyndham Alleyn Daubeny Evanson, Eng. rugby
William James Forsyth, Scotland rugby
William Gilbert Grace, test cricket
Richard Lyon Geaves, England soccer
Joseph Fletcher Green, England rugby
Ernest Harwood Greenhalgh, England soccer
William Joseph Hamilton, Ireland rugby
George Hubert Hugh Heron, Scotland soccer
James Heron, Ireland rugby
Arnold Frank Hills, Scotland soccer
Thomas Charles Hooman, England soccer

Alfred Neilson Hornby, test cricket and Eng. rugby
Robert William Irvine, Scotland rugby
Henry Halcro Johnston, Scotland rugby
Henry Edward Kayll, England rugby
William Kelly, Irish rugby
Gilbert George Kennedy, Scotland soccer
Arnold Kirke-Smith, England soccer
William Lindsay, England soccer
Alfred Lyttelton, test cricket and England soccer
Reginald Heber Macaulay, England soccer
John Lisle Hall MacFarlane, Scotland rugby
William Henry MacLaren, England rugby
Edward Rowland Nash, England rugby
Richard Robinson Osborne, England rugby
Alfred Clunies Ross, Scotland rugby
George Robertson Turner, England rugby
Thomas C Vallance, Scotland soccer
Andrew Watson, Scotland soccer
David Henry Watson, Scotland rugby
Andrew Ramsay Don Wauchope, Scotland rugby
Sam Weller Widdowson, England soccer
Edward John Wolfe, Ireland rugby
John George Wylie, Scotland soccer

Not Who They Seem

Some famous names you may find in the lists:
Actors: Harry Andrews, Robert Lindsay, James Stewart, Robert Taylor.
Cowboys: William Boyd.
Explorers: David Livingstone, Robert Scott.
Footballers: John Aston, William (Billy) Bremner, Duncan Ferguson, George Young.
Magicians: John Dee
Politicians: Henry Brooke, D.Cameron, W.Hague, George Osborne, Harold Wilson.
Royal connections: John Brown, Macbeth.
Scientists: William Armstrong, Alexander Fleming, James Watt.
Tennis Players: James (Jamie) Murray.
Writers: Henry James, Walter Scott.
Others: J.R.Hartley, Mark Shearman

Victorian Innovations

In addition to the performances noted in the lists, much else of lasting importance in athletics was initiated in the period 1866-80.

International Meetings
A match between teams from Ireland and England on 5 June, 1876 was the world's first international athletics meeting. England won by 9 events to 4. A return match in London in 1877 resulted in England winning again by 11 events to 2. Illustrations opposite.

The England team that met Ireland in the first ever international match, in Dublin on 5 June 1876. Back row from left: James Waddell (manager), Tom Stone (shot put), Montague Shearman (sprints), William Waddell (manager), William Fuller (4 miles), Gerard Blathwayt (high jump), Walter Chinnery. Middle row: Charles Mason (4 miles), William Winthrop (shot & tug-of-war), Harry Venn (3 miles walk), Walter Slade (880y & 1M), Alfred Powles (sprints), Charles Lockton (high jump & long jump), Henry Hill (440y & 880y). Reclining: Nat Perry and Bob Rogers (trainers).

The return match at Stamford Bridge on 26 May 1877. Note Maurice Davin (IRL) winning the hammer with a one-handed throw; and a novel event, the solo tug-of-war, won for Ireland by Patrick Hickey.

Multi-event competitions

As early as 1862 the German Gymnastic Society started holding 'general competitions' in athletic events, awarding points for events. On 10 August, 1867 at Crystal Palace the number of events was fixed at five: 880yds, high jump, long jump, two-handed 36lb shot put and rope climbing. The overall winner was Henry Brooke.

On 15/16 August, 1877, a pentathlon was held over two days at the National Olympian Association meeting at Shrewsbury, consisting of 440yds, high jump, long jump, pole vault and shot put. In the 440 yards one point was scored for each 2 seconds short of 70sec, so that a run of 50 sec scored 10. In the high jump, one point was scored for each 3 inches above 4 feet. The same principle applied in the other field events. The winner was John G.Wylie (Shrewsbury), with 32 1/3 points.

On 20 and 27 October of the same year, London AC organised a 'general competition' at Stamford Bridge spread over two days separated by one week, involving 12 events: 100, 220, 440 and 880yds, 1 mile, 120yds hurdles, 2 mile walk, high jump, long jump, shot put, hammer and single-handed tug-of-war. The points system was 12 for a win, 6 for second and 3 for third. The winner was Herbert Sturt, with 78 points.

By the late 1870s general competitions were being held in Caledonian games in America and one professional four-hander at Baltimore in 1879 was billed as Scotland vs Ireland. Duncan C Ross and E W Johnston defeated James C Daly and James T Maloney.

Tug of War

This ancient sport began to appear in athletics meetings in the 1870s. The Sporting Gazette reporting the Woolwich Garrison Sports of 18/19 August, 1874: 'The rope pulling game was *the* contest of the meeting and heartily each team tugged to try and drag its opponent over the ditch. This game in my schooldays used to be known as "French and English" and is a capital test of strength between two sides of a school or dormitory.' The sport was given rules by the AAA at its AGM of 1887.

Ultra Running

The running of very long distances underwent a transformation in 1878 after the American walker, Edward Payson Weston, had toured Britain and competed in a six-day race against Irishman Dan O'Leary during 1877. The style of walking was considered by some as not 'fair heel and toe' so Sir John Astley had the idea of offering a championship belt and cash prizes for a six-day 'go-as-you-please' contest, starting Monday 18 March, 1878, at the Agricultural Hall, Islington. It was won by O'Leary with 520 miles 2 laps. The vast hall was crowded for the finish and from that time go-as-you-please was established as a popular event in Britain and America. By 1888 the record had been improved to 623¾ miles by George Littlewood of Sheffield at Madison Square Garden, New York. Numerous other records were set in the course of such races. Six-day events were revived in the 1980s and are still staged.

However, not all the new ideas were successful.

Automatic Timing

'The celebrated firm of watchmakers, Messrs Benson, have erected a clock opposite the winning post at Lillie Bridge Ground which is to be set going by electricity at the start of a race and the act of breasting the tape is to stop it.' *Bell's Life in London*, 21 March, 1874.

'For the purpose of timing the races a new electric clock by Benson, of Ludgate Hill, was for the first time brought into use, but unfortunately, owing to the wire being broken in three places after the Hundred Yard race, it did not have a fair trial.' *Bell's Life in London,* 28 March, 1874.

Floodlighting

'Lillie Bridge, October, 1876: The lamplight mile was not a success. There was hardly anyone there and the stink of the naphtha which reminded the spectators of the costermongers' barrows in the New Cut materially interfered with the comfort of the runners.' *Sporting Gazette*, October, 1876.

Video Board

The Telegraph Board – the performance whereon of Nat Perry of Kennington in the way of copperplate writing – being indeed wonderful. *Sporting Gazette*, on the 1875 AAC Championships.

In Their Own Words

Victorian athletes on the challenges of the sport

Francis O Philpott, on the first Oxford v Cambridge mile (1864): 'The Mile Race was won for Cambridge by C.B.Lawes with some ease after A.H.Hannam had made a gallant fight . . . Lawes was in tights and light blue silk hip-drawers – smacking to my boyish prejudice too much of the circus – while Hannam was encumbered with long flannel trousers bagging about his ankles and clinging to his knees. The easy freedom of the university costume, as it used to be called, was unknown in 1864, and Hannam was but dressed as others were; it was Lawes who was singular in his get-up, though it was quite professionally correct at that date and of undoubted advantage to him.'

Montague Shearman, co-founder of the AAA, on E.J.Colbeck's 440 yards record: 'The tale of Colbeck's celebrated quarter mile at the championship meeting at the old Beaufort House grounds in 1868 is one that has been often told. Coming along at a great pace, he led all the way round the ground and was winning easily when a sheep found its way upon the path and stopped still there, being presumably amazed at the remarkable performance which the runner was accomplishing. The athlete cannoned against the sheep, broke its leg, and then went on and finished his quarter in 50 2/5 seconds. This time was never equalled until J.Shearman in 1877 covered the distance in exactly the same time at Lillie Bridge and was never surpassed in England by an amateur until Myers paid his first visit to England in 1881.'

Clement N. Jackson, first record holder for 120 yards hurdles: 'Marston Moor . . . where your humble servant, just at his best, brought to an untimely end a promising career by spiking a hidden oyster shell when going "full bat" in a hurdle handicap after the seven-leagued legs of W.G.Grace. From that day forth I have never run again, never tasted an oyster, never spoken to W.G. the Great!'

Pat Davin (Ireland) on his 23ft 2in long jump record (1883): 'The ground on which I jumped was anything but favourable, the run up being rather uphill and the grass four or five inches high. My three jumps measured 22ft 3ins, 23ft, 23ft 2ins. I expect to do better and probably may before the end of the season.'

Alfred Lubbock, cricketer and pole vaulter: 'I was very sorry not to be able to play in the Canterbury week this year (1867), as, while jumping for the pole jump in the Amateur Athletic Meeting, I had broken a bone in my foot, and had in consequence to spend two or three months on the sofa.'

Richard F. Webster, AAA President, on the first Oxford v Cambridge match (1864): 'To our surprise, when the competitors arrived from Oxford they proposed to throw the weight with both hands. This was, of course, not putting the weight at all as understood in Scotland and in other places where this form of competition was in vogue, and the fact that they proposed to use both hands shows how little some branches of athletic sports were understood at that date. We were in a dilemma as to what to do, but finally determined that as the Oxford men claimed the right to use both hands, both methods of throwing should be used – that is to say, putting in the proper way with one hand and throwing with both hands. In the result Cambridge won quite easily. They were very little, if at all, behind the Oxford men in putting with both hands, and far superior in putting in the orthodox manner.'

Walter Rye, AAC champion, 7 mile walk (1868): 'To such a stage of apathy had the club (the AAC) sunk in 1876 that an unfriendly critic declared it had only three active members – the secretary, the pony and the roller.'

Donald Dinnie, durable Scottish all-rounder: 'Before this season (1872) was more than halfway through an unfortunate accident befell me at Buffalo Caledonian Club Games, where I contested in the pole-vaulting competition. By losing my balance when crossing the bar I sprained my left hand and wrist very severely, thus spoiling my work to a considerable extent for the remainder of that season . . . My friend Fleming had to take my place . . . at Toronto, where he met the great R.R.McLennan, of Glengarry, who won the heavy hammer by some 6ft . . . With my left arm still in a sling, I tried only the light hammer with one hand, for which McLennan did not compete, and I won easily by 7ft.'

RULES FOR COMPETITIONS.

1.—No attendant to accompany a competitor on the scratch, or in the race.

2.—Any competitor starting before the word, to be put ——— yards, at the discretion of the starter; on a repetition of the offence, to be disqualified. At the Champion Sports, starting before the word to disqualify the competitor.

3.—All Level races to start by word of mouth, Handicaps by pistol.

4.—In Hurdle races, each competitor to keep his own hurdles throughout the race.

5.—In Sprint racing, each runner to keep his own side of the course. To prevent jostling, it is advisable to stake and string off a course for each runner.

6.—Jostling or running across, or wilfully obstructing another, so as to impede his progress, to disqualify the offender from any further competitions held by the Club.

7.—All cases of dispute to be referred to the Committee of Management at the time.

8.—The decision of the Judges to be final.

9.—In Pole Leaping and High Jumping, 3 tries at each height allowed. Each height to be determined by the majority of the competitors, displacing the bar only to count as a try.

10.—In Broad Jumping, Putting the Stone, and Throwing the Hammer, three tries only allowed: the best three competitors of the first trial to be allowed three more tries each for the final: the farthest Throw, Put, or Jump, of the six attempts, to win.

*11.—In Throwing the Hammer the length of the run not limited; the throw to be measured from the nearest footprint at the delivery to the edge of the pitch of the ball.

12.—"No Throws" to count as a try.

13.—Crossing the Scratch-line in the attempt, to count as "No Throw." This rule applies to Putting the Stone, and Broad Jumping.

14.—The weight of the Hammer and Stone to be 16 lbs. respectively.

15.—The height of the hurdles to be 3 ft. 6 in.

16.—The Stone to be delivered from the shoulder with either hand; seven feet run allowed; no "Put" to count, if delivered or followed with any part of the body touching the ground over the mark; all throws to be measured from the nearest point of the scratch, continued in a straight line on either side until opposite the edge of the pitch.

DEFINITION OF AN AMATEUR.

Any person who has never competed in an open competition or for public money, or for admission money, or with professionals for a prize, public money or admission money, and who has never at any period of his life taught, pursued, or assisted in the pursuit of Athletic Exercises as a means of livelihood.

All objections against a Competitor's qualification to contend must be made to the Committee of the Club.

* The accuracy of the measurement is facilitated by sprinkling ashes, sawdust, or sand at the point of delivery. The footprints of the competitors must be effaced after each throw.

The complete AAC Rules For Competitions from 1867, a far cry from the nearly 300 pages of IAAF rules today